Social Science Literature
A Bibliography
for International Law

Social Science Literature
A Bibliography
for International Law

By Wesley L. Gould and Michael Barkun

Published for The American Society of International Law

Princeton University Press, Princeton, New Jersey

016.3
G 698

LCC 70-39328

ISBN 0-691-09225-7 .

Published for the American Society of International Law

Printed in the United States of America
by Princeton University Press

PREFACE

From time to time members of the American Society of International Law, chiefly practicing lawyers and teachers of law, have indicated that they would like to make use of the findings of social scientists that are relevant to their own work. But each found himself without time to search the unfamiliar social science literature in addition to the familiar and extensive legal literature. As one lawyer put it, he could hardly search through a hundred issues of a journal in order to find perhaps the one sociological treatment of the problem before him.

Early in 1964 these suggestions, together with what amounted to pleas for help in the form of an annotated bibliography of relevant literature, received expression at a meeting of a panel at the offices of the American Society of International Law. Shortly thereafter a proposal was made and the Society supported both the production of this bibliography and, as matters developed, a companion expository volume, International Law and the Social Sciences (Princeton, N.J.: Princeton University Press, 1970).

International Law and the Social Sciences dealt with a representative sample of the more important literature annotated in this bibliography. It undertook to set the sample in a framework of social science concepts that give promise for future development of international legal studies in harmony with the main currents of social science thought. Conversely, it endeavored to show how social science research itself could take better account of the legal dimension of international relations.

However, the discursive style of the earlier volume could not accommodate the mass of social science literature. The original need for a bibliography remained. As may be seen from a comparison of the two volumes, they are complementary. Among the annotations here are those that indicate the relevance of the concepts or methods employed in a particular research project to potential international law research.

Not all annotations indicate the potential for adaptation. Such suggestions are unnecessary for those articles, books, and monographs that provide only factual or descriptive information. In many other cases what could have been suggested had already been set forth under a prior entry and where this has happened, we have tried not to burden the user with nonessential repetition.

Our selections for inclusion fall chiefly in the decade 1955-1965, that is, in the post-World War II period when experimentation with new social science methods was gaining momentum. This does not mean that we have ignored earlier years or the following half-decade during which (as

i

entry No. 69-A indicates) there was a doubling of the percentage of behavioral articles on the United Nations published in eighteen journals.

Our tendency to be more restrictive in selecting pre-1955 items is
in part because some of that literature is of chiefly historical interest
now and because some, e.g., Harold Lasswell's many studies, are too well
known to scholars to require listing. For the literature after 1965 we
have tended to exclude what for our purposes would be little more than
repetitious demonstrations of technical proficiency.

We have made no effort to confine our selections to the "behavioralist" literature, however defined, even though much historical literature, including many useful memoirs, has had to be excluded in order to
make way for the basic social science focus. But a considerable number
of entries employ historical and other traditional approaches. For reasons that vary according to the subject matter, some law journal articles
have also been included. Certainly, there is room to quarrel with our
selections, to argue that we have included some items of secondary importance and excluded those that others cherish. To such arguments we
can only reply that we have tried to include items useful to scholars
of varied interests and may have overlooked that which is beyond the
capacities of two men to find.

We have tried, up to the last available moment, to insert some of
the more useful studies that have come to our attention since September
1969. Such interpolations will be readily apparent by the addition of
a letter to the preceding citation number, for we chose not to indulge
in a renumbering that might work havoc with our cross-reference scheme.

While this bibliography is primarily the work of two men, we have
had valuable assistance that should be acknowledged. We are particularly grateful to Alan and Hanna Newcombe, editors of the Peace Research
Abstracts Journal, published by the Canadian Peace Research Institute,
for making many of their abstracts available to us prior to publication.
By doing so, they provided a big lift, particularly through coverage of
the psychological literature, without which our task would have taken
much longer. Among the political science graduate students at Purdue
University who have been helpful, the following deserve special acknowledgement: Mary Lou Kelleher, Andrea Eisenstein, and Anne Ross. At
Wayne State University, Paul Shui was particularly helpful. As in the
case of International Law and the Social Sciences, our appreciation is
due the following individuals: Richard C. Snyder and Victor G. Rosen-
blum, to whom we owe the opportunity for collaboration; Brunson Mac-
Chesney, who played a vital role in the initiation of the project;
H.C.L. Merillat and Stephen M. Schwebel, successive Executive Directors
of the American Society of International Law; and, Richard W. Edwards,
Jr., the Society's former Assistant Director.

Finally, we owe an unbounded debt to two of our typists: Patricia
Anne Woodruff, who converted the often ungrammatical scribbling on 4 x 6

cards into an organized, usable manuscript; and Judith Mitchell, who produced the final copy, indexed it, and demonstrated an awesome capacity to ferret out our omissions and inconsistencies. Naturally, for those errors that remain we bear sole responsibility.

Wesley L. Gould

Michael Barkun

TABLE OF CONTENTS

Social Science Literature
A Bibliography
for International Law

I. SOCIAL SCIENCE CONCEPTS AND METHODS

A. BIBLIOGRAPHIES AND SURVEYS OF RESEARCH

1. Albert, Ethel, and Kluckhohn, Clyde. A Selected Bibliography on Values, Ethics, and Aesthetics in the Behavioral Sciences and Philosophy, 1920-1958. Glencoe: Free Press, 1959, pp. xviii, 342.
        Contains 2,000 annotated items from several disciplines, all dealing with values. Coding is by discipline, subject matter, and geographic area.

2. Arms Control and Disarmament. Arms Control and Disarmament Bibliography Section, General Reference and Bibliography Division, Reference Department, Library of Congress. Washington: Government Printing Office, 1965- .
        Quarterly journal of annotated materials on arms control and disarmament.

3. Beardsley, Seymour, and Egdell, Alvin. Human Relations in International Affairs: A Guide to Significant Interpretations and Research. Washington: Public Affairs Press, 1956, pp. vi, 40.
        A bibliography of books covering human relations as they relate to international problems. The choice of books is interdisciplinary but limited to English language publications since World War II. Single articles in periodicals, specific area studies, publications with sections pertinent to international affairs or of implicit and not explicit relevance to international affairs have been omitted.

4. Bibliography of Social Science Periodicals and Monograph Series. Foreign Demographic Analysis Division, Bureau of the Census. Edited by Frederick A. Leedy. Washington: Government Printing Office, 1961- .
        Appearing at irregular intervals, this annotated bibliography covers periodicals and monograph series using the so-called difficult languages, with entries in each issue limited to a specific country.

5. Bulletin analytique de documentation politique, économique et sociale contemporaine. Edited by Jean Meyriat. Paris: Presses Universitaires de France, 1946- .
        Provides descriptive annotations of articles from over 1,000 French and other periodicals that deal with social, economic, and political questions and also of documents of international organizations and national governments.

6. Canadian Peace Research Institute. Peace Research Abstracts Journal. Edited by Alan G. and Hanna Newcombe. Oakville, Ontario. Vols. 1- . 1964- .
        A monthly publication of abstracts of articles, books, reports, and unpublished papers in the social and natural sciences that deal with the following topics: (1) the military situation; (2) arms

control and disarmament; (3) tension and conflict; (4) ideology and issues; (5) decision-making; (6) communications; (7) international institutions; (8) international law, economics, and diplomacy; (9) nations and national policies; (10) pairs of countries and crisis areas; (11) methods of study; (12) science and society. Approximately 9,000 items are abstracted annually.

7. de Grazia, Alfred (ed.). Universal Reference System: Political Science Series. 10 vols. Quarterly and Annual Supplements. Princeton: Princeton Research Publishing Co., 1965-   .
       Each of these ten volumes contains 2,000-4,000 annotations of books, articles, papers, and documents in the political and behavioral sciences. Quarterly supplements permit continuous updating. Most useful to specialists in international law are Volume I, International Affairs, and Volume VII, Law, Jurisprudence, and Judicial Process.

8. Department of State: Foreign Service Institute. Bibliography on Science and World Affairs. Washington: Government Printing Office, November 1964.
       Contains over 2,000 entries relevent to the impact or potential impact of science and technology on world affairs.

9. Deutsch, Karl W., and Rieselbach, Leroy N. "Recent Trends in Political Theory and Political Philosophy." 360 Annals of the American Academy of Political and Social Science (July 1965), 139-162.
       Review of recent literature in political and social science that sees as the first among three suggested goals for political theory the development of a political theory of peace.

10. Gray, Charles H., Gray, Leslie B., and Gregory, Glenn W. A Bibliography of Peace Research: Indexed by Key Words. Eugene, Oregon: General Research Analysis Methods, 1968, pp. 170.
       Employing the Key Word In Context format, this bibliography includes over 7,800 entries for over 1,300 articles, books, and anthologies chiefly from the period 1957-1967.

11. Hoselitz, Bert F. (ed.). A Reader's Guide to the Social Sciences. Rev. ed. New York: Free Press, 1970, pp. 448.
       Essay introductions to the standard literature of each of the social sciences, plus the somewhat marginal cases of geography and history.

12. Index of Selected Publications of The RAND Corporation. Vol. I: 1946-1962. Santa Monica: RAND Corporation, August 1962, pp. xi, 767. Supplement: February 1963, pp. 71.
       Contains abstracts of unclassified RAND Technical and social science papers, memoranda, and books to 1962.

13. International Political Science Abstracts. Edited by Serge Hurtig. Oxford: Basil Blackwell for the International Political Science Association, 1951-
       Abstracts of periodical literature in political science, with

abstracts averaging 150 words and with non-English language articles abstracted in French.

14. Newcombe, Hanna, and Newcombe, Alan. Peace Research Around the World. Oakville, Ontario: Canadian Peace Research Institute, 1969, pp. 275.
A review of studies that can be classified under the rubric, peace research, and that can be further categorized under the following headings: international systems; crisis; conflict; attitudes; research on the future; integration; economics; international law; disarmament; protest; nonviolence. The review is followed by sections on theoretical conclusions, policy recommendations found in the studies, and research recommendations.

15. Pehrsson, Hjalmar, and Wulf, Hanna. The European Bibliography-- La bibliographie européenne. Leiden: Sijthoff, 1965, pp. viii, 472.
Lists general works and technical literature related to current economic and political events reflecting the idea of creating a Europe conscious of its traditions.

16. Saul, Leon J. (compiler). "Hostility: A Bibliography in the Psychological Sciences with Supplementary References from Other Social Sciences." 4 American Behavioral Scientist (supplement, June 1961), pp. 46.
An interdisciplinary bibliography with contributions from the following fields: animal behavior studies; child behavior studies; physiology; psychiatry; psychoanalysis; psychosomatics. Less inclusive citations are drawn also from: anthropology; criminology; neurology; sociology; social psychology; political science; economics; and therapeutics.

17. Selected RAND Abstracts. Vols. 1- . 1963- . Santa Monica: RAND Corporation, 1964- .
Annual compilation of annotations of unclassified RAND papers and research memoranda in the natural and social sciences together with an indication of availability and of those items that have been openly published as articles or books.

18. Shubik, Martin. "Bibliography on Simulation, Gaming, Artificial Intelligence and Allied Topics." 55 American Statistical Association Journal (1960), 736-751.
A useful guide to the literature on gaming and related topics.

19. Smith, Bruce Lannes, Lasswell, Harold D., and Casey, Ralph D. Propaganda, Communication and Public Opinion: A Comprehensive Reference Guide. Princeton: Princeton University Press, 1946, pp. vii, 435.
Bibliography on public opinion and communications research.

20. Smith, Bruce Lannes, and Smith, Chitra M. International Communication and Political Opinion: A Guide to the Literature. Princeton: Princeton University Press, 1956, pp. xi, 325.
Bibliography on communications research that extends the 1946 bibliography by Smith, et al.

21. Wasserman, Paul, with Silander, Fred S. <u>Decision-Making: An Annotated Bibliography</u>. Ithaca: Graduate School of Business and Public Administration, Cornell University, 1958, pp. vi, 111.
>   Covers materials chiefly since 1945 and up to September 1957.

22. White, Carl M., <u>et al</u>. <u>Sources of Information in the Social Sciences</u>. Totowa, N.J.: Bedminster, 1964, pp. xiii, 498.
>   A heavily annotated overview, covering the following subjects: the literature of social science; history; economics and business administration; sociology; anthropology; psychology; education; political science. Contains for each field a selection of substantive works plus a bibliography of bibliographies.

23. Zawodny, J.K. <u>Guide to the Study of International Relations</u>. San Francisco: Chandler, 1966, pp. xii, 151.
>   Annotated guide to abstracts, U.S. archives, library holdings, bibliographies, biographies, dictionaries, documents, encyclopaedias, dissertation lists, films, periodicals and the literature in major fields including newspapers, interviews and oral histories, and compilations of statistics.

B. ENCYCLOPAEDIAS AND DICTIONARIES

24. Gould, Julius and Kolb, William L. (eds.). <u>A Dictionary of the Social Sciences</u>. New York: Free Press, 1964, pp. xvi, 761.
>   An attempt to bring order out of conceptual chaos.

25. Hadik, Lazlo (ed.). <u>Trilingual Glossary of Strategic Terminology</u>. Geneva: Institut Universitaire des Hautes Études Internationales, 1964, pp. 260.
>   A useful aid to students that constitutes what a reviewer calls "depressing evidence of the rapid escalation of professional unintelligibility in a subject still barely ten years old" (Michael Howard in <u>Year Book of World Affairs</u>, 1966, p. 387).

26. Haensch, G. (compiler). <u>Dictionary of International Relations and Politics</u>. Amsterdam: Elsevier, 1965, pp. 638.
>   A systematic and alphabetic dictionary in four languages (German, English/American, French, Spanish).

27. <u>International Encyclopedia of the Social Sciences</u>. 17 vols. New York: Crowell-Collier, 1968.
>   Entries on various topics reflecting more recent research and efforts to build empirical theory, with stress on the behavioral sciences and with the elimination of a number of topics embraced in the earlier <u>Encyclopedia of the Social Sciences</u>, e.g., intervention.

28. Pei, Mario (ed.). <u>Language of the Specialists: A Communications Guide to Twenty Different Fields</u>. New York: Funk & Wagnalls, 1966, pp. xii, 388.
>   Collection of brief descriptive essays about the basic concepts

of various fields. Following the information given about each field, a list of words most frequently used and their definitions is presented.

C. METHODS

1. Law and Social Sciences

29. Association of American Law Schools. Program and Reports of Committees, 1963.
Includes a report on the work of the Joint Committee on Political Science and International Law of the American Political Science Association and the Association of American Law Schools. The Committee, composed of five lawyers and five political scientists, expressed the hope that financial support could be found to permit legal and behavioral scholars to engage in joint research "to provide a basis for evaluating Professor Grundstein's thesis that administrative law has much to learn from behavioral science." The report quotes extensively from the Grundstein article (infra, no. 38). A partial dissent by Kenneth Culp Davis was subsequently expanded into an article (infra, no. 34) published as a commentary to the Grundstein article.

30. Barkun, Michael. "Bringing the Insights of Behavioral Science to International Rules." 18 Western Reserve Law Review (1967), 1639-1660.
A part of a symposium that looks at international legal developments since the founding of Western Reserve's School of Law in 1892 and makes some projections to 1992, this article examines the development of the behavioral sciences and their relevance to the needs of international law in the contemporary and future world that differs from the world in which international law developed. The need for a breakdown of barriers between disciplines and development of interdisciplinary syntheses is stressed in terms of relevance to the contemporary and future requirements for international order.

31. Boulding, Kenneth E. The Impact of the Social Sciences. New Brunswick: Rutgers University Press, 1966, pp. vi, 117.
Exploration of the effects of modern social science on such areas as international relations, ethics, and law.

32. Colliard, C.A. "Science juridique et science politique." Revue de l'enseignement superieur (No. 4, 1965), 37-46.
Dealing with the relations between law and political science, the author sees the two tendencies of political science, the one toward observation and analysis and the other toward systemization and synthesis, as leading legal scholars to a better appreciation of their own discipline through attention to methodology and to efforts to synthesize.

33. Cowan, Thomas A. "What Law Can Do for Social Science." In William M. Evan (ed.), _Law and Sociology_. New York: Free Press, 1962, pp. 91-123.

Provocative discussion of the research potential of a blend of legal and social science approaches that invites the social scientist to venture into the law as the nearest thing to an orderly system of value judgments.

34. Davis, Kenneth Culp. "Behavioral Science and Administrative Law." 17 _Journal of Legal Education_ (1965), 137-154.

A professor of law, who states (p. 137) that he requested the publication of an article by Nathan Grundstein (_infra_, no. 38) "and have committed myself to write this commentary on it, because law professors should be informed about both the claims and the accomplishments of behavioral science," finds the Grundstein article to be empty and some of its conclusions to be unsound. The author is disturbed about those aspects of behavioral science that are "pretending to use the methods of natural science where they are clearly a misfit" (p. 154). Reviewing (pp. 138-147) a few behavioral works, chiefly efforts to evaluate accomplishments of behavioral science, he finds nothing useful for administrative law research.

35. de Grazia, Alfred. "Law and Behavior: A Unified Approach to Their Study." 3 _Prod_ (1960), 3-7.

A theoretical framework for relating verifiable human behavior with the law.

36. Delos, Joseph Thomas. _Le problème de civilisation--la nation._ 2 vols. Montreal: Editions de l'Arbre, 1944.

A seldom mentioned theoretical treatise by a teacher of international law. Volume I attempts a sociological analysis of the nation and volume II deals with nationalism and legal order. The ideas bear the imprint of World War II and the French collapse of 1940, but are suggestive both of potential approaches to problems of international law and of potential bridges between more traditional scholarship and the newer social science scholarship that was to come to the fore in the next decade.

36-A. Dror, Yehezkel. "Law as a Tool of Directed Social Change: A Framework for Policy-Making." 13 _American Behavioral Scientist_ (1970), 553-559.

Part of a special issue on "Law and Social Change" edited by Stuart S. Nagel, this article, based on the Lasswell-McDougal approach, argues for the study of law as an instrument of directed social change by going beyond both jurisprudence and the social sciences to employ the policy sciences and policy analysis, the latter regarded as an extension of systems analysis.

37. "Frontiers of Legal Research." Coordinated by Charles L. Ruttenberg. 7 _American Behavioral Scientist_ (December 1963). Entire issue, pp. 55.

Papers on law and the social sciences, covering, among others, the following topics: researches in the sociology of law; scientific method and the judicial process; a primer of psychological theories holding implications for legal work; innovators in the study of the legal process; an annotated bibliography of recent innovative studies in the law.

38. Grundstein, Nathan D. "Administrative Law and the Behavioral and Management Sciences." 17 Journal of Legal Education (1965), 121-136.

This article by a political scientist examines possible uses of behavioral methodologies in a field that in the past has been dominated by practitioner-oriented problems. The author sees decision and organization theory as offering, in respect to concerns within the traditional scope of administrative law research, a better methodology and a richer set of conceptual schema than have so far been applied. Experimental control of regulatory processes through simulation, particularly simulation dealing with a relatively high order of organization complexity and with decision problems that are not trivial, is viewed as a means whereby more rigorous conceptualization may be compelled and whereby the conceptual may displace the priority of the operational in the research orientation of administrative law. For full exploitation of potential contributions of the behavioral sciences, administrative law would, in the author's opinion, have to shift from an essentially procedure- or process-oriented approach to a predominantly outcome or decision-consequences approach. At the same time, because the technology relevant to management of regulatory organizations is now a primary concern, an area exists in which management science is more relevant than behavioralism, particularly since the latter does not share the professional responsibility for the character and quality of regulatory agencies that is carried by law-based research.

39. Hall, Jerome. "Unification of Political and Legal Theory." 69 Political Science Quarterly (1954), 15-28.

Legal theory and political theory are artificially separated largely due to the far-ranging influence of formal theories of law and by specialization and vocationalism. It would be advantageous to unify the two disciplines that would extend to unification of the theorist's thinking in terms of a problem, organization of the knowledge thus acquired, and a reordering and classification of social science.

40. Lundberg, George A. "Conflicting Orientation in Law and National Policy." In Richard A. Taylor, Life, Language, Law: Essays in Honor of Arthur F. Bentley. Yellow Springs, Ohio: Antioch Press, 1957, pp. 168-203.

Concerned with the split in the social thinking of this generation, more particularly with the influence of what he calls the Natural Law faction on public policy, the author presents the hypothesis that the Natural Law viewpoint is incompatible with coherent and successful public policy. Thus the basic cleavage referred to is the legalistic-moralistic vs. the "scientific" approach. The author

posits a causal relationship between the evolution of industrial society and the development of the natural sciences.

41. Mayo, L.H., and Jones, E.M. "Legal-Policy Decision Process:
Alternative Thinking and the Predictive Function." 33 George Washington
Law Review (1964), 318-456.
    Discusses the need of legal policy-making to predict and sug-
gests new techniques available for that purpose among them systems
analysis, operations research, and simulation.

42. Podgorecki, Adam. "Law and Social Engineering." 21 Human Organization (1962), 177-181.
    Concerned with the uses of law in planning, the Polish author
(University of Warsaw) presents a brief outline of the nature of a
science of legal policy and makes some brief suggestions concerning
types of research that could produce useful guides for legislators.

43. Riesman, David. "Toward an Anthropological Science of Law and
the Legal Profession." 57 American Journal of Sociology (1951), 121-135.
    Anthropologists and sociologists who have studied primitive law
have not applied their method to contemporary law in the United States.
An anthropological study must go beyond both the glamorous and the social reform aspects of law and study the unique structure of the law,
the type of people it attracts, their training, and the role the law
has played in shaping present day society.

44. Redford, Emmette Shelburn. General Passenger Fare Investigation.
Inter-University Case Programs. No. 56. Indianapolis: Bobbs-Merrill,
1960, pp. 56.
    An example from the area of administrative law of a study by a
political scientist of nonsequencing potentialities for action, con-
cealed within administrative procedure, upon information behavior
and decision outcomes. Realizing that, while procedure as sequence
can be dealt with by consideration of functional and structural formalities and responsibilities of position-holders, nonsequencing aspects require accounting for perceptions, motivations, and utilities
of decision-makers, the author develops from his data a set of propositions about the interplay of information and decision within a
regulatory agency.

45. Shapiro, Martin. "Political Jurisprudence." 52 Kentucky Law
Journal (1964), 294-295.
    A political scientist's explanation to lawyers of the rationale
for extending the findings of other areas of political science into
the public law area and for rounding out political science by integrating the law and courts into portrayals of political life.

46. Sherwood, Foster H. "The Role of Public Law in Political Science." In Roland Young (ed.), Approaches to the Study of Politics.
Evanston: Northwestern University Press, 1958, pp. 86-96.
    Public law is here conceived as a body of relevant political
data and so as a subject within political science rather than on
its periphery.

47. Stjernquist, P. "Gränsområden mellan rättsvetenskap och
samhällsvetenskap (Borderland between Jurisprudence and Social Sciences)."
61 Statsvetenskaplig Tidskrift (1958), 141-150.
   Holding that jurisprudence is essentially normative and the social sciences essentially causative, the author denotes a bridge area
in causal studies of the relations between law and society. He en-
visages studies both of the political, economic, and social influences upon law and of the political, economic, and social effects of
norms. He recommends the employment of sociological methods but with
a truly juridical frame of mind.

48. Stone, Julius. Law and the Social Sciences in the Second Half
Century. Minneapolis: University of Minnesota Press, 1965, pp. 121.
   Reviews the contributions and interrelations of the bodies of
knowledge bearing upon the study of law and shows how ideas in jurisprudence have been stimulated and clarified by work in the social
sciences.

2. Methods: Surveys and Commentaries

49. Allott, A.N. "Methods of Research into Customary Law." 5 Journal
of African Administration (1953), 172-177.
   Concern is for African customary law and the methods of research
to deal with problems of distortion in European courts and lack of
records of native proceedings. The author seeks to assist the lawyer
in dealing with rules enforced or enforceable rather than to promote
what he perceives to be the anthropologist's task, namely, to investigate the social purpose of customary rules.

50. Bell, Daniel. "Twelve Modes of Prediction--A Preliminary Sorting
of Approaches in the Social Sciences." 93 Daedalus (1964), 845-880.
   An illustration of the range of approaches to conjecture, i.e.,
first explanation and then prediction, that outlines the following
approaches: social physics; trends and forecasts; structural certainty; operational code; operational system; structural requisites;
overriding problem; prime mover; sequential development; accounting
scheme; writing "fictions"; decision theory. Research called for is
in the problem areas of the planning process, standardization of social indicators, and modeling of political structures.

51. Boasson, Ch. Approaches to the Study of International Relations.
Assen: Van Gorcum, 1963, pp. 100.
   A critical review of various models for the study of international relations, including (pp. 50-57) legal conceptions of the
international community. Although regarding the concept of world
community as essential for a useful study of international relations
and for assertion of the existence of international law, the author
is particularly critical of the primitive community model and of the
model limiting membership to states, thereby manifesting a club-
membership mentality.

52. Cartwright, D. "The Strategy of Research on International Conferences." 5 _International Social Science Bulletin_ (1953), 278-286.

   One of the contributions to the issue on the "Technique of International Conferences," this is one of the more useful articles in that it discusses the possibilities of employing objective techniques and of manipulating variables. In particular, the author suggests minimizing the "international" aspect of conferences and working from a general scheme for classifying conferences.

53. Deutsch, Karl W., and Isard, Walter. "A Note on a Generalized Concept of Effective Distance." 6 _Behavioral Science_ (1961), 308-311.

   Explains why effective distance between two places, objects, or individuals must be measured not just in miles but also in terms of economic, communication, and social distances, each of which may differ from the others. A method for computing effective distance and suggestions for further investigation of the concept are made.

54. Devereux, George. _From Anxiety to Method in the Behavioral Sciences_. New York: Humanities Press, 1968, pp. 376.

   The author asserts that the data of the behavioral scientists arouse anxieties that are warded off by a "counter-transference inspired pseudo-methodology" that accounts for most of the defects found in behavioral science.

55. Duverger, Maurice. _An Introduction to the Social Sciences with Special Reference to Their Methods_. Translated by Malcolm Anderson. New York: Praeger, 1964, pp. 342.

   Review of the social sciences and their methods that serves as a relatively nontechnical inventory of techniques and some of their applications.

56. Edwards, David V. _International Political Analysis_. New York: Holt, Rinehart and Winston, 1969, pp. xiii, 366.

   With scant attention to international law and considerable attention to crisis, war, and alliance, this volume deals with social science methods of analysis, explanation, and theory building, and with applications in the forms of prediction and control of events. A chapter entitled "Studying Cooperative Control" is devoted to arms control.

57. Galtung, Johan. "The Social Sciences: An Essay on Polarization and Integration." In Klaus Knorr and James N. Rosenau (eds.), _Contending Approaches to International Politics_. Princeton: Princeton University Press, 1969, pp. 243-285.

   Concerned essentially with history, anthropology, and sociology, the article examines why different methods of dealing with space and time developed--_diachronic_ analysis (a point found in space and a cut made parallel to the time axis); _synchronic_ analysis (a point found in time and a cut made parallel to the space axis); the _ideographic_ approach (a contiguous space-time region is selected and investigation preserves the unity of action, space, and time); the _nomothetic_ approach (data is collected from various scattered space-time points or regions). Possible syntheses of these methods are suggested, e.g., ideographic studies using nomothetic substudies, nomothetic studies using ideographic substudies.

58. Galtung, Johan. Theory and Methods of Social Research. New York: Columbia University Press; London: Allen & Unwin; Oslo: Universitetsforlaget, 1967, pp. 534.
    Integration of techniques of data collection, techniques of analysis, statistical methods, and some philosophy of science in an effort to show how the theory and method of social research can be enriched by simultaneously bringing to the fore the concepts and methods of several disciplines.

59. Gaudemet, P.M. "L'Apport de la science financière à la science politique." 15 Revue française de science politique (1965), 629-644.
    Discussion of the potential uses of financial documentation and methods and rules of interpretation of such data for the study of politics and political forces.

60. Golembiewski, Robert T., Welsh, William A., and Crotty, William J. A Methodological Primer for Political Scientists. Chicago: Rand Mc-Nally, 1969, pp. ix, 484.
    With a tendency to reinforce similarities and interdependence among basic approaches, this volume attempts to supply orderly guidelines for empirical research. It includes chapters on inter-nation simulation and on the study of the international political system.

61. Hassner, P. "Violence, rationalité, incertitude--tendances apocalyptiques et iréniques dans l'étude des conflits internationaux." 14 Revue française de science politique (1964), 1155-1178.
    A criticism of studies of conflict that treats Schelling's work as avoiding three errors to be found in the works of a number of other authors: (1) indulging the belief that violence is impossible because no one wishes it; (2) assuming that, once unleashed, violence becomes uncontrollable and must go to the limit; (3) believing that if violence can be a signal or a message, it can be like other signals or messages. In the United States the tendency of scholarship is either toward a utopia of integral rationalization or toward an apocalyptic vision of pacifist origin. After comments on certain French studies, the author proposes that rationality and foresight be clearly distinguished and that there be no confusion between the prospective rationality of the theoretician who expounds possible choices and strategies, the active rationality of the participant who makes his choices amid uncertainty and risk, and the retrospective rationality of the historian-philosopher who finds an interaction of decisions during conflict that was unknown to the decision-makers.

62. Hoffmann, Stanley. "Une théorie quantitative du nationalisme." 4 Revue française de science politique (1954), 401-405.
    A criticism of Karl W. Deutsch's work on nationalism, the main point of which is that the idea of communication is too material and too mechanistic to account for the whole of nationalism.

63. Kaplan, Morton A. (ed.). New Approaches to International Relations. New York: St. Martin's, 1968, pp. 534.

Product of a 1966 conference at the University of Chicago, this volume includes the following essays, among others: Wohlstetter, "Theory and Opposed-Systems Design"; Kahn, "The Alternative World Futures Approach"; Burns, "Quantitative Approaches to International Politics"; Falk, "New Approaches to the Study of International Law"; Chi, "The Chinese Warlord System as an International System"; Franke, "The Italian City-State System as an International System"; Reinken, "Computer Exploration of the 'Balance of Power': A Project Report."

64. Knorr, Klaus, and Rosenau, James N. (eds.). Contending Approaches to International Politics. Princeton: Princeton University Press, 1969, pp. 297.

Presents articles debating the merits of the scientific and traditional approaches to international politics, three of them originally published in World Politics. For the most part, the articles illustrate the futility of this type of debate except to the extent that it may induce a scholar to reexamine his own efforts and to introduce more rigor into his methods. As methodological guides, the most useful contributions are by J. David Singer, Richard A. Brody, and Johan Galtung.

65. Mathisen, Trygve. Research in International Relations. Oslo: Universitetsforlaget, 1963, pp. x, 238.

A guide to the planning of research projects, the collection of data, and the use of data in the field of international relations.

65-A. Mueller, John E. (ed.). Approaches to Measurement in International Relations. New York: Appleton-Century-Crofts, 1969, pp. 311.

On the study of the arms race, the calculus of deterrence, uses of public opinion data, certain bargaining games, voting studies of international organizations, uses of aggregate data, content analysis, and mathematical and statistical models.

66. Platig, E. Raymond. International Relations Research: Problems of Evaluation and Advancement. Santa Barbara: Clio Press for the Carnegie Endowment for International Peace, 1967, pp. xiv, 211.

A valuable review of the development of international relations as a field of research, with attention to various approaches including interdisciplinary efforts, the research infrastructure, research needs, criteria for the evaluation of research and suggestions for improved evaluative procedures.

67. Ransom, Harry Howe. "International Relations." 30 Journal of Politics (1968), 345-371.

Critical review of eight approaches to the study of international relations, with dangers seen in the two chief concerns of the last 20 years, namely, (1) the aim for more theoretical and scientific research that limits itself to that which can be tested empirically and (2) the urgency to prevent nuclear war that contains the built-in confusion between what ought to be and what is.

68. Raser, John R. "Deterrence Research: Past Progress and Future Needs." 3 <u>Journal of Peace Research</u> (1966), 297-327.

Examines the development of thought on nuclear deterrence in 1945-1957, proposes an analytic framework for the study of deterrence that would include sociological and psychological variables, reviews and evaluates the research since 1958 that fits this framework, and suggests directions for future study.

69. "Research Approaches to the Study of War and Peace." 11 <u>Journal of Social Issues</u> (1955), 1-57.

A psychologically oriented symposium, including such topics as: the peaceful adjustment of international relations; problems and research approaches; research to establish the conditions for peace; the possibility of predicting reactions to international events; psychoanalytic hypotheses in the study of war; governments and people as foci for peace-oriented research; societal, attitudinal, and structural factors in international relations.

69-A. Riggs, Robert E., Hanson, Karen Feste, Heinz, Mary, Hughes, Barry B., and Volgy, Thomas J. "Behavioralism in the Study of the United Nations." 22 <u>World Politics</u> (1970), 197-236.

An analysis and evaluation of behavioral studies of the United Nations as exemplified by articles appearing in 18 English-language political science and international relations quarterlies in which the behavioral articles accounted for 2% of all articles on the United Nations in 1950-1951 and 21% in 1968-1969.

70. Rosenau, James N. (ed.). <u>International Politics and Foreign Policy: A Reader in Research and Theory</u>. New York: Free Press, 1961, pp. xii, 511.

Anthology that provides a representative picture of research and theory in international relations. Major topics: international politics and foreign policy as a subject of study; the international system; the actions of states; theories and approaches; the actions and interactions of states; research techniques and orientations. A number of the essays are individually annotated.

71. Rosenau, James N. (ed.). <u>International Politics and Foreign Policy</u>. Rev. ed. New York: Free Press, 1969, pp. xx, 740.

Fifty-one of the fifty-seven selections are new to this edition and include five previously unpublished articles. Among the selections included are the following: Coplin, "International Law and Assumptions about the State System"; Levi, "The Relative Irrelevance of Moral Norms in International Politics"; Jervis, "Hypotheses on Misperceptions"; Kissinger, "Domestic Structure and Foreign Policy"; Hermann, "International Crisis as a Situational Variable"; Brams, "The Structure of Influence Relations in the International System".

71-A. Rosenau, James N., Davis, Vincent, and East, Maurice A. (eds.). <u>The Analysis of International Politics</u>. New York: Free Press, 1970, pp. 450.

Eighteen original articles on theoretical problems, conceptual foci, and empirical concerns by the editors and fifteen other writers, among them Robert Gilpin who considers the impact of technology on international politics, Richard A. Falk, Charles F. Hermann, Raymond Tanter, Charles A. McClelland, Dina Zinnes, and Cyril E. Black. The essays deal with such matters as explanation, prediction, forecasting, the actors, the external environment, national capabilities, sources of conflict, the development of consensus in the General Assembly, and Russian interpretations of world history.

72. Schwartz, Leonard E. "Social Science and the Furtherance of Peace Research." 9 American Behavioral Scientist (March 1966), 24-28.
Review of types of research relevant to international affairs being supported by government agencies that helps to explain why certain areas of research such as economic matters, military affairs, methods of arms control inspection, and crisis situations--but not factors productive of crisis--dominate the social science literature.

73. Sherif, Muzafer, and Sherif, Carolyn W. (eds.). Interdisciplinary Relationships in the Social Sciences. Chicago: Aldine, 1969, pp. xvi, 360.
Concerned about the difficulties impeding interdisciplinary collaboration and about the failure of the separate disciplines to understand the basis on which collaboration is necessary and possible, the several authors demonstrate means of coordination and delineate promising areas for cooperative research. Among the papers are the following: Muzafer and Carolyn W. Sherif, "Interdisciplinary Coordination as a Validity Check"; Stanley Milgram, "Interdisciplinary Thinking and the Small World Problem"; John Paul Scott, "Biological Basis of Human Warfare"; Sidney H. Aronson, "Obstacles to a Rapprochement between History and Sociology"; Donald T. Campbell, "Ethnocentrism of Disciplines and the Fish-Scale Model of Omniscience."

74. Singer, J. David. "Data Making in International Relations." 10 Behavioral Science (1965), 68-80.
Discusses the difficulty of converting facts into data and focuses on two data-analysis techniques, content analysis and laboratory simulation.

75. Snyder, Richard C. "Some Recent Trends in International Relations Theory and Research." In Austin Ranney (ed.), Essays on the Behavioral Study of Politics. Urbana: University of Illinois Press, 1963, pp. 103-171.
Systematic overview of theory and research in international relations.

76. Snyder, Richard C. "Toward Greater Order in the Study of International Politics." 7 World Politics (1955), 461-478.
Critique of some of the traditional concepts employed in the field of international relations, particularly in five textbooks

serving as the basis of this review article. Seven directions are suggested for research that might lead toward more orderly study of international relations.

76-A. Stone, Anthony R. "The Interdisciplinary Research Team." 5 Journal of Applied Behavioral Research (1969), 351-365.
Analyzes intrateam statuses, rewards, leadership and followers' roles, and inner and outside stress.

77. Stroup, M. Jane. "Problems on Research on Social Conflict in the Area of International Relations." 9 Journal of Conflict Resolution (1965), 413-417.
Discussion of eight approaches to the study of international conflict: (1) historical approach; (2) political analysis; (3) case study; (4) field theory; (5) conflict episode analysis (an adaptation of case study); (6) economic models of conflict; (7) decision theory; (8) game theory.

78. Thompson, Kenneth W. "The Study of International Politics: A Survey of Trends and Developments." 14 Review of Politics (1952), 433-467.
The article includes suggestions concerning the inadequacies of early international law research and a suggestion for research on social forces affecting the likelihood of observance of international law.

79. Ward, Robert E., Bonilla, Frank, Coleman, James S., Hyman, Herbert H., Pye, Lucian W., and Weiner, Myron. Studying Politics Abroad: Field Research in the Developing Areas. Boston and Toronto: Little, Brown, 1964, pp. vii, 245.
Addressed chiefly to political scientists undertaking research in developing areas, this volume attempts to sensitize potential field researchers to the ways in which earlier researchers have coped with methodological and practical problems encountered in documentary research, survey research, interviewing, and observation.

80. Wright, Quincy. A Study of War. 2nd ed. with a commentary on war since 1942. Chicago: University of Chicago Press, 1965, pp. xlii, 1637.
A reissue of the 1942 pioneering study of conflict that not only led the way toward systematic efforts at measurement in international relations but also, by example, points to the goal of integration of historical, legal, behavioral, statistical, and mathematical evidence.

81. Wright, Quincy. "Design for a Research Project on International Conflicts and the Factors Causing Their Aggravation or Amelioration." 10 Western Political Quarterly (1957), 263-275.
Proposes a series of research projects on international conflict to inquire into the relations between conflicting states, their internal structures and policies, processes and procedures of adjustment, and the condition of the entire field of international relations

at the time, e.g., the general level of tension and unrest, degree of interdependence in its several forms, general standards of value and law, and conditions of population, resources, consumption and production, ideology, and world politics.

82. Wright, Quincy. The Study of International Relations. New York: Appleton-Century-Crofts, 1955, pp. 642.
    Excellent examination of the substance and methods of international law and relations, with clear indications of a number of approaches, including interdisciplinary approaches, and their limitations and uses. More importantly, Wright presents his own verbally structured field theory relevant to international relations.

3. Classification and Definition

83. Deutsch, Karl W. "On Theories, Taxonomies, and Models as Communication Codes for Organizing Information." 11 Behavioral Science (1966), 1-17.
    Concerning evaluation of theories, taxonomies, models, and schemes for classification and retrieval of information and suggesting that performance tests of information organizing capacity should include organizing power, predictive range, average error margin, economy of categories, operating rules and social cost of adoption, originality, fruitfulness, and probability of transcending itself. Examples presented are from theories of nationalism, power, and value.

84. Gibbs, Jack P. "The Sociology of Law and Normative Phenomena." 31 American Sociological Review (1966), 315-325.
    An analysis and reformulation of Hohfeld's fundamental legal conceptions to produce a taxonomy of legal relations and laws that is then expanded into a social evaluation of acts in terms of both legal and extra-legal norms. The reformulation is designed to facilitate expression of the divergence between legal and extra-legal norms. The author suggests that his taxonomy can be used to designate the referents of the normative aspects of social integration and anomie.

85. Hartshorne, R. "Suggestions on the Terminology of Political Boundaries." 26 Annals, Association of American Geographers (1936), 56-57.
    An important attempt to clarify geographical terminology and to introduce usages that might retain some consistency, reflect accumulated knowledge, and bear close relationship to the cultural landscape, economic and political functions, and the exercise of state functions.

86. Lasswell, Harold D., and Kaplan, Abraham. Power and Society: A Framework for Political Inquiry. New Haven: Yale University Press, reprinted 1957, pp. xxiv, 295.
    General political theory through the utilization of systematic

techniques of conceptual definition. Major headings: persons; perspectives; groups; influence; power; symbols; practices; functions; structures; processes.

87. van Doorn, J.A.A. "Sociology and the Problem of Power." 1 Sociologia neerlandica (1962-1963), 3-51.
An attempt to classify definitions and forms of power, to comprehend the problem of establishing a lasting order through the acknowledgement of power by its subject, and to identify the directions of evolution of power.

See also nos. 716, 910, 1209, 2230, 2231.

4. Systems Analysis

88. Ashby, W.R. Design for a Brain. New York: Wiley, 1954, 2nd rev. ed. 1960, pp. 286.
Applies a steady state theory to living systems generally, including the brain.

89. Ashby, W. Ross. "The Application of Cybernetics to Psychiatry." 100 Journal of Mental Science (1954), 114-124.
Of heuristic value for the study of social networks, this article includes discussion of the problem of overstability and a statement of "the fundamental law that when a whole system is composed of a number of subsystems, the one that tends to dominate is the one that is least stable. . . ." The article also deals with instability and the probability of a runaway, the memory, and the problem of how the component parts of a nervous system are modified during learning so that the whole can produce integrated rather than chaotic behavior.

90. Bertalanffy, Ludwig von. "Der Organismus als physicalisches System betrachtet." 28 Die Naturwissenschaften (1940), 521-531.
Sets forth the principle that steady states of open systems depend upon system constants more than upon environmental conditions while the environment has a surplus of essential inputs--a principle modified by James G. Miller to take account particularly of the individuality of each system's history. The importance of Bertalanffy's principle is that purposive activities can be explained as open system characteristics rather than by addition of a teleological interpretation such as is often found in legal theory.

91. Bertalanffy, Ludwig von. "General System Theory." 1 General Systems (1956), 1-10.
A concise statement by a mathematical biologist, generally recognized as the intellectual father of the systems orientation in integrated science, of the aims of general system theory as a device for dealing with organized complexity, for integrating the natural and social sciences, for aiming at exact theory in the nonphysical

fields of science, and for integration in scientific education. Attention is accorded the limitations of the closed systems of physical science, the problems of information, entropy, and feedback, causality and teleology in living organisms, and the potential of general system theory as a step toward the unity of science.

92. Bertalanffy, Ludwig von. General System Theory: Foundations, Development, Applications. New York: Braziller, 1969, pp. xvi, 290.
    Ten essays, all but one previously published, restating the general character of system theory in an effort to restore its potential for unification of disciplines in the face of what the author perceives as a tendency of system theory to become just another specialty and even, through centering system science in computer technology, cybernetics, automation, and systems engineering, another technique to shape man and society into a "megamachine."

93. Boulding, Kenneth E. "General Systems Theory--The Skeleton of Science." 2 Management Science (1956), 197-208. Reprinted in 1 General Systems (1956), 11-17.
    Discusses the objective of general systems theory of providing a framework or structure of systems on which to hang the flesh and blood of particular disciplines and particular subject matter in an orderly and coherent manner.

94. Buck, R.C. "On the Logic of General Behavior Systems Theory." In H. Feigl and M. Scriven (eds.), Minnesota Studies in the Philosophy of Science. Vol. I. The Foundations of Science and the Concepts of Psychology and Psychoanalysis. Minneapolis: University of Minnesota Press, 1956, pp. 223-238.
    Contains some criticisms of general systems theory and raises the question of whether a nonhomeostatic system might exist.

95. Buckley, Walter (ed.). Modern Systems Research for the Behavioral Scientist. Chicago: Aldine, 1968, pp. xxv, 525.
    This collection of articles on general systems theory and research begins with an overview and then explores the application of the principle of homeostasis by focusing on the complementary duality of self-regulation and self-direction on the one hand and adaptation and evolution on the other. Such facets of self-regulation and self-direction of psychological systems as the perceptual, the cognitive, and the motivational are examined and followed by assessment of the usefulness of a systems model for studying sociocultural systems.

96. Burgers, J.M. "On the Emergence of Patterns of Order." 69 Bulletin of the American Mathematical Society (1963), 1-25.
    Although limited to the appearance of patterns of order in such manifestations of nonliving nature as crystal structures, fluid motion, and a simplified case of gas motion--in the last case treating the writings of Alfred North Whitehead as a counterpart to statistical work in physics--the article suggests the possibility of a broader point of view that would provide a more complete realization of the concept of order.

97. Burton, J.W. Systems, States, Diplomacy and Rules. New York: Cambridge University Press, 1968, pp. xii, 251.

Arguing that world society should not be considered as made up of separate states but of states that cluster in systems that cut across national boundaries, the author holds that such an approach permits sharper analysis not only of relations among states but also of relations and conflicts between systems and states. Examination of internal interactions and processes of the modern state is followed by examination of the place of power and force in international behavior. A norm is postulated that abnormal behavior occurs when states take actions that either do not satisfy system needs or do not assist adaptation to environmental change.

98. Campbell, Donald T. "Common Fate, Similarity and Other Indices of the Status of Aggregates of Persons as Social Entities." 3 Behavioral Science (1958), 14-25.

With reference to Herbert Spencer's contention that political units or social organizations are organism-like units, the author seeks indices for empirically testing whether an aggregate qualifies as an entity and whether an entity meets the criteria of being an organic system. Use is made of Wertheimer's principles of proximity, similarity, common fate, and pregnance, good continuation, or good figure. The problem of system boundaries is dealt with and multiple diagnosability recommended. Particularly interesting is the suggestion that successive temporal observations might permit development of coefficients of common fate to deal with entativity as a matter of degree. Common fate refers to movement of elements in the same direction permitting their perception as parts of the same organization, and hence what is sought is a more precise statement of the search for common interests and common good that Cicero viewed as the essential bond of any community.

99. Cannon, W.B. Wisdom of the Body. New York: Norton, 1939, pp. xviii, 19-333.

Writing about the concept to which he gave the name "homeostasis," the author raises the question of whether there are not general principles of stabilization applicable on a cross-level basis to organizations of various sorts.

100. Caplow, Theodore. "Organizational Size." 1 Administrative Science Quarterly (1957), 484-505.

Categorization of groups by size that endeavors to relate size to such characteristics as basic form of organization types of interrelationships among members of organizations, and participation of individuals. The article serves as a tentative guide to possible consequences of variance in the number of actors in social systems including the international.

101. Churchman, C. West. The Systems Approach. New York: Delacorte, 1968, pp. xii, 243.

A presentation of the systems approach largely in terms of the arguments of its supporters and detractors that revolve around the objectives or performance measures of a total system, fixed environmental constraints, system resources, components (goals, activities, and measures of performance), and system management.

102. Coleman, James Covington. Personality Dynamics and Effective Behavior. Chicago: Scott, Foresman, 1960, pp. 566.
Textbook in psychology that embodies a conceptualization of living systems.

103. Coppock, Joseph David. International Economic Instability: The Experience after World War II. New York: McGraw-Hill, 1962, pp. 184.
Uses statistical data from 83 countries in an effort to measure differing degrees of instability in post-World War II international economic relations.

104. East, Maurice A., and Gregg, Phillip M. "Factors Influencing Cooperation and Conflict in the International System." 11 International Studies Quarterly (1967), 244-269.
An undertaking, partially successful but raising more questions than it answers, to ascertain whether a nation's domestic conditions or its international conditions account for the greater proportion of its international action and whether the types of conditions that account for its international conflict behavior also account for its cooperative behavior. Among the indices employed are number of treaties, number of threats, number killed in domestic violence, press censorship, ethnic homogeneity, amount of technical assistance received, and number of embassies and legations.

105. Easton, David. A Systems Analysis of Political Life. New York: Wiley, 1965, pp. xvi, 507.
A Dynamic Response Model is used to examine political life. Seven systems are listed as constituents of the total environment: (1) ecological; (2) biological; (3) personality; (4) social; (5) international political; (6) international ecological; (7) international social. Systems 1-4 comprise the intrasocietal environment and systems 5-7, the extrasocietal environment. The flow of effects from the environments generate inputs into, demands upon, and supports for the political system in which authorities use information feedback to convert inputs into outputs affecting the total environment. The model appears rather more like a self-regulating mechanistic model than is necessary, this appearance resulting from underemphasis on the psychological features implied in the inclusion of personality systems among the environmental components.

106. Easton, David. "Limits of the Equilibrium Model in Social Research." 1 Behavioral Science (1956), 86-104.
Considers the applicability of steady state or equilibrium theory to social systems.

107. Goodman, Jay S. "The Concept of 'System' in International Relations Theory." 8 Background (1965), 257-268.
Examines three uses of "system"--system-as-description, system-

as-explanation, and system-as-method--as used by international relations theorists. Confusion of these three uses are examined and the difficulties attendant on intermingled usage are carefully analyzed.

108. Hanrieder, Wolfram F. "Actor Objectives and International Systems." 27 Journal of Politics (1965), 109-132.

An undertaking to deal with the level-of-analysis problem whereby one approach emphasizes the internal predispositions of international actors and a second approach stresses external determinants of goal formation. The author seeks to deal with the problem through frames of reference in the form of sets of internal, external, and systemic referents, not only in respect to states but also to international organizations, which then require correlation.

109. McClelland, Charles A. "Access to Berlin: The Quantity and Variety of Events, 1948-1963." In J. David Singer (ed.), Quantitative International Politics: Insights and Evidence. New York: Free Press, 1968, pp. 159-186.

Examination of data derivable from the New York Times Index on events regarding Berlin, separated into 18 categories and analyzed both in terms of volume and by a measure of relative uncertainty, in an effort to determine whether a "change of state" can be detected in a system's activities in the transition from a noncrisis to a crisis period, whether a designated subsystem (really an events or activity subsystem) that is part of a more general system of action can be discovered to be responsive to significant disturbances of the general system, whether the available data show crises to be "short burst" affairs to be dealt with in progressively routinized form with the passage of time, and whether the level of violence rises during a crisis.

110. McClelland, Charles A. "Applications of General Systems Theory in International Relations." 12 Main Currents in Modern Thought (1955), 27-34.

Reviews von Bertalanffy's exposition of general systems theory and, with reference to Wright's observation that any conceptual framework seeking to reconcile the various approaches to international relations must supply a world view, indicates how general systems theory can perform an integrating function, thereby permitting piecemeal approach to knowledge and encouraging the borrowing from other disciplines without yielding to a planless eclecticism.

111. McClelland, Charles. "Systems and History in International Relations: Some Perspectives for Empirical Research and Theory." 3 General Systems Yearbook (1958), 221-247.

Deals with some aspects of the study of history and of international relations, some of their larger relationships at the present stage of methodological development and prospectively, and the coordinating potential of the idea of dynamic and open systems.

112. Menegazzi, Guido. I Fondamenti dell'ordine vitale dei popoli (Fundamentals of the Vital Order of Nations). Milan: A. Giuffre, 1962.

Analysis of the subjective and objective strengths of various economic and social systems.

113. Miller, James G. "Living Systems: Basic Concepts." 10 Behavioral Science (1965), 193-237. "Living Systems: Structure and Process." Ibid, 337-379. "Living Systems: Cross-Level Hypotheses." Ibid, 380-411.

Three essays on living systems from cell to supranational organization that define terms, distinguish concrete and abstracted systems, identify subsystems and fundamental processes, and generate cross-level hypotheses.

114. Nettl, P. "The Concept of System in Political Science." 14 Political Studies (1966), 305-338.

A general discussion of the status of concepts in social science followed by comparison and contrast of four categories of uses of system concepts: (1) the functional system; (2) system as analogy; (3) system as specific performance structure; (4) system as a problem-solving concept. Some criteria of preference are enunciated and the author's preference for a functional concept not requiring an equilibrium postulate is stated.

115. Parsons, Talcott, and Shils, Edward A. (eds.). Toward a General Theory of Action. Cambridge: Harvard University Press, 1951. Torchbook ed. New York: Harper & Row, 1962, pp. xi, 506.

Besides the basic Parsonian model of an abstracted system that is set forth in the core section by Parsons and Shils on "Values, Motives, and Systems of Action," this volume includes a psychological model elaborated by Edward C. Tolman and essays on the theory of action and its application by Gordon W. Allport, Clyde Kluckhohn, Henry A. Murray, Robert R. Sears, and Samuel A. Stouffer.

116. Powers, W.T., Clark, R.K., and McFarland, R.I. "A General Feedback Theory of Human Behavior." 11 Perceptual and Motor Skills (1960), 71-88. Reprinted in Alfred G. Smith (ed.), Communication and Culture: Readings in the Codes of Human Interaction. New York: Holt, Rinehart and Winston, 1966, pp. 333-343.

Based on the concepts of a system as a collection of functions, of a function as the direct relationship of two or more variables corresponding to physical events that are related by operation of a physical device such as a neural network or a chemical reaction, of a variable as a combination of two classes of percepts one of which does not vary while the other does, and of percepts as basic units of experience self-evident as the taste of salt, a model is constructed of a general feedback control system, the model being intended to help to understand human behavior. A hierarchical concept dominates explanation of the model's operation.

117. Radcliffe-Brown, Alfred R. A Natural Science of Society. Glencoe: Free Press, 1957, pp. 156.

An anthropologist's approach to systems dynamics that constitutes a major contribution to the growth of general systems theory and structural-functional analysis.

118. Robinson, T.W. _Systems Theory and the Communist Orbit_. P-3812. Santa Monica: RAND Corporation, March 1968, pp. 68.

An attempt, using the Banks and Textor data, to analyze the Communist international system that leads to an assessment of the strengths of that approach and its limits when seeking details.

119. Rosecrance, Richard N. _Action and Reaction in World Politics: International Systems in Perspective_. Boston: Little, Brown, 1963, pp. x, 314.

An undertaking to identify nine international systems said to have existed since 1740. A common framework of analysis is employed, providing two sources of actor disturbance, a regulator, environmental constraints, and a pattern of international outcomes as the major elements. The descriptions of the systems, and even their identification and dates of duration, are open to question, a point which the author concedes. A more serious defect lies in the limitation of historical data to what is contained in secondary works, almost exclusively in the English language, thereby leaving the analysis biased by the judgment, preferences, and slogans of historians. Nevertheless, the author's conviction that history is the greatest source of data leads him to a technique for explanation that, with methodological improvement, gives promise for the ultimate employment of historical data to extend knowledge rather than myth.

120. Scott, Andrew M. _The Functioning of the International System_. New York: Macmillan, 1967, pp. xi, 244.

Development of a set of interrelated propositions on international relations that represent an application of general systems theory while also making use of communications theory, perception theory, and conflict analysis.

121. Simon, Herbert A. "The Architecture of Complexity." 106 _Proceedings of the American Philosophical Society_ (1962), 467-482.

Discussion of the desirability and basic nature of a theory of a hierarchical arrangement of interrelated subsystems.

121-A. Singer, J. David. _A General Systems Taxonomy for Political Science_. New York: General Learning Press, 1971, pp. 22.

An argument for a taxonomy based on the general systems concept and employing not particular variables but classes of variables that could aid longitudinal analysis, build a cumulative discipline by permitting constructs to match and mesh, and encourage description prior to attempting explanation.

122. Smoker, Paul. "Nation State Escalation and International Integration." 4 _Journal of Peace Research_ (1967), 61-75.

The author suggests that two systems are currently operative: (1) the internation system in which states are the only actors; (2) the international system that includes international governmental and nongovernmental organizations. Collapse of the weak integrative subsystem in 1914 had no effect on the arms race escalation because integration at that time was an insignificant part of the overall

system. In the 1930s integration had proceeded far enough to matter
and collapse of the subsystem further accelerated the arms race. The
1951-1952 drop in the rate of formation of international nongovernmental organizations is treated as being a result of rising tension
but the stage of integrative development is seen as having been
strong enough to resist and to react back on the escalation system
to slow the arms race.

123. Weiss, P. "Animal Behavior as System Reaction." 4 General Systems (1959), 1-44. Translated and revised from "Tierisches Verhalten als
'Systemreaktion'." 1 Biologia generalis (1925), 167-248.
 Includes a definition of a system as a complex tending to retain
its constancy as a whole, notwithstanding changes in its parts, by
means of active changes in some parts of opposite sign to changes
which have occurred in other parts.

124. Wiener, Norbert. "Cybernetics." 179 Scientific American
(November 1948), 14-18.
 An adaptation from the author's well-known book of the same
title, this article presents a concise statement of the concept of
feedback.

See also nos. 259, 381, 505, 512, 513, 708, 1125, 1130, 1135, 1214,
1783.

5. Structural-Functional Analysis

125. Almond, Gabriel. "A Developmental Approach to Political Systems." 17 World Politics (1965), 183-214.
 Advocates a systematic examination of comparative history, based
on the use of common categories and hypotheses, as an aid to the
study of political development. Social structures are treated as
performers of functions, the latter constituting three categories:
capabilities, conversion functions, and system-maintenance and adaptation functions. Conversion functions are designated as articulation of interests, aggregation, rule-making, application of rules,
adjudication, information. Capability functions are categorized as
extraction of human and material resources, regulation, distribution,
symbolic, and responsive. The author regards functional categories
as permitting comparison of complex political systems and of such
systems with simpler systems.

126. Almond, Gabriel A., and Coleman, James S. (eds.). The Politics
of the Developing Areas. Princeton: Princeton University Press, 1960,
pp. xii, 591.
 Important for its suggested ideas concerning political culture,
given further development by Almond and Verba in The Civic Culture,
and for the exposition of the functional approach that receives further exposition in relation to political development in Almond and
Powell, Comparative Politics: A Developmental Approach.

127. Almond, Gabriel A., and Powell, G. Bingham, Jr. Comparative
Politics: A Developmental Approach. Boston: Little, Brown, 1966, pp.
xv, 348.
      Adaptation of structural-functional analysis and systems theory
to politics, treating political systems at the levels of (1) interaction of the political system, treated as a unit, with the domestic
and the international environment, (2) conversion structures and
processes, and (3) system maintenance and adaptation. Political development receives historical treatment with reference to the experiences in building states and nations and to the development of political participation and concern for welfare. Attention is also focused on the development problems of new and modernizing states. The
work is pointed toward development of a theory of political development.

127-A. Becker, Theodore L. Comparative Judicial Politics: The Political Functionings of Courts. Chicago: Rand McNally, 1970, pp. xvi, 407.
      An application of structural-functional analysis to the study of
judicial politics that includes a plea for the understanding of variation in judicial output as a function of structural variations in
decision processes. Survey research and laboratory experiments are
recommended as devices permitting explicit building of this variation
into research designs.

128. Davis, Kingsley. "The Myth of Functional Analysis as a Special
Method in Sociology and Anthropology." 24 American Sociological Review
(1959), 757-772.
      Demonstrates that the "functional method" is not separate from
prevailing methodologies in sociology and anthropology by tracing
the history of the "functional" concept. The functional method appears to be separate because of the historical separateness of the
two disciplines.

6. Ecological Approaches

129. Caldwell, Lynton K. "Biopolitics: Science, Ethics, and Public
Policy." 54 Yale Review (1964), 1-16.
      Employing the term "biopolitics" to designate political efforts
to reconcile biological facts and popular values, notably ethical
values, the author calls attention to the problem of the relation of
the total organism to the total environment and physiological issues
such as the biochemical control of personality and the amount of
positive harm or deprivation one nation may lawfully inflict upon
the rest of the world while pursuing its "sovereign rights." Wide
gaps between the biological sciences and public policies are regarded
as unlikely to be bridged until a comprehensive biological foundation
is established to permit society to deal effectively with its problems before they become compelling issues. While a technical version
of science may be suitable for lower and more routinized levels of
administration, the science suitable at the higher executive and

legislative levels must be conceptual and expressed in terms meaningful to political and administrative practitioners. The necessary development, with biology central because its concern with life has
made it the integrator of the sciences, requires a continued development of new disciplines to interpenetrate the older ones and thereby
to carry forward the beginnings of needed syntheses as represented by
the behavioral sciences, ecology, regional economics, and biometeor-
ology.

130. Caldwell, Lynton K. "Environment: A New Focus for Public Policy?" 23 Public Administration Review (1963), 132-139.
    A plea for a systematic approach to formulate a comprehensive
environmental policy to guide legislative, administrative, and judicial decision-makers in order to avoid the waste and confusion that
have hitherto resulted from fragmented action and policies affecting
natural resources and man-environmental relationships.

131. Duncan, Otis Dudley, and Schnore, Leo F. "Cultural, Behavioral,
and Ecological Perspectives in the Study of Social Organization." 45
American Journal of Sociology (1959), 132-146.
    A critical comparison of three approaches to the study of social
organization that emphasizes the level-of-analysis problem and suggests that, in employing a framework of human ecology, social structure can be viewed as the dependent variable influenced by population,
environment, and technology. However, the authors prefer a more
sophisticated view of reciprocal relationship of organization to the
other three variables and suggest the use of the term "ecosystem" to
emphasize interrelatedness.

132. Gjessing, Gutorm. "Ecology and Peace Research." 4 Journal of
Peace Research (1967), 125-139.
    Defining ecology in Ernst Haeckel's sense as the interrelated-
ness and transactions of organisms within their geographical environment and thereby excluding the specifically sociological concept, the
author presents a sketch of the ecological background of conflicts in
terms of the conversion of energy through plants and animals. Adherence to habitat (or territory) is treated as prehuman, emotional rather than rational, creating cohesion and, under certain situations
and conditions, structure and rank within groups and maximizing hostility toward the enemy in territorial conflicts. This concept is
joined to Broch and Galtung's assertion (3 Journal of Peace Research
(1966)) that the white race is without comparison the most warlike
and with the economic theory of conflict as related to need for raw
materials, migration from exhausted land, and population pressures.
Acquisition of new instruments is seen as promoting belligerence and,
in our time, undermining the principle of reciprocity and the primitive rituals that once delimited conflicts.

133. Hawley, Amos H. "Ecology and Human Ecology." 23 Social Forces
(1944), 398-405.
    An outstanding exposition of the content and approach of human
ecology, including a critique of several interpretations of ecology.

Ill-suited to direct study of the psychological counterpart of symbiosis, ecology, as a description of communal structure in terms of its overt and visible features, has its distinctive feature in its conception of the adjustment of man to habitat as a process of community development.

134. Huntington, Ellsworth. Mainsprings of Civilization. New York: Wiley, 1945, pp. xii, 660.
Summation of a lifetime's work on the effects of environment on human conduct, with attention also given to heredity.

135. Ivanoff, Dimitry, and Harrison, Daniel. International Environmental Analysis Panel: International Environment, 1965-1975. 2 vols. Santa Monica: Douglas Aircraft Company, 1965.
Report on continuing research by the Douglas Aircraft Company into the nature of the international environment with reference to United States policy objectives. The first volume summarizes political and military environmental trends to be expected in the next decade, while the second volume provides a more detailed treatment of the environmental approach to weapons and space systems requirements.

135-A. Krader, Lawrence. "Environmental Threat and Social Organization." 389 Annals of the American Academy of Political and Social Science (May 1970), 11-18.
With particular attention to water resources, the author takes account of the change from the early American settlers' belief that nature will provide for man's wants to the current feeling that environmental problems threaten social existence. A comparison is made with older Central Asian civilizations where water was not a threat but a blessing and its scarcity was dealt with by practical legal and technical means.

136. McElrath, Dennis C., Grant, Daniel R., and Wengert, Norman. Political Dynamics of Environmental Control. In Lynton K. Caldwell (ed.), Environmental Studies: Papers on the Politics and Public Administration of Man-Environment Relationships. No. I. Bloomington, Indiana: Institute of Public Administration, Indiana University, January 30, 1967, pp. iv, 62.
Three essays on the politics affecting environmental control. Grant's sees little difference between attempts to control environmental change and attempts to produce other changes in the status quo and finds stronger governmental and national leadership to be essential to overcoming resistance at state, local, and personal levels. Wengert's paper on "Perennial Problems of Federal Coordination" notes that natural resources are discrete but the environment a unity and that natural resource policy tends to ignore that unity. Dealing primarily with problems of interagency coordination, Wengert takes note of basic value orientations that impede integration of approach and notes that the problem-solving approaches of American governmental programs impede planning and are in part a reflection of the culture's emphasis on techniques and technology and its low

regard for the planner and the generalist. McElrath's paper on "Public Response to Environmental Problems" emphasizes the failure of the political culture to keep pace with changing environmental relationships, thereby impeding development of a concept of public responsibility for the quality of the physical environment and changes in the political structure needed for meaningful formulation of comprehensive environmental issues essential to legal and policy changes.

137. Mills, Clarence Alonzo. Climate Makes the Man. New York: Harper, 1942, pp. vi, 320.
    A medical expert's discussion of the relation between man and his environment.

138. Odum, Eugene P. "The Strategy of Ecosystem Development." 164 Science (1969), 262-270.
    An examination of ecological development and succession, reviewing the most important concepts and research findings, that stresses the conflict between the "maximum protection" strategy of nature and the "maximum production" strategy of man, the latter suitable for pioneer society but at later stages requiring replacement by symbiosis, birth control, and recycling of resources. The article treats the restriction of land use as an analogue of territoriality.

138-A. Orians, Gordon H., and Pfeiffer, E.W. "Ecological Effects of the War in Vietnam." 168 Science (1970), 544-554.
    Description of the effects of defoliation, bombing, and other military activities on the ecology of Vietnam. Attention is given, among other things, to the formal procedures for requesting defoliation missions, accidental defoliations of rubber plantations near targets, the killing of rubber trees despite the claim of the Chemical Operations Division, US Army, that defoliants cannot kill rubber trees, problems of compensation for defoliation, potential ecological consequences of an estimated 848,000 bomb craters of 1967 and 2,600,000 of 1968, and the consequences of rapid urbanization.

139. Sprout, Harold and Margaret. An Ecological Paradigm for the Study of International Politics. Research Monograph No. 30. Princeton: Center of International Studies, Princeton University, March 1968, pp. 65.
    Around the three integral concepts of environment, environed entities, and entity-environment relationships, the authors construct an ecological paradigm for thought about human affairs in general and about international relations in particular.

140. Sprout, Harold and Margaret. Man-Milieu Relationship Hypotheses in the Context of International Politics. Princeton: Center of International Studies, Princeton University, 1956, pp. 101.
    Important critical examination of theories concerning the relationship of man to his environment that are of particular concern for the study of international affairs.

141. Sprout, Harold and Margaret. The Ecological Perspective on Human Affairs with Special Reference to International Politics. Princeton: Princeton University Press, 1965, pp. xi, 236.

Re-examination of issues discussed in <u>Man-Milieu Relationship</u> in an effort to clarify and set straight a number of semantic and conceptual issues related to theories of politics, particularly the ascription of psycho-ecological behavior to abstract entities. Dealing with such topics as environmental determinism, free-will environmentalism, possibilism, probabilistic models, general theories of explanation, and prediction, the book is an excellent guide to the limits of various approaches that can be employed to discuss relationships between man and environment and serves also as a set of markers of channels of clear thought and exposition.

142. Strausz-Hupé, Robert (ed.). "Society and Ecology." 11 <u>American Behavioral Scientist</u> (July-August 1968), entire issue, pp. 48.
Among others, the following articles are included: Robert L. Pfaltzgraff, Jr., "Ecology and the Political System"; Britton Harris, "A Technology of Social Progress"; Aurelio Peccei, "World Problems in the Coming Decades"; John McHale, "Global Ecology: Toward the Planetary Society"; Robert Rienow, "Manifesto for the Sea".

142-A. Wilson, Thomas W., Jr. <u>International Environmental Action: A Global Survey</u>. New York: Dunellen, 1971, pp. 366.
A survey of the political, legal, social, and economic aspects of the environmental crisis and national and international efforts to manage it.

7. Anthropological Approaches

143. Alger, Chadwick F. "Comparison of Intranational and International Politics." 57 <u>American Political Science Review</u> (1963), 406-419. Also in R. Barry Farrell (ed.), <u>Approaches to Comparative and International Politics</u>. Evanston: Northwestern University Press, 1966, pp. 301-328.
Suggests bridges between international relations and anthropology to deal more adequately with political socialization and recruitment, interest articulation and aggregation, and political communication. Anthropological writings emphasize the importance of political roles, challenge assumptions that force and certain kinds of governmental institutions are necessary for social order, and suggest the stages of political development when such roles can be introduced. The author seeks to avoid erroneous distinctions between intranational and international politics that result from biased samples of both, failure to see nations as multiple actors, and the assumption that international systems have no environment.

144. Barkun, Michael. "International Norms: An Interdisciplinary Approach." 8 <u>Background</u> (1964), 121-130.
Reviews some of the recent literature that points in directions linking international law and other facets of international relations more closely together. More importantly, the objective of a genuinely

cross-cultural and cross-historical theory of law is set forth and
certain anthropological studies are employed to suggest the possibility of developing an ethnography of international relations and
international law.

145. Barkun, Michael. Law without Sanctions: Order in Primitive
Societies and the World Community. New Haven: Yale University Press,
1968, pp. 179.
        Amalgamation of concepts and findings from studies of anthro-
pology, social psychology, jurisprudence, and international law in
an effort to develop a theoretical framework to embrace such decentralized systems as primitive law and international law. Attention
is accorded models of segmentary lineage and of international structure, manipulation of symbols and facts, the concept of jural community, the relation of law to perception, the function of law as a
model, and transformation from dyadic to triadic interactions entailing both implicit and explicit mediation.

146. Beattie, John. Other Cultures: Aims, Methods and Achievements
in Social Anthropology. New York: Free Press, 1964, pp. xii, 283.
        Description and analysis of method and substance in social an-
thropology including chapters on "Social Control: Political Organization" and "Social Control: Law and Social Sanctions."

147. Bohannan, Paul. Justice and Judgment Among the Tiv. London:
Oxford, 1957, pp. xiii, 221.
        Standard work on judicial procedure in a segmentary society.

148. Bohannan, Paul. Social Anthropology. New York: Holt, Rinehart and Winston, 1963, pp. 421.
        Sets up cross-culturally applicable framework for legal analy-
sis through the study of "event sequences". Includes discussions
of primitive feud and international war and diplomacy.

149. Campbell, Donald T. "The Informant in Quantitative Research."
60 American Journal of Sociology (1955), 339-342.
        The anthropological use of the informant is distinguished from
the social survey in that the respondents are selected not for their
representativeness but rather on the bases of informedness and ability to communicate with social scientists. As such, the method seems
to have general social science utility.

150. Easton, David. "Political Anthropology." In B. Siegel (ed.),
Biennial Review of Anthropology, 1959. Stanford: Stanford University
Press, 1959, pp. 210-262.
        A political scientist seeks politically significant anthropo-
logical materials, particularly on stateless political systems.
Easton also presents an analytic framework for primitive and complex
systems, together with a well-annotated bibliography.

151. Foster, George McClelland. Traditional Cultures: And the Impact of Technological Change. New York: Harper & Row, 1962, pp. 292.

Cultural, social, and psychological aspects of technical aid and technological change, especially in traditional rural communities.

152. Gluckman, Max. Politics, Law, and Ritual in Tribal Society. Chicago: Aldine, 1965, pp. xxxii, 339.

A comprehensive presentation of the author's work and the most comprehensive treatment to date of political anthropology. Data from 41 non-Western societies, 27 of them African, are employed in a search for "invariant relations" in economic life, politics, law, and ritual. Among other things, civil strife, dispute settlement, and ritual adjustment receive attention.

153. Gluckman, Max. The Ideas in Barotse Jurisprudence. New Haven: Yale University Press, 1965, pp. xx, 299.

Draws Barotse concepts into the wider field of legal theory to show that the more important the legal issues, the more imprecise become their definitions, thereby rendering the definitions applicable to very wide ranges of problems. The analysis is stimulated by Glanville Williams' five articles in volumes 61 and 62 of the Law Quarterly Review (1945-1946). Gluckman's work calls particular attention to the Barotse objective of reconciliation of the litigants in the circumstance of crosscutting allegiances in which judicial solutions at the expense of one litigant would endanger parts of the whole structure. The study is in part comparative in that it identifies parallels in fundamental issues of early British and Roman law, in other African systems, and in some Polynesian and Southeast Asian native systems.

154. Kluckhohn, Clyde. "Anthropology in the Twentieth Century." In Guy S. Metraux and François Crouzet (eds.), The Evolution of Science. New York: Mentor, 1963.

Of interest for its critique of social anthropology.

155. Kluckhohn, Clyde. "Common Humanity and Diverse Cultures." In Daniel Lerner (ed.), The Human Meaning of the Social Sciences. New York: Meridian, 1959, pp. 245-284.

Author treats anthropology in general and cultural anthropology in particular in this essay. He notes in what ways the anthropological viewpoint is a source of disturbance to many, and includes a treatment of both the limitations and strengths of the anthropological method. He shows how the discipline has its roots in linguistics and notes certain tools anthropology has drawn from linguistics. He treats the question of cultural relativity and draws an analogy between culture and personalities: each is distinct yet similar and comparable.

156. Llewellyn, Karl N., and Hoebel, E. Adamson. The Cheyenne Way. Norman: University of Oklahoma Press, 1941, pp. ix, 360.

Includes the first explicit formulation of ideas derivable from Gierke and Ehrlich, namely, that within a society there is a multiplicity of legal systems and points up the erroneous impression that can result when the focus is upon a society as an undifferentiated entity that possesses an all-embracing legal system.

157. Murdock, George P. Culture and Society. Pittsburgh: University of Pittsburgh Press, 1965, pp. xii, 376.
    Essays in cultural anthropology that deal with such topics as anthropology's relationship to other disciplines, nature of culture, social organization, cross-cultural comparisons, and the dynamics of cultural change.

158. Nader, Laura (ed.). "The Ethnography of Law." 67 American Anthropologist (December 1965), entire issue.
    Special publication, providing an introductory historical review and a brief summary of the sociology of law and anthropological studies of conflict.

159. Scarritt, James R. Political Change in a Traditional African Clan: A Structural-Functional Analysis of the Nsits of Nigeria. Monograph Series in World Affairs. Monograph No. 3, 1964-1965. The Social Science Foundation and Graduate School of International Studies, University of Denver, 1965, pp. 54.
    Review of the traditional system of the Nsits, the impact of changes attempted by the colonial power, and the persistence of traditionalism and parochialism in independence with reference to the judicial as well as to the political system. The problems of lack of common values and differing British and indigenous views of legitimacy are discussed and their effects illustrated.

160. Schapera, Isaac. Government and Politics in Tribal Societies. London: Watts, 1956, pp. 238.
    On the ground that communities such as the Bergdama and the Bushmen enjoy an orderly existence without courts and without their chiefs being able to punish in other ways, the author rejects the possibility of defining "political organization" as something inevitably associated with the monopoly or the legitimate use of force. Instead, political organization is treated as that aspect of the total organization that establishes and maintains internal cooperation and external independence--functions treated as the only ones common to all governments. However, order without organized physical force is restricted to small communities. Cooperative activities are presumed to precede organized exercise of coercive authority which is viewed as emerging only in a widened range of activity and complexity.

161. Swartz, Marc J., Tuden, Arthur, and Turner, Victor W. (eds.). Political Anthropology: An Introduction. Chicago: Aldine, 1966, pp. viii, 309.
    Includes three insightful articles on conflict control and resolution that employ some of the newer anthropological concepts.

See also nos. 600, 997, 1148, 1152, 1215, 1254, 1668, 1673, 1676, 1679, 1681, 1682, 1800, 1833, 1835, 2417.

8. Comparative Methods

162. Apter, David E. "A Comparative Method for the Study of Politics." 44 American Journal of Sociology (1958), 221-237.

Proposes a model of three dimensions--social stratification, political groups, and government--each dimension composed of a set of variables, with empirical clustering of the variables being the expected outcome of comparative study.

163. Finer, S.E. "Metodo, ambito e fini dello studio comparato dei sistemi politici." 3 Studi politici (1954), 26-43.

Criticisms of comparative approaches do not apply to the construction of generalizations establishing the formal fact that reciprocal causal relations exist between a determinate number of factors, i.e., to a general theory of functional interdependencies. Such a theory establishes only formal relationships and leaves individual values to be established only ad hoc and uniquely.

164. Gregg, Phillip M., and Banks, Arthur S. "Dimensions of Political Systems: Factor Analysis of A Cross-Polity Survey." 59 American Political Science Review (1965), 602-614.

Using aggregate data primarily from A Cross-Polity Survey, 68 variables, some making use of qualitative data treated in the form of nominal scales, are factor-analyzed to produce seven factors related to types of political systems.

165. Gurr, Ted. New Error-Compensated Measures for Comparing Nations: Some Correlates of Civil Violence. Research Monograph No. 25. Princeton: Center of International Studies, Princeton University, May 1966, pp. v, 126.

Proposes an "optimal interval" technique for reducing the effects of error in cross-national comparisons employing aggregate data. A demonstration is given in the form of new measures of government fiscal performance, group discrimination and separatism, labor unionization, and size of internal security forces. The measures employed, dealing with 119 polities, are intended for use in comparative study of the origins of civil violence.

166. Haas, Michael. "Aggregate Analysis." 19 World Politics (1966), 106-121.

Review article, based on Banks and Textor, A Cross-Polity Survey, Ginsburg, An Atlas of Economic Development, and Russett, et al., World Handbook of Political and Social Indicators, that deals with the uses of aggregate data and problems arising when aggregate data is employed, particularly in cross-national work seeking generalization.

166-A. Holt, Robert T., and Turner, John E. (eds.). The Methodology of Comparative Research. New York: Free Press, 1970, pp. 352.
Studies on such matters as the comparison of whole political systems, cross-cultural surveys, linguistic methods, and diachronic methods.

167. Kalleberg, Arthur L. "The Logic of Comparison: A Methodological Note on the Comparative Study of Political Systems." 19 World Politics (1966), 69-82.
Research note intended to clarify the logical requirements of classification and comparison: (1) careful distinction between classification and comparison; (2) properly defined comparative concepts; (3) specification of operational definitions of the criteria or dimensions employed in the conceptual framework.

167-A. Merritt, Richard L. Systematic Approaches to Comparative Politics. Chicago: Rand McNally, 1970, pp. xiii, 264.
Reviews the uses and limitations of quantitative data in comparative research, types and analysis of aggregative data, cross-national content analysis and survey research, elite studies, and such related matters as surveys with limited samples, political anthropology, and the cross-cultural study of personality.

168. Merritt, Richard L., and Rokkan, Stein (eds.). Comparing Nations: The Use of Quantitative Data in Cross-National Research. New Haven: Yale University Press, 1966, pp. xv, 584.
Conference papers discussing the most significant projects using quantitative data in international social science research.

169. Mohanna, Mohamed Fouad Ismail. Le rôle du juge dans le droit anglais et dans le droit de l'Islam comparés. Paris: Rousseau, 1930.
A helpful examination of judicial roles in quite different legal systems, based essentially on secondary sources. Above all, the volume suggests a topical organization for a deeper penetration of the subject, with less reliance on secondary sources and traditional conceptualizations. The study is not really comparative but rather a study composed of two sections.

170. Sartori, G. "Lo studio comparato dei regimi e sistemi politici (considerazioni introduttive)." 3 Studi politici (1954), 7-25.
This introductory article in an issue devoted to comparative research problems insists upon the noninterchangeability of the concepts "state" and "government". The former is an abstract notion while the latter relates to concrete political problems. Comparative political studies imply a convergence of these two currents through two preoccupations, one tending to open a window on the world and the other tending to provide an instrument of control in the development of general theory. It is important to bear in mind that comparison is a middle road between analogy and contrast, to define relations between practice and scientific investigation, to specify whether a general theory precedes or follows comparison of given facts, and to distinguish particularist methods of comparison and the generalist methods of political science.

171. Scarrow, H.A. "The Scope of Comparative Analysis." 25 Journal of Politics (1963), 565-577.

Two aspects of the comparative approach can be identified: (1) comparative research, and (2) comparative description. Comparative research takes the forms of attribute survey, trend analysis, attribute uniformities and sequential regularities, cross-unit testing of behavior hypotheses, variable analysis, and analytical schemes. Comparative description may be merely parallel description or, at a higher level, analysis of two or more systems in terms of a particular focus. Although unfashionable, comparative description is the logical outgrowth of comparative research.

172. Sjoberg, Gideon. "The Comparative Method in the Social Sciences." 22 Philosophy of Science (1955), 106-117.

The author surveys obstacles to a comparative science of society. He notes the ethnocentricity of American social scientists and a need for invariant points of reference, i.e., universal categories which should permit the testing of hypotheses in a cross-cultural setting. On the question of whether social scientists should choose concrete or abstract categories, he suggests a compromise somewhere between these two extremes. Invariant points of interest need to be integrated into a logically consistent system which could develop from the logico-mathematical tradition. Sampling-process problems also exist--there is a need to standardize observations. It is necessary to gather contradictory evidence, including both deviant and unique cases, to reformulate the supposedly invariant points of reference and the hypotheses being tested.

9. Cross-Cultural Approaches

173. Banks, Arthur S., and Textor, Robert B. A Cross-Polity Survey. Cambridge: MIT Press, 1963, pp. x, 1476.

Quantitative comparisons of states along a number of dimensions including the type of legal system.

174. Bharucha-Reid, R.P. "Appearance and Reality in Culture." 57 Journal of Social Psychology (1962), 169-193.

Cautions against acceptance of experimental results in the cross-cultural field owing to inept performance of experiments. One study is analyzed at length to reveal insufficient preliminary acquaintance with the culture, inadequate theoretical framework, and faulty experimental design. The author remarks that such studies and the inferences drawn from them increase misunderstanding of cultures.

175. Campbell, Donald T. "Cooperative Multinational Opinion Sample Exchange." 24 Journal of Social Issues (1968), 245-256.

Finding that much too much multinational social psychology research bears an American stamp, the author calls for research machinery to distribute initiative among all nations and presents a model for low budget research that can overcome the asymmetrical distribution of research funds that stands in the way of true multinational comparisons.

176. Crow, Wayman J., and Raser, John R. <u>A Cross-Cultural Simulation Study</u>. A Report to Project Michelson under Contract #N60530-10134, NOTS, China Lake, California. Ditto. La Jolla: Western Behavioral Sciences Institute, November 20, 1964, pp. 18.

  Replication of the WINSAFE II study (Raser and Crow, <u>infra,</u> no. 423), employing Mexican subjects in two runs conducted at the National University of Mexico. Similarities and differences in response of U.S. and Mexican participants are reported. Differences included the following: much greater exchange of messages by Mexican participants; more emphasis by Mexicans on such international issues as peace, disarmament, and the international organization; less emphasis, almost neglect, of internal economic growth by the Mexicans; more sharing of power with other cabinet members by the Central Decision Maker in the Mexican runs; more emphasis upon the form of communication, for the most part ignored by participants in the U.S. runs, as opposed to content; systematic differences in response to the questionnaire that appeared to be related to a culturally based Mexican predisposition to respond passively to frustration and stress by accommodation to environmental features, as contrasted with a tendency of U.S. participants to respond actively by attempting to change the frustrating or stress-inducing aspect of the environment.

177. Eisenstadt, S.N. "Primitive Political Systems: A Preliminary Comparative Analysis." 61 <u>American Anthropologist</u> (1959), 200-220.

  Objects to the Fortes-Evans-Pritchard approach that distinguishes "segmentary" and "centralized" primitive societies and to the Colson-Gluckman-Peristiany approach that endeavors to show that basic common mechanisms for social control exist in all primitive societies. The author prefers to distinguish societies on the basis of the extent to which different types of political functions are performed by different specialized units determined by multiple variables, i.e., by laws of social differentiation, societal goals, and available resources.

178. Hanna, William John. "Image-Making in Field Research: Some Tactical and Ethical Problems of Research in Tropical Africa." 9 <u>American Behavioral Scientist</u> (1965), 15-20.

  Report on problems of presenting oneself to the people of Nigeria and Uganda in a manner that will elicit responses to interviews. Exposition brings to the fore and clarifies points related to attitudes toward Europeans and Americans that differ from attitudes attributed to Africans by non-Africans, thereby raising the question of perception.

179. Hoffmann, M. "Recherches sur les opinions et les attitudes en Afrique occidentale." 15 <u>Revue internationale des sciences sociales</u> (1963), 61-71.

  On the basis of three attitude surveys conducted in West Africa between 1958 and 1961 the author identifies basic problems encountered in the conduct of such surveys, including the inevitable presence of the village chief at interviews.

180. Hunt, W.H., Crane, W.W., and Wahlke, J.C. "Interviewing Political Elites in Cross-Cultural Comparative Research." 70 American Journal of Sociology (1964), 59-68.

       Recital of factors affecting access and response in three nations. Among those interviewed were a high number of American, French, and Austrian legislators.

181. Siegman, A.W. "A Cross-Cultural Investigation of the Relationship between Ethnic Prejudice, Authoritarian Ideology, and Personality." 63 Journal of Abnormal and Social Psychology (1961), 654-655.

       Employing subjects at an Israeli university, the author concludes that the outcome of the tests provided validation of the major conclusions in Adorno, et al., The Authoritarian Personality, and that ethnocentrism is a generalized trait.

182. Theodorson, George A. "The Feasibility of International Co-operation in Conducting Cross-Cultural Research." 12 Journal of Human Relations (1964), 309-311.

       A brief report on a sociological study begun in 1957 and entailing the cooperative efforts of scholars in the United States, Burma, India, Singapore, and Costa Rica in the administration of a basically identical 80-item questionnaire.

183. "Transcultural Studies in Cognition." Edited by A. Kimball Romney and Roy Goodwin D'Andrade. 66 American Anthropologist (No. 3, Part 2, June 1964). Entire issue, pp. 253.

       Linguistic, anthropological, and psychological approaches to the knowledge-gathering processes in different societies.

184. Wilson, E.C., and Armstrong, L. "Enquêtes et enquêteurs en Inde." 15 Revue internationale des sciences sociales (1963), 49-60.

       Problems of preparing interviewers in India in the absence of specialization of research personnel and in the face of the need to prepare to meet the difficulties of getting clear responses expressive of the individual opinions of those interviewed.

185. Wülker, G. "Les questionnaires en Asie: organisation et possibilités de sondages d'opinion." 15 Revue internationale des sciences sociales (1963), 36-48.

       Problems of designing questionnaires suitable for survey research among the various peoples of Asia.

See also nos. 1681, 1682, 2417.

10. Intertemporal Approaches

186. Bozeman, Adda B. Politics and Culture in International History.
Princeton: Princeton University Press, 1960, pp. xiii, 560.
        A most important study in international politics and law, inter-
cultural relations, and the backgrounds of nations that today are
probing into their past in an effort to rediscover principles that
supported their cultures, which brings to Western students of international affairs not only information about the Graeco-Roman and medieval past up to 1500 A.D. but also about the ancient Near East,
China, the Muslim Empire, Sino-Indian relations, and Byzantium.

187. Naroll, Raoul. Method of Study: Northridge Deterrence Project,
Report No. 34. Report to Project Michelson, U.S. Naval Ordnance Test Station, China Lake, California. Mimeo. Northwestern University, June 15,
1964, pp. ii, 84, 84a-c.
        Report on the method of procedure employed in the study of de-
terrence in history in various parts of the world during decades a
century apart from 376-367 B.C. to 1776-1785 A.D. Problems encountered, including those related to historian's accounts, are
dealt with in an instructive manner.

188. Ruiz Moreno, Isidoro. El derecho internacional publico antes
de la era christiana. Buenos Aires: Faculty of Law and Social Sciences,
1946, pp. 554.
        Rests proof of the existence of pre-Christian systems of inter-
national law and relations on analysis of religious, literary, and
scientific works and on archeological evidence. Ancient systems are
treated as affording bases for comparative analysis and as evidence
that international law, in some form or other and with a number of
rules that are similar despite systematic differences, is as old as
human culture.

189. Warriner, Doreen (ed.). Contrasts in Emerging Societies:
Readings in the Social and Economic History of South-Eastern Europe in
the Nineteenth Century. Selected and translated by G.F. Cushing, E.D.
Tappe, V. de S. Pinto, and Phyllis Auty. London: The Athlone Press,
University of London, 1965, pp. xx, 402.
        Translation of a wide range of selections from 18th and 19th
century writers, including Hungarian, Rumanian, Bulgarian, and Yugoslav economists and historians and German, French, Italian, and English travelers in Eastern Europe. These selections provide guides
to identification of that which is recurrent in economic development
and even in emergence from subordination to an imperial overlord and
to further probing of the nature of the recurrent without confusion
with that which is unique to particular societies and particular
cultures.

11. Historical Sociology

190. Aron, Raymond. "Une Sociologie des rélations internationales".
4 Revue française de sociologie (1963), 307-320.
Aron notes the spontaneous antinomy between a sociologist of
social systems and one of international relations. The former, when
he approaches international relations, tries to find there the equivalent of a social system, i.e., social consensus and roles, without
always realizing that the originality of international relations consists precisely in that they do not take place in a system in the
sense that there is a social system in a civil state. He discusses
the relationship between two propositions: that of the novelty introduced by industrial society in the progressive reduction of profit-
earning as a result of conquest in comparison to the rentability of
productive work; and the optimistic conclusion that peace rather than
war will prevail as a result of this condition. The danger involved
here is that of forgetting that as long as there is a plurality of
political sovereignties, each in the last analysis being judge of war
or peace, there cannot be a common civilization, in the sense of a
single social system. For Aron, the specific character of international relations consists of the relations between men who kill each
other. He notes that an element of recognition of the humanity of
the enemy always appears. One of the aspects which to him appears
the most interesting is that of looking in each diplomatic system
for the total of nonwritten rules, of values more or less respected
by the combatants. He poses the question of whether the competition
of rival sovereignties suffices to conserve an international system
which in essence is not different from the international system of
the past and answers in the affirmative. He concludes that as long
as the essence of international relations (the plurality of sovereignties) exists, the central point of study will be the theory of
decision. The limit of sociology as applied to international relations is that it is possible only to suggest what the rational conduct is--it cannot be imposed.

191. Cahnman, Werner J., and Boskoff, Alvin (eds.). Sociology and
History: Theory and Research. New York: Free Press, 1964, pp. xix, 596.
The several authors argue for a humanistic sociology based upon
awareness of the processes of history. After a survey of efforts in
these directions, areas for future collaboration between sociologists
and historians are suggested. International law specialists may be
able to find inspiration for generation of studies in their own field
that would contribute to a more adequate history of international law
and its place in world affairs.

192. Hoffmann, Stanley. The State of War: Essays in the Theory and
Practice of International Politics. New York: Praeger, 1965, pp. x, 276.
Includes an appraisal of modern theoretical analyses of international politics and an argument for an historical sociology of world
politics and international law.

192-A. Johnson, Harry M. "The Relevance of the Theory of Action to Historians." 50 Social Science Quarterly (1969), 46-58.

The question of relevance to historians is based on analyses of the hierarchy of control, levels of social structure, functional interchanges, equilibrium and change, and the progressive synthesis.

See also no. 525.

12. Quantitative Historical Analysis

193. Aydelotte, William O. "Quantification in History." 71 American Historical Review (1966), 803-825.

A stylistically easy review of the uses and limitations of quantitative methods, correcting some common misconceptions among historians including confusion between methodological and data deficiencies, and calling attention to some of the relatively few uses of quantitative methods by historians. The author notes that for most historical studies descriptive statistics will suffice.

194. Berkhofer, Robert F. A Behavioral Approach to Historical Analysis. New York: Free Press, 1969, pp. ix, 339.

A study of the theoretical bases for the derivation and synthesis of facts from historical evidence that integrates concepts from the social sciences and philosophies of history. Particularly useful are the chapters on systems analysis and the organization of the observer's viewpoint and on historical explanation and synthesis in behavioral perspective.

195. Braudel, Fernand. "History and the Social Sciences: The Long Duration." 3 Prod Translations (February 1960), 3-13.

Analysis of the relationship (or lack of one) between history and the social sciences, indicating potential points of useful contact. Untranslated, the article appears in: Annales: Économies, Sociétés, Civilisations (No. 4, October-December 1958), 725-753.

196. Crozier, Dorothy. "History and Anthropology." 17 International Social Science Journal (1965), 561-570.

On the relationships between historical and anthropological approaches and the limits thereof in light of the statistical noncomparability of historical data and anthropological field-work data, despite the utility of anthropological concepts for historical studies.

197. Davis, Lance E., Hughes, Jonathan R.T., and McDougall, Duncan M. American Economic History: The Development of the National Economy. Homewood, Illinois: Irwin, 1961, pp. 408.

American economic history is presented through a model cast in terms of the process of economic growth and development. Quantitative measures of production increases are not of themselves regarded as criteria of economic growth and development. Changes in the processes of production are the preferred criteria. Nonindustrialization

and underdevelopment are not regarded as synonymous, New Zealand and
Denmark, for example, being essentially nonindustrial but hardly
underdeveloped. Thus, building factories is not regarded as a precondition of development, even though many new countries make the
mistake of believing that development requires factories. The account then proceeds on the basis of the model, concern with law being confined to United States law. The chapter on foreign trade
calls attention, among other things, to the contradiction between
the policies of protectionism and of multilateralism when pursued
simultaneously. For students of international law, the primary
value of the book lies less in its substance than in the adaptability of the model for use in more precise analysis than heretofore of
the impact of international economic developments upon the growth of
international law and of international norms and procedures upon international economic development and of the interrelations of both
with national economic policies and special interests.

198. Deane, Phyllis, and Cole, W.A. British Economic Growth, 1688-
1959: Trends and Structure. New York: Cambridge University Press, 1962,
pp. xvi, 348.
       With acute awareness of the pitfalls, the authors undertook to
establish the main quantitative features of the British economy over
as long a period as the available statistics would allow, thereby
opening a way to a better use of data concerning the past and, for
the field of international law, helping to account for the nature
and intensity of British influence at various periods upon that law
with greater precision than by generalized references to economic
power, overseas enterprise, and naval strength.

199. Deluz-Chiva, Ariane. "Anthropology, History and Historiography."
17 International Social Science Journal (1965), 571-582.
       Discusses variations in relations between anthropology and his-
tory, as well as different anthropological trends and schools, such
as evolutionism, diffusionism, functionalism, and structuralism.
Anthropologists have contributed their data to the historian for
peoples whose traditional outlook did not include the idea of "objective" history. The author feels that the anthropologist must put
himself at the service of historiography.

200. Dovring, Folke. History as a Social Science. The Hague:
Nijhoff, 1960, pp. 97.
       Includes the suggestion that by the use of appropriate tech-
niques history can identify key empirically determinable variables
in social processes and can model their interaction over time.

201. Lewis, I.M. The Modern History of Somaliland: From Nation to
State. New York: Praeger, 1965, pp. xi, 234.
       An anthropologist turned historian presents an excellent exam-
ple of the potential for synthesis of anthropological with traditional historical data as he deals with the history of the Somali
nation in search of a country. National consciousness was aroused
in 1900-1920 in consequence of Sayyid Muhammed's unsuccessful holy

war against a Christian threat but today is frustrated by the general African position that nation-building must take place within the state boundaries established by European imperialists rather than in pursuit of irridentist policies such as that of the Somali Republic.

202. Lorwin, V.R. "The Comparative Analysis of Historical Change: Nation-Building in the Western World." 17 International Social Science Journal (1965), 594-606.

    On the need for cooperation between historians and other social scientists to study the processes of nation-building and integration in Western Europe, together with some reminders of the characteristics of the work done by most professional historians that the author wants taken into account in order to minimize the illusions that could impede cooperation.

203. McRandle, James H., and Quirk, James P. "An Interpretation of the German 'Risk Fleet' Concept." Mimeo. Paper delivered at the Econometric Society meetings, December 30, 1960, pp. 48. Abstract in 29 Econometrica (1961), 475-476.

    An attempt to explore the possibilities of probabilistic models in interpreting problems of historical analysis, this paper by an historian and an economist makes use of statistics on naval power in 1899-1914 to analyze the naval arms race between Great Britain and Germany. Probability of German victory at various points in time are calculated through use of a model of naval warfare, "Lanchester's square law" as modified by probabilitiy analysis. The model, which is applicable only to forces composed of homogeneous units, is justifiable since the measure employed by political and naval leaders in estimating naval strength was numbers of battleships to 1910 and of dreadnaughts thereafter.

204. North, Douglass C. The Economic Growth of the United States, 1790-1860. New York: Prentice-Hall, 1961. Norton Paperback ed., 1966, pp. xv, 304.

    Quantitative study of United States economic history over a 70-year period that includes two chapters on the international economic setting and international economic flows for the periods 1790-1814 and 1815-1860. Included are surveys of shipping and data in the form of a United States shipping activity index and a table comparing the net earnings of U.S. and foreign ships.

205. Rashevsky, N. Looking at History Through Mathematics. Cambridge: MIT Press, 1968, pp. xiii, 199.

    On the application of mathematical tools and models to the study of history.

206. Rudin, S. Argument for a Psychology of History. Paper presented at the annual meeting of the American Psychological Association, Cincinnati, 1959.

    An appeal for a reexamination of historical events that makes use of psychological tools and findings.

13. Mathematical Models and Methods; Other Formal Models

207. Alker, Hayward R., Jr. Mathematics and Politics. New York: Macmillan; London: Collier-Macmillan, 1965, pp. viii, 152.
An illustration of ways in which certain important ideas in mathematics may increase our understanding of politics.

208. Arrow, Kenneth J., Karlin, Samuel, and Suppes, Patrick (eds.). Mathematical Methods in the Social Sciences, 1959; Proceedings. Stanford Symposium on Mathematical Methods in the Social Sciences. Stanford: Stanford University Press, 1960, pp. viii, 365.
A collection of mathematical models proposed by several authors. The models relate to economics (efficiency of resource allocation, stability, capital accumulation, consumer behavior), management science (inventory problems, nonlinear programming), and psychology (learning theory, theory of measurement, testing).

209. Boudon, R. "Methodes d'analyse causale." 6 Revue française de sociologie (1965), 24-43.
Discussion of certain statistical methods for causal analysis. Multivariate analysis is seen as permitting treatment only of relatively simple causal structures. Statistical techniques such as regression analysis permit only consideration of particular structures and permit only analysis of causality related to those structures. More powerful is analysis of dependence which represents an extension of regression analysis, which has a basis in causal models used by economists and provides grounds for classification on the basis of formal characteristics of structures of causality.

210. Charlesworth, James C. (ed.). Mathematics and the Social Sciences. Philadelphia: American Academy of Political and Social Science, 1964, pp. vi, 121.
Paired essays on the uses and limitations, respectively, of mathematics in economics, political science, and sociology.

211. Claunch, John M. (ed.). Mathematical Applications in Political Science. Dallas: The Arnold Foundation, Southern Methodist University, 1965, pp. vi, 85.
Four essays, circulated to a National Science Foundation conference on uses of mathematics, deal with (1) stochastic process models and their fit to Supreme Court decisions, Senate roll calls, and state election returns, (2) the conversion of assumptions about international political processes to arithmetical statements, (3) the application of set theory to voting or decision-making in legislatures or committees, and (4) a statistical model adopted to fit data on the relationship of publics to representation in Congress. Harold Guetzkow's essay on international processes is perhaps the most valuable contribution from the point of view of benefit to the uninitiated since it illustrates initial steps in building descriptive models for formal theory or for simulation and describes choices and compromises in early stages of research that are seldom reported.

212. Coleman, James S. Introduction to Mathematical Sociology. New York: Macmillan, 1964, pp. xiv, 554.

One of the essential guides to the uses of mathematical methods. The study includes the most extensive and most imaginative treatment (especially pp. 103-240) of multiple relationships among qualitative attributes of nations and of foreign policy makers. The volume thus provides foundations for extension of the techniques, appropriately adapted, to international legal studies.

213. Fagen, Richard R. "Some Contributions of Mathematical Reasoning to the Study of Politics." 55 American Political Science Review (1961), 888-899.

In the course of a bibliographical essay, Fagen covers normative theory and the democratic process, social choice and individual values, the study of power, international politics and strategy, and judicial behavior.

214. Johnston, John. Econometric Methods. New York: McGraw-Hill, 1963, pp. 300.

Includes explanation (pp. 221-229) of ways of changing qualitative attributes of nations or of foreign policy makers into "dummy variables" of an either-or, 1 or 0, type in a standard linear regression analysis.

215. Kaplan, Abraham. "Sociology Learns the Language of Mathematics." In James R. Newman (ed.), The World of Mathematics. New York: Simon and Schuster, 1956, vol. II, pp. 1294-1313.

Discusses promising leads and disappointing results in attempts to apply mathematical models to social behavior.

216. Orcutt, Guy H., Watts, Harold W., and Edwards, John B. "Data Aggregation and Information Loss." 58 American Economic Review (1968), 773-787.

On the problem of aggregation before analysis with resultant loss of information, the consequent compatibility of aggregated data such as national accounts with all sorts of models, and the desirability of using less aggregated data to deal with small sample biases, improve the precision of estimates of parameters in macroeconomic models, and enhance chances of detecting misspecifications and of choosing correctly between alternative formulations.

217. Singer, J. David (ed.). Quantitative International Politics: Insights and Evidence. New York: Free Press, 1968, pp. xiii, 394.

A set of quantitative studies ranging in subject-matter from the psychology of individual decision-makers to the behavior of nations and alliance systems. A number of the contributions are separately annotated.

14. Factor Analysis

218. Cattell, Raymond B. "The Principal Culture Patterns Discoverable

in the Syntal Dimensions of Existing Nations." 32 <u>Journal of Social Psychology</u> (1950), 215-253.

Report of a systematic factor analytical study of culture patterns that sought a more precise measurement of cultural change. "Syntality" refers to the characteristics of a particular group, and the research design elaborated entailed measurement of 69 nations on the basis of their individual syntalities and the search for common patterns across a wider range of dimensions than had theretofore been attempted.

219. Cattell, Raymond B., Breul, H., and Hartman, H. Parker. "An Attempt at More Refined Definition of the Cultural Dimensions of Syntality in Modern Nations." 17 <u>American Sociological Review</u> (1951), 408-421.

In a refinement of earlier work on 69 nations, the authors attempt by factor analysis the correlation of 72 quantifiable variables for 40 nations, chiefly industrial nations and to resolve the variables, according to the correlations, into 12 independent factor entities or underlying influences. Most directly pertinent to international law are the interrelation under the "Cultural Pressure" factor of, among other things, large number of clashes with other countries, great number of treaties contracted, large number of secret treaties contracted, and frequent involvement in war. The findings, in agreement with those made in small experimental groups, suggest interpretation of Cultural Pressure at the population level, as a culture pattern primarily defined by a population personality characteristic dimension of "long-circuiting of dynamic expression," rather than at either the structure or the syntality level.

219-A. Rummel, Rudolph J. <u>Applied Factor Analysis</u>. Evanston: Northwestern University Press, 1970, pp. 617.

Concerned with social variables rather than psychological tests, this book presents a nontechnical approach to the methodological and philosophical context of factor analysis, deals with structure, matrices, and research design, gives attention to preparation of data and the derivation of factors from the data, and considers factor results in detail and the techniques for comparing the results of different factor analyses. The problem of interpretation of results is dealt with, as are alternative models for presenting results.

220. Rummel, Rudolph J. "Understanding Factor Analysis." 11 <u>Journal of Conflict Resolution</u> (1967), 444-480.

Something of a preview of the author's <u>Applied Factor Analysis</u>, this article presents the fundamentals of the technique of factor analysis and indicates several of its uses. At the same time, the article displays the dependence of the technique on the quality of the data employed, for international lawyers might be inclined to take exception to an indicator labelled "Acceptance of International Law" restricted to two values: "0= does not subscribe to Statute of International Court of Justice; 1= subscribes with reservations"-- apparently meaning not acceptance of the Statute but of the Optional Clause.

220-A. Russett, Bruce M., and Lamb, W. Curtis. "Global Patterns of Diplomatic Exchange, 1963-64." 6 Journal of Peace Research (1969), 37-55.
Employs factor analysis to identify groups of nations linked by relatively high levels of mutual diplomatic representation and finds support for two hypotheses: (1) high diplomatic exchange will be maintained with states with which there are bonds of common interest; (2) many diplomats will be sent to potential enemies and major neutrals. Comparison with groupings derived from other variables shows the closest approximation to be with groups based on trade or shared memberships in international organizations, while poorer fits exist with socio-cultural similarity, UN voting, and geographical proximity.

See also nos. 458, 547, 548, 686, 723, 1029, 1030, 1032, 1129, 2765.

15. Roll-Call Vote Analysis

221. Anderson, Lee F., Watts, Meredith W., Jr., and Wilcox, Allen R. Legislative Roll-Call Analysis. Evanston: Northwestern University Press, 1966, pp. ix. 203.
Handbook reviewing the several statistical techniques for analyzing roll-call votes.

222. Russett, Bruce M. "Discovering Voting Groups in the United Nations." 6 American Political Science Review (1966), 327-339.
Disturbed about the use of geographic or other pre-selected groups to explain United Nations voting and dissatisfied with the limits of Guttman scaling and of tabular and graphic representations of particular levels of agreement, the author recommends the use of the Q-technique of factor analysis to find similar actors (as contrasted with the similar variables identified by R-analysis). The author argues that the technique has the merits of being inductive (thereby avoiding pre-selection) readily interpretable, displaying gradations in agreement, identifying all groupings, and applicable either to a selected set of issues or to all roll-call votes of a session. He illustrates by means of an analysis of the roll-call votes in the 18th Session (1963) of the U.N. General Assembly.

See also nos. 690, 700, 2029.

16. The Study of Judicial Behavior

223. Baade, Hans W. (ed.). Jurimetrics. New York: Basic Books, 1963, pp. 270.
Papers on the mathematical study of the legal process, covering, among others, the following topics: the utility of computers in the judicial process; simultaneous equations and Boolean algebra in the analysis of judicial decisions; the analysis of judicial decisions through modern logic.

224. Becker, Theodore L. "Inquiry into a School of Thought in the Judicial Behavior Movement." 7 Midwest Journal of Political Science (1963), 254-266.

Views the approach of Glendon Schubert as accomplishing only description and prediction but not explanation of the psychological and sociological factors responsible for judicial action as is purported to be the goal of the movement headed by Schubert.

225. Becker, Theodore L. Political Behavioralism and Modern Jurisprudence. Chicago: Rand McNally, 1965, pp. xii, 177.

Critical survey of the main currents of judicial behavioralism that accords attention to the relationship between role-playing and decision-making and develops a working theory of judicial decision-making susceptible to empirical testing.

226. Bernard, Jessie. "Dimensions and Axes of Supreme Court Decisions: A Study in the Sociology of Conflict." 34 Social Forces (1955), 19-27.

Guttman scale techniques were applied to Supreme Court decisions to determine whether differences of opinion among the judges were of degree, kind, or both.

227. Blawie, J.L., and Blawie, M.J. "The Judicial Decision: A Second Look at Certain Assumptions of Behavioral Research." 18 Western Political Quarterly (1965), 579-593.

Expresses concern about the jump from earlier excellent behavioral inquiries into the judicial decision, based on limited and valid data, to intricate reworking of the same basic material with sophisticated statistical and psychological tools. This tendency is seen as obscuring the realities of socio-judicial behavior and failing to recognize lawyer-type public policy alternatives, e.g., in regard to diversity jurisdiction. A different frame of reference is suggested in place of what the authors regard as the inadequate characterization of cases as involving political and constitutional law.

228. Boehm, Virginia Ruth. Legal Attitudes and Legal Decision-Making. Ph.D. Dissertation. New York: Columbia University, 1966; Ann Arbor: University Microfilms, Inc., Order No. 67-817, pp. 132.

A Legal Attitudes Questionnaire was employed to develop scores on authoritarianism, anti-authoritarianism, and equalitarianism. Then a pencil-and-paper approximation of a jury system, together with both a guilty version and an innocent version of the case, was used with the result that authoritarians tended to convict and anti-authoritarians to be lenient without regard for the evidence. Verdicts were justified by resort to irrelevant information, by sheer conjecture, and by ignoring strategic points of evidence. Equalitarians alone appeared to follow lines of reasoning logically related to the case presented and so to be unpredictable as compared with the other two groups. Authoritarians appeared to be most certain of their own correctness regardless of actual correctness of a verdict.

229. Clarkson, G.P.E., and Tuggle, F.D. "Toward a Theory of Group-Decision Behavior." 11 Behavioral Science (1966), 33-42.

Report of experimental work exploring the possibility that group decision behavior in regard to a specific task can be explained or predicted from knowledge of the decision processes of the individual participants. This study is preliminary to the exploration of the problems of the manner and the procedures by which the process of reaching a group decision affects or influences the decision processes of the individuals involved. This study is relevant to the process of collegial judicial decision-making and should be considered together with studies that have been made of the predispositions of individual judges and of bloc alignments, particularly on the United States Supreme Court.

230. Daiches, Lionel. Russians at Law. London: Michael Joseph, 1960, pp. 208.

A Glasgow lawyer's report of conversations with Soviet lawyers on the operation of the Soviet judicial system.

231. Danelski, David J. "The Influence of the Chief Justice in the Decisional Process." In Walter F. Murphy and C. Herman Pritchett (eds.), Courts, Judges and Politics. New York: Random House, 1961, pp. 497-508.

An analysis of task and social leadership in the Taft, Hughes, and Stone courts and of the impact of the caliber of leadership by the Chief Justice upon the output of the Supreme Court.

232. Goldman, Sheldon. "Voting Behavior on the United States Courts of Appeals, 1961-1964." 60 American Political Science Review (1966), 374-383.

One of relatively few voting behavior studies of Courts of Appeals, this study, like most studies of judicial behavior, does not touch upon cases involving international law issues but deals with civil liberties, criminal, government regulation, fiscal, labor, private economic, and related cases that permit ranking on a traditional liberal-conservative continuum.

233. Harding, T. Swann. "Social Technology and the Courts of Modern Times." 10 American Sociological Review (1945), 746-751.

Argument to withdraw questions of social and economic policy, in which technical knowledge is a necessity, from a body of non-experts, specifically the Supreme Court. Numerous cases are cited to demonstrate the conflicts that arise when technical aspects are underplayed.

234. Howard, J., Jr. "On the Fluidity of Judicial Choice." 62 American Political Science Review (1968), 43-56.

Employing data drawn from the personal papers of Justices Burton, Frankfurter, Murphy, and Stone, the article examines intervening variables between attitudes and behavior of Supreme Court justices to suggest that such variables, e.g., socialization, strategy, and style, account for the disparity between the fluid choices of judges and the rigid ideological appearances of their opinions. The

article is critical of current research procedures that infer attitudes from votes and opinions without giving sufficient attention to
the group interaction that intervenes and may modify both attitude
and action.

235. Kort, Fred. "A Nonlinear Model for the Analysis of Judicial
Decisions." 62 American Political Science Review (1968), 546-555.
    With digital computers making it possible to go beyond the ini-
tial assumptions that the combinations of facts on which judicial
decisions are dependent are linear and to explore for nonlinear relationships, new insights have been reached on how different facts
combine to influence judicial decisions and indications have appeared
to suggest that linear and nonlinear models may provide a criterion
for distinctions of decisions between Anglo-American and Continental
legal systems.

235-A. Krislov, Samuel, with the assistance of Malcolm Feeley and
Susan White. "Manual for the Judicial Behavior Laboratory." Mimeo.
Minneapolis: University of Minnesota, Department of Political Science,
Fall 1969, pp. 172.
    A manual on the analysis of the judicial process that gives
primary attention to scaling. The manual includes an introduction
to data sources and exercises designed to train the students in the
types of questions that can be asked and methods of handling data
on the judicial process. This is one of a series of eight manuals
that are to be published by Little, Brown and Company.

236. Lasswell, Harold D., and Almond, Gabriel. "Twisting Relief
Rules." 13 Personnel Journal (1935), 338-343. Reprinted in Lasswell,
The Analysis of Political Behavior. New York: Oxford University Press,
1949, pp. 261-267.
    A pioneering and neglected field experiment demonstrating that
differences in claim-granting were related to differences in personality characteristics of welfare grants as these characteristics in-
teracted with characteristics of clients.

237. Murphy, Walter F. Elements of Judicial Strategy. Chicago:
University of Chicago Press, 1964, pp. xiii, 249.
    An inquiry into role and role perception, employing a "capa-
bility analysis," that deals with the capacity of policy-oriented
judges to make the most of the choices available to them.

238. Newland, Chester A. "Legal Periodicals and the United States
Supreme Court." 3 Midwest Journal of Political Science (1959), 58-74.
    Examination of Supreme Court reliance in 1924-1956 on articles
in over 100 legal periodicals, noting that the most frequently cited
periodicals were the Harvard Law Review, the Yale Law Journal, and
the Columbia Law Review, that the most frequently cited writers were
Felix Frankfurter and Charles Warren.

239. Schmidhauser, J.R. "Judicial Behavior and the Sectional Crises
of 1837-1860." 23 Journal of Politics (1961), 615-640.

Voting responses of Supreme Court Justices are employed in a
search for evidence to identify variables influencing the decision-
making process. The responses can be compared with those of President and Congress to similar or identical issues. Insight is sought
concerning the behavior of Justices as participants in a highly institutionalized small group process. Results include determinations
that Justices voted on the basis of attitudes related to policy consequences of decisions, that fundamental divisions represented party
rather than regional divisions, and that judicial responses differed
from legislative responses due to apparent generational differences
in issue presentation and to differences in perceptions of institutional role. While the approach employed cannot be transferred directly for use in the analysis of tribunals preserving the anonymity
of judges, the analytical techniques employed suggest possible indirect methods of approach to the study of judicial decision-making in
systems preserving anonymity but susceptible of comparison with
legislative or executive responses.

240. Schubert, Glendon. "Behavioral Jurisprudence." 2 Law and Society Review (1968), 407-428.
Outlines a behavioral model of adjudicatory decision-making and
indicates directions that future research can take, e.g., the study
of stare decisis as a function of psychological variables such as
commitment and identification and of sociopsychological variables
such as reinforcement and reference group behavior.

241. Schubert, Glendon. "Behavioral Research in Public Law." 57
American Political Science Review (1963), 433-445.
Surveys methodological and substantive developments in the application of social science to public law during 1955-1963. A summary description of political science research into judicial behavior indicates the relations of this research to group interaction,
courts conceptualized as small groups, political socialization of
judges, and the social psychology of judicial attitudes.

242. Schubert, Glendon. Judicial Policy-Making: The Political
Role of the Courts. Chicago: Scott, Foresman, 1965, pp. 212.
Although concentrating on domestic policies, particularly upon
economic, social, and political rights, the volume presents a concise descriptive survey of the structure, functions, and procedures
of the Supreme Court, a chapter analyzing policy-making in terms of
inputs, conversion, and outputs, and outlines a functionalist theory
of the Court's policy-making and its exercise of the power of judicial review. A final chapter is devoted to an unnecessary defense
of the behavioralist approach to judicial decision-making against
the attacks of Becker and others. From the point of view of the international lawyer, the unrewarding feature of Schubert's approach is
its inattention to international issues.

243. Schubert, Glendon. The Judicial Mind: The Attitudes and Ideologies of Supreme Court Justices, 1946-1963. Evanston: Northwestern
University Press, 1965, pp. xiii, 295.

Examines the Supreme Court's record between 1946 and 1963, subjects it to factor analysis and cumulative linear scaling, and constructs a composite multidimensional model of the Court's group decision-making.

244. Schubert, Glendon A. "The Study of Judicial Decision-Making as an Aspect of Political Behavior." 52 The American Political Science Review (1958), 1007-1025.

Examples of some methods for the study of the behavior of judges, namely, bloc analysis, scalogram analysis, content analysis, and game analysis. A fuller exposition appears in the author's Quantitative Analysis of Judicial Behavior.

245. Schubert, Glendon, and Danelski, David J. (eds.). Comparative Judicial Behavior: Cross-Cultural Studies in Political Decision-Making in the East and West. New York: Oxford, 1969, pp. 350.

The best-known pioneer in the contemporary study of judicial behavior has in this volume brought together papers by political scientists and lawyers that extend to the cross-cultural level the theories and methods now employed to analyze judicial decision-making. The selections deal with judicial behavior in Japan, Australia, Canada, India, Korea, and the Philippines.

246. Schubert, Glendon (ed.). Judicial Decision Making. New York: Free Press, 1963, pp. ix, 278.

A collection of essays on judicial behavior at the levels of the Supreme Court and state courts in the United States and of military courts and the Supreme Court in Norway. Perhaps most useful to the scholar concerned with the judicial process and its function in the development of international law are the essays by Stuart S. Nagel, "Off-the-Bench Judicial Attitudes," by Fred Kort, "Content Analysis of Judicial Opinions and Rules of Law," and by Ulf Thorgersen, "The Role of the Supreme Court in the Norwegian Political System." Although the primary concern of the authors is not with the judicial process as it relates to international law, their work, besides providing methodological guides, falls into the category of studies of judicial behavior that permit generalizations of consequence to international law.

247. Snyder, Eloise C. "Political Power and the Ability to Win Supreme Court Decisions." 39 Social Forces (1960), 36-41.

On the basis of a study of 8,724 cases before the Supreme Court in 1921-1953 that involved amendments to the Constitution, it was found that the litigant with the superior political power won nearly twice as many cases as the inferior litigant. The hierarchy employed was federal government, state government, local government, business corporations, trade unions, individuals. A trend for corporations and unions to become more powerful and a tendency of the court in 1946-1953 to favor the politically inferior litigant were observed.

248. "Social Science Approached to the Judicial Process--Symposium." 79 Harvard Law Review (1966), 1551-1628.

Presents a sampling of social science methods of analyzing judicial behavior: Joel B. Grossman, "Social Backgrounds and Judicial Decision-Making"; Walter F. Murphy, "Courts as Small Groups"; Joseph Tanenhaus, "The Cumulative Scaling of Judicial Decisions"; Samuel Krislov, "Theoretical Attempts at Predicting Judicial Behavior"; Fred Kort, "Quantitative Analysis of Fact-Patterns in Cases and Their Impact on Judicial Decisions."

249. Tanenhaus, Joseph. The Uses and Limitations of Social Science Methods in Analyzing Judicial Behavior. Mimeographed. Presented at the Annual Meeting of the American Political Science Association, September 7, 1956.

Particularly useful for its discussion of the sample survey and for the examples given of its application to the study of judicial behavior.

250. Thurstone, Louis L., and Degan, James W. "A Factorial Study of the Supreme Court." 37 Proceedings of the National Academy of Science (1951), 628-635.

A study to ascertain by factorial methods whether the voting records of the individual judges give evidence of any groupings in the Supreme Court. The present study was made on voting records of the judges during 1943-1944 and 1944-1945 terms of the Court on 115 cases in which there were at least 2 dissenting votes.

See also nos. 378, 383, 385, 1774, 1940, 1964.

17. Measurement of Power

251. Dahl, Robert. "The Concept of Power." 2 Behavior Science (1957), 201-215.

Unusually lucid discussion of the problems associated with the measurement and definition of "power".

252. German, F. Clifford. "A Tentative Evaluation of World Power." 4 Journal of Conflict Resolution (1960), 138-144.

An attempt to determine national power objectively through assessment of (1) national economy, (2) land, (3) population, and (4) military forces. Downward corrections of land area are made for sparse population and lack of communication, as well as of population itself if there are food deficits and low morale. National economy is corrected for material shortages and for the benefits of a directed economy. Military forces are corrected for possession of atomic weapons. Data is given to permit change of weightings, etc., by other researchers.

253. Simon, Herbert A. "Notes on the Observation and Measurement of Political Power." 15 Journal of Politics (1953), 500-516.

Objects to defining power in terms of personal resources or potential resources on the ground that these are only an indices of power and need not indicate its exercise. Observing conditions for the exercise of power, especially attitudes and expectations of persons submitting to authority, provide indirect evidence of distribution of power. Acceptance of power rather than power resources may lead to the best measure, with the concept of partial ordering among sets being a possible means of measurement.

18. Tension Measurement and Analysis

254. Gross, Feliks. "Tension Areas Analysis." 28 Il Politico (March 1963), 45-60.
A typology of tensions which allows the world to be mapped in terms of tensions which vary by type, class, and degree.

255. Holsti, Ole R. "The Value of International Tension Measurement." 1 Journal of Arms Control (1963), 702-711.
Inventory of methods of measuring international tensions, with attention paid to the need for qualitative as well as quantitative measures, that presumes a need to make available to decision-makers adequate devices for measuring so crucial an influence upon decisions as tensions and perception thereof.

256. North, Robert C., Triska, Jan F., Brody, Richard A., Holsti, Ole R., Armour, Anne, and Cohen, Elizabeth. The Analysis of International Tensions. Report to Project Michelson, U.S. Naval Ordnance Test Station, China Lake, California. Studies in International Conflict and Integration, Stanford University, June 15, 1964, pp. vi, 207.
Six papers based on use of an adaptation of the General Inquirer system of content analysis to test some hypotheses confirmed by a study of the 1914 crisis. Situations of high tension (Cuba, October 1962), of medium tension (Cuba, April 1961), and of low tension (Krushchev visit, September 1959) were studied along with comparisons of Soviet and Chinese reactions, of Soviet and American self-perceptions, and of the behavior of the 1914 decision-makers. The last paper, by Anne Armour, presents a Balgol program for a quantitative format in automated content analysis that was used to analyze the documents examined in the study.

See also no. 1661.

19. Communication Research and Communication Models;
Human Information Processing

257. Ackoff, R.L. "Towards a Behavioral Theory of Communications." 4 Management Science (1958), 218-234.
The fundamental idea of this paper consists of the analysis of communication with three components--the transmission of information, instruction, and motivation, and the definition of these in terms of a purposeful state.

258. Bauer, Raymond. "The Communicator and the Audience." 2 _Journal of Conflict Resolution_ (1958), 67-77.

This report of some of the ideas which have emerged from work of the Program of International Communications at MIT notes that a high proportion of individual pieces of research are so inconclusive that they have forced the development of more elaborated models of the communication process. Study of informed communication has been combined with basic psychological research on interpersonal influence and sociological studies of the primary group. The author offers three propositions concerning the role of the audience in communications: (1) audience influences the way in which the communicator organizes new information; (2) a communication once completed has an existence external to the originator; (3) a statement once made constitutes some degree of personal commitment; (4) secondary audience or reference groups are important targets of communication.

259. Beauregard, O.C. de. "Sur l'equivilance entre information et entropie." 11 _Sciences_ (1961), 51-58.

Important discussion of the relationship between information and entropy that notes a difference in meaning between negentropy $\rightarrow$ information and information $\rightarrow$ negentropy, information in the former meaning acquisition of knowledge and in the latter, power of organization.

260. Boulding, Kenneth E. _The Image: Knowledge in Life and Society._ Ann Arbor: University of Michigan Press, 1956, paperback ed., 1961, pp. 175.

An exposition of the image, or subjective knowledge, of communication and information, of meaning as the change produced in the image, and of the dependence of behavior on the image.

261. Carson, John J. "The Role of Communication in the Process of Administration." 4 _Public Administration Review_ (1944), 7-15.

The author discerns three principal purposes for which administrators use communication: to convey instructions, i.e., policy decisions, down the line of authority; to transmit suggestions of employees (reverse communication); to create common understanding of the group's purpose. Problems involved in communication include decentralization and its impediments to effective communication, distortion, differing interpretation of the written word according to the background of the individual. To illustrate these central principles and problems the author gives a picture of the communications system of a relatively typical governmental unit, the Bureau of Old Age and Survivors Insurance.

262. Chapman, R.C., Kennedy, J.L., Newell, A., and Biel, W.C. "The Systems Research Laboratory's Air Defense Experiments." 5 _Management Science_ (1959), 250-269.

Work on a simulated air defense system that shows, among other things, a general rise in information processing capacity along with increased load up to an asymptote, at which point information inputs were ignored or stacked up on a waiting list. At moderately high inputs the simulated air defense systems engaged in a flurry of creative perceptual integrations (cf. no. 284).

263. Cherry, Colin. On Human Communication: A Review, A Survey, and a Criticism. 2nd paperback ed. New York: Wiley, Science Edns., 1970, pp. xiv, 337.

An examination of the range of communications studies that covers such aspects as the following: communication and organization; signs, language, and communication; the analysis of signals, including speech; the statistical theory of communication; the logic of communication (syntactics, semantics, and pragmatics); cognition and recognition. A 411-item bibliography is included.

264. Cooper, Joseph B. "Perceptual Organization as a Function of Politically Oriented Communication." 41 Journal of Social Psychology (1955), 319-324.

The author reports on the study of two hypotheses: in reporting crucial events, communicators evidence their biases to the extent that peers are capable of identifying such biases significantly above chance, peers tend significantly above chance to evaluate the objectivity of such communications in terms of their own biases. Results of study indicate that a message sender not only purveys information about the event but also gives information about the way he has cognated the event. The fact that receivers are able to identify the biases of the senders indicates that, even in non-face-to-face communication processes, considerable information about the sender is purveyed by the sender. There is a need to send information in such ways as to protect the ego. Clear, too, is the fact that receivers perceive messages in the light of their own needs.

265. Damle, Y.B. "Communication of Modern Ideas and Knowledge in Indian Villages." 20 Public Opinion Quarterly (1955), 257-270.

Distance from the city has to do with communication of ideas and knowledge, but the social structure also determines the quantitative and qualitative content of the communications. Information more relevant to the people is more widespread than such matters as foreign affairs, but in foreign affairs facts concerning one's own country are more widespread than are facts about others. Also, that which is visible is more readily received by the people.

266. Davison, W. Phillips. "On the Effects of Communication." 23 Public Opinion Quarterly (1960), 343-360.

The purpose of the article is to suggest another method of interpreting the existing body of knowledge about the effects of communication, one that sees communication as serving as a link between man and his environment. The author assumes that all human actions are directed toward satisfaction of needs and that man's wants and needs are dependent on his environment for their satisfaction. Communication can lead to adjustive behavior by reporting an actual or expected change in the environment, by serving as a reminder of conditions in the environment or about needs, or by bringing to a person's attention a new way of patterning his relationship to the environment. The author concludes that this approach to communication involves bargaining, i.e., a two-way relationship in which the audience requires something from the manipulator and vice-versa.

267. Davison, W. Phillips, and George, Alexander L. "An Outline for the Study of International Political Communication." 16 Public Opinion Quarterly (1952-1953), 501-511.

When dealing with international communications one must work according to his country's policies and according to what particular characteristics are in the country as far as what they will accept and reject. It is also the case that propaganda not backed by power is unlikely to achieve its goal.

268. Deutsch, Karl W. "On Communications Models in the Social Sciences." 16 Public Opinion Quarterly (1952), 356-380.

Communications models serve four functions: organizing, heuristic, predictive, and measuring. They should also be original, simple, and realistic. There is a tendency toward trouble when mathematical models are used in social science areas, but models in general suggest lines of study of organizations, their memory problems, their information channels, and their secondary symbols that are related to the primary information used by the organization.

269. Deutsch, Karl W. The Nerves of Government: Models of Political Communication and Control. New York: Free Press, 1963, pp. xviii, 316.

Stimulating book, emphasizing channels of communication and highly suggestive of research directions utilizing conceptualizations set forth that treats government as more a problem of steering than of power. Among the provocative suggestions is one related to sovereignty that suggests that states, actually not being unlimited, need to be aware of limit probabilities in international affairs, to be sensitive to limit signals but such signals apparently are of low status, and should but do not store limit images since they teach the rejection of constraints on their own decisions and behavior. Also of some consequence is a provisional definition of the core area of politics as, roughly, the area of enforceable decisions. Its discussion of preferential treatment of messages and claims thereto is of considerable importance to comprehension of the communication function of law. Furthermore, although the study is centered upon the state, its concepts are applicable to the analysis of international organizations.

270. Dorsey, J.T. "A Communication Model for Administration." 2 Administrative Science Quarterly (1957), 307-324.

Decisions are treated as communication phenomena in that they occur on receipt of communication, consist of a complex combining of communications from various sources, and result in transmission of further communication. Administration is defined as consisting of decisions and so as a communication process. A "self-modifying communication net" is suggested as a suitable model--self-correcting through feedback as results are observed and corrections made, self-modifying by adopting internal relationships and processes after comparing present with past experiences. Purposiveness of the model tends to exclude communications such as individual purposes and goals unconnected with the organization, although some extraneous, sometimes conflicting, information is always present and is a condition of survival of the communication net.

271. Dovring, Karin. "Change of Attitude in Global Communication: The Ideology's Role in Salesmanship and Public Relations." 15 Journal of Communication (1965), 250-269.
      An examination of communications and ideology, communications clashes, and the problem of analysis of communications such as the seemingly democratic communications intended as sales pitches to other countries, that includes the hypothesis that "the more interdependent our societies become, the more communication realms are likely to clash". It might be noted that the author reaches a similar conclusion to that in Robert L. Friedheim's analysis of the Law of the Sea Conferences, namely, that more thought should be given to communicative relations with underdeveloped countries.

272. Driver, Michael J., and Streufert, Siegfried. Group Composition, Input Load and Group Information Processing. Institute Paper No. 142. Institute for Research in the Behavioral, Economic, and Management Sciences. Herman C. Krannert Graduate School of Industrial Administration, Purdue University. Lafayette, Indiana, July 1966, pp. 28.
      Outline of a model of information processing for systems of all types--individuals, groups, and organizations--together with discussion of recent experiments testing the model. The model postulates that each system alters its internal integrative capacity in a curvilinear fashion as input complexity increases. It is argued that each system should react with a predictable curvilinear pattern of output complexity as input complexity changes, so that a whole family of curves would be necessary to represent the operations of information processing systems. The experiments showed that in perceptual integration high integrative complexity groups and individuals differed most from those of low complexity. Distinguishing between delegated information search requests and self-initiated information search, the latter being preferred by high complexity subjects and the former by low complexity subjects, beyond optimal input loads the amount of increased information dropped, but more input was still requested, perhaps because a crucial input was still sought or perhaps because of social desirability to appear to want more information. Further consideration of the experimental data also suggested the possibility that both a perceptual subsystem and an executive subsystem are operative in information processing, each with a different optimal level, perhaps related to filtering of information from the perceptual to the executive subsystem.

273. Ennis, P.H. "The Social Structure of Communication Systems: A Theoretical Proposal." 3 Studies of Public Communication (1961), 120-144.
      The paper suggests that some of the centrifugal elements of the communications tradition may be recombined by subsuming the key

elements of a communication subsystem (key elements being audience, channel, producers, distributors and medium content) within the sociological rubric of a social group.

274. Fagen, Richard R. Politics and Communication: An Analytic Study. Boston: Little, Brown, 1966, pp. x, 156.
    Introductory analysis of the relation between politics and communication, of the structure of communication networks, and of the relation between communication and political development. The uses of communication networks in various political systems are described. With a measure of translation, it is possible to apply this and/or other communications approaches to the analysis of the social functions of law.

275. Feld, M.D. "Political Policy and Persuasion: The Role of Communications from Political Leaders." 2 Journal of Conflict Resolution (1958), 78-89.
    The author suggests that politics might be defined as "that aspect of society in which the objective of persuasion dominates all attempts at communication." Political communication is designed to affect the attitudes of parties whose free choice determines the form the political system takes. Policy statements represent the reaction of political actors to their environment. The intellectual habits of the audience determine, in the long run, the persuasiveness of the policy communication. A political decision is a determination on the part of political actors to bring about a qualitative change in the composition of the political environment. They must indicate that the point of view of the opposition is taken into consideration and the decisions being considered are in their interest.

276. Festinger, Leon, Riecken, Henry W., and Schachter, S. When Prophecy Fails. Minneapolis: University of Minnesota Press, 1956, pp. vii, 256.
    Application and exposition of the theory of cognitive dissonance and the information processing by means of which individuals try to cope with the internal conflict.

277. Grinspoon, Lester. "The Truth is Not Enough." In Roger Fisher (ed.), International Conflict and Behavioral Science: The Craigville Papers. New York: Basic Books, 1964, pp. 272-281.
    Raises the question of why people seem not to listen and respond to the truth, i.e., that the existence of a whole civilization is threatened. The author says the reason why it is not accepted is that people cannot and do not wish to be overwhelmed by the anxiety which would accompany true comprehension of the situation. He notes that the individual employs active psychological processes by means of the ego. These mechanisms include denial, isolation, displacement, rationalization, intellectualization, and dogmatism. The truth is not enough when the individual feels he lacks the means of influencing a given situation. It is when this is the case that the protective mechanisms are employed. The author notes two models for making disturbing "truths" acceptable: (1) the psychotherapy

relationship and (2) a program or activity which promises to modify unacceptable facts.

278. Holsti, Ole R., Brody, Richard A., and North, Robert C. "Measuring Affect and Action in International Reaction Models: Empirical Materials from the 1962 Cuban Crisis." Peace Research Society (International), Papers. Ghent Conference, 1964, Vol. II (1965), pp. 170-190. Also in 1 Journal of Peace Research (1964), 170-190.
    Suggests ways of analyzing the 1962 Cuban crisis and then employs a two-step mediated stimulus-response model treating acts of one nation as inputs for other nations.

279. Hunt, J. McV. "Motivation Inherent in Information Processing and Action." In O.J. Harvey (ed.), Motivation and Social Interaction. New York: Ronald, 1963, pp. 50-73.
    Suggests that classical motivational constructs such as drives and effects can no longer be regarded as prime sources of behavior and so, with some researchers on animal behavior, postulates biological "cognitive motivations" inherent to information processing itself rather than offspring of other motives.

280. Hurley, W.V. A Mathematical Theory of the Value of Information. Report 63-3. New York: Port of New York Authority, Engineering Dept., Research and Development Division, May 1963.
    Mathematical theory on calculation of the value of relevant but not necessarily reliable information obtained for the decision process.

281. Jacobsen, E., and Deutschmann, Paul J. "Introduction /to Issue on Communications and Information/." 14 International Social Sciences Journal (1962), 251-256.
    Review of articles in the issue and identifies three lines of research as important: (1) differences and similarities in cognitive organizations of various cultures; (2) controlled experiments attempting to measure the effectiveness of propaganda; (3) studies that treat mass and interpersonal communications as an integrated combination of forces.

281-A. Jervis, Robert. The Logic of Images in International Relations. Princeton: Princeton University Press, 1970, pp. 296.
    An undertaking to show how states try to get others to accept desired images of themselves. In addition to distinguishing between readily controlled signals and substantial acts that can be seen as indicators of a state's intentions, the author examines the uses of ambiguity and the coupling and decoupling of signals and indices. The analysis is then applied to the Vietnam War.

282. Kirk, John R., and Talbot, George D. "The Distortion of Information." 17 ETC: A Review of General Semantics (1959), 5-27.
    A discussion of three forms of distortion of information: (1) stretch distortion in which no information is lost but is changed or recorded in an orderly or systematic way and so can be corrected by applying a transformation rule; (2) fog distortion in which information

is lost, masked out, or fogged over due to the transducer's inability to respond to the smallest or largest differences of the input or, in language, through the loss of distinctions; (3) mirage distortion in which one sees what isn't there, that is, obtains information that should be unwanted but which many people desire and even construe as pertinent information.

283. Mavis, Melvin. "The Interpretation of Opinion Statements as a Function of Message Ambiguity and Recipient Attitude." 63 Journal of Abnormal and Social Psychology (1961), 76-81.

The goal of the study was to assess the proposition that in interpreting an ambiguous statement of opinion, the average person would be more strikingly influenced by his own views than when interpreting a nonambiguous statement. The subjects were three groups of college students who varied in their attitude toward college fraternities. By presenting to them ambiguous forms of messages, subjects were asked to estimate the writer's attitude toward fraternities. Data revealed there was a curvilinear relationship between attitude and judgment for both the pro- and anti-fraternity message, for in both cases the committed subjects perceived the communicators as occupying more extreme positions than did neutral subjects. Neutral positions showed an essentially linear relationship between attitude and judgment.

284. Miller, James G. "Information Input Overload and Psychopathology." 116 American Journal of Psychiatry (1960), 695-704.

Finds that as the complexity (i.e., rate and amount) of information input increased, both individuals and groups increased their handling capacity in a linear fashion up to an asymptote, at which level a system would begin to omit inputs or to "queue" them (cf. no. 262).

285. Miller, James G. "The Individual as an Information Processing System." In William S. Fields and Walter Abbott (eds.), Information Storage and Neural Control. Springfield, Illinois: Charles C. Thomas, 1963, pp. 301-328. Reprinted in part in J. David Singer (ed.), Human Behavior and International Politics: Contributions from the Social-Psychological Sciences. Chicago: Rand McNally, 1965, pp. 202-212.

An examination of five information processing systems ranging from neurons in the frog sciatic nerve to a small social institution. The findings include evidence that there is a hierarchical, cross-level difference in maximum channel capacity, capacity dropping with increased complexity, and that at higher levels the adjustment processes for dealing with increased information input are both more numerous and more complex.

286. Mills, Judson, Aronson, Elliot, and Robinson, Hal. "Selectivity in Exposure to Information." 62 Journal of Abnormal Psychology (1959), 250-253.

Report of a study which tested the hypotheses: (1) that following a decision, people tend to seek out information that favors the chosen alternative and to avoid information that favors the rejected alternative and (2) the more important the decision, the greater the subsequent selectivity in exposure to information. Using college students, the hypotheses were tested by means of a choice of type of examination to be given them. The data did not support the prediction concerning the importance of the decision, as the importance of the decision did not influence selectivity. Results were explained by two tendencies: (1) individuals tend to seek out information that supports their choice and to avoid discrepant information; (2) individuals seek more information about the alternative they have chosen.

287. Newcomb, Theodore M. "An Approach to the Study of Communicative Acts." 60 Psychological Review (1953), 393-404.
Employs the concept of coorientation as the basis of human communication. Coorientation means a simultaneous orientation of communicators toward each other and toward objects of communication. The concept is analogous to that of coding in the mathematical theory of communication and to the idea of coupling or matching of systems in electronic engineering. Coorientations are treated as changeable, thereby producing a dynamic view of human communication. Note is taken of three kinds of group properties: (1) homogeneity of orientation toward objects; (2) homogeneity of perceived consensus, i.e., of judgments of homogeneity of orientation; (3) attraction among group members concerning which the proposition is set forth that interpersonal attraction varies with the degree to which demands of coorientation are met by communicative acts. The article has relevance both to communications theory and to undertakings to ascertain the nature of consensus.

288. Rapoport, Anatol. "What Is Information?" 10 ETC: A Review of General Semantics (1953), 247-260.
Restates the concepts of information, signal, code, and entropy, and shows how these concepts are definable in terms of probability and statistics to give expression to degrees of order and disorder in communication. Communication is seen as requiring a measure of regularity and orderliness, some structure in the code, and a degree of disorder and of the unexpected that provides a message with a surprise value. In a broader, more philosophical vein the author treats life as dependent essentially on ordering process that repels a general trend toward chaos seen as ever present in the nonliving world. Increasing the degree of order is treated as making a portion of the world describable or more comprehensible with less information or less effort. Evolution is treated as an ordering process in which gross changes of structure, physiology, and behavior are possible because biological structures, physiological process, and behavior patterns are always being organized into assemblies.

289. Schroder, Harold M., Driver, Michael J., and Streufert, Siegfried. Human Information Processing: Individuals and Groups Functioning in Complex Social Situations. New York: Holt, Rinehart and Winston, 1967, pp. viii, 224.
Employing the theoretical orientation of O.J. Harvey, D.E. Hunt, and H.M. Schroder, Conceptual Systems and Personality Organization

(New York: Wiley, 1961), the authors concern themselves with how
people use conceptual structures for adaptive purposes. Norms are
viewed, along with roles, etc., as information-processing structures,
with lower level, less integratively complex, conceptual structures
generating less diversity, fewer alternative perspectives, rigidly
constricted norms, and fixed role relationships. Evidence from the
literature and from the authors' experiments is brought to bear to
note differences in capacities to tolerate noxity (severity of the
adverse consequences of behavior) and information load, among other
things, between concrete or simple and more abstract or complex cognitive structures. Noting tendencies in mass society and in mass
education to employ content criteria rather than structural criteria,
the authors call attention to the tendency to react to other groups
and nations primarily in terms of their norms, beliefs, and attitudes.
Policies, strategies, and actions tend to be guided by the degree to
which the other's beliefs differ from one's own. The authors suggest
that it might be more relevant to base actions on the structure of
the other's attitudes, since attitude structure and group or political structure appear to be very closely related.

290. Shannon, C.E., and Weaver, W. The Mathematical Theory of Communication. Urbana: University of Illinois Press, 1949, pp. vii, 117.
    First development, intended for communication engineering, of
the basic concepts, theorems, and measures that constitute information theory and that have been extended to other fields.

291. Smith, Alfred G. (ed.). Communication and Culture: Readings
in the Codes of Human Interaction. New York: Holt, Rinehart and Winston,
1966, pp. xi, 626.
    Reprints of articles on human communications, the first part of
the book representing the three approaches of the mathematical theory
of communication, social psychology, and linguistic anthropology,
while the remainder of the book deals with the three dimensions of
human communication, namely, syntactics, semantics, and pragmatics.

292. Smith, Bruce L. "Trends in Research in International Communication and Opinion." 20 Public Opinion Quarterly (1956), 182-195.
    The author noted that the term international communication in-
cludes not just campaigns of information conducted by governments
but negotiations of diplomats, activities of international news
agencies, tourist impact, impact of books, movies distributed in
foreign countries, international business activities, etc. He noted
one of the striking trends in 1945-1955 decade, namely, the willingness of the U.S. government to commission important research on international communications and opinion (Smith-Mundt Act, 1948). Attention is also called to a wealth of nationally sponsored survey
research here and abroad.

293. Streufert, Siegfried, and Driver, Michael J. "Conceptual Structure, Information Load and Perceptual Complexity." 3 Psychonomic Science
(1965), 249-250.
    Employing a simulated decision-making environment, it was found

that differentiation and integration in perception increases with increasing information load until a criterion of optimal perception is reached. Thereafter, differentiation and integration in perception decreases with further increases in information load. Differences in perceptual integration that are related to differences in complexity of cognitive structure are noted.

294. Streufert, Siegfried, Driver, Michael J., and Haun, Kenneth W. "Components of Response Rate in Complex Decision-Making." 3 Journal of Experimental Social Psychology (1967), 286-295.
    A simulated decision-making environment was employed to investigate experimentally the effect of changes in information load on response rate and its components. The experimental situation permitted both integrated and unintegrated decision-making responses. Findings were (1) that with increasing information load, strategic integrated decision-making first increases and then decreases; (2) with increasing information load, general unintegrated decision-making first decreases and then increases; and (3) with increasing information load, simple retaliatory decision-making increases.

295. Streufert, Siegfried, Suedfeld, Peter, and Driver, Michael J. "Conceptual Structure, Information Search, and Information Utilization." 2 Journal of Personality and Social Psychology (1965), 736-740.
    Employing a complex decision-making task in order to provide opportunity for differences in the handling of information, the experimenters find that generally information search decreases as information load increases, and that subjects scoring high on measures of complexity of conceptual structure are less affected by information load changes than lower scoring subjects. Structurally simple persons (or groups composed of such persons) respond more directly to immediate environmental information and under suboptimal information loads would require more information to meet their tendency to relate one stimulus to one response rather than reutilize information for complex integrated decisions. Structurally complex persons (or groups) tend to respond in more integrated strategic fashion and to require additional relevant information no matter what the information load, even when superoptimal except possibly to an extreme, may happen to be.

296. Triandis, Harry C. "Some Determinants of Interpersonal Communication." 13 Human Relations (1960), 279-287.
    An empirical study on the relation of similarity of cognitive structure to the ability to communicate effectively.

297. Weaver, Warren. "The Mathematics of Communication." 181 Scientific American (July 1949), 11-15.
    Reporting on the work of Claude E. Shannon, this article presents a general mathematical model of communications developed for telecommunications engineering. The model represents a linear process from source to destination. An expanded and more technical version of the article appears in Shannon and Weaver, The Mathematical Theory of Communication (supra, no. 290).

298. Zajonc, Robert B. "The Process of Cognitive Tuning in Communication." 61 Journal of Abnormal and Social Psychology (1960), 159-167.

Two experiments on the cognitive effects of the individual's role in the communication process indicated that persons expecting to transmit information activate cognitive structures which are more differentiated, complex, unified, and organized than those activated by those expecting to receive information. But decreased differences between transmitters and receivers appeared when groups dealt with incongruent, as compared with congruent, information.

299. Zeman, J. "Le Sens philosophique du terme 'Information'." 3 La Documentation en France (1962), 19-29.

Examination of the meaning of "information" that provides valuable clarifications helpful to any effort to make use of information theory.

See also nos. 120, 124, 683, 696, 703, 1283, 1794, 1855, 2172, 2355, 2373, 2376, and sec. III, C, 5, e.

a. Semantics and Linguistics

300. Bazelon, David T. The Paper Economy. New York: Random House, 1963, pp. 467.

In the spirit of Alfred Korzybski's Manhood of Humanity (1921), which called for considerable revision of many notions of classic social science including wealth, capital, and money, The Paper Economy raises serious questions about the future of an economic system based on paper values derived from ritualistic activities such as budget-balancing, devotional stability of the dollar, fear of inflation, etc. The treatise thus focuses on some semantic problems including time-binding (although not using that term), entrapment in symbols that cloud analysis of the economic system, and economic "maps" that overlook some of the most significant economic problems of our time.

301. Glenn, Edmund S. "Meaning and Behavior; Communication and Culture." 16 Journal of Communication (1966), 248-272.

A well-illustrated semantic analysis, supplemented by other research, that indicates problems of meanings arising in routine phraseology when several languages are used as in the Security Council, related politico-economic behavioral differences, and the problem of transmitting not just immediate meanings but also latent meanings.

301-A. Grimshaw, Allen D. "Sociolinguistics and the Sociologist." 4 American Sociologist (1969), 312-320.

On four theoretical perspectives concerning relationships between language and social structure, some sociological questions that require speech data if they are to be dealt with, and language as a barrier to research across cultural boundaries. This article from the sociologist's perspective can be helpful in approaching the linguistic aspect of law.

302. Koebner, Richard. _Empire_. New York: Cambridge University Press, 1961, pp. 393.

In this study of the term "empire," particularly in relation to the British Empire, the author traces the meaning to the emergence by the Napoleonic Period of a clear concept of the territorial British Empire. The book constitutes a warning against research based upon stereotypes, abuse of words, and lack of examination of the historical validity of classical passages in speeches. Hence, its chief value may well be as a model of a method for the attainment of historical precision.

303. Koebner, Richard, and Schmidt, Helmut Dan. _Imperialism: The Story and Significance of a Political Word, 1840-1960_. New York: Cambridge University Press, 1964, pp. xxv, 432.

An important study prepared by Schmidt from Koebner's notes for the second volume of _Empire_, of an extended and evolving case of communication and perception. Imperialism is a polemicist's epithet. It appears in the English language as a pejorative word referring to Louis Napoleon's empire. It was not used in relation to the British Empire until Gladstone's attack on Disraeli's overseas undertakings in the late 1870s. Modern connotations stem from Hobson and "scholarly criticism was unable to prevent the forming of an international communis opinio for which economic imperialism has become an accepted fact." The authors regard the identification of the West with imperialism as providing shape for Communist concepts of the background against which their world system would arise, contributing to United States, European, and British mutual distrust, and both inspiring and embittering African and Asiatic nationalist movements.

304. Nathan-Chapotot, Roger. _Les Nations Unies et les réfugiés: le maintien de la paix et le conflit de qualifications entre l'Ouest et l'Est_. Paris: Pedone, 1949, pp. xii, 292.

The importance of adequate communication through legal instruments is stressed in this study of problems resulting from different definitions in Europe of such terms as "displaced person," "refugee," and "political exile."

305. Vigotsky, L.S. "Thought and Speech." 2 _Psychiatry_ (1939), 29-54.

Rejects the two analyses of (1) treating the whole (thinking-in-words) as divided into speech and thinking, neither of which contain the qualities inherent in the whole; and (2) the analysis which refers to thinking-in-words as a whole and to all its separate qualities in an equal manner. The author prefers an analysis which separates a complex whole of thinking-in-words into units, which, as distinguished from the elements, do not lose the qualities inherent in the whole but contain them in a simple primary form. One fundamental thesis is that the meaning of a word represents the unity of word and thought. From this unity the meaning of words develops.

See also nos. 1185, 1675, 1782, 1879, 1885, 1944, 2078.

20. Content Analysis

306. Budd, Richard W., Thorp, Robert K., and Donohew, Lewis. Content Analysis of Communications. New York: Macmillan, 1967, pp. x, 142.
    Contains valuable recipes for content analysis, employing a step-by-step approach, but with content analysis by computer limited to a last chapter of five pages.

307. Dovring, Karin. "Troubles with Mass Communication and Semantic Differentials in 1744 and Today." 9 American Behavioral Scientist (January 1965), 9-14.
    A case study of an early content analysis by the Orthodox Swedish religious leadership to determine why the symbols used by some preachers and in a particular hymnal produced disobedience.

308. Holsti, Ole R. Content Analysis for the Social Sciences and Humanities. Reading, Massachusetts: Addison-Wesley, 1969, pp. xvi, 235.
    An exposition of content analysis that gives attention to research designs, uses of content analysis, coding, sampling, reliability, validity, and computer programs.

309. Jansen, B. Douglass. "A System for Content Analysis by Computer of International Communications for Selected Categories of Action." 9 American Behavioral Scientist (March 1966), 28-32.
    The author describes a system, related to earlier groundbreaking work, for computer content analysis that was applied to three five-day periods of the Bosnian crisis of 1908, the crisis period preceding the outbreak of World War I, and the U-2 crisis of 1960.

309-A. Korobejnikov, V.S. "Analizis soderžanija v massovoj kommunikacii." Voprosy Filosofii (No. 4, 1969), 100-110.
    A Soviet article on content analysis of mass communications, interesting for its argument that Lasswell and his followers have severely limited the effectiveness of the instrument. The author argues that content analysis should not be used only to describe mass communication processes but also certain trends in societal development and that not models of individual or "subjective" events but models of objective events, immanent in mass-communication data, are the proper units of analysis.

310. La Forge, Rolfe. Media Content and Elite Values: A Critical Review of "A Comparison of Soviet and American Values and Foreign Policies" /a report by Robert C. Angell, NOTS Contract N123 (60530) 24904A.7 ORI Research Monograph, Vol. 2, No. 2. Eugene: Oregon Research Institute, April 1962, pp. 49.
    Criticism of content analysis as used in the first version of the Angell Report to Project Michelson, that highlights deficiencies in the method and makes some suggestions for improvements.

311. Namenwirth, J. Zvi, and Brewer, Thomas L. Elite Editorial Comment on the European and Atlantic Communities in Four Countries. Mimeo. Yale University, 1965.

Content analysis of samples of editorials on integration and arms control of 1953 and 1963 that can be found in the New York Times, Le Monde, the Frankfurter Allgemeine Zeitung, and The Times (London) that shows a significant divergence between the New York Times and the three European newspapers. The New York Times views European integration in ideal terms and in a military context emphasizing NATO and similar institutions and the danger of Soviet aggression; the European papers stress legal and technical aspects of integration and concrete values, e.g., "food" rather than "unity".

312. North, Robert C., Holsti, Ole R., Zaninovich, M. George, and Zinnes, Dina A. Content Analysis: A Handbook with Applications for the Study of International Crisis. Evanston: Northwestern University Press, 1963, pp. xv, 182.
Handbook on content analysis, with examples drawn from Stanford studies of World War I and of Soviet attitudes, that gives attention to such matters as documents as a source of data, quantitative analysis of content, measurement of intensity of attitudes and behavior, "pair comparison" scaling, and methods of analysis.

313. Stone, Philip J., Bales, Robert F., Namenwirth, J. Zvi, and Ogilvie, Daniel M. "The General Inquirer: A Computer System for Content Analysis and Retrieval Based on the Sentence as a Unit of Information." 7 Behavioral Science (1962), 484-498.
Describes the first program developed for computer content analysis that entails employment of a dictionary useful for the theoretical framework employed, limited editing of the text, and transfer to punchcards and magnetic tape. The computer sorts words into tagged categories, prints out frequency distribution of words and tagged concepts, and performs analysis of variance, factor analysis, and other statistical operations. If the researcher finds that another theoretical framework would have been more appropriate, he need only employ another dictionary and resubmit the data to the computer, using the same programs.

314. Stone, Philip J., Dunphy, Dexter C., Smith, Marshall S., and Ogilvie, Daniel. The General Inquirer: A Computer Approach to Content Analysis. Cambridge: MIT Press, 1966, pp. xx, 651.
A full discussion of computer-aided content analysis, presentation of the procedures of the General Inquirer, some applications illustrating different theoretical orientations, text problems, and research designs, and discussion of the evolution of and planned changes in the system. Technical details, including programs and necessary information related thereto, are presented in a separate User's Manual.

See also no. 1471.

21. Decision-Making

315. Back, Kurt W. "Decisions under Uncertainty: Rational, Irrational and Non-Rational." 4 <u>American Behavioral Scientist</u> (1961), 14-19.

Rational decision models are valid only for situations in the middle range of importance, while irrational models, although accounting for psychodynamic processes, cannot embrace the entire range of decision processes. Hence, the author proposes a nonrational model, the sources of which are neither the structure of the situation (as in rational models) or that of the person (irrational models) but rest more on analyses of experience by phenomenologists and existentialists. The advantage of the nonrational model is asserted to be its applicability to situations of which little is known of relevant facts. It is meaningful only in situations not susceptible to analysis on the basis of a deterministic or a probabilistic system. The article thus highlights the difficulty of employing present conceptualizations of the decision process to account for the mixture of the rational, the nonrational, and the irrational in decisions.

316. Back, Kurt W., and Gergen, Kenneth J. "Individual Orientations, Public Opinion and the Study of International Relations." 11 <u>Social Problems</u> (1963), 77-87.

In this article the authors utilize the approach to international relations which considers decisions about war and peace to be a reflection of the feelings of significant segments of a nation's population. They use public opinion data to explore some of the psychological dimensions leading to decisions about international conflict. Interpretation of data indicates that time and space orientation are highly related to preferences for absolutist or realist solutions to conflict in international relations. Uses suggested for the concept of personal orientation include application of this concept to the actions of nations by examining the actions of decision-makers (i.e., comparing the characteristic decisions of national leaders who differ in age). By concentration on underlying personal dimensions or orientations it would be possible to classify solutions to various problems on the basis of the amount of time or space considered.

317. Bross, Irwin D.J. <u>Design for Decision</u>. New York: Macmillan, 1953, pp. 276.

A largely nonmathematical introduction to decision theory: choice among alternative futures and conflicting values; prediction; probability; calculated risks; uncertainty; sequences of decisions; statistical inference.

318. Bullinger, Clarence E. "The Estimating Function in Decision-Making: Its Development Characteristics and Use." 13 <u>Journal of Industrial Engineering</u> (1962), 3-7.

Notes two routines, scientific method and operations research procedure, and gives the steps for each to determine key element which, for both, is found to be either hypothesis or model. Examination of situations in which this factor influenced or affected decision-making leads to the extraction of suggestions for estimating functions to be used as models in decision-making.

319. Cantril, Hadley. The Human Dimension: Experiences in Policy Research. New Brunswick: Rutgers University Press, 1967, pp. x, 202.

Advocacy of consideration of psychological factors in decision-making, description of the author's rapid sampling methods, and suggestions as to how their application for prediction of human reactions could reduce the chances of disasters such as the Bay of Pigs.

320. Collins, Barry E., and Guetzkow, Harold. A Social Psychology of Group Processes for Decision-Making. New York: Wiley, 1964, pp. x, 254.

Built around a series of interrelated propositions and the empirical evidence related thereto, this contribution to the study of decision-making in organizations and groups includes consideration of factors contributing to leadership and power, control of punishment and reward, the impact of the social weighting given to the majority opinion (conformity), differences in conditions that affect the outcomes of substantive conflict as contrasted with affective conflict, the impact of conditions of common fate, and the effect of influence attempts outside the scope formally designated. Some of the propositions warrant consideration in terms of their possible relevance to international relations as determinable by data from that arena.

321. Edwards, Ward. "Utility, Subjective Probability, Their Interaction, and Variance." 6 Journal of Conflict Resolution (1962), 42-51.

Reviews three models of decision-making: (1) a model assuming that the course of action chosen is that which maximizes one's subjectively expected utility; (2) a model assuming overestimation of the likelihood of desirable events and underestimation of the likelihood of undesirable events; and (3) one assuming the placing of higher values on outcomes of which the probability of occurrence is low.

322. Fishburn, P.C. "Analysis of Decisions with Incomplete Knowledge of Probabilities." 13 Operations Research (1965), 217-237.

Primary concern is with the way "imprecise" measures of probability information may help determine some ordering of utilities anticipated in various strategies.

323. Gournay, B. "L'Étude des décisions politiques--Note introductive." 13 Revue française de science politique (1963), 348-352.

A warning of some of the difficulties to be encountered in analysis of the decision process, ending with the suggestion that the analysis include measures of implementation and the manner of reception by society, a suggestion which in the context of legal studies could be carried to analysis of reception of appeals to law or to Charter principles.

324. Holt, Robert T., and Van de Velde, Robert W. Strategic Psychological Operations and American Foreign Policy. Chicago: University of Chicago Press, 1960, pp. x, 243.

A study of the place psychological considerations should have in the activities of diplomats and decisions-makers. Includes case studies of the use of propaganda in international relations.

325. Lasswell, Harold D. "Strategies of Inquiry: The Rational Use of Observation." In Daniel Lerner (ed.), The Human Meaning of the Social Sciences. New York: Meridian, 1959, pp. 89-113.

Lasswell is here concerned with the notion of strategy and choice as related to policy-making. He treats what he calls the "Map of Knowledge" and how routine and technical (i.e., methodological) gaps are filled. He emphasizes the forward-looking character of thought that has to do with policy (all choices refer to future events), and enumerates limitations of our traditional patterns of problem-solving. Lasswell suggests what he calls the "social planetarium technique" and shows by analogy to astronomy how such a technique can provide a total environment for the observer by bringing together the past and the potential future.

326. Lasswell, Harold D. The Decision Process: Seven Categories of Functional Analysis. College Park, Maryland: Bureau of Government Research, 1956, pp. iii, 23.

Sets forth seven functional categories for the analysis of any decision, a framework developed from work in jurisprudence and having its most important influence in international law in the series of publications by McDougal and associates, in which work Lasswell has collaborated.

327. Patchen, M. "Decision Theory in the Study of National Action: Problems and a Proposal." 9 Journal of Conflict Resolution (1965), 164-176.

Questions whether decision-making models consider nonconscious and nonpractical motives, or serve to separate the effects of separating situational and personal variables. The author suggests Atkinson's theory of motivation as an alternative as it is more susceptible to quantification, thus being more fruitful.

328. Robinson, James A., and Snyder, Richard C. "Decision-Making in International Politics." In Herbert C. Kelman (ed.), International Behavior: A Social-Psychological Approach. New York: Holt, Rinehart and Winston, 1965, pp. 435-463.

Reviews literature related to decision-making within the framework of three major factors, occasion for decision, characteristics of individual decision-makers, and organizational context.

329. Robinson, James A., and Wyner, Alan J. Information Storage and Search in Inter-Nation Simulation. Mimeo. Columbus: Ohio State University, May 28, 1965, pp. 20, appendix.

Report of an inter-nation simulation seeking to test two theories of decision-making, "satisficing" by which a sequential search for alternatives ends when the first alternative meeting minimal criteria is found and "maximizing" by which the alternative most likely to maximize goals is selected from a wide range of alternatives and while in possession of all relevant information. The data did not clearly substantiate either theory.

330. Scodel, A.P., Ratoosh, P., and Minas, J.S. "Some Personality Correlates of Decision Making under Conditions of Risk." 4 Behavioral Science (1959), 19-28.

This study asserts the need for considering personality variables in risk-taking situations as part of the formal mathematical models of decision-making for better predictions. In this study a gambling situation was arrange and observed. The authors concluded that "low payoff betters as compared to high payoff betters are a more other-directed, more socially assimilated, more middle-class oriented group."

331. Sidjanski, D. "Décisions closes et décisions ouvertes." 15 Revue française de science politique (1965), 251-269.

Proposes a threefold classification of decisions to facilitate study: (1) closed decisions, made by a public authority without consultation with or participation of others; (2) open decisions, made by a decisional process that associates representative elements with the responsible authority; (3) mixed decisions, such as those that associate a government and an international organization.

332. Simon, Herbert A. "Rational Choice and the Structure of the Environment." 63 Psychological Review (1958), 129-138.

The central problem of paper was to construct a simple mechanism of choice that would suffice for the behavior of an organism confronted with multiple goals. The author uses equations to illustrate parameters describing the organism and the environment, for example, range of vision, storage capacity of the organism, etc. His most important conclusion is that blocks of the organism's time can be allocated to activities related to individual needs without creating any problem of coordination, since time can be stored by the organism. The author notes that the analysis is static--one should not readily postulate for human beings elaborate mechanisms for choosing among diverse needs. The model suggests that current economic and statistical theories of national behavior are inadequate and that more emphasis should be placed on psychological theories of perception and cognition.

333. Simon, Herbert A. "Theories of Decision-Making in Economics and Behavioral Science." 49 American Economic Review (1959), 253-283.

The article treats of the gap between economics and psychology and how the methods of the latter have repercussions on the assumptions of classical economic theory. Classical theory presents a picture of a man choosing among fixed and known alternatives, for which the consequences are known. Now one must recognize that perception and cognition enter between the decision-maker and his objective environment. Exploring areas where economics has interests common with the other behavioral sciences, the author notes the implications of complexity and change on the assumption that economic man is a maximizing animal and suggests that he is, instead, a satisficing animal whose problem-solving is based on search activity to meet certain aspiration levels.

334. Snyder, Richard C., and Robinson, James A. National and International Decision-Making. New York: Institute for International Order, 1961, pp. 228.

Outline of 56 major research projects on decision-making processes. Interwoven through the research projects are comments on decision-making literature from many social science disciplines.

335. Snyder, Richard C., Bruck, H.W., and Sapin, Burton (eds.). Foreign Policy Decision-Making: An Approach to the Study of International Politics. New York: Free Press, 1962, pp. vii, 274.

Contains the Snyder-Bruck-Sapin monograph of 1954, Decision-Making as an Approach to the Study of International Politics, setting forth a conceptual scheme for the study of decision-making, a commentary by Herbert McClosky, the essay by Snyder and Glenn D. Paige undertaking to apply Snyder's analytical scheme to the U.S. decision to resist North Korea's aggression, and Richard A. Brody's discussion of three conceptual schemes for studying international relations. The Snyder-Bruck-Sapin monograph is an essential aid to the establishment of an appropriate framework for analysis of political decision-making and permits inclusion of legal aspects of the decision process both in terms of setting relevant norms in their proper position in the process, e.g., as information or as constraints, and in terms of the role of legal advisers in the decision process.

336. Starbuck, William H. The Aspiration Mechanism. Institute for Quantitative Research in Economics and Management. Institute Paper No. 50. Lafayette, Indiana: Herman C. Krannert School of Industrial Administration, June 1963, pp. 42.

Centering on maximum utility as a decision target, this paper deals with aspiration level as a subjectively defined criterion of success or failure linking the affective, cognitive, and conative modes of behavior. The element of time enters the discussion in relation to a lowering of compatibility between an organism's needs and its environment to note that if needs or environment is complex, the behavior of fast-changing variables can be approximated by assuming slow-changing variables to be constants, although at the cost of error that can render fatal an approximate forecast in the wrong circumstances. To minimize transition time is to maximize slow-changing variables, but for long periods problem-solving mechanisms require adjustment to compensate for slow-changing variables. The discussion then deals with problems of feedback design, social institutions (including some laws) that help individuals cope with transient states by providing information beyond that obtained by personal experience, and the possibility of lingering too long in transient safe states. A theory similar to Simon's "satisficing" model of decision-making but permitting a problem-solver to move from success to failure as a target in preference to a success state of longer transition time.

336-A. White, D.J. Decision Theory. Chicago: Aldine, 1970, pp. ix, 185.

Brings together the many aspects of decision theory in a cohesive focus on the meaning of "best" decisions, how to attain the "best" in practice, and the implications of theory for practical decisions.

See also nos. 262, 272, 280, 282, 284, 293-295, 341, 380, 450, 703, 1558, and sec. III, C.

22. Role Theory

337. Biddle, Bruce J., and Thomas, Edwin J. Role Theory: Concepts and Research. New York: Wiley, 1966, pp. xiv, 453.
Four original essays and 48 reprinted selections on significant theory and research on major specialized topics. The book also contains a comprehensive bibliography of 1,500 items.

338. Levinson, Daniel J. "Role, Personality, and Social Structure in the Organizational Setting." 58 Journal of Abnormal and Social Psychology (1959), 170-180.
Includes discussion of "role" in the organizational setting in a manner that permits integration of the concept of role within the meaning of subsystem process. Applicable to explanation of the behavior of international civil servants and international judges, the concept of "role" is dealt with both in terms of prevailing expectations about duties in a role incumbent's environment and in terms of the incumbent's own expectations.

See also nos. 1232, 1236, 1237, and 1264.

23. Issue-Area Orientation

339. Rosenau, James N. "The Functioning of International Systems." 7 Background (1963), 111-117.
Argument for dividing the aggregate of global relationships into "issue-areas" subjected to systematic treatment. The author suggests that a typology of issue areas, sufficiently generalized to embrace past and future as well as present areas, might include such entries as "predominant Great Power participation" areas, "internal war" areas, and "international organization involvement" areas.

340. Spiro, Herbert J. "Comparative Politics: A Comprehensive Approach." 56 American Political Science Review (1962), 577-595.
A theoretically-oriented essay that includes the assumption that issues generate structurally and functionally significant political differences.

341. Wildavsky, Aaron B. "The Analysis of Issue-Contexts in the Study of Decision-Making." 24 Journal of Politics (1962), 717-732.
An empirically-oriented article that attempts to determine relevance, strength, and boundaries of issue-areas as they affect decision-making.

24. Organization Behavior

342. Blau, Peter M., and Scott, W. Richard. Formal Organizations: A Comparative Approach. San Francisco: Chandler, 1962, pp. x, 312.
A study of organization behavior that includes pertinent chapters on relations with clients, experiments and field studies of communications and communication patterns, interorganizational processes, and the function and position of the professional expert and his reference group as contrasted with that of the bureaucrat.

343. Cangelosi, V.E., and Dill, W.R. "Organizational Learning: Observations Towards a Theory." 10 Administrative Science Quarterly (1965), 175-203.
Analyzes the learning process of a seven-man team during a complex management decision exercise and identifies four stages: (1) initial stage; (2) searching stage; (3) comprehending stage; (4) consolidating stage. After comparing the observations of how the team learned with three recent discussions of organizational learning processes (Chapman et al., Cyert and March, Hirschman and Lindblom), a synthesis is proposed that views organizational learning as a product of interactions among three kinds of stress, as sporadic and stepwise, and as entailing a close relationship between the learning of goals and preferences with the learning of how to achieve them.

344. Kaufman, Herbert. "Organization Theory and Political Theory." 58 American Political Science Review (1964), 5-14.
On a number of parallels between classic formulations of political theory and the formulations of modern organization theory.

345. March, James G., and Simon, Herbert A., with the collaboration of Harold Guetzkow. Organizations. New York: Wiley, 1958, pp. xi, 262.
An outstanding book on organization behavior, replete with propositions, that for purpose of study of the various aspects of international affairs as affected by both national and international agencies, are particularly relevant as they deal with intraorganizational and interorganizational conflict, organizational reaction to conflict, perception, communication, and information processing.

346. Tuckman, B. "Personality Structure, Group Composition and Group Functioning." 27 Sociometry (1964), 469-487.
Finds that, under conditions of stress, power hierarchies in the groups studied became simplified.

346-A. Yarmolinsky, Adam. "Bureaucratic Structures and Political Outcomes." 23 Journal of International Affairs (1970), 225-235.
On the differences in organization and tasks that give the Department of Defense advantages over the Department of State in recommending policies and getting them adopted and executed.

See also nos. 320, 601, 602, and sec. III, C, 6.

25. Economic Analogies

347. Buchanan, James M., and Tullock, Gordon. The Calculus of Consent: Logical Foundations of Constitutional Democracy. Ann Arbor: University of Michigan Press, 1962, paperback ed., 1965, pp. xi, 361.
    Application of the concepts, methodology, and analytics of the study of economic organization of society to the study of democratic political organization, which contains chapters on a generalized economic theory of constitutions, the costs of decision-making, various decision-making rules, and democratic ethics.

348. Curry, Robert L., and Wade, Lawrence. A Theory of Political Exchange: Economic Reasoning in Political Analysis. Englewood Cliffs: Prentice-Hall, 1969, pp. 156.
    An important example of the use of economic concepts to analyze political phenomena.

349. Russett, Bruce M. (ed.). Economic Theories of International Politics. Chicago: Markham, 1968, pp. ix, 542.
    Twenty-nine selections employing economic approaches potentially relevant to the analysis of international relations, including the following: Mancur Olson, Jr., and Richard Zeckhauser, "An Economic Theory of Alliances"; John G. Gross, "Some Theoretic Characteristics of Economic and Political Coalitions"; Oliver E. Williamson, "A Dynamic Theory of Interfirm Behavior"; Martin McGuire, "The Arms Race: An Interaction Process"; Albert O. Hirschman, "The Stability of Neutralism: A Geometric Note"; Russett, "Is There a Long-Run Trend Toward Concentration in the International System?"; Harry G. Johnson, "A Theoretical Model of Nationalism in New and Developing States"; E.R. Livernash, "The Relation of Power to the Structure and Process of Collective Bargaining"; Clark Kerr and Abraham Siegel, "The Inter-industry Propensity to Strike--An International Comparison"; Alfred E. Kahn, "The Tyranny of Small Decisions: Market Failures, Imperfections, and the Limits of Econometrics."

See also no. 492.

26. Psychological Approaches

350. Bjerstedt, Ake. "'Ego-Involved World-Mindedness', Nationality Images, and Methods of Research: A Methodological Note." 4 Journal of Conflict Resolution (1960), 185-192.
    Advocates sentence-completion tests to get at intensity of attitudes and extent of their stereotype or differential and employs as example the tests for national images of a Swedish group, a Syrian group, and a Children's International Summer Village reunion group. The test suggests one method for probing attitudes toward international law, basic segments thereof, and related matters.

351. Christiansen, Bjørn. Attitudes Towards Foreign Affairs as a
Function of Personality. Oslo: Oslo University Press, 1959, pp. 283.
    A review of personality centered and social norm centered theo-
ries concerning the basis of different reaction patterns toward foreign affairs precedes the analysis of data collected in 1952 and
1954 by administering questionnaires to samples of subjects drawn
from the Norwegian Military and Naval Academies. All international
situations referred to entailed threats to Norwegian interests and
include hypothetical issues such as fishing limits, freedom of movement of diplomats, and the sinking of a tanker by Viet Minh forces
that are related to international law as well as to politics. Answers to international questions could be correlated with answers to
a second questionnaire dealing with reactions to everyday occurrences to permit analysis relating attitudes toward foreign affairs
to personality. The questionnaires administered are reproduced in
an appendix.

352. Coombs, Clyde Hamilton. A Theory of Data. New York: Wiley,
1964, pp. xviii, 585.
    Analyzes psychological measurement and scaling foundations and
provides a construction for a comprehensive system of interrelations
of four types of data relevant to measurement and scaling theories:
preferential choice data; stimuli comparison data; similarities data;
single stimulus data.

353. Greenstein, Fred I. "The Impact of Personality on Politics:
An Attempt to Clear Away Underbrush." 61 American Political Science Review (1967), 629-641.
    A useful review of the role of personality in political affairs
that sets forth propositions that are applicable to foreign as well
as to domestic politics both for purposes of scientific analysis and
for assessment of responsibility as when the issue of war crimes is
raised. Although formulated as a defense of psychological approaches,
the footnotes provide guides to opposing views, e.g., Karl Popper's
argument (The Open Society and Its Enemies, 1963, II, 97) that psychological evidence is often of limited relevance, as compared to
situational evidence, in explanation of behavior--an issue which may
really be a question of what is obtainable as well as one of range
of choice.

354. Louch, A.R. Explanation and Human Action. Berkeley: University of California Press, 1967, pp. viii, 243.
    Holds that the lack of adequate theory of human or social behav-
ior stems from psychologists' greater concern with form than with
content. Explanations of human behavior are treated as inseparable
from moral assessments.

355. Newcomb, T.M. "Autistic Hostility and Social Reality." 1
Human Relations (1947), 69-86.
    On the changing of certain types of interpersonal attitudes held
by individuals either as individuals or as members of groups. The
focus is upon the conditions under which hostile impulses develop

into persistent attitudes. Although dealing with the individual, the article by its nature suggests the desirability of further exploration of an approach to the development of persistent hostile attitudes at the international level.

356. Rubinstein, S.L. "Problems of Psychological Theory." In Psychological Research in the U.S.S.R. Vol. 1. Moscow: Progress Publishers, 1966, pp. 46-66.
An attempt, possibly helpful for communications theory and learning theory, to establish a theoretical basis for psychological theory that would unite the physiological and psychological aspects of thinking in terms of the mental as a process or activity connecting the individual with the world.

357. Singer, J. David (ed.). Human Behavior and International Politics: Contributions from the Social-Psychological Sciences. Chicago: Rand McNally, 1965, pp. xiii, 466.
Selections from the behavioral sciences, particularly from studies of social attitudes, interpersonal relations, small groups, and such fields as decision-making, conflict, and conflict management within groups, together with the editor's commentary indicative of insights that such studies may provide for the understanding of international affairs.

358. Singer, J. David. "Man and World Politics: The Psychological Interface." 24 Journal of Social Issues (1968), 127-156.
An argument that cultural properties of subnational, national, and extranational entities are subject to assessment through the psychological properties of individuals constituting a particular system and that the emergent effects that may result from interaction of individual properties within and among single humans must be either structural or behavioral or, if cultural, can be observed as individual psychological properties.

359. Tedeschi, James T., and Malagodi, E.F. "Psychology and International Relations." 8 American Behavioral Scientist (October 1964), 10-13.
A defense against challenges to the relevancy and adequacy of the application of psychology to international problems. The problems of generalizations based on individual cases, speculation and empirical investigation, and laboratory experiments are discussed.

360. Therre, Paul. La psychologie individuelle et collective dans l'éfficacité du droit international public. Paris: Pedone, 1946, pp. 168.
An undertaking, virtually contemporaneous with Ranyard West's, to relate aspects of individual and collective psychology to the efficacy of international law. The book deals with individuals occupying decision-making posts, presents case studies relevant to their obligations and to the resort to citations of law, and discusses the roles of parliaments and of public opinion that have an effect on efficacy.

361. West, Ranyard. Conscience and Society: A Study of the Psychological Prerequisites of Law and Order. New York: Emerson Books, 1945, pp. 261.

Review of philosophical theories of human nature, the state, and law, followed by a search among psychological findings for a principle to reconcile and correct conflicting theories and opinions. The work is the first deep psychological probe into the basis of obedience to international law.

See also nos. 1289, 1340, 1629.

27. Sociological Approaches

362. Bosc, Robert. "Où en est la sociologie des relations internationales?" Projet (No. 7, July-August 1966), 786-804.

Reviews the postulates of behavioral sociology and of historical sociology and presents, as examples of the state of the sociology of international relations, Johan Galtung's structural theory of aggression, Herbert Kelman's concern with social-psychological analysis of the behavior of "actors," Ernst Haas' work on international integration, and John Burton's effort to develop a general theory of international relations.

363. Horowitz, Irving L. "A Formalization of the Sociology of Knowledge." 9 Behavioral Science (1964), 45-55.

Distinguishes between ideology and propaganda on the basis of true belief. A table of social-psychological characteristics of each is worked out, and then a matrix of basic systems of utopian constellations, using a threefold classification of utopial as (1) coercive (Caesaristic), (2) permissive (hedonistic), and (3) libertarian (economistic). A footnote objects to Shils' typology as regarding only "right" and "left" as ideology bound and suggests it worthy of examination as to why a theory of consensus should be less authoritarian than a theory of conflict.

364. Kriesberg, Louis (ed.). Social Processes in International Relations: A Reader. New York: Wiley, 1968, pp. xi, 577.

Readings, illustrative of a variety of methods and substantive topics, that illustrate sociological and social science perspectives as applied to the study of international relations.

365. Yakemtchouk, Romain. "Droit des gens positif et sociologie des relations internationales." Revue de l'Institut de Sociologie (1958), 335-390.

Calls for a sociology of international relations which would examine positive international actions in their function as international juridical acts, thereby tending to attack the problem of the lag between the movement of social reality and precise juridical regulation.

See also nos. 1136, 1138, 1966.

28. Survey Research and Interviewing

366. Backstrom, Charles H., and Hursh, Gerald D. Survey Research. Evanston: Northwestern University Press, 1963, pp. xxi, 192.
Handbook on survey research that deals with the mechanics of such matters as the planning of a survey, selecting a sample, preparing questions and designing questionnaires, training interviewers, coordinating field work, and processing data.

367. Becker, Theodore L. "Surveys and Judiciaries, or Who's Afraid of the Purple Curtain?" 1 Law and Society Review (1966), 133-143.
Taking the position that, with the proper approach, interview techniques and mail questionnaires can be useful tools for investigation of the judicial process, the author focuses on three studies to describe the techniques employed to elicit responses from significant percentages of the judges approached.

368. Fink, R. "Formation et direction des enquêteurs au Laos." 15 Revue internationale des sciences sociales (1963), 21-35.
Problems of conducting survey research in Vientiane and certain small Laotian towns and villages.

369. Gorden, Raymond L. Interviewing: Strategy, Techniques, and Tactics. Homewood, Illinois: Dorsey, 1969, pp. xiii, 388.
A recent, useful guide to the use of the interview and questionnaire techniques for gathering data.

370. Gough, Harrison G., and di Palma, Guiseppe. "Attitudes Toward Colonialism, Political Dependence, and Independence." 60 Journal of Psychology (1965), 155-163.
On a measuring instrument, involving an 18-item index, for research on anti-colonial attitudes that was validated in English, French, and Italian versions.

371. Hanna, W.J., and Hanna, J.L. "The Problem of Ethnicity and Factionalism in African Survey Research." 30 Public Opinion Quarterly (1966), 290-294.
On the need to match interviewers and respondents on the basis of ethnic group and faction before giving attention to two other factors important in Africa, namely, age and sex.

372. Hunt, William H., Crane, Wilder W., and Wahlke, John C. "Interviewing Political Elites in Cross Cultural Comparative Research." 70 American Journal of Sociology (1964), 59-68.
Concerning the experiences of researchers applying similar survey instruments in studying legislators in three nations. Although cultural differences affected the interviewers' capacities to handle such problems as gaining access to respondents, cooperation, and respondents' candor, variation in the institutional context was found to be more important.

373. International Directory of Sample Survey Centers Outside the U.S. Paris: UNESCO, 1965.
     Useful guide to foreign centers engaging in survey research.

374. Mitchell, Robert Edward. "Barriers to Survey Research in Asia and Latin America." 9 American Behavioral Scientist (November 1965), 6-12.
     Obstacles to the development of survey research lie in the organizational background to research in the countries of Asia and Latin America. Universities emphasize teaching over research, administrative ability over teaching. University research groups are without political or administrative independence. Methodological standards are of poor quality and preclude reliable results. Insertion of ideology results in poor research.

375. Richardson, Stephen A., Dohrenwend, Barbara Snell, and Klein, David. Interviewing: Its Forms and Functions. New York: Basic Books, 1965, pp. 380.
     Questions established methods of interviewing and suggests several methods empirically tested in order to raise efficiency of social science research interviewing.

376. Rieselbach, Leroy N. Personality and Political Attitudes: Available Questionnaire Measures. Mimeo. Mental Health Research Institute, University of Michigan, Ann Arbor, 1964.
     Surveys more than 100 sources, many from the late 1950s and early 1960s and lists instruments for personality assessment.

377. Robinson, James A. "Survey Interviewing Among Members of Congress." 24 Public Opinion Quarterly (1960), 127-138.
     Congressional interviewing may take numerous callbacks, but the necessary number of appointments may be expected. Resistance is greater to giving appointments than to giving satisfactory interviews, although the more difficult the appointment to make, the more difficult it is to avoid response failures. Congressmen are more difficult to interview than state legislators. Interviews are easier to obtain at the beginning of the year, except for the Appropriations Committee for which late July is best.

378. Zeisel, Hans. "The Uniqueness of Survey Evidence." 45 Cornell Law Quarterly (1960), 330-346.
     A comprehensive study of the problem of introducing survey evidence into legal proceedings. The most important obstacles to acceptance are: (1) the base in a sample rather than the whole population; (2) drawing of inferences from hearsay evidence; (3) reluctance of the researcher to set aside the anonymity of his informants. It may be noted that data bearing some of these characteristics, e.g., the census, receives judicial notice due to the disinterested character of the data and the presumed expertise employed in its collection.

29. Small Group Research

379. Bales, Robert F. Interaction Process Analysis. Cambridge: Addison-Wesley, 1950, pp. xi, 203.

Presents a theory of small groups, but the most important part of the book is a scheme for systematically observing and recording what happens in observable small groups, whether in the laboratory or in real life. The scheme provides four major categories, positive reactions, negative reactions, answers, and questions, that break down into subcategories covering the actions of the several members of small groups.

380. Holden, Matthew, Jr. "Committee Politics under Primitive Uncertainty." 9 Midwest Journal of Political Science (1965), 235-253.

Finds that normal committee behavior tends to be consistent with pressure toward internal harmony as suggested by small group theory, that greater environmental uncertainty is associated with a greater likelihood of looking inward for bases of decision, that ignoring of external demands tends toward irrationality when decisions must be ultimately validated by external audiences, and that the pressure group can improve the rationality of decision by forcing decision-makers to do more than rely upon received prejudices and the predilections of their own personalities.

381. Homans, George C. Social Behavior: Its Elementary Forms. New York: Harcourt, Brace, 1961, pp. 404.

A modification of the author's system theory of small groups (infra, no. 382) by using behavioral psychology and economics in order to deal with motivation. One proposition suggests that introduction of a third person into a two-person situation sharply increases available alternatives and reduces satiation as a factor affecting activity. The proposition that satiation is less operative underscores the idea that expansion beyond two members renders relationships exceedingly complex--a point implied by advocates of a flexible balance-of-power in preference to international bipolarity in a view of major international actors that amounts to an analogue of small groups, the validity of which has had no systematic test.

382. Homans, George C. The Human Group. New York: Harcourt, Brace, 1950, pp. xxvi, 284.

A system theory of small groups based on three elementary forms of behavior, activity, interaction, and sentiment, the social system being the character and state of relations among the three and consisting of an external system and an internal system with relative dominance varying. The theory, which in its elaboration deals also with such concepts as role, rank, and norms, was modified in an article co-authored with Henry W. Riecken that was published in Gardner Lindzey (ed.), Handbook of Social Psychology (Cambridge: Addison-Wesley, 1954), and in Homan's Social Behavior: Its Elementary Forms (supra, no. 381).

383. Murphy, Walter F. "Courts as Small Groups." 79 Harvard Law Review (1966), 1565-1572.

On the utility of small group research techniques and concepts for the study of courts and the judicial process that indicates how many of the newer techniques for the study of courts entail small group approaches.

384. Shepherd, Clovis R. Small Groups: Some Sociological Perspectives. San Francisco: Chandler, 1964, pp. xi, 130.
Exposition of the basic objectives and uses of small group research and a review of the essentials of some of the more important projects undertaken and their findings. Particular attention is accorded the approaches and theories of Lewin, Bales, Homans, Thibault and Kelley, Festinger, Kelman, Blau, and Bion.

385. Snyder, Eloise. "The Supreme Court as a Small Group." 36 Social Forces (1958), 232-238. Reprinted in S. Sidney Ulmer (ed.), Introductory Readings in Political Behavior. Chicago: Rand McNally, 1961, pp. 238-248.
Study of alignments within the Supreme Court from 1921 to 1953 that treats the Court as a small group, the replacement of a member having the effect of instituting a new group. This study, restricted to cases concerning Amendments to the Constitution, finds most new members tending to associate with the "pivotal clique" and later become a member of a clique with less effective power.

386. Verba, Sidney. Small Groups and Political Behavior: A Study of Political Leadership. Princeton: Princeton University Press, 1961, pp. 273.
Contributions of small group research to empirical political theory and a discussion of the small group as an analogue of larger political systems.

See also nos. 1269, 1778.

30. Simulation

387. Abelson, Robert P., and Bernstein, Alex. "A Computer Simulation of Community Referendum Controversies." 27 Public Opinion Quarterly (1963), 93-122.
Computer simulation of a fluoridation campaign that not only exposes the individuals in the simulated community to arguments but also allows them to hold conversations with each other. Conversational rate depends upon degree of interest in the issue which is itself dependent on previous exposure to argument and information and on outcomes of earlier conversations.

388. Abelson, Robert P., and Carroll, J. Douglass. "Computer Simulation of Individual Belief Systems." 8 American Behavioral Scientist (1965), 224-230.
Computer simulation of the belief system of a right-winger that used the published remarks of the individual concerned to establish a memory structure, to evaluate statements according to credibility,

and to enable the computer to "rationalize" away statements not credible according to the belief system. The program permitted interaction of statements put into the system and responses to change the system itself.

389. Abt Associates, Inc. Survey of the State of the Art: Social, Political, and Economic Models and Simulations. Report prepared for the National Commission on Technology, Automation, and Economic Progress, Washington, D.C. Cambridge, November 26, 1965, pp. 82.
    Among other things, this survey notes fundamental differences between economic and political-social simulations. The former, usually of the computer type, are generally designed for policy relevance and tend to be cast in terms of regression equations of aggregate relationships as derived from economic data. Political-social simulations, usually of the gaming type, tend to be cast in terms of behavioral micro-processes, are employed chiefly for research and teaching, and are of less value for short-range forecasting than for experimental theory building.

390. Abt, Clark C. "War Gaming." 32 International Science and Technology (August 1964), 29-37.
    General discussion of uses of simulated conflict, of inclusion of political, military, and cultural-ideological factors, and the advantages of computer simulation of models of conflict. TEMPER, a strategic model of international conflict, is described and explained, particularly in regard to its capacity to simulate economic, military, and political interactions in bargaining between East, West, and Neutral nations and blocs. Limitations on the inferences about the real world that can be drawn from games are dealt with.

391. Abt, Clark C., and Gorden, Morton. "Report on Project TEMPER." In Dean G. Pruitt and Richard C. Snyder (eds.), Theory and Research on the Causes of War. Englewood Cliffs: Prentice-Hall, 1969, pp. 245-262.
    Describes the all-computer TEMPER simulation of international relations conducted first at Raytheon Co. and subsequently at Abt Associates in Cambridge, Massachusetts.

392. Alker, Hayward R., Jr., and Brunner, Ronald D. "Simulating International Conflict: A Comparison of Three Approaches." 13 International Studies Quarterly (1969), 70-110.
    A comparison of the MIT Political-Military Exercise (PEM), Northwestern University's Inter-Nation Simulation, and the TEMPER simulation of Clark C. Abt and associates. The PEM scenario was adapted to the other simulations to permit comparisons through runs of the same problem. The findings provide some useful guides to the strengths, weaknesses, and usefulness of each of the three simulations. A useful critique by Edwin H. Fedder follows the article.

393. "ARPA/COIN Model." In Abt Associates, Inc., Some Examples of Completed Work. Mimeo. Cambridge, Massachusetts: 1965, pp. A-1-A-14.
    Simulation by manual gaming based upon examination of some 20 case histories of insurgencies suggesting that the principle variables are "loyalty," information, and effective military force, all

mutually interdependent and presenting quite complex interactions. These three types of interaction, concentrated on to the exclusion of a number of other variables that may appear during insurgencies, were present in various mixtures among three types of actor groups, namely, villagers, insurgents, and government forces, the latter two competing for the loyalties of uncommitted villagers who could be subjected to various cross-pressures or "double-binds." The game structure was intended to simulate one kind of "terror" phase, namely, the transition from Mao Tse-tung's "Phase I" to "Phase II", i.e., from subversion to guerrilla warfare. Such economic factors as food control, civic action, and bribery were excluded from the game because they were not basic to every case history. The article then indicates problems in shifting from a manual game through man-machine simulation to a computer simulation, e.g., the problem of going from an implicit to an explicit structure to include the un-written, unspoken, and perhaps unthought of constraints and bounds, conventions and rituals of human interaction of which the computer can have no more knowledge than is explicitly programmed.

394. Barringer, R.E., and Whaley, Barton. "The MIT Political-Military Gaming Experience." 9 Orbis (1965), 437-458.
Gaming exercises held at MIT since 1958 are discussed. The report analyzes the participants' reactions and concludes that gaming of this type is a learning experience of diffuseness and intensity and with personal involvement.

395. Bloomfield, Lincoln P., and Whaley, Barton. "The Political-Military Exercise: A Progress Report." 8 Orbis (1965), 854-870.
Report on a simulation of foreign policy decision-making in a mock policy session held during a hypothetical crisis situation. The script is loosely defined. Various teams represent nations, with a control group serving to introduce inputs in the form of un-expected events and representing "nature," an international organi-zation, or a nation. The article contains detailed descriptions of methodology and of results of the exercises.

396. Benson, Oliver. "A Simple Diplomatic Game." In James N. Rosenau (ed.), International Politics and Foreign Policy: A Reader in Research and Theory. New York: Free Press, 1961, pp. 504-511.
Description of a use of the computer for simulation purposes, the human user in this game being able to select from 729 possible combinations of actor, action, and target. The game employs a power distribution derived from Kaplan's balance of power, loose bipolar, and tight bipolar systems. Some tentative findings are listed, in-cluding infrequent change in the nature of the universe and the re-tention of a residue of the balance principle within a tight bipolar world.

397. Boguslaw, Robert, and Davis, Robert H. "Simulating National Policy Formation." 8 SDC Magazine (April 1965), 5-16.
Concerned with the long-range impact of disarmament on the American society, the authors simulated national policy formation primarily through the pressures of six interest groups, Business,

Labor, Civil Rights, Military, Internationalists, and Nationalists.
Two pilot experiments are described, and certain faults of design
mentioned. It is also noted that the experienced administrators and
scientists who served as participants in the first pilot run employed negotiating methods strikingly different from those of the
graduate students participating in the second run. A two-page chart
of the sociometric model of the United States that was employed is
suggestive of a method whereby internation simulations might be developed in depth to take better account of the internal dimensions,
conflicts, and constraints affecting foreign policies.

398. Boguslaw, Robert, Davis, Robert H., and Glick, E.B. "A Simulation Vehicle for Studying National Policy Formation in a Less Armed World."
11 Behavioral Science (1966), 43-61.
    Presents a simulation instrument designed to aid national policy
planning and negotiation, together with a report of experiments employing that instrument.

399. Chadwick, Richard Waller. Developments in a Partial Theory of
International Behavior: A Test and Extension of Inter-Nation Simulation
Theory /with/ Supplement: Technical Notes. Evanston: Northwestern University, 1966; Ann Arbor: University Microfilms, Order No. 66-13, pp. 311.
    Report on a comparison of the Brody-Driver simulation with Dimen-
sions of Nations data to ascertain whether the patterns are isomorphic.
Six of the ten two-variable associations employed in constructing the
simulation were not supported by the referent system data.

400. Chadwick, Richard W. Theory Development Through Simulation:
A Comparison and Analysis of Associations Among Variables in an International System and an Inter-Nation Simulation. Paper presented at the
American Political Science Association, New York, September 1966, pp. 41.
    Examination of associations among variables both programmed and
unprogrammed in the Brody-Driver simulation at Northwestern University that concludes (1) that INS theory needs to be restructured to
remove programmed assumptions that appear to be empirically invalid
and adding new assumptions providing indirect linkages between programmed and unprogrammed variables, (2) that in the absence of operation of a revised simulation, no positive demonstration of the usefulness of simulation or theory development is possible, and (3)
that the usefulness of simulation as a heuristic does not appear
great.

401. Cloonan, James B. "Simulation: Techniques and Applications."
6 University of Missouri Business and Government Review (November-December 1965), 18-26.
    A review of the basic techniques of simulation, including
references to Simscript and other simulation languages, and a
survey of various uses of simulation in the social sciences,
medicine, and business and industrial administration.

402. Coleman, James S., Boocock, Sarane S., and Schild, E.O. (eds.).
"Simulation Games and Learning Behavior." 10 American Behavioral Scientist (October and November 1966), pp. 36, 32.

Two issues containing ten articles on the impact of simulation
on learning behavior. Articles of possibly greatest interest to
students of international affairs are that by E.O. Schild on "The
Shaping of Strategies" and that by Holly J. Kinley on "Development
Strategy in a Simulation of Internal Revolutionary Conflict." Appendices include a selective bibliography on simulation in relation
to learning and a list of six centers engaging in simulation and of
the games employed by each.

403. Coplin, William D. "Inter-Nation Simulation and Contemporary
Theories of International Relations." 60 American Political Science Review (1966), 562-578.
    Compares assumptions of the Northwestern simulation with current
    verbal theories and finds much convergence between the two. Some
    simulation assumptions were at variance with the verbal assumptions,
    but many not only were compatible with verbal theory but also raised
    theoretical issues not adequately examined by verbal theorists.

404. Coplin, William D. (ed.). Simulation in the Study of Politics.
Chicago: Markham, 1968, pp. x, 365.
    Papers presented at a conference at Wayne State University in
    May 1967 on uses of simulation in research on international rela-
    tions, urban affairs, elections, political recruitment, organiza-
    tion behavior, and political development.

405. Crow, Wayman J. "A Study of Strategic Doctrines Using the
Inter-Nation Simulation." 7 Journal of Conflict Resolution (1963), 580-
589; 1 Journal of Arms Control (1963), 674-683.
    Report of a pilot run of an Inter-Nation simulation on the
    Northwestern model that includes discussion of the ease of ex-
    perimental intervention through a confederate central decision-
    maker and also a discussion of the eventually successful reduc-
    tion of tension, after initial suspicion and hostility, through
    having the confederate employ Charles Osgood's GRIT strategy.

406. Crow, Wayman J. Simulation: The Construction and Use of
Functioning Models in International Relations. In K.R. Hammond (ed.),
Egon Brunswik's Psychology. New York: Holt, Rinehart and Winston, 1966,
pp. 340-358.
    This paper reviews some major simulation efforts in interna-
    tional relations and then relates simulation research to Brunswik's
    probabilistic functionalism and to his requirements for objectivity.
    The result is a clear, readable exposition both of the requirements
    to be met in the design of a simulation in order to produce accept-
    able results and of methods of validation.

407. Crow, Wayman J., and Noel, Robert C. The Valid Use of Simulation Results. La Jolla: Western Behavioral Sciences Institute, 1965,
pp. 29, 50.
    A useful examination of what may properly be derived from
    simulation studies at the present stage of development of the
    technique.

408. "Empire." In Abt Associates, Inc., Some Examples of Completed Work. Cambridge, Massachusetts: October 1965, pp. E-1 - E-7.
  Example of an undertaking to simulate an historical situation, namely, the situation of colonial America of the 18th century and of the British Customs in the matter of duties on the shipment of goods to and from the Colonies.

408-A. Friedman, Monroe Peter. "Using Simulation Techniques to Predict the Behavioral Effects of New Laws: The Case of Truth-in-Lending Legislation and the Consumer." 54 Journal of Applied Psychology (1970), 297-301.
  Report on the use of a laboratory simulation of the lending environment of a small midwestern city to explore experimentally the probable effects on behavior of "truth-in-lending" legislation. The simulation did not indicate that a sharp short-term decline in consumer credit utilization would result.

409. Goldhamer, Herbert, and Speier, Hans. "Some Observations on Political Gaming." 12 World Politics (1959), 71-83.
  Description of a simulation developed at the RAND Corporation to analyze Cold War situations. Players were area specialists who acted as they thought the country they represented would act except in the case of the United States team which was to pursue policies judged to be optimal. The objective was to test strategies by confronting expert with expert. Variations included the test of the impact of domestic considerations upon foreign policy-makers by including an internal U.S. political game. Another variation had all teams follow optimal policies.

410. Gorden, Morton. International Relations Theory in the TEMPER Simulation. Mimeo. Cambridge: Abt Associates, October 1, 1965, pp. 25.
  Contrasts the TEMPER computer simulation with verbal theory, noting that the computer requires treating as continua terms and concepts that verbal theorists employ in discrete categories. Aggregated concepts such as power, balance of power, public opinion, and national security may be useful to summarize the results of a computer run but not to simulate. Computer simulation requires delving into the components of such concepts and to specify the dynamics of interaction among the component parts.

411. Guetzkow, Harold, Alger, Chadwick F., Brody, Richard A., Noel, Robert C., and Snyder, Richard C. Simulation in International Relations: Developments for Research and Teaching. Englewood Cliffs: Prentice-Hall, 1963, pp. viii, 248.
  Papers on the Northwestern University simulation experiments that include a review of varieties of simulations in international relations.

412. Guetzkow, Harold (ed.). Simulation in Social Science: Readings. Englewood Cliffs: Prentice-Hall, 1962, pp. xv, 199.
  A collection of articles providing a general introduction to simulation and describing some simulation projects in psychology, sociology, political science, economics and business management,

education, industrial engineering, and military operations. An article by the editor, reprinted in part from 4 Behavioral Science (1959), 183-191, describes an early effort to employ inter-nation simulation for the development of theory and for instructional purposes.

412-A. Hermann, Charles F. Crises in Foreign Policy: A Simulation Analysis. Indianapolis: Bobbs-Merrill, 1969, pp. 246.
    With focus on simulated crisis situations within the format of the Northwestern Inter-Nation Simulation design, this study provides insights into the strengths and limitations of man-computer simulation for the study of international politics.

413. Hermann, Charles F., and Hermann, Margaret G. Validation Studies of the Inter-Nation Simulation. Studies in Deterrence, X. U.S. Naval Ordnance Test Station, China Lake, California. NOTS TP 3351. December 1963.
    Report of two simulation runs of the outbreak of World War I in which an attempt was made to match personalities, although not political attitudes. In the run with the greater percentage of matched personalities there was a closer approximation to the July 1914 influence and decision patterns than in the other run. But the matched personalities also engaged in more role playing or imitation, despite efforts to disguise the historical situation. Suggestions are made for possible improvements in simulation of historical situations. A discussion of validation includes a typology of validation and consideration of some major prediction problems.

414. Hermann, Margaret Gladden. Stress, Self-Esteem, and Defensiveness in an Inter-Nation Simulation. Ph.D. Dissertation. Evanston: Northwestern University, 1965; Ann Arbor: University Microfilms, Order No. 65-12,099, pp. 144.
    Study of certain personality factors affecting the coping behavior of naval petty officers serving as subjects in an Inter-Nation Simulation of crisis decision-making on foreign policy. A test was also made of a pre-existing model conceptualizing stress. The association of four behaviors with self-esteem, defensiveness, and negative effect are reported, as are also the responses of four types of personalities distinguished by the possible combinations of low or high self-esteem with low or high defensiveness.

415. Howard, Edward P. "Principles of Simulation." 9 American Behavioral Scientist (September 1965), 6-10.
    Although restricted to simulations of economic systems, this article is a lucid explanation of simulation as a means of dealing with questions that begin with "What difference would it make if. . . ."

416. Kress, Paul F. On Validating Simulation: With Special Attention to Simulation of International Politics. Mimeo. Evanston: Northwestern University, April 1966, pp. 26.
    A useful paper on the problem of ascertaining isomorphism between a simulation and its referent system, with six validation strategies suggested.

417. Naylor, Thomas H., Balintfy, Joseph L., Burdick, Donald S., and Chu, Kong. Computer Simulation Techniques. New York: Wiley, 1966, pp. xiii, 352.

A combination of both theoretical and practical considerations, this volume deals with the planning and building of models for computer simulation, the design of simulation experiments, simulation languages, and the problem of verification. It also presents a collection of computer models based on economic theory.

418. Noel, Robert C. A Simplified Political-Economic System Simulation. Ph.D. Dissertation. Evanston: Northwestern University, 1963, pp. 162.

Contains stimulating suggestions for introducing a more pluralistic economy model that would serve to introduce more of the complexity that confronts decision-makers in the referent system.

419. "Politica." In Abt Associates, Inc., Some Examples of Completed Work. Mimeo. Cambridge, Massachusetts: October 1965, pp. P-1 - P-22.

Description of a simulation of the processes of internal national conflict leading to democratic change, revolutionary change, or reaction. The game, set in a simulated Latin American country, does not cover out-and-out military action and so comes to an end prior to the time limit if the circumstance of armed insurgency in the field arises. It is sufficient for the purposes of the investigators to be able to identify the human and societal variables giving rise to the condition of armed insurgency.

420. Pool, Ithiel de Sola, and Kessler, Allan. "The Kaiser, the Tsar, and the Computer: Information Processing in a Crisis." 9 American Behavioral Scientist (May 1965), 31-38.

Computer simulation of information processing by decision-makers in the 1914 crisis that concentrates on the messages between Wilhelm II and Nicholas II during the week preceding the outbreak of World War I.

421. Pool, Ithiel de Sola, Abelson, Robert P., and Popkin, Samuel. Candidates, Issues and Strategies: A Computer Simulation of the 1960 and 1964 Presidential Elections. Rev. ed. Cambridge: MIT Press, 1965, pp. xi, 193.

Computer simulation of two presidential campaigns, conducted during the campaigns, making use of sample surveys of years prior to the election to break down the population into 480 categories of voter-types and making shrewd guesses as to issues. Likely state-by-state voter reactions and voter shifts to particular stands that could have been taken on major issues were predicted. In the 1960 campaign the sponsor, the Democratic National Committee, was advised in August to meet the religious issue head-on and to play down foreign policy issues.

422. Raser, John R. Simulation and Society: An Exploration of Scientific Gaming. Boston: Allyn and Bacon, 1969, pp. xi, 180.

A highly readable exposition of philosophical and methodological considerations related to simulation, the intellectual and historical roots of social science simulations, the uses of simulation for the development of theory, the types of research conducted by resort to particular games, games used for teaching, and the criteria of validity for research games.

423. Raser, John R., and Crow, Wayman J. WINSAFE II: An Inter-Nation Simulation Study of Deterrence Postures Embodying the Capacity to Delay Response. A Report to Project Michelson under Contract #N 123 (60530) 35639A, NOTS, China Lake, California. Ditto. La Jolla: Western Behavioral Sciences Institute, July 31, 1964, pp. xiii, 95, 102. Condensed as "A Simulation Study of Deterrence Theories," in Dean G. Pruitt and Richard C. Snyder (eds.), Theory and Research on the Causes of War. Englewood Cliffs: Prentice-Hall, 1969, pp. 136-149.

A simulation of an international system in which one nation has the capacity to delay response with strategic weapons. Data obtained indicate that such a nation is perceived as stronger than if the same nation lacked a delaying capacity, but that nation is also perceived as more threatening, i.e., more likely to precipitate war. When capacity to delay response existed, a significant number of participants shifted their responses in a direction that reduced the probability of accidental war. A later report (supra, no. 176) compares the results of this experiment with the findings of a replication with Mexican subjects.

424. Robinson, James A., Anderson, Lee F., Hermann, Margaret G., and Snyder, Richard C. "Teaching with Inter-Nation Simulation and Case Studies." 60 American Political Science Review (1966), 53-65.

On simulation as a teaching device, this article reviews the Northwestern University comparison of the teaching of international relations by case study and by simulation, the findings in respect to each method, the conclusion that simulation produced small but important departures from the "set" that students brought to courses as compared with case study, and a recommendation for further research and replication.

425. Scott, Andrew M., Lucas, William A., and Lucas, Trudi. Simulation and National Development. New York: Wiley, 1966, pp. ix, 177.

A report on simulations of underdeveloped countries in the form of a generalized "Simuland," a simulation of Brazil in 1965-1967 centering on the Congress, the Presidential election, and a weighted representation of interests, and a simulation of Chile in May-September 1965, and 1969-1970, with focus upon legislative implementation of presidential policy and the impact upon the politics of the next election.

426. Smoker, Paul. Analyses of Conflict Behaviours in an International Processes Simulation and an International System 1955-60. Mimeo. Evanston: Northwestern University, August 1968, pp. viii, 137.

Compares simulation data and Dimensions of Nations (Rummel-Tanter) data in a manner indicating distortions in the Northwestern University Inter-Nation Simulation, revealing some of the questionable aspects of the Dimensions of Nations data, and making reference to some of the interpretations of the referent system by theorists.

426-A. Terhune, Kenneth W., and Firestone, Joseph M. "Global War, Limited War, and Peace: Hypotheses from Three Experimental Worlds." 14 International Studies Quarterly (1970), 195-218.

Use was made of the Princeton Internation Game to generate eight hypotheses and their corollaries about the overall international system, conflict, and causal relationships.

427. Terhune, Kenneth W., and Firestone, Joseph M. Psychological Studies in Social Interaction and Motives (SIAM); Phase 2: Group Motives in an International Relations Game. CAL Report No. YX-2018-G-2. Buffalo: Cornell Aeronautical Laboratory, Inc., March 30, 1967, pp. 131.

Report on an international relations simulation in which nations were three-man groups each homogeneously composed of individuals dominant in the achievement, affiliation, and power motives, with findings that achievers initiated cooperation the most but also were high in initiating conflict, power groups were moderately cooperative and highly conflictive, while affiliation groups were lowest in both cooperation and conflict.

428. Tomkins, Silvan S., and Messick, Samuel (eds.). Computer Simulation of Personality: Frontier of Psychological Theory. New York: Wiley, 1962, pp. x, 325.

Reports several attempts at computer simulation of human personalities.

429. Zinnes, Dina A. "A Comparison of Hostile Behavior of Decision-Makers in Simulate and Historical Data." 18 World Politics (1966), 474-502.

Comparison of Stanford data on the perception and expression of hostility during the 1914 crisis with comparable data from the pre-nuclear spread period of the Northwestern simulation of the Nth-country problem to test, among other things, the isomorphism of the international system and its laboratory stimulate. Thirteen hypotheses were tested and the high school students in the simulate behaved similarly to the 1914 statesmen in respect to nine of the hypotheses. In the case of the four hypotheses in respect to which there was discrepancy between the historical and the simulate data, the discrepancy is probably explained by differences between the simulate model and the 1914 international world, in particular the presence of two nuclear powers in the simulate and the absence of a pattern of communication through ambassadors. Unlike the statesmen of 1914, the decision-makers in the simulate behaved in a manner like that displayed in small group experiments--an effect resulting from assembly in the laboratory as contrasted with the real life diplomatic activity between geographically separated national capitals.

See also nos. 176, 458, 683, 1270, 1889, 2653, 2654, and sec. VI, A, 5, b.

31. Gaming and Game Theory

430. Bernard, Jessie. "The Theory of Games of Strategy as a Modern Sociology of Conflict." 59 American Journal of Sociology (1954), 411-424.
    Criticizes the "model of man" implicitly utilized by game theory.

431. Deutsch, Karl W. "Game Theory and Politics: Some Problems of Application." 20 Canadian Journal of Economics and Political Science (1954), 76-83.
    Notes advantages of game theory in the form of the requirement of clear definitions and explicit assumptions but finds a lack of changes in behavior in those parts of the game that correspond to changes in political behavior, a neglect of growth of new resources, and insufficient consideration to dynamic factors and value judgments. Game theory cannot deal with the problem of finding relevant solutions quickly enough.

432. Gerasimov, G. "War Savants Play Games." International Affairs (Moscow) (No. 7, 1964), 77-82.
    A Soviet writer's criticism of American uses of game theory (also of systems analysis) in relation to strategic problems of the Cold War. The argument is that game theory holds considerable promise for the social sciences and needs defense against its mutilation by militarists whose unscientific use of game theory threatens serious political miscalculations. The potential of game theory is held to be subject to remembering that many political problems cannot be translated into the formal language of mathematics.

433. Harsanyi, John C. "Game Theory and the Analysis of International Conflicts." 11 Australian Journal of Politics and History (1965), 292-304.
    Game-theoretical analysis rests on the principle that rationality requires each player to have a set of consistent policy objectives rather than to try to go in two directions at once. Rationality also requires that the choices of each player be based on expectations rationally entertainable about other players' behavior. Application of game theory to international politics is based on the fact that a state's basic policy goals are quite stable and consistent over long periods despite occasional inconsistencies and mistakes.

434. Harsanyi, John C. "Some Social-Science Implications of a New Approach to Game Theory." In Kathleen Archibald (ed.), Strategic Interaction and Conflict: Original Papers and Discussion. Berkeley: Institute of International Studies, University of California, 1966, pp. 1-18.
    Sets forth his postulates in the realm of game theory, the postulates being urged as providing a framework for analyzing society in terms of the partly conflicting and partly complementary interests of different individuals and social groups and in terms of their relative bargaining positions.

435. Hopkins, R.F. "Game Theory and Generalization in Ethics." 27 Review of Politics (1965), 491-500.
    Treats game theory as a special type of utilitarianism that calculates "ought" behavior and so can prescribe prudent strategies

which may also be the most ethical strategies in situations lacking normative structure.

436. Kaplan, Morton, Burns, Arthur Lee, and Quandt, R.E. "Theoretical Analysis of the Balance of Power." 5 Behavioral Science (1960), 240-252.

Describes a competitive international-political board game intended to test hypotheses on the stability of a balance-of-power system, the tendencies toward wars and toward alliances, and the relationship of the number of nations in the system to its stability.

437. Kuhn, Harold W. "Game Theory and Models for Negotiation." 6 Journal of Conflict Resolution (1962), 1-4.

A mathematician's attempt to answer Schelling's criticism (The Strategy of Conflict, p. 119) that game theory is too abstract and Maccoby's criticism (Social Psychology of Deterrence, p. 280) that the game theorist does not always appreciate the power of his "hidden variables." The author's attempt to point out directions of development for game theory in order to meet the criticisms calls attention to three needs previously encountered: (1) the need for a form adequate to describe the temporal sequence of negotiations; (2) the need for a theory of preferences encompassing both the objectives of the participants and their estimation and modification through negotiation; (3) the need for concepts of solution that take account both of the dynamic character of negotiations and the lack of information about objectives.

438. Luce, R. Duncan, and Raiffa, Howard. Games and Decisions. New York: Wiley, 1957, pp. 509.

One of the best introductory works on game and decision theory.

439. Lumsden, Malvern. "Perception and Information in Strategic Thinking." 3 Journal of Peace Research (1966), 257-277.

Presents a theoretical discussion of the relationship of information and perception to strategic thinking and then reports on an experiment employing certain games with a finding that would not have emerged if only one kind of game had been employed. The experiment indicates that analysis of strategic behavior cannot be made without recourse to psychological factors as game theory had led many to hope. The context in which strategic behavior occurs was shown to affect strategic behavior itself, but this context includes perception of "self" and of "other." A problem remains to find ways to measure values put by people upon possible outcomes of their actions before much progress can be made in deciding which logical considerations determine choices.

440. Quandt, R.E. "On the Use of Game Models in Theories of International Relations." 14 World Politics (1961), 69-79. Also in Klaus Knorr and Sidney Verba (eds.), The International System. Princeton: Princeton University Press, 1961, pp. 69-76.

Contends that game models are of little predictive value because too much necessary information is unobtainable by either the researcher or the decision-maker. Attention is given to difficulties inherent in Schelling's analysis if one attempts to equate his model with the realities of international relations.

441. Rapoport, Anatol. "Critique of Strategic Thinking." In Roger Fisher (ed.), <u>International Conflict and Behavioral Science: The Craig-ville Papers</u>. New York: Basic Books, 1964, pp. 211-237.
    This essay discusses some tendencies prevalent among strategists: oversimplification of problems; assessment of a situation by numerical values instead of by attempting to determine the actual inherent values; treating non-zero sum games as if they were zero-sum games, i.e., not considering the presence of an opponent but assuming "nature" as a neutral force. The psychological aspects of decision-making are virtually ignored because they complicate assessment of a problem and detract from the desired characteristic of rationality. Not enough attention is given to the formulation of problems--the role of human interaction is ignored. It is to the formulation of problems that more time and effort should be devoted.

442. Rapoport, Anatol. "Strategic and Non-Strategic Approaches to Problems of Security and Peace." In Kathleen Archibald (ed.), <u>Strategic Interaction and Conflict: Original Papers and Discussion</u>. Berkeley: Institute of International Studies, University of California, 1966, pp. 88-134.
    Discussion of the theory of rational decision with reference to game theory and to the idea behind Schelling's concept of the "prominent solution," that is, the hypothesis that the opponent is like oneself. Comments by Paul Diesing and Albert Wohlstetter, together with Rapoport's rejoinders, are included, the reply to Wohlstetter including a statement concerning the immorality of treating war as a normal phase of international relations, thereby bypassing the moral issue and introducing the perceptual defect of visualizing war from the point of view of its designers rather than from that of its victims.

443. Rapoport, Anatol. "Systemic and Strategic Conflict." 40 <u>Virginia Quarterly Review</u> (1964), 337-368.
    An uncomplicated exposition of the essential theory of Richardson's work and of game theory. Richardson's theory is praised as opening a view of large-scale human affairs that does not assume the goals and strategies of states to be prime movers. The theory, therefore, calls attention to the limitations within which decision-makers may be operating. Game theory's importance lies in its providing a conceptual framework for a theory of rational conflict that restored nobility and glamor to war in the guise of profound intellectual exercise. But game theory presupposes thinking in the strategic mode, and strategic thinking must be transcended if a form of reasoning having survival value is to be attained. This requires thought in terms of pairs of actors rather than of single actors, so that primary importance is attached to the survival of the pair of which each individual is a part, e.g., by both lowering their guns simultaneously.

444. Rapoport, Anatol. Two-Person Game Theory: The Essential Ideas. Ann Arbor: University of Michigan Press, 1966, pp. 214.
Clearly written explanation of the fundamentals of game theory.

445. Sawyer, Jack, and MacRae, D., Jr. "Game Theory and Cumulative Voting in Illinois: 1902-1954." 56 American Political Science Review (1962), 936-946.
A large-scale test of a game theory model that specified the number of candidates each party should have run, given the expected vote distribution, in three-member districts of the Illinois House of Representatives. For elections between 1902 and 1954 the model predicted 69 percent of the actual decisions.

446. Shubik, Martin (ed.). Game Theory and Related Approaches to Social Behavior--Selections. New York: Wiley, 1964, pp. xi, 390.
Articles on the nature of game theory and various applications thereof, some of which are separately annotated.

447. Shubik, Martin. "Some Reflections on the Design of Game Theoretic Models for the Study of Negotiation and Threats." 7 Journal of Conflict Resolution (1963), 1-12.
Discussion of problems of gaming and problems of design that may impede understanding of reality.

448. Snyder, Richard C. "Game Theory and the Analysis of Political Behavior." In Research Frontiers in Politics and Government: Brookings Lectures, 1955. Washington: Brookings Institution, 1955, pp. 70-103.
A clear, relatively brief, explanation of game theory that includes some reference to international and domestic political situations to supply a measure of concreteness to the discussion.

449. Von Neumann, John, and Morgenstern, Oskar. Theory of Games and Economic Behavior. 2nd ed. Princeton: Princeton University Press, 1947, pp. xviii, 641.
Basic volume on game theory and its application to economic, sociological, and strategic problems.

See also nos. 701, 707, 1757, 2128, 2150, 2170.

32. Assumptions of Rationality

450. Simon, Herbert A. "A Behavioral Model of Rational Choice." 69 Quarterly Journal of Economics (1955), 99-118.
The author suggests a revision of "economic" (and thereby, "rational") man by turning to psychology. He inquires into the properties of the choosing organism and gives some general features of rational choice. Terms essential to models of rational behavior are defined in equation form. The "classical" concepts of rationality include the minimax rule, the probabilistic rule, and the certainty rule. The author suggests that these rules are not operative in actual human situations. His aim, in constructing definitions of

"approximate" rationality, is to have them applied to a theory of human individuals behavior in an organizational context (i.e., if an organism having limited knowledge and ability is substituted for concept of "rational man").

451. Verba, Sidney. "Assumptions of Rationality and Non-Rationality in Models of International Systems." 14 World Politics (1961), 93-117.
    Discussion of the place of assumptions and theories about individual decision-making in models of the international system (which is conceived as interaction of two or more nation-states). Notes that both the rational and the nonrational models make a simplifying assumption about the way individuals act in international situations. In most cases neither model represents a complete description of actual behavior. The rationality model is useful only if its limitations are recognized. There is a need to consider the complex ways in which policy is formulated.

See also nos. 61, 315, 442.

D. ELECTRONIC DATA PROCESSING; INFORMATION RETRIEVAL; DATA ARCHIVES; USES OF COMPUTERS

452. Alker, Hayward R., Jr. "An IBM Program for the Gross Analysis of Transaction Flows." 7 Behavioral Science (1962), 498-499.
    An IBM program based upon the Savage-Deutsch model of transaction flows which was originally designed for use with a desk calculator.

453. Arnold, Robert R., Hill, Harold C., and Nichols, Aylmer V. Introduction to Data Processing. New York: Wiley, 1966, pp. ix, 326.
    A useful introduction to a variety of data processing methods, their advantages, and their limitations.

454. Beshers, James M. (ed.). Computer Methods in the Analysis of Large-Scale Social Systems. Rev. ed. Cambridge: MIT Press, 1968, pp. 266.
    An updating of the proceedings of a 1964 conference at the Joint Center for Urban Studies of MIT and Harvard, the papers display three major themes: (1) control over computer processes by the social scientist; (2) the implications of time with reference to complex feedback relationships; (3) the level of aggregation.

455. Bisco, Ralph L. "Social Science Data Archives: A Review of Developments." 60 American Political Science Review (1966), 93-109.
    A guide to 17 undertakings in the United States and Western Europe to collect social science data and make it available to scholars.

456. Bisco, Ralph L. "Social Science Data Archives: Technical Considerations." 4 Social Science Information (1965), 129-150.

Reviews technical problems related to the establishment and maintenance of a data archive.

457. Bobrow, Davis B., and Schwartz, Judah L. (eds.). Computers and the Policy-Making Community. Englewood Cliffs: Prentice-Hall, 1968, pp. vii, 374.

Combines analysis of the ways in which computers can aid the study of international relations with nontechnical discussions of how computers work and what functions they can serve.

458. Borko, Harold (ed.). Computer Applications in the Behavioral Sciences. Englewood Cliffs: Prentice-Hall, 1962, pp. /xvii/, 633.

Written for the social scientist who is not a specialist in computers, this volume not only sets forth what the computer can do but includes the following chapters, among others: E. Lowell Kelly and James C. Lingoes, "Data Processing in Psychological Research"; Benjamin Fruchter and Earl Jennings, "Factor Analysis"; Julian Feldman, "Computer Simulation of Cognitive Processes"; Sydney C. and Beatrice K. Rome, "Computer Simulation Toward a Theory of Large Organizations"; Oliver Benson, "Simulation of International Relations and Diplomacy."

459. Brown, W.S., Pierce, J.R., and Traub, J.F. "The Future of Scientific Journals." 158 Science (1957), 1153-1159.

A proposal, based on the Mercury system employed at Bell Telephone Laboratories, for improving the distribution system of journal articles by employing a computer-based system to make available those articles that a researcher wants rather than those few plus the unwanted excess in bound journals and to assist in keeping researchers up-to-date by making preprints available through a less difficult system than that of restricted mailing lists based on exchanges.

460. Cades, J. Russell. "Jurimetrics and General Semantics." 22 ETC: A Review of General Semantics (1965), 279-292.

Reviews developing computer retrieval projects and their relationships to such semantic problems confronting lawyers as analysis of syntactically ambiguous sentences.

461. Converse, P.E. "A Network of Data Archives for the Behavioral Sciences." 28 Public Opinion Quarterly (1964), 273-286.

Reports on present and projected efforts to solve the problems of data accumulation and preservation and to make such data available for secondary analysis. Attention is called to the need to avoid duplication of effort and to secure collaboration on problems of data format, machine conventions, and retrieval systems to permit rapid data interchangeability among American archives and between American and European archives.

462. Goodman, Leo A. "A Short Computer Program for the Analysis of Transaction Flows." 9 Behavioral Science (1964), 176-186.

Computer program generalizing the Savage-Deutsch model of transaction flows that helps to cover situations not fitting the original model.

463. Goodman, Leo A. "Statistical Methods for the Preliminary Analysis of Transaction Flows." 30 _Econometrica_ (1963), 197-208.

A generalization of the original Savage-Deutsch model of transaction flows to include cases where entries in off-diagonal cells in the matrix of actual transaction flows equal zero. A subsequent application of the model to social mobility data (70 _American Journal of Sociology_ (1965), 564-585) was to show a fit between model and data.

464. Hastings, P.K. "The Roper Public Opinion Research Center: An International Archive of Social Science Data." 16 _International Social Science Journal_ (1964), 90-97.

On the services provided scholars by the Roper Public Opinion Research Center.

465. Janda, Kenneth (ed.). "Advances in Information Retrieval in the Social Sciences." 10 _American Behavioral Scientist_ (January and February 1967), pp. 32, 32.

Two issues that contain 14 articles on social science information retrieval, including a report on the Northwestern University program for selective dissemination of information.

466. Janda, Kenneth. _Data Processing: Applications to Political Research_. Evanston: Northwestern University Press, 1965, pp. xv, 288.

A handbook on electronic data processing for political science research that deals with procedural matters such as collecting, coding, and managing punch card data, correlations, information retrieval, cross-classification, and correlation. Appendices present illustrative uses in regard to several matters including county election returns, political variables for national governments, roll call voting, and legislative history of bills.

467. Janda, Kenneth. _Information Retrieval: Applications to Political Science_. Indianapolis: Bobbs-Merrill, 1968, pp. xxiii, 230.

Case study approach to information retrieval problems for political science that shows how widely available programs can be used relatively inexpensively to solve important and immediate retrieval problems.

468. Levien, Roger, and Maron, M.E. _Relational Data File: A Tool for Mechanized Inference Execution and Data Retrieval_. Memorandum RM-4793-PR. Santa Monica: RAND Corporation, December 1965, pp. 102.

Description of a RAND project for the development and testing of logical techniques for data retrieval and inference making that includes sections on the reasons for not storing information in ordinary language as in some systems, the theory of relations, typical data retrieval requests, key problems of inference, techniques for practical realization of the data file, literature searching, and steps to be taken to extend the capability of the system.

469. Merritt, Richard L. _Political Science and Computer Research_. Paper presented at the conference on Humanistic Studies and the Computer, Georgetown University, Washington, October 21-22, 1965.

Review in nontechnical language of various uses of the computer
in political science research. The paper deals with the fundamentals
of mathematical thinking in political research, factor analysis,
transaction flow analysis, content analysis, gaming and simulation,
and future needs.

470. Miller, Warren E., and Converse, Phillip E. "The Inter-University Consortium for Political Research." 16 International Social Science
Journal (1964), 70-76.
 Reviews the activities of the Consortium and the aids to research
which it provides.

471. Mitchell, Robert Edward. "The Survey Research Center, University
of California, Berkeley." 16 International Social Science Journal (1964),
86-89.
 On the activities of the Survey Research Center at Berkeley and
the services provided for scholars.

472. Murdock, George P., et al. Outline of Cultural Materials. 4th
ed. New Haven: Yale University, Human Relations Area Files, 1961, pp. xxv,
164.
 On the Human Relations Area Files that employs categories for
its data that are often applicable to contemporary societies as well
as to the primitive societies for which the categories were designed.

473. Robinson, Jane, and Marks, Shirley. Parse: A System for Automatic Syntactic Analysis of English Text. Memorandum RM-4654-PR (Parts I
and II). 2 vols. Santa Monica: RAND Corporation, September 1965, pp.
207, 270.
 Interim report providing a detailed technical description of a
system for computer receipt of natural English sentences and converting them into formal structures for further machine manipulation. The system, developed at RAND, was submitted to SHARE, a
voluntary organization of IBM equipment users whereby knowledge
about equipment, programs, routines, etc., is cooperatively pooled.

474. Rohn, Peter H. "The United Nations Treaty Series Project." 12
International Studies Quarterly (1968), 174-195.
 Describes the origin and development of the United Nations
Treaty Series data bank at the University of Washington, the types
of information already produced including treaty profiles of nations
that help to map the legal segment of the international system as
well as functional segments related to treaty subject-matter, the
services performed by the UNTS Project for scholars and professional
organizations, and plans for the extension of the treaty base to the
League of Nations Treaty Series and other published treaties.

474-A. Rohn, Peter H. "Turkish Treaties in Global Perspective." 6
Turkish Yearbook of International Relations (1965), 119-160.
 This is one in a series of national treaty studies using the
computerized data bank of the University of Washington's Treaty
Information Project as well as some available national treaty records

for comparison. For other published studies see 474-B and 474-C, on Canada and the U.S.S.R. For up-to-date information on yet unpublished studies (Australia, China, Japan, Norway, Philippines, Spain, and others) write to Treaty Information Project. Each study analyzes the "gap" between national and U.N. treaty records, and usually concludes that the gap (while variable and sometimes large) does not badly distort national treaty patterns. Hence, treaty studies based only on U.N. records, while incomplete, render a reasonable national, regional, and global image of total treaty patterns. In this perspective, the treaty pattern of Turkey appears quite typical of a medium-sized, medium-developed country in the Western alliance. It bulges heavily toward the U.S.A. and slightly toward Great Britain and Turkey's regional neighbors. It is generally oriented more toward the big and rich partners than toward the small and poor, even if the latter are added together. It reflects local and temporary disputes, and especially the one with Greece over Cyprus. Turkey shows an above-average and slightly growing reliance on international institutions and a normal distribution of treaty topics. All in all, Turkey's general international status is quite well reflected in its treaty pattern, and hence post-dictable from it.

474-B. Rohn, Peter H. "Canada in the United Nations Treaty Series: A Global Perspective." 4 Canadian Yearbook of International Law (1966), 102-130.

This is part of a series of national treaty studies described generally in 474-A. Canada's international status is well postdictable from its treaty pattern, especially with regard to the overwhelming relation with the U.S.A. and the secondary but important linkage with the Commonwealth. U.S.A.-Canada is by far the largest dyad among bilateral treaty-makers in the world. Compared to most countries of its size and status Canada shows a clear preference for the more informal modes of treaty-making, including a lesser involvement of international institutions.

474-C. Rohn, Peter H. "A Computer Search in Soviet Treaties." 2 The International Lawyer (1968), 661-680.

This is related to the series of national treaty studies described generally in 474-A. Again, the country's international position is well mirrored in its treaty pattern. The growth of the Bloc, the loss of Yugoslavia, the partial gain of Cuba, the estrangement of China and especially the globally unique low-water mark in Soviet reliance on international courts and other institutions--all these matters are visible and post-dictable from Soviet treaty patterns. Even Stalin's death (or some major renovation of Soviet governmental procedures) might be post-dicted from the fact that in the mid-1950s Soviet treaty registration suddenly changed from a capriciously erratic pattern to a fairly steady course near the world average. The study puts these substantive findings in the context of a test of computerized legal research and related questions of methodology and research strategy.

475. Rokkan, Stein (ed.). Data Archives for the Social Sciences. Paris: Mouton for the International Social Science Council, 1966, pp. 213.

Proceedings of the Paris Conference on Data Archives for the Social Sciences, September 28-30, 1964. The essays deal with types of archives in existence and foreseeable, the survey data produced in the United States, Great Britain, and Continental Europe, and the training functions of a data library.

476. Savage, I. Richard, and Deutsch, Karl W. "A Statistical Model of the Gross Analysis of Transaction Flows." 28 Econometrica (1960), 551-572.

Postulates a special kind of interaction or partnership occurring when the actual level of transactions is significantly higher than would result from a purely random distribution of transactions. The model develops a matrix resulting from purely random distribution of any type of transaction. Comparison of actual distribution with "expected" distribution produces an index of "relative acceptance" that indicates both the extent and the direction of divergence from expected patterns. This gives an idea of whether a pair or group of states is increasing or decreasing the examined transactions beyond what would be expected from normal shifts and, perhaps, provide a measure of whatever integration may be occurring.

477. Sharp, John R. Some Fundamentals of Information Retrieval. New York: London House and Maxwell, 1965, pp. 224.

Concerned with several aspects of information retrieval: classification, types of systems, indexing language control, correlation and coordination, auto-indexing and auto-abstracting.

478. Vickery, B.C. On Retrieval System Theory. 2nd ed. Washington: Butterworth, 1965, pp. xii, 191.

Comprehensive and clear presentation of modern concepts of information retrieval and their applications to date.

See also no. 539.

E. LOCATION AND USE OF UNPUBLISHED PRIMARY MATERIALS

479. Brooks, Philip C. Research in Archives: The Use of Unpublished Primary Sources. Chicago: University of Chicago Press, 1969, pp. 160.

This manual on the location and proper use of unpublished source materials, including official archives and historical manuscripts, is based upon the author's experience of over 30 years with the National Archives and Records Service.

F. THEORY AND THEORY-BUILDING

480. Alker, Hayward R., Jr. "The Long Road to International Relations Theory: Problems of Statistical Nonadditivity." 18 World Politics (1966), 623-655.

Deals with criticisms by certain writers, particularly Stanley Hoffmann, of mathematically structured theories of international politics by suggesting methods for taking nonadditivity into account in view of the reliance of frequently used statistical procedures on additivity assumptions said by critics to prevent formalizing relationships that are greater or less than the sum of their parts. Remedial procedures suggested are regional factor analysis, mixed or multiplicative equations as well as analysis of variance and covariance procedure, and a set of procedures called "confluence analysis."

481. Bosc, Robert. La Société internationale et l'église: Sociologie et morale des relations internationales. Paris: Spes, 1961, pp. 416.
Particularly important is Chapter 6 which delves into the problem of the incompatibility between the undertaking to build a science of international relations and indoctrination with relativistic beliefs that are represented as moral behavior.

482. Boulding, Kenneth. "Defense and Opulence: The Ethics of International Economics." 41 American Economic Review (1951), 210-228.
The author's thesis is that the principal ethical confusions of the last 100 years are due to a confusion of the public-private value scale with the coercive-noncoercive value scale. There is a tendency toward "publicness"--i.e., organizations devoted to general welfare have high value placed upon them, while private organizations do not. Boulding notes the virtual absence of theory of the state and the consequence that international relations is still studied almost entirely at the level of high-class journalism, without either theoretical foundations or empirical superstructure. He advocates the development of public, noncoercive organizations and comments that if the techniques of, e.g., group dynamics, child psychology, industrial relations, etc., can be applied to international relations, hope prevails for redeeming the nation-state in a union of defense and welfare. Such a union is mandatory in a world where distances are as small as they are today.

483. Burns, Arthur Lee. "The International Consequences of Expecting Surprise." 10 World Politics (1958), 512-536.
The author's concern is with surprise in terms of invention of instruments of war, but he approaches the topic more in an economic and political than a psychological manner. The several dimensions of surprise and their technological and scientific foundations are discussed. Surprise is treated as cheaper than its antidote, the antidote said to be best being countersurprise. Attention is given to the technical features that may prematurely reveal a surprise undertaking, the difficulties imposed by a foreign policy seeking to minimize surprise and types of theory that may be used to study surprise.

484. Burton, John W. International Relations: A General Theory. Cambridge: Cambridge University Press, 1965, pp. ix, 288.
A mixture of analysis and prescriptions about foreign policies, somewhat shallow in its survey of contemporary theories of

international relations, antagonistic toward theories of power, and finding nonalignment and noninvolvement in the affairs of other states to be the basic prescription for a peaceful world.

485. Burton, John W. Peace Theory: Preconditions of Disarmament. New York: Knopf, 1962, pp. xii, 201.
     Argument for the study of peaceful international relations that would make use of some of the developments in sociology that result from investigation of cooperation but would exclude such conflict-laden areas of study as law, foreign policy, military affairs, balance of power, prevention of war, etc. The author, between 1947 and 1951 Secretary of the Australian Department of External Affairs and more recently Research Fellow at the Australian National University at Canberra and then a Senior Lecturer at the University of London, employs the Dollard work on frustration and aggression to express the opinion that enforcement efforts, sanctions, and discriminatory policies do not lead to peace but, through frustration, to aggression. Hence, the chief prescription for a route to a more peaceful world is to drop negotiations in areas that are so competitive as to lead to deadlock and aggravation, shift negotiations to areas where agreement is possible, widen the area of agreement, and return at a later date to the discussion of topics about which no headway proved possible.

486. Cox, Richard. "The Role of Political Philosophy in the Theory of International Relations." 29 Social Research (1962), 261-292.
     The purpose of the article is to question the assumption that every significant aspect of political life necessarily has a theory of its operations only waiting to be discovered or created and to show the relationship of this assumption to modern political philosophy.

487. Dubin, Robert. Theory Building. New York: Free Press, 1969, pp. ix, 298.
     An overall picture of the construction and testing of theoretical models within an operational framework. Attention is given to the units of a theory, distinctions among them, their interaction, boundaries, system states, propositions, empirical indicators and hypothesis.

488. Field, G. Lowell. "Law as an Objective Political Concept." 43 American Political Science Review (1949), 229-249.
     The logical characteristics and contradictions of normative systems.

489. Hinsley, F.H. Power and the Pursuit of Peace: Theory and Practice in the History of Relations Between States. New York: Cambridge University Press, 1963, pp. 416.
     Treats the present century as merely elaborating on concepts of international relations expressed in the 18th century. However, the author himself analyzes attempts to achieve peace in terms of 18th century ideas in that he attributes the peace sometimes achieved to stability in the distribution of power among nations. Neither international law nor arbitral tribunals nor international organizations are regarded as having achieved peace.

490. Hoffmann, Stanley. "International Relations: The Long Road to Theory." 11 World Politics (1959), 346-377.

Critical analysis of the approaches of Morgenthau, Morton Kaplan, Liska, and Snyder. On the constructive side the essay suggests employing Raymond Aron's historical sociology as an initial step toward international relations theory. This would permit identification and description of the dynamics of change from one system to another, definition of types of systems, and comparison of domestic and international systems. The writings of theorists and statesmen, including theories of international law, should be used as tools for analyzing actual systems and situations.

491. Holsti, Kalevi J. International Politics: A Framework for Analysis. Englewood Cliffs: Prentice-Hall, 1967, pp. xv, 505.

An integrated approach to the analysis of international politics with attention to internal restraints on actions and to resolution of international conflicts. Use is made of recent theoretical and empirical studies. Analysis of various systems of the past permits comparison with the present international system.

492. Homans, George C. "Social Behavior as Exchange." 63 American Journal of Sociology (1958), 597-606.

To consider social behavior as an exchange of goods may clarify the relations among four bodies of theory: behavioral psychology; economics; propositions about the dynamics of influence; propositions about the structure of small groups.

493. Jouvenel, Bertrand de (ed.). Futuribles: Studies in Conjecture. Geneva: Droz, 1963-____.

Selected papers from the Ford Foundation's Futuribles project, an opportunity for social scientists to frankly speculate on the shape society will take over the short-run future. Volume II (1965) includes papers on the federative and supranational aspects of Europe at the time of publication and in the 1970s and on the probable foreign policy of a united Europe.

494. Jouvenel, Bertrand de. The Art of Conjecture. Translated by Nikita Lary. New York: Basic Books, 1967, pp. x, 307.

Reminder to political theorists of their task to aid foresight in the political realm in the manner of economists who often lack tools any better than those available to political scientists.

495. Kaplan, Morton A. "Problems of Theory Building and Theory Confirmation in International Politics." 14 World Politics (1961), 6-24.

Problems of theory confirmation in international relations are compared with those in (a) the physical sciences and (b) the other social sciences.

496. Landau, Martin. Political Theory and Due Process of Inquiry. Paper presented at the Annual Meeting of the American Political Science Association, Chicago, September 1964.

Outlines a set of canons for the use of models, warning that models from alien fields become metaphors, that clarity can be lost

when transfer to another field occurs, that vagueness results when
different models are intermingled, that the rules and language of a
model's original field should be adhered to, etc.

497. Lerner, Daniel (ed.). Evidence and Inference: The Hayden Colloquium on Scientific Concept and Method. Glencoe: Free Press, 1959, pp.
164.
    A Daedalus symposium on the development of generalizations in
history, law, clinical psychology, nuclear research, social research,
and medicine.

498. MacIver, Robert M. Power Transformed. New York: Macmillan,
1964, pp. 244.
    After a review of the changing character and role of power in
society the author portrays the rule of force as waning. The remainder of the volume deals with the nature of power.

499. Maruyama, Masao. "Patterns of Individuation and the Case of
Japan: A Conceptual Scheme." In Marius B. Jansen (ed.), Changing Japanese Attitudes Toward Modernization. Princeton: Princeton University
Press, 1965, pp. 489-531.
    One of an important series of articles on one people's attitudes
toward modernization and changes therein. This particular article is
deserving of attention because of its rich theoretical possibilities.
It starts from the relatively simple scheme resting on the two variables of associative or dissociative attitudes of individuals toward
each other and their attitudes toward political authority. Such attitudes can be characterized as centripetal or centrifugal. Many combinations can be generated from this simple beginning and connected
with historical, social, and biographical evidence, as the author
demonstrates with reference to Japan's historical, social, and political development.

500. Maurseth, Per. "Balance-of-Power Thinking from the Renaissance
to the French Revolution." 1 Journal of Peace Research (1964), 120-136.
    This review of balance-of-power thinking concludes with emphasis
upon the great similarity between balance of power in the 18th century and current debate on international affairs, which may suggest
skepticism toward today's revival of the idea both as descriptive
theory and as political doctrine. The article includes discussion
of the dilemma faced by writers on international law as they approach
the problem of whether it is legitimate to intervene to restore the
balance when legitimate actions of a state, e.g., its efforts at internal development, upset the balance of power and threaten its
hegemony.

501. McClelland, Charles A. "The Function of Theory in International
Relations." 4 Journal of Conflict Resolution (1960), 303-336.
    A valuable inventory of approaches to international relations
and identification of numerous tasks that can usefully be undertaken
to develop useful theory. The article is more sympathetic to recent
efforts than is Hoffmann's, but stresses the need to move beyond
analysis to synthesis.

502. McClelland, Charles A. _Theory and the International System_.
New York: Macmillan, 1966, pp. vi, 138.
     An exposition of the place, function and uses of theories of the
international system with particular attention to transformations of
the international system, power and influence, system analysis (including interaction analysis, decision-making analysis, and research
on conflict and conflict resolution), and international communication.

503. Mukerji, K.P. "The Problem of the Psychological Proletariat."
14 _Indian Journal of Political Science_ (1953), 279-289.
     A suggestive discussion of the meaning of the word "proletariat"
which the author contends has come to mean "all persons who suffer
from a sense of frustration born of exploitation." The proletarian
mind being the frustrated mind, the class is not economic but psychological in nature. The proletarian philosopher, bourgeois by origin,
is a frustrated power-hunter. Although its philosophy is one-sided
in its stress on economics (the author does not mention the offshoot
from bourgeois stress on economics), it reflects the undemocratic
privilege that the bourgeois politician, emphasizing peace and democracy because profitable, has failed to see. Communism _versus_ democracy is a psychological struggle within the bourgeois fold that
employs the economic proletariat as a pawn. In world affairs Marxism tends to unite not the property-less but the world's opportunity-
less frustrated.

504. Peckert, Joachim. _Die grossen und die kleinen Mächte: Möglich-
keiten der Weltpolitik Heute_. Stuttgart: Deutsche Verlags-Anstalt, 1961,
pp. 192.
     Analysis by a West German diplomat of the rapid changes occurring
in concepts of world affairs and the situations of Great Powers and
less powerful countries.

505. Rummel, Rudolph J. "A Field Theory of Social Action with Application to Conflict within Nations." 10 _General Systems_ (1965), 183-211.
     With reference to data of July 1, 1962-June 30, 1964, on various
forms of internal violence, the author undertakes to go beyond factor
analysis to develop a social field theory that treats social reality
as a field made up of all attributes and interactions of social units
--a field susceptible of division into attribute spaces and behavioral
spaces. The two types of spaces are spanned by finite and empirically
determined dimensions which generate the spaces. Social units are located as vectors in attribute space and are coupled in behavioral
space into dyads that display a direction and movement over time. By
defining social forces as vectors, equilibrium concepts are incorporated into the theory. Change is incorporated as the movement of social
units or dyads as attributes and resultant interactions change.

506. Rummel, Rudolph J. "A Social Field Theory of Foreign Conflict
Behavior." _Peace Research Society (International), Papers_. Cracow Conference, 1965, Vol. IV (1966), pp. 131-150.
     A report of the author's test of his social field theory by
using his Dimensions of Nations data on foreign conflict.

507. Russell, Frank M. <u>Theories of International Relations</u>. New York: Appleton-Century, 1936, pp. viii, 651.

Thorough chronological review of the essential concepts of international relations as expressed by publicists and, although referred to less frequently, by policy-makers. The study covers the Western world from ancient times to the 1930s and includes short summaries of ancient Hindu and Chinese concepts.

508. Said, Abdul A. (ed.). <u>Theory of International Relations</u>. Englewood Cliffs: Prentice-Hall, 1968, pp. xii, 191.

A collection of essays presented at American University's School of International Service in 1966-1967. Although examining exertive influences, operational hypotheses, and emerging directions in the study of international relations, the degree of focus on theory is uneven. Included are essays by William D. Coplin on the impact of simulation on the theory of international relations, by Karl W. Deutsch on the impact of communications on theory, and by Said on the impact of the non-Western world.

509. Wight, Martin. "Why There is No International Theory." In Herbert Butterfield and Wight (eds.), <u>Diplomatic Investigations: Essays in the Theory of International Politics</u>. London: Allen & Unwin, 1966, pp. 17-34.

In an attempt to ascertain the reason for a lack of international theory except, perhaps, such as is included in philosophies of history, the author concludes that the difficulty lies in the need to theorize in the language of political theory and law, both relevant to man's control of his social life, that is, to systems of action within the realm of normal relationships and calculable results. Instead of the theory of the good life, international theory must be the theory of survival in which the regular case is what for political theory is the extreme case. Comparing the newer methodologies with works on international history, the author finds the latter to do a better job of conveying the nature of foreign policy and the working of the state system because historical studies (1) do the job with more judiciousness and modesty and (2) accord closer attention to the record of international experience.

See also nos. 400, 403, 719, 1140, 1763, 1953.

II. PATTERNS, STRUCTURES, AND UNITS

A. SYSTEMS AND SUBSYSTEMS

1. Models of Systems

510. Boserup, Anders, and Iversen, Claus. "Demonstrations as a Source of Change: A Study of British and Danish Easter Marchers." 3 <u>Journal of Peace Research</u> (1966), 328-348.

Among other things, finds that peace demonstrators tend to hold a two-level model of the world, clearly differentiating the national and international levels with minimum interaction at a given level. Their preferred solution is a world state, that is, a world without nations but with peaceful individuals. But this preferred state of peace is not attainable without violation of their model of the world. Hence, the authors conclude that the peace demonstrators are compelled by their own views to settle for second best, namely, a world of peaceful nations.

511. Casanova, Pablo González. "Internal and External Policies of Underdeveloped Countries." In R. Barry Farrell (ed.), Approaches to Comparative and International Politics. Evanston: Northwestern University Press, 1966, pp. 131-149.

Sketches a model of the international system that most leaders of underdeveloped countries consider the true one and which differs from those commonly employed by researchers from the developed Western countries.

512. Kaplan, Morton A. "Some Problems of International Systems Research." In International Political Communities--An Anthology. Garden City: Doubleday (Anchor Books), 1966, pp. 469-501.

Besides a nontechnical account of some of Kaplan's models of international systems and indications of some theoretical problems raised by the models, the article reviews some preliminary tests being made of the models at the University of Chicago. Computer simulation of the balance-of-power model has been undertaken with such objectives as testing the impact of differing numbers of major actors, changing formulae for figuring imbalance and for determining battle exchanges, and determining the effects of various degrees of distaste for or liking of foreign imbalance. Historical studies are also being made, the three referred to being studies of the Italian city-state system and the mercenary system of that period, the Chinese warlord system between disruption of Yuan Shih-kai's national system and reunification under the Kuomintang, and the breakup of Alexander's Empire. Aside from what may be learned about the formation and disruption of empires, the historical studies make possible a continuous feedback learning process and integration of data linking historical studies, computer simulation, and system theories.

513. Kaplan, Morton A. System and Process in International Politics. New York: Wiley, 1962, pp. xxiv, 283.

Abstract approach to international relations, starting from a set of terms, definitions, and axioms that serve as foundations on which to construct six international systems: balance of power, loose bipolar, tight bipolar, universal international, hierarchical international, and unit veto. The first two models alone approach systems known in history. Attention is accorded regulatory processes and integrative and disintegrative processes which are treated as regulatory in character. Concluding sections deal with values, game theory, and strategy. The study is conceptual, not descriptive, but when employed with awareness of its limitations can be very helpful in ordering and integrating the data of international relations.

514. Tolman, E.C. "Cognitive Maps in Rats and Men." 55 Psychologi-cal Review (1948), 189-208.

On the carrying of cognitive maps of the organization of one's environment, such maps being of varying degrees of accuracy but es-sential for effective life in the environment.

See also nos. 119, 1136, 2224, 2338.

2. System Structure; System Mapping

515. Alexander-Alexandrowicz, C.H. "Vertical and Horizontal Divi-sions of the International Society." 1 Indian Year Book of International Affairs (1952), 88-96.

Hypothesis that international cooperation requires promotion of common functional interests of primary importance through organiza-tion by groups having genuine motives for forming horizontal strata. Alliance of such groups with the state, as in the case of trade un-ions, is seen as impeding attempts at international cooperation. Therefore, promotion of horizontal strata may require sacrifice of certain social and economic policies which also strengthen the state and so strengthen vertical barriers.

516. Alger, Chadwick F., and Brams, Steven J. "Patterns of Repre-sentation in National Capitals and Intergovernmental Organizations." 19 World Politics (1967), 646-663.

Correlation of numbers of diplomatic representatives sent from and received in national capitals, shared memberships in 161 inter-governmental organizations (excluding the UN and the specialized agencies), and international trade that finds a stronger relation-ship between states' patterns of trade and diplomatic representation than between either and shared memberships. Rankings on the basis of diplomatic representation and shared memberships are also provided-- with note taken of the possibly foreboding position of the four Asian Communist countries at the bottom of the table of shared memberships. Differences between the number of diplomats sent and the number re-ceived are regarded, if a positive difference (25% of the states), as balance toward seeking information about the world and, if nega-tive, as less expenditure of human resources to observe and report on the world than the world expends observing and reporting on the state concerned. The addition of data on treaty relations (see Rohn, supra, no. 474) and its correlation with the data on which this arti-cle is based would help to map the international legal system and the degree to which it coincides with other systems.

517. Banks, Arthur S., and Gregg, Phillip M. Grouping Political Sys-tems: Cluster Analysis of A Cross-Polity Survey. Mimeo. Carnegie-IDRC Joint Study Group on Measurement Problems. Indiana University, April 1965, pp. 8.

Finding that Russett's paper, "Delineating International Regions," does not define political regions but regions demarcated by social and economic variables, the authors employ a Q-technique to analyze 68 political variables for 115 countries, chiefly from Banks and Textor, A Cross-Polity Survey. Using the inflection point criterion, the first five factors were selected for rotation, the nations clustering under the factors labelled polyarchic (generally democratic), elitist (5 new Asian and 25 new African states), centrist (including all Communist states), personalist, and traditional.

518. Blühdorn, Rudolf. Internationale Beziehungen: Einführung in die Grundlinien der Aussenpolitik. Vienna: Springer, 1956, pp. xiii, 391.
    One of the first German efforts to produce a text on international relations rather than on diplomatic history or international law. International relations are treated in terms of psychological and sociological propositions about individuals and groups. Different types of states and foreign policy alternatives are examined along with their ideological and philosophical foundations. Despite some tendency toward diffusion, the book represents an important effort to draw on the findings of the various social sciences. For example, in dealing with the influence of domestic affairs on international relations the author takes up the problems of frustration and the consequences of social frustration. Attention is given to such matters as propaganda and mass psychology, the foundations of nationality and nationalism, forces making for internal cohesion of states, the function of language and forms of thought and their impact on human relations, the functions of war, various aspects of nuclear warfare and its impact on international relations before and after 1954, the conduct of foreign policy, and various forms of peaceful, or at least nonviolent, relations among states.

519. Boggs, S. Whittemore. "Geographic and Other Scientific Techniques for Political Science." 42 American Political Science Review (1948), 223-238.
    The purpose of the author's paper is to suggest concepts for utilizing in political problem-solving an objective geographical study in which changing planetary patterns of economic and social activity, influenced by science and technology, are compared with changing patterns of political activity. Studies are suggested on world-code, area, individual and governmental, and individual-in-society levels. Specific techniques are listed.

520. Brams, Steven J. "Measuring the Concentration of Power in Political Systems." 62 American Political Science Review (1968), 461-475.
    Political systems, conceptualized as "partly ordered structures" in which some pairs of actors are connected in either symmetrical or asymmetrical influence relationships, are analyzed by using the theory of directed graphs (digraphs) to group actors into "mutual influence sets" and assign the sets to unique hierarchical levels in an influence structure. A quantitative index to measure the concentration of power between any two hierarchical levels is applied to analyze Communist bloc power relationships in 1956-1959.

521. Brams, Steven J. "The Structure of Influence Relationships in the International System." In James N. Rosenau (ed.), International

Politics and Foreign Policy: A Reader in Research and Theory. Rev.
ed. New York: Free Press, 1969, pp. 583-599.
    Employs digraph theory to analyze visits in 1964 and 1965 between
heads of state and other high-level government officials and, on the
assumption that the nation more often visited is the more influential,
in an attempt to develop a hierarchy of influence relationships aiding
in explanation of some aspects of state behavior. Several tentative
findings are presented and matters about which additional research is
needed are identified. The effort to ascertain and delineate a hierarchy of influence relationships, if further developed and the reliability of potential indicators of influence compared, could conceivably provide a better guide to the question of influence upon the
content of international law than present sweeping statements about
past European dominance and current Afro-Asian numbers in the United
Nations.

    522. Brams, Steven J. "Transaction Flows in the International Sys-
tem." 60 American Political Science Review (1966), 880-898.
    Employing data on diplomatic exchanges, trade, and shared mem-
berships in intergovernmental organizations, the author starts with
the Savage-Deutsch transaction flow model to measure deviation of the
three types of transactions from an ideal type. A battery of decomposition programs was applied to the salient and coincidentally salient linkage matrices for the three types of transaction in order to
obtain maps of the international system indicative also of subgroups
of nations and their interrelationships.

    523. Burns, Arthur Lee. "From Balance of Power to Deterrence: A
Theoretical Analysis." 9 World Politics (1957), 494-529.
    The author attempts to show that international relations form a
system and that a general theory of that system may be possible. He
uses the game theory approach to interpret international conflicts,
recognizing that the mathematical approach cannot by itself explain
or resolve international conflicts. Relations of alliance and of
pressure or opposition are designated as those which constitute the
international system. Burns sums up their system-building propensities in a series of propositions.

    524. Cohen, Saul Bernard. Geography and Politics in a Divided World.
New York: Random House, 1963, pp. xxiii, 347.
    A geopolitical exposition that includes some useful analyses and
data of interrelationships, primarily regional in geostrategic and
geopolitical terms, that help to illuminate some of the bases of international order. While the volume must be used with the same caution that applies to other geopolitical works, a part of its utility
lies in the author's recognition, illustrated by his references to
the differences in Mackinder's views in 1904, 1918, and 1943, of the
dependence of geographic analysis upon other variables.

    525. Eberhard, Wolfram. "Concerns of Historical Sociology." 14
Sociologus (New series, 1964), 3-17.
    The author discusses some reservations concerning current socio-
logical research. He observes that the concept of social system has

its limitations for the historical sociologist, for it implies interaction between units and a political-geographical area with clear-cut
borders. The problem is that in the same geographical area several
"societies" can exist side by side without functional social relations
and without acculturation or assimilation. Political boundaries, even
linguistic boundaries, do not limit such societies. Another type of
"society" consists of widely scattered members who share values and
behavior over large distances and belong socially only peripherally
to their actual environment. A model depicting multiple social units
in this sense as, e.g., the co-existing Indian farmers and the merchants in Moghul India who were in part geographically overlaid by
other units, would consist of more than four or five such layers,
each, as a rule, hierarchically structured. Such a model would facilitate the formation of a historical theory of social change, a
problem that functionalists have not been able to study successfully.
Conceivably, change could spread across political borders and continents but inside a particular layer.

525-A. Fisher, Dana D. "National Socialist Germany (1933-1939) and
International Law." Paper presented at the International Studies Associa-
tion-West meeting, San Francisco, March 31-April 1, 1970, pp. 44, ix.
    Against the background of the international law theory of Nazi
Germany, the author presents analyses of the number and types of
Nazi treaties, the distribution among treaty partners, and a brief
comparison with the treaty practice of some other states studied
under the guidance of Peter Rohn at the University of Washington.

526. Gluckman, Max. Custom and Conflict in Africa. Glencoe: Free
Press, 1955, pp. 173.
    The author gives careful attention to cross-cutting memberships
that hold societies together by permitting friends on one basis or
system of alliance to be enemies in another--a matter also of concern to such sociologists as Edward A. Ross (The Principles of Sociology), Georg Simmel (Conflict and the Web of Group Affiliations),
and Lewis Coser (The Functions of Social Conflict).

527. Hanrieder, Wolfram F. "International Organizations and International Systems." 10 Journal of Conflict Resolution (1966), 297-313.
    Relying on Inis Claude's exposition of the nature of balance of
power, collective security, and peaceful settlement systems, upon
Richard Rosecrance's analysis of 18th and 19th century systems, and
upon recent analyses of bipolarity and of the UN, the article seeks
to clarify the nature of the present system of international organization and to identify some similarities with the post-Napoleonic
system. Claude's three systems are treated as representing a continuum of systems, with peaceful settlement in the middle and ambiguous in the sense of possessing attributes of both the balance of
power and the peaceful settlement systems. Some indications are
given of the forces that move a system from one type to another along
the continuum.

528. Horowitz, Irving L. Three Worlds of Development: The Theory and Practice of International Stratification. New York: Oxford, 1966, pp. xii, 475.

On the structure of the international system and the interactions of the United States and its allies, the Soviet Union and the Eastern bloc, and the third world of developing nations.

529. Isard, Walter, and Wolpert, Julian. "Notes on Social Science Principles for World Law and Order." Peace Research Society (International), Papers. Ghent Conference, 1964, Vol. II (1965), pp. 242-251. Also in 1 Journal of Peace Research (1964), 242-251.

An attempt to demonstrate that social science analysis and sound world law are inextricably bound together. Without attaching weight to the findings of their oversimplified analysis, the authors illustrate their contention by means of a model of world hierarchical structure of central places and service areas. A chart is made of vectors of influence and flow (communication, migration, etc.) to and from the world primary node to major and subregional primary nodes and to local community nuclei. Steel production is suggested as being organized in regional nodes, while elementary schools illustrate a local service function. The impact of political boundaries dividing regional nodes is discussed. A system of world law is viewed as requiring criteria for adjudication, by governmental and other personnel with decision-making competence, on the basis of multipliers or other bases for programmed decisions that would permit at least reasonable approximations as to the relative importance of participation in decision-making, efficiency, and equality. World law would then provide the weights, e.g., for determining the point of substitution between participation potential and efficiency--in other words, establish bases for compromise.

530. Joxe, A. "Logique des relations de préférence et nombre de protagonistes." 4 Stratégie (April-May-June, 1964), 41-58.

Regarding hypotheses concerning risks in a multiplication of powers whose voices would be heard in East-West negotiations as far from demonstrated, the author attempts to demonstrate the implications of the logic of simple numbers of actors--the logic of two, three, and four actors--in a system of international relations.

531. Klingberg, Frank L. "Studies in the Measurement of the Relations among Sovereign States." 6 Psychometrika (1941), 335-352. Reprinted in James N. Rosenau (ed.), International Politics and Foreign Policy. New York: Free Press, 1961, pp. 483-491.

Develops indices of hostility among nations by having students of international relations rank pairs of major nations in terms of hostility in an effort to gauge the degree of friendliness and hostility and so to determine the probability of war.

532. Landheer, Bart. "State-mobility as a Sociological Concept." 1 Internationales Recht und Diplomatie (1960), 53-62.

Sociological conceptualization of the state as a group transmitting social innovation and characterized by behavioral rules and patterns of communication. The author believes that the current structure of international society is based upon ideological or cultural blocs.

533. Michaely, Michael. <u>Concentration in International Trade</u>. Contributions to Economic Analysis. No. XXVIII. Amsterdam: North-Holland Publishing Company, 1962, pp. 167.
   A study based upon measurement of commodity concentration of trade of 44 countries and of geographic concentration. Only in eight countries (France, Italy, Japan, Netherlands, Norway, the United Kingdom, the United States, and Yugoslavia) is commodity concentration of imports higher or just slightly lower than of exports, while geographic concentration is roughly equal. Other findings provide a clearer view of international economic relations and include some findings of special significance for underdeveloped countries. The study is an aid in the identification of economic variables that can strain noneconomic, including legal, relations between states.

534. Michaely, Michael. "Multilateral Balancing in International Trade." 52 <u>American Economic Review</u> (1962), 685-702.
   A quantitative analysis of multilateral balancing by 65 countries and territories that, among other things, finds the following patterns: (1) a rise in multilateral balancing between 1938 and 1948 and a decline thereafter; (2) little change in multilateral balancing in non-Soviet Europe between 1948 and 1954-1958 and an apparent decline for Germany; (3) no single country outside the Soviet bloc with as low a level of multilateral balancing as any country within the Soviet bloc; (4) relatively bilateral balancing for the United States, Canada, the Latin American dollar countries, the United Kingdom, and Continental Western Europe; (5) relatively high multilateral balancing for the nondollar Latin American countries, the Overseas Sterling Area, and the rest of the world. The attributes of countries with relatively high multilateral balancing were: (1) export of primary goods (except Japan); (2) underdevelopment (except Australia); (3) relatively small foreign trade (except Japan); (4) location outside Europe. The U.K. and U.S., two of the most bilateral non-Soviet countries, were by far the leading multilateral balancing agents, while India was found to be an important agent of multilateral balancing.

535. Parsons, Talcott. "Order and Continuity in the International Social System." In James N. Rosenau (ed.), <u>International Politics and Foreign Policy</u>. New York: Free Press, 1961, pp. 120-129.
   Treating order as a normative control that keeps action within limits essential to stability, the article attempts to identify the principal elements of normative order in contemporary international affairs. Normative components are regarded as institutionalized when it is in the interest of acting units to do what they ought to do. Increasing differentiation of the nontotalitarian modern state is seen as making for greater independence of the controllers of force and so as increasing relations across national boundaries. Not states but alliances or communities of interest make up the

world. Pluralism is increased as solidarities between states cross-cut each other. The U.N. is viewed as performing a legitimizing function while polarization, although entailing the risk of war, is seen as an analogue of a two-party system. The two conditions that can promote stability are cross-cutting solidarities inhibiting polarization and a constitutional order in which each party sees the other as legitimate. Problems of integration of Western and other cultures are mentioned and processes that could extend the range of normative order are noted.

536. Parsons, Talcott. "Polarization of the World and International Order." In Quincy Wright, William M. Evan, and Morton Deutsch (eds.), Preventing World War III: Some Proposals. New York: Simon and Schuster, 1962, pp. 310-331.
        Making use of a general systems approach, this article deals with the possibility that there is a two-party system emerging in international politics with the United States and the Soviet Union acting as leaders of the contending parties and the developing countries playing the role of the electorate.

537. Perroux, François. La coexistence pacifique. 3 vols. Paris: Presses Universitaires de France, 1958, pp. xi, 666.
        An essentially economic approach to coexistence under hostile conditions and the possible consequences thereof, as well as of forces and actions pointing toward the emergence of global authority. The core thesis expounded in the second volume is that of "poles of development," that is, that the growth of an economy depends on the existence of poles created by a key industry and those industries that are related to it, the emergence of which is conducive to the creation of a "growth mentality." The concept is applied to the examination of the Western and the Soviet bloc economies with reference to differences between the growing global economy and the traditional international economy and to contradictory elements in the global situation.

538. Perroux, François. L'Économie du XXième siècle. Paris: Presses Universitaires de France, 1961, pp. 598.
        A collection of 27 papers written over a period of ten years. Perhaps most important from the point of view of influences upon international law is the discussion of the place of the dominating firm in a growing economy. This discussion leads into an examination of power relations on the international plane, with "dominating effect" not referring only to greater bargaining power but also involving significant repercussions on trade and on capital flow. Attention is called to the role of international companies in economies dependent on industrial nations and in the shaping of international trade flows. The "poles of development" concept appears also in this volume.

539. Rohn, Peter H. "A Legal Theory of International Organization." 5 Turkish Yearbook of International Relations (1964), 19-53.

Revised and condensed version of a 1958 doctoral dissertation which developed a method of comparing the constituent instruments of different international organizations so as to measure the legal powers conferred on these institutions. To maximize the range of comparability the sample is not limited to the usual major organizational types (United Nations, NATO, Common Market, Benelux, etc.) but includes also such extreme cases as a true federal government (U.S.A.) and a largely symbolic institution (Commonwealth) as well as some minor and defunct types (Balkan Assembly and European Payments Union) and even a hypothetical case (European Defense Community). A concluding tabulation ranks 20 organizations separately on each of 10 dimensions of legal power, e.g., purpose of constituent instrument, power to interpret or amend it, number of organs created, treaty-making power, decisional procedure, enforcement, budget, etc., as well as various subcategories. The overall rankings confirm non-quantitative professional opinion. There are three clusters in the degree to which legal power is transferred from states to institutions: (1) most powerful, clearly, is the federal government; (2) intermediate are the supranational communities of the Western European Six; and (3) least powerful are all the other international institutions, and rather similarly so, whether global or regional, functional or political. The study thus identifies and quantifies the most and least likely legal means which states use to transfer power to joint institutions, and it explores critical combinations, thresholds and other relationships among such integrative means.

539-A. Rohn, Peter H. Institutions in Treaties: A Global Survey of Magnitudes and Trends from 1945 to 1965. Syracuse: Maxwell School, 1970, pp. 92.

Designs an empirical test for the general notion that 20th-century international law increasingly relies on international institutions for its development and implementation. The study postulates theoretically that institutionalism (like any other major fact of public international life) would be mirrored in the world's treaties. The unit of measurement is a textual reference in any treaty to any international organization. The universe consists of all 8,641 treaties in U.N. Treaty Series Volumes 1-550. The major source is the computerized data bank of the University of Washington's Treaty Information Project (see 474), of which the author is director. Substantive findings confirm the general notion that, indeed, institutions do play a major and increasing role in contemporary treaties. The world-wide average for the 20-year period from 1945 to 1965 amounts to one institutional reference for every two treaties, with a slight but fairly consistent upward trend. However, the average distributes quite unevenly over the various signatories, topics, and institutions. Typical high and low scores (above or below average reliance on institutions per treaty) include the following. Rich and strong countries score low; poor and new countries score high. The Soviet Bloc scores quite low, and the Soviet Union lowest of all. The only Western country scoring anywhere nearly as low as the Soviet Bloc is the United States. The U.N., the I.C.J., and the general category of ad hoc commissions score high; regional institutions score low. Multilaterals score more than twice as high as bilaterals. Treaties on transport and communication score about three times as high as those on diplomatic and administrative matters. The overall finding on the growth of institutionalism will please the optimists but many of the details will confirm the cynics. In any case, the study supplies concepts and facts for system-wide analyses of international law and institutions.

539-B. Rosenau, James N. (ed.). Linkage Politics: Essays on the Convergence of National and International Systems. New York: Free Press, 1969, pp. xii, 352.
 A set of essays by such authors, in addition to the editor, as J. David Singer, William G. Fleming, Bernard C. Cohen, Richard L. Merritt, R.V. Burks, and Michael O'Leary, among others, that seek systematic approaches to the links between national and international systems.

540. Sawyer, Jack. "Dimensions of Nations: Size, Wealth, and Politics." 73 American Journal of Sociology (1967), 145-172.
 Factoring 236 characteristics of the 82 then-independent nations of more than 800,000 population in 1955 indicates that three practically uncorrelated dimensions--size, wealth, and politics, closely indexed, respectively, by the variables population, G.N.P., per capita, and political orientation as Communist, neutral, or Western--account for 40% of the variance, sort nations into relatively homogeneous groups, and predict several other national characteristics.

541. Schlesinger, J.R. The Strategic Consequences of Nuclear Proliferation. RAND Report P-3393. Santa Monica: RAND Corporation, June 1966, pp. 20.
 Drawing a distinction between political and strategic consequences, the author contends that it is a mistake to view the problem of proliferation in quantitative terms of numbers of nations and that in any confrontation the central strategic balance of the United States and the Soviet Union could continue to provide stability in regional conflicts.

542. Swingle, Paul G. "Illusory Power in a Dangerous Game." 22 Canadian Journal of Psychology (1968), 176-185.
 Report on a bargaining game which, under one condition giving one player illusory power while the weaker power retained the capacity to inflict mutual loss, produced the result that, as compared with the equal power condition, illusory power delayed cooperation until the stronger player became aware of the power structure--a circumstance not unlike some recent superpower involvements, including Vietnam.

542-A. Union of International Associations. "Schematic Relationship between Organizations in the World System." 21 International Associations (no. 1, 1969), 31.
 Table of relationships between nongovernmental, nonprofit, governmental, and business organizations from the local to the international level, together with estimates of the numbers of these types of organizations at each level.

543. Wiley, Jay W. "Issues in International Economics: Gold, the Dollar, and CRU." 10 (N.S.) Indiana Academy of the Social Sciences, Proceedings, 1965 (1966), 28-36.

Discusses the differences between a world with a single financial center such as England in the 19th century and the United States in 1945-1958 and a world of many financial centers. Sheer economic power of England and the United States, not gold, is identified as the reason for dominance and is contrasted with today's diffusion of economic power. A composite reserve unit (CRU) of currency is viewed as having limited utility, the limitations being specified. It is noted that redeemability and economic power are tied up with the notion of sovereignty, while a CRU entails mutual interdependence among and some surrender of sovereignty by the subscribing nations. In the relation of sovereignty to redeemability lies a hitherto inescapable junction of national politics and economics.

544. Woolley, Herbert B. Measuring Transactions Between World Areas. National Bureau of Economic Research. Studies in International Economic Relations. No. 3. New York: Columbia University Press, 1966, pp. xviii, 157.

Detailed record of such types of transactions between major world areas in 1950-1954 as merchandise, services, and unilateral transfers.

545. Young, Oran R. "Political Discontinuities in the International System." 20 World Politics (1968), 369-392.

An argument for new ways of conceptualizing the international system in light of the increasing interpenetration of the global political axes and the emergence of widely divergent regional subsystems.

See also nos. 252, 452, 462, 463, 474, 476, 513, 977, 1084, 1201, 1556, 1650, 1759, 1793, 1883, 1966, 2689.

a. Subsystems

545-A. Atal, Y. "Subordinate State System and the Nation-Set: Tools for the Analysis of External Milieu." 3 South Asian Studies (Jaipur, July 1968), 40-53.

Objecting to Brecher's concept of the "subordinate state system" as inapplicable to countries having multiple orientations, the author proposes the concept of the "nation-set" in which a nation's complement of role relationships with other nations constitutes its nation-set in a particular field. Analysis should include (a) intensity of interaction between a nation and the members of the nation-set, (b) bilateral relationships, (c) the influence of the nation-set of a partner, the pattern of conflicting demands, and the size of the nation-set. The four types of nation-sets tentatively identified are (1) the contiguous boundary set, (2) the common interest set, (3) the membership-role set, and (4) nonmembership nations.

546. Bell, Philip Wilkes. <u>The Sterling Area in the Postwar World</u>.
New York: Oxford University Press, 1956, pp. xxvi, 478.
Detailed study of the sterling area, its problems in the
first ten postwar years, and its cohesiveness.

547. Berry, Brian J.L. "A Method for Deriving Multi-factor Uniform
Regions." 33 <u>Polish Geographer</u> (1961), 263-279.
Employs a discriminant function analysis applied to Q-factor
loadings to examine countries' scores on economic development and
demographic scales. Results obtained are quite similar to those
obtained by Russett who employed a different method in the effort
to delineate international regions. Other articles by Berry that
resulted from the employment of this method are found in two volumes by Norton Ginsburg, <u>Essays on Geography and International</u>
<u>Development</u> (University of Chicago Press, 1960) and <u>Atlas of Eco-</u>
<u>nomic Development</u> (University of Chicago Press, 1961).

548. Berry, Brian J.L. "Basic Patterns of Economic Development."
In Norton Sydney Ginsburg (ed.), <u>Atlas of Economic Development</u>. Chicago:
University of Chicago Press, 1961, pp. 110-119.
Focusing not on patterns among variables but upon regional
variations, 95 countries are rank-ordered on 43 economic and demographic variables. Factor analysis then indicated that four factors described patterns underlying the 43 variables. Some common-
sense notions about regional levels of economic development were
then tested, some confirmed, some not--e.g., tropical location
apparently has little to do with stage of economic development,
while poverty does not appear to be explained by political
colonialism.

548-A. Berton, Peter (ed.). "International Subsystems." 13 <u>Inter-</u>
<u>national Studies Quarterly</u> (Special Issue, December 1969), 329-434.
Contains the following articles: Michael Banks, "Systems
Analysis and the Study of Regions"; Louis J. Cantori and Steven
L. Spiegel, "International Regions: A Comparative Approach to
Five Subordinate Systems"; John H. Sigler, "News Flow in the
North African Subsystem"; Thomas W. Robinson, "Systems Theory
and the Communist System"; Donald C. Hellmann, "The Emergence
of an East Asian International Subsystem."

549. Bhagat, Ajit. "Working of the Sterling Area Gold and Dollar
Pool--1948-1958: An Essay in Regional Multilateral Payments System." 9
<u>Indian Economic Journal</u> (1961-1962), 199-218.
A study of a Commonwealth institution as it operated among
former components of an Empire.

550. Bigosinski, Jerry T. <u>The Swiss Money Market</u>. Ph.D. Dissertation. New York: New York University, Graduate School of Business Administration, 1963.

Based upon primary sources and direct contacts with Swiss authorities and experts, the study undertakes an assessment of the Swiss money market (not a money market in the terms of reference applied to New York and London) on the international system, in light of the noneconomic character of much of the funds moving through Switzerland and Switzerland's role as the world's ultimate hoarding place. Despite positive contributions made by the Swiss market for long-term funds, the Swiss market has had basically unsettling effects on the international financial system due to some not too sound foundations that are identified by the author.

551. Binder, Leonard. "The Middle East as a Subordinate International System." 10 World Politics (1958), 408-429.
     Employs the concepts of subordination and of system in analysis of the Middle East.

552. Brecher, Michael. "International Relations and Asian Studies: The Subordinate State System of South-Eastern Asia." 15 World Politics (1963), 213-235.
     Proposal for a new "level of analysis" of international relations. To analysis limited to states as units in the political system has been added analysis starting from the existence of an international political system, but this entails "an almost pathological concern with Soviet-American relations." Hence, it is suggested that a third level of analysis, that of the "subordinate state system," be employed. As an example, the Southeast Asian system is analyzed as manifesting the characteristics of low power concentration, suffering from underdeveloped organizational integration, displaying lack of contacts between states, and continually penetrated by the dominating world system.

553. Brecher, Michael. "The Middle East Subordinate System and Its Impact on Israel's Foreign Policy." 13 International Studies Quarterly (1969), 117-139.
     Centering on Israel as a part of the "Near East core" of a three-segment subordinate state system (core, periphery, outer ring) that is semi-geographical in terms of distance as a criterion for inclusion in a segment (e.g., Tunisia and Morocco are placed in the outer ring and Algeria in the periphery), this paper assesses the designated subsystem in terms of, among other things, level of power, power stratification, penetration of and by subordinate systems, level of communications, homogeneity of values, and commonality of political systems.

554. Burr, Robert N. By Reason or Force: Chile and the Balancing of Power in South America, 1830-1905. University of California Publications in History. Vol. 77. Berkeley, October 9, 1965, pp. 322.
     On the problem of the regional balance of power in South America and of a regional balancer during the 19th century. The situation has three elements of similarity with today's non-European regional systems, namely (1) the subsystem members were new states; (2) their economies were underdeveloped; (3) their land transportation systems were poorly developed.

555. Caprariis, Vittorio di. Storia di un'alleanza: Genesi e significato del Patto Atlantico. Roma: Opere Nuove, 1958, pp. 185.

Concentration on the common substratum of Atlantic Community institutions that proceeds from an effort to identify the spiritual values to analysis of foreign policy developments and East-West dissent. This is a particularly useful volume in that it can be used to give another, non-Anglo-American, view of the common substratum problem and its relation to the question of identification of the European content of "the general principles of law recognized by civilized nations," as well as of treaty norms and norms of customary international law.

555-A. Connor, Walker F. "Myths of Hemispheric Continental, Regional, and State Unity." 84 Political Science Quarterly (1969), 555-582.

An overview and critique of assumptions that common interests and traits are to be found among peoples joined by territorial contiguity, including some comments on the uses of foreign territory as sanctuaries for rebels and the expectation that anti-revolutionary governments will observe the traditional sanctity of borders.

556. Curcio, Carlo. Europa--storia di un'idea. 2 vols. Firenze: Vallecchi, 1958, pp. 1003.

A vast, finely elaborated mosaic dealing with the idea of Europe as it developed through the centuries and as its spirit and character changed within the wider Atlantic framework. Discussion of East and West treats these notions as historical and so as subject to change with time. The volumes can thus be useful in linking the "family of nations" concept more accurately "with the general principles of law recognized by civilized nations."

557. Fisher, F.M., and Ando, A. "Two Theorems on 'Ceteris Paribus' in the Analysis of Dynamic Systems." 56 American Political Science Review (1962), 108-113.

Describes two recent theorems concerning large systems that can almost, but not completely, be divided into subsystems. The theorems permit far-reaching statements concerning the behavior over time of the subsystems and of the entire system. Although the theorems were intended to deal with problems frequently encountered in economics, the paper suggests their applicability to situations in other social sciences and presents two examples, one concerning armaments races and another concerning the voting strength of political parties.

558. Galtung, Johan, Mora y Araujo, Manuel, and Schwartzman, Simon. "El sistema latinoamericano de naciones: un análisis estructural." 9 América latina (January-March 1966), 59-93.

An examination of the Latin American system along the four dimensions of extent of territory, distribution of income, social structure, and ethnic composition and in terms of six variables permitting study of the interactions among the Latin American states. Although rank along the four dimensions does not appear to affect relations even with the United States, the introduction of the United States discloses a different system, the Interamerican, in which the rank of the United States has an impact upon the system's relations with the outside world.

559. Good, Robert C. "Changing Patterns of African International Relations." 58 American Political Science Review (1964), 632-641.
Discusses the relationships (1) between radicals, moderates, and conservatives, (2) between the new states themselves, (3) between the new states and the mother countries, and (4) between the new states and the Communist world. The author treats the fragile quality of the new governments as productive of a common concern to assure the legitimacy of the present state system but not necessarily the legitimacy of each national regime.

560. Gordon, Bernard K.   The Dimensions of Conflict in Southeast Asia. Englewood Cliffs: Prentice-Hall, 1966, pp. xv, 201.
Deals with conflict and cooperation in Southeast Asia. A brief but important section on "Western Legalisms and Ancient Empires" calls attention to the lack of defined territorial limits of ancient empires, the absence of Western concepts of sovereignty and independence, special relations with China, and the absence of imperial rule beyond the maritime outposts of certain empires. Application of Fred W. Riggs' concept of a prismatic system, in which achievement-oriented norms superimposed upon a traditional system create a contradiction between formal prescription and accepted practice, serves as an introduction to Southeast Asian territorial conflicts. A chapter on personality in Southeast Asian politics produces some tentative suggestions for theory. Cooperation in Southeast Asia is treated as permitting application of Southeast Asian data in an effort to determine whether hypotheses drawn from European integration experiences have wider application or merely reflect a unique European experience. Particular attention is given to some generalizations of Harold Guetzkow and Ernst B. Haas.

561. Gray, Richard B. (ed.).   International Security Systems. Itasca, Illinois: F.E. Peacock, 1969, pp. xi, 227.
With attention to both theoretical models and actual global and regional systems that have security as their objective and operate systematically, these essays examine, among other things, processes, concepts, and institutions in the framework of general systems theory.

562. Hamilton, W.B., Robinson, Kenneth, and Goodwin, C.D.W. A Decade of the Commonwealth, 1955-1964. Durham: Duke University Press, 1966, pp. xx, 567.
Changes in the Commonwealth since 1955 are examined by 25 scholars concerned with the interrelationship of its members, its institutions, its international relations, etc.

563. Hartshorn, J.E.   Politics and World Oil Economics: An Account of the International Oil Industry in its Political Environment. New York: Praeger, 1962. English ed. Oil Companies and Governments: An Account of the International Oil Industry and its Political Environment. London: Faber and Faber, 1962, pp. 364.

Careful analysis of the evolving pattern of organization, the pressures on the international industry that have been brought by the producing states, and the consequences of the upsurge of nationalism.

564. Hodgkin, Thomas. "The New West Africa State System." 31 University of Toronto Quarterly (1961), 74-82.
A treatment of West Africa as a distinguishable state system.

565. Hoffmann, Stanley. "Discord in Community: The North Atlantic Area as a Partial International System." 17 International Organization (1963), 521-549.
Development of a typology of interstate interactions and the types of tension produced by each.

566. Lindberg, Leon N. "The European Community as a Political System: Notes Toward the Construction of a Model." 5 Journal of Common Market Studies (1967), 344-387.
An employment of David Easton's systems-analytic framework to develop a model of the European Community.

567. Megee, Mary. "Problems in Regionalizing and Measurement." Peace Research Society (International), Papers. Cracow Conference, 1965. Vol. IV, 1966, pp. 7-35.
An undertaking to employ factor analysis to develop a system of world regions. Four factors were extracted: (1) industrial development; (2) social overhead and government expenditures; (3) domestic and foreign trade; (4) social dimensions. Euclidean space concepts, Cartesian coordinate systems, and simple distance models were employed in the effort to derive more objective systems of regions. Note is taken of the propositions of writers on development that appear to have been confirmed. Reference is made to the grouping problem and a need for more complex methods of measurement if geographically contiguous regions are to be derived rather than only homogeneous economic and social groupings. The latter are seen as of value when the interest is not in contiguity but in need for economic aid. Isolated cases are said to warrant study as possible examples of development that might guide neighbors. The method of factor analysis is treated as a first rough approximation of theory about regions opening the door to more direct experimentation. More refined distance formulae are regarded as necessary for delineation of more than rough groups of countries.

568. Modelski, George. "International Relations and Area Studies: The Case of South-East Asia." 2 International Relations (1961), 143-155.
On the use of area studies as a means for studying international subsystems, particularly for the following classes of problems: foreign policies of subsystem members; influence of the international system on subsystems; particular subsystem relationships; the subsystem and its functions.

569. Nye, Joseph S. (ed.). International Regionalism: Readings. Boston: Little, Brown, 1968, pp. xvi, 432.

Brings together a number of articles that discuss the role, value, and prospects of a number of regional groupings, including those in underdeveloped areas.

570. Penrose, E.F. "Political Development and the Intra-Regional Balance of Power." 1 Journal of Developmental Studies (1964), 47-70.
Discussion of the practical importance of the idea of regional balance of power in the Afro-Asian-Latin American world.

571. Perkins, J.O.N. Sterling and Regional Payments Systems. Melbourne: Melbourne University Press; New York: Cambridge University Press, 1957, pp. xv, 171.
Examination of the sterling area and the European Payments Union as regional systems in the postwar years prior to EEC.

572. Perroux, François. L'Europe sans rivages. Paris: Presses Universitaires de France, 1954, pp. vii, 668.
Stimulating study of the role imposed on Europe by the mid-20th century world economy in which viable economic spaces transcend national and limited regional units, the two dominant poles of attraction being the United States economy in the "Euratlantic orbit" and the Soviet economy in the "Eurasian orbit." Basic economic data and trends of the two orbits and the relations of continental Europe with them are discussed, with emphasis upon the long-standing material and cultural relations of the Atlantic community that have been emphasized by the threat of war.

573. Polk, Judd. Sterling: Its Meaning in World Finance. New York: Harper for the Council on Foreign Relations, 1956, pp. xvii, 286.
A former U.S. Treasury official's exposition of broader economic and political aspects of the sterling system.

574. Reid, A.J.S. "The Economic Background to Indonesia's 'Confrontation'." 16 Political Science (Wellington) (no. 2, September 1964), 3-6.
On "confrontation" as part of Indonesia's effort to withdraw the country's foreign trade from the entrepôts of Singapore and Penang and from the hands of Chinese merchants in those two cities.

575. Rhode, Gotthold. "Politische und soziale Probleme einer Integration in den Ostblocksländern Ostmitteleuropas." In Erik Boettcher (ed.), Ostblock, EWG und Entwicklungsländer. 3rd ed. Stuttgart: W. Kohlhammer, 1964, pp. 22-50.
An exposition of social and political problems in Eastern Europe with attention accorded to the existence and effects of division into three culture areas: (1) areas experiencing little or no Russian or Turkish domination; (2) the area (Congress Poland) controlled for a century by Russia; (3) the area under Turkish control for three to four centuries.

576. Russett, Bruce M. "Delineating International Regions." In J. David Singer (ed.), Quantitative International Politics: Insights and Evidence. New York: Free Press, 1968, pp. 317-352.

Employing a factor analysis of data in Russett, et al., World Handbook of Political and Social Indicators, four factors, economic development, communism, Catholic culture, and intensive agriculture, are derived to produce groupings of nations given the following labels: Afro-Asia, Western Community, Latin America, semi-developed Latins (Uruguay, Puerto Rico, Cuba, Spain, Portugal, Chile), Eastern Europe, and "unclassifiable" (Haiti, Jamaica, British Guiana, South Africa, China). A further analysis, based upon a relative accept- ance index employing trade data, is employed in an effort to deline- ate regions of interdependence, which breaks the world down into more and smaller regions than does the author's test of sociocultural homogeneity.

577. Russett, Bruce M. International Regions and the International System: A Study in Political Ecology. Chicago: Rand McNally, 1967, pp. xvi, 252.
Exploration of some relations between political systems and their social and physical environment that undertakes to delineate regions, cohesiveness among states, to examine theories of politi- cal integration, conditions of peaceful change, formation and de- composition of coalitions, and the uses of ecological data for testing hypotheses and developing better taxonomies descriptive of national attributes and behavior. Methodological problems are dis- cussed throughout the book which relies chiefly upon factor analysis of several types of data.

578. Schwartzman, Simon, and Mora y Araujo, Manuel. "The Images of International Stratification in Latin America: A Reputation Study Based on Social Science Students." 3 Journal of Peace Research (1966), 225-243.
Report on questionnaire administered to 327 Argentinian, Bra- zilian, and Chilean social science students and to a control group of Norwegian students productive of a rank-ordering of the 20 Latin American states. The students were asked to distribute the 20 states in three levels of prestige and importance. Other questions con- cerned their knowledge of Latin America, their perception of rank positions on some relevant rank-dimension, and the criteria used in distributing the countries on the three levels. Besides being able to obtain a stratification with composite rankings from 1 to 20, the experimenters analyzed the indicated determinants of the image of stratification to find that the image derived from the generalized rank-roles played by the countries as a function of their power and development, not from specific knowledge of the countries.

579. Sovani, N.V. Economic Relations of India with South-East Asia and the Far East. New Delhi: Indian Council of World Affairs and Oxford University Press, 1949, pp. 137.
Approximately half of the book consists of statistics of India's bilateral trade with Southeast Asian countries, China, Japan, Aus- tralia, New Zealand, and the Philippines from 1911 to World War II. The other half consists of commentary upon potential developments in independence. The two sections of the book help to illuminate the nature of the economic ties left by imperialism and throw light upon the limitations of economic relations as one basis on which to rest

a Southeast Asian regional system extending into the legal and political spheres.

580. Szalai, Alexander. "Cohesion Indices for Regional Determination." Peace Research Society (International), Papers. Cracow Conference, 1965. Vol. IV (1966), pp. 1-6.
    A Corresponding Member of the Hungarian Academy of Sciences, at this writing Deputy Director of Research, UNITAR, deals with measurements of regional cohesion based on "spatial flow" analyses, which are contrasted with other measurements obtainable from a regional "activity specialization" approach. In his concluding remarks the author briefly discusses the problem of which flows to measure, the problem of whether there is a "best type" of flow for the study of any particular regional problem, the use of a components analysis to reduce a combination of measures to a single measure, the possibility of treating several measures at once through reformulation as vector-valued quantities, and the prerequisites of an approach to the problem of how cohesive regions should be with respect to various activity spheres.

581. Wheare, Kenneth Clinton. The Constitutional Structure of the Commonwealth. New York: Oxford, 1961, pp. xiv, 201.
    Analysis of rules, understandings, and practices that serve to regulate interrelationships of the members of the Commonwealth.

582. Whitaker, Arthur P. The Western Hemisphere Idea: Its Rise and Decline. Ithaca: Cornell University Press, 1954, pp. 194.
    Tracing of the idea of a Western Hemisphere united by geography and common political ideas and what the author regards as the decline of the concept in the 1940s.

583. Zartman, I. William. International Relations in the New Africa. Englewood Cliffs: Prentice-Hall, 1966, pp. xiv, 175.
    Excellent review, rich in traditional-type data, on the international system of Africa, particularly West Africa and the Maghreb, designated by the author as a "mobile system" as distinct from a supranational, balance-of-power, or bipolar system. Among the topics of special interest to international lawyers are those of the "international relations rules" of legitimization of states and territories, legitimation of colonial boundaries, nonintervention (opposition to political assassination, subversion, and interference in internal affairs), opposition to war except against colonialism and neocolonialism, and peaceful settlement. Attention is given to actual instances of subversion, territorial disputes, attempts to employ boundary closings to produce political pressures on a neighbor, actions against nationals of other African states, alliances and counter-alliances, transportation problems, problems in allocation of resources, river regimes, restoration of the Tunisian-Algerian electricity grid, special purpose and multipurpose international organizations and commissions, the foreign policy structures and decision processes, and the ideological element in foreign policy decision-making. Attention is called to the presence of oil fields in an area

disputed by Algeria and Tunisia and placed under joint sovereignty or condominium by bilateral agreement. The relation of the African subsystem to the global system as affected by the Cold War is examined, and the retained police role of certain West European military forces, including French control of ammunition supplies in certain areas, is seen as a factor keeping political conflicts from becoming military conflicts.

See also nos. 218, 219, 749, 1135, 1654, 1925, 2644, 2645, 2647-2649, 2778, 2788, 2799, 2846.

(1) Special Bilateral Bonds

584. Clark, S.D. "Canada and Her Great Neighbor." 1 Canadian Review of Sociology and Anthropology (1964), 193-201.
   Treats Canadian national feelings as entailing rejection of opportunity to participate in the large free market produced by union south of the border and political and social upheavals in Canada as resulting from efforts to change policies limiting freedom of movement and denying opportunities offered by the expanding community of North America.

585. Deener, David R. (ed.). Canada-United States Treaty Relations. Durham: Duke University Press, 1963, pp. xiv, 250.
   A collection of papers by political scientists and lawyers that deal with such matters as boundary waters, military cooperation, commercial relations, metals and energy fuels, and the need for continental management of resources.

586. Meyer, Milton Walter. A Diplomatic History of the Philippine Republic. Honolulu: University of Hawaii Press, 1965, pp. 321.
   Reviews Philippine foreign policy with attention to relations with the United States, frequent departures from the Afro-Asian consensus, and the derivation of Philippine policy from its Western supraculture and its Asian infraculture. Some problems of state succession are discussed.

587. Munro, John M. Trade Liberalization and Transportation in International Trade. Toronto: University of Toronto Press, 1969, pp. x, 203.
   This volume deals with the transportation aspects of the flow of goods within North America and with policy in Canada and in the United States with attention to provincial and state as well as national policies concerning rail, highway, and water transportation. Attention is given to the potential impact of North American free trade on Canadian transportation. Recommendations are made for the easing of transport problems resulting from the separate policies of sovereign authorities.

588. Piper, Don C. "The Role of Intergovernmental Machinery in Canadian-American Relations." 62 South Atlantic Quarterly (1963), 551-574.

Analysis of the nature and scope of joint commissiones and committees concerned with the conservation and development of shared resources or facilitating bilateral cooperation in economics and defense.

589. Reuber, Grant L. The Growth and Changing Composition of Trade Between Canada and the United States. (Washington and Montreal): Canadian-American Committee, 1960, pp. xii, 87.

Discussion of various aspects of Canadian-American trade, including petroleum and the adaptation of 1957 when Venezuelan supplies were diverted to Europe while the Suez Canal was closed.

590. Russett, Bruce M. Community and Contention: Britain and America in the Twentieth Century. Cambridge: MIT Press, 1963, pp. 252.

Analysis of bonds and strains within the Anglo-American alliance, notable for its dispute-settling capacity, that undertakes to test the effects of communication, attention, and mutual identification upon international relationships, together with policy recommendations for reversing a discerned trend toward a weakening of the alliance. Evidence for decline, probably strongest in case of importance of the United Kingdom to the United States, is found in such measures as volume of exports, tourists, movies, literature, student exchange, migration, first-class letters, telephone and telegraph communications, etc., plus evidence from more conventional sources. The alleged decline is relative, that is, a decline in responsiveness relative to that toward other countries in the 20th century.

591. Tilton, John E. "The Choice of Trading Partners: An Analysis of International Trade in Aluminum, Bauxite, Copper, Lead, Manganese, Tin, and Zinc." 6 Yale Economic Essays (1966), 416-474.

A study of nonprice factors in the metals trade that finds that international ownership ties, political blocs, government interference and regulation, the heterogenous nature of ores and metals, and traditional buyer-seller ties have greater influence on the course of the ore and metal trade than do transportation costs, total export supplies, or total import requirements.

592. Wonnacott, Ronald J. Canadian-American Dependence: An Interindustry Analysis of Production and Prices. Contributions to Economic Analysis. No. XXIV. Amsterdam: North-Holland Publishing Co., 1961, pp. 143.

An econometric study of interdependence of Canada and the United States, the most significant suggestion for the analysis of underlying economic interrelations being that a reverse absolute index may reveal certain aspects of the effect in one country of change in demand in another--particularly in large-small country situations--that may be missed by reliance only on the more commonly employed relative index.

See also nos. 681, 2587, 2670, 2673, 2728, 2783, 2846.

(2) Economic Landscapes and Company Regions;
Spatial Relationships

593. Gottmann, Jean. "Geography and International Relations." 3
World Politics (1951), 153-173.
On differentiations between "compartments of space" and the
study of international relations and the importance of traffic,
trade, transportation, and exchanges to understanding the relationships between geography and international relations.

594. Gottmann, Jean. "The Political Partitioning of Our World: An
Attempt at Analysis." 4 World Politics (1952), 512-519.
An exposition of the "circulation" theory arising from French
geographic concepts that emphasize the "movement factor."

595. Jackson, W.A. Douglas. Politics and Geographic Relationships:
Readings on the Nature of Political Geography. Englewood Cliffs: Prentice-Hall, 1964, pp. xii, 411.
Book of readings drawn from some of the more important theoretical writings on geography of recent times and covering such
subjects as boundaries, location, nationality, transportation, access to the sea, international rivers, the functional geography of
the business firm, the economic landscape, the territorial state
and its conflicts with international firms and with economic landscapes, and natural resources.

596. Lösch, August. The Economics of Location. New Haven: Yale
University Press, 1954, pp. xxviii, 520.
Includes a section comparing states and "economic landscapes"
and calls attention to dissimilarities, the influence of economic
areas on states, coincidences of economic and political boundaries,
and transformations of economic areas by changes in state boundaries. Attention is also given to national boundaries as factors in
determining the location of industries and also to the tariff as a
device for inducing foreign industries to establish branches within
a particular state.

597. McNee, Robert B. "Centrifugal-Centripetal Forces in International Petroleum Company Regions." 51 Annals, Association of American
Geographers (1961), 124-138. Reprinted in W.A. Douglas Jackson (ed.),
Politics and Geographic Relationships: Readings on the Nature of Political Geography. Englewood Cliffs: Prentice-Hall, 1964, pp. 257-274.
An adaptation of Hartshorne's centrifugal-centripetal concept
to deal with the problem of the relationship of the transnational
firm with the nationalistic territorial state. The concept is applied to analyze the Jersey Standard regional corporate system.

598. McNee, Robert B. "Functional Geography of the Firm, with an Illustrative Case Study from the Petroleum Industry." 34 Economic Geography (1958), 321-337.

Development of the concept of functional geography of the firm in an effort to explain its spatial relationships and organization, the petroleum industry serving as the example.

(3) Normative Subsystem Structure

599. Georgopoulos, B.S. "Normative Structure Variables and Organizational Behavior." 18 Human Relations (1965), 155-169.

Tests of a hypothesis that the behavior of a social system is significantly related to the noncontent character of its normative structure, i.e., normative complementarity, internal normative consistency, normative congruence, normative consensus, and normative member attractiveness.

600. Pospisil, Leopold. "Legal Levels and Multiplicity of Legal Systems in Human Societies." 11 Journal of Conflict Resolution (1967), 2-26.

Employing comparisons among the legal systems of the United States, pre-Communist China, the Incan Empire, the Kalinga of Northern Luzon, and the Kapauku Papuas of West New Guinea, among whom the author has done field work, a case is made for the conceptualization of legal systems as reflections of the patterns of subgroups of a society so that what is displayed is a multiplicity of legal systems--as many as there are functioning social units. These systems may be in conflict, with no guarantee that the center of power, which may move upward or downward in response to circumstances, is necessarily at the level of the more inclusive social group.

601. Rome, Beatrice, and Rome, Sydney. Communication and Large Organizations. Professional paper SP-1690/000/00. Santa Monica: System Development Corporation, September 4, 1964, pp. 108.

Two lectures on the Project Leviathan simulation of large organizations based on the conceptual approach that the most important feature of large social organizations is hierarchy. The several conditions under which the organization was allowed to operate and varying instructions to subjects are indicated. The most important findings are of consequence to both constitutional law and international law. (1) Only when a normative element was present were the participants able to run the organization effectively. (2) Like a constitution, the normative prescriptions had to clearly establish relationships of authority and responsibility between levels of commands and within particular levels in order to obtain well-structured feedback data usable to satisfy both component and system requirements. (3) The most important major value scheme may be summed up in the norm "Take the system perspective," that is, subordinate subsystem objectives to system accomplishments. In international affairs the comparable norm would subordinate national--and, presumably, regional --goals to global objectives, thereby mitigating the rigor of sovereignty and according the international aspect of dédoublement fonctionnel an effectiveness greater than achieved to date. In the Leviathan experiment, taking the system perspective alone produced more than 300% improvement in performance.

602. Rome, Beatrice, and Rome, Sydney. "Leviathan." 8 SDC Magazine (April 1965), 17-25.
    A more recent report on Project Leviathan, containing a more complete account of the findings of the 1964 experiments to the effect that a normatively structured, value-laden culture provides a more effective and continuous evaluative feedback, providing information needed for long-range planning and near-optimal strategies, than when there is a relative lack of norms. This article and the paper of September 4, 1964, provide findings rich in their implications and highly suggestive of further basic research, particularly in the area of norms, their interpretation, and their application under various conditions of organization.

603. Sherif, Muzafer. "Superordinate Goals in the Reduction of Intergroup Conflict." 63 American Journal of Sociology (1958), 349-356.
    Report on that part of the Robbers Cave experiment in which superordinate goals were introduced with the effect of reducing intergroup friction and increasing intergroup friendship choices as measured by observational and sociometric techniques. In the absence of superordinate goals, mere intergroup contact proved ineffective in reducing conflict and, instead, served as opportunities to display hostility. The findings in terms of superordinate goals are similar to the Romes' findings about the importance of the system perspective in a normative sense.

See also nos. 1187, 1285, 1783, 1901.

b. Public Units or Entities

(1) International Personality

604. Aspaturian, Vernon V. The Union Republics in Soviet Diplomacy: A Study of Soviet Federalism in the Service of Soviet Foreign Policy. Geneva: Droz; Paris: Minard, 1960, pp. 228.
    Survey of Soviet uses of its 1944 constitutional amendments that accorded foreign relations powers to the Union Republics.

605. Hartman, R.S. "La nación: reliquia feudal." 23 Cuadernos americanos (May-June 1961), 33-61.
    A comparison of the nation with feudal units that tends to ignore differences but still serves as a useful reminder both of some

relics from the past and of the possibility that the state is but a stage in an incomplete integration process.

605-A. McNemar, Donald W. "Participatory Internationalism: The Role of the Individual in International Relations." Prepared for the International Studies Association Convention, Pittsburgh. Mimeo. Hanover, N.H.: April 1970, pp. 23.

> Argues for study of interdependence by shifting the level of analysis from the state to the individual as actor in international relations and for the encouragement of "participatory internationalism."

605-B. McNemar, Donald W. "World Student Unrest and the Future of the U.N." Prepared for the Conference on the Future of the United Nations, World Order Research Institute, Villanova University. Mimeo. May 1969, pp. 19.

> Developing the concept of "participatory internationalism" from its roots in current demands for "participatory democracy," the author includes some suggestions for United Nations initiative, e.g., by establishment of a "Peacekeeping Academy," to increase the involvement of youth in projects around the globe of internationalist rather than purely national nature.

See also nos. 1764, 1965, 2058, 2410.

(a) Penetrated Systems

606. Feld, Werner J. "National-International Linkage Theory: The East European Communist System and the EEC." 22 Journal of International Relations (1968), 107-120.

> Applying Rosenau's national-international linkage theory, the author examines the interaction of Soviet policymakers, the Italian and French Communist parties, and EEC, with particular attention to the efforts of the Italian Communists to gain representation on EEC organs, prevent supranational measures that impede democratic reforms in particular countries, keep power over EEC in national parliaments, and revise the Rome Treaty for the benefit of the East European states.

607. Rosenau, James N. "Pre-theories and Theories of Foreign Policy." In R. Barry Farrell (ed.), Approaches to Comparative and International Politics. Evanston: Northwestern University Press, 1966, pp. 27-92.

> An argument for a pre-theory for foreign policy analysis that would provide a means for similar processing of raw data, render it comparable, and thereby permit theorizing. The author prefers an issue-area orientation, each issue-area seen as requiring a special type of decision-making treatment. Analytic dimensions would embrace the idiosyncratic, role, governmental, societal, and systemic dimensions. A horizontal-vertical system dichotomy is intended to

distinguish sets of interdependent procedures through which a geographic unit or functional institution allocates values and mobilizes support in issue-areas (horizontal political systems) from sets of interdependent procedures whereby clusters of values within particular issue-areas are allocated by a single horizontal system or a fusion of such systems (vertical political system). Most interesting is the elaboration of the concept of a "penetrated system" in which nonmembers of a society participate in the decision process without converting that society into a protectorate or other entity of the traditional semisovereign type. Several examples of such penetration, e.g., Vietnam, occupied Germany, U.S. participation in India's post-1962 defense planning, are given.

See also nos. 1052, 1216, 1217, 2376.

(b) Divided or Partitioned States

608. Cho, Soon Sung. "Japan's 'Two Koreas' Policy and the Problems of Korean Unification." 7 Asian Survey (1967), 703-725.
On disagreement between rightists and leftists in Japan over the meaning of the third point in Japan's "two Koreas" policy: (1) recognition of South Korea as the only lawful government; (2) future recognition of North Korea not automatically precluded; (3) maintenance of some formal or informal relations with North Korea.

609. Cho, Soon Sung. "The Politics of North Korea's Unification Policies, 1950-1965." 19 World Politics (1967), 218-241.
Review of a problem confronting the divided state of Korea, namely, that of unification propaganda with focus on that of North Korea as influenced until 1960 by internal economic problems and politics in North Korea and after 1960 by changes occurring in South Korea and by the Communist Chinese ideology of wars of national liberation.

610. Fall, Bernard B. "Sociological and Psychological Aspects of Viet-nam's Partition." 18 Journal of International Affairs (1964), 173-187.
Review of the impact of ten years' partition upon Vietnam that finds that some social differences have developed but without changing the proportion of peasants which has remained at 80% of the population in both areas. On the psychological side, the North is deemed to be better off in that it not only can claim a prior existence and military victories but also legitimacy through Bao Dai's transfer of all his instruments of power to it in 1914, while South Vietnam is a product of defeat and revolt, lacking a national raison d'être.

611. Fall, Bernard B. The Two Viet-Nams: A Political and Military Analysis. 2nd rev. ed. New York: Praeger, 1966, pp. xii, 507.
The outstanding analytic history of Vietnam, including the events since the fall of Diem and the escalation of the conflict.

612. Feld, Werner. <u>Reunification and West German-Soviet Relations:</u> <u>The Role of the Reunification Issue in the Foreign Policy of the German</u> <u>Federal Republic, with Special Attention to Policy toward the Soviet</u> <u>Union, 1949-57</u>. The Hague: Nijhoff, 1963, pp. 204.

  An attempt to assess the consequences of partition of Germany in terms of the importance of the reunification issue to West German politics, its relation to other West German goals, and as a factor in Soviet-West German relations.

613. Gordenker, Leon. <u>The United Nations and the Peaceful Unifica-</u> <u>tion of Korea: The Politics of Field Operations, 1947-1950</u>. The Hague: Nijhoff, 1959, pp. 306.

  Study of the work of the United Nations field commission during the three years preceding the outbreak of the Korean War.

614. Haggard, M.T. "North Korea's International Position." 5 <u>Asian</u> <u>Survey</u> (1965), 375-388.

  North Korea has made a sustained effort to improve its international position since 1953. It has been achieved in Asia and Africa where South Korea's representatives are thinly spread. Its recovery from war destruction and its relatively independent position within the Communist world has enhanced its position. Its main objective of foreign policy has been to undermine the existing South Korean government and eventually to reunify Korea under communism.

615. Hartmann, Frederick A. <u>Germany Between East and West: The</u> <u>Reunification Problem</u>. Spectrum Books. Englewood Cliffs: Prentice-Hall, 1965, pp. x, 181.

  Review of the politics of the partition decision, of subsequent Soviet and American policies, and of the reunification issue in German politics.

616. Honey, P.J. <u>Communism in North Viet Nam: Its Role in the Sino-</u> <u>Soviet Dispute</u>. Cambridge, Mass.: MIT Press, 1963, pp. xiii, 207.

  Discussion of North Vietnam's relations with China and the Soviet Union before the nuclear test ban and the probabilities, as of 1963, of moving toward China as a result of the test ban treaty.

617. Lee, Chong-sik. "Korean Partition and Unification." 18 <u>Journ-</u> <u>al of International Affairs</u> (1964), 221-233.

  Review of the growing gulf between North and South Korea and the growing impediments to development of a sense of national identity conducive to reunification.

618. Martinez-Agulló, L. "L'État divisé." 91 <u>Journal de droit in-</u> <u>ternational</u> (1964), 265-284.

  An attempt by a lawyer to develop the concept of the divided state in an effort to differentiate the phenomenon represented by Germany, Korea, China, Vietnam, and Berlin from such situations as civil war, military occupation of part of a territory, <u>debellatio</u>, dismemberment, annexation, federalism, and zones of influence or interest. Division into two systems of full sovereign powers, reflecting East-West as well as national tensions, is examined in respect to both the internal and the international system.

619. McInnis, Edgar, Hiscocks, Richard, and Spencer, Robert. The Shaping of Postwar Germany. New York: Praeger, 1960, pp. 195.
Useful study of the process of partitioning a state and the consequences of and responses to partition.

620. Mendershausen, Horst. Interzonal Trade in Germany--Part I: The Trade and the Contractual Relations. Part II: Interaction with Early Berlin Conflicts. RAND Report RM-3686-PR. Santa Monica: RAND Corporation, July, November, 1963, pp. 45, 69.
Part I deals with the general setting of interzonal trade, with constraints on commerce as a balancing element in hostile political relationships and as a safeguard against both Western defeat and armed conflict, and with the interaction between constraints and efforts to evade them in relation to the post-1958 Berlin crisis. Part II deals with the beginnings of interzonal trade and its relations with the Berlin conflicts in 1948-1952.

621. Merkl, Peter H. The Origin of the West German Republic. New York: Oxford, 1963, pp. xviii, 269.
Story of the division of Germany, the establishment of the Federal Republic, and the transition of the occupation regime.

622. Pounds, N.J.G. "History and Geography: A Perspective on Partition." 18 Journal of International Affairs (1964), 161-172.
An examination of the ten instances of partition in the preceding 25 years, with reference to the territorial nature of the state and the balance of power among the partitioning states. Instances of partition, which can be grouped within an existing classification for the territorial bases of the state, are treated as entailing consequences that may be worth enduring in order to avoid strife and, perhaps, civil war.

623. Prittie, Terence. Germany Divided. Boston: Little, Brown, 1960, pp. 381.
One of the better studies of the consequences of the division of Germany.

624. Scalapino, Robert A. (ed.). North Korea Today. New York: Praeger, 1963, pp. 141.
Contributions of several authors, previously published in a special edition of The China Quarterly, dealing with such matters as North Korean policy before and after the Korean War, its foreign policy, industrial development, judicial and administrative structure, army, and party.

625. Scigliano, Robert. South Vietnam: Nation under Stress. Boston: Houghton Mifflin, 1963, pp. ix, 227.
A short discussion of political personalities and the party system in South Vietnam and of American involvement that treats the United States as having failed to recognize the nationalistic-revolutionary character of South Vietnamese insurgents.

626. Sheehy, Michael. _Divided We Stand: A Study of Partition_.
New York: Putnam, 1956, pp. 104.
     A study of partition and its effect on Irish history since 1912.
Criticism of Southern Irish leadership highlights some of the consequences of concentration upon particular dramatic issues and of public commitment to rectification.

627. Sievers, Bruce. _The Divided Nations: International Integration and National Identity--Patterns in Germany, China, Viet-Nam, and
Korea_. Stanford Studies of the Communist System. Research Paper No. 11.
Stanford University, March 1966, pp. 43.
     Results suggest that the four divided nations are on the basis
of data on trade, foreign aid, mail flow, and treaties, among the
most highly integrated members of their respective international systems. Yet they show no signs of losing their sense of identity with
the traditional national units, thereby creating apparently unresolv-
able fundamental "identity crises". To the extent that integration
of international political communities requires stable national identities, these divided nations can be expected to remain the most unsettling factor for both Communist and Western systems. The monograph includes a number of pertinent tables such as one showing that
the younger West Germans show stronger interest in reunification than
do older age groups. Among its conclusions are the following: (1)
that true integration depends on successful identification of international systems with nationalist causes, found to be most likely for
China and North Vietnam and least likely for East Germany and South
Vietnam; (2) that predictions of reduction of interest in reunification with the passage of time are based on a false premise that identity is a function of interaction. The last suggests that it might
be useful to investigate further by reference to peoples who suffered
apparent linguistic decline only to reassert themselves at a later
historical period.

628. Vali, Ferenc A. _The Quest for a United Germany_. Baltimore:
Johns Hopkins Press, 1967, pp. xii, 318.
     Includes discussion of the reunification issue in international
politics and of the role of Berlin as a microcosm of the larger reunification issue.

629. Wilcox, Wayne. "The Economic Consequences of Partition: India
and Pakistan." 18 _Journal of International Affairs_ (1964), 188-197.
     Although dealing with the partition of a colony rather than of
a dependent state, the article calls attention to some problems that
exist also in the latter case, particularly when the geographical
boundary is also a psychological boundary of hostility, namely, duplication of productive facilities, competition in the world market
with the same crops, financial and transport problems, uneconomic
utilization of capital, and larger military budgets as each unit
ascribes hostile intent to the other.

See also no. 2295.

(c) Associations of States

630. Butwell, Richard. "Malaysia and Its Impact on the International
Relations of Southeast Asia." 4 Asian Survey (1964), 940-946.
     The impact of Malaysia upon international politics in Southeast
Asia is largely seen in its contribution to interaction among Southeast Asian countries. It caused much controversy concerning its establishment, legitimacy, and future, and aroused open hostility on
the part of some Southeast Asian countries. The limited role of the
great powers in Southeast Asia is noted.

631. Foltz, William J. From French West Africa to the Mali Federation. New Haven: Yale University Press, 1965, pp. xiv, 235.
     West African politics from 1956-1960. Political leaders at-
tempted to use the Mali Federation as means to guarantee and increase
control over their own states. These leaders withdrew their states
when the federation threatened their control.

632. Holmes, John. "The Impact on the Commonwealth of the Emergence
of Africa." 16 International Organization (1962), 291-302.
     Review of changes in the nature of the Commonwealth as a conse-
quence of the growth in membership, particularly of African states.

See also nos. 562, 581, 788, 801, 1175.

(d) Governments-in-Exile

633. Beněs, Eduard. Memoirs: From Munich to New War and New Victory. Translated by Godfrey Lias. Boston: Houghton Mifflin; London:
Allen & Unwin, 1954, pp. xi, 346.
     American edition of a work originally published in Czech in
1947 and providing some insights into the nature and problems of
governments-in-exile.

634. Raczyński, Edward, Count. In Allied London. English ed.
London: Weidenfeld, 1963, pp. xiv, 318.
     Wartime diaries by the acting Polish Foreign Minister from 1941
to 1943 that casts light upon the nature and problems of governments-
in-exile.

(2) State Succession

635. Aaronovitch, Sam. The Ruling Class: A Study of British Finance
Capital. London: Lawrence and Wishart, 1961, pp. 192.
     Although polemical in defense of the Marxian concept of class,
the volume provides a helpful discussion of the involvement of political and economic elites with emphasis upon Cabinet Committees
and foreign policy as key areas of dominance of economic over

political elites. Not all class institutions are studied, nor are all the intricacies of relationships between the elites made clear. Large British groups are examined against an international rather than a purely national background to identify the links between national groups. A problem of succession that is raised is that of the transformation of such groups in the decolonization process for, despite the claim of foreign status, it is possible analytically to treat them either as nationals of new states or as stateless.

636. Das Gupta, Jyoti Bhusan. Indo-Pakistan Relations: 1947-1955. Amsterdam: Djambatan, 1958, pp. xii, 254.
Although the author's commitments prevent balanced treatment, the volume is of value particularly in providing some information on the canal waters dispute and on the evacuee property problem.

637. Jeffries, Sir Charles Joseph. Transfer of Power: Problems of the Passage to Self-Government. New York: Praeger, 1961, pp. 148.
Deals with problems encountered in the course of change from colonial status to independence, such problems including or affecting those that are generally discussed in legal treatises on state succession. Formerly Deputy-Undersecretary of the Colonial Office, the author writes from a background of personal experience.

638. Lancaster, Donald. The Emancipation of French Indochina. London: Oxford University Press, 1961, pp. xii, 445.
The author, who became a member of Prince Sihanouk's governmental secretariat, deals, among other things, with a number of succession problems such as (1) the status of Vietnamese resident in Cambodia and of Cambodians in Vietnam and (2) the dispute over funds left over from the banking institution established by France for all Indochina, originally apportioned by the Pau agreements of 1950 that were abrogated by the Geneva Conference of 1954 which did not settle the issue.

639. Leigh, L.H. "Rhodesia After U.D.I.: Some Aspects of a Peaceful Rebellion." Public Law (Summer 1966), 148-160.
Treating the Rhodesian declaration of independence as rebellion, the article deals with the obscurity of the constitutional position of the territory, the rights and liabilities of the colonial armed forces, civil service, and police, the legal liability of members of the de facto government, and the future of the society.

See also nos. 586, 1923, 2108, 2109, 2268, 2384, 2524, 2552, 2561.

(3) Semisovereign States

640. Alexandrowicz, C.H. "India's Himalayan Dependencies." Year Book of World Affairs (1956), 128-143.
On India's relations with and policies toward Tibet, Sikkim, Bhutan, Nepal, Ladakh, and Kashmir.

641. Aron, Robert. Histoire de Vichy: 1940-1944. Paris: Fayard, 1954, pp. 766.

As nearly objective and thorough a chronicle of the Vichy regime as can be found. An abridged translation appeared under the title, The Vichy Regime, 1940-1944 (New York: Macmillan, 1958).

642. Ginther, K. "Der Satellitenstaat." 9 Österreichische Zeitschrift für Aussenpolitik (1969), 3-14.

On the basis of a comparison between the Caribbean states in 1900-1940 and the states of Eastern Europe since World War II, the author arrives at a definition of satellite states in terms of their geographic location, of the vital interests of a world power, and of the employment of force without change of the territorial status quo.

642-A. Hay, R. "The Impact of the Oil Industry on the Persian Gulf Shaykdoms." 9 Middle East Journal (1955), 361-372.

Brief description of Kuwait, Bahrain, and Qatar under the treaty regime that provided for British conduct of their foreign relations.

See also nos. 893, 972.

(4) Satellite and Puppet States

643. Murphy, George G.S. Soviet Mongolia: A Study of the Oldest Political Satellite. Berkeley: University of California Press, 1966, pp. ix, 224.

Economic and political history of the Mongolian People's Republic from 1921 to 1960 that relies principally on Russian source materials. Guidance of Mongolia's 1921 "revolution" by the Comintern, the subordination of Mongolian aspirations to the Soviet national interest, and the changes in policy after Communist China began a competition for influence, are among the subjects dealt with.

644. Skilling, H. Gordon. "The Soviet Impact on the Czechoslovak Legal Revolution." 6 Soviet Studies (1955), 361-381.

Because of the Soviet impact, the Czech legal system is now one whose purposes are to support the regime and maintain order and discipline. The rights of the individual are strictly subordinated to these collective purposes, not only in official theory and in the provisions of the new Czech codes, but also in the judicial and semi-judicial procedures for their implementation.

See also nos. 853, 981, 1039, 2299.

(5) Nonsovereign Entities

(a) Internationalized Territories

645. Stuart, Graham H. <u>The International City of Tangier</u>. 2nd ed. Stanford: Stanford University Press, 1955, pp. xv, 270.
Narrative of the formation of the Tangier regime, changes made, and the operation of the international regime until the mid-1950s, just before Moroccan independence.

646. Ydit, Meir. <u>Internationalised Territories</u>. Leyden: Sijthoff, 1961, pp. 323.
Study of the theory and practice of internationalization of territories since the Napoleonic Wars. Case studies are made of Cracow, Tangier, Danzig, Trieste, Jerusalem, and Berlin.

(b) Dependent Entities

(i) Colonies and Dependencies

646-A. Abshire, David M., and Samuels, Michael A. (eds.). <u>Portuguese Africa: A Handbook</u>. New York: Praeger, 1969, pp. 466.
Among the topics dealt with by this multidisciplinary collection of essays are international issues affecting Angola, Mozambique, Portuguese Guinea, and some island groups.

647. Curcio, Carlo. "Il problema coloniale." 2 <u>Studi politici</u> (1953-1954), 462-479.
Draws attention to the change in European values that now reject the 19th-century position that colonialism was a civilizing mission. Reference is also made to the status of the colonial problem in the ensemble of world problems. Attention to the European aspect is vital both in regard to the introduction of anticolonial norms and also to the European reaction to the accusation of neo-imperialism and to Europe's sometimes less cooperative reaction to revisionist demands concerning international law than was manifest at the time of grant of independence. However, besides the psychological problem, that of the European internal political struggle and attendant ideological commitment must be considered.

648. Duffy, James. <u>Portugal in Africa</u>. Cambridge: Harvard University Press, 1962; Baltimore: Penguin, 1963, pp. 240.
Traces Portuguese activities in Angola and Mozambique to the summer of 1961, with analysis of the theories and philosophies undergirding policies and policy statements.

649. Duffy, James. <u>Portuguese Africa</u>. Cambridge: Harvard University Press, 1959, pp. 389.
Well-documented sociological, political, and economic history of Portuguese Africa.

650. Silvera, V. "Du régime beylical à la République tunisienne." 22 <u>Politique étrangère</u> (1957), 594-611.

Review of the role of France as protector of the power of the
Bey of Tunis from 1881 to 1955 and of the deterioration of the Bey's
regime after French recognition of Tunisian independence removed the
French capacity to act against the introduction of a constitutional
regime and the proclamation of the Republic.

651. Wainhouse, David W. Remnants of Empire: The United Nations
and the End of Colonialism. New York: Harper & Row for the Council on
Foreign Relations, 1964, pp. 153.
On the status and development of the remaining Spanish, Portuguese, British, Australian, New Zealand, and American colonial territories, together with a chapter on South-West Africa.

652. Wohlgemuth, Patricia. "The Portuguese Territories and the
United Nations." International Conciliation. No. 545. November 1963,
pp. 68.
Review of the issue of Angola, Mozambique, and Portuguese Guinea
before the United Nations, with some reference to internal war in
Angola and Portuguese Guinea and to the problem of refugees and political exiles from the three territories.

See also nos. 896, 1610, 1993, 2298.

(ii) Mandates and Trusteeships

653. Chidzero, B.T.G. Tanganyika and International Trusteeship.
London: Oxford for the Royal Institute of International Affairs, 1961,
pp. x, 286.
Survey by a Rhodesian of African descent of the political and
constitutional developments in Tanganyika under the mandate and trusteeship systems.

654. Choudhuri, R.N. International Mandates and Trusteeship Systems: A Comparative Study. The Hague: Nijhoff, 1955, pp. xv, 328.
Excellent undertaking that sets side-by-side the League of Nations and United Nations experiences in dealing with common problems. The focus is overly narrow only in the sense that, like
earlier studies of mandates and trusteeships, it pays relatively
little attention to other forces working toward colonial reform and
independence.

655. Coulter, John Wesley. The Pacific Dependencies of the United
States. New York: Macmillan, 1957, pp. 388.
Deals with the administrative system and the economy of all
Pacific territories, including trust territories, under United
States control and with the circumstances of the indigenous
populations.

656. de Smith, Stanley A. Exceeding Small: The Future of the U.S.
Trust Territories. New York: New York University Press, 1969.

A useful study of the problems and prospects of the trust territories that came under United States control after World War II.

657. Fishel, Murray I. "The International Aspects of South West Africa: The Historical Perspective." 13 Journal of Human Relations (1965), 196-207.

Historical treatment of the South-West African mandate question and analysis of the failure of the UN to resolve the question.

658. Gardinier, David E. Cameroon: United Nations Challenge to French Policy. London, New York, and Nairobi: Oxford University Press for the Institute of Race Relations, London, 1963, pp. x, 142.

Narrative of events in the Cameroons under the trusteeship system, of armed uprisings in 1955, 1957, and after, of intervention of Guinea and Ghana by shipping Soviet bloc arms and supplies, partial reunification after plebiscites, and of relations with France in the first years of independence. The effects of boundary restrictions after the fall of France and the establishment of the Vichy Regime that continued into the postwar period are discussed.

659. Giniewski, P. "Un nouveau problème international: Le sort du Sud-Ouest africain." 30 Politique étrangère (1965), 280-286.

Review of economic and administrative developments in South-West Africa aiming toward internal autonomy of each of 12 ethnic groups, with some attention to the probability that such developments may represent irreversible steps on the route to independence.

660. Meller, Norman. The Congress of Micronesia: Development of the Legislative Process in the Trust Territory of the Pacific Islands. Honolulu: University of Hawaii Press, 1969, pp. x, 480.

Provides information on some aspects of the evolution of those Pacific islands that are under United States trusteeship.

661. Thullen, George. Problems of the Trusteeship System: A Study of Political Behavior in the United Nations. Geneva: Droz, 1964, pp. 217.

Examination of the background of the trusteeship system, the establishment of the system as part of the U.N. arrangements, procedures and issues, and the Ewe and Togoland unification problems.

662. Wellington, John H. South West Africa and Its Human Issues. New York: Oxford, 1967, pp. xxiv, 461.

A student of South West Africa for over 40 years, the author discusses pre-1919 history of the area, the mandate period, the defiance of the United Nations, and the legal struggle over South West Africa. A useful section is devoted to the International Court of Justice judgment of 1966.

663. Wiens, Herold J. Pacific Island Bastions of the United States. Searchlight Books. Princeton: Van Nostrand, 1962, pp. 124.

Historical and geographical review of the Pacific trust territories, with reference to administrative, economic, and sociological problems and to the islands' position in the United States security system.

See also nos. 1720, 1777, 2194.

(c) Enclaves; Rights of Passage

664. Burckhardt, Carl Jacob. Meine Danziger Mission--1937-1939.
Munich: Callwey, 1960, pp. 366.
    Account of the Danzig issue as seen by the last League of Nations
Commissioner to that city.

665. Fijalkowski, Jürgen, Hauck, Peter, Holst, Axel, Kemper, Gerd-
Heinrich, and Mintzel, Alf. Berlin--Hauptstadtanspruch und Westintegra-
tion. Köln and Opladen: Westdeutscher Verlag, 1967.
    On the de facto integration of West Berlin into the political
and economic systems of the Bundesrepublik.

666. Franklin, William M. "Zonal Boundaries and Access to Berlin."
16 World Politics (1963), 1-31.
    Reviews the plans for the drawing of zonal boundaries for the
occupation of Germany, the lack of coordination in the United States
Government and between Washington and London, concerns for the occupation of other parts of Germany that took attention away from the
Berlin access problem, and the evidence of clear Soviet understanding
that the right of transit was assured.

667. "Le Problème des enclaves territoriales." 18 Revue française
de science politique (1968), 315-374.
    Five articles on Hongkong, Gibraltor, Aden, Ifni, and Moroccan
enclaves, and French stations in India.

668. Peretz, Don. "Jerusalem--A Divided City." 18 Journal of International Affairs (1964), 211-220.
    Review of the separate development of the two portions of Jeru-
salem from 1948 to the time of writing prior to the 1967 war. Attention is given to the increased gap between the two ethnic segments as each enclave has spread beyond its prewar borders.

669. Plischke, Elmer. Government and Politics of Berlin. The
Hague: Nijhoff, 1963, pp. xiv, 119.
    Deals with allied authorities, constitutional system, govern-
ment, and political parties, with the last chapter devoted to the
juridical and political status of Berlin. The volume includes consideration of the modifications made in the Kommandatura decision
process and de facto revisions of the formal status after Soviet
withdrawal in June 1948. The positions of West Berlin and East Berlin are compared.

670. Plischke, Elmer. "Integrating Berlin and the Federal Republic
of Germany." 27 Journal of Politics (1965), 35-65.
    On the development of West Berlin's de facto institutional
integration into the government of the Federal Republic while maintaining the legal fiction of separation.

671. Schlier, O. "Berlins Verflechtungen mit der Umwelt früher und heute." 11 Geographische Rundschau (1959), 125-151.
     Comparison of the economic influence of Berlin in such matters as services, food supplies, and employment before and after World War II.

672. Verdun, L.G. "Les relations Sénégal-Gambie." 20 Revue juridique et politique (1966), 477-488.
     On Gambia as an enclave in Senegal and the need of each for association with the other, the need being met by agreements for cooperation in foreign affairs, defense, and management of the basin of the Gambia River.

673. Warren, Roland. "The Conflict Intersystem and the Change Agent." 8 Journal of Conflict Resolution (1964), 231-241.
     A combination of participant-observer's report and social scientist's theorizing about relationships between East and West Berlin.

See also no. 620.

(6) Religious Organizations

674. Alix, Christine. La Saint-Siège et les Nationalismes en Europe, 1870-1960. Paris: Sirey, 1962, pp. ix, 367.
     Relation of the Catholic Church to the nationalisms of 19th and 20th century Europe and the course of diplomacy under the impact of nationalism.

675. Graham, Robert A., S.J. Vatican Diplomacy: A Study of Church and State on the International Plane. Princeton: Princeton University Press, 1959, pp. xii, 440.
     Treats of the origins of diplomatic missions beginning with representation of non-Catholic states at the Roman Court, the organs of papal diplomacy, some questions of papal sovereignty, and recent foreign relations of the Vatican.

676. Plavsic, W.S. "La diplomatie pontificale, heir et aujourd'hui." 6 Res publica (1964), 286-298.
     A short description of papal diplomatic practice with reference to the Secretariat of State, the Congregation of Extraordinary Ecclesiastic Affairs, and the function of papal nuncios.

(7) Alliances, Blocs, and Coalitions

677. Abt, Clark C., O'Sullivan, Thomas, Kessler, Melvin H., and Dadrian, Vahakn. Theoretical Aspects of Unilateral Arms Control. Report, Raytheon Company, Bedford, Massachusetts, January 1963.
     Analysis of arms control doctrine including assumptions about the nature of military and international conflict. Operational

distinctions between intrinsic and reciprocal unilateral arms control. A theory of alliance formation is discussed, together with the significance of alliances for the initiation, escalation, and termination of war.

678. Brzezinski, Zbigniew K. The Soviet Bloc: Unity and Conflict. Rev. ed. Cambridge: Harvard University Press, 1967, pp. 599.
A narrative and analysis of the relations of Soviet bloc members with each other and with the Soviet Union that includes a consideration of the political uses of treaties in the maintenance of the bloc.

679. Burgess, Philip M., and Robinson, James A. "Alliances and the Theory of Collective Action: A Simulation of Coalition Processes." 13 Midwest Journal of Political Science (1969), 194-218.
A simulation experiment is employed to test Mancur Olson's theory of collective action as elaborated by the authors with specific reference to alliances as a form of voluntary international association that can dispense a mixture of collective and private benefits with possibility of varying the proportions.

680. Coleman, James S., and James, J. "The Equilibrium Size Distribution of Freely-Forming Groups." 24 Sociometry (1961), 36-45.
Deals with freely-forming peaceful groups in various public situations, the groups being closed systems in that all individuals remain in the system although with a joining and leaving of groups. Observed size distribution, treated as the outcome of a probabilistic process of joining and leaving, provided an extremely good fit with their model, the truncated Poisson distribution.

681. Dawson, Raymond, and Rosecrance, Richard. "Theory and Reality in the Anglo-American Alliance." 19 World Politics (1966), 21-51.
Holds that the proposition of conventional alliance theory that calculation, not sentiment traceable to ideology, cultural ties, and common historical traditions, determines original combinations and that interest of members determines breakdowns of alliances does not explain the Anglo-American alliance. Major events since World War II are presented as evidence that history, tradition, and affinity have been crucial in maintaining the Anglo-American alliance and that a number of actions which were taken were not particularly of benefit to either partner but were beneficial to the alliance.

682. Dib, G. Moussa. The Arab Bloc in the United Nations. Amsterdam: Djambatan, 1956, pp. 128.
An attempt to fit the Arab states into the wider framework of the United Nations and into the power situation up to July 1956. A substantial number of cases are examined in an effort to analyze Arab attitudes on East-West issues and solidarity is found to have lasted only through the Second Assembly. The author attributes the loss of bloc unity on East-West issues to a need for scientific know-how and different views as to how it is to be obtained.

683. Driver, Michael J. <u>Conceptual Structure and Group Processes in an Inter-Nation Simulation. Part I: The Perception of Simulated Nations.</u> Princeton: Educational Testing Service, 1962, pp. xiv, 266, 89.

Report on a simulation experiment that, among other things, notes a probable curvilinear relationship of stress to efficiency of problem-solving, reduction in dimensionality of thinking under stress, a tendency under stress to oversimplify the portrayal of objects such as other nations, and reduction of internal conflict. Differences in the behavior of concrete and abstract personalities receive attention to indicate the apparent behaviors of different cognitive structures under stress. Stress tended to focus attention chiefly on alliances in apparent support of Donald Campbell's notion of common fate as basic to the perception of social groups (<u>supra</u>, no. 98). Power appeared to be a secondary dimension. The economic dimension became quite unimportant or even moved outside perception as stress increased, although this may have been either an artifact of the simulation design or a consequence of high school student subjects' limited experience. Even so, the primary concern about alliances--a concern comparable to Paul Cambon's fear that England would not honor her commitment of 1912 --suggests that useful integration of laboratory and historical data may tell us a great deal about alliance behavior under stress, systemic processes at the international level, and the psychological foundations of the effectiveness of this type of treaty obligation.

684. Emerson, Richard M. "Power-Dependence Relations: Two Experiments." 27 <u>Sociometry</u> (1964), 282-298.

Data presented from an experiment on conformity and "status insecurity" include an unforeseen curvilinear relation between conformity and sociometric status, conformity being found at status extremes. An attempt to explain this finding within the rationale of the study appears forced, and a theory of balancing processes in power-dependence relations is offered as a tentative explanation for these data. A second experiment is reported, designed specifically to test hypotheses concerning balance in power relations. Conformal tendencies of high status group members in the first study, and differential allocations of rewards within coalitions in the second study appear to be explainable as two very different manifestations of a single generic balancing operation in power relations. What appears to be a pertinent finding is the one termed balancing operation #3 in the theory, which increases the dependence of the stronger party through increasing his motivational investment in the relation.

685. Farajallah, Samaan Boutros. <u>Le groupe afro-asiatique dans le cadre des Nations Unies.</u> Geneva: Droz, 1963, pp. xii, 511.

Careful study of the behavior of African and Asian states and of cohesive tendencies in regard to issues raised at the United Nations.

686. Friedheim, Robert L. "Factor Analysis as a Tool in Studying the Law of the Sea." In Lewis M. Alexander (ed.), <u>The Law of the Sea: Offshore Boundaries and Zones.</u> Columbus: Ohio State University Press, 1967, pp. 47-69.

Uses factor analysis to determine positions and groupings of states on (1) the territorial sea and contiguous zone, (2) fishing, (3) supranational proposals such as procedures for compulsory settlement of disputes, (4) legal conservatism, and (5) rights of land-locked states. The most important issues are given graphical representation that highlight differences in positions and make clear some of the differences within and between blocs that can be overlooked when facile generalizations are indulged.

687. Galtung, Johan. "East-West Interaction Patterns." 3 Journal of Peace Research (1966), 146-177.
   Examination of the system of the 15 NATO nations and the 8 Warsaw Pact nations to see to what extent the nations defined as big powers rank high on all other dimensions. A test is made of the hypothesis that interaction between the two blocs will be largely interaction between the big powers, less between big powers and small powers, and very little between small powers. On the basis of data concerning 15 types of interaction, the hypothesis is confirmed in almost all cases involving governmental initiative and partly disconfirmed for cases involving nongovernmental initiative.

688. Groennings, Sven, Kelley, E.W., and Leiserson, Michael (eds.). The Study of Coalition Behavior: Theoretical Perspectives and Cases from Four Continents. New York: Holt, Rinehart and Winston, 1969.
   Twenty-five original articles on the importance and ubiquity of coalition processes and on ways of explaining coalition behavior.

689. Horvath, William J., and Foster, Caxton C. Stochastic Models of War Alliances. Preprint 92. Ann Arbor: Mental Health Research Institute, University of Michigan, September 1962, pp. 13.
   Compares the equilibrium distribution of the numbers of nations in war alliances with a particular class of skew distribution functions derived from a simple stochastic process, and interprets the mechanism at work in the formation and dissolution of war alliances as a type of random process occurring in many natural and social phenomena. The observed data on the number of sides in each war in the period 1820-1939 agree quite well with a Yule Distribution which postulates that nations join alliances of a given size at a rate proportional to the total number of nations in alliances of that size and that alliances break up at a constant rate independent of size. This differs from the conclusion of Coleman and James concerning freely-forming small groups in various peaceful public situations, which deals only with closed systems in which all individuals remain within the system. The authors conclude that Richardson was correct in his conjecture that there was a difference between peaceful groups and aggregations for aggressive purposes but that, on the basis of their tests, the difference lies in the particular rules by which members join and leave the groups.

690. Hovet, Thomas, Jr. Bloc Politics in the United Nations. Cambridge, Mass.: Harvard University Press, 1960, pp. xx, 197.
   Quantitative analysis of bloc voting patterns and bloc cohesion, with attention to voting on international legal questions.

690-A. Iatrides, John O. <u>Balkan Triangle: Birth and Decline of an Alliance Across Ideological Boundaries</u>. The Hague: Mouton, 1968, pp. 211.
    Useful in part because of its examination of the stimuli that brought Yugoslavia, Greece, and Turkey into alliance in 1953 and 1954, despite ideological differences, and the portrayal of the decline of the alliance, despite its existence on paper, as the external threat receded after 1955.

691. Laredo, I.M. "Latinamérica en las Naciones Unidas." 16 <u>Foro internacional</u> (1964), 571-611.
    Review of the Latin American bloc, its stand on certain issues before the United Nations, and the erosion of its influence as a regional group with the admission of the many Afro-Asian states. The author considers the loss of position in the United Nations to be accompanied by gradual weakening of the Panamerican movement.

692. Lieberman, B. "<u>i</u>-Trust: A Notion of Trust in Three-Person Games and International Affairs." 8 <u>Journal of Conflict Resolution</u> (1964), 271-280.
    A concept of trust based on interest that was derived from an experimental three-person, zero-sum, majority game situation. The concept is regarded as akin to that of maximizing gain and as relevant to situations in which coalition structure is important, hence, to alliances.

693. Lijphart, Arend. "The Analysis of Bloc Voting in the General Assembly." 57 <u>American Political Science Review</u> (1963), 902-917.
    Use of votes on colonial issues to determine the extent to which differences exist between voting groups and caucusing groups.

694. Liska, George. <u>Nations in Alliance: The Limits of Interdependence</u>. Baltimore: Johns Hopkins Press, 1962, pp. x, 301.
    Theory of alliances--their structure and dynamics, formation, effectiveness, and dissolution.

695. Meskill, Johanna Menzel. <u>Hitler and Japan: The Hollow Alliance</u>. New York: Atherton, 1966, pp. x, 245.
    On the nature of an alliance that had a fragile basis, saw the partners resort to deception and secretiveness as do enemies, was based upon at least one party's underestimation of the other's ambitions and overestimate of its strength, and had the primary consequence of embroiling the Axis against the US and the USSR at the same time. Particularly useful is the analysis of the Tripartite Pact of September 1940, which publicly committed Japan to an anti-American policy but through secret addenda actually released Japan from anti-American obligations. Numerous documentary sources are used, including the records of corporations involved in the Axis equivalent of Lend-Lease and the war journals of the German naval staff.

696. Modelski, George. <u>SEATO: Six Studies</u>. Melbourne, Canberra, and Sydney: F.W. Cheshire for the Australian National University, 1962, pp. xxxiii, 302.

A well-coordinated collection of papers by five Australians that deal with the organization and functions of SEATO, economic relationships, India and the security pact, Australia and the alliance, Communist China and SEATO, and the Asian states participation, the last being an outstanding paper by the editor on the relationship of small to large states.

697. Modelski, George. "The South-East Asia Treaty Organization." 5 Australian Journal of Politics and History (1959), 24-40.
  Examines SEATO and its activities in terms of three conditions posited as favoring the emergence of permanent organization: (1) relatively large number of allies, (2) duration, and (3) relative equality of members' contributions.

698. Mulder, Mauk. "The Power Variable in Communication Experiments." 13 Human Relations (1960), 241-257.
  Not satisfied with some previous experiments on communications structures in groups, the author devised and here describes his own experiments and their results which confirm a hypothesis that there is a tendency of individuals toward identification with the more powerful and toward separation from the less powerful--a hypothesis then discussed in terms of psychological distance. In reference to some experiments of Thibault and Kelley that showed no preference for the more powerful persons on the part of the less powerful, the author suggests that when the distance between the more powerful and the person himself becomes too great, the preference, and the striving for the goal that might bring satisfaction, decreases and striving for the goal ceases.

699. Olson, Mancur, Jr. The Logic of Collective Action: Public Goods and the Theory of Groups. Cambridge: Harvard University Press, 1965, pp. 176.
  The author develops an economic theory of "public goods" that permits classification of associations in terms of the types of benefits they produce, namely, collective benefits that cannot be denied any potential consumer and private benefits that are available only to the members of the association. The theory is applicable to associations of nations.

700. Rieselbach, Leroy N. "Quantitative Technique for Studying Voting Behavior in the United Nations General Assembly." 14 International Organization (1960), 291-306.
  Suggests some possible quantitative techniques for the study of the voting patterns of the United Nations.

701. Riker, William H. The Theory of Political Coalitions. New Haven: Yale University Press, 1962, pp. x, 292.
  Employs a model of political and social dynamics that is derived from the n-person zero-sum game and draws from the general theory that is expounded in the proposition that, when rational players have perfect information, only minimum winning coalitions emerge. This proposition is applied to the dissolution of the victorious coalitions after 1815, 1918, and 1945.

702. Ritchie, Ronald S. NATO: The Economics of an Alliance.
Toronto: Ryerson Press for the Canadian Institute of International Af-
fairs, 1956, pp. 147.
Economic base for NATO and burden-sharing therein.

702-A. Russett, Bruce M. "An Empirical Typology of International
Military Alliances." 15 Midwest Journal of Political Science (1971),
262-289.
A study of military alliances from 1920 to 1957 on the basis
of factor analysis of a variety of background and output variables.
The characteristics of pre-World War II alliances are found to be
little different from those alliances formed since the war. While
dominated alliances seem to be most effective as deterrents, multilateral alliances among equals are found to be most likely to display the members fighting on the same side.

703. Shaw, Marvin E., Rothschild, Gerald H., and Strickland, John
F. "Decision Processes in Communication Nets." 54 Journal of Abnormal
and Social Psychology (1957), 323-330.
Report of experiments attempting to determine the effects of
certain communication nets upon group performance and satisfaction
when the task is to solve a "human relations" problem. From the
results, the following conclusions were drawn: (1) the central
more than the peripheral subject tries to change the opinion of
those who disagree, but if he fails, he himself changes more, presumably because of his greater vulnerability to direct pressure;
(2) the presence of one supporter strengthens the resistance of a
subject relatively more than the mere reduction of the size of opposition and more than the simple fact that the opposition is not
unanimous; (3) member satisfaction is a joint function of central-
ity and the amount of support by other group members.

704. Singer, J. David, and Small, Melvin. "Alliance Aggregation
and the Onset of War, 1815-1945." In J. David Singer (ed.), Quantitative International Politics: Insights and Evidence. New York: Free
Press, 1968, pp. 247-286.
A stage in an undertaking to find the relationships between
alliance aggregation and war, the study finds that both alliance
aggregation and bipolarity covary strongly with the amount of war
following within three years in the 20th century but inversely to
almost the same degree in the 19th century. For the 19th century,
as alliance aggregation or bipolarity increases, the amount of war
experienced by the international system goes down, while in the
20th century it goes up. These relationships hold whether one measures the number of wars, the nation-months involved, or battle
deaths. However, it should be noted that the correlations may be
interpreted as accounting for between 6.8% and 8.4% of the variance in the 19th and 20th centuries, indicating that other factors
may well account for more of the variance related to war than do
alliances. The authors call attention to other questions requiring investigation in an effort to explain the onset of war.

705. Teune, Henry, and Synnestvedt, Sig. "Measuring International Alignment." 9 Orbis (1965), 171-189.

Seeks to assess the importance of a set of foreign policy decisions that appear to indicate a general foreign policy position concerning the United States and the Soviet Union. The authors find the best indicators to be military commitments, U.N. votes, patterns of diplomatic recognition, and diplomatic visits by heads of states. They seek to calculate from a series of decisions and acts the trends of foreign policy and to distinguish patterns from miscellaneous decisions. Data on hand and to be collected would then be used to investigate alignment as a major structural characteristic.

706. Travis, Tom A. "Foreign Policy Communications in the NATO-Warsaw International System." Paper presented at the 66th Annual Meeting of the American Political Science Association, Los Angeles, September 8-12, 1970, pp. 20.

A study of the gross bivariate relationships between the NATO and Warsaw Pact nations, aggregating the communications data for the several national members to reflect the hostile and friendly behaviors of the two blocs during 1953-65.

707. Triska, Jan F., and Koch, Howard E., Jr. "The Asian-African Coalition." In Leonard Freedman and Cornelius Cotter (eds.), Issues of the Sixties. San Francisco: Wadsworth, 1961, pp. 371-376.

An essentially historical treatment of the development of the Asian-African coalition, beginning with noting nationalism as the impetus to political independence followed by considerations of the role played by socialism as a means of adapting to economic and political realities. Nehru's policy of neutralism is assessed from the viewpoints of the Asian-African states, the Soviet Union, and the United States.

708. Vinacke, W. Edgar. "Intra-Group Power Relation, Strategy and Decisions in Inter-Triad Competition." 27 Sociometry (1964), 25-39.

Ten pairs of triads of each sex engaged for monetary rewards in a multiplication game and a matching game. In each of these games there were 12 contests, four for each of the three power-patterns. In each event, the two groups separately cast two votes, (1) which of three alternatives to enter into competition against the choice of the other group, (2) how to allocate a bonus, if they won. Players had the number of votes represented by their weights in the power pattern for that event. These triads reached a very high proportion of "triple alliances," typically arriving at consensus without regard to power differences. A comparison of winning and losing groups strongly suggests that skill and decision-making efficiency are both highly significant factors in winning.

709. White, H. "Chance Models of Systems of Casual Groups." 25 Sociometry (1962), 153-172

An elaborate discussion of the arrival and the departure of persons in relation to casual groups, a discussion of the factors of size, degree of isolation, proportion of isolation, and the type of system used. Various models are used to show these factors at work. The author then uses these models in relation to open and closed systems, and comes up with an equilibrium size distribution. The approach may have some value in suggesting a method of evaluation of ad hoc state alignments and their impact upon international rules not based on enduring alignments.

See also nos. 583, 844, 860, 866, 1134, 1204, 1501, 1502, 1759, 1932, 2029.

(a) Nonalignment (Neutralism)

710. Anabtawi, S.N. "Neutralists and Neutralism." 27 Journal of Politics (1965), 351-361.
Noting that neutralism lacks a code of behavior equivalent to that of neutrality, the article, among other things, examines what neutralists believe neutralism to be and distinguishes between two major types, i.e., "withdrawal" as for Switzerland and Austria, and "self-interest" as for India, Indonesia, and the U.A.R., with attention to the conditions and risks attending each type.

711. Choucri, Nazli. "The Perceptual Basis of Nonalignment." 13 Journal of Conflict Resolution (1969), 57-74.
A comparison of statements by major nonaligned leaders through content analysis to test hypotheses concerning similarity of perceptions, the hypotheses being derived from a model of nonalignment.

712. Lyon, Peter. Neutralism. Leicester, England: Leicester University Press, 1963, pp. 215.
Essay on the political nature of neutralism and its significance in the Cold War.

712-A. Rubinstein, Alvin Z. Yugoslavia and the Nonaligned World. Princeton: Princeton University Press, 1970, pp. 376.
On the manner of Yugoslavia's establishment of close relationships with the new African and Asian nations and on the nature of those relationships as manifest in interactions in the United Nations, the relationship between Tito and Nasser, and the role played by Yugoslavia in the Sino-Soviet dispute.

See also nos. 1251, 2101, 2139, 2204.

c. Intergovernmental Organizations

(1) International Organizations in General

713. Akzin, Benjamin. New States and International Organizations. Paris: UNESCO for the International Political Science Association, 1955, pp. 200.

Problems of newly independent states in their relations with international organizations. The book deals with the experiences of India, Pakistan, Lebanon, Israel, the Philippines, and Indonesia.

714. Angell, Robert C. "An Analysis of Trends in International Organizations." Peace Research Society (International), Papers. Chicago Conference, 1964. Vol. III (1965), pp. 185-195.
One of a series of studies on trends in international participation, this article employs the data to be found in the sixth (1956-57) and ninth (1962-63) editions of the Yearbook of International Organizations to ascertain growth in numbers and percent of international organizations in terms of membership base and of orientation, changes in country involvement, and frequency of various patterns of country involvement.

714-A. Cosgrove, Carol Ann, and Twitchett, Kenneth J. (eds.). The New International Actors: The United Nations and the European Economic Community. New York: St. Martin's, 1970, pp. 272.
A collection of 12 articles on the UN and EEC that attempts to show the extent to which the two organizations play significant international roles. A comprehensive introduction sets forth a series of tests designed to assist identification of the qualities that enable international organizations to be actors with impacts that are significant yet differ from the impacts of states.

714-B. Dam, Kenneth W. The GATT: Law and International Economic Organization. Chicago: University of Chicago Press, 1970, pp. 544.
An effort to ascertain the role of rules, particularly procedural rules, in international affairs with focus upon the international organization that deals day by day with the many dimensions of international trade.

715. Haas, Ernst B. Beyond the Nation-State: Functionalism and International Organization. Stanford: Stanford University Press, 1964, pp. xii, 595.
Careful study, focused primarily but not exclusively on the ILO. It seeks the relationships between the normal aims and expectations of states and the process of international integration. Some propositions are developed about the relationship between integration, systems theory, and functional analysis. The theory that emerges is reexamined in the light of findings about the ILO. Succeeding chapters deal with the ILO's organizational ideology, clients, international labor standards, international collective bargaining, human rights, and freedom of association. Aided by a convenient tabular presentation, analysis of the record of compliance permits a later characterization of C. Wilfred Jenks' version of human rights law as a parade of "a body of aspirations." The author's somewhat uncritical reliance on Stanley Hoffmann's views, although not wholly unjustified in respect to some matters dealt with in detail, risks a generalization not yet supported by superficial, anecdotal evidence. Haas's legal prescription calls for a functional law that does not impose centralized institutions before the emergence of a consensus on needs. Judges should apply this law by resort to a functional jurisprudence that

stresses the needs apparently overwhelmingly experienced by their society, with the interpretation of texts based on a consensus discovered by the judges themselves. Haas's formula, although essentially
a generalized retreat from law, is suggestive of approaches to legal
development that could be usefully applied if rendered more selective
to distinguish untenable positions from the tenable and thereby formulate a concept of strategic retreat and advance.

716. Haas, Michael. "A Functional Approach to International Organization." 27 Journal of Politics (1965), 498-517.
    An attempt to articulate fundamental terms and expressions to
serve as bases for a theory of international organization viewed as
a phase of a broader structural-functional theory of international
relations. Besides its basic undertaking to define and to categorize,
the article suggests, among other things, that most functions performed by major actors (city-states, empires, or nation-states) are
performed outside international structures within each particularistic unit, that institutionalization within particularistic structures
is likely if there are only one or two power centers, and that universalistic structures are most likely to contain functionally specific structures when there is a diffusion of power throughout an
international system.

717. International Political Communities--An Anthology. Garden City:
Doubleday (Anchor Books), 1966, pp. viii, 512.
    Collection of previously published articles on international
organizations in Western Europe, Latin America, Africa, and Eastern
Europe, together with a portion of the book by Deutsch, et al., on
Political Community and the North Atlantic Area and an article, appearing for the first time, by Morton Kaplan providing a nontechnical account of some of the models used in System and Process in International Politics, indicating some theoretical problems raised by
the models, and giving a preliminary account of some research efforts
to test the models.

718. Mitrany, David. A Working Peace System. London: Royal Institute of International Affairs, 1943, pp. 56.
    Best-known argument for a functional approach to international
organization by concentrating on nonpolitical exchanges to construct
patterns of shared interests and values.

719. Monaco, Riccardo. Lezioni di organizzazione internazionale--I
--Diritto delle istituzioni internazionali. Torino: G. Giappichelli,
1957, pp. 354.
    An attempt to lay foundations for a scientifically systematized
theory of international organizations, with concern for characteristics, function, organization and structure, and legal character.
This study of organizations on the universal level and on the regional European level represents an effort by the writer of a treatise on
public and private international law to establish foundations that
will blend legal elements with historical, social, and political

factors. The approach is to an important degree intuitive and expressive of inference from "soft" data, as well as often including
legalistic argumentation. Its importance lies in its exploratory
effort to systematize and synthesize in a manner conducive to the
construction of a general theory of international organizations.

720. Schiffer, Walter. The Legal Community of Mankind: A Critical
Analysis of the Concept of World Organization. New York: Columbia University Press, 1954, pp. x, 368.
    Theoretical investigation of the conflicting concepts underly-
ing the League of Nations and the United Nations. The study focuses
on the League. Due attention is accorded writers on international
law with particular reference to their concepts of the legal nature
of war.

721. Scott, William G. The Management of Conflict: Appeal Systems
in Organizations. Homewood, Illinois: Dorsey, 1965, pp. ix, 129.
    Systematic study of the managerial judicial function based on
the official records and documents of four nonbusiness organizations
and on an empirical study of nearly 800 business firms. Attention
is given to the issue of judicial criteria in appeal practices. The
volume should be of particular value to students of administrative
law at the international level as it relates to the management of
international organizations.

721-A. Wallace, Michael, and Singer, J. David. "Intergovernmental
Organization in the Global System, 1815-1964: A Quantitative Description."
24 International Organization (1970), 239-287.
    A quantitative study of the growth and proliferation of inter-
governmental organizations that, although only descriptive, provides
a basis for the asking and investigation of questions having theoretical impact.

See also nos. 269, 527, 1066, 1069, 1109, 1228, 1752, 2436.

    (2) United Nations

722. Alger, Chadwick F. "Interaction in a Committee of the United
Nations General Assembly." In J. David Singer (ed.), Quantitative International Politics: Insights and Evidence. New York: Free Press, 1968,
pp. 51-84.
    A study of interactions in the Fifth Committee of the United
Nations, based upon recorded observations. The study seeks to
identify high interactors, to relate interaction rate to writing
and sponsorship of resolutions and amendments and to public speak-
ing. It also seeks relationships between interaction rate and
length of General Assembly service, capabilities, and information
level as perceived by other delegates.

723. Alker, Hayward R., and Russett, Bruce M. World Politics in the
General Assembly. New Haven: Yale University Press, 1965, pp. xxvi, 326.

That the voting patterns in the UN are affected by the bipolar conflict between East and West and that these patterns are also affected by aid or alliances of a nation with the US or Russia is quantitatively confirmed. Overshadowing all this are self-determination, UN supranationalism, Palestine, the Cold War, and intervention in Africa. The volume both provides descriptive parameters of international politics and demonstrates some of the things that are possible with quantitative methods despite some unresolved problems. A review by Davis B. Bobrow (60 American Political Science Review (1966), 690-691) sets forth some of the basic problems including the issue of whether an index actually measures the concept which an investigator has assigned to it.

724. Goodrich, Leland M. "Geographical Distribution of the Staff of the United Nations." 16 International Organization (1962), 465-482.
Deals with the concept of wide distribution of positions on a geographical basis, the scope of application of the principle, and the various ways that staff members are chosen. The third section deals with the determination of national quotas and the final part with the actual practice of distribution of these United Nations positions.

725. Gordenker, Leon. "Policy-Making and Secretariat Influence in the U.N. General Assembly: The Case of Public Information." 54 American Political Science Review (1960), 359-373.
Shows the influence of the U.N. Office of Public Information on policy-making and the results of attacks on the Office by the General Assembly.

726. Keohane, Robert Owen. "Political Influence in the General Assembly." International Conciliation, No. 557, February 1966, pp. 64.
On strengths, cohesiveness, and voting patterns of regional groups in the General Assembly, the ways in which states attempt to exercise influence, and the characteristics that tend to make one state more influential than another.

727. Van Wagenen, Richard W. "The Concept of Community and the Future of the United Nations." 19 International Organization (1965), 812-827.
Suggests that there are three main approaches to study of "the concept of community" in a divided world: (1) unstructured judgment based on the assumption that whatever seems to strengthen the UN builds community and generally advances integration; (2) application of research findings on integration in certain other international contexts by use of rough judgment and by ignoring the fact that conditions underlying and surrounding the research are different and may render application to the UN unreliable; (3) development and application of a framework intended specifically for study of the UN system. The author suggests exploration of the first two approaches, the first very briefly, in the realization that development of the framework specifically designed to study the integrative function of the UN system cannot be accomplished in a short time.

728. Wadsworth, James J. The Glass House: The United Nations in Action. New York: Praeger, 1966, pp. xiv, 224.
Draws liberally on personal experiences to illustrate the functioning of the UN.

See also 614, 651, 652, 690, 691, 693, 1087, 1090, 1103, 1108, 1109, 1129, 1143, 1356, 1593, 1753, 1769, 1770, 2029, 2039, 2060, 2486, 2488, 2718, 2721.

(3) Specialized Agencies and Administrative Unions

729. Asher, Robert E., et al. The United Nations and the Promotion of the General Welfare. Washington: Brookings Institution, 1957, pp. xvi, 1216.
Extensive review of major UN activities in the fields of economics and social cooperation, human rights, and advancement of dependent peoples.

730. Berkov, Robert. The World Health Organization: A Study in Decentralized Administration. Geneva: Droz; Paris: Minard, 1957, pp. x, 173.
Essentially a study from the point of view of public administration and administrative theory, with emphasis upon the nature of the organization, the development of programs, and the consequences of decentralization.

731. Codding, George A., Jr. The International Telecommunications Union: An Experiment in International Cooperation. Leiden: E.J. Brill, 1952, pp. xvi, 505.
Study, based on primary sources, of the self-adaptation of an international organization developed to meet practical problems. The author gives attention to the tendency of telecommunications experts to disregard legal formalities and to the difficulties that result, as well as, in consequence, in avoidance of many of those types of political machinations that result from resort to legal formalities.

732. Codding, George A., Jr. The Universal Postal Union: Coordinator of the International Mails. New York: New York University Press, 1964, pp. ix, 296.
Review of the activities of the Universal Postal Union with reference both to the use of international conventions to produce changes and to adaptation through practice while dealing with specific problems.

733. Hambidge, Gove. The Story of FAO. New York: Van Nostrand, 1955, pp. 303.
Review of the work of FAO to the mid-1950s.

734. Holborn, Louise W. The International Refugee Organization, A Specialized Agency of the United Nations: Its History and Work, 1946-1952. New York: Oxford for the Liquidation Board of the International Refugee Organization, 1956, pp. xiv, 805.

Official account of the activities and achievements of the organization from 1946 to its termination in 1952.

735. Krause, Günther B. Internationaler Fernmeldverein. Frankfurt-am-Main: Metzner, 1960, pp. 184.

A study of the International Telecommunications Union.

736. Malinowski, W.R. "Centralization and Decentralization in the United Nations Economic and Social Activities." 16 International Organization (1962), 521-541.

Reviews what institutional framework and administrative arrangements have been made and their development in the last ten years. The article then discusses the financing of these agencies and the development of the various regional groups.

737. Menon, M.A.K. "Universal Postal Union." International Conciliation. No. 552, March 1965, pp. 64.

Brief review of the organization and activities of the Universal Postal Union and regional unions, with reference to some problems dealt with by international agreement.

738. Schenkman, Jacob. International Civil Aviation Organization. Geneva: Droz, 1955, pp. viii, 410.

Extensive study of international aspects of civil aviation with particular concern for the role and functions of ICAO.

739. Schloss, Henry Hans. The Bank for International Settlements: An Experiment in Central Bank Cooperation. Amsterdam: North-Holland Publishing Co., 1958, pp. xi, 184.

Origins, structure, and operations of the Bank.

740. Sewell, James Patrick. Functionalism and World Politics: A Study Based on United Nations Programs Financing Economic Development. Princeton: Princeton University Press, 1966, pp. xii, 359.

Evaluates the argument for a functional approach to international organization by reference to such agencies for economic development as the International Bank for Reconstruction and Development, the International Finance Corporation, the International Development Association, and the United Nations Special Fund.

741. Wightman, David. Economic Co-operation in Europe: A Study of the United Nations Economic Commission for Europe. New York: Praeger; Toronto: British Book Service (Canada) Ltd., 1956, pp. xi, 288.

Study of an entity that has achieved reputation for reliable analysis and for achieving coordination through technical committees, including facilitation of the evolution and functioning of ECSC. The volume emphasizes the manner in which the supply of reliable data to the members of technical committees aids achievement of consensus on methods of conducting business and leads to patterns of production, distribution, and consumption that constitute important subjects of international agreements.

742. Wightman, David. Toward Economic Cooperation in Asia: The United Nations Economic Commission for Asia and the Far East. New Haven: Yale University Press for the Carnegie Endowment for International Peace, 1963, pp. 400.
    On the structure, purpose, and development of ECAFE and its effort among other things, to stimulate economic cooperation in Asia.

See also nos. 715, 1068, 1106, 2486.

(4) The European Communities

743. Alker, Hayward, Jr., and Puchala, Donald. "Trends in Economic Partnership: The North Atlantic Area, 1928-1963." In J. David Singer (ed.), Quantitative International Politics: Insights and Evidence. New York: Free Press, 1968, pp. 287-316.
    Making use of relative acceptance coefficients as measures of transactions and of indices of trade flows in A. Sturmthal's 1964 manuscript, National Income and Growth Rates in Western Europe, the authors find (1) a notable structural change in North Atlantic economic interaction between the inter-war and post-war periods, (2) as much economic disintegration in Western Europe since 1951 as integration, (3) a noticeable increase of interaction in the normally weak non-EEC countries in the post-war period, (4) a failure of the EEC countries to grow any closer structurally in their economic relations in the early 1960s than in the early 1950s, and (5) some spill-over effects in the form of faster growth for the EEC countries than for the United States or EFTA, increase in the European share of world trade, and increasing economic independence of the Common Market countries.

744. Alting von Geusau, F.A.M. European Organization and Foreign Relations of States: A Comparative Analysis of Decision-Making. Leiden: Sijthoff, 1962, pp. xiii, 290.
    Analysis of foreign policy decision-making processes and the changes therein as a result of the formation of multilateral organizations among European states.

745. Barzanti, Sergio. The Underdeveloped Areas Within the Common Market. Princeton: Princeton University Press, 1965, pp. 437.
    Thorough examination of the problems of underdevelopment in Southern Italy and Central and Southwest France that provides essential data for an understanding of Common Market negotiations. Particular attention is given to agriculture and freedom of movement of workers, with somewhat less space devoted to transportation, power, industry, and tourism. In respect to efforts to redress the situation, the author notes the effects of habits and

customs of the people upon governmental efforts and also indicates
what is possible within the terms of the EEC treaty.

746. Clark, W. Hartley. The Politics of the Common Market. New
York: Praeger, 1967, pp. x, 180.
     Drawing on hitherto unavailable documents, the author examines
the Common Market as a political institution with attention to the
distribution of power and to the influence of Cold War politics on
Community decisions.

747. Collins, Norman R. "The Development of a Coordinated Food Production and Distribution System in Western Europe." 45 Journal of Farm
Economics (1963), 263-272.
     Discussion of problems affecting the development of a Western
European food production and distribution system, including problems of markets, scale, and methods.

748. Cosgrove, C.A. "Agriculture, Finance and Politics in the European Community." 3 International Relations (1967), 208-225.
     On the intense interaction of national and Community interests
during the negotiations that culminated in the 1966 decisions governing the financing of the common agricultural policy of EEC.

749. Dell, Sidney. Trade Blocs and Common Markets. New York: Alfred A. Knopf, 1963, pp. xviii, 384, x.
     An analysis that views economic groupings as emerging to correct
the excessive economic forces of other areas. Conflicts within EEC,
which influence the growth of Community law, are given appropriate
attention as are also conflicts created outside the Community in a
world economy characterized, among other things, by conflict and
collaboration and by constant regrouping and reorganizing.

750. Deniau, J.F. The Common Market: Its Structure and Purpose.
Translated by Graham Heath. New York: Praeger, 1960, pp. 167.
     A brief treatise on the theory, history, and economics of large
markets followed by a discussion of the Common Market and its treaty
with an emphasis on political and economic aspects.

751. Diebold, William. The Schuman Plan: A Study in Economic Cooperation. New York: Praeger, 1959, pp. xviii, 750.
     Detailed study of what was done in the 1950s about trade bar-
riers, transportation, prices, cartels, and other matters, with particular concern for the interplay of business, labor governments,
and community organs.

752. Feld, Werner. The European Common Market and the World. Englewood Cliffs: Prentice-Hall, 1967, pp. vii, 184.
     Reviews EEC structure, its problems, its effects on American
foreign policy, and its relations with EFTA, and examines the political, economic, and trade policies of EEC toward nonmember nations, developing nations, and the Communist satellite countries.

753. Gaudet, Michael. Euratom. London: Pergamon, 1959.
Study of Euratom now most useful in combination with more recent studies taking account of developments since the first year of the organization.

754. Haas, Ernst B. The Uniting of Europe. Stanford: Stanford University Press, 1958, pp. 552.
Excellent study of the integration process in Europe based on intensive study of ECSC activities and interrelationships.

755. Henderson, William O. The Genesis of the Common Market. Chicago: Quadrangle, 1962, pp. 201.
The historian of the Zollverein reviews efforts and achievements in international economic union since the late 18th century.

756. Homan, J. Linthorst. "The Merger of the European Communities." 3 Common Market Law Review (1966), 397-419.
On the possible nature of a merger of the three Communities following the merger of the Executives.

757. Houben, P.-H.J.M. De associatie von Suriname en de Nederlandse Antillen met de Europese Economische Gemeenschap. Leiden: Sijthoff, 1965, pp. 124.
While the association of important parts of Africa with EEC is well known, it is sometimes forgotten that some segments of the Western Hemisphere are also associated with the six integrating countries of Europe. This volume examines the nature of the relationship of two parts of the Western Hemisphere, parts of the Dutch association, with EEC.

758. Houben, P.-H.J.M. "Merger of the Executives of the European Communities." 3 Common Market Law Review (1965), 37-89.
On the history and provisions of the Treaty Establishing a Council and a Commission Common to the European Communities, signed in Brussels, April 8, 1965. The French text is appended.

759. Institut d'Études Juridiques de la Faculté de Droit de l'Université de Liège. La Fusion des Communautés Européennes--Colloque organisé à Liège les 28, 29 et 30 Avril 1965. The Hague: Nijhoff, 1965.
Papers and proceedings of a colloquium on the possible comprehensive merger of the three Communities.

760. Jensen, Finn B., and Walter, Ingo. The Common Market: Economic Integration in Europe. Philadelphia: Lippincott, 1965, pp. vii, 278.
Essentially economic account of the Common Market.

761. Kapteyn, Paul. L'Assemblée Commune de la Communauté Européenne du Charbon et de l'Acier: Un essai de parlementarisme européenne. Leiden: Sijthoff, 1962, pp. 270.
Account of the workings of the Common Assembly by a Dutch Socialist whose group played an important role in the organization of the Assembly by party groups and who himself played an important

role in the Assembly's assertion of influence in regard to transport and to energy policy.

762. Kitzinger, U.W. The Politics and Economics of European Integration. New York: Praeger, 1963, pp. 246.

A short study of the strategy of European federalists, particularly the belief in "snowballing" integration created by successive economic integration and interdependence moves.

763. Leites, Nathan. The "Europe" of the French. Memorandum RM-4584-ISA. Santa Monica: RAND Corporation, June 1965, pp. ix, 41.

On French and particularly Gaullist reactions to the prospect of European unity as reflected in political vocabulary and opinion polls. The author finds almost unanimous acceptance of a Europe of shared facilities but rapid or systematic progress toward a unified Europe being regarded as neither urgent nor acceptable.

764. Limits and Problems of European Integration. The Conference of May 30-June 2, 1961. Stichting Grotius Seminarium. The Hague: Nijhoff, 1963, pp. iv, 144.

Papers by Haas (also in 15 International Organization (1961), 366-392), Mitrany, van der Goes van Naters, Claude Durand-Prinborgne and François Borella, and J. Alting von Geusau, among others, that deal with the necessity of fitting European integration into a wider framework of international cooperation, the dangers of overlapping structures and related enforcement problems, and the intermingling of law and politics in the European integration process.

764-A. Lindberg, Leon N., and Scheingold, Stuart A. Europe's Would-Be Polity: Patterns of Change in the European Community. Englewood Cliffs: Prentice-Hall, 1970, pp. 256.

Incorporates diverse findings and competing theories into a focus on coalition formation as the agent of community growth to posit a model of system change and to identify patterns of growth and decline as a result of operation of the European Community system.

765. Liska, George. Europe Ascendant: The International Politics of Unification. Baltimore: Johns Hopkins Press, 1964, pp. x, 182.

A highly projective long essay, best understood when read in conjunction with the author's Nations in Alliance, that treats the present as a parallel to the Victorian era as it makes liberal use of analogies from the Victorian and other pre-1945 periods to speculate upon Europe's future, its potential relations with the non-European world and particularly with the Maghreb, and the impact of a united Europe upon international affairs, allowing for various forms of possible European association and for a variety of European and non-European policies.

766. Lister, Louis. Europe's Coal and Steel Community: An Experiment in Economic Union. New York: Twentieth Century Fund, 1960, pp. 495.

Careful, detailed study of constitutional and political aspects of ECSC.

767. Ljubisavljevic, Bora. Les problèmes de la pondération dans les institutions européennes. Leiden: Sijthoff, 1959, pp. 199.

Deals with problems related to voting and its relations to equality of states and of majorities in European institutions, with reference to problems of retaining a balance among states and interests. By getting to the issues of majority and other forms of decision-taking, including both equal and weighted voting that have also been a feature of discussion of United Nations decision-making, the book, on the level of a particular region, gets at organizational mechanics in a sort of transfer of the argument related to individual enfranchisement as expressed in earlier centuries. Like most discussions of this type that are rooted in intuition and preference, this monograph is actually more a pondering upon possibilities than a systematic exposition of the mechanics of interest-balancing decision.

768. Mayne, Richard. The Community of Europe. New York: Norton, 1962, pp. 192.

Study of the political and economic backgrounds and narration of events leading to the formation of the European Communities. The problem of Britain is accorded attention as are also the problems of relations with nonmember states and of GATT obligations.

769. Meade, J.E., Liesner, H.H., and Wells, S.J. Case Studies in European Economic Union. New York: Oxford, 1962, pp. vii, 424.

Compares the Belgium-Luxembourg Economic Union, Benelux, and ECSC to determine requirements for effective economic integration.

770. Merkl, Peter H. "European Assembly Parties and National Delegations." 8 Journal of Conflict Resolution (1964), 50-64.

The setting, organization, and voting behavior of community-wide parties within various European parliamentary assemblies are examined on the basis of the formation and growth of these parties that compete with the national delegations which are the original representation units.

771. Namenwirth, J. Zvi. Changing Editorial Concerns with Atlantic and European Politics. Appendix 5. Arms Control in the European Political Environment. New Haven: Yale University, Political Science Research Library, January 1966.

Content analysis of a random sample of editorials of the New York Times, The Times of London, the Frankfurter Allgemeine Zeitung, and Le Monde during 1953 and 1963 that deal with Atlantic and European matters. The report deals with the 30 categories of words, out of 99 categories initially employed, that displayed a difference in frequency over the years or between papers. These categories were statistically reduced to four dimensions: (1) NATO perspective vs. EEC perspective; (2) idealized future vs. concrete issues and difficulties; (3) costs of supranational alliances vs. domestic French and German political controversies; (4) American pressures for integration vs. legal temporizing and restraint. Differences among the four papers and changes over time along these four dimensions are identified.

772. Namenwirth, J. Zvi, and Stone, Philip J. "Plannism and the Advent of European Unification." 23 Acta Psychologica (1964), 247-248.
      Content analysis of speeches of leading politicians and administrators in Europe to identify attitudes toward "plannism" and European unification.

773. Nichols, R.T. The Common Market and European Unification. Memorandum RM-4640-PR. Santa Monica: RAND Corporation, December 1965, pp. x, 117.
      Review of the effect of the Common Market on development of the economic potential of Europe.

774. Nieburg, H.L. "Euratom--A Study in Coalition Politics." 15 World Politics (1963), 597-622.
      On American and British policy toward Euratom, Continental nuclear technology, American desire for inspection, French desire for the use of enriched uranium and plutonium for armaments, and the British countermove in the form of ENEA.

775. Polach, Jaroslav G. Euratom: Its Background, Issues and Economic Implications. Dobbs Ferry: Oceana, 1964, pp. xxiv, 232.
      Broader than its title indicates, this volume includes discussion of problems related to the division of authority and lack of comprehensive regulation and policy for the vital field of energy production and utilization. Difficulties in erecting a satisfactory legal structure, as well as the important effects upon an integrating system of the maintenance of diverse systems of energy-flow, suggest possibilities of systems conflict--as a system of diversity overlays a system of integration. Except in regard to nuclear energy, the study does not undertake to delve into the problem of the desirability of European-wide coordination of energy policy, e.g., in regard to utilization of North Sea natural gas resources, should the Inner Six develop a common energy policy but not expand its membership.

776. Scheinman, Lawrence. "Euratom: Nuclear Integration in Europe." International Conciliation. No. 563, May 1967, pp. 66.
      On the problems of Euratom and on the ways in which it differs from other supranational undertakings, especially EEC.

777. Spinelli, Altiero. The Eurocrats: Conflict and Crisis in the European Community. Translated by C. Grove Haines. Baltimore: Johns Hopkins Press, 1966, pp. xi, 229.
      On the bureaucratic politics of European integration with attention to the lesser executives, the Common Market Commission, relations between the Commission and national bureaucracies, special interest groups, and relations with national politicians, political parties, and European movements.

778. van Oudenhove, Guy. The Political Parties in the European Parliament: The First Ten Years (September 1952-September 1962). Leiden: Sijthoff, 1962, pp. 268.

On the formation of political groups at the international level
in the Common Assembly of ECSC and on their further development in the
European Parliament. Both legal and political aspects are dealt with
exhaustively, as is also the institutionalization of the parties and
the clearly discernible force that they have been able to exert.

779. Walter, Ingo. The European Common Market: Growth and Patterns
of Trade and Production. New York: Praeger, 1967, pp. xv, 212.
    An attempt to map the volume and direction of intra-community
trade during the first eight years of the Common Market.

780. Westerterp, T.E. "Europese fractievorming, een eerste experiment." 12 Internationale Spectator (1958), 359-378.
    Review of the functions of party groups in the European Parlia-
ment, particularly the formulation of basic principles on which policy can be rested and the harmonization of national points of view
be attained.

See also nos. 493, 566, 1065, 1071, 1073, 1074, 1078, 1080-1082, 1086,
1102, 1105, 1238, 1325, 1391, 1392, 1400, 1403-1405, 1464, 1526, 1594, and
sec. III, A, 3.

(5) Other European and North Atlantic Organizations

781. Allais, Maurice. L'Europe Unie--Route de la prospérité. Paris:
Calmann-Levy, 1960, pp. 368.
    Awarded the Grand Prix de la Communauté Atlantique, this argu-
ment for a convention to explore the possibilities of a real Atlantic Community emphasizes economic integration of Western Europe as
a first step toward Atlantic Community. Some useful discussion of
the impact of the ECSC treaty and of the Common Market treaty in its
first years leads into consideration of such questions as the eventual dependence of economic integration upon a measure of political
unification. Numerous annexes set out more fully certain economic,
statistical, and political theories and data on which the author's
arguments are based. An excellent classified bibliography is
included.

782. Anderson, Stanley V. The Nordic Council: The Study of Scandinavian Regionalism. Seattle: University of Washington Press, 1967,
pp. xvi, 194.
    A description of the structure and procedures of the Nordic
Council that assumes "amalgamation" to be a higher form of life
but sheds little light on the integration process.

783. Andrén, N. "Nordic Integration." Cooperation and Conflict
(1967), 1-25.
    Examines the background and nature of Nordic integration in
the context of current theories of integration and offers a redefinition and conceptual framework of facilitate analysis of the
dynamics, ideology, strategy, and limitations of Nordic integration.

784. Barclay, G. St. J. "Background to E.F.T.A.: An Episode in Anglo-Scandinavian Relations." 11 Australian Journal of Politics and History (1965), 185-197.

Notes that associations of the EFTA countries were often older, closer, and more amicable than those of the EEC countries and goes on to examine how EFTA, by preserving freedom from advance commitments, permitted Scandinavians, whose attitudes were conditioned by Swedish neutrality, to preserve their association with Sweden.

785. Bonsdorff, G. von. "Regional Cooperation of the Nordic Countries." 1 Cooperation and Conflict (1965), 32-38.

Deals with the Nordic community of interests and with the political and organizational aspects of the Nordic Council.

786. Dolan, P. "The Nordic Council." 12 Western Political Quarterly (1959), 511-526.

Description of the Nordic Council and its work.

787. Etzioni, Amitai. "Atlantic Union, the Southern Continents, and the United Nations." In Roger Fisher (ed.), International Conflict and Behavioral Science: The Craigville Papers. New York: Basic Books, 1964, pp. 178-207.

The author concentrates on the idea of Atlantic Union--an idea which has yet to be actualized. He discusses the economic, political, and military aspects of the desired union, which he describes as "a vague expression of fairly clear political needs." Etzioni visualizes a bloc organization having two regional bases: a united Europe and a North American base. One of his main concerns is with the problem of distribution of authority in interunit relations. The major drawback of the Atlantic Union is said to be its semi-imperial relationship to the less developed countries. To counteract this effect he suggests the formation of a Commonwealth of the Free, a grouping which would include the "have-not" nations which would, however, have to meet certain minimal economic and political standards. The United States would play a unique role, cast as the historic balancer instead of being predominantly tied with Europe.

788. Eyck, F. Gunther. The Benelux Countries: An Historical Survey. Anvil Books. Princeton: Van Nostrand, 1959, pp. 192.

An outline history of the Low Countries tracing the main lines of divergence and later of convergence that led to the Benelux economic union. An appendix includes 20 pertinent documents.

789. Fischer, Per. Europarat und parlamentarische Aussenpolitik. Munich: Oldenbourg, 1962, pp. 134.

A discussion of the idea of "European parliamentary foreign policy" and of the implications of the Council of Europe in the growth of such a system.

790. Haas, Ernst B. Consensus Formation in the Council of Europe. Berkeley: University of California Press, 1960, pp. 70.

Seeks an operational definition of "consensus," and investigates the role of organizational norms in consensus-formation. Roll call votes in the Consultative Assembly show that there is no overall trend away from nationality toward some other dominant basis of cohesion among groups of parliamentarians, that nationality is not consistently dominant, and that cohesion oscillates from session to session and with the issues. Lack of substantive issues is offered as one explanation of the absence of consensus in the sense of national party politics.

791. Harnwell, Gaylord. "Science, Technology and the North Atlantic Community." 2 Orbis (1958), 209-221.
    Joining of science and technology with a common culture can serve to bind the Atlantic Community and permit negotiation from a position of strength.

792. Lambrinidis, John S. The Structure, Function, and Law of a Free Trade Area: The European Free Trade Association. New York: Praeger, 1965, pp. xxii, 303.
    One of the few books on EFTA, this volume deals with its structure, function, and law in the light of the first years of the Area's operations. Actually, the approach is somewhat more general in that it treats EFTA as the paramount example of a free trade area and considers EFTA against the background of other free trade schemes and multilateral economic institutions.

793. Lindgren, R.E. "International Co-operation in Scandinavia." Year Book of World Affairs (1959), 95-114.
    Review of Scandinavian cooperation including the promotion of joint civil and criminal laws and the conferring of the benefits of the legislation concerning individuals upon all Nordics.

794. Meyer, F.V. The European Free Trade Association: An Analysis of "the Outer Seven". New York: Praeger, 1960, pp. viii, 140.
    An essentially economic study that includes analysis of the Convention of Stockholm. Background discussion of earlier free trade efforts, of Commonwealth procedures, and of the circumstances among the Outer Seven differing from those of the EEC countries helps to place the Stockholm arrangements in a perspective aiding system analysis. Discussion of rules of origin elaborates upon the differences between positively and negatively phrased rules and throws light upon the problem of selecting at the lawmaking stage the most viable of the several choices perceived as susceptible of governing foreseeable situations.

795. Miller, Arthur S. "The Organization for Economic Co-operation and Development." Year Book of World Affairs (1963), 80-95.
    A brief survey of the structure purposes, activities, and problems of OECD.

796. Padelford, Norman J. "Regional Co-operation in Scandinavia." 11 International Organization (1957), 597-614.
    Exposition of Scandinavian cooperation in such matters as passports, equality of treatment of each other's citizens, common

labor market, mutual arrangements for social security, hospital and ambulance services, economic cooperation, peaceful uses of atomic power, and educational and cultural affairs.

797. Palmer, Michael, Lambert, John, et al. A Handbook of European Organizations. New York: Praeger, 1968, pp. 519.
This volume revises and updates Political and Economic Planning (P.E.P.), European Organizations (1959). Both principal authors of the original volume contributed to the revision which includes chapters on EFTA and OECD. The original volume dealt with the origins, structure, techniques of cooperation, methods of work, and principal activities of ECE, OEEC, the Council of Europe, NATO, WEU, ECSC, EEC, and Euratom. This coverage is updated by the present Handbook.

798. Petren, G. "Nordiska radet." 58 Statsvetenskaplig Tidsskrift (1955), 287-305.
Description of the organs of the Nordic Council, based not on a ratified treaty but on a uniform text adopted by each national legislature, together with a review of the functions allocated to each organ.

799. Radovanovitch, Lj. "L'Assemblée consultative balkanique." 29 Questions actuelles du socialisme (1955), 31-40.
Description of the Balkan Consultative Assembly established by the agreement of March 2, 1955.

800. Robertson, Arthur H. The Council of Europe: Its Structure, Functions and Achievements. 2nd ed. New York: Praeger, 1961, pp. xv, 288.
A comprehensive study of the Council of Europe since 1949 that concentrates on structure and function and records activities in promotion of the European ideal.

801. Valentine, A. "Benelux: Pilot Plant of Economic Union." 44 Yale Review (1954), 23-32.
In democracies it is essential to conciliate group pressures, but to protect special interests postpones economic union. Benelux escaped the static circle of providing protection in an effort to eliminate protection by first putting goods into free circulation with provisions for post-factum adjustment. Traditional controversies such as the Netherlands-Belgium waterways issues required settlement to create a general good will essential for durable union. Legislation alone cannot achieve economic union but must be buttressed by public discussion and conferences between economic groups within and between states.

802. Wendt, Frantz Wilhelm. The Nordic Council and Cooperation in Scandinavia. Translated from the Danish. Copenhagen: Munksgaard, 1959, pp. 247.
Survey, by the Secretary General of the Danish Delegation to the Nordic Council, of all aspects of cooperation among the Scandinavian countries.

See also nos. 572, 1074, 1088, 1099, 1105, 1211, 1583, 2440, 2486, 2487, and sec. III, A, 3.

(6) The Organization of American States

803. Caudill, Orley Brandt. The Inter-American Economic and Social Council: Instrument of Peaceful Revolution. Ph.D. Dissertation. College Park: University of Maryland, 1968; Ann Arbor: University Microfilms, Inc., Order No. 69-713, pp. 335.
On the OAS economic organization, its development from a purely technical organization to one concerned with policy, and its relations with the Alliance for Progress.

804. Mecham, J. Lloyd. The United States and Inter-American Security, 1889-1960. Austin: University of Texas Press, 1961, pp. xii, 514.
Comprehensive narrative of the development of the Western Hemisphere security system.

805. Poppino, Rollie. International Communism in Latin America: A History of the Movement, 1917-1963. New York: Free Press, 1964, pp. viii, 247.
History of Latin American communism, with chapters on party organization and on the role of the Soviet Union and of Castro, that provides important data relevant to the problem of the effectiveness and even the survival of the present legal order and regional organization of the Americas. Since communism has produced among its effects a reaction in the attempt to establish a normative underpinning for effective protection of non-Communist regimes (with dichotomous tendency by bringing rightist dictatorships under the democratic umbrella), the Communist impact requires analysis as an organizational as well as an ideological impact.

806. Stoetzer, O. Carlos. The Organization of American States: An Introduction. New York: Praeger, 1965, pp. viii, 213.
A concise, essentially chronological account of the structure and activities of the OAS, originally published in German in 1964 for the Institute of Ibero-American studies in Hamburg.

See also nos. 1064, 1072, 1510, 1592, 1595, 2236, 2335, 2486, 2489, and sec. III, A, 3.

(7) Other Inter-American Organizations

807. Babbar, M.M. "Economic Integration of the Central American Countries and Their Agriculture." 14 Monthly Bulletin of Agricultural Economies and Statistics (November 1965), 1-9.

Provides data on the agricultural sector and the impact thereon of the Central American Common Market at the stage of integration reached by 1965.

808. Busey, James L. "Central American Union: The Latest Attempt." 14 Western Political Quarterly (1961), 49-63.
    Somewhat pessimistic in tone, the article reviews activities of the Organización de Estados Centroamericanos (ODECA) and raises an important question concerning conflict between the institutionalized interests of separate political entities and functional collaboration. This question goes to the foundation of the legal framework for integration and, as the tone of the article indicates, can too readily be subjected to emotionalism, pessimistically projecting the present into tomorrow or optimistically reading today's hopes as tomorrow's realities, instead of employing rigorous scientific analysis of the interrelation of institutional interests and functional interaction to assist identification of variables and combinations thereof that have potential influence, positive or negative, on the course of integration.

809. Cale, Edward G. The Latin American Free Trade Association: Progress, Problems, Prospects. Prepared for the Office of Research and Analysis for American Republics, Department of State Publication 8448. Washington: Department of State, Office of External Research, 1969, pp. 64.
    Discusses the several obstacles to reorientation of Latin American trade including the opposition of protection-minded industrialists, the reasons for slowness in reducing trade barriers, the April 1967 decision of the Latin American Presidents to establish by 1985 a Latin American Common Market built from LAFTA and the Central American Common Market, the consequences of Latin American manufactured products not being competitive on the world market, indications that there may be little correlation between tariff rates and imports of manufactured goods despite concessions to imports from LAFTA countries, and the probability that slow liberalization of trade is congenial to countries stressing either internal development or trade with non-LAFTA countries.

810. Castillo, Carlos M. Growth and Integration in Central America. Englewood Cliffs: Prentice-Hall, 1966, pp. x, 188.
    On the creation of the Central American Common Market, its nature and scope, the growth of investment and commodity flows, and the need for a concerted policy of development of productive capacity.

811. Dell, Sidney. A Latin American Common Market? New York: Oxford University Press, 1966, pp. ix, 336.
    Review of steps toward economic integration that have been taken by the Latin American Free Trade Association and by the Central American Common Market. Attention is given to obstacles encountered and possible methods of overcoming them.

812. Duncan, Julian S. "Demographic Factors and Economic Integration in Central America." 5 Journal of Inter-American Studies (1963), 533-543.

   Contains vital statistics important in attempting to assess the demographic basis on which the Central American Common Market rests.

813. Griffin, Keith B. "The Potential Benefits of Latin American Integration." 17 Inter-American Economic Affairs (Spring 1964), 3-20.

   Emphasizes economic and some political impediments to regional development through the Latin American Free Trade Area.

814. Gutíerrez Olivas, Sergio. Subdesarrollo, integración y Alianza. Buenos Aires: EMECE, 1963, pp. 189.

   On economic development and integration in Latin America in the first years of LAFTA and the Alliance for Progress.

815. Haas, Ernst B., and Schmitter, Philippe C. The Politics of Economics in Latin American Regionalism: The Latin American Free Trade Association After Four Years of Operation. Monograph series in World Affairs. Vol. III, No. 2. The Social Science Foundation and Graduate School of International Studies, University of Denver, 1965-1966, pp. 78.

   Reviews the first four years of LAFTA, its discouraging features and such integrative efforts as have been made, makes certain comparisons with the West European integration process, and finds the norm of reciprocity and the role of the técnicos to be substitutes for factors in Western Europe making for integration. The Herrera Plan, which aimed to speed integration, is briefly outlined. The monograph at the least highlights difficulties to be overcome in the Latin American integration process, including that of competition with ECLA, IDB, OAS, the Instituto Latinoamericano de Planificación Económica y Social, CEMLA, and Alliance for Progress organs for regional expertise and for program priority in Latin America.

816. Karnes, Thomas L. The Failure of Union, Central America, 1824-1960. Chapel Hill: University of North Carolina Press, 1961, pp. xii, 277.

   Study of the efforts made down to 1960 to unite or, after the collapse of the early union, to bring closer together the Central American Republics.

817. Keller, Frank L. "ODECA: Common Market Experiment in an Under-Developed Area." 5 Journal of Inter-American Studies (1963), 267-276.

   Deals in broad strokes with the Common Market movement in Central America.

818. Lagos, Gustavo (ed.). "Intégration Latino-Américaine: Symposium." 6 Tiers-Monde (July-September 1965), 601-775.

   Useful symposium on problems of economic integration in Latin America.

819. Lauterbach, Albert. "Comportement économique en Amérique Latine Occidentale." 15 Économie appliquée (1962), 263-288.

Finds that there are intraregional differences among Latin
American businessmen that correlate roughly with the extent of industrialization of the several countries.

820. Lauterbach, Albert. "Objectives de la administratión de em-
presas y requerimentos del desarrollo en la América Latina." Revista de
economiá latinoamericana (January 1963), 119-174.
A study of Latin American businessmen that calls attention to
intraregional differences, something very much of consequence to
the course and outcome of attempted integration.

821. López-Ortiz, F. "El Mercado Commun, un rato para América
Latina." 31 Foro internacional (1968), 302-316.
On the obstacles to attainment of the Common Market proclaimed
as a goal by the Latin American Presidents in April 1967.

822. Macdonald, N.P. "The Continental Policy of President Perón."
604 Quarterly Review (1955), 192-205.
Describes the attempt, of which Perón was principal architect,
to join Argentina, Chile, Paraguay, Bolivia, and Equador in a form
of economic union designed to ease trade restrictions and that
looked forward to the abolition of customs duties.

823. Nystrom, J. Warren, and Haverstock, Nathan A. The Alliance
for Progress: Key to Latin America's Development. Princeton: Van
Nostrand, 1966, pp. 126.
A brief review of the formation of the Alliance for Progress,
the problem of leadership, operational problems, and successes and
setbacks to the time of writing.

824. Pincus, Joseph. The Central American Common Market. Regional
Technical Aids Center, Agency for International Development. Mexico,
September 1962, pp. 231.
Thorough study of the Central American Common Market, its eco-
nomic and organizational aspects, and its political potential.

825. Schmitter, Philippe C., and Haas, Ernst B. Mexico and Latin
American Integration. Research Series No. 5. Berkeley: Institute of
International Studies, University of California, 1964, pp. 43.
Concise study of Mexico's decision to join LAFTA with particular attention accorded to economic and ideological aspects, reciprocity and complementarity, tactics, the process of integration,
the theory of integration in relation to underdevelopment, and the
satisfaction of immediate expectations.

826. Sosa-Rodriguez, Raul. Les problèmes structurels des relations
économiques internationales de l'Amérique latine. Geneva: Droz, 1963,
pp. 252.
Examines the history of Latin America's economic relations
with Europe and the United States, giving attention to such matters as the decline of British and French financial hegemony, to
the penetration by North American capital, to commercial relations
with Japan after World War II, to Latin America's association with

such dominant economies as EEC (with attention to the impact of associate status for former colonies), the USSR, and the United States, to the efforts to integrate under the Treaty of Montevideo and the Central American Common Market, and to such current aspects of financial relations as North American and European investments, foreign aid from Western states and from the Soviet Union, convertibility, governmental policy toward foreign investments, and aid problems under the Alliance for Progress.

827. Urquidi, Victor L. Trayectoria del Mercado Commun Latinoamericano. Mexico City: Centro de Estudios Monetarios Latinoamericanos, 1960, pp. 178.

Contains a brief history of various plans for economic cooperation up to the LAFTA undertaking.

828. Vernon, Raymond. The Dilemma of Mexico's Development. Cambridge: Harvard University Press, 1963, pp. xi, 226.

In this examination of Mexico's development problems attention is given to the técnicos and their objectives which are not to be confused with those of the políticos but which helped bring Mexico into LAFTA to prevent that organization from becoming subregional rather than regional in extent.

829. Wardlaw, Andrew B. Achievements and Problems of the Central American Common Market. Department of State Publication 8437. Washington: Department of State, Office of External Research, February 1969, pp. vi, 46.

Reviews the activities and accomplishments of the organs of the Central American Common Market, their relations with the Organization of Central American states, the growth of intraregional trade, the directions of extraregional trade, tariff problems, difficulties in the area of agriculture, the System of Integrated Industries, the Special System for the Promotion of Production, and the obstacles to expansion of the Common Market toward closer ties with Panama, Mexico, and LAFTA.

830. Wionczek, Miguel S. (ed.). Integración de América Latina--Experiencias y perspectivas. Mexico City: Fondo de Cultura Economica, 1964, pp. xxxi, 381. Latin American Economic Integration: Experiences and Prospects. New York: Praeger, 1966, pp. xiv, 310.

Nineteen essays on theoretical approaches, experiences, and hopes, and United States opinions on ECLA, LAFTA, and the Central American Common Market. Particularly important is the editor's discussion of the concept of economic distance and its consequences in Latin America. Also of special interest are the editor's article on the background of the Treaty of Montevideo, Sidney Dell's review of the way in which the treaty provisions were dealt with during the organization's first year and Plácido García Reynoso's examination of problems of industrialization.

See also nos. 1050, 2757, 2764, 2827, and sec. III, A, 3.

(8) The Communist International System
     and Organizations

831. Agoston, István. Le Marche Commun Communiste--Principes et
pratique du COMECON. 2nd ed. Geneva: Droz, 1965, pp. xii, 353.
          Chiefly an economic analysis by an author whose doctorate is in
     political science, this book is a very thorough study of COMECON in
     terms of the economies of the East European countries and of their
     economic relations with each other and with the non-Communist world.
     A wealth of economic statistics is presented in relatively easily
     understood form. An appendix includes, among other things, a record
     of meetings of COMECON committees, problems treated, and recommenda-
     tions or decisions made through 1962. Political aspects are more
     lightly dealt with than economic aspects and the chapter on organiza-
     tion is essentially a paraphrase of formal treaty provisions concern-
     ing structure. Relationship to Communist parties is not dealt with.
     The author sees more a multilateral tendency, although of doubtful
     efficacy, in the economic cooperation system of Eastern Europe and
     the USSR than do a number of other analysts. However, the author
     notes a lack of dynamism, particularly as compared with EEC. More-
     over, resistance of a number of East European states to efforts to
     execute CEMA recommendations casts doubts upon the likelihood of
     realizing objectives, at least through methods and procedures em-
     ployed to date.

832. Cattel, David T. "Multilateral Cooperation and Integration in
Eastern Europe." 13 Western Political Quarterly (1960), 64-69.
          Reports that the information that is published concerning the
     multilateral cooperation and integration in Eastern Europe is mostly
     propaganda. All evidence strongly suggests that relations remain
     bilateral with Soviet leaders giving the orders.

833. Gehlen, Michael P. "The Integrative Process in East Europe:
A Theoretical Framework." 30 Journal of Politics (1968), 90-113.
          Examines seven states in terms of their respective levels of
     integration into an East European community and in terms of depend-
     ence on the USSR, and finds that the potential for sustained inte-
     grative action has not been realized.

834. Gehlen, Michael P. The Politics of Coexistence: Soviet Methods
and Motives. Bloomington and London: Indiana University Press, 1967, pp.
334.
          Includes an analysis of Soviet relations with other Communist
     parties and other Communist states. The book treats Soviet foreign
     policy as much less a product of ideology than a function of con-
     flicting interests in which, internally, the military establishment
     and industrial interests are most important, changing military tech-
     nology has an impact, and political caution stemming from careful
     assessments of other nations' capabilities dominates external
     relations.

835. Griffith, William E. _The Sino-Soviet Rift_. Cambridge: MIT Press, 1964, pp. xiv, 508.
Analysis of the Sino-Soviet conflict, together with complete texts of or excerpts from 16 documents. The analysis in part relates the conflict to change in the power base of the Communist system similar to that in the Western system stemming from the rise of Western Europe.

836. Grzybowski, Kazimierz. _The Socialist Commonwealth of Nations: Organizations and Institutions_. New Haven: Yale University Press, 1964, pp. xvii, 300.
Detailed description of formal Communist international institutions and of formal procedures based essentially on the available public policies and upon the writings of Soviet legal theorists. Analysis is relatively brief, legalistic, and intuitive. A chapter deals with the settlement of disputes in the Communist system.

837. Hoffmann, Emil. _Comecon, der gemeinsame Markt in Osteuropa_. Opladen: C.W. Leske, 1961, pp. 174.
Study of economic integration in the European Communist bloc.

838. Hopmann, P. Terry. "International Conflict and Cohesion in the Communist System." 11 _International Studies Quarterly_ (1967), 212-236.
With reference to two periods of crisis and two periods of relative détente, computer content analysis is used to measure the orientations of members of the Communist coalition toward the United States. The study finds that tendencies toward unity of attitude in relation to external threat and divergence of attitude when threat declines appears both in the Sino-Soviet dyad but also in the relations among nine of the Communist states. Shortcomings of the method are noted as well as the needs to add study of decision-making and to replicate the study for other coalitions such as NATO.

839. Hsia, R., and Chin, S.K. "Soviet Loans and Repayment." 1 _China Mainland Review_ (1965), 1-12.
On the Chinese Communist effort to repay debts to the Soviet Union, accomplished by 1964, and the human cost of the effort rooted in politics, ideology, and Chinese custom and tradition. The loan aspect of Sino-Soviet economic relations both before and after repayment may be treated as part of the more general system structure among Communist countries.

840. Hübbenet, Georg von. _Die Rote Wirtschaft Wächst--Aufbau und Entwicklungsziele des COMECON_. Düsseldorf: Econ Verlag, 1960, pp. 283.
Includes an exposition of the path of a COMECON decision that illustrates organizational limitations on decisions that may be viewed either as a specific manifestation of the general or as a piece of empirical evidence from which generalization may be built.

841. Jaster, Robert S. "CMEA's Influence on Soviet Policies in Eastern Europe." 14 _World Politics_ (1962), 505-518.

Describes the transformation of COMECON, after Stalin's death, from a transmission apparatus of the Soviet bureaucratic system into an organization of major importance in Communist affairs. The author sees COMECON as growing in authority and this growth as related to or an accompaniment of change in Soviet policy toward Eastern Europe and of fragmentation in the Communist movement.

841-A. Kanet, Roger E. (ed.). The Behavioral Revolution and Communist Studies: Applications of Behaviorally-Oriented Political Research on the Soviet Union and Eastern Europe. New York: Free Press, 1970, pp. 350.
　　Includes a study by Robert Sharlet on law in the political development of a Communist system, a research note by Charles Gati on Soviet elite perspectives of international regions, and an article by P. Terry Hopmann on the effects of conflict and détente on cohesion in the Communist system.

842. Kaser, Michael. COMECON: Integration Problems of the Planned Economies. London: Oxford, 1965, pp. vii, 215.
　　History of COMECON, its institutional reinforcement, and its trade problems, with attention to the contrast between mutual technical assistance and limited progress in multilateralism through the transferable ruble not convertible to outsiders, as well as limited progress in development of Soviet-type central planning. Appendices include summary lists of sessions of the Council, meetings of the Executive Committee and of Communist Parties of Member Countries, and a list of committees and their subcommittees or working parties.

843. Korbonski, Andrzej. "COMECON." International Conciliation. No. 549, September 1964, pp. 62.
　　Concise review of the evolution, structure, and policies of COMECON, together with a brief survey of attitudes of Communist countries, particularly China, Rumania, and Yugoslavia, toward the organization.

844. Korbonski, Andrzej. "The Warsaw Pact." International Conciliation. No. 573, May 1969, pp. 73.
　　A sketch of the development of the Warsaw Pact, its institutional framework, its accomplishments, the attitudes of individual member states, and Rumania's changing position.

845. Krengel, Rolf. "Die wirtschaftliche Integrationsbestrebungen und Hindernisse im Ostblock." In Erik Boettcher (ed.), Ostblock, EWG und Entwicklungslander. Stuttgart: W. Kohlhammer, 1964, pp. 51-79.
　　Includes an analysis of the essentially independent nature of policy decisions of the COMECON executive council even though representatives may act in accordance with higher party directives.

846. Loeber, Dietrich Andre. "The Legal Structure of the Communist Bloc." 27 Social Research (1960), 183-202.
　　Stresses nature of the intra-bloc treaty system and its lack of supranational organs as contrasted with links at the party level that have some supranational characteristics.

847. Menahem, H. "Le marche commun de l'Est: le Conseil d'assistance économique mutuelle." 30 _Politique étrangère_ (1965), 410-438.
On the history, structure, and evolution of COMECON and the
results obtained by it particularly in respect to commercial relations with the West.

848. Miles, Edward L., and Gillooly, John S. _Processes of Interac-_
tion Among the Fourteen Communist Party-States: An Exploratory Essay.
Research Paper No. 5. Stanford Studies of the Communist System, March
1965, pp. 60.
Employment, insofar as collected available data permitted, of
economic, social-cultural-technical, treaty, and political-military-
diplomatic indices of interaction. Economic indices indicated two
subsystems within the Soviet system. The cultural area shows blurred
boundaries, while the political-military-diplomatic area shows the
clearest boundaries. Trade and cultural interaction appear to pro-
ceed somewhat independently of political conflict. Inhibitions on
further integration appear to include differing emphasis on various
economic development criteria, lack of supranational planning on the
basis of system interests, developing political cleavage, and possibly the extent of resort to bilateral treaties.

849. Mitchell, R. Judson. _A Theoretical Approach to the Study of_
Communist International Organizations. Research Paper No. 3. Stanford
Studies of the Communist System, Ditto, 1964, pp. 30.
Suggestions as to modifications of coalition theory and general
organization theory for study of Communist international organizations. Organizational concepts of CEMA are seen as designed to secure control by the organizer, i.e., the Soviet Union, but lack of
clear indication of the binding authority of specific organizational
decisions and of methods of enforcement is seen as inhibiting complete analysis of authority-responsibility relationships.

850. Modelski, George. _The Communist International System_. Research
Monograph No. 9. Princeton University: Center of International Studies,
1960, pp. 78.
Treats the Communist system as it stood at the time of writing
as a potentially universal, therefore potentially international system, possessing all the qualities and mechanisms of such a system.

851. Neuberger, Egon. "International Division of Labor in CEMA:
Limited Regret Strategy." _Papers and Proceedings of the Seventy-sixth_
Meeting of the American Economic Association (1963). 54 _American Economic_
Review (1964), 506-515.
A survey of progress made by the Soviet bloc toward specialization of production in the face of three sets of inhibiting obstacles:
sensitivity of the sovereignty issue; insistence on diversified development; inability to use actual or shadow prices and costs as
guides to decision-making in the planning process.

852. Pryor, Frederick L. _The Communist Foreign Trade System_. Cambridge: MIT Press, 1963, pp. 296.

This study includes material provided by interviews with East German foreign trade officials, but in developing an index of multilateralism the author was not able to take full account of Michael Michaely's study and so could not undertake an explanation of discrepancies between his and Michaely's results (supra, no. 534). Moreover, some of the tabular and statistical material requires a check for reliability. Nevertheless, the study does contribute to an understanding of some of the important features of the Communist bloc and its relations with the West.

853. Thornton, Thomas Perry. "Foreign Relations of the Asian Communist Satellites." 35 Pacific Affairs (1962-1963), 341-352.
A brief review of the status of Mongolia, North Vietnam, and North Korea in the wider international scene and among Communist states. The author seeks to throw light upon the question of whose satellites the Asian satellites are.

853-A. Tretiak, Daniel. "Cuban Relations with the Communist System: The Politics of a Communist Independent, 1967-1970." ASG Monograph No. 4. Waltham, Massachusetts: Westinghouse Electric Corporation, Advanced Studies Group, June 1970, pp. 49.
An examination of Cuba's relations with the USSR, Communist China, and the Asian party-states of Korea and Vietnam that makes use of such indicators as Cuban attendance at COMECON meetings, attention paid to Cuba in the World Marxist Review and in Chinese articles, and Cuban statements about North Korea and North Vietnam.

854. Triska, Jan F. (ed.). Communist Party-States: International and Comparative Studies. Indianapolis: Bobbs-Merrill, 1969, pp. 512.
A collection of the Stanford Studies of the Communist System, several of which are separately annotated as issued earlier by Stanford University.

855. Triska, Jan F., and Finley, David D. Soviet Foreign Policy. New York: Macmillan, 1968, pp. xiii, 541.
After giving attention to the Soviet foreign policy decision-making process in terms of role structure, the belief system, and events, this book then examines Soviet policy regarding international organization and international law. The decision-making process is dealt with in terms of role structure, personality, belief system, and events analysis.

856. Triska, Jan F. "Stanford Studies of the Communist System: The Sino-Soviet Split." 8 Background (1964), 143-160.
A review of the approaches being employed (coalition theory, cost and coalition equilibrium theory, decision-making theory, etc.) by the scholars collaborating on the Stanford studies. One section of this article presents a brief outline of the Communist international system including reference to the absence of dispute-settling machinery and to resort to the passive denial of the right of participation and sharing in community endeavor and benefits as a substitute for active enforcement of obligations.

857.   Triska, Jan F., with Beim, David O. and Roos, Noralou.   "The
World Communist System." Stanford Studies of the Communist System, Mimeo,
1964.
        Discusses four principal unifying elements of the Communist in-
ternational system: (1) the parties, (2) the Marxist-Leninist belief
system; (3) Soviet military strength; (4) geographical contiguity.
The impact of these elements, in the face of many disputes, are analyzed, with attention accorded the European-Asian and the advanced-
backward divisions in the system. Dependence upon agreement and persuasion and upon denial of participation and benefits are identified
as the bases of rule implementation. The Sino-Soviet rift is treated
as a symptom of difficulties in coalition formation and community
building at the international level.

858.   Uschakow, Alexander. Der Rat für gegenseitige Wirtschaftshilfe
(COMECON). Cologne: Verlag Wissenschaft und Politik, 1962, pp. 199.
        Substantial documentary account of the Council for Mutual Eco-
nomic Assistance.

859.   Wiles, P.J.D. Communist International Economics. Oxford:
Blackwell, 1968, pp. xiv, 566.
        A useful analysis of Communist international economics with at-
tention to invisible as well as visible trade and to the political
nature of foreign economic relations.

860.   Wolfe, Thomas W. The Evolving Nature of the Warsaw Pact. RAND
Report RM-4835-PR. Santa Monica: RAND Corporation, December 1965, pp. 47.
        Examines changes in the Warsaw Pact Alliance since 1960. At-
tention is given to political reasons for changes in the alliance
from the institutionalization of existing arrangements for the East
European countries to be a Soviet defensive zone against the West
into a system in which the East European contribution of forces
would be more thoroughly integrated into Soviet operational plans.
The result was an increased interdependence counterbalanced by assertion of separate national interests and a greater East European
role in decision-making.

861.   Wszelaki, Jan. "Economic Developments in East-Central Europe."
4 Orbis (1961), 422-451.
        An examination of the potential of East Central Europe for
development under COMECON direction, the probability of increased
economic interdependence between East Europe and the USSR, the
possibility of a lag in food production compared with industrial
progress, and the likelihood of increasingly large gaps in standards of living among the COMECON countries.

862.   Zybenko, Roman. "The Economic Problems of COMECON Integration."
2 Studies of the Soviet Union (1963), 60-70.
        Shows the problems of COMECON, the main one being the lack of
an efficient system of integration.

See also nos. 118, 575, 709, 805, 892, 981, 1066, 1084, 1558, 1851,
2742, 2759, and sec. III, A, 3.

(9) Other Regional Organizations

863. Boutros-Ghali, Boutros. "The Addis Ababa Charter." _Interna-_
tional Conciliation. No. 546, January 1964, pp. 62.
    Commentary on the Addis Ababa Charter, the institutions of the
Organization of African Unity, and some non-African reactions to the
Charter.

864. Braums-Packenius, Otfried. "The Nature of Restricted Postal
Unions." 87 _Union Postale_ (April 1962), 55A-58A.
    Discussion of regional postal unions, the advantages afforded
members particularly when some countries are unable to accept additional and optional UPU agreements on a global basis, and the advantages, particularly to developing states, of being able to pool resources in order to present a case at a UPU congress.

865. Burns, Creighton L. "The Colombo Plan." _Year Book of World_
Affairs (1960), 176-206.
    On the origins, organization, pattern of aid, and economic and
political functions of the Colombo Plan for Co-operative Economic
Development in South and Southeast Asia.

866. Ferris, J.P. "Organization for Regional Economic Development
Projects: A Middle East Experience." 25 _Public Administration Review_
(1965), 128-134.
    On the use of the Central Treaty Organization structure, es-
pecially its Economic Committee, by the United States, Turkey, Iran,
and Pakistan in 1956-1964 to achieve effective joint action on technical plans, adjustment of national-regional issues, and coordination of financing and contracts in the planning and building of the
Turkey-Iran-Pakistan telecommunications projects as a regional system.

867. Gopalan, M.P. "The Launching of ASA." 33 _Far Eastern Economic_
Review (September 21, 1961), 548-553.
    Summary of the circumstances leading to the establishment of the
Association of Southeast Asia and the immediate reactions it aroused.

868. Hoskyns, Catherine. "Trends and Developments in the Organization of African Unity." _Year Book of World Affairs_ (1967), 164-178.
    A review of the first several years' activities and achieve-
ments of the OAU, of the development of partial and subregional
organizations and groups to act where OAU cannot, of the inadequacy of the Secretariat as a center for ideas and action, and of
the lack of prestige in OAU service of a type that in Europe and
Central America produced politically minded technocrats with positive impact on integration.

869. Islam, Nurul. "Regional Co-operation for Development: Pakistan, Iran and Turkey." 5 _Journal of Common Market Studies_ (1967), 283-
301.
    On the RCD experiment in regional cooperation--its organiza-
tion, objectives, undertakings, and problems, including Turkey's
orientation toward EEC.

870. Joyaux, F. "L'Association des États Asiatiques." 30 *Politique étrangère* (1965), 98-107.

On the limited activities in the realms of communications and commerce that are carried on by the organization established in Southeast Asia.

871. Legum, Colin. *Pan-Africanism: A Short Political Guide.* Rev. ed. New York: Praeger, 1965, pp. 326.

History of Pan-Africanism and samples of some basic statements related to ways of organizing African states and attempts to assert the existence of ties of culture and of common interest, together with a collection of basic documents and statements on inter-African groupings or blocs.

872. Liebenow, J. Gus. "Which Road to Pan-African Unity? The San-niquellie Conference, 1959." In Gwendolen M. Carter (ed.), *Politics in Africa: 7 Cases.* New York: Harcourt, Brace and World, 1966, pp. 1-32.

Deals with the confrontation of Tubman with Nkrumah and Touré in which Tubman expressed favor for the functionalist approach to African cooperation and for the maintenance of existing state boundaries.

873. MacDonald, Robert W. *The League of Arab States: A Study in the Dynamics of Regional Organization.* Princeton: Princeton University Press, 1965, pp. xiii, 407.

Discussion, with particular reference to the Arab League, of the role of functional integration in cultural, social, and scientific affairs, of regional security and peaceful settlement, and of interaction between the League and the United Nations. Attention is also accorded the techniques of cooperation with the UN and its specialized agencies and such policies as the boycott of Israel.

874. Newlyn, W.T. "Gains and Losses in the East African Common Market." 17 *Yorkshire Bulletin of Economic and Social Research* (1965), 130-138.

Analysis of the effort of Kenya, Uganda, and Tanzania to implement a Common Market agreement in the circumstance of imbalance resulting from the preference of industry for the Nairobi location.

875. Rifaat, M.A. "Afro-Asian Organisation for Economic Cooperation (Afrasec)." 15 *Civilisations* (1965), 73-78.

Review of the goals of AFRASEC, programs undertaken to implement those goals, plans for "sectoral cooperation," and impediments to economic cooperation.

876. Wallerstein, Immanuel. "Pan-Africanism as Protest." In Morton A. Kaplan (ed.), *The Revolution in World Politics.* New York and London: Wiley, 1962, pp. 137-151.

A review of Pan-Africanism as a protest against the past and a vision of the future.

See also nos. 583, 2832, and sec. III, A, 3.

d. Nonpublic Units or Entities

(1) International Nongovernmental Organizations

877. Dechert, Charles R. "The Christian Democratic 'International'."
11 Orbis (1967), 106-127.
    Traces the development of regional organizations of Christian
Democratic parties in Western Europe, Latin America, and Eastern
Europe, the holder of World Conferences of the three regional organizations beginning in 1956, and the formation of the World Union
of Christian Democrats in 1964.

878. Gardner, Mary A. "The Inter-American Press Association." 42
Journalism Quarterly (1965), 547-556.
    A brief history of a professional organization that traces
its roots to the First Pan-American Congress of Journalists (Washington, 1926), held under the auspices of the Pan American Union.
The organization has been both vilified and highly praised, and a
number of journalists have credited it with saving their lives as
well as defending the freedom of the press.

878-A. Galtung, Johan. "Non-Territorial Actors and the Problem of
Peace." Paper presented at the International Peace Research Association
meeting, Karlovy Vary, Czechoslovakia. September 20-23, 1969, pp. 31.
    Speculative paper that posits an international system composed
of two parts or structures, a territorial system based on states
and a nonterritorial system made up of international governmental
organizations, international nongovernmental organizations, and
business international nongovernmental organizations. The author
develops a scenario of an international system of the future in
which the nonterritorial system gains a salience in people's minds
that becomes equal to and, later, greater than that of the territorial system.

879. Lador-Lederer, J.J. International Non-Governmental Organizations and Economic Entities: A Study in Autonomous Organization and Ius
Gentium. Leiden: Sijthoff, 1963, pp. 403.
    Although a legal treatise with considerable concern for the
legal nature of NGO's, this is the best available survey of NGO's
and their role in the international arena.

880. Lorwin, Lewis Levitzki. The International Labor Movement.
New York: Harper, 1953, pp. xviii, 366.
    Review of labor's attempts to organize and cooperate interna-
tionally and the resultant struggle between ICFTU and WFTU.

881. Merle, M. "Los Grupos de presion y la vida internacional."
107 Revista de estudios politicos (Spain), 101-114.
    A brief article on the methods of operation of international
pressure groups at international organizations and in their relations with national governments.

882. Ridgeway, George L. **Merchants of Peace: The History of the International Chamber of Commerce.** Rev. ed. Boston and Toronto: Little, Brown, 1959, pp. 291.

A sympathetic narrative providing a handy guide to the efforts of an international nongovernmental entity seeking to bridge conflicting business interests and to produce a framework of international public order.

883. Rodgers, Raymond Spencer. **Facilitation Problems of International Associations.** Brussels: Union of International Associations, 1960, pp. 167.

Deals with legal, fiscal, and administrative facilities and problems of nongovernmental organizations.

884. Schevenels, Walter. **Forty-Five Years, 1901-1945: International Federation of Trade Unions, A Historical Precis.** Brussels: IFTU, 1956, pp. 442.

The General Secretary of the IFTU from 1929 to 1945 traces the history of the organization from its origin to its dissolution and succession by the World Federation of Trade Unions.

884-A. Skjelsbaek, Kjell. "Development of the Systems of International Organization." Paper presented at International Peace Research Association meeting, Karlovy Vary, Czechoslovakia. September 20-23, 1969, pp. 45.

Quantitative description of the development of international governmental and nongovernmental organizations through the use of the following system theory concepts: domain (number of members or organizations); scope (number of functions); intensity (size of budget, number of employees, number of meetings, etc.); political implications; interconnectedness (number and frequency of interactions); entropy (unevenness of regional distribution); and isomorphism (similarity of national distribution of governmental and nongovernmental organizations).

885. White, Lyman C. **International Non-Governmental Organizations.** New Brunswick: Rutgers University Press, 1951, pp. xi, 325.

Survey of functions and accomplishments of international nongovernmental organizations.

886. Windmuller, John P. **American Labor and the International Labor Movement, 1940 to 1953.** Ithaca: Institute of International Industrial and Labor Relations, Cornell University, 1954, pp. xvi, 243.

American labor's interest and influence in foreign affairs with particular attention to the issues concerning WFTU and the formation of ICFTU.

See also nos. 1087, 1089, 1091, 1468, 2140, 2436.

B. PROTECTION OF UNITS

1. Nonrecognition of Conquest or Absorption

887. Seraphim, P.H. "Bevölkerungsverschiebungen im baltischen Raum." 25 Zeitschrift für geopolitik (1954), 405-411.
Brief review of displacement of populations of the Baltic States, including the influx of Russians, which are of consequence to the character of those areas. The summarized information is of consequence to the problem of nonrecognition of absorption of the Baltic States, to the refugee problem that resulted, and to the question of nationality of refugees that has on occasion presented legal issues to courts in non-Communist countries.

2. Nonintervention--Protection of Government or Protection of State?

888. Ball, M. Margaret. "Issue for the Americas: Non-Intervention vs. Human Rights and the Preservation of Democratic Institutions." 15 International Organization (1961), pp. 21-37.
Discussion of the conflict between the old principle of nonintervention and the newer principle of multilateral action to protect human rights and to support democratic institutions. Examination of the disputes between Venezuela and the Dominican Republic and between Cuba and the United States and resultant oblique OAS action in 1961 leads the author to the conclusion that the human rights approach, together with economic development programs, is more likely to be acceptable than intervention in favor of democracy.

889. Graber, Doris A. "The Truman and Eisenhower Doctrines in the Light of the Doctrine of Non-Intervention." 73 Political Science Quarterly (1958), 321-334.
Interprets the limited interventionism of the Truman and Eisenhower Doctrines as consistent with the American tradition in which nonintervention was not unconditional and, apart from a short span of imperialism at the turn of the century, intervention was a last resort employable only when vital objectives were otherwise unattainable.

890. Hatta, Mohammed. "Indonesia Between the Power Blocs." 36 Foreign Affairs (1958), 480-490.
Although including some remarks about Indonesia's loyalty to the United Nations that are at odds with developments in 1965, this article by the former Vice President, Prime Minister, and Foreign Minister of Indonesia is interesting in that it treats coexistence as another side of the coin of nonintervention so that "Moscow loses the right to interfere with a democratic government's action against the Communist movement within its borders."

891. Wood, Bryce. The Making of the Good Neighbor Policy. New York: Columbia University Press, 1961, pp. x, 438.

Traces the development of the policy of nonintervention after the 1920 intervention in Nicaragua. The Good Neighbor Policy is judged to have been more reflective of wearying of an unprofitable and embarrassing task than of moral reform. Amicable settlement of expropriation crises were facilitated when the United States (1) shifted its focus from company (subnational) interest to national interest and (2) shifted from demands for arbitration to political negotiations.

See also nos. 913, 1010, 1013, 1892, 2236.

C. INTERNATIONAL SYSTEMS; COMPARATIVE APPROACH

892. Ames, Edward. "Economic Integration in the European Soviet Bloc?" 49 American Economic Review (1959), 113-124.

This article contributes to the comparative study of international systems by indicating a route for the assessment of the international system of Communist states, identification of the rules conducive to integration of the system, and establishment of a basis for comparison with a market economy. By the standard of market economies the Soviet bloc could not be regarded as integrated. Proper assessment of the Soviet bloc requires recognition that enterprises of the bloc countries seek to maximize output, subject to prices not falling below a stated sum called "planned profits," rather than to maximize profits. By taking account of a "control system," that is, a set of parameters consisting of "price rules" (rates of marginal cost, the values assumed to be either nondecreasing or nonincreasing functions of quantity) and of "plans" (values at which discontinuities occur on the ground that changes in rates of marginal revenue or cost occur at the point where indices contained in official economic plans are attained), a general equilibrium system can be mathematically derivable. This system is subject to discussion in terms of "industry" (a set of enterprises, all transactions of which are subject to the same price rules) as the equivalent of "commodity" in a market economy.

See also nos. 399, 400, 429, 491, 1139, 1759.

1. Extinct and Archaic Systems (Inter-Nation
    and Inter-Tribal)

893. Cady, John F. Southeast Asia: Its Historical Development. New York: McGraw-Hill, 1964, pp. xvii, 657.

Five chapters deal with pre-European conflict over control of trade in given commodities, of routes for trade, and of cities and entrepôts serving as centers of trade. A good account is given of the nature of claims to imperial control with resultant receipt of tribute rather than Western-type territorial control.

894. Crowder, Michael. The Story of Nigeria. London: Faber and Faber, 1962, pp. 307.

A history of Nigeria, insofar as it can be established or inferred from documentary, archeological, and other currently available evidence, that includes accounts of war between states and empires and of civil war prior to the establishment of British rule. Reference is made to treaties (pp. 44, 79), embassies (pp. 44, 60), and to some still surviving diplomatic correspondence of 1391 and of the first decade of the 19th century (pp. 36, 84). The book also deals with commercial relations, the slave trade, colonization, and the coming of independence.

895. Edwardes, S.M., and Garrett, H.L.O. Mughal Rule in India. 2nd Indian reprint. New Delhi: S. Chand & Co., 1962, pp. vii, 260.

Concise review of Mughal history that provides glimpses of external relations, foreign trade, diplomacy, and anecdotal evidence that the obligation of a treaty rested on the personal integrity of the other party.

896. Fage, J.D. An Introduction to the History of West Africa. 3rd ed. Cambridge: The University Press, 1962, pp. xiii, 233.

A concise narrative of the known history of pre-European West African states and Empires, of their wars, of the beginnings of European trade and imperialism along the West African coast, of the slave trade and its abolition, of the establishment of colonies, and of the coming of independence. Of particular interest are the sections dealing with the commercial, political, and military relations of the states and empires, including the maintenance of ambassadors at Fez by Mansa Musa (1307-1332), emperor of Mali at the peak of its power.

897. Fürer-Haimendorf, Christof von. The Apa Tanis and Their Neighbors. New York: Free Press, 1963, pp. viii, 166.

Virtually unknown to the outside world, not yet subject to any administration, and still totally free from modern influences when the author visited them in 1944 and 1945, this archaic society on India's North-East Frontier represents a cultural type different from both the Hindu civilization of the Assam plains and the Lamaist civilization of Tibet. The author's observations of the Apa Tanis' internal social structure, of their institution of slavery, of their system of raids and ransoms, and of their political and economic relations with their neighbors provides valuable data on the status of law and of the nature of war and peace at the stage of societal development reached by the Apa Tanis.

898. Hall, D.G.E. A History of Southeast Asia. 2nd ed. London: Macmillan, 1964, pp. 955.

Particularly useful for its exposition of the nature of pre-European empires, lacking Western concepts of sovereignty, and of

pre-European international conflict in Southeast Asia in the form
of conflict not over territorial boundaries as much as over control
over a particular commodity trade, trade routes, and cities and
entrepots that were centers of trade and of income.

899. McShane, Roger B. The Foreign Policy of the Attalids of Per-
gamum. Illinois Studies in the Social Sciences (Vol. 53). Urbana: University of Illinois Press, 1964, pp. ix, 241.
    Analysis of interstate relationships that contributed to the
maintenance of peace and order in the Mediterranean world in 281-
133 B.C. The study deals with such matters as leagues and alliances, peace agreements and armistices, claims, arbitration, coin-
age ententes and monetary union, trade relations, piracy and efforts to suppres it, and the payment of tribute.

900. Modelski, George. "Kautilya: Foreign Policy and International
System in the Ancient Hindu World." 58 American Political Science Review
(1964), 549-560.
    A systematic rather than a historical analysis. Draws fully
on the insights of international relations, sociology, and social
anthropology and applies them to the classic Indian work of political theory, the Arthasastra.

901. Oliver, Roland, and Fage, J.D. A Short History of Africa.
Baltimore: Penguin, 1962, pp. 280.
    Contains summary accounts of African states and empires, their
commercial relations and wars, the slave trade and its abolition,
the establishment of colonies, and the coming of independence.

902. Sastri, K.A.N. "Inter-State Relations in India." 2 Indian
Year Book of International Affairs (1953), 133-153.
    An example of a non-Western article displaying pride in
indigenous institutions and portraying an Asian family of nations
with established laws, customs, and practices that long antedated
the European law of nations. Instances of treaty relations with
conquered vassals and other states are presented.

903. Walker, Richard Louis. The Multi-State System of Ancient China.
Hamden, Connecticut: Shoe String Press, 1953, pp. xii, 135.
    Summarizes research on the international relations of pre-Han
China, including development of interstate norms and the resolution
of conflicts within alliances.

See also nos. 63, 186, 188, 491, 507, 512.

D. CHANGES WITHIN UNITS

1. Recognition; Seating at International Organizations

904. Albinski, Henry S. <u>Australian Policies and Attitudes Toward China</u>. Princeton: Princeton University Press, 1965.

Includes discussion of the recognition issue and ultimate non-recognition, the original inclination to follow the British lead being delayed by general elections and the assumption of power by a new government, thereby providing time to learn that the interests and investments of non-Communist states were not protected by representation in Peking. The Korean War's impact on the recognition issue is also dealt with. Attention is also given to such matters as trade with China and permissiveness in respect to travel to mainland China.

905. Betancourt, Romulo. <u>Hacia America Latina democratica e integrada</u>. Caracas: Editorial Senderos, 1967, pp. 212.

Includes a detailed defense of the author's policy, while President of Venezuela in 1959-1964, of refusing to recognize any Latin American government that had gained office unconstitutionally. Details of Betancourt's correspondence with the Argentine, Costa Rican, and Mexican Presidents and with President Kennedy are presented. The author also discusses the Fidelista campaign to foment guerrilla wars, United States intervention in the Dominican Republic, and the details of the effort which he, José Figueres, and Luis Munoz Marin made to act as mediators of the Dominican civil war.

906. Deutsch, Julius. <u>Wesen und Wandlung der Diktaturen</u>. Vienna: Weg-Verlag, 1953, pp. 316.

Survey by an Austrian socialist of dictatorships from Tiberius Gracchus to Stalin in an effort to identify social conditions fostering the emergence of dictatorships.

907. Dozer, Donald Marquand. "Recognition of Contemporary Inter-American Relations." 8 <u>Journal of Inter-American Studies</u> (1966), 318-335.

On vacillations of recognition policy in inter-American affairs and on new uses for nonrecognition, particularly those of the 1960s of extracting assurances from military juntas seizing power that they would respect civil liberties, allow freedom of political action, and hold elections.

908. Duverger, Maurice. <u>De la dictature</u>. Paris: Julliard, 1961, pp. 211.

An attempt to classify types of dictatorships that produces the "sociological" and the "technical" types as the basic groups.

909. Fabela, Isidro. <u>Historia diplomática de la Revolución Mexicana (1912-1917)</u>. 2 vols. Mexico City: Fondo de Cultura Económica, 1958, 1959, pp. xv, 390; 438.

Based upon the author's experiences as participant, for a time in charge of the Foreign Office, and on original documents and copies preserved in his private archive, the second section of the study casts light from the Mexican viewpoint on such matters of concern to international law as the recognition problem and the ABC mediation after the Vera Cruz incident.

910. Hallgarten, George Wolfgang Felix. Why Dictators? The Causes and Forms of Tyrannical Rule Since 600 B.C. New York: Macmillan, 1954.
An attempt to classify dictatorships historically and by type, the most useful effort being the three-fold classification as classical, ultra-revolutionary, and counter- or pseudo-revolutionary.

911. Joktik, Ong. "A Formosan's View of the Formosan Independence Movement." 15 China Quarterly (1963), 107-114.
History of the origins, expansion, and split of the Formosan independence movement and comments on its situation and possible role.

912. Khopkind, A.D. Moral and Political Considerations in the Debate in Britian on Recognition of the Peking Government. M. Sc. (Econ.) Thesis. London School of Economics, 1960-1961.
Available in microfilm and Xerox copies, this thesis deals with those considerations that came to the fore in a country that reached a different decision from that of the United States on the question of whether to recognize the Communist government of China.

913. Kleine-Ahlbrandt, William Laird. The Policy of Simmering: A Study of British Policy During the Spanish Civil War, 1936-1939. The Hague: Nijhoff, 1962, pp. xii, 161.
Includes discussion of the nonintervention policy, the problem of recognition of the Franco regime prior to its final success, and the appeasement of Franco essential to preventing a feared accrual to the strength of the Axis.

913-A. Mehrish, B.N. "India's Recognition Policy Towards the Divided States: Korea and Viet Nam." 1 Journal of African and Asian Studies (Delhi, 1968), 238-254.
On India's refusal to recognize the South and North Korean Governments on the ground that a government must be based on a substantial declaration of the will of a nation and on India's contradictory policy in recognizing the regimes of both South and North Vietnam on the grounds of expediency.

914. Meisner, Maurice. "The Development of Formosan Nationalism." 15 China Quarterly (1963), 91-106.
Discussion of the emergence of a Formosan sense of their existence as a separate nation with its own historical, ethnic, and cultural experience and the nature of the present relationship between native Formosans and refugee mainlanders.

915. Mertens, P. "La reconnaissance de la Chine populaire par la France à la lumière de la doctrine récente." Revue de l'Institut de Sociologie (No. 1, 1965), 25-50.
Analysis of the doctrine adopted by the French Government in 1964 in regard to its recognition of Red China, the time chosen for recognition being related in the analysis to the Vietnam crisis.

916. Newman, Robert P. Recognition of Communist China? New York: Macmillan, 1961, pp. xii, 318.

Thorough exposition of the various arguments that have been put
forward on the issues of recognition of the Communist Government of
China and of its being seated at the United Nations. The author, although far from partial to the Communist Chinese, finds recognition
to be an essential step toward American political maturity. A bibliography of 352 entries is included.

917. Nguen Tuyet Mai. "Electioneering: Vietnamese Style." 2 Asian
Survey (1962), 11-18.
    On election practices in South Vietnam that, as in other places
and times, throw into doubt the criterion of the popular will as a
basis for determining whether to recognize a government.

918. Reynolds, J. "Recognition by Trade: The Controversial Wheat
Sales to China." 18 Australian Outlook (1964), 117-126.
    Discusses the novel situation between Australia and China whereby
a statutory body could be encouraged to enter into important commercial transactions with an unrecognized government. The author calls
attention to speculation that has followed concerning possible changes
in procedure in conducting certain phases of the relations among states

919. Vinacke, Harold M. United States Policy Toward China. Occasional Papers--No. 1. Cincinnati: Center for the Study of U.S. Foreign
Policy of the Department of Political Science, University of Cincinnati,
1961, pp. 52.
    This descriptive-analytical discussion of the China recognition
problem emphasizes the limitations imposed upon bargaining potential
by positions and commitments made either in treaty form or in unilateral policy pronouncements. Attention is drawn to the British
view that no commitment to return Taiwan to China was made in 1945
and to the absence of stipulations to that effect in the Japanese
Peace Treaty.

See also nos. 1764, 2145.

2. Secession; National Self-Determination

920. Baker, Ross K. "The Emergence of Biafra: Balkanization or
Nation-Building." 12 Orbis (1968), 518-533.
    Examines the divisions and diversity of Nigeria, traces events
leading to Biafran secession, and seeks to draw a distinction between particularism and pluralism with regard to their respective
impacts on the viability of states.

921. Barber, James. Rhodesia: The Road to Rebellion. London: Oxford for the Institute of Race Relations, 1967, pp. xii, 338.
    Reviews political developments between 1960 and Rhodesia's uni-
lateral declaration of independence in 1965.

922. Bull, Theodore (ed.). Rhodesian Perspective. London: Michael
Joseph, 1967, pp. viii, 184.

Articles by former contributors to the <u>Central African Examiner</u> that deal with several facets of the background of the Rhodesian issue.

923. Castles, A.C. "Law and Politics in the Rhodesian Dispute." 21 <u>Australian Outlook</u> (1967), 165-178.
Deals primarily with the internal problems of the legality of the Unilateral Declaration of Independence, lack of effective British power after 1961, and the judicial problem of questionable legality of the 1965 Constitution and resultant efforts to apply the Smith regime's measures as far as possible in harmony with the 1961 Constitution.

924. Cefkin, J. Leo. "The Rhodesian Question at the United Nations." 22 <u>International Organization</u> (1968), 649-669.
A useful review of the Rhodesian issue with attention to propagandistic uses of the General Assembly and the Colonial Committee and to the more tempered Security Council approach that led to three actions applying sanctions.

925. Decker, Günter. <u>Das Selbstbestimmungsrecht der Nationen</u>. Göttingen: Schwartz, 1955, pp. x, 435.
National self-determination is examined at length in its historical and theoretical aspects and efforts to apply the principle are examined.

926. Gérard-Libois, Jules. <u>Katanga Secession</u>. Translated by Rebecca Young. Madison: University of Wisconsin Press, 1967, pp. vi, 377.
Against its social, economic, and political background, the secession of Katanga is set forth in terms of its Katangan, Congolese, and Belgian aspects. Use is made of the minutes of the Katangan Council of Ministers meetings, security police reports, testimony of those involved, and scattered public documents. The author, Director of the Center for Socio-Political Research and Information in Brussels, published the French edition, <u>Sécession au Katanga</u>, in 1963.

927. MacFarlane, J.L. "Justifying Rebellion: Black and White Nationalism in Rhodesia." 6 <u>Journal of Commonwealth Political Studies</u> (1968), 54-79.
Examines the cases of the whites favoring the unilateral declaration of independence, those supporting the objectives but opposing the declaration, and the African nationalist case, questioning its rejection of the 1961 Constitution and instances of resort to violence.

928. Panter-Brick, S.K. "The Right to Self-Determination: Its Application to Nigeria." 44 <u>International Affairs</u> (1968), 254-266.
Examines the question of the applicability of the principle of self-determination to the Biafran situation.

929. Perham, Margery. "The Rhodesian Crisis: The Background." 42 <u>International Affairs</u> (1966), 1-13.

Reviews the background of the deviant case of Rhodesia in which not the continuation of a dependent status but unilateral declaration of independent statehood became the cause of collective action to prevent the exercise of international personality.

930. Post, K.W.J. "Is There a Case for Biafra? 44 _International Affairs_ (1968), 26-39.

Discursive evaluation of the Biafran secession effort in terms of the viability of a Nigeria without Biafra, of Biafra's capacity to sustain itself under conditions of peace, and the possible lot of the non-Ibo minority groups whose land would contain much of Biafra's oil. Comparison is made with the Katanga secession in terms of timing, foreign backing (Britain and the oil companies compared with Belgium and the _Union Minière_), and the financial impact on the central governments of Nigeria and the Congo.

931. Young, Crawford. "The Politics of Separatism: Katanga, 1960-63." In Gwendolen M. Carter (ed.), _Politics in Africa: 7 Cases_. New York: Harcourt, Brace & World, 1966, pp. 167-208.

Traces the tangled events of the Katanga secession that raised issues about the proper uses of U.N. forces, the activities of expatriate enterprise, and the limits of self-determination.

932. Young, Kenneth. _Rhodesia and Independence_. London: Eyre and Spottiswoode; New York: James H. Heineman, 1967, pp. xv, 567.

A presentation of the Rhodesian state of mind chiefly through the reflections over time of Ian Smith.

932-A. Zacklin, Ralph. "Challenge of Rhodesia: Toward an International Public Policy." _International Conciliation_. No. 575, November 1969, pp. 72.

Includes consideration of the background of Rhodesia's unilateral declaration of independence from the point of view of constitutional history and of the making and enforcement of sanctions.

See also nos. 639, 2488.

3. Coups d'État

933. Barber, Willard F., and Ronning, C. Neale. _Internal Security and Military Power: Counterinsurgency and Civic Action in Latin America_. Columbus: Ohio State University Press, 1966, pp. ix, 338.

Providing a good deal of information not readily available, this book deals with the effort to use Latin American armies for counterinsurgency purposes and for military civic action against governmental actions not wanted by the military. An important segment of the book deals with expenditures incurred and training provided by the United States to prepare officers and enlisted men for military civic action.

934. Carril, Bonifacio del. *Crónica interna de la revolución lib-eratadora*. Buenos Aires: Talleres de la Compañía Impresora, 1959, pp. 277.

Study of the anti-Perón uprisings in Cuyo province in September 1955.

935. De Grazia, Sebastian. *The Coup d'État: Its Political and Mili-tary Significance*. Report to Project Michelson, U.S. Naval Ordnance Test Station, China Lake, California. Mimeo. Princeton: Metron, Inc., November 27, 1961.

The coup d'état is distinguished from revolution and factors contributing to modern coups are identified. Among other things it is noted that in some areas the coup is an established institution for changing governments and receives de facto recognition in in-ternal and international law by means of such legal concepts as asylum and exile--the author might have added abdication. Attention is called to the nature of the coup as not being necessarily a dis-turbance or at least as great a disturbance as it sometimes seems to Western eyes. References to this feature and to the continued ef-fective working of government through acceptance by bureaucracy and public, particularly politically neutral sections of the public and by economic interests wanting to avoid disruption of trade flow, are made in the paper on techniques of coups. Identification is made of military as well as of political uses of coups.

936. De Grazia, Sebastian. *The Coup d'État: Modern Techniques and Countermeasures*. Report to Project Michelson, U.S. Naval Ordnance Test Station, China Lake, California. Mimeo. Princeton: Metron, Inc., November 30, 1961, pp. 55.

A study of the techniques of the coup d'état, with general dis-tinction from revolution, that sheds light about this method of changing government without election. The paper treats it as a mis-take to be overly concerned about the visible part of a coup, such as demonstrations, and to defend against them instead of concentrat-ing on the invisible part aimed at key points.

937. Fluharty, Vernon Lee. *Dance of the Millions: Military Rule and the Social Revolution in Colombia, 1930-1956*. Pittsburgh: University of Pittsburgh Press, 1957, pp. 336.

Useful in that it makes available information about and provides some insights into the nature of coups d'état and various forms of internal violence.

938. Goodspeed, Donald James. *The Conspirators*. New York: Viking, 1962, pp. xii, 252.

Study of six 20th-century coups d'état or attempted coups: Belgrade (1903), Dublin (1916), Petrograd (1917), Berlin (1920), Rome (1922), and the 1944 effort to assassinate Hitler.

939. Greenfield, Richard. *Ethiopia: A New Political History*. New York: Praeger, 1965, pp. viii, 515.

Deals, among other things, with the unsuccessful coup of 1960 and the effort to reduce the weight of the Ethiopian past and produce a greater similarity to the modernization efforts occurring else-where in Africa.

940. Gross, Feliks. The Seizure of Political Power in a Century of Revolutions. New York: Philosophical Library, 1958, pp. xxvii, 398.
On the transfer of political power by violent means, particularly with reference to Russian and Communist strategy and tactics since 1825, and on the opposition to such seizures expressed through either an underground movement or political emigration.

941. Huntington, Samuel P. "Patterns of Violence in World Politics." In Huntington (ed.), Changing Patterns of Military Politics. New York: Free Press, 1962, pp. 32-40.
Treats coups d'état aimed at change of policies as a nonconstitutional equivalent of elections as a means of periodic change of party in control.

942. Kaplan, Morton A. The Communist Coup in Czechoslovakia. Princeton: Center of International Studies, January 1960, pp. 40.
A careful study of perhaps the most important coup d'état of the post-World War II period in the sense that it raises questions about forms of intervention and in the sense of its stimulus to Western European coalescence.

943. Mazrui, Ali A., and Rothschild, Donald. "The Soldier and the State in East Africa: Some Theoretical Conclusions on the Army Mutinies of 1964." 20 Western Political Quarterly (1967), 82-97.
In dealing with the role of the army in the several states of East Africa, the author, among other things, calls attention to the difficulty confronting native troops who, under conditions of independence, are expected to be loyal to the nationalists against whom they had earlier fought, e.g., in Kenya.

944. Meisel, James Hans. The Fall of the Republic: Military Revolt in France. Ann Arbor: University of Michigan Press, 1962, pp. 309.
Examination of the role of the army in producing the fall of the Fourth French Republic and of the implications of this form of political action.

945. Nun, J. "Amérique latine: la crise hégémonique et le coup d'État militaire." 9 Sociologie du travail (1967), 281-313.
Undertakes to distinguish types of Latin American coups d'état in terms of a liberal model that attributes a reactionary character to the military, a developmentalist model that treats the officer corps as an intelligentsia in uniform, and a socialist model that separates the technical and the political aspects of the military machine.

946. Özbudan, Ergun. The Role of the Military in Recent Turkish Politics. Occasional Papers in International Affairs. No. 14. Cambridge: Harvard University Press, 1966, pp. 54.

On the role of the Turkish military with special reference to the 1960 coup led by the National Unity Committee that ousted the Menderes Government and the ruling Democratic Party.

947. Payne, James. "Peru: The Politics of Structured Violence." 27 Journal of Politics (1965), 362-374.

Deals with political decision-making in Peru and the function of the coup d'état when leadership is strongly centralized, the patronage system is under presidential control, a party-controlled communications system exists, and only the president's removal may seem to offer hope of dealing with problems. The struggle between president and opposition, with violence structured into the Peruvian political system, is treated as a consequence of the opposition's view of politics not as a gentlemen's game but as entailing an outcome more significant than constitutional norms, moral injunctions, or personal safety.

948. Rapoport, David C. "Coup d'État: The View of Men Firing Pistols." In Carl J. Friedrich (ed.), Revolution: Nomos VIII. New York: Atherton, 1966, pp. 53-74.

Outline of a more sophisticated view of the coup d'état than that of Kelsen, which tends to link revolutions and coups d'état in terms of legal consequences, and that of Huntington which does not identify those coups d'état which may not be simply nonconstitutional substitutes for elections. The analysis, noting several political and legal effects, makes much use of Gabriel Naudé's Considérations politiques sur les coups d'état (1667 ed.), but attempts to deal with some aspects not covered in Naudé's work. The author indicates that he has done additional preliminary work on the specific immediate consequences of coups d'état in selected underdeveloped states.

949. Tixier, G. "Les coups d'Etat militaries en Afrique de l'Ouest." 66 Revue de droit publique et de la science politique (1966), 1116-1132.

A review of West African military coups d'etat that relates events to the inadequacies of the constitutions of African presidential regimes as instruments for dealing with political and related problems and to difficulties to be met in attempting to replace presidents by nonmilitary procedures.

950. Tosti, S. "Movimenti rivoluzzionari contemporanei." 3 Studi politici (1954), 128-132.

An attempt to distinguish the coup d'état and revolution with reference to elements of the coup that resemble revolution, particularly in Communist coups. Such a distinction suggests that discussions of the recognition problem need to probe deeper, as the successful coup eliminates the issues of whether to recognize insurgency or belligerency. It also raises the question of the frequency of resort to the policy of nonrecognition of regimes that come to power through revolution compared with the frequency in cases of coups. It is not inconceivable that the coup d'état may have been treated as a more acceptable route to power than revolution.

951. Trager, F.N. "The Failure of U Nu and the Return of the Armed Forces in Burma." 25 Review of Politics (1963), 309-328.

A review of the circumstances productive of General Ne Win's coup d'état of March 1962.

952. von der Mehden, Fred R. Politics of the Developing Nations. Englewood Cliffs: Prentice-Hall, 1964, pp. xi, 140, iii.

Contains some data on coups d'état, secessionist threats, intervention of the military in politics, alien elites, and minorities in the developing nations of Africa, Asia, and Latin America. The treatment of each topic is brief, supported usually by briefly cited examples and some tabular representations of aggregative data.

953. Weiker, Walter F. The Turkish Revolution 1960-1961: Aspects of Military Politics. Washington: Brookings Institution, 1963, pp. 172.

A useful study of the overthrow of a regime without much of the external aid and stimuli that have characterized revolutions and coups d'état since 1945.

954. Whitaker, Arthur Preston. Argentine Upheaval: Perón's Fall and the New Regime. New York: Praeger, 1956, pp. x, 179.

Deals with the five months' crisis of 1955 that culminated in Perón's overthrow and his replacement by Lonardi, who in turn was replaced by Aramburu.

See also nos. 907, 998, 1026, 1039, 1050, 1053, 1119, 1121, 1329, 1610.

4. Internal War

955. AlRoy, Gil Carl. "Insurgency in the Countryside of Underdeveloped Societies." 26 Antioch Review (1966), 149-157.

Resulting from the undertaking of the Center of International Studies at Princeton University to study internal war, this article undertakes to set forth some of the main features of insurgency in the backlands: (1) lack of transportation and communications facilities enabling national governments to control either the populace or outlying officials; (2) the similarity of insurgents to brigands and the frequent incorporation of brigands into guerrilla forces; (3) the contribution of revolutionaries to pre-existent anti-government forces by bringing skills of large-scale organization; (4) adoption of the passive peasants' craving for land as a part of the revolutionary program together with co-option of those peasants seeking to flee the land and to acquire modernity; and (5) ideological fervor comparable to the religious fervor of the past.

956. AlRoy, Gil Carl. The Involvement of Peasants in Internal Wars. Research Monograph No. 24. Princeton: Center of International Studies, June 1966, pp. 38.

Reviews historical examples of peasant involvement from inchoate riots to revolutionary wars and proposes a new conceptual framework in the hope of systematizing propositions put forward to date and of encouraging the formulation of new propositions. The author suggests treating peasant involvement as an aspect rather than as a type of internal war such as was done under such older designations as "peasant rebellion." The concept "involvement" would be broad enough to include the several varieties of involvement including victimization. Problems encountered in dealing with three principle variables--participation, goals, setting-- are discussed.

957. Anber, Paul. "Modernization and Political Disintegration: Nigeria and the Ibos." 5 Journal of Modern African Studies (1967), 163-179.
    Raises the question of why the Ibos could separate as Biafra on May 30, 1967, and then undertakes a descriptive analysis in terms of the stimulus to strengthened tribal loyalty provided by intellectual and economic development in a pluralistic, underdeveloped society, particularly when a minority tribe advances more rapidly than other tribes in the state and so develops convictions of superiority combined with a sense of being frustrated by a "backward" majority. That modernization should produce a change from a nationalistic to a tribalistic viewpoint expressed in political behavior is treated as a phenomenon likely to recur and so as one requiring rethinking of our longitudinal models of modernization and its relationship with political behavior.

958. Anderson, Charles W., von der Mehden, Fred R., and Young, Crawford. Issues of Political Development. Englewood Cliffs: Prentice-Hall, 1967.
    Employing depth comparisons and elaborate descriptive examples from Asian, African, and Latin American countries, the book deals with such matters as subnational loyalties, endemic violence and civil strife (with case studies of Burma, Colombia, and the Congo), and the meaning of revolution in the developing world.

959. Bjelajac, S.N. "Principles in Counterinsurgency." 8 Orbis (1964), 655-669.
    Attempts to identify some of the errors of counterinsurgents such as failure to detect and evaluate a revolutionary movement before an outbreak, failure to identify leaders, lack of understanding of the nature of conflict, excessive reliance on the administrative, police, and military machinery, overemphasis of economics, and inadequate psychological and propagandistic undertakings.

960. Black, Cyril E., and Thornton, Thomas P. (eds.). Communism and Revolution: The Strategic Uses of Political Violence. Princeton: Princeton University Press, 1964, pp. 467.
    Among the subjects considered by this symposium on guerrilla warfare and domestic violence are: the Communist ideological framework for the use of violence; case studies of Communist revolutionary experiences in Eastern Europe, Finland, Southeast Asia, Vietnam, and Korea; and Communist strategies in the underdeveloped countries.

961. Chandler, Geoffrey. The Divided Land: An Anglo-Greek Tragedy. New York: St. Martin's Press, 1959, pp. 214.
    Chronicle by a British officer providing useful information on the civil war in Greece after the Germans withdrew in 1944.

962. Chassin, Lionel Max. The Communist Conquest of China: A History of the Civil War, 1945-1949. Translated by Timothy Osato and Louis Gales. Cambridge: Harvard University Press, 1965, pp. xiii, 264.
    First published in French in 1952 and based in part on intelligence reports, this study by a former vice-chief of the French General Staff deals with the military and strategic aspects of the civil war, with the social (particularly the agrarian) situation, and with schisms among both Nationalists and Communists.

963. Chou Shun-sin. The Chinese Inflation, 1937-1949. New York: Columbia University Press, 1963.
    Analytical treatment, together with economic history of the period, of the inflation that ultimately imposed the cost of war upon recipients of fixed incomes to undermine morale of the functionaries upon whom the Kuomintang Government depended if it were to retain power.

964. Crozier, Brian. The Rebels: A Study of Post-War Insurrections. London: Chatto & Windus, 1960, pp. 256.
    Broad review of post-World War II uprisings that seeks to identify origins, causes, leaders, techniques, etc., and to ascertain whether there were alternative courses of action that might have averted rebellion.

965. Davies, James C. "Toward a Theory of Revolution." 27 American Sociological Review (1962), 5-19.
    Develops a thesis, with some historical evidence in support, that revolutions are most likely when a prolonged period of economic and social development is followed by a short period of sharp reversal that generates the subjective fear that the ground gained will be lost.

966. Denno, B.F. "Sino-Soviet Attitudes Towards Revolutionary War." 11 Orbis (1968), 1193-1207.
    Examines disagreements between the Soviet Union and China on where and when revolutionary wars should be fought, how they should be fought, and the degree of risk of escalation to be tolerated, with reference to the comparative dependence of the two countries on revolutionary war as an instrument of policy.

967. Eckstein, Harry. "On the Etiology of Internal Wars." 4 History and Theory (No. 2, 1965), 133-163.
    Commentary suggesting criteria to guide the development of theory about internal war.

968. Eckstein, Harry (ed.). Internal War: Problems and Approaches. New York: Free Press; London: Collier-Macmillan Ltd., 1964, pp. x, 399.
    Symposium dealing with such matters as the theoretical study of internal war, the place of force in the social process, external

involvement in internal war, the political framework of internal war, the roots of insurgency, and the economic aspects of revolutions. A number of the papers are separately annotated. This volume and Rosenau's symposium, International Aspects of Civil Strife, emerged from a general inquiry carried on at the Princeton Center for International Studies.

969. Enos, J.L. An Analytic Model of Political Allegiance and Its Application to the Cuban Revolution. RAND Report P-3197. August 1965, pp. 34.

Develops a simple model susceptible of analytic solution but sufficiently complex to include major factors underlying political change. The model, permitting successive solutions to reveal changes in the political environment, is applied to Cuba during the period that culminated in the overthrow of the Batista regime.

970. Gagula, David. Counter-Insurgency Warfare: Theory and Practice. New York: Praeger, 1964.

Written by a graduate of the French military academy, St. Cyr, the volume sees revolutionists' success as a consequence of gaining popular support and counterinsurgency as successful only through establishment or re-establishment of a political apparatus mobilizing popular support.

971. Galíndez, Bartolomé. Apuntes de tres revoluciones--1930, 1943, 1955. Buenos Aires: Castro Barrera, 1956, pp. 188.

Perceptive observations on the nature of three Argentine revolutions.

972. Ginsburgs, George, and Mathos, Michael. Communist China and Tibet, The First Dozen Years. The Hague: Nijhoff, 1964, pp. 218.

On the relations of China and Tibet after the de facto independence of Tibet was ended and the century-long suzerainty of China was formalized by the 1951 agreement, with attention to the rebellion of 1959.

973. Guelzo, Capt. Carl M. "The Communist Long War." 40 Military Review (December 1960), 14-22.

Survey of Chinese Communist ideas of war, with reference to the carrying on of the ideological struggle in international politics in terms of the guerrilla warfare principles of concentrating forces for momentary superiority but avoiding a decisive engagement except when victory is certain.

974. Gurr, Ted Robert. The Genesis of Violence: A Multivariate Theory of the Preconditions for Civil Strife. Ph.D. Diss. New York: New York University, 1965; Ann Arbor: University Microfilms, Inc., Order No. 66-5728, pp. 708.

Develops an explanatory theory of systemic violence in the form of 40 hypotheses derived from frustration-aggression theory and from literature on collective violence. The objective is the specification of independent variables capable of predicting the magnitude of violence in any policy or period, using multiple regression techniques.

974-A. Gurr, Ted Robert. Why Men Rebel. Princeton: Princeton University Press, 1970, pp. 407.
On psychological causes of violence, including socio-economic discontent and attitudes that justify and condone violence.

975. Holt, Edgar. Protest in Arms: The Irish Troubles, 1916-1923. New York: Coward-McCann, 1961, pp. 328.
Valuable account, despite controversial aspects, of the Irish revolt against Britain and of subsequent bitter conflict within Ireland.

976. Horowitz, Irving L. Revolution in Brazil: Politics and Society in a Developing Nation. New York: Dutton, 1964, pp. xiv, 430.
Suggests that America views Brazil biasedly because it is uninformed. The internal situation of Brazil, including revolutionary forces and socio-economic conditions, are discussed. Attention is also given to Brazil's international position in relation to all other nations and in relation to the Great Power struggle.

977. Janne, Henri. "Un modèle théorique du phénomène révolutionnaire?" 15 Annales (1960), 1138-1154.
The structure of all comprehensive societies includes a vertical stratification (industry, army, etc.) and a horizontal stratification (hierarchical layers). Each horizontal culture exercises a pressure on the vertical culture. When such tension exceeds the margins of tolerance of system equilibrium, the phenomenon of revolution appears and may grow until it can break the state's monopoly of force, which is controlled by a higher layer in the hierarchy. Such a process tends to be generated (1) when social stratification is more strongly integrated along the horizontal than the vertical or (2) when the quantum of action consisting of the sum of negative social relations (unfavorable to integration and to continuity of structures) exceeds the quantum of action consisting of the sum of positive social relations. Revolution is thus an expression of disintegration, its form differing according to the social region of global society in which it is localized.

978. Johnson, Chalmers. Revolution and the Social System. Stanford: Hoover Institution on War, Revolution, and Peace, 1964, pp. vii, 68.
An attempt to synthesize theoretical writings on the sources of revolution.

979. Johnson, Chalmers A. Revolutionary Change. Boston: Little, Brown, 1966, pp. vx, 191.
Blends findings and hypotheses in the literature of anthropology, social psychology, and political theory to describe the structure and function of coups d'état, guerrilla wars, peasant rebellions, and other types of armed uprisings. A model of the social system is employed to analyze the causes of revolution. An attempt is also made to provide a synthetic approach to social integration and social violence.

980. Kecskemeti, Paul. _Insurgency as a Strategic Problem_. RAND Report RM-5160-PR. Santa Monica: RAND Corporation, February 1967, pp. 49.

Examining recent historical examples of insurgency, the author finds the chief causes to lie not in economic deprivation but in such political factors as alien rule and foreign invasion, while nationalist and peasant-populist aspirations provide incentives to join insurgent forces. Removal of political causes of insurgency is viewed as beyond the capacity of any single administrative agency and incapable of remedy from outside the country. But insurgency resting on nationalist or populist origins is not considered to be fatal to the United States security posture in relation to "undeterrable" forms of Communist aggression.

981. Kecskemeti, Paul. _The Unexpected Revolution: Social Forces in the Hungarian Uprising._ Stanford: Stanford University Press, 1961, pp. 178.

Analyzes the Hungarian Revolution of 1956 in terms of political and social forces, data being obtained through interviews and documentary analysis.

982. Klieman, Aaraon S. "Bab al-Mandab: The Red Sea in Transition." 11 _Orbis_ (1967), 758-771.

An article on four tension areas near Bab al-Mandab, namely, Yemen and Aden, both caught in civil war at the time of writing, Eritrea and its separatist movement, and French Somaliland and the efforts of its nationalists to gain independence.

983. Kling, Merle. "Towards a Theory of Power and Political Instability in Latin America." In John H. Kautsky (ed.), _Political Change in Underdeveloped Countries: Nationalism and Communism._ New York: Wiley, 1962, pp. 123-139.

Suggests that when land is concentrated in a few hands, revolution may be a means of gaining wealth through the political process as what one might call a prior condition of renewed social and political development.

984. Kornhauser, William. "Rebellion and Political Development." In Harry Eckstein (ed.), _Internal War: Problems and Approaches_. New York: Free Press, 1964, pp. 142-156.

Regards rebellion as a way of performing political functions in the absence of structures that can accommodate political demands. It may be noted that this view is not out of line with the Marxist and older views, even Locke's institutionalization of revolution as a procedure based on constitutional criteria.

985. Kousoulas, D. George. _Revolution and Defeat: The Story of the Greek Communist Party_. New York: Oxford, 1965, pp. xiv, 306.

Study of various forms of revolutionary activity by the Greek Communists. In many of the events discussed, the author was personally involved.

986. Ladhari, N. "L'Abdication." 12 <u>Revue internationale d'histoire politique et constitutionnelle</u> (1953), 329-337.

Includes reference to the employment of abdication as a means of facilitating resolution of conflicts with other states. Abdication being a less likely event than before so many monarchies gave way to nonmonarchical forms of government, its implications may receive too little attention whereas, as a venerable form of change of regime, it warrants consideration à propos such matters as the interaction of foreign and domestic politics and legalities, intervention and coercion, internal war and recognition.

986-A. Leites, Nathan, and Wolf, Charles, Jr. <u>Rebellion and Authority: An Analytic Essay on Insurgent Conflicts</u>. Chicago: Markham, 1970, pp. xii, 174.

Two RAND Corporation authors attempt to develop a method of analysis of insurgent conflicts by use of such concepts as "demand" and "supply" of rebellion, "inputs" and "outputs" associated with rebellion, "damage-limiting" and "profit-maximizing" influences on population behavior, and principles of target-selection. The authors seek to approach the rigor which they regard as achieved in the analysis of strategic nuclear conflicts. They apply their concepts to certain recent instances of insurgency.

987. Marcum, John A. <u>The Angolan Revolution.</u> Vol. I. <u>The Anatomy of an Explosion (1950-1962)</u>. Cambridge: MIT Press, 1969.

Reviewing events in Angola and Lisbon from 1950 to 1962, the author gives attention to the numerous views of the origins of the Angolan rebellion, the means by which it was carried out, and the inadequacy of organization that took the form often of flimsy coalitions or of groups openly competing with each other. A second volume, to be published later, will carry the story from 1962 to 1968.

988. McAlister, John T., Jr. "The Possibilities for Diplomacy in Southeast Asia." 19 <u>World Politics</u> (1966), 258-305.

Lengthy review article based on eight books on Southeast Asia with particular attention to Vietnam and Laos but with attention also to Thailand and Cambodia. The article is a handy guide to many of the intricacies of the Southeast Asian situation including the tribal divisions of Laos and Vietnam.

989. Meadows, Paul. "Sequence in Revolution." 6 <u>American Sociological Review</u> (1941), 702-709.

The author outlines theories of revolution including developmental constructs that tried to trace the sequential pattern of revolutionary social movements, inductive generalizations from studies of many different contexts, and delineations of selected phases of revolution. One school of thought states that sequence is a cycle of institutionalization and that revolution occurs with the emergence of a new felt need. Another interpretation of revolutionary sequence is in terms of psycho-social factors. The key is in the idea of adjustment in terms of conditioning of responses. In a diagram, author attempts to integrate these theories into a comprehensive conception of sequence in revolution.

990. Meisel, James H. Counterrevolution: How Revolutions Die. New York: Atherton, 1966, pp. xiii, 236.

Blends historical and sociological approaches, including resort to biography, to view history as a process of revolution and counter-revolution, with attention to cases in which revolution has been aborted or preceded by counterrevolution. When the focus is upon second-echelon figures it is because the author believes that their lives tell more about the natural process of revolution than do the atypical "men of destiny."

991. Millares, Edgar. Las Guerrillas: Teoría y práctica. Sucre: Biblioteca, Universidad de San Francisco Xavier, 1968.

Although not going into any theme in depth, this volume, of which only 1,000 copies were printed in 1968, some of which were sent to political scientists and major quarterlies in the United States, provides valuable information about political groups related to the guerrillas of 1967 that previously was virtually unavailable outside Bolivia.

992. Miller, Linda B. "Regional Organization and the Regulation of Internal Conflict." 19 World Politics (1967), 582-600.

An attempt to ascertain the potential roles of regional organizations in three types of internal conflicts: (1) colonial wars; (2) internal conflicts involving a breakdown of law and order; (3) proxy wars and internal conflicts involving charges of subversion or external aggression. Attention is given to the internal and external limitations on the responses of regional organizations, potential compatibilities and incompatibilities of regional and global (UN) approaches to internal conflicts, and the importance of the perceptions of leaders of third-party states in determination of the classification of internal conflicts.

993. Mus, Paul. Viêt-Nam: Sociologie d'une guerre. Paris: Seuil, 1952, pp. 373.

Study of sociological problems related to the Vietnamese uprising against France.

994. Nairn, R.C. "Counterguerrilla Warfare in Southeast Asia." In Morton A. Kaplan (ed.), The Revolution in World Politics. New York and London: Wiley, 1962, pp. 411-466.

Considerations on counterguerrilla techniques that include consideration of the circumstances in which partition of a territory may represent a desirable power equation, even if not laudable. However, desirability is couched in terms of potential for consolidating a pro-Western regime and threatening the pro-Communist segment of the territory, not in terms of producing a relatively durable settlement.

995. Newbold, Stokes. "Receptivity to Communist-Fomented Agitation in Rural Guatemala." 5 Economic Development and Cultural Change (1955), 338-361.

On the lack of "ideological awakening" among the Indians in the rural areas and a presentation of evidence that the Indians voted to fill their pocketbooks.

996. O'Connor, James. "On Cuban Political Economy." 79 _Political Science Quarterly_ (1964), 233-247.

Explanation of the Cuban revolution in terms of a forcing-out of the agrarian middle class by foreign capital, a popular support of Castro, a transfer of political power from one small group to another, and introduction of class conflict after the ouster of Batista.

996-A. Ohonbaumu, O. _The Psychology of the Nigerian Revolution_. Ilfracombe, England: Stockwell, 1969, pp. 224.

A review of Nigerian political history in 1960-66 to set forth the events leading to the eventually unsuccessful fight for the independence of Biafra which received a few states' recognition (statement of Julius Nyerere in _The Observer_ (London), April 28, 1968).

997. Otterbein, Keith F. "Internal War: A Cross-Cultural Study." 70 _American Anthropologist_ (1968), 277-289.

Employs a sample of 50 societies to test hypotheses relating variables drawn from three categories--social structure, political organization, and intersocietal relations--to the frequency of internal war defined as warfare between culturally similar political communities.

998. Pettee, George. "Revolution--Typology and Process." In Carl J. Friedrich (ed.), _Revolution: Nomos VIII_. New York: Atherton, 1966, pp. 10-33.

Employs a typology that distinguishes private palace revolutions, public palace revolutions, rebellion of an area against the rule of another country, great national revolutions, and systemic revolutions entailing widespread change in the system of state organization. An attempt is made to identify processes associated with each type, the role of actors' intentions, and the consequences as identified after the event. The article is suggestive of other studies that need to be undertaken in order to advance understanding of and to correct or improve classification of revolutions and also of the function and, perhaps, the necessity of great wars in the process of systemic revolution.

999. Pike, Douglas. _Viet Cong: The Organization and Techniques of the National Liberation Front of South Vietnam_. Cambridge: MIT Press, 1966, pp. 490.

Emphasizing the organizational complexity and discipline of Viet Cong and providing a survey of the origins of the NLF in the clandestine societies that developed in Vietnam during the period of French rule, this volume provides perhaps more information about the South Vietnamese insurgent movement than any other single volume.

1000. "Political Conflict: Perspectives on Revolution." 23 _Journal of International Relations_ (1969), entire issue, pp. 118.

The articles deal with various aspects of revolution, particularly with respect to internal political conflict.

1001. Polsky, Anthony. "Himalayan Battleground." 61 Far Eastern Economic Review (1968), 511-514.

A discussion of the border regions of India, Burma, and China that concentrates on the trouble being given by the hillsmen to India and Burma, Chinese encouragement of their activities, India's mountain troops in border areas, and China's troubles in Tibet.

1002. Powell, Ralph L. The Rise of Chinese Military Power, 1895-1912. Princeton: Princeton University Press, 1955, pp. x, 383.

Deals with the growth of the system of war lords and their armies in China between 1895 and 1912, the introduction to a protracted period of internal conflict.

1003. Pye, Lucien W. Guerrilla Communism in Malaya: Its Social and Political Meaning. Princeton: Princeton University Press, 1956, pp. 369.

Examines political and social forces contributing to the development of Malayan guerrilla communism and uses interview data to analyze experiences of former members prior to recruitment, during membership, and at the time of disaffection.

1004. Rosenau, James N. (ed.). International Aspects of Civil Strife. Princeton: Princeton University Press, 1964, pp. vii, 322.

Symposium dealing with such matters as the international relations of internal war, intervention in internal war, international settlement of internal war, and the international law of internal war. A number of the papers are separately annotated.

1005. Sanders, R. "Mass Support and Communist Insurrection." 9 Orbis (1965), 214-231.

Discusses Communist insurrectionists' efforts to mobilize masses as an effort to overcome the technological power of governments and the failure of nonelite minorities to subvert the military elite.

1006. Sarkisyanz, E. Buddhist Backgrounds of the Burmese Revolution. The Hague: Nijhoff, 1965, pp. xxix, 248.

As a study in revolution this volume is less concerned with political processes and organization than with the cultural backgrounds productive both of unrest and of socialist leanings in Burma.

1007. Stanley, Manfred. "The Turn to Violence: A Sociological View of Insurgency." 8 International Journal of Comparative Sociology (1967), 232-244.

Regarding the concept of insurgency as important in international law and politics but sociologically an artificial construct, the author seeks the sociological foundations of insurgency and of the readiness to perceive violence as a "solution."

1008. Stone, Lawrence. "Theories of Revolution." 18 World Politics (1966), 159-176.

Critical review by a historian of recent models of revolution that indicates their usefulness and their limitations.

1009. **Tauras, K.V. (pseud.).** Guerrilla Warfare on the Amber Coast.
New York: Voyages Press, 1962, pp. 110.
Account of anti-Soviet guerrilla activities in Lithuania after
World War II.

1010. Thomas, Hugh. The Spanish Civil War. New York: Harper & Row,
1961, pp. 720; Colophon ed., 1963, pp. xxix, 720.
Comprehensive and well-documented history of the Spanish Civil
War that places the major issues of international law in a setting
of detailed political and military events. A 25-page bibliography
is included.

1011. Thompson, Sir Robert. Defeating Communist Insurgency: Experiences from Malaya and Vietnam. New York: Praeger, 1966, pp. 171.
The author, 23 years a member of the Malayan Civil Service and
also former chief of the British Advisory Mission to the Republic
of Vietnam (1961-1965), provides a careful analysis of the start of
insurgency in terms of a popular cause or symbol (e.g., the presence of a foreign power), exploitation of societal conflicts and
cleavages not resolved by existing institutions, the types of people attracted to insurgency, and the breakdown in rural administration. Counterinsurgency being treated as primarily an administrative and judicial reconstruction and adaptation, the discussion
thereof becomes a devastating critique of the American military
approach in Vietnam.

1012. Tilly, Charles, and Rule, James. Measuring Political Upheaval.
Research Monograph No. 19. Princeton University: Center of International
Studies, June 1965, pp. iii, 113.
Discussion of problems of categorizing and measuring internal
political upheaval and explanation of the methods being employed
in a study of uprisings and disturbances in France from 1830 to
1960.

1013. van der Esch, Patricia A.M. Prelude to War: The International
Repercussions of the Spanish Civil War (1936-1939). The Hague: Nijhoff,
1951, pp. xi, 190.
Deals with the diplomatic maneuvers related to the Civil War
in Spain which marked the first confrontation of consequence with
the boundary issue between the national and the international in
an internal struggle characterized by active foreign intervention
and by the threat of an accrual to the strength of the anticipated
international aggressors.

1013-A. von Lazar, Arpad, and Beadle, Vi Ann. "National Integration
and Insurgency in Venezuela: An Exercise in Causation." 24 Western Political Quarterly (1971), 136-145.
An examination of six Venezuelan states that have been inflicted with guerrilla warfare. The study finds a definite relationship between lack of integration and insurgency but notes
that other variables need to be considered in order to properly
ascertain which variables have a positive effect on insurgency
and which ones have a negative effect.

1014. Weinert, Richard S. "Violence in Pre-Modern Societies: Rural Colombia." 60 <u>American Political Science Review</u> (1966), 340-347.
Analysis of the long and intense violence experienced by Colombia from 1946 to 1953 and finds the case to be unique in that it occurred in rural areas as peasant fought peasant in a situation in which the Liberal and Conservative parties were well established and depended upon traditional loyalties rather than organizational structure to maintain their positions. The result was a violent defense of traditional ways by the Conservative peasantry against the Liberal peasantry supporting their party's modernization program. In the late 1950s and early 1960s looting and revenge killing became a way of life for orphans of the earlier violence. The author suggests that the fidelista-inspired violence of January 1965 may herald a third stage in Colombia's evolving conflict.

1015. Wilson, David A. "Nation-Building and Revolutionary War." In Karl W. Deutsch and William J. Foltz (eds.), <u>Nation-Building</u>. New York: Atherton, 1963, pp. 84-94.
Comments on the nature of revolution and the critical role of organization of rural populations with guerrilla forces employable as the major organizational core. The author's focus is upon the Southeast Asian countries, but with some reference to the Chinese experience. A paper of the same title appeared as a RAND Corporation paper, P-2624 (September 1962).

1016. Wolf, C., Jr. <u>Insurgency and Counterinsurgency: New Myths and Old Realities</u>. RAND Report P-3132. Santa Monica: RAND Corporation, May 1965, pp. iii, 23.
Treats the doctrine that popular support is essential to insurgency or counterinsurgency as untested and suggests that the main task of either side is to influence the behavior, not the attitudes of the populace.

1016-A. Wolf, Eric R. <u>Peasant Wars in the Twentieth Century</u>. New York: Harper & Row, 1970, pp. 364.
On the role of peasants in revolutions in Mexico, Russia, China, Vietnam, Algeria, and Cuba.

1017. Wulfften, Palthe, P.M. van. <u>Psychological Aspects of the Indonesian Problem</u>. Leiden: Brill, 1949, pp. 58.
An attempt to find psychological roots for the political unrest in Indonesia after World War II.

1018. Young, Crawford. "The Congo Rebellion." 10 <u>Africa Report</u> (April 1965), 6-11.
Perceptive analysis of the civil war in the Congo.

1019. Zasloff, J.J. <u>Political Motivation of the Viet Cong: The Vietminh Regroupees</u>. RM-4703/2-ISA/ARPA. Santa Monica: RAND Corporation, May 1968, pp. 197.
On the nationalism of those 30,000 South Vietnamese who first fought the French and now are part of the Viet Cong.

1020. Zinner, Paul. <u>Revolution in Hungary</u>. New York: Columbia University Press, 1962, pp. ix, 380.
Based upon documentary records and extensive interviewing of refugees, this volume traces the Hungarian uprising back to the seizure of power by the Communists. The book is notable for its integration of information from various kinds of sources.

See also nos. 165, 393, 419, 503, 611, 625, 905, 913, 940, 1056, 1062, 1329, 1509, 1601, 1610, 1620, 1621, 1689, 1806, 2514, 2517, 2522, 2570.

a. Colonial War

1021. Bernard, Stéphane. "Considérations sur la théorie des conflits coloniaux." <u>Revue de l'Institut de Sociologie</u> (1958), 71-101.
Reviews three approaches to decolonization: (1) the formal political approach that views political authority as a function of force and of consent; (2) the psycho-social approach based upon distinguishing the French minority, Moroccan notables, and the Moroccan masses; (3) the functional approach, viewing colonialism as a succession of problems and the fall of colonialism as due to the failure of colonial regimes to resolve social and political problems resulting from their own efforts to reform institutions and maintain public order. The author prefers the third approach.

1022. Bernard, Stéphane. <u>Le Conflit franco-marocain 1943-1956</u>. 3 vols. Brussels: Éditions de l'Institut de Sociologie de l'Université Libre de Bruxelles, 1964, pp. 389, 286, 402. <u>The Franco-Moroccan Conflict, 1943-1956</u>. Translation of Vols. I and II of the French ed. New Haven: Yale University Press, 1968, pp. xxxvi, 680.
The second volume of this study, entitled in the French original, <u>Mécanisme de la decolonisation du protectorat; Contribution à la théorie du système politique</u>," presents a theory of colonial conflicts based on structural-functional analysis. Concern is with variance in the authority of a political regime as a function of attitudinal variables and of the conditioning situation and also with the accomplishment by the regime of its social function in putting to work its potential to resolve social problems confronting it. For the author the problem of decolonization is one of disaggregation of that local authority of metropolitan origin. The theory is applied to the Moroccan situation to illuminate important aspects of events there.

1023. Fistié, Pierre. <u>Le réveil de l'Extrême-Orient: Guerres et révolutions, 1834-1954</u>. Paris: Presses Universelles, 1956, pp. 435.
History of the wars and revolutions related to Western penetration of the Far East from the initial contacts with Japan and China to the struggles in Southeast Asia in the early 1950s.

1024. Mansur, Fatma. <u>Process of Independence</u>. London: Routledge, 1962; New York: Humanities Press, 1963, pp. xvi, 192.
A Turkish sociologist's comparison of stages in achievement of independence and of groups taking the lead at each stage.

Comparison is made of five countries: India, Pakistan, Indonesia, Ghana, and Nigeria.

1025. Nasution, Abdul Haris. Fundamentals of Guerilla Warfare and the Indonesian Defense System--Past and Future. (Djakarta): Information Sirvice (sic) of the Indonesian Armed Forces, 1953, pp. 338. Der Guerilla-krieg--Grundlagen der Guerillakriegführung aus der Sicht des indonesischen Verteidigungssystems in Vergangenheit und Zukunft. Cologne: Brückenhauer, 1961, pp. 148.
An exposition of the fundamentals of guerrilla warfare in the light of the Indonesian experience of 1945-1949.

5. Riots, Demonstrations and Other Violent Domestic Protests

1026. Ashford, Douglas E. "Politics and Violence in Morocco." 13 Middle East Journal (1959), 11-25.
The experience in Morocco testifies to the importance of violence as a way of influencing political behavior. The higher incidence of violence in new countries means that analytical tools need revision and elaboration before being applied to new nations. In the Moroccan situation, in reference to certain defined goals, violence is by no means completely dysfunctional; in some cases it may be essential to change.

1027. Blanksten, George. "The Politics of Latin America." In Gabriel Almond and James S. Coleman (eds.), The Politics of the Developing Areas. Princeton: Princeton University Press, 1960, pp. 455-531.
Suggests that political riots, in contrast to coups, general strikes, demonstrations, and assassinations, may indicate a serious malfunctioning of the political system.

1028. Feierabend, Ivo K., and Feierabend, Rosalind L. "Aggressive Behaviors Within Polities, 1948-1962: A Cross-National Study." 10 Journal of Conflict Resolution (1966), 249-271.
An attempt to employ data on internal conflict behaviors and the frustration-aggression model to obtain, among other things, rankings of nations on the basis of political stability, systemic frustration, and relationships between modernity level and rates of change in such matters as ecological variables and national income.

1029. Rummel, Rudolph J. "Dimensions of Conflict Behavior Within Nations, 1946-59." 10 Journal of Conflict Resolution (1966), 65-73.
Application of factor analysis to internal conflicts from 1946 to 1959.

1030. Tanter, Raymond. "Dimensions of Conflict Behavior Within Nations, 1955-60: Turmoil and Internal War." Peace Research Society (International), Papers. Chicago Conference, 1964. Vol. III (1965), pp. 159-184.

A study of 74 nations to compare dimensions of internal conflict in 1955-1960 with other studies. One result is an indication that the theoretical significance of the basic variable, revolution, lies in terms of the rising expectations and role demands of the masses that are followed by challenges to the social structure and the efforts of revolutionary elites to seize power in an apparent lack of political structures allowing orderly succession. An appendix provides tabulations of raw data.

1031. Thornton, Thomas Perry. "Terror as a Weapon of Political Agitation." In Harry Eckstein (ed.), Internal War: Problems and Approaches. New York: Free Press, 1964, pp. 71-99.
Analysis of terror as a deliberately employed weapon that distinguishes enforcement terror, employed by those in power, and agitational terror, employed by aspirants to power, and that accords careful attention to the relations between terror, guerrilla warfare, and conventional warfare.

See also nos. 503, 937, 1220-1223, 2230, 2231.

6. Intervention; Subversion

1032. Allardt, Erik. "Social Sources of Finnish Communism: Traditional and Emerging Radicalism." 5 International Journal of Comparative Sociology (1964), 49-72.
In view of the failure of Finnish Communists to furnish, during Finland's wars with the USSR and after, the expected support that would have added Finland to the list of Communist countries, the findings of this factor analysis of aggregate data is of value in the search for explanation of Finland's capacity to escape the fate of East European countries bordering on or near the Soviet Union.

1033. Baddour, Abd-el-Fattah Ibrahim el-Sayed. Sudanese-Egyptian Relations: A Chronological and Analytical Study. The Hague: Nijhoff, 196 pp. xiii, 264.
Defense of the Egyptian position in respect to the status of the Sudan under the Condominium and, more important, in the first years of independence that entailed efforts to bring the Sudan under Egyptian sovereignty via the pro-Egyptian segment of the Sudanese population. Vital to the whole issue is utilization of Nile waters.

1034. Baldwin, David A. "Foreign Aid, Intervention, and Influence." 21 World Politics (1969), 425-447.
Focussing on links between (a) aid and influence, (b) aid and intervention, and (c) trade and intervention, this article indicates various forms of intervention that can result from loans, bilateral aid, multilateral aid, and private investment. "Non-aid" is treated as a means of influence. Following Andrew Scott in The Functioning of the International Political System (1967), the doctrine of

nonintervention is treated as a relic of a day when nations were more distant in time-space, when countries had little significant interaction, and when no countries were so powerful that they "intervened" merely by existing and acting.

1035. Blackstock, P.W. The Strategy of Subversion: Manipulating the Politics of Other Nations. Chicago: Quadrangle, 1964.
    Programmed subversion, its control, management and policy problems and dangers are analyzed. Several cases are compared: US, Czarist, German, and Soviet cases and the Bay of Pigs case. The State Department-military-CIA power struggle is described.

1036. Calvocoressi, Peter. World Order and New States: Problems of Keeping the Peace. New York: Praeger, 1962, pp. ix, 133.
    Disorders since World War II, resulting from internal quarrels, incompetent governments, ideological differences, and the intrusion of the Cold War, will make intervention a frequent occurrence both at present and in the foreseeable future. Restraints exist in the form of fear of provoking larger wars and in that of practical impediments to effective intervention.

1036-A. Dimitrijevic, Vojin. "Intervention and Aggression." 19 Review of International Affairs (Belgrade) (December 5, 1968), 23-26.
    A Yugoslav writer's discussion of intervention with particular regard for the Soviet intervention of 1968 in Czechoslovakia.

1037. Henderson, K.D.D. Sudan Republic. New York: Praeger, 1966, pp. 256.
    Includes a perceptive account of the Sudan under the Condominium as well as of the problems under independence including that of Egyptian objectives that raise questions about the nature of intervention and subversion.

1038. "Intervention and World Politics." 22 Journal of International Affairs (1968), entire issue.
    Includes the following articles: James N. Rosenau, "The Concept of Intervention"; I. William Zartman, "Intervention Among Developing States"; Andrew M. Scott, "Nonintervention and Conditional Intervention"; Adam Yarmolinsky, "American Foreign Policy and the Decision to Intervene."

1039. Kantor, Harry. The Costa Rican Election of 1953: A Case Study. Gainesville: University of Florida Press, 1958, pp. xii, 68.
    Excellent study of the election of 1953 and of its background in the events of the preceding years in the form of attempted coup d'état by the party in power in 1948, the civil war that followed, and intervention by other Central American states.

1040. Korbel, Josef. The Communist Subversion of Czechoslovakia, 1938-1948: The Failure of Coexistence. Princeton: Princeton University Press, 1959, pp. 258.
    Personal interviews by the author, former head of Jan Masaryk's Cabinet, and Communist materials published shortly after the seizure

of power, form much of the basis of this study of the Communist
takeover in Czechoslovakia.

1041. Langer, P.F., and Zasloff, J.J.   Revolution in Laos: The
North Vietnamese and the Pathet Lao.   RM-5935-ARPA.   Santa Monica: RAND
Corporation, September 1969, pp. 252.
    An analysis of the role of the Vietnamese Communists in the
    Pathet Lao insurgency, including a consideration of the North
    Vietnamese view of the relation of the Laos border regions to
    their security.

1042. Langer, P.F., and Zasloff, J.J.   The North Vietnamese Military
Adviser in Laos: A First Hand Account.   RM-5688-ARPA.   Santa Monica:
RAND Corporation, June 1968, pp. 49.
    Based on the testimony of Captain Mai Dai Hap, a military ad-
    viser in Northern Laos from February 1964 until his defection in
    December 1966, this study analyzes the organization and work of
    North Vietnamese political and military advisory, logistic, and
    training activities for the Pathet Lao.

1043. Martz, John D.   Central America--The Crisis and the Challenge.
Chapel Hill: University of North Carolina Press, 1959, pp. 356.
    Lively, but pessimistic account of the politics of Central
    America and Panama that includes details of the Figueres-Somoza
    rivalry and the efforts of the latter to aid Calderonista inva-
    sions from Nicaragua in the late 1940s and in 1955 in opposition
    to the National Liberation Party of Costa Rica.

1043-A. Mitchell, C.R.   "Civil Strife and the Involvement of External
Parties."   14 International Studies Quarterly (1970), 166-194.
    Sets forth a framework for the study of civil strife and the
    behavioral, attitudinal, and structural factors that underlie and
    lead up to intervention.

1044. Morley, James William.   The Japanese Thrust into Siberia, 1918.
New York: Columbia University Press, 1957, pp. xiii, 395.
    Provides data derived from Japanese and Russian sources on
    Japan's decision to intervene in Siberia in the summer of 1918.

1045. Morrison, Joseph L.   "Editor for Sale--A World War II Case History."   43 Journalism Quarterly (1966), 34-42.
    On the situation in which The Living Age, with a history dat-
    ing to 1844, fell into the hands of an editor, Joseph Hilton Smyth,
    who was financed by the Japanese from July 1938 to August 1941, the
    Japanese Consulate in New York in 1937 starting the payments which
    made possible the purchase of the magazine (circulation 3,000) in
    June 1938, on condition that at least one pro-Japanese article ap-
    pear each month and that occasional pieces supplied by the Consul-
    ate be run.

1046. Nyerere, Julius K.   "Rhodesia in the Context of Southern Africa."   44 Foreign Affairs (1966), 373-386.

Presents the African arguments against the position that intervention is wrong and for the transfer of power to the African majority--an argument that mixes the idea of the majority, a matter of number, with that of skin color.

1047. Parker, Franklin D. The Central American Republics. New York: Oxford, 1964, pp. x, 348.
Excellent treatment of the political aspects of each of the Central American countries that provides basic information on the attempted coup d'état by President Picado and the Calderonistas who attempted to nullify the 1948 election and the subsequent uprising by José Figueres and his followers who, still later, were to resist invasions of Calderonistas from Guatemala despite abolition of standing military forces.

1048. Qubain, Fahim Issa. Crisis in Lebanon. Washington: Middle East Institute, 1961, pp. 243.
Detailed study of the background, domestic occurrences, and international aspects of the crisis in Lebanon in 1958 and United States intervention to try to still the reaction to what amounted to an attempted coup d'état by President Chamoun.

1049. Ramsey, P. "The Ethics of Intervention." 27 Revue of Politics (1965), 287-310.
Regards decisions to intervene politically or militarily as resting on understandings of politics that can be summarized in terms of the just war theory.

1050. Rodríguez, Mario. Central America. Englewood Cliffs: Prentice-Hall, 1965, pp. xi, 178.
Historical survey of Central America that deals with such international affairs as U.S. intervention, efforts to unite the area, Communist infiltration particularly in Guatemala, several facets of the Panama Canal Zone issue, and the attempted coup d'état and successful uprising of José Figueres and followers in Costa Rica during which President Alévaro of Guatemala supported the Ulate-Figueres group while Nicaragua and Honduras aided the Picado-Calderón-Communist coalition, the latter effort being followed by others from Nicaragua seeking to oust the National Liberation Party.

1051. Ronning, C. Neale. Intervention in Latin America. New York: Knopf, 1969, pp. 288.
On the politics and diplomacy of intervention in Latin America and the relations thereof with the evolution of the relevant portion of international law.

1052. Scott, Andrew M. The Revolution in Statecraft. New York: Random House, 1965, pp. 194.
Presents the history and varieties of informal penetration of states by superpowers competing indirectly with each other by means of direct concern with the Third World, the presentation including systematization of tools and concepts employed in the study of

informal penetration and hypotheses about the conditions and preconditions for successful informal penetration.

1053. Taylor, Phillip B. "The Guatemalan Affair: A Critique of United States Foreign Policy." 50 American Political Science Review (1956) 787-806.
    Analysis of U.S. policy toward Guatemala and the anti-Communist coup d'état of 1954.

1053-A. Van Ness, Peter. Revolution and Chinese Foreign Policy: Peking's Support for Wars of National Liberation. Berkeley: University of California Press, 1970, pp. 275.
    On the theory and practice of Communist China's support for wars of national liberation.

1054. Whitaker, A.P. "Cuba's Intervention in Venezuela: A Test of the OAS." 8 Orbis (1964), 511-536.
    Narrative of the 1963 Cuban intervention in Venezuela and the difficulties facing the OAS when Latin American opinion is divided. Both internal matters, as in Mexico, Brazil, and Chile, and geographical proximity appear to have been factors helping to divide the Latin American states into "hard-line" and "soft-line" blocs in the effort to impose sanctions.

1055. Zabih, Sepehr. The Communist Movement in Iran. Berkeley and Los Angeles: University of California Press, 1966, pp. vii, 279.
    A case study of the Communist doctrine of revolution in colonial and "semi-colonial" countries.

1056. Zasloff, J.J. The Role of the Sanctuary in Insurgency: Communist China's Support to the Vietminh, 1946-1954. RAND Memorandum RM-4618-PR. Santa Monica: RAND Corporation, May 1967, pp. 93.
    On the role of China as both sanctuary and provider of aid and psychological reinforcement during the Vietminh's struggle against the French.

1057. Zorgbibe, C. "De l'intervention à Saint-Domingue." 31 Politique étrangère (1966), 291-307.
    A view of the intervention in the Dominican Republic as both a unilateral intervention and a collective police action.

See also nos. 583, 611, 625, 658, 905, 960, 981, 995, 1004, 1010, 1013, 1020, 1252, 1329, 1821, 1849, 1851, 1965, 1971, 2057, 2236, 2266, 2501, 2674, 2714.

a. Irredentism

See nos. 1876, 2321, 2364, 2378, 2499.

7. Impact of National Modernization on
   International System Structure

1058. Cressey, George B. Soviet Potentials: A Geographic Appraisal.
Syracuse: Syracuse University Press, 1962, pp. xvii, 232.
   Analysis leads to the conclusion that the USSR probably lacks
the environmental potential to become the world's leading state.

1059. Hax, Karl. Japan: Wirtschaftsmacht des Fernen Ostens--Ein
Beitrag zur Analyse des wirtschaftlichen Wachstums. Cologne: Westdeutscher
Verlag, 1961, pp. 632.
   Massive study of the background, resources, and stages of
Japan's industrial advance that helped to extend the international
power structure to global proportions. Indeed, this growth of
Japan is probably the most important step in making major conflict
and war in the 20th century into something other than a European
struggle, possibly involving also the United States, whether fought
in Europe or in Asia.

1060. Hoffmann, Walther G. Das Wachstum der deutschen Wirtschaft
seit der Mitte des 19. Jahrhunderts. Berlin: Springer, 1966, pp. xxvi,
842.
   A study of the growth of the German economy which, after the
middle of the 19th century, by development within the German region altered the European balance of power through accretion to
Prussian strength.

1061. Lockwood, William Wirt. The Economic Development of Japan:
Growth and Structural Change, 1868-1938. Princeton: Princeton University
Press, 1954, pp. xv, 603.
   An important study of Japan's economic growth between the
Meiji Restoration and World War II and so of the internal changes
that altered the European balance-of-power system to make of it
a global system.

1062. Pletcher, David M. Rails, Mines, and Progress: Seven American
Promoters in Mexico, 1867-1911. Ithaca: Cornell University Press for the
American Historical Association, 1958, pp. 321.
   Study of the activities of seven American entrepreneurs in
Mexico, of the security of their investments, and of the effect
of economic development in producing that measure of social
progress that brings new leadership groups to the fore to upset
old land and class structures and thereby to render obsolete
policies of support of existing regimes that earlier were the
only route to investment and economic growth.

1063. Rosovsky, Henry. Capital Formation in Japan, 1868-1940. New
York: Free Press, 1961, pp. xiii, 358.
   Focuses on a major aspect of internal development in Japan
that contributed to Japan's capacity to bring change into the international system and to compel international law to seek for
broader than European foundations.

See also nos. 1162, 1922, 2724, and sec. VIII, D, 2.

E. INTERSYSTEM RELATIONS, CONFLICTS
    AND ADJUSTMENTS

1. Relations between States and International
    Organizations

1064. Anglin, Douglas G. "United States Opposition to Canadian Membership in the Pan American Union: A Canadian View." 15 International
Organization (1961), 1-20.
       Review of United States policies toward inclusion of Canada
       in the Pan American Union that concentrates on the period from
       1926 until after World War II.

1065. Erdman, Paul, and Rogge, Peter. Die Europäische Wirtschaftsgemeinschaft und die Drittländer. Basel: Kyklos, 1960, pp. xii, 337.
       Investigation of the relationship of the Common Market to
       third countries.

1066. Gajzágó, Olivér von. "Ungarns Stellung im COMECON." 8 Der
Donauraum (1963), 200-230.
       A view of Hungary's relations with COMECON.

1066-A. Granfil, Toma. "Yugoslavia and the EEC." 21 Review of International Affairs (Belgrade, April 5, 1970), 1-3.
       On the economic relations between Yugoslavia and the EEC as
       set forth in the agreement of March 19, 1970, that entered into
       force on May 1, 1970. The article also makes reference to Yugo-
       slavia's participation in the work of COMECON commissions, the
       joint working group with EFTA, and the Yugoslav-EEC Mixed Committee.

1067. Hoffmann, Stanley. Organisations internationales et pouvoirs
politiques des états. Paris: Colin, 1954, pp. 427.
       Examination of the impact of state sovereignty upon the rela-
       tions of the Concert of Europe, the League of Nations, and the United
       Nations.

1068. Maullin, R.L. The Colombia-IMF Disagreement of November-
December 1966: An Interpretation of Its Place in Colombian Politics. RAND
Report RM-5314-RC. Santa Monica: RAND Corporation, June 1967, pp. 61.
       Analyzes the interplay of politics and economics in Colombia
       by focusing on President Carlos Lleras Restrepo's handling of
       Colombia's foreign exchange crisis and his dealings with the In-
       ternational Monetary Fund in light of the internal conflict be-
       tween the classical, conservative political subsystem and the
       pragmatic, industrial segment of the political public. Disagree-
       ment with IMF is seen as exploited by the President to provide a
       route of escape from restraints and compromises ordinarily im-
       posed by party politicians.

1069. Morawiecki, Wojciech. "Institutional and Political Conditions of Participation of Socialist States in International Organizations: A Polish View." 22 International Organization (1968), 494-507.

Discusses the weighing of rights and advantages against the duties and disadvantages of membership in an international organization, membership policies, voting arrangements, and the reasons for the withdrawal of Poland and other Socialist countries from the World Bank, FAO, WHO, and UNESCO.

1070. Prieur, Raymond. Les relations internes et externes de la Communauté Européenne du Charbon et de l'Acier. Paris: Éditions Montchrestien, 1958, pp. 311.

Study of ECSC in terms of relations among constituent entities, between those entities and Community organs, and, perhaps most importantly, in terms of external relations of the Community.

1071. Reboud, Louis. Systèmes fiscaux et Marché Commun. Paris: Sirey, 1961, pp. iv, 374.

Analysis of the difficulties involved in attempting to bring diverse fiscal systems into harmony with each other and with the provisions of the Common Market treaty.

1072. Roussin, Marcel. Le Canada et le système interaméricain. Ottawa: Éditions de l'Université d'Ottawa, 1959, pp. ix, 285.

Well-documented study of Canada and the Inter-American system that finds United States opposition to be the chief reason for Canada's remaining outside the OAS.

1073. Zdziechowski, Stanislas. "The Impact of the Common Market on the Soviet Union." 2 Studies on the Soviet Union (1963), 50-59.

The Common Market's influence on Africa and Europe and Russia's failure to organize COMECON effectively. Russia fears the influence of the Common Market, and has almost no grounds to fight it.

See also nos. 713, 714, 744, 748, 752, 757, 768, 774, 777, 822, 828, 1356, 2451, 2690.

2. Interregional Relations

1074. Benoit, Emile. Europe at Sixes and Sevens. New York: Columbia University Press, 1961, pp. 275.

Deals with the relations between EEC and EFTA and the implications of these groupings for Europe and for the United States. The analysis is more pertinent to the problem of relations between groups of states than to relations between regional organizations.

1075. Gamson, William A., and Modigliani, Andréa. "Soviet Responses to Western Foreign Policy, 1946-53." Peace Research Society (International), Papers. Chicago Conference (1964). Vol. III (1965), pp. 47-78.

Deals with 31 major Soviet bloc actions in 1946-1953 when
"major" or "significant" in terms of the size of New York Times
headlines and treats Soviet actions as the dependent variable,
i.e., as responses to Western actions treated as the independent
variable, thereby producing a classification of Soviet actions as
either refractory or conciliatory. Western actions being scaled
as more or less average in conciliatory magnitude, the predictability of three Western belief systems was tested. One, a more
aggressive policy toward the Soviet Union, predicted well in confrontation periods. A second, a more accommodating policy toward
the Soviet Union, did well in nonconfrontation periods. A third,
a mix of firmness and flexibility, did poorly for both periods.
A commentator at the Chicago Conference, whose remarks are not
reproduced in a volume limited to papers themselves, demonstrated
that there was a consistent pattern in terms of sequence of conciliatory and refractory acts if a premise were reversed and
Western actions were treated as the dependent variable or response
and Soviet actions as the independent variable.

1075-A. Gamson, William A., and Modigliani, Andrea. Untangling the
Cold War: A Strategy for Testing Rival Theories. Boston: Little, Brown,
1971, pp. 222.
 A continuation of the preceding study to cover the New York
Times for 1946-1963 that compares various well-known competing
theories attempting to explain the Cold War with the authors'
data on interaction units, the overall success rates of prediction being used to evaluate the explanatory power of each theory.

1076. Heuss, Ernst. Wirtschaftsysteme und internationaler Handel.
Zürich: Polygraphischer Verlag, 1955.
 Treatise on economic theory dealing with problems of trade
between relatively free market economies and planned economies
that sees the bridge between systems, particularly the East-West
bridge, as the use of a foreign trade monopoly by the Western
economies.

1077. Lazarcik, Grégor. Le Commerce en matière agricole entre l'Europe de l'Ouest et l'Europe de l'Est. Paris: Rivière, 1959, pp. 278.
 Comparison of trade in agricultural commodities between East
and West Europe before and after World War II.

1078. Lerdau, Enrique. "The Impact of the EEC on Latin America's
Foreign Trade." 1 Economia Latinamericana (1963), 93-126.
 Thorough discussion, expressive of Latin American fears,
of the economic grounds for conflict between Latin America and
EEC and between Latin America and the Associated Overseas States
of Africa arising from EEC discrimination favoring the AOS and
from protection of less efficient producers of nontropical foodstuffs.

1079. Mikesell, Raymond Frech, and Behrman, Jack N. Financing Free
World Trade with the Sino-Soviet Bloc. Princeton: Princeton University
Press, 1958, pp. viii, 109.

Study of the financial and trading practices involved in trade with Communist countries, which is approached essentially on a bilateral basis.

1080. Pan American Union. The Effects of the European Economic Community on the Latin American Economies. Washington, 1963. Originally published for the First Annual Meeting of the Inter-American Economic and Social Council, with the classification: OEA/Ser. H/X, 3, Doc. 10, September 10, 1962.
Review of the unfavorable situation of Latin American trade and of the potentially serious effects of discrimination in favor of Associated Overseas States of Africa and their tropical foodstuffs, particularly if price and subsidy policies stimulating production of such crops were continued. The economic grounds for potential conflict between Latin America and the African AOS are clarified.

1081. Ramazani, Rouhollah K. The Middle East and the European Common Market. Charlottesville: The University Press of Virginia (1964), pp. xii, 152.
Study of a facet of international affairs that presents the paradoxical feature of disapproval of EEC by Arab states that have suffered least by and could gain much as a result of establishment of the Common Market and greater favor on the part of non-Arab states that have encountered some economic dislocation. The study looks at the various sectors of Middle Eastern economies, the impact of EEC and the potential impact of British entry, and Middle Eastern attitudes and policies, including the fear of Israeli collaboration with EEC.

1082. Rivkin, Arnold. Africa and the European Common Market: A Perspective. 2nd rev. ed. The Social Science Foundation and Department of International Relations, University of Denver. Monograph Series in World Affairs: Monograph No. 4, 1965-1966. Denver: 1966, pp. 65.
Analysis of the pattern of Eurafricanism after the Addis Ababa negotiations isolated Nkrumah's version of Pan-Africanism and tended to promote, instead, the idea of an "Africa of the Fatherlands," with discussion of the implications of the Nigeria-EEC agreement.

1083. Silcock, T.H. The Commonwealth Economy in Southeast Asia. Duke University Commonwealth-Studies Center. Publication No. 10. Durham: Duke University Press, 1959, pp. xvii, 259.
A view of an international economic system with emphasis upon one region of the Commonwealth and with consideration particularly in Chapter 4 of potential effects upon it in consequence of formation of EEC and EFTA.

1084. Simon, Maurice David. Communist System Interaction with the Developing States, 1954-1962: A Preliminary Analysis. Stanford Studies of the Communist System. Research Paper No. 10. Stanford University, January 1966, pp. 94.

Employing data on trade, economic and military aid, cultural relations, and treaties, the article traces the Communist patterns of interaction with developing states to find that (1) states clustering at the top of a composite scale were the smallest and least developed of the 26 countries examined, (2) high interaction with noncontiguous states, and (3) increases in interaction following difficulties between developing states and either the West or other developing states leaning toward the West. Another finding of potential methodological consequence is that only one state, Yemen, had a high economic interaction but low frequency of treaty engagements with Communist states. Otherwise, generally economic, military, and cultural interaction were about the same, thereby suggesting (a) that treaties are indicative of more than surface relations and (b) that systems may be susceptible to at least rough mapping by reference to the numbers of treaties between states.

1085. Stonham, P.E. "Intra-Regional Trade Co-operation in Developing Asia." 6 Journal of Common Market Studies (1967), 197-210.
On neglect of intra-regional trade possibilities by the developing countries of Asia and on the extra-regional ties through tariff preferences and other arrangements that tend to take precedence over intra-regional effort.

1086. Wilkinson, Joe R. Latin America and the European Economic Community: An Appraisal. Monograph No. 4, 1964-1965. The Social Science Foundation and Graduate School of International Studies, University of Denver, 1965, pp. 61.
On the threat to Latin America from EEC's preferential arrangements with the Associated Overseas States of Africa, protective tendencies regarding temperate zone agricultural commodities, and high tariffs on partially processed industrial raw materials and foodstuffs. Nationalistic obstacles to a coordinated regional response are indicated. Attention is also given to the development, beginning in 1961, of permanent channels of communication between EEC and OAS. In addition, the author notes a tendency of Latin Americans favoring a regional approach to economic problems to associate with the técnicos and of those favoring continuing stress on individual country effort to associate with the políticos.

See also nos. 559, 620, 826, 1073, 2145.

3. Relations between Public and Private Systems

1087. Bock, Edwin A. Representation of Non-Governmental Organizations at the United Nations. (Chicago): Public Administration Clearing House, 1955, pp. 43.
A study of interorganization relations in terms of relations between public and private organizations. This is about as close to a study of lobbying by private interests, comparable to such studies in regard to domestic legislatures, as has been made in regard to international organizations.

1088. Evan, William M. "Public and Private Legal Systems." In Evan (ed.), Law and Sociology. New York: Free Press, 1962, pp. 165-184.
Although Evan is concerned with the interaction of governmental and nongovernmental legal systems, he presents a model applicable to other cases of the interaction of two or more legal systems.

1089. Rohn, Peter H. Relations between the Council of Europe and Non-Governmental Organizations. Brussels: Union of International Organizations, 1957, pp. 79.
Careful study of the relations between the Council of Europe and organized European interests.

1090. Spencer, Daniel L. India, Mixed Enterprise and Western Business: Experiments in Controlled Change for Growth and Profit. The Hague: Nijhoff, 1959, pp. xi, 252.
Deals with problems of Western participation in India's mixed economy which entails the problem of differences between the relationships between foreign and domestic private sectors and those between the foreign private and domestic public sectors.

1091. Stošić, Borko D. Les organisations non-gouvernementales et les Nations Unies. Geneva: Droz, 1964, pp. 367.
An exposition of the relations between international nongovernmental organizations and the United Nations.

See also nos. 881, 1726, 2135, 2140, 2436, 2668, 2674, 2799.

4. Interactions of Social, Legal, Technological and Other Systems

1092. Azad, John. Der politische Faktor in den internationalen privaten Kapitalwanderungen. Geneva: Descombes, 1961.
An undertaking to identify the influences of both internal policies and external policies on international capital movements, of the investor upon policies, and of trends toward internationalization of domestic policies.

1093. Fridman, G.H.L. "Lawyers' Law and Politicians' Law." 26 Australian Quarterly (1954), 64-70.
Example of an overly rigid separation of lawyers and politicians while maintaining that the era of lawyers' law has passed. The author asserts that, in general, principles formulated by lawyers still govern and that scope remains for further development of those principles. Even so, the era of politicians' law is held to be with us in that the rules for conducting daily life now go beyond elementary moral principles, anthropomorphized in valid law. Today's statutes, rules, orders, and regulations are viewed as controlling activities formerly regarded as outside the purview of law. Their purpose is seen not as fulfilling underlying concepts of law but as canalizing into legal rules the political, economic, or social

prejudices that rest upon the philosophical concepts of one section
of the community. Although differing from those views that restrict
law's scope to secondary matters by omitting the question of scope
and creating a distinction between lawyers' law and politicians' law,
the article, besides displaying shallow and imprecise analysis, shows
little comprehension of the nature of law and of social and legal
evolution.

1094. Gardner, Lloyd C. Economic Aspects of New Deal Diplomacy.
Madison: University of Wisconsin Press, 1964, pp. xi, 409.
Review of New Deal diplomacy that highlights the relationship
between the economic and the political aspects of international
affairs.

1095. Nicolai, André. Comportement économique et structures sociales.
Paris: Presses Universitaires de France, 1960, pp. 322.
In this theoretical study of the relationship between economic
behavior and social structures, the author (1) examines the nature
of systems and coherent complexes of structures, (2) reconsiders
the significance of economic behavior, and (3) explains and seeks
to evaluate the dynamic union of structures and behavior. In doing
so, he treats economics as a broad discipline for the analysis of
dynamic social systems, maintained by individuals in groups as supports of the structures and perpetuated by conscious behavior in
connection with the satisfaction of wants. Economic fluctuations
are signals of tension and of structural transformation. The broad-
ness of Nicolai's theory permits its adaptation for use as a bridge
between, on the one hand, more exclusively economic literature and,
on the other, the literature on law and social systems, domestic
and international.

1096. Vandenbosch, Amry. "The Small States in International Politics." 26 Journal of Politics (1964), 293-312.
Treats the weakness of small states as an important element
accounting for their role in the development of international
law. Recent increase in the number of small states while the
number of large states has remained stable, together with opposition among the large states, is seen as having the effect of concentrating military power while diffusing political power. The
position of the small states is seen as aided also by nuclear
neutralization of Great Power threats and by politicization of
the office of the UN Secretary-General.

1097. von der Mehden, Fred R. "Southeast Asian Relations with Africa." 5 Asian Survey (1965), 341-349.
Provides basic information on the potential of political
relations and trade relations to differ greatly, e.g., the absence of Southeast Asian embassies in the white-dominated countries of southern Africa even though over half of Southeast
Asian trade with Africa is with those countries.

1098. Weiner, Myron. The Politics of Scarcity: Public Pressure and
Political Response in India. Chicago: University of Chicago Press, 1962,
pp. 251.

The book addresses itself to the effects on political processes of operating in a setting of economic scarcity. The same
question can be asked about international affairs and the norms
generated. Two routes of investigation might be travelled: (1)
investigating, on a regional or other basis potentially having
its own norms, the effects of differing levels of subsystem
wealth; (2) simulate such subsystems. For the lower economic
levels the investigation might lead to further understanding of
underdevelopment and of its norm-producing tendencies independent of cultural values of a more aesthetic and philosophical
nature.

See also nos. 129, 130, 524, 525, 808, 819, 820, 826, 828, 829, 1157,
1181, 1214, 1654, 1885, 2033, 2222, 2357, 2363, 2365, 2371, 2381, 2386,
2416, 2644, 2672, 2674.

5. International and Municipal Law

1099. Anderson, S.V. "Supranational Delegation Clauses in Scandinavian Constitutions." 18 Western Political Quarterly (1965), 840-847.
On the 1953 Danish and 1962 Norwegian constitutional changes
to permit delegation of expressly defined national authority to
supranational organizations, together with discussion of the more
flexible Finnish, Icelandic, and Swedish amending procedures that
make advance authorization of supranational delegation unnecessary
for these three countries.

1100. Blamont, E. "Le respect de la loi par les Parlements." 3
Informations constitutionnelles et parlementaries (Genève, 1953), 197-216.
In the course of discussion of parliamentary violations of
law, the author devotes some attention to the uncertainty as to
whether the modification of a treaty by Parliament is equivalent
to a denunciation, thereby calling attention to a complexity that
can only be dealt with by uniting nonlegal and legal reasoning
based upon the pertinent situation and upon probabilities concerning long-range effect and acceptance. Rephrased, the problem is whether and to what extent legislative authorities are
exempt from international regulation. This is a slight modification of Blamont's somewhat more comprehensive phrasing related
to violations of the several areas of law other than grand traditions or imprecise natural law which are hardly violable.

1101. Gaudet, Michel. "The Challenge of the Changing Institutions."
3 Common Market Law Review (1965), 143-157.
Particularly pertinent in that it raises (pp. 151-154) the
issue of inducing national institutions to act also as authorities of the European Communities in the execution of Community
law.

See also nos. 715, 1110, 1112, 1569, 1867.

a. International and European Community Law

1102. van Panhuys, Jonkheer H.F. "Conflicts Between the Law of the
European Communities and Other Rules of International Law." 3 Common Market Law Review (1965-66), 420-449.
    Cautious attempt to systematize the problems involved in
conflicts between Community law and general international law
that includes an undertaking to view the various conceivable
projects from the points of view of the "mandates" of the European judges and of the national judges of the member countries.

6. Interorganizational Relations and Conflicts

1103. Goodwin, Geoffrey L. "The Commonwealth and the United Nations."
19 International Organization (1965), 678-694.
    On the varied effects of thrusting some divisive Commonwealth
problems into the United Nations arena, thereby undermining the
old doctrine that intra-Commonwealth relations are different in
international law. The author suggests that another consequence
of the Commonwealth presence in the United Nations, even though
not as a unit, has been a strengthening of United Nations potential for mediation and conciliation.

1104. Heinrichs, Armin. Die auswärtigen Beziehungen der Europäischen
Gemeinschaft für Kohle und Stahl, insbesondere ihr Verhältnis zur OEEC.
Bonn: Bouvier, 1961.
    A study of the foreign relations of ECSC that, because of
its particular attention to the relations ECSC had with OEEC,
is in part a study in interorganizational relations.

1105. Socini, Roberto. Rapports de conflits entre organisations
européennes. Leiden: Sijthoff, 1960, pp. 168.
    A monograph dealing with the problem of coordination of the
activities and interests of the several Western European organizations and with the problem of conflict between and among the
organizations.

1106. Whetten, Laurence Lester. The Relations of the International
Atomic Energy Agency with Other International Organizations. Ph.D. Diss.
New York: New York University, 1963; Ann Arbor: University Microfilms,
Inc., Order No. 64-1789, pp. 390.
    On the relations of IAEA with the Specialized Agencies,
regional intergovernmental organizations, and nongovernmental
organizations.

1107. Wilcox, Francis O. "The Atlantic Community and the United Nations." 17 International Organization (1963), 683-708.
    UN impingement upon the Atlantic Community is examined in
light of the lack of organic relationships between the two.

1108. Wood, Bryce, and Morales, M. Minerva. "Latin America and the United Nations." 19 International Organization (1965), 714-727.

Deals with the Latin American states' insistence on their right to carry disputes to the United Nations in the event of unsatisfactory OAS action, particularly in the case of disputes with the United States, and with the opportunities presented by ECLA and UNESCO to discuss Latin American problems without the participation of the United States.

1109. Yalem, Ronald. Regionalism and World Order. Washington: Public Affairs Press, 1965, pp. 160.

Examines the relations between regional and universal international organizations and, finding that the trend is not in the direction of subordination of regional to universal organizations, suggests the possibility of a continuation of the present trend leading to a substitution of a struggle for power among regions for the struggle for power among states.

See also nos. 746, 752, 768, 774, 777, 809, 815, 829, 1439-A.

7. Internal Effects of International Commitments

1110. Aligwekwe, E. "The Cyprus Situation." 1 International Review of History and Political Science (1964), 60-80.

Review of the Cyprus situation that deals, among other things, with weaknesses set in the Cyprus constitution by incorporating international agreements into it.

1111. Baade, Hans W. Das Verhältnis von Parlament und Regierung im Bereich der auswärtigen Gewalt der Bundesrepublik Deutschland: Studien über den Einfluss der auswärtigen Beziehungen auf die innerstaatliche Vefassungsentwicklung. Hamburg: Hansischer Gildenverlag, Joachim Heitmann & Co, 1962, pp. 247.

Excellent study, employing both legal and political science approaches and techniques, of the impact of foreign affairs on the relations between executive and legislature in West Germany.

1112. Bahramy, A.A. La législation internationale du travail et son influence sur le droit iranien--Aspects internationaux du problème du développement économique et social. Geneva: Droz, 1963, pp. xi, 299.

The problem of economic development in Iran is examined in terms of the impact of international labor legislation on Iranian law. The book develops more fully in respect to one country what Haas has examined more broadly in respect to compliance and to the related problem of the authority of international organizations.

1113. Conséquences d'ordre interne de la participation de la Belgique aux organisations internationales. Par une commission d'étude interuniversitaire de l'Institut royal des relations internationales. The Hague: Nijhoff, 1964.

An examination of the principal powers of the Belgian state and of certain private and semi-public institutions to ascertain the competences lost and the influences gained as a result of Belgium's participation in international organizations.

1114. Deutsch, Karl W. "External Influences on the Internal Behavior of States." In R. Barry Farrell (ed.), Approaches to Comparative and International Politics. Evanston: Northwestern University Press, 1966, pp. 5-26.

Employs a rough model to illustrate linkages between national and international realms to show the basic communications channels permitting the environment to influence the domestic system and also to indicate the ways in which communications from outside the nation can be interrupted or can be prevented from having significant domestic effect even when received.

1115. Goriely, G. "Du lien entre l'évolution du sentiment national en Belgique et la position internationale du pays." Revue de l'Institut de sociologie (No. 1, 1954), 41-87.

Account of the relations between international and domestic affairs, particularly the relation of the 1920 alliance with France to the development of the Flemish national movement and the relation between the 1936 return to neutrality to development of the Walloon national movement. Although alliance and neutrality, each invoking its own particular set of international obligations, may relate more to the political then the legal arena, domestic effects are not unrelated to the nature of the obligations assumed. Perhaps a more important aspect of the article is that it deals with the causal relationship in the international-to-domestic direction rather than in the domestic-to-international direction.

1116. Matecki, Bronislaw Eugene. Establishment of the International Finance Corporation and United States Policy. New York: Praeger, 1957, pp. 194.

Influence of an international institution on American foreign economic policy.

See also nos. 2406, 2408, 2646.

8. External Effects of Domestic Commitments

See secs. III, C; V, B, 8; VI, A, 5, m.

9. Politicization

1117. Bagdikian, Ben H. "Washington Letter: The Morning Line." 1 Columbia Journalism Review (Fall 1962), 26-28.

This article deals with the capacity of the press to disturb the order of importance of issues and to create situations that receive official attention. An example is given of the thrusting of an issue on Secretary of State Rusk. Because of the capacity of the press to insert a political or a conflict element into a situation, the author concludes that, regardless of the extent of agreement of officials among themselves, the newspaper story removes initiative from specialists and forces a decision either by politicians or by men who have to take account of politics.

1118. Duclos, P. "La politification: trois exposés." 14 _Politique_ (1961), 23-72.

Politicization is treated as accession to a political condition characterized by the idea that social relations are transformed by the existence of a particular arrangement for cohesion. Concepts such as opinions, values, and juridical rules, as well as institutions and rulers, are essential elements of politicization. In nonpolitical societies social relations continue to be established and freely exercised in relations between members. International organization is regarded as a substitute for a political solution. Duclos' thesis gives a structural meaning to "political," a limitation it shares with Morton Kaplan's definition of a political system.

1119. Grimm, Friedrich. _Politische Justiz--Die Krankheit unserer Zeit_. Bonn: Scheur, 1953, pp. 184.

A German defense attorney's concern about politicization of justice, particularly in his own country, that has developed in recent decades. The concern about Germany reminds us of the international as well as the domestic strains that affect internal political justice, particularly in the more acute forms related (a) to postwar occupation of the defeated and its aftermath and (b) the aftermath of revolution and _coup d'état_.

1120. Khouri, F.J. "The Jordan River Controversy." 27 _Review of Politics_ (1965), 32-57.

Review of the controversy over uses of the Jordan River and the entanglement of the issue in Arab-Israeli political differences that prevents dealing with the matter as a technical problem.

1121. Kirchheimer, Otto. _Political Justice: The Use of Legal Procedure for Political Ends_. Princeton: Princeton University Press, 1961, pp. xiv, 452.

Power mechanisms functioning through courts in Western Europe and the United States are analyzed to ascertain their role in the development of modern nations. The organization of what is essentially a series of case studies deprives the volume of a measure of continuity. Even so, the analysis is useful, particularly since some of the cases are of consequence to international law.

1121-A. Lanyi, Anthony. "Political Aspects of Exchange-Rate Systems." Paper presented at the 66th Annual Meeting of the American Political Science Association. Los Angeles, September 8-12, 1970, pp. 19.

An examination of alternative exchange-rate systems that makes use of game theory, considers the implications of alternative systems on both integration of the political decision-making process and integration of markets, and the normative aspects in terms of whether integration is always a good thing from the point of view of the economic welfare of a particular country or region.

1122. Peretz, Don. "Development of the Jordan Valley Waters." 9 Middle East Journal (1955), 397-412.

Reviews three rival plans for the development of the Jordan Valley, and the course of negotiations that at the time of writing left the author with some hope that unified international development might result. The article is of particular interest in that in the spring of 1955 it apparently was possible to identify three technical matters as the remaining principal issues requiring resolution.

1123. Pye, Lucian W. Politics, Personality, and Nation-Building: Burma's Search for Identity. New Haven: Yale University Press, 1962, pp. xx, 307.

Examination of political, economic, and social problems of a new, underdeveloped state that includes, in a chapter entitled "The Sovereignty of Politics" a comparison of development under the British and with that after independence. The latter uncovered political and submerged economic concepts of enterprises and traditional views of agriculture that inhibited economic development and even produced declines. In an observation (pp. 91-92) relevant to motivations in many countries prompting nationalization of foreign enterprises, Pye notes that foreign firms are viewed as discrediting governments when they provide enclaves that more effectively maintain law and order than does a government.

1124. Röpke, W. "La dimension politique de la politique économique." 113 Revue de travaux de l'Académie des Sciences morales et politiques (1960), 221-232.

Commentary on the task of economists to defend economic logic in a perilous situation characterized by an unprecedented politicization of economics.

1125. Schlesinger, James A. "Systems Analysis and the Political Process." 11 Journal of Law and Economics (1968), 281-298.

Although restricting its meaning of systems analysis to the set of analytical procedures that feature cost-benefit calculations, this paper is useful for the attention it gives to the quality of the information base, methodology, bias, and the impact of highly politicized environments on analytical efforts and analytical results.

See also nos. 543, 774, 828, 1743, 1744, 1746, 2137, 2138, 2644.

III.   INTERNATIONAL SOCIETAL DEVELOPMENT

A.   GROWTH, COMPLEXITY, AND INTERDEPENDENCE

1.   "Family of Nations" Doctrine

1126.   Hurewitz, J.C.   "Ottoman Diplomacy and the European State System."   15 Middle East Journal (1961), 141-152.
Part of a larger research project, this exploratory inquiry deals with the major lines of development whereby the Ottoman Empire became the first non-Christian state to participate in the European state system. The grounds of the original diplomatic actions--nonreciprocation by the Sultan and discussions on home grounds in the Turkish language--are outlined. The evolution of unilateralism into the reciprocal system adopted at the start of the 19th century, although not adopting French as the principal language of communication until after the Crimean War, is traced and related to the contraction of the empire. While the process of Ottoman inclusion in the European system--ultimately leading to Ataturk's policy of deliberately Europeanizing--manifests some similarities to the conduct of today's new states--e.g., pride in language--the circumstances, including the Ottoman presence in Europe and its early power status vis-à-vis Europe, give the Ottoman inclusion in the European regional system a quite different impact upon system evolution than the inclusion of former colonies in the global system of the 20th century, despite the European roots of the global system.

1127.   Meng, S.M.   The Tsungli Yamen: Its Organization and Functions. Cambridge: East Asian Research Center, Harvard University, 1962, pp. v, 146.
Somewhat less thorough than Banno's study (infra, no. 1965), this volume deals with the organization, operation, and influence of the Tsungli Yamen from its formation until it was replaced in 1901. The volume thus adds to our knowledge of China's early efforts to adapt to and maintain its identity and values in a world dominated by Europe and European international norms.

See also nos. 556, 1965, 2689.

2.   Evolution of International Society; System-Level Change

1128.   Alker, Hayward R., Jr.   "Dimensions of Conflict in the General Assembly."   58 American Political Science Review (1964), 642-657.

Factor analysis of roll-call votes from the 16th General
Assembly Session (1961-62) that finds nine factors underlying
83% of the total voting variance. The author suggests that important changes in the international system are ascertainable
from changing factor loadings of particular issues and regression coefficients for variables influencing conflict alignments.

1129. Allen, George Cyril, and Donnithorne, Audrey Gladys. Western
Enterprise in Far Eastern Economic Development: China and Japan. New York:
Macmillan for the International Secretariat, Institute of Pacific Relations,
1954, pp. 291.
    Impact of Western trade and business upon China and Japan
and of their differing responses. The study provides data that
should be studied along with that in Norman Jacobs' examination
of differing responses of the two countries in regard to the
formation of a capitalist society (infra, no. 1149).

1130. Berrien, F. Kenneth. General and Social Systems. New Brunswick: Rutgers University Press, 1969, pp. vii, 231.
    An application of general systems theory to problems in so-
cial psychology, based on the evolutionary concept, applicable
to the chemical evolution of the universe, biological evolution,
and social evolution, that primitive randomness evolves into
organized complexity.

1131. Bloomfield, Lincoln P. Evolution or Revolution? Cambridge:
Harvard University Press, 1957, pp. 220.
    Includes, particularly in Chapter 5, consideration of the
nature of peaceful change.

1132. Blumer, Herbert. "The Idea of Social Development." 2 Studies
in Comparative International Development (St. Louis: Social Science Institute, Washington University, 1966), 3-11.
    Critique of contemporary sociological approaches to social
development that distinguishes the generic process that may take
place in any society, culture, or institution from the restricted
meaning of bringing underdeveloped nations abreast of the advanced nations of the current moment in time. In terms of the
latter, sociologists are criticized for failing to formulate criteria of modernization, for assuming that what happened in an
earlier day in the West is relevant to the present, and for assuming that unrelated comparative studies will automatically produce a body of generic knowledge on social development. Similar
considerations are valid in respect to the possibilities for international societal development which is too easily and too often visualized as development toward some form of present-day
organization, e.g., a federation.

1132-A. Cobb, Roger, and Elder, Charles. International Community:
Regional and Global Study. New York: Holt, Rinehart and Winston, 1970,
pp. 160.
    Review of integration theory and its antecedents and a test-
ing of hypotheses found in integration theory by examination of

(1) public opinion polls on attitudes toward other countries, (2) transactional exchange derived from data on international trade, mail, student exchange, telephone calls, and telegrams, and (3) treaty arrangements.

1133. Dinerstein, Herbert S. "The Transformation of Alliance Systems." 59 American Political Science Review (1965), 589-601.

An historical-analytical examination of alliances that examines the differences among alliance types of three periods, namely, pre-1914, 1919-1939, and post-1945. The greater part of the essay is devoted to the post-1945 alliances and differences between the Western and Communist alliance systems. Transformation is dealt with in terms other than those of process. Primary reference is to environmental and situational factors related to alliances in the three periods under consideration.

1134. Friedrich, Carl J. "Political Pathology." 37 Political Quarterly (1966), 70-85.

On the possibilities that corruption, secrecy, betrayal and treason, violence, and propaganda may play an organic, e.g., interdependent, role in the body politic. When not at pathological levels that are dysfunctional and perhaps threaten the existence of the political system, corruption, secrecy, etc., may be important factors in conflict resolution. They may aid the adaptation of formal rigid structures to evolving communal values and permit bargaining and decision-making that assists manipulation of highly dynamic situations.

1135. Lamer, Mirko. The World Fertilizer Economy. Stanford: Stanford University Press, 1957, pp. xvi, 715.

Extensive examination focusing on the changes that began during World War II as a result of employment of different forms of commercial fertilizers and of resort to different uses of such fertilizers. The study is a useful reminder of the ways in which changes introduced in one area of human activity can have widespread systemic effects.

1136. Landheer, Bart. On the Sociology of International Law and International Society. The Hague: Nijhoff, 1966, pp. ix, 118.

Attempts a distinction between the coercive political society represented by the national state of the 19th century and a world society which is an industrial, structured, complex, noncoercive society, yet to be established on the international level and yet seen as the only route out of the power mentality that produces a gap between an international law based on 19th century political concepts and analogies and the social reality now emerging in mid-20th century but only in an early, unevenly evolved form.

1137. Landheer, Bart. "The Image of World Society and the Function of Armaments." Peace Research Society (International), Papers. Ghent Conference, 1964. Vol. II (1965), pp. 232-241. Also in 1 Journal of Peace Research (1964), 232-241.

On the incompatibility of the image of world society as having essentially national and global levels, the need to establish a complex, multilevel superstructure if a complex world society is to achieve functionality, and the desirability of institutionalizing bloc organization and policies expressing the international hierarchy rather than the ideal of a hundred self-determining states. The author sees the evolutionary process as one of growth rather than of exclusively purposive development and calls attention to both the need for the West to accept historical processes of social evolution in other parts of the world and for industrial societies to think in terms of restraints rather than exclusively in terms of expansion, including expansion of production.

1138. Landheer, Bart. "The Sociological Approach to International Problems." 6 Higher Education and Research in the Netherlands (Summer, 1962), 3-14.

In an address given on the occasion of his inauguration as a part-time professor at the University of Groningen, the author calls for new modes of thinking about international affairs and world society that would entail a growth of individual consciousness rather than emphasis on the state. Treating social evolution as identical with the growth of consciousness, a number of needs are identified, e.g., emphasis on growth rather than development which is seen as produced from outside, more emphasis on permanence and continuity and less upon technical and economic change.

1139. Liska, George. "Continuity and Change in International Systems." 16 World Politics (1963), 118-136.

Search for structural continuities that exist independently of ideological flux and changes in weaponry. Cf. Ruiz Moreno, supra, no. 188.

1140. Lucifero, Roberto. Il ritorno di Cristoforo Colombo. Roma: Tipografia del Senato, 1949.

A remarkable speech to the effect that a process is taking place that consists in the overcoming of the national state, which is not a constant factor in history but only a phase in the evolution of international organization. Today this phase is being overcome in order to enter into a wider system based not on nationality but on a kind of common civilization. Lucifero saw two such systems in existence, an Eastern system already constituted and a Western system, composed of the democracies of Western Europe and America, in the process of formation. The approach is intuitive but the conceptualization is one that warrants serious consideration when trying to develop frameworks for the ordering of empirical data concerning international institutional growth, regional societal development, and identification of the characteristics of inter-nation systems.

1141. Maslow, Abraham H. "A Theory of Human Motivation." In Philip Lawrence Harriman (ed.), Twentieth Century Psychology: Recent Developments in Psychology. New York: Philosophical Library, 1946, pp. 22-48.

Offers five basic goals or needs (physiological comforts, safety, love, esteem, and self-actualization) that are conceived as existing in a hierarchy of prepotency in which the most prepotent dominates until fairly well satisfied, then the second most prepotent, and so on. At lower political status positions physiological needs dominate. Only with an upward movement in status do citizens realize the importance of their political system as a fulfiller of demands for material comforts. Its significance in this regard may later diminish if the impetus to esteem or affection takes on a different dimension and arises from demands for citizenship and participation. Maslow's exposition does not extend to the international system and, therefore, does not get at this aspect of the loyalty problem. Yet there is need for even quantitative data on the individual's dependence on the international system and on the extent of his awareness thereof, if not yet affection and esteem.

1142. Ong, Walter J. "Nationalism and Darwin: A Psychological Problem in our Concept of Social Development." 22 Review of Politics (1960), 466-481.
Open structure models of evolution (e.g., pairing and branching structures; interlacing and bushing structures) have replaced the cyclic version of evolution. Hence, the author argues that nations should be conceived as open to one another not so much by concession as by their very nature.

1143. Platt, John R. "Social Chain Reactions." 17 Bulletin of Atomic Scientists (1961), 365-369.
Changes in social institutions can be produced by an individual who amplifies his intelligence by a social change reaction that entails an exponential increase in the reaction initiated by the new idea. Emphasis is placed on "feedback tokens," among them money, as reinforcement to people along the chain. So, too, is the use of beneficial runaway chains to combat malignant runaway chains. This last concept is related to belligerency among nations and to a suggestion that reduction in international tension may require a party structure in the chain to convert international tension into party tension. This leads into a recommendation on reforming the system of choosing representatives to the U.N. General Assembly. The important point of the article is less the recommendation, which may be treated as only an illustration, than the relation of organization to law not directly as in an Austinian arrangement related to legislation and enforcement but indirectly in terms of linkage between actual socioeconomic substructure and institutions established by internation negotiations.

1144. Russett, Bruce M. Trends in World Politics. New York: Macmillan; London: Collier-Macmillan, 1965, pp. 156.
A concise attempt to ascertain trends through rough measures and, where in order, to project to 1975. Attention is upon trends within the North Atlantic community, in UN politics, and in world inequality. Explanation of trends in UN voting is in terms of international cross-pressures. An attempt is made

to identify broad aspects of political consequences of economic and social change. Measures employed include GNP, direction of trade, tourism, and letter mail, speeches and votes in the General Assembly, inhabitants per hospital bed, adult literacy, radios, government revenues, and population distribution including urban population. Far from all the conclusions rest upon hard data, and the volume's value depends upon recognition of the role of intuition and preconception in the interpretation of the data presented.

1145. Vickers, G. "Is Adaptability Enough?" 4 Behavioral Science (1959), 219-234.
    A conceptual model of the adaptation of a system, pointing out the essential features of adaptation, helps in our understanding of the problems of rapid industrialization. The author investigates the role of regulatory machinery in countering disruption in the form either of a breakdown in the system or of an impoverishment or change in the value system.

1146. Waskow, Arthur I. Quis Custodiet? Controlling the Police in a Disarmed World. 2 vols. A Peace Research Institute Report Submitted under ACDA Grant ACDA/IR-8. Washington: Peace Research Institute, Inc., 1963.
    On the problem of disarmament and subsequent control of international forces that includes discussion of the potential situation in which disarmament would occur in the absence of sufficient political consensus to establish control of a "world army" by international political institutions. A proposal is then made for a police force of small size but capable of escalating responses to violations of a disarmament agreement, e.g., graduated deterrence, while also offering opportunities for peaceful pursuit of national interests. One assumption related to the size of the deterrent force is the more international consensus that came into being, the greater the force that could be used. Included in these volumes are collaborative studies by Lincoln P. Bloomfield and others.

1147. Worsley, P.M. "Millenarian Movements in Melanesia." Rhodes-Livingstone Institute (1957), 18-31.
    Description of movements that break down existing social systems.

See also nos. 527, 631, 715, 749, 788, 1237, 1501, 1654, 1759, 1842, 1884, 1922, 2689.

a. Stages and Processes

1148. Jackson, Merrill. A Study of the Evolution of Social Control: The Organization, Theory and Practice of Jurisprudence and Medicine. Preprint 99. Ann Arbor: Mental Health Research Institute, The University of Michigan, July 1962, pp. ix, 195.

A study of the development of juridical and medical organization, differentiation, theory, and practice in 24 societies falling in five ranges, namely, band, tribe, chiefdom, primitive state, and archaic state. The theory on which the study proceeded holds that greater social structural complexity creates problems demanding increased juridical and medical effectiveness, with juridical and medical agencies becoming more complex internally and more specialized with relation to each other. In general, the several hypotheses tested through a judgment and scaling procedure followed by appropriate statistical analysis were confirmed. In certain instances there was confirmation only if the band were excluded, since a lack of statuses prevented resort to lowering of status as a sanction, while economic necessity or lack of institutions prevented punishments that rendered an individual's presence a liability. One tribe, the Kikuyu, ranked above a chiefdom, the Siuai, to suggest that higher tribes may be better integrated and structurally more complex than lower chiefdoms. Not unrelated to the problem of liability without fault, it was noticeable that above the band, where the problem of fault could not be adequately taken into account, the more complex the society the greater the tendency to judicially assign individual responsibility without concern for intent. In jurisprudence the intentionality mode is established, while later medicine, perhaps in reaction to the juridical approach to deviance, develops an unintentionality mode. Besides a careful elaboration of his procedures with warnings as to pitfalls, the author suggests several complementary projects for future research.

1149. Jacobs, Norman. The Origin of Modern Capitalism and East Asia. Hong Kong: Hong Kong University Press, 1958, pp. 243.
A suggestive comparative sociological approach in an effort to ascertain why Japan but not China became a modern industrial society. It is not inconceivable that partnership capacity in a system may be related to receptivity or capacity to absorb capitalistic forms and that lack of absorptive capacity in respect to capitalism may explain the efforts of some states since 1917 to skip the capitalist stage of evolution on the Marxian single-track continuum.

1150. Nagel, Stuart S. "Culture Patterns and Judicial Systems." 16 Vanderbilt Law Review (1962), 147-157.
A statistical analysis of the judicial systems of ten societies: Ashanti, Cheyenne, Eskimo, Ifugao, Trobriand, United States, pre-Communist China, pre-Nasser Egypt, French Fourth Republic, Soviet Union. Attention is given to such salient societal characteristics as whether a country was manufacturing or nonmanufacturing, democratic or dictatorial, and collectivist or individualist.

1151. Organski, A.F.K. The Stages of Political Development. New York: Knopf, 1965, pp. xiii, 229.
Sees nation-building as entailing four stages of political development: (1) the politics of primitive unification; (2)

the politics of industrialization; (3) the politics of national welfare; (4) the politics of abundance, linked to automation. Each of the first three stages is discussed and illustrated by what has happened in countries that have industrialized or are industrializing, while the fourth stage is dealt with on the basis of provocative speculation.

1152. Schwartz, Richard D., and Miller, James C. "Legal Evolution and Societal Complexity." 70 American Journal of Sociology (1964), 159-169.

Examines the relationship between the institutions of mediation, police, and counsel and the degree of societal complexity in 51 societies. Establishes mediation-police-damages as apparent sequence of development in harmony with the folk-urban continuum set by Durkheim that represents a society's increasing complexity. Questions are raised about international legal evolution and note is taken of such differences between domestic and international society as the presence or absence of a common interest against a hostile environment and of a multiplicity of units from which to borrow for survival purposes.

1153. Service, Elman R. Primitive Social Organization: An Evolutionary Perspective. New York: Random House, 1962, pp. xii, 211.

An undertaking to relate rules, social structure, and statuses to successive levels of social organizations, namely, primate sociality, bands, tribes, and chiefdoms.

b. Positive Feedback

1154. Dechert, Charles R. "Positive Feedback in Political and International Systems." 9 American Behavioral Scientist (March 1966), 8-14.

Reviews basic concepts relevant to systems analysis, develops a meaning of "mutual causal processes" in terms of negative and positive feedback, and indicates some of the consequences of positive feedback, both beneficial and detrimental. A special effort is made to indicate types of positive feedback that may lead to a true world community and a more fully agreed-upon ius gentium. An important position of the author is that it is the philosophers of history who have done the most to identify major recurrent processes akin to deviation-amplifying mutual causal processes.

1155. Maruyama, Magoroh. "The Second Cybernetics: Deviation-Amplifying Mutual Causal Processes." 51 American Scientist (1963), 164-179.

Noting that what he calls the "first cybernetics" concerns itself with self-regulating and equilibrating systems, i.e., with deviation-compensating mechanisms or negative feedback loops, the author calls for more attention to the "second cybernetics," i.e., deviation-amplifying mechanisms or positive feedback loops. Deviation-amplifying mechanisms are viewed as violating the law of causality in that a small "initial kick" can

change the course of events. They also appear to violate the
second law of thermodynamics since inhomogeneities accumulate.
Interactions produce networks of loops, some positive and some
negative. The author derives a rule that a loop with an even
number of negative influences in deviation-amplifying while one
with an odd-number of negative influenced is deviation-counter-
acting.

1156. Wender, Paul H. "Vicious and Virtuous Circles: The Role of
Deviation-Amplifying Feedback in the Origin and Perpetuation of Behavior."
31 Psychiatry (1968), 309-324.
    The concept of deviation-amplifying, i.e., positive, feed-
back is treated as having greater explanatory usefulness than
simple unidirectional cause, particularly since an initial impetus may be trivial and easily forgotten. This leads the author to suggest that in relation to conflicts it is more important to focus on what is going on than on who started it. The
author suggests that a stabilization process intermingling positive and negative feedback renders behavior induced by deviation-
amplifying feedback exceedingly difficult to change.

See also no. 1603, 1842.

c. Impact of Science and Technology

1157. Allen, Francis R., Hart, Hornell, Miller, Delbert C., Ogburn,
William F., and Nimkoff, Meyer. Technology and Social Change. New York:
Appleton-Century-Crofts, 1957, pp. 529.
    Deals with acceleration in technology and cultural lag, a
theme that permits Ogburn to define the world crisis as the
strain between two correlated parts of a culture that change at
unequal rates and Hart and Allen to deal with the problem in
terms of contact between nations of differing cultural and technological states.

1158. Braunias, Karl, and Meraviglia, Peter (eds.). Die modernen
Wissenschaften und die Aufgaben der Diplomatie (Les Sciences modernes et
les taches de la diplomatie; Modern Science and the Tasks of Diplomacy).
Beiträge aus dem Internationalen Diplomatenseminar Klessheim. Graz:
Styria Verlag, 1963, pp. 238.
    A collection of papers presented at the 1962 session of a
seminar at Klessheim. The papers, most of them superficial, at-
tempt to examine the problems confronting diplomacy as a result
of scientific advances. Some of the more interesting papers are
the following: F. Asinger, "Der heutige Stand der technischen
Chemie und die neuen Aufgaben der Diplomatie"; Donald Darnley
Reid, "Medicine, Population and the New Tasks of Diplomacy"; B.R.
Sen, "Food and Population"; Sigvard Eklund, "The Supply of Energy
in the Future"; David A. Davies, "Geophysics and Its Impact on
International Affairs"; Marcel Golay, "La recherche spatiale et
la collaboration européenne"; John Goormaghtigh, "Les sciences
sociales et les relations internationales."

1159. Cottrell, Fred. <u>Energy and Society: The Relation Between Energy, Social Change, and Economic Development</u>. New York: McGraw-Hill, 1955, pp. xix, 330.

Examination of the impacts on society and on international affairs of development and use of energy forms from wind, water, and human being to nuclear energy.

1160. Fourastié, Jean, and Laleuf, André. <u>Révolution à l'Ouest</u>. Paris: Presses Universitaires de France, 1957, pp. 285.

Analysis of human causes and consequences of economic and technical progress as revealed in reports of about 500 French professional and technical productivity missions to the United States in 1949-1957. Technical progress is seen as the determinant factor in social progress. France is viewed as being in an intermediate stage between societies like Great Britain and the United States (so technically advanced as to show an almost total decline of traditional civilization) and underdeveloped countries.

1161. Haas, Ernst B. "Toward Controlling International Change--A Personal Plea." 17 <u>World Politics</u> (1964), 1-12.

Concerned about the unchecked rate of scientific and technological innovation, about the potential for cumulative, systematic, and destabilizing change in coming years, and about dictation of the rate of innovation by values and motives that run behind socioeconomic development, the author proposes that an arrangement be made under the United Nations for the discussion of desirable innovations, consideration of their likely impact on the international system, and establishment of priorities.

1161-A. Miller, Arthur Selwyn. "Science Challenges Law: Some Interactions Between Scientific and Legal Changes." 13 <u>American Behavioral Scientist</u> (1970), 585-593.

On the subordination of law and lawyers to the furtherance of scientific and technological change as ends in themselves, without regard to consequences, and with disregard of humanistic values. This article is part of a special issue on "Law and Social Change" edited by Stuart S. Nagel.

1162. Somers, J.C. "Impact of Technology on International Trade." 21 <u>American Journal of Economics and Sociology</u> (1962), 69-76.

This article sets forth the economic framework of several technological developments and the corresponding results in the area of international business, working on the assumption that industrial development creates more foreign commerce and becomes more and more industrial up to some critical point. Attention is given to the impact of the Benelux customs union of 1948, the addition of France, West Germany and Italy in 1952, and the creation of the Atomic Energy Commission in fields of technological adaptation, marketing, and development. Somers states that because the relative volume of export and import depends on a country's internal development, growth, and production, technology is significant because it creates opportunity and is an avenue to wealth.

See also nos. 129, 130, 136, 138, 151, 483, 1559, 2381, 2785.

d. International Socialization

1163. Alger, Chadwick F. "Participation in the United Nations as a Learning Experience." 27 Public Opinion Quarterly (1963), 411-426.
Delegates were interviewed before and after a General Assembly session to determine the socialization effects. Attitudes generally changed in the direction of a greater and more significant acceptance of UN processes and purposes.

1164. Alger, Chadwick F. "Personal Contact in International Organizations." In Herbert C. Kelman (ed.), International Behavior: A Social-Psychological Approach. New York: Holt, Rinehart and Winston, 1965, pp. 523-547.
Employs material from interviews and from personal observations at the United Nations to indicate the impact of more frequent contacts and communications and of the performance of nonnational roles on the conduct of international affairs, with some contrasts made with more traditional diplomatic processes.

1165. Cory, Robert H., Jr. "Images of United States Disarmament Negotiating System." 1 Journal of Arms Control (1963), 654-662.
Employing confidential interviews with individual diplomats and informal group discussions, the author obtained information that is known to persons familiar with United Nations workings and published it in this article. In respect to images of United States disarmament policy, Soviet bloc delegates were best informed and their private views were on a sophisticated level that sharply contrasts with the oversimplified stereotype they employ for public presentation. Representatives of the eight "new" nations at the Disarmament Conference were not so well informed and suffered from inadequate depth of their staffs. Diplomats of nations active only at the UN level were poorly supplied with technical advice. They viewed both the Soviet Union and the United States as giants, each with capacities endangering civilization.

1166. Debrun, Michel. "Nationalisme et politiques du développement au Brésil." Sociologie du travail (No. 3, July-September 1964), 235-257.
Among other things, gives attention to the role of the técnicos whose efforts toward development include promotion of economic integration and who, perhaps, come closest of any Latin American group to forming a transnational elite holding similar values.

1167. Greenstein, Fred I. Children and Politics. New Haven: Yale University Press, 1965, pp. viii, 199.

Employing a sample of New Haven children between the ages
of nine and thirteen in an effort to ascertain what political
ideas children hold, from whom the ideas come, variance between
boys and girls and between upper and lower socioeconomic classes, and the relation of children's political development to their
later participation, this study suggests an approach by which to
ascertain the extent to which norms of international accommodation enter into the political socialization processes of various
countries, as contrasted with or in mitigation of conflict-laden
ideas. In other words, studies of this type can help to map the
early underpinning of ideas and subsequent overlays related to
the degree of support accorded international law by elites and
by publics.

1168. Murphy, Roy E., Jr. Adaptive Processes in Economic Systems.
New York: Academic Press, 1965, pp. xvi, 209.
Discussion of conditions under which the adaptive process
always improves the behavior of decision-makers, what controls
the rate of improvement of behavior, and whether the adaptive
process can explain diversity in the observed behavior of supposedly rational decision-makers without appeal to the existence of individual utility functions.

3. Integration Processes

1169. Binkley, Robert C. Realism and Nationalism, 1852-1871. New
York: Harper, 1935, pp. xx, 337; reprinted 1963, pp. xvi, 338.
Contains a significant but neglected discussion of attempts
at international integration and federalism in Europe, utilizing
a concept of "federative polity."

1170. Collins, Doreen. "Towards a European Social Policy." 5 Journal
of Common Market Studies (1966), 26-48.
On the development of the various aspects of social policy
under the Treaty of Rome and the problem of harmonization of
relevant laws.

1171. Deutsch, Karl W. Political Community at the International
Level. Garden City: Doubleday, 1954, pp. x, 70.
A model of the integration process, including both conceptual
and operational definitions. Defines "community" in terms of mea-
surable transactions.

1172. Deutsch, Karl W., Edinger, Lewis J., Macridis, Roy W., and Merritt, Richard L. France, Germany, and the Western Alliance: A Study of
Elite Attitudes on European Integration and World Politics. New York:
Charles Scribner's Sons, 1967, pp. xi, 324.
Analysis of public opinion surveys from 1954 to 1963 and of
interviews of French and German elites conducted in 1964, together with a systematic content analysis of the postwar press
in four countries, that examines, among other things, trends in

French and West German domestic politics that affect foreign policy, trends in the West European integration movement, and the
relation of Western alliance policies to French and West German
attitudes concerning arms control and disarmament.

1173. Deutsch, Karl W., et. al. Political Community and the North
Atlantic Area. Princeton: Princeton University Press, 1957, pp. xiii,
228.
        The process of international integration as evidenced by a
series of historical case studies within the North Atlantic area.

1174. Etzioni, Amitai. "A Paradigm for the Study of Political Unification." 15 World Politics (1962), 44-74.
        A groping for common terms and concepts to cover future in-
vestigations of international integration. In revised and expanded form, the article constitutes Chapters 1 and 2 of the author's Political Unification (q.v.).

1175. Etzioni, Amitai. Political Unification: A Comparative Study
of Leaders and Forces. New York: Holt, Rinehart and Winston, 1965, pp.
xx, 346.
        Important study of the process of political unification with
reference to international organizations (monofunctional and mul-
tifunctional), blocs, empires, and political communities (states).
The discussion proceeds in terms of properties of the preunifica-
tion state; integrating power and integrated sectors in the unification process, and the termination state or leveling off period,
the last occurring before additional unification or regression sets
in, that allow classification of unions. Four unions are analyzed:
the United Arab Republic, the Federation of the West Indies, the
Nordic Council, and EEC.

1176. Etzioni, Amitai. "The Epigenesis of Political Communities at
the International Level." 68 American Journal of Sociology (1963), 407-
421.
        "Epigenesis" deals with the formation of units that acquire
functions not previously serviced by the unit--in other words,
what Ernst B. Haas has denoted as "task-expansion." Epigenesis
(accumulation) models are concerned with inputs from and articulation with external units. The concept has relevance for international relations, which itself has gradually become more amenable to sociological analysis. In juxtaposition to epigenesis
the author places "preformism," i.e., the assumption that the
"primitive" social unit contains in embryonic form all the basic
models of social relations that later become structurally differentiated. Etzioni treats social units and their change as
multilayer phenomena, including at least a performance, a power
(or control), and a communication layer. Attention is also given
to the role of coercion in successful integration.

1177. Feldstein, Helen S. "A Study of Transaction and Political Integration: Transactional Labour Flow Within the European Economic Community." 6 Journal of Common Market Studies (1967), 24-55.

Deals with EEC policy on worker mobility, migration of workers within the Common Market in 1956-1965, assimilation problems in terms of the development of social communication and perception of Community ties vis-à-vis labor from outside the Community, and responsiveness at the Community level.

1178. Gamson, William A., and Modigliani, Andrea. "Tension and Concessions: The Empirical Confirmation of Belief Systems About Soviet Behavior." 11 Social Problems (1963), 34-48.
The authors discuss some of the conceptual and methodological problems that they have encountered in the search for empirical assumptions underlying different belief systems (a term they prefer to "theories" of international relations). Tension is defined as a social system property which may be but is not necessarily correlated with the anxiety felt by members of the system. It is the ratio of disintegrative forces to integrative ties existing between two nations or blocs of nations at any given point in time. An increase in integrative ties will lower tension more in a system where tension is high and existing integrative ties are few. Manifestations of integrative ties are found in institutional form: (1) mechanisms for the handling and resolution of disagreement, e.g., UN General Assembly, Security Council, World Court, Summit Conferences; (2) mechanisms for the implementation of common goals: economic, political, military, educational, social and cultural, e.g., UNESCO.

1179. Gregg, Robert W. "The U.N. Regional Economic Commissions and Integration in the Underdeveloped Regions." 20 International Organization (1966), 208-232.
Treats the Economic Commission for Europe as having the task of preventing the collapse of an earlier community and that of the Economic Commissions for Asia and the Far East, Latin America, and Africa as the development of a sense of community. An attempt is made to rate the effectiveness of each of the three commissions for the underdeveloped regions.

1180. Haas, Ernst B. "International Integration, the European and the Universal Process." 15 International Organization (1961), 366-392.
European integration compared with attempts at integration in other regional groupings.

1181. Haas, Ernst B., and Schmitter, Phillippe C. "Economics and Differential Patterns of Political Integration: Projections About Unity in Latin America." 18 International Organization (1964), 705-736.
Treating the relationship between economic and political union as a continuum in which each attempt at economic integration has political consequences of a functional nature resting on "dialectical relations between antagonistic purposes," the authors analyze the Latin American Free Trade Association through the use of pattern variables. Automatism is a concept underlying the analysis, that is, high-scoring economic units are visualized as transformed into political units even against their will. LAFTA is seen as either likely to stagnate by remaining within

the free trade organization framework or, with the impetus of a
serious crisis, as failing and making way for a wider based
organization.

1182. Haberler, Gottfried. "Integration and Growth of the World
Economy in Historical Perspective." 54 American Economic Review (1964),
1-22.
        A review of influences toward and impediments to economic
integration, including reference to a veritable revolution in
the form of a cheapening of world transport costs.

1183. Hansen, Roger D. "Regional Integration: Reflections on a
Decade of Theoretical Efforts." 21 World Politics (1969), 242-271.
        Essentially a critique of functionalism and a contrast of
the Haas-Schmitter model with Stanley Hoffmann's approach, together with some questions for directions that might be usefully
asked by integration theorists.

1184. Hazlewood, Arthur (ed.). African Integration and Disintegration: Case Studies in Political and Economic Union. New York: Oxford
for the Royal Institute of International Affairs, 1967, pp. xii, 414.
        With concern for the size of the cash market of most Afri-
can countries which is no larger than that of a European town
of moderate size, this book deals with economic integration as
a vital need and covers such subjects as the Equatorial Customs
Union, the East African common market, the defunct Federation
of Rhodesia and Nyassaland, and pan-Africanism.

1185. Honigmann, John J. "Intensional Orientation and National Unity:
A Case Study from Pakistan." 13 ETC.: A Review of General Semantics (1955-
1956), 108-115.
        On the use of words meaninglessly (intensional orientation)
in order to overcome diversity, with emphasis on the political
functions and dysfunctions of the tactic, especially in Pakistan.

1186. Hovey, J. Allan, Jr. The Superparliaments: Interparliamentary Consultation and Atlantic Cooperation. New York: Praeger, 1966, pp.
xiv, 202.
        Critical analysis of interparliamentary assemblies and their
role in Atlantic affairs, with reference to the NATO Parliamentarians' Conference, the European assemblies, and to proposals
for rationalizing interparliamentary consultation. The author
concludes that, despite shortcomings, interparliamentary assemblies have influenced in salutory manner both the formulation
and the popularization of international policy.

1187. Jacob, Philip E. "The Influence of Values in Political Integration." In Philip E. Jacob and James V. Toscano (eds.), The Integration
of Political Communities. New York and Philadelphia: Lippincott, 1964,
pp. 209-246.
        An individual's own personality structure as it emerges
from the socialization process, specific expectations of what
should be done in social roles, and characteristic behavior

patterns of the culture to which an individual belongs introduce
a normative component into human decision-making. The normative component is an imperative to make choices in terms of standards of what the individual has come to regard as legitimate or
proper. Normative values are a determinant in policy-making and
a strong influence upon community response. At the policy level,
decisions may reflect an attempted integration of divergent normative values in a way tending to sustain the policy-makers'
leadership while also contributing to society's cohesion. Social norms contribute to political integration within a community but are a major impediment to integration among communities.
The implications for decision-making analysis of the phylogenetic
view, field theory, and social role theory are indicated as prelude to elaboration of the above-mentioned propositions. An important section of the essay sets forth the essence of the problem of measuring values, with preference indicated for the "self-
anchoring" approach of Hadley Cantril as extended toward "culture-
anchored" scales of the Kluckhohns and David McClelland.

1188. Jacob, Philip E., and Toscano, James V. (eds.). The Integration of Political Communities. Philadelphia and New York: Lippincott,
1964, pp. x, 314.
An interdisciplinary seminar held at the University of Pennsylvania in the winter of 1961-1962 undertook an assessment of
integrated political behavior from the metropolitan to the international level. Four of the essays are by Karl W. Deutsch and
include an essay outlining communications theory and its relevance to the study of political integration and an essay on
"Transaction Flows as Indicators of Political Cohesion." An
essay by Henry Teune on "Models in the Study of Political Integration" summarizes some uses and misuses of models. Most immediately adaptable to international law research is Professor
Jacob's essay on "The Influence of Values in Political Integration" annotated above.

1189. Lamfalussy, Alexander. "Europe's Progress: Due to Common
Market?" In Laurence B. Krause (ed.), The Common Market: Progress and
Controversy. Englewood Cliffs: Prentice-Hall, 1964, pp. 90-107.
Employs trade statistics and statistics on gross national
product and industrial production of both EEC and EFTA countries
and reaches the conclusion that the big growth of the European
economy occurred before the Common Market was formed and that up
to 1960 there had been no change in the rate of growth traceable
to the Common Market. Comparison of EEC with EFTA shows that
divergence of trends in 1958-1961 was already apparent in the
preceding five years, and that the reasons for Britain's slower
rate of progress, a major factor in EFTA's divergence from EEC,
are connected with the periods 1950-1952 and 1955-1958 rather
than with the first years of EEC. Furthermore, the Belgian figures show that membership in the Common Market does not automatically insure rapid economic growth, although it might be that
the Belgian record would have been less impressive without EEC.

These findings should be compared with those of Karl W. Deutsch, et al. (supra, no. 1172).

1190. Lemberg, Eugen. Geschichte des Nationalismus in Europa. Stuttgart: Curt E. Schwab-Verlag, 1950, pp. 319.
    Although much irreplaceable material was lost during the author's flight to the West, this book by a former professor at the German Hochschule in Prague treats European nationalism as a comprehensive phenomenon. Conceptualization rests on the sociopsychological ground of man's struggle for social integration and the corresponding urge to find the organizational and intellectual form most suited to the current situation. Regarding nationalism as an "ambivalent means of integration," the author holds the tragedy of the national attitude to lie in the incapacity of Herderian humanity to enable the concept of a people seeking civilized aims to gain the upper hand over Darwinian "integral nationalism" which made all values relative or restricted them to one's own people. The latter reduced European nationalism to absurdity and made room for supranational bases of integration ranging from the race concept of the Third Reich to the "idea" or "ideology" of the present situation.

1191. Lijphart, Arend. "Tourist Traffic and Integration Potential." 2 Journal of Common Market Studies (1964), 251-262.
    The measure of the international tourist flow among Western European countries is treated as a significant indicator of potential for integration. The limits of this measure are discussed and also its correlation with such other variables as religion and language.

1192. Meynaud, Jean, and Sidjanski, D. "Science Politique et integration européenne." 10 Bulletin du Centre européen pour la Culture (No. 6, January-March 1965), 1-81.
    Review of approaches taken to date in the study of European integration that concludes that the essential need is for an interdisciplinary method concentrating on a single topic, namely, the diverse types of integration in Europe.

1193. Mitchell, R. Judson. World Communist Community Building. Stanford Studies of the Communist System. Research Paper No. 6. Stanford University, August 1965, pp. 20.
    Examines forces making for integration under an organizer, giving particular attention to leadership, organization, interests, values, the bargaining process, and the communication system. Seven propositions are advanced as a partial model of community formation.

1194. Mitrany, David. "The Prospect of Integration: Federal or Functional." 4 Journal of Common Market Studies (1965), 119-149.
    Argument, with special reference to Europe, that authority need not be coupled with territory and that the functional approach to integration, linking activities and interests one by one, is preferable to a federal approach.

1195. Norro, Michel. Le rôle du temps dans l'integration économique. Louvain: Nauwelaerts, 1962, pp. 259.

A philosophical approach to the problem of the time dimension in relation to economic integration.

1196. Nye, Joseph S. "Patterns and Catalysts in Regional Integration." 19 International Organization (1965), 870-884.

Applies to British East Africa the Haas-Schmitter pattern in an attempt to determine the usefulness of pattern analysis of political integration of underdeveloped regions. The author finds a need for a weighting of the nine Haas-Schmitter variables which are not of equal importance, feels that the variables may establish preconditions for political integration but may need the stimulus of an outside factor or event, and concludes that the Haas-Schmitter framework is inadequate.

1197. Pirages, Dennis C. Socio-Economic Development and Political Change in the Communist System. Stanford Studies of the Communist System. Research Paper No. 9. Stanford University, January 1966, pp. 87.

Based upon the ideas of Abraham Maslow, T.H. Marshall, and Amitai Etzioni, this paper attempts to relate economic development and compliance systems, employing three hypotheses related to the major theme that as economic development proceeds, compliance systems move from the coercive of Etzioni's typology toward the remunerative and the normative. Ranking 35 non-Communist countries by G.N.P. per capita and employing an aggregate index of four attributes denoting compliance structure and six indicating elite responsiveness, an expected inverse relationship between economic development and coercive compliance was found. However, when applied to the Communist countries of Eastern Europe, the reverse effect obtained with highly developed East Germany and Czechoslovakia being high on the coercion level and low on responsiveness and underdeveloped Yugoslavia and Rumania at the other extreme. The results for Eastern Europe suggests a need for further investigation to explain the course of development of the Communist system and unevenness therein, as well as re-examination of the method proposed to explain societal development in the light of whatever explanations for East European deviance from an apparent global pattern might be uncovered.

1198. Plischke, Elmer (ed.). Systems of Integrating the International Community. Princeton: Van Nostrand, 1964, pp. ix, 196.

Five authors discuss international integration, the United Nations and state sovereignty, the European Communities, international federalism, and integration in Communist sphere.

1199. Puchala, Donald J. "The Pattern of Contemporary Regional Integration." 12 International Studies Quarterly (1968), 38-64.

Making use, among other things, of the stimulus-response theory of learning, the article sets forth a view of the integration process that gives special attention to processes of international social assimilation leading to a regional population linked by bonds of mutual understanding and confidence and to processes of international political development toward regional government and a supranational polity.

1200. Sannwal, Rolf, and Stohler, Jacques. Economic Integration: Theoretical Assumptions and Consequences of European Unification. Translated from the German by Herman F. Karriman. Princeton: Princeton University Press, 1959, pp. xvi, 260.
  Illuminating study of the many aspects of economic integration in the light of the European experience in the 1950s.

1201. Schmitt, Hans O. "Capital Markets and the Unification of Europe." 20 World Politics (1968), 228-244.
  Treating the spillover process as one that is not inexorable, the author examines developments in the European Common Market in terms of the Community's need for its own capital market instead of separate national relations with the New York market or with a Euro-dollar market in London, the related need for a common currency, and the consequences thereof in the surrender of national control over exchange rates and investments. He also examines the French aspiration for making Paris the financial center of Europe and the potential German capability not only of functioning as the economic center but also of gaining acceptance of that position, despite the German past that gave rise to integration not to rely upon but to control the core area, the Ruhr. Attention is given to the lack of clarity as to whom, in a situation of diffused responsibility for exchange and interest rate policy, the sovereignty of national monetary authorities was to pass. Suggesting that the urge to draw back may be strongest at the point of creating a common currency, the author holds that if political unification is finally rejected, the customs union may also be endangered.

1202. Schokking, J.J., and Anderson, N. "Observations on the European Integration Process." 4 Journal of Conflict Resolution (1960), 385-410.
  Review of the European integration process that, among other things, attributes the formation of the Communities more to potential economic gains as the motivator of negotiation and accommodation than to ideals of integration.

1203. Shoup, Carl S. (ed.). Fiscal Harmonization in Common Markets. 2 vols. New York: Columbia University Press, 1967, pp. xli, 1411.
  One volume being devoted to theory and the other to practice, this set of essays is a most useful contribution to the understanding of a very difficult aspect of the process of integration among sovereign entities.

1204. Stikker, Dirk V. Men of Responsibility. New York: Harper & Row, 1966, pp. xii, 418.
  Personal memoir of the former Secretary-General of NATO that spells out the difficulties in trying to fit the ideal of unity to the reality of dissension in Western Europe and the North Atlantic area.

1205. Tinbergen, Jan. <u>International Economic Integration</u>. 2nd ed. Amsterdam: Elvesier, 1965, pp. xix, 142.

Explanation of main forces tending toward international economic integration, as well as a description of integration to date.

1206. Zawodny, J.K. (ed.). <u>Man and International Relations</u>. Vol. I, <u>Conflict</u>; Vol. II, <u>Integration</u>. San Francisco: Chandler, 1966.

An extensive collection of essays dealing with conflict and integration at the individual, group, and nation-state levels.

See also nos. 122, 476, 560, 715, 1085, 1214, 1238, 1558, 1605, 1615, 1878, 2499, 2738, 2742, 2744, 2761, 2764, and secs. II, A, 2, c (4-9).

B. CENTRIFUGAL FORCES--SOVEREIGNTY, NATIONALISM, AND SECURITY

1. <u>Sovereignty and the Preservation of Independence</u>

1207. Aventur, J. "Régimes économiques et relations internationales-Application à la Communauté économique européenne." 11 <u>Revue juridique et économique du Sud-Ouest, Série juridique</u> (1960), 85-109.

Sees a relationship between the form of international economic relations and the "régime d'une économie des correspondances." A nation's economy being strongly affected or even determined by its international commercial exchanges, the author endeavors to show the impact of international relations upon the organization form and the functioning of capitalist economies. He finds the latter to be a function of the former, with predictable consequences for the national economies of Common Market members when, after integration, the Community adjusts and articulates its position in world commerce.

1208. Benedict, Burton (ed.). <u>The Problems of Smaller Territories</u>. Commonwealth Papers No. 10. New York: Oxford University Press, 1967, pp. 153.

The material for this collection was developed in an exhaustive two-year seminar held at the Institute of Commonwealth Studies, University of London. The papers deal with such matters as the sort of independence, the means of self-defense, economic survival, self-administration, and the possibility of maintaining or improving standards of living that are possible for small territories.

1209. Efimenco, N.M. "Categories of International Integration." 16 <u>India Quarterly</u> (1960), 259-269.

Identifies four categories of integration as bridges between the reality of the state and the concept of world community: (1) accommodation by such techniques as negotiation and mediation, limited because never destructive of sovereignty; (2) legal universalism, supporting the state system due to the inadequacies

of legislative and enforcement procedures; (3) institutionalization, most successful in the economic area but with no assurance
that international economic institutions have developed better
than national economies; (4) transformation, which assumes that
loyalties can be shifted from the state to a world government
and the possibility of developing common standards of law and
government.

1210. Hall, Daniel George Edward. A History of South-East Asia.
New York: St. Martin's, 1955, pp. xvii, 955.
    A general history seven-eights of which deals with events
prior to 1900. A good overview is provided of cultural intermingling and of the successive international systems that preceded the importation of the Western concept and meaning of
independence.

1211. Lerner, Daniel, and Gorden, Morton. Strategic Thinking of the
European Elites. Report to Project Michelson, U.S. Naval Ordnance Test
Station, China Lake, California. Cambridge, Massachusetts: Center for
International Studies, Massachusetts Institute of Technology, Ditto, June
1964, pp. 110.
    Report on the fifth (1961) of a series of interviews of
French, German, and British industrial, commercial, political,
administrative, labor, professional, military, cultural, journalistic, and intellectual leaders on strategic problems. Among
findings of interest to international lawyers are those on disarmament and deterrence and those on the necessity and aggressive
nature of the U-2 flights, only the British panel including a majority regarding the flights as aggressive, albeit necessary. A
majority of all panels believed the nation-state to be obsolete
and its passing to be a good thing. About 80% of all panels
favored limitation on national sovereignty, the French giving
the largest support (43%) to wholehearted movement toward international association, while responses to a question given only
in France and Germany showed small majorities favoring a federal
system in Europe. However, British and German elites tended to
prefer an Atlantic connection including the United States while
the French preference was for a European orientation. It may be
noted that the French alone tended to view the European Communities as a counterpoise to the United States and not just to Russia.

1212. Marshall-Cornwall, J.H. Geographic Disarmament: A Study of
Regional Demilitarization. London: Oxford, 1935, pp. xii, 207.
    Includes discussion of buffer-states in Asia that includes
some examples, among them Sikkim and Bhutan, that are better
classified as protectorates. Even with these questionable examples the study is a useful one on the principle of the buffer-
state and guarantees of the independence of such states in an
arena other than Europe.

1213. Sayegh, Fayez A. (ed.). The Dynamics of Neutralism in the Arab
World: A Symposium. San Francisco: Chandler Publishing Co., 1964, pp.
xiv, 275.

A symposium presenting views of eight Arab scholars on various aspects of neutralism as a manifestation of sovereignty during the Cold War.

See also nos. 136, 269, 601, 602, 715, 778, 1067, 1203, 1232, 1237,
1883, 1901, 2413, 2432, 2501, 2872.

a. Territorialism

1214. Dia, Mamadou. The African Nations and World Solidarity. Trans
lated by Mercer Cook. New York: Praeger, 1961, pp. 145.
        In an essentially economic exposition, the Prime Minister
of Senegal applies Francois Perroux's theory of mutual development to the problem of the relations of African states with other
states and, in particular, with France and the Common Market. An
epilogue on the rupture of the Mali Federation embraces some interesting hypotheses concerning the strength of territorialism as
against legal structures, which can be related to Boulding's remarks on the image produced by territorial demarcations.

1215. Dowling, John H. "Individual Ownership and the Sharing of Game
in Hunting Societies." 70 American Anthropologist (1968), 502-507.
        On patterns of ownership as conflict-suppressing mechanisms,
with reference particularly to acquisition of an animal that each
hunter would like to have and to supporting evidence from social
situations in which a pattern of property ascription is absent
and conflict is present. What is said in this article appears
also to be relevant to the African states' effort to suppress
conflict by retaining colonial boundaries, but does not include
the problem of conflicting patterns of property ascription as
displayed, e.g., in the nationalization issue.

1216. Herz, John H. International Politics in the Atomic Age. New
York: Columbia University Press, 1959, paperback ed. 1962, pp. viii, 360.
        Centering upon the impact of nuclear weapons and the conse-
quences for the defensive capabilities of states, this book constitutes an elaboration upon the theme of the article published
earlier, "The Rise and Demise of the Territorial State," on the
several ways in which the once "hard-shelled" state has become
penetrable.

1217. Herz, John H. "The Rise and Demise of the Territorial State."
9 World Politics (1957), 473-493.
        An interpretation of international history centering upon
its military facets to identify the state as a territorial unit
surrounded by a "hard-shell" defensive perimeter. Traditional
international law is viewed as reflecting the European system
of impermeable "hard-shell" states by means of such rules as
those defining jurisdictional limits, proclaiming nonintervention, and outlawing in Europe the obliteration of states by
conquest. "Hard-shell" protection can now be bypassed and the

impermeable state can no longer be the symbol of security. The
article embraces the greater part of Chapters 1-6 of the author's
International Politics in the Atomic Age (1959).

1218. Herz, John H. "The Territorial State Revisited: Reflections
on the Future of the Nation-State." 1 Polity (1968), 12-34.
A revision of the author's earlier forecast that technology
was leading to the demise of the territorial state and replacement of territoriality--assuming a rational outcome--by global
universalism protecting a mankind regarding itself as a single
unit. Finding that international developments of the 1900s indicate not universalism but retrenchment, not interdependence but a
new self-sufficiency, and not a loss but a regaining of its impact by territoriality, the author attempts an analysis of newer
trends, gives attention to the concepts of territoriality expressed by Konrad Lorenz and Robert Ardrey but suggests that not
biological drives but competition for scarce resources accounts
for intergroup conflicts and territorial defense, and foresees a
"neo-territoriality" in which the future polity would provide
group identity, protection, and welfare. Israel and Switzerland
are suggested as models of genuine, legitimate nations that are
units of their own protection. The author now sees raw chaos as
the current alternative to the territorial or nation-state system.

See also nos. 132, 138, 583, 872, 1246, 1556, 1861, 1965, 2020, 2431.

2. Responsibilities to Other States

1219. Hall, Harvey P. (ed.). The Evolution of Public Responsibility
in the Middle East. Washington: Middle East Institute, 1955, pp. 118.
A series of lectures by Americans who consider the problems
of general responsibility to the world but then focus on the narrow United States policy objective of preventing Communist aggression. The more generalized comments on responsibility warrant consideration in terms of national responsibility for the
effectiveness of international norms.

See also nos. 129, 130, 1898, 2562, 2575, 2580, 2586, 2588, 2594, 2644,
2774.

a. Responsibility for Hostile Acts of Crowds

1220. Canetti, Elias. Crowds and Power. New York: Viking, 1962,
pp. 495.
Builds the idea of crowds and more structured pluralities
upon the concept of a single bio-psychological drive and group
satisfaction therein, with power relationships an extrapolation
of the basic instinctive process of pursuing, killing, and consuming animals.

1221. Lasswell, Harold D. "The Impact of Crowd Psychology upon International Law." 1 <u>Philippine International Law Journal</u> (1962), 293-309.

Examination in essentially broad stroke fashion of collective psychological factors and their impact in precipitating international legal controversies. National decision-makers must be relied on to vindicate <u>inclusive</u> rather than <u>exclusive</u> claims, and both doctrines and adaptations of international law are in many cases directed toward providing incentive for support of inclusive claims rather than exclusive interests popular with crowds. However, crowd formation can cross some national boundaries, with the result that the security of both governments and social systems can be threatened. The author prefers the free forum approach to crowd control and recommends proceeding internationally toward an effective free forum embracing the key powers of the current continuing crisis.

1222. Mason, Henry L. <u>Mass Demonstrations Against Foreign Regimes: A Study of Five Crises</u>. Tulane Studies in Political Science. Vol. 10. New Orleans: Tulane University, 1966, pp. vi, 98.

Case studies of three demonstrations during the German occupation of the Netherlands during World War II (the February Strike of 1941 in Amsterdam against anti-semitism, the April-May 1943 strikes against forced labor drafts, and the railroad strike of 1944-45), the Hungarian uprising of 1956, and the Panamanian demonstrations of January 1964.

1223. Smelser, Neil J. <u>Theory of Collective Behavior</u>. New York: Free Press, 1962, pp. xi, 436.

Application of sociological insights in an attempt to unify under a single theory the subject of collective behavior. In attempting to explain why collective actions occur where, when, and in the ways they do, the author gives attention to accompanying social conditions, and to beliefs. The theoretical scheme is designed to permit classification and analysis of such social strains as ambiguity, deprivation, conflicts of norms, and conflicts of values.

See also no. 1869.

3. The National Role

1224. Breton, Albert. "The Economics of Nationalism." 72 <u>Journal of Political Economy</u> (1964), 376-386.

Development of a hypothesis based upon an economic view of nationality as a form of capital and of nationalism as entailing encouragement of the investment of present scarce resources for the alteration of the interethnic or international distribution of ownership. The study sheds light upon the problem of nationalization of foreign enterprises. Other implications of the hypothesis are dealt with in the light of recent acts of English-Canadian nationalism in the form of claims and demands on the

United States and of acts of French-Canadian nationalism in the form of claims and demands on English Canada.

1225. Cattell, Raymond B. "Concepts and Methods in the Measurement of Group Syntality." 48 Psychological Review (1955), 48-63.
Develops seven theorems on the dynamics of syntality or "togetherness" of groups that are intended to facilitate further research through factor analysis of the results of sampling a wide range of group characteristics.

1226. Cattell, Raymond B. "The Dimensions of Culture: Patterns of Factorization of National Characters." 44 Journal of Abnormal and Social Psychology (1949), 443-469.
Report of a study which takes national groups as its units and seeks to discover the psychological dimensions which must be utilized in defining national cultural patterns. A test experiment was conducted using 21 groups of six people each and using 40 variables. Of the 70 nations studied, 12 dimensions for measurement of national cultures were found.

1227. Cole, J.A. Lord Haw-Haw--and William Joyce: A Full Story. London: Faber and Faber, 1964, pp. 316.
Biography of the American who, going to Germany under British passport, broadcast German propaganda to Britain.

1228. Guetzkow, Harold. Multiple Loyalties. Publication No. 4. Princeton: Center for Research on World Political Institutions, 1955, pp. 62.
Discussion of the sources, expression, and conflicts among national and international loyalties.

1229. Jahoda, Gustav. "Nationality Preferences and National Stereotypes in Ghana Before Independence." 50 Journal of Social Psychology (1959), 165-174.
An undertaking to discover the extent to which Ghanaians differentiate among non-African nationalities and how they feel about each of those they know. Interviews of 214 Ghanaians were conducted by honor students in sociology who were natives of the informants' villages. Similarities to social distance scores obtained in the United States a generation earlier were found. Similarities to British stereotypes were also found. Attitudes toward non-Africans appear to have originated in the education system developed by the British and to have been modified by African nationalist propaganda and by personal contacts. The role of scapegoat was accorded Syrian merchants.

1230. Kulischer, Eugene M. "Displaced Persons in the Modern World." 262 Annals of the American Academy of Political and Social Science (March 1949), 166-177.
Deals with the problem of the International Refugee Organization prior to mid-1948 as it attempted to give expression both to Western humanitarian idealism and also to serve as an instrument of totalitarian government policy by assisting in the

repatriation of Eastern European nationals, many against their
will--a factor that raises the issues of whether, at least for
the individual, nationality is properly imposed upon him and
whether he can be bound when beyond the national jurisdiction
and, under stress, alienated from his native land.

1230-A. Mendershausen, Horst. "The Diplomat as a National and Transnational Agent: Dilemmas and Opportunities." P-4158. Santa Monica: RAND
Corporation, August 1969, pp. 28.
     Explores the diverse commitments under which diplomats func-
tion: e.g., representing states and international organizations,
Great Powers and revisionist regions, complex governments or more
than one government at a time. Attention is accorded to situations with maximal congruity of loyalties, governmental restraints
that sharpen the agent's conflict between national and transnational interests, and functioning in multiple national diplomacy,
among unequal power alliances, and as viceroy for a Great Power
that dominates a collectivity.

1231. Mozingo, D.P. <u>Sino-Indonesian Relations: An Overview, 1955-
1965</u>. Memorandum RM-4641-PR. Santa Monica: RAND Corporation, July 1965,
pp. 94.
     Includes a chapter on the dispute over the status of over-
seas Chinese triggered in 1959 by two Indonesian decrees, one
banning aliens from the retail trade in rural areas and the other
ordering aliens to terminate residence in West Java. Peking considered the Indonesian decrees to be in violation of the 1955
Dual Nationality Treaty whereby China would relinquish jurisdiction, based on the <u>ius sanquinis</u>, over overseas Chinese choosing
Indonesian nationality, although the exchange of ratifications
did not take place until January 1960. The dispute was ironed
out in 1960 through Indonesian restraint of the anti-Chinese
military and through negotiations of the Joint Committee on Methods of Implementing the Dual Nationality Treaty.

1232. Perry, Stewart E. "Notes on the Role of the National: A Social-psychological Concept for the Study of International Relations." 1
<u>Journal of Conflict Resolution</u> (1957), 346-363. Reprinted in James N.
Rosenau (ed.), <u>International Politics and Foreign Policy</u>. New York: Free
Press, 1961, pp. 87-97.
     The author suggests focusing on the role of the national in
an effort to avoid personification of the state. He regards
nation-state as a consensus of affective or motivational behavior in a collection of individuals viewing themselves as living
together. Personification, i.e., expectations of the communicative value of one's own behavior and one's image of the other
actor, could be applied to state behavior with high probability
of validity only if based on a wide variety of observations of
extra-national behavior, that is, wide enough to demonstrate the
existence of a collective consensus. The national role mobilizes members of one society against another, displays its strength
in attitudes toward traitors, and takes precedence even over family in time of national crisis. It can indulge almost any

personality pattern. Official representation of one's country
is treated as the most rigid definition of the national role,
the most difficult in which to attempt modifications, and the
most misunderstood by the extra-national.

See also nos. 1236, 1237, 1287, 1333, 1480, 1565, 1704, 2372, 2463,
2466, 2501.

4. National Symbols, National Self-Respect,
National Self-Realization

1233. Barritt, Denis P., and Carter, Charles F. The Northern Ireland
Problem: A Study in Group Relations. New York: Oxford, 1962, pp. 163.
Includes evidence of the capacity of a religion to be valued more as a symbol of differences between peoples than as a
system of beliefs and practices. It may be suggested that the
national law may also be such a symbol and that the promotion of
the rule of law in international affairs is in part faced with
the obstacle that one of the foundations on which international
law must rest, and without which it has no raison d'être, is the
existence of differences. In another respect the book is of interest in that it deals with the accommodations that are necessary when fully one-third of a society does not accept the legitimacy of the government but was not prepared to act directly
to change the government.

1234. Elfin, Mel, and Zweig, Leonard. "The Battle of Political Symbols." 18 Public Opinion Quarterly (1954), 205-209.
A survey showing how certain words are used or involved with
both the American ideals and with communism. It found (1) a tendency to identify groups as Communistic when the words "peace,"
"equal rights," and "world" were used in the group's name, (2) a
lesser tendency to call a group Communistic if the word "Women's"
was used, (3) men and women did not differ greatly in identifying
groups, and (4) a high percentage of people identified non-Communist groups as Communists.

1235. Hassner, Pierre. "Nationalisme et relations internationales."
15 Revue française de science politique (1965), 499-528.
Analysis of the problem of nationalism and its international
effects in the modern world.

1236. Katz, Daniel. "Nationalism and Strategies of International Conflict Resolution." In Herbert C. Kelman (ed.), International Behavior: A
Social-Psychological Analysis. New York: Holt, Rinehart and Winston, 1965,
pp. 354-390.
Deals in general terms with the functions of states, types
of nationalist ideology, generic dimensions of nationalism, the
dynamics of four types of national systems, arousal of nationalism and assumption of national roles, types and sources of international conflict, and the forms of conflict resolutions

appropriate to economic, ideological, and power differences. Identified forms of conflict resolution are: (1) force, threats, and deterrence; (2) conflict denial, conflict restriction and control, including limited war; (3) nonviolence; (4) bargaining and compromise, including arbitration; (5) problem-solving and creative integration. Arbitration is treated as an aid to negotiation and without clear distinction from conciliation, for international arbitration is treated as similar to the settlement of labor-management conflict in which a third party, umpire or arbiter, facilitates settlement by communicating to each party information about the other. Adjudication is not mentioned except to indicate that sovereignty is an obstacle to use of the World Court.

1237. Katz, Daniel, Kelman, Herbert, and Flacks, Richard. "The National Role: Some Hypotheses about the Relation of Individuals to Nation in America Today." Peace Research Society (International), Papers. Chicago Conference, 1963. Vol. I (1964), pp. 113-127.

Hypotheses, partly tested in Ann Arbor, on symbolic, normative, and functional commitment. Symbolic commitment, essential in an early stage of existence and during crises but inherently weak and unstable, cannot be maintained on a prolonged basis as a foundation of conformity. Hence, norms and sanctions are developed. In the United States, normative commitment, persuasive among the lower middle and working classes, is pictured as entailing little interest in international affairs and so as accepting any policy seeming to generate a consensus. Functional integration being deemed essential to the existence of a national system, functional commitment is seen as a characteristic of the highly educated and the middle and upper classes. The functionally committed see the maintenance of their own positions or the institutions to which they are tied as dependent upon effective functioning of the national system. Highly interested in international affairs, these people find themselves compelled to conform to the national administration's foreign policy.

1238. Kriesberg, Louis. "German Public Opinion and the European Coal and Steel Community." 23 Public Opinion Quarterly (1959), 28-42.

The opinions collected about ECSC varied and did so because of party adherence, relevant predisposition, and a need for coal. After it was established, ECSC received support based upon habituation to what exists and transference of feeling about authority and the sacredness of laws.

1239. Mark, Max. Beyond Sovereignty. Washington: Public Affairs Press, 1965, pp. 178.

Analysis of the contemporary international system in terms of the crisis of nationalism and of the traditional national state, together with an argument that transnationalism based on the value of survival is bound to affect the policies of the superpowers with the probability that their relations will be governed less by power than by their capacity to command the loyalty and allegiance of others.

1239-A. Mendel, Douglas. The Politics of Formosan Nationalism. Berkeley: University of California Press, 1970, pp. 320.

Focuses primarily on the attitudes of the Formosans about the claims of both Nationalist and Communist China that Formosa is an integral part of China.

1240. Noble, Roberto J. Argentina: A World Power. Translated by Marisa Martínez Corvalán. Buenos Aires: Ediciones Arayú, 1960, pp. xviii, 206.

Highly optimistic view of Argentina's role in the world that is of value in efforts to assess nationalism and of problems impeding progress toward internationalism.

1241. Rupen, Robert A. Mongols of the Twentieth Century. 2 vols. Paris: Mouton, 1964.

Discusses the leading Mongols of the 20th century and the degree of their opposition to Russia and China. Attention is given to cultural influences on politics and the changing degree and content of the culture itself in respect to education, national feeling, and sense of identity. Note is taken of the effects on the Mongols of the Russian and Chinese revolutions. Volume 2 is a bibliography.

1242. Silvert, Kalman H. "The Strategy of the Study of Nationalism." In Silvert (ed.), Expectant Peoples. New York: Random House, 1963, pp. 3-38.

Important for what it says about different degrees and types of nationalism, with particular attention to Latin America.

1243. Smith, E.E. "Individual Versus Group Goal Conflict." 58 Journal of Abnormal and Social Psychology (1959), 134-137.

Employing the task of forming squares from simpler pieces which the members of groups could exchange, an experiment was run with high and low individual motivation. It was found that when the choices of individuals were overt rather than secret, the group goal was chosen more often than individual goals when there was conflict between individual and group goal attainment. The group goal was chosen even under high individualistic motivation.

1244. Touval, Saadia. Somali Nationalism: International Politics and the Drive for Unity in the Horn of Africa. Cambridge: Harvard University Press, 1963, pp. x, 214.

Examination of the foundations and validity of the Somali claim for unity, including the problem of the nomads that has given rise to territorial and boundary issues. The case is of particular interest because of the elements of ethnic and cultural homogeneity based on segmentary lineage and genealogies according to which, at the highest genealogical level, all Somalis belong to one of six major clan families.

1245. Weilenmann, Hermann. "The Interlocking of Nation and Personality Structure." In Karl W. Deutsch and William J. Foltz (eds.), Nation-Building. New York: Atherton, 1963, pp. 33-55.

A Swiss scholar and leader in citizenship and education combines historical study and participant observation to develop a theory of democracy based upon the opportunity of individuals to choose small group affiliations which indirectly entail the choice of what they want their own personality structures and personal identities to become. The directions of the theory are indicated in this article and are also suggested in the author's Pax Helvetica: Die Demokratie der kleinen Gruppen (Zürich: Rentsch, 1951). Book length exposition of the theory is in preparation. It should be noted that this viewpoint, essentially that political choices of groups and parties are made more on the basis of what people want to be rather than upon what they want to get, is one of the basic conceptions that Angus Campbell and his associates expressed in the theoretical section of The American Voter.

1246. Znaniecki, Florian. Modern Nationalities: A Sociological Study. Urbana: University of Illinois Press, 1952, pp. xvi, 196.

Examines the origins of national culture societies, the spread of national cultures through the use of such symbols as the national land, heroes, saints, intellectual heroes, etc., sources of conflict between nationalities, and cooperation between national culture societies.

See also nos. 363, 1190, 1252, 1964, 2338, 2379, 2460, 2779.

5. Inequalities of the Doctrine of Equality

1247. Fox, Annette Baker. The Power of Small States: Diplomacy in World War II. Chicago: University of Chicago Press, 1959, pp. ix, 211.

Analyzes the foreign policies of Turkey, Finland, Norway, Sweden, and Spain in World War II to determine their maneuverability vis-à-vis the major powers.

1248. Fox, Annette Baker. "The Small States of Western Europe in the United Nations." 19 International Organization (1965), 774-786.

On the distaste of the small Western European states for use of the UN as a propaganda forum and on their desire for adoption only of such resolutions as are likely to be put into effect. Their position on these matters is contrasted with the positions of other small states and of the superpowers.

1249. Lagos, Gustavo. International Stratification and Underdeveloped Countries. Chapel Hill: University of North Carolina Press, 1963, pp. xii, 302.

The author, on leave from the University of Chile while serving as an official of the Inter-American Development Bank, stresses the unequal distribution of power in international relations and the consequences thereof. He views states as

comprising a great social system of interacting groups occupying
various positions on a status scale. Economic status, power, and
prestige are the ingredients of status, the first being the most
important because underlying the development of an adequate power
base. Stratification on the international level is regarded as
having become visible at about the time that the doctrine of the
legal equality of states became firmly established. The author's
model of rational international behavior for underdeveloped states,
including improvement of economic stature, power, and prestige,
presumes that such behavior is suitable for situations of tension
stemming from the coexistence of international stratification and
the legal principle of equality.

1250. Rummel, Rudolph J. "Some Dimensions in the Foreign Behavior
of Nations." 3 Journal of Peace Research (1966), 201-224.
    Factor analysis and orthogonal rotation of data for the mid-
1950s related to 94 variables and 82 nations that finds many correlated activities susceptible of structuring in terms of several
uncorrelated dimensions, many diverse activities forming independent patterns of relationships, and certain basic indicators serving as indexes of some of the independent clusters of relationships. The main conclusions offered are that the magnitude of a
state's participation in international affairs is a consequence
of its economic development and power capability while its conflict behavior is dependent on its relation to other states.

1251. Smith, Roger M. Cambodia's Foreign Policy. Ithaca: Cornell
University Press, 1965, pp. x, 273.
    Investigation of the influence of a new state, dispropor-
tionate to its size and military strength, and of its uses of
nonalignment to further its interests in dealing with both East
and West.

1252. Thompson, Laura. "Core Values and Diplomacy: A Case Study of
Iceland." 19 Human Organization (1960), 82-85.
    An anthropological approach, focusing on social structure
and land-use pattern, is employed in an effort to explain the
attitudes of Icelanders toward foreign affairs, their resistance
to foreign interference in national affairs, and to the need to
relate her international capacities and potential acceptance of
responsibilities to the assets that Iceland can bring to bear
that may not be a function of either size or political strength.

1253. Vital, David. The Inequality of States: A Study of the Smaller
Power in International Relations. New York: Oxford University Press, 1968, 198.
    Analysis of the problems that limited resources present to
small powers in respect to national defense and foreign affairs
and an examination of the passive, active, and defensive policies
that small states can employ.

See also nos. 504, 552, 696, 1096, 1208, 1212, 1256, 2095, 2501, 2689.

6. Self-Help; Self-Defense

1254. Masters, Roger D. "World Politics as a Primitive Political System." 16 World Politics (1964), 595-619.

Except for Maine's perception of the parallel between ancient jurisprudence and international law, the author, for some reason not extending his study to include Vinogradoff and Kelsen and a number of anthropologists who published in the earlier decades of this century, proposes the relative novelty of a comparison between stateless primitive systems and the international system. In a clear and well-refined presentation, he reviews primitive vengeance, including its degeneration (or escalation) into the feud. Quite conscious of differences such as the scope and powers of units in the two kinds of systems, he points to the parallels in international politics and in decision-making.

1255. Richardson, Lewis F. "Threats and Security." In T.H. Pear (ed.), Psychological Factors of Peace and War. New York: Philosophical Library, 1950, pp. 219-235.

The author notes that a threat from one group of people to another may result in reactions of contempt, submission, negotiation, avoidance, or retaliation. Examples are drawn from history and include the League of Nations' attempt at economic sanctions vis-à-vis Italy and the Agadir incident. He shows that arms races are best described in quantitative terms and illustrates this fact by his mathematical analysis of the arms race from 1909 to 1914.

1256. Schaffer, B.B. "Policy and System in Defense: The Australian Case." 15 World Politics (1963), 236-261.

The article identifies the following special characteristics of the Australian system: (1) sheer lack of dimension, (2) high dependence on decisions elsewhere, and (3) notably poor parliamentary performances by the Australian legislature and by the Opposition in particular. The study is useful in pointing up some problems faced by countries that simply cannot afford to provide adequate expenditures for defense.

1257. Schlesinger, James R. "Quantitative Analysis and National Security." 15 World Politics (1961), 295-315.

The economics profession at last dropped its neglect of the military establishment. Economics helps to select and frame the questions that should be asked, but the data for the decision-maker must come from elsewhere. The military allocation problem has two parts: (1) how much resources to devote to defense, and (2) how to use such resources. Total security is unobtainable, and the real question is one of trading more or less military security for other goals.

1258. Sen, Chanakaya. Against the Cold War. Bombay: Asia Publishing House, 1962, pp. 288.

Discussion of the dilemma of Asian, African, and Latin American countries in formulating a policy to deal with the Cold War contenders. Stress is placed upon the positive objectives of nonalignment.

See also nos. 1834, 1875, and secs. IV, A, 2, and D, 5, 6; VII, A, 3.

C. INTERNAL DECISION-MAKING

1. Foreign Policy Decision-Making

1259. Baumol, W.J., and Quandt, R.E. "Rules of Thumb and Optimally Imperfect Decisions." 54 American Economic Review (1964), 23-46.
An investigation of methods of designing and evaluating rules of thumb which are regarded as among the more efficient pieces of decision-making equipment. Simple algebraic functions and simulation are employed to generate rules of thumb that may plausibly be expected to yield fair approximations to true maxims. Although the context in which the experiments were conducted was that of the business firm and the price-setting decision, the authors' approach in their effort to open up a new area of investigation can be employed to investigate the place of international law in rules of thumb for certain types of foreign policy decisions and decision-making situations.

1260. Beichman, Arnold. The "Other" State Department: The United States Mission to the United Nations--Its Role in the Making of Foreign Policy. New York: Basic Books, 1968, pp. 221.
Employs hitherto unpublicized information in a study of the US Mission to the UN that, among other things, gives attention to the successes of the heads of that Mission in pressing their views over initial objections of the Department of State and the White House.

1261. Birnbaum, K.E. "The Formation of Swedish Foreign Policy." 1 Cooperation and Conflict (1965), 6-31.
Description of the primary and secondary agencies participating in the making of Swedish foreign policy, including administrators, interest groups, and parliamentary agencies such as the Advisory Council on Foreign Affairs, the Parliamentary Committee on Foreign Affairs, and conferences of party leaders.

1262. Blechman, Barry M. "The Quantitative Evaluation of Foreign Policy Alternatives: Sinai, 1956." 10 Journal of Conflict Resolution (1966), 408-426.
An undertaking, employing a probabilistic model, to evaluate the courses of action open to Israel at the time of the Suez crisis in terms of payoffs and degrees of uncertainty or, conversely, safety of the alternatives.

1263. DeRivera, Joseph H. <u>The Psychological Dimension of Foreign Policy</u>. Columbus: Charles E. Merrill, 1968, pp. 441.

Four actions in American foreign policy are employed to study the behavior of formulators of foreign policy by application of contemporary psychological concepts.

1264. Edinger, Lewis J. "Political Science and Political Biography." 26 <u>Journal of Politics</u> (1964), 423-439, 648-675.

Treats political leadership as a cognitive role, not as an office or behavior. This leads to analysis of the role as aspiration, not just as function, and to a compartmentalization of the various segments of an individual's political activity in terms of role-sets.

1265. Fisher, Roger. "Defects in the Governmental Decision Process." In Fisher (ed.), <u>International Conflict and Behavioral Science: The Craigville Papers</u>. New York: Basic Books, 1964, pp. 248-253.

The author describes his essay as an "attempt to identify some institutional features which may be causing good people to reach bad decisions." They include: lack of attention to fundamentals, i.e., attention is paid to short-range in preference to long-range goals; inadequate consideration of improbable alternatives; effect of a decision upon the decision-maker, i.e., on his personal future; effect of one decision on the ability to make another because of the interrelation of subject matter. Institutional inertia can preclude reconsideration of issues. Finally, a government is unable by its nature to take private action, even when that is the best course in a given situation. Fisher suggests that private individuals and corporations should operate in the spheres and in the manner in which government is incapable of acting.

1266. Gregg, Phillip M. <u>A Test of Systemic International Behavior: The Case of Conflict and Cooperation</u>. Carnegie-IDRC Joint Study Group on Measurement Problems. Mimeo. Bloomington: Indiana University, April 1965, pp. 22.

A multiple regression technique is employed to try to determine whether universal processes underlie national decision-making or whether the uniqueness of each nation prevents relationships from being systematic from nation to nation. A test is made of a model of the impact of the international situation the domestic condition upon each other, with the decision process an intervening variable. One test indicated both the international situation and the domestic condition to be highly influential, thereby producing the interpretation of regularity in the decision process in different nations. A second test, showing slightly more covariance between action and the international situation than between action and the domestic condition, was deemed inconclusive. Other tests were thought to identify particular measures accounting for much of the variance and to indicate that different characteristics of both the international situation and the domestic condition determine conflict and cooperation. The author asserts that a high level of diplomatic action and power politics tends to engage government officials in conflict while the engagement of nongovernmental organizations reduces conflict.

1267. Grinspoon, Lester. "Interpersonal Constraints and the Decision-Maker." In Roger Fisher (ed.), International Conflict and Behavioral Science: The Craigville Papers. New York: Basic Books, 1964, pp. 238-247.

The author is concerned with constraints on the decision-maker that are a consequence of attaining high office, particularly the tightening of his circle of friends and business contacts, with a consequent danger of sycophancy.

1268. Gross, Feliks. Foreign Policy Analysis. New York: Philosophical Library, 1954, pp. 179.

This effort to develop a methodology for the analysis of foreign policy includes an argument that logical determination and analysis of foreign policy alternatives is possible without distortion by national bias. The point is illustrated by reference to the secret minutes of 1939 in which the Russians and the British, unknown to each other, agreed on the alternatives open to Russia. Gross' broader concept is that foreign policy is a social process in which three basic concepts are distinguishable --ideology including policy objectives as both a part and a result of ideology, factors as elements of power, and policies as courses of action.

1269. Guetzkow, Harold. "An Exploratory Empirical Study of the Role of Conflict in Decision-Making Conferences." 5 International Social Science Bulletin (1953), 286-300.

This exploratory study led to the conclusion that substantive conflicts, related to problems under discussion, tend to be resolved by agreements emphasizing factors positively promoting agreement while affective conflicts, entailing interpersonal struggle, tended to be resolved by reducing forces making for disagreement through the use of such devices as withdrawal and isolation. Observation of business and governmental conferences in the United States provided data.

1270. Hermann, Charles Frazer. Crises in Foreign Policy-Making: A Simulation of International Relations. Ph.D. Dissertation. Evanston: Northwestern University, 1965; Ann Arbor: University Microfilms, Order No. 65-12,098, pp. 321.

Report on a simulation experiment in foreign policy decision-making at various levels of stress and crisis. Naval petty officers were employed as subjects. Among the findings were increased likelihood of action if situations were initiated by actors previously perceived as hostile, if situations were perceived as deliberately initiated, and if national survival was perceived to be threatened. Action was less likely when situations were initiated by actors previously perceived as responsive. Some other findings tend to confirm hypotheses about reduced search for alternatives, increased search for support, and increased consensus on endangered goals at higher crisis levels.

1271. Hilsman, Roger. "The Foreign Policy Consensus: An Interim Research Report." 3 <u>Journal of Conflict Resolution</u> (1959), 361-382.

Employs a model of conflict and consensus-building that treats foreign policy-making as similar to labor-management relations and international relations. The model in action and some of the effects of conflict and accommodation on the President are discussed. With reference to foreign aid policy, military policy, and East-West relations, consideration is given to participation and the differences thereof in crisis policy, program policy, and anticipatory policy, to roles, and to the working of the policy-making system.

1272. Hilsman, Roger. <u>To Move a Nation: The Politics of Foreign Policy in the Administration of John F. Kennedy</u>. Garden City: Doubleday, 1967, pp. xxii, 602.

On the bureaucratic and legislative politics, international negotiations, intelligence operations, and some public relations problems of the foreign policy process with special reference to Laos, the Cuban missile crisis, the Congo, Communist China, the Indonesia-Malaysia confrontation, and Vietnam. Particularly useful is a chapter that summarizes and systematizes the anecdotal material about decision-making circles, the public arena, the information leak, oversimplification of the policy debate, incrementalism in policy formulation, overselling policies, group decision-making, and the sources of power. Some reference to the use of informal channels for intergovernmental communications is included.

1273. Holsti, Ole R. "Perceptions of Time, Perceptions of Alternatives, and Patterns of Communication as Factors in Crisis Decision-Making. <u>Peace Research Society (International), Papers</u>. Chicago Conference, 1964. Vol. III (1965), pp. 79-120.

Employs the quantifiable data of the messages of the Triple Entente and the Dual Alliance between the assassination of the Archduke and the outbreak of World War I in order to test a number of propositions concerning crisis decision-making. The article includes a useful set of references to reports of experimental studies of decision-making and of the impact of crisis.

1274. Holsti, Ole R. "The Belief System and National Images: A Case Study." 6 <u>Journal of Conflict Resolution</u> (1962), 244-252.

Analyzes John Foster Dulles' statements in 1953-1959 about the Soviet Union, employing Osgood's "evaluative assertion analysis" for coding, and develops the postulate that Dulles interpreted information about the Soviet Union to render it consistent with his belief system.

1275. Hubert, Jacques. <u>Les relations extérieures d'un état nouveau le Senegal</u>. Dakar: Faculté de Droit, 1963.

Presents a view of policy outputs as well as staffing problems and other variables that affect the foreign policy decision process in Senegal.

1276. Husler, Angelo. <u>Contribution à l'étude de l'élaboration de la politique étrangère britannique, 1945-1956</u>. Geneva: Droz, 1961, pp. 236.
  A partly theoretical study of the foreign policy decision-making process in Britain.

1277. Johnstone, William C. <u>Burma's Foreign Policy</u>. Cambridge: Harvard University Press, 1963, pp. ix, 340.
  Examines Burma's policies toward the West, the Communist states, and states of Southeast Asia with some indications of the forces, mechanisms, and processes that produce particular policies.

1278. Kennedy, Robert F. <u>Thirteen Days: A Memoir of the Cuban Missile Crisis</u>. New York: Norton, 1969, pp. 224.
  The late Senator's account of the handling of the 1962 missile crisis, which can be fitted in and compared with other accounts, particularly those by Sorensen, Schlesinger, Hilsman, Acheson, and Salinger.

1279. Lindblom, C.E. "The Science of Muddling Through." 19 <u>Public Administration Review</u> (1959), 79-88.
  Contrasts the rational-comprehensive method of decision-making with the method of successive limited comparisons. The former, appearing in formalized accounts of decision-making, is treated as being, for complex problems, too demanding on human intelligence and unable to cope with conflicts in objectives or values. Successive limited comparison, often held to be the method usually employed by decision-makers, is seen as a method of simplification that reduces problems to manageable complexity and that is able to cope with conflicts in values. Coordination of decision-makers employing successive limited comparison is regarded as attainable through mutual adjustment of partisan individuals and groups within and outside government.

1279-A. Mack, Ruth P. <u>Planning on Uncertainty: Decision Making in Business and Government Administration</u>. New York: Wiley, 1971, pp. 264.
  Dealing with the problem of keeping uncertainty to a minimum, the author describes the fundamentals of statistical decision theory, develops a typology for a realistic range of decision situations for choices by "natural man," and deals with real life situations in which a decision is only one link in a chain of behavior. A checklist of over 50 specific ways to reduce the cost of uncertainty is included.

1280. Maruyama, Masao. <u>Thought and Behavior in Modern Japanese Politics</u>. Edited by Ivan Morris. New York: Oxford, 1963, pp. xix, 344.
  A collection of essays by a Japanese scholar. Among them is "Thought and Behavior Patterns of Japan's Wartime Leaders," a highly original analytical study that has important consequences for the building of a model of a national foreign policy decision system that produces unintended outcomes.

1281. McClelland, Charles A. "Decisional Opportunity and Political Controversy: The Quemoy Case." 6 Journal of Conflict Resolution (1962), 201-213.

Using the Quemoy crisis of 1958 as an example, behavior during international crises are examined. From interaction analysis of this type, three identifications are possible: (1) means of handling crisis; (2) determining a country's foreign policy; (3) reactions of domestic opposition to the Administration.

1282. McClosky, Herbert. "Perspectives on Personality and Foreign Policy." 13 World Politics (1960), 129-139.

On personality as a dimension relevant to understanding foreign policy to account for belief, conformity, deviation, consensus, ways of perceiving and organizing experience, likes and dislikes, affection and hostility.

1283. Miller, James G. "Information Input, Overload, and Psychopathology." 116 American Journal of Psychiatry (1960), 695-704.

Finds that under conditions of perceived threat or of information overload some subjects of attitude tests tended to reduce the number of categories employed to classify statements.

1284. Paige, Glenn D. The Korean Decision, June 24-30, 1950. New York: Free Press, 1968, pp. xxv, 394.

Application of the Snyder-Bruck-Sapin framework to produce a detailed analysis of the United States decision to intervene in Korea in 1950. The study is as well documented as is presently possible. It leads to a set of useful hypotheses, some of which are similar to hypotheses independently derived from other case studies (infra, no. 1451).

1285. Rabow, Jerome, et al. "The Role of Social Norms and Leadership in Risk-Taking." 29 Sociometry (1966), 16-27.

Based on earlier studies, the experiment described tends to confirm the hypothesis that, in decisions involving risk, groups are likely to choose more risky alternatives than are individuals. The data also suggest that the most influential group members tend personally to support the normatively strongest position, thereby suggesting that, to understand decisions involving risk, the nature of the relevant norms should be considered.

1286. Rapoport, Anatol. Strategy and Conscience. New York: Harper and Row, 1964, pp. xxvii, 323.

Criticizes defense strategists as more concerned with abstract alternatives than with human lives and as treating self-selective concepts as "hard analyses," even though they have the effect of inhibiting understanding of the complexities of international politics. Attention is accorded pressures for simplification, simulation of interaction motivated by trust and suspicion, and attempts to escape from the zero-sum trap.

1287. Renouvin, Pierre, and Duroselle, Jean-Baptiste. Introduction à l'histoire des relations internationales. Paris: Librairie Armand

Colin, 1964, pp. 520. An Introduction to the History of International Relations. Translated by Mary Ilford. New York: Praeger, 1967, pp. xiii,
432.

The first part, by Professor Renouvin, deals with the forces
profondes of international relations: geography, economics, nationalism, etc. Professor Duroselle's part is less conventional
in that, with a fine blend of theoretical insight and historical
knowledge, it deals with the statesman and his personality, his
relation to the national interest, interaction between forces
profondes and the statesman, and the nature of the statesman's decision. Quite important, whether as antidote or as a potentially
modifying supplement to recent American decision-making studies,
are the discussion of the typology of statesmen and of the irrational nature of the political decision, irrationality being seen
as a function of the complexity of the political world. Hence,
Duroselle thinks little of the undertaking to reduce political
complexities to abstract and often mathematical propositions.

1288. Reynolds, Philip Alan. British Foreign Policy in the Inter-War
Years. New York: Longmans, Green, 1954, pp. xi, 182.
Concise survey of British foreign policy of particular value
in what it brings out about the difficulties of maintaining traditional policies when the environment has changed.

1289. Rutherford, Brent M. "Psychopathology and Political Involvement." 10 Journal of Conflict Resolution (1966), 387-407.
A study showing, among other things, a tendency of manic-
depressive and schizophrenic-paranoid types to be overrepre-
sented in leadership positions and of paranoic types to be selected as leaders in proximate democratic groups as well as of
totalitarian systems. Attention is called to the apparent existence of a paranoid style of politics as a continuing part of
the American political scene. The author feels that the evidence that he presents, particularly that of the background of
patients in the Elgin State Hospital, tends to support Lasswell's
view of political man as a displacer and externalizer. Suggestions for further research include the paranoid personality's
effort to control the flow of communications, organizational
concern for secrecy, paranoia as an intervening variable in
decision-makers' perceptions and misperceptions of public opinion, the possibility that absence of widespread paranoia may be
a requisite for societal development requiring a general distribution of trust while societal paranoia may be both a correlate
of development and an obstacle to continued advance, and the
impact of paranoia upon the ability of organizations to enter
into trustful relations with other organizations.

1290. Ruthnaswamy, M. Principles and Practice of Foreign Policy.
Bombay: Popular Book Depot, 1961, pp. 384.
An Indian study in systematic form on the principles and
organization of foreign policy, and the art and techniques of
diplomacy.

1291. Sapin, Burton M. Making United States Foreign Policy. Washington: Brookings Institution, 1966, pp. xi, 415.

Examines the structure, processes, procedures, and personnel of the American foreign policy machinery.

1292. Sforza, Carlo. Cinque anni a Palazzo Chigi (La politica ester italiana dal 1947 al 1951). Roma: Atlante, 1952, pp. 586.

A detailed account, accompanied by various documents, including memoranda and confidential letters, of important Italian foreign policy problems during Count Sforza's five postwar years as Foreign Minister.

1293. Snyder, Richard C., and Paige, Glenn D. "The United States Decision to Resist Aggression in Korea: The Application of an Analytical Scheme." 3 Administrative Science Quarterly (1958), 341-378.

The article presents a conceptual scheme for the analysis of decision-making and applies the scheme to a particular crisis decision or set of decisions. Several tentative hypotheses are set forth and the critical role of values in structuring the decision process is set forth. Perhaps the most important feature of the article is the clarity with which it identifies the several components of a decision and the components of the decision-making process.

1294. Sondermann, Fred A. "The Linkage Between Foreign Policy and International Politics." In James N. Rosenau (ed.), International Politics and Foreign Policy: A Reader in Research and Theory. New York: Free Press, 1961, pp. 8-17.

Distinguishes the areas of foreign policy and international politics, emphasizes the linkage between the two areas, and argues for organization of analysis around the concept of an international system. The linkage between foreign policy and international politics as separate processes lies in terms of factors considered in initial foreign policy decisions and of repeated revisions of those calculations after interaction between or among implementors of two or more states' foreign policy decisions.

1295. Sorensen, Theodore C. Decision-Making in the White House: The Olive Branch or the Arrows. New York & London: Columbia University Press 1963, pp. xvii, 94.

Several references to the Cuban crisis indicate in general form several features of presidential foreign policy decision-making. Brief enumeration and explanation of restraints on presidential choice include international law as a restraint which in the smaller world of today's transportation and communication "cannot be dismissed as quickly as some claim."

1296. Sorensen, Theodore C. Kennedy. New York: Harper & Row, 1965 Paperback ed., New York: Bantam Books, 1966, pp. xii, 881.

An account of the Kennedy Administration in which the late President's Special Counsel deals, among other things, with foreign policy issues, decision processes, and international negotiations as viewed from his vantage point.

1297. Thiam, Doudou. The Foreign Policy of African States. New York: Praeger, 1965, pp. xv, 134.

Among other things, the Foreign Minister of Senegal brings up the possibility of "an embryo-system of international law" (p. 44) among the African states that gives rise to the possibility of the growth of an idea comparable to that of inter-American law. The volume, originally published in French in 1963, also analyzes the principal concepts and ideologies that have encouraged both unity and division among African states as each state has formulated and carried out the policies seemingly most appropriate to its interests.

1298. Triska, Jan F., and associates. Pattern and Level of Risk in Soviet Foreign Policy-Making: 1945-1963. Final Report to Project Michelson, U.S. Naval Ordnance Test Station, China Lake, California. September 10, 1964, pp. 268.

Examination of 29 situations in which the Soviet Union could have or did take a degree of risk due to (a) direct US-Soviet opposition, (b) involvement of a major Soviet ally in a quarrel, (c) civil war with overt or covert Soviet aid, (d) perception of a Western diplomatic move or one by another Communist party-state as a threat to the USSR, (e) uprising in a party-state that threatened the USSR, or (f) opportunity for Soviet political or ideological gains. Soviet policy is found to be a low-risk policy, thus confirming what some other authors had concluded by more intuitive analysis.

1299. Vandenbosch, Amry. Dutch Foreign Policy Since 1815. The Hague: Nijhoff, 1959, pp. 318.

Valuable for the information provided on the foreign policy-making procedures in the Netherlands and for its discussion of debates over policy in the States General and among the electorate.

1300. Whiting, Allen S. China Crosses the Yalu: The Decision to Enter the Korean War. New York: Macmillan, 1960, pp. x, 219.

A reconstruction of the course of Chinese Communist decision on the basis of four general types of evidence: (1) official Chinese statements for foreign consumption; (2) official Chinese statements and publications for domestic consumption; (3) United States intelligence estimates, Chinese unit histories, and interrogations of prisoners; (4) formal diplomatic activity indicated in public records.

1301. Zartman, I. William. "Characteristics of Developing Foreign Policies in Former French Africa." In William H. Lewis (ed.), French-Speaking Africa: The Search for Identity. New York: Walker, 1965, pp. 179-193.

On ideological divisions, unstable alliances, and relations with the Organization of African Unity in the former French African colonies.

1302. Zartman, I. William. "Decision-Making Among African Governments on Inter-American Affairs." 2 Journal of Development Studies (1966), 98-119.

On the central position of the president in North and West African national decision-making, influences from lieutenants, councils, and advisors, and the relatively small influence of representative groups.

See also nos. 176, 256, 275, 414, 443, 583, 744, 822, 855, 1168, 1644 1760, 1852, 1898, 1927, 1930-A, 2037-2041, and secs. I, C, 19, 21.

2. Pursuit of Domestic Objectives

1303. Friedrich, Carl J. "International Politics and Foreign Policy in Developed (Western) Systems." In R. Barry Farrell (ed.), Approaches to Comparative and International Politics. Evanston: Northwestern University Press, 1966, pp. 97-119.
On the increasing obliteration of the boundary between the national and the international, reasons for the lack of inte-grated foreign policies in democracies, and the impact of party and pressure politics in producing policy discontinuities. For-eign policy decisions are seen as operating on (1) the technical and bureaucratic level, (2) the level of particular interest groups, and (3) the level of broad popular participation seldom activated but involved in dramatic turns and even reversals of foreign policy. Consideration is given to interactions of the three and the difficulties of generalization concerning foreign policy when the problem exists of whether a response to an issue occurs on the first, second, or third level. The author suggests that a functional approach to policy processes requires (1) treating foreign policy as an interdependent collection of ap-proaches to concrete problems having both foreign and domestic dimensions and (2) visualizing foreign affairs both as external aspects of self-contained systems and as internal aspects of supranational systems.

1304. Gehlen, Michael P. "The Politics of Soviet Foreign Trade." 1 Western Political Quarterly (1965), 104-115.
Treats political motives as playing a relatively small role in the Soviet trade program with the West and with underdeveloped states. Trade with the West is viewed as designed to obtain aid in domestic economic development, gold and oil being expendable in exchange for chemical plants, technical equipment, and steel pipe. In the case of trade with underdeveloped states, the po-litical motive enters with the goal of reducing such states' de-pendence on the West and that of increasing Soviet prestige and influence.

1305. Good, Robert C. "State-Building as a Determinant of Foreign Policy." In Laurence W. Martin (ed.), Neutralism and Nonalignment. New York: Praeger, 1962, pp. 3-12.
On the impact of one form of domestic political policy upon foreign policy that for new states provides one link rendering foreign policy a continuation or extension of domestic policy.

1306. Joseph-Barthélémy. <u>La Conduite de la politique extérieure dans les démocraties</u>. Paris: Publications de la Conciliation Internationale, 1930, pp. 174.

An early study of the problem of democratic polities and their efforts to conduct foreign affairs that recognizes the impact of internal issues and the difficulties of preventing internal issues from determining the course of foreign policy.

1307. Nurkse, Ragnar. "International Monetary Policy and the Search for Economic Stability." 37 <u>American Economic Review</u> (1947), 569-594.

A consideration of the international implications of national policies aimed at maintaining high and stable levels of employment and of how the system can be operated to agree rather than conflict with the domestic objective of stability at full employment.

1308. Rosenau, James N. (ed.). <u>Domestic Sources of Foreign Policy</u>. New York: Free Press, 1967, pp. xiv, 340.

A series of papers on domestic influences on foreign policy, chiefly related to United States policy, that includes the following: Herbert McClosky, "Personality and Attitude Correlates of Foreign Policy Orientation"; Milton J. Rosenberg, "Attitude Change and Foreign Policy in the Cold War Era"; Bernard C. Cohen, "Mass Communication and Foreign Policy"; Lester W. Milbrath, "Interest Groups and Foreign Policy"; Kenneth N. Waltz, "Electoral Punishment and Foreign Policy Crises"; Theodore J. Lowi, "Making Democracy Safe for the World: National Politics and Foreign Policy."

See also nos. 518, 2814, 2838, 2855, 2861.

3. <u>Legislative Influences</u>

1309. Carroll, Holbert N. <u>The House of Representatives and Foreign Affairs</u>. Rev. ed. Boston: Little, Brown, 1966, pp. xii, 386.

Comprehensive descriptive study of the behavior of the House of Representatives in foreign affairs, with concern, among other things, for leadership, interaction of committees concerned with foreign affairs, relations with the Senate and the Executive, and the place of political parties and interest groups. A chapter is devoted to the politics of the Committee on Foreign Affairs and another to committees concerned with foreign economic policy.

1310. Elder, N. "Parliament and Foreign Policy in Sweden." 1 <u>Political Studies</u> (1953), 194-206.

Description of Swedish parliamentary powers and machinery in the foreign policy field, including the Foreign Affairs Council which is consulted prior to reaching agreements, even secret agreements, and which can be bound to secrecy, and the Foreign Affairs Committee, established in 1937, which includes the members of the Council and which has the task of scrutinizing treaties and reporting to Parliament.

1311. Farnsworth, David N. The Senate Committee on Foreign Relations
Urbana: University of Illinois Press, 1961, pp. vi, 189.

The most directly relevant portion of this study of the Foreign Relations Committee in 1947-1956 is Chapter 4 on treaties.
Attention is called to forms of Committee action, particularly to
the "smothering" or delaying techniques and to the technique of
withdrawal by the Executive at the request of the Committee, perhaps on the ground of obsolescence resulting from long delay in
the Committee, or on Executive preference for avoiding a possible
rebuff in committee or on the Senate floor. Preference of both
the Executive and the Committee for indirect disposition of unacceptable treaties means that the Senate may be expected to ap-
prove that which passes the Committee, which amounts to a decision before the hearing stage is reached.

1312. Hughes, Christopher. The Parliament of Switzerland. London:
Cassell for the Hansard Society, 1962, pp. 203.

At several points throughout the description of parliamentary institutions and procedures the role of the Swiss legislature
and, since 1936, that of the Foreign Affairs Committee in the development of foreign policy, particularly the policy of neutrality,
are discussed. An appendix includes an opinion in administrative
law distinguishing ordinary neutrality from permanent neutrality
and attempting to delimit economic neutrality. A biographical
sketch of Max Huber is presented as illustrative of "the various
strands from which the Establishment in Switzerland is spun."

1313. Mathews, Donald R. U.S. Senators and Their World. Chapel Hill
University of North Carolina Press, 1960, pp. xvi, 303.

Most important as a background volume because of its penetrating exposition of the folkways of the Senate and for its
revealing statistical analyses of such matters as committee
prestige and effectiveness, the volume does little with foreign
affairs and nothing with the ratification process. The chapter
on committees is most important for what it indicates of the
types of men who prefer Foreign Relations Committee and other
prestige committee assignments, the status of the Foreign Relations Committee as the most united committee of the Senate, the
tendency of the Foreign Relations Committee to be sympathetic
to the Department of State, and the relationship between committee unity and effectiveness on the Senate floor.

1314. Nikolitch, Georges. L'Effet du controle parlementaire de la
politique étrangère sur le développement du droit international. Paris:
Pierre Bossuet, 1939, pp. 190.

One of the few analyses of representative government and of
the effects and consequences of parliamentary control upon the
content and form of international law and upon international
procedures.

1315. Paul, John, and Laulicht, Jerome. In Your Opinion: Leaders'
and Voters' Attitudes on Defence and Disarmament. Vol. I. Clarkson, Ontario: Canadian Peace Research Institute, 1963, pp. xiv, 140.

An attitude survey dealing with defense and disarmament issues. The sample consisted of 1,000 voters, 150 teenagers, 100 contributors to the Canadian Peace Research Institute, 48 leading businessmen, 48 union leaders, and 48 political leaders including 43 Members of Parliament and three senior advisers to Cabinet Ministers. All groups felt that every nation should take its disputes to the International Court of Justice and accept its decisions, the business leaders (61%) providing the lowest favorable response.

1316. Richards, Peter G. Parliament and Foreign Affairs. London: Allen & Unwin; Toronto: University of Toronto Press, 1967, pp. 191.
Deals with public opinion and foreign policy, political pressures from constituencies and pressure groups, political pressures within the British Parliament, parliamentary debates with particular attention to the debates of 1962-1963, the influence of Parliament on foreign policy, the role of the Opposition, and the sources of information and the gaps in information available to Members of Parliament. Attention is given to the Royal Prerogative as it relates to the treaty-making procedure.

1317. Rieselbach, Leroy N. "The Basis of Isolationist Behavior." 24 Public Opinion Quarterly (1960), 644-657.
A study of roll-call votes in the House of Representatives in 1939-1941 and 1949-1952 was analyzed in terms of an index of isolationism. Independent variables were percent of population classed as rural in each district, percent of first or second generation German or Irish in each district, and percent of roll calls answered by a Republican Congressman. Rank order correlations indicate Republicanism to be a far more important factor than rural residence or ancestry.

1318. Robinson, James A. Congress and Foreign Policy-Making: A Study in Legislative Influence and Initiative. Rev. ed. Homewood, Illinois: Dorsey, 1967, pp. xii, 254.
Interviews and other appropriate techniques are employed for an invaluable study of the influence of Congress on the foreign policy process. The first edition deals with the 85th Congress, while the second edition deals also with the 87th Congress. The second edition includes suggestions concerning ways in which Congress can improve its procedures particularly toward orientation on long-range objectives and goals.

1319. van Campen, S.I.P. The Quest for Security: Some Aspects of Netherlands Foreign Policy, 1945-1950. The Hague: Nijhoff, 1958, pp. xv, 308.
Concentrating on a five-year period, this volume on the security of the Netherlands develops quite clearly the European aspects of the security problem and casts light on various important political developments related to the negotiations for the Brussels Treaty, NATO, and the Council of Europe. Particularly informative is the issue of European cooperation about which the Second Chamber was quite vocal in its dislike of the

Government's hesitancy and was able to bring about a change in policy toward a more thorough-going collaboration and, although beyond the time period covered by this book, bring about the constitutional revisions of 1953 that eased the path of Dutch participation in European integration.

1320. van Raalte, E. The Parliament of the Kingdom of the Netherlands. London: The Hansard Society for Parliamentary Government, 1959, pp. 216.

A short section (pp. 151-157) deals with the role of Parliament in foreign policy matters and in approval of international agreements. Attention is called to the far more frequent and more meaty conferences, although the matters dealt with remain secret, between the Foreign Ministry and the Standing Committee for Foreign Affairs since 1945 than were held in the years between 1919 and World War II.

1321. Wheare, K.C. Legislatures. New York: Oxford, 1963, pp. vii, 247.

A short comparative study of legislatures of the United States, Western Europe, and the Commonwealth, Chapter 7 of which is devoted to the roles and influence of legislatures in foreign and military affairs. The problem of secrecy is made the focus of evaluation of probable influence of legislatures and of foreign affairs committees in foreign policy-making and so in treaty-making. Two complementary hypotheses are of interest in that they suggest a research topic on the relationship of information to policy-making: (1) where a country pursues a policy of neutrality, the legislature and its committee may be well informed about that country's foreign affairs; (2) where a country wishes to use its influence and its power continuously in pursuit of an "active" foreign policy, the legislature and its committee will be less well informed.

See also nos. 1261, 1272, 1299, 1867, 2108, 2109, 2311, 2716, 2812, 2861.

4. Political Party Conflict and Influences

1322. Armstrong, J.A. "The Domestic Roots of Soviet Foreign Policy." 41 International Affairs (1965), 37-47.

Deals with the subordination of Soviet interests abroad to the demands of the domestic power struggle while noting that, since the manipulation of foreign policy issues stops when a power struggle ends, the West can make no gains by concessions to aid a contestant.

1323. Belknap, George, and Campbell, Angus. "Political Party Identification and Attitudes Toward Foreign Policy." 15 Public Opinion Quarterly (1951-1952), 601-623.

The attitude toward foreign policy was found to be dependent upon party lines even among the well-informed individuals and despite Catholic-Protestant, economic, and urban-rural differences. The authors suggest that this result obtains because people tend to seek a party that proclaims what they feel and then associate themselves with it.

1324. Berner, W. "Nasser und die Kommunisten." 20 Europa-Archiv (1965), 569-578.
On the impact on Nasser's neutralist policy of integration of the Communists in Nasser's single party.

1325. Bung, Hubertus. Die Auffassungen der verschiedenen sozialistischen Parteien von den Problemen Europas. Saarbrücken: Karl Funk, 1956.
An exposition of expressed attitudes of socialist parties in Europe concerning issues of European integration to 1956. Included are socialist positions on the relation of Europe to Africa.

1326. Epstein, Leon. British Politics in the Suez Crisis. London: Pall Mall, 1964, pp. viii, 220.
Study of the function of party cohesion in the formation of foreign policy decisions leading to armed conflict affecting the status and international legal obligations related to the Suez Canal.

1327. Farrell, R. Barry. "Foreign Politics of Open and Closed Political Societies." In Farrell (ed.), Approaches to Comparative and International Politics. Evanston: Northwestern University Press, 1966, pp. 167-208.
A broad-stroke comparison of foreign policy organization and processes in the Communist countries, the United States, the United Kingdom, and, occasionally, Canada that is particularly valuable for its discussion of the probable relationship between the party machinery and the foreign ministries in European Communist countries in part indicated by data on the membership in the politburos of first party secretaries (all), defense ministers (5 of 9), foreign ministers (1--Poland), and foreign trade ministers (0). Data is also presented on the education of senior political leaders, foreign ministers, and defense ministers of the European Communist countries (only one political leader with a university degree but five foreign ministers) and of nine Western countries (only one political leader and one foreign minister without a university degree) as of July 1, 1965.

1328. García-Cantú, G. "Las dos políticas exteriores de México." 18 Cuadernos americanos (1959), 41-55.
A treatment of Mexican foreign policy as a reflection of internal conflicts.

1328-A. Hellmann, Donald C. Japanese Domestic Politics and Foreign Policy: The Peace Agreement with the Soviet Union. Berkeley: University of California Press, 1969, pp. ix, 202.

A study of the impact of factionalism within Japanese political parties, particularly the party in power, on the formulation of Japanese foreign policy with focus on the Peace Agreement of 1956 with the Soviet Union. Attention is also given to
the opposition Socialist Party, issue and policy groups, business
interest groups, and the press which had little influence because
it buried significant information in an excess of detailed trivia
about faction leaders. Of particular interest in this account is
the use by the Soviet Union of an alleged conservation measure to
induce the Japanese fishing industry to bring influence to bear
in favor of the Soviet objective of early agreement after negotiations had been suspended over territorial issues.

1329. Kantor, Harry. "Tambien hay democracia en el Caribe." Combate
(No. 9, March-April 1960), 56-67.
    A fine, concise article for the Spanish-speaking public on
the subject of the contention between the Calderón and Figueres
factions in Costa Rica that reached the stages of civil war and
of intervention coming from elsewhere in Central America.

1330. Weber, E. "Political Language and Political Realities." 7
Cambridge Journal (1954), 408-423.
    Holds that in the 18th century political opinion was that
of a narrow circle, but that the ever-growing, politically naïve
electorate of the 19th century had to be wooed through a new political language. At the same time organization gained ascend-
ancy over language so that, as structure became more sophisticated,
language became less so. Stiffening party structure came to control political structure, but the author believes that political
sophistication is increasing to permit foreseeing the possibility
of bypassing party machinery.

1331. Westerfield, H. Bradford. Foreign Policy and Party Politics:
Pearl Harbor to Korea. New Haven: Yale University Press, 1958, pp. x,
448.
    Richly documented case studies of foreign policy issues in
the arena of American party politics which itself entails a cutting across party lines in that the true division between internationalism and nationalism (or, in its manifestation of withdrawal symptoms, isolationism) is not identical with party divisions.

See also nos. 1261, 1435, 1867, 1871, 2108, 2109, 2143, 2398, 2476.

5. Influence of Elite and Mass Opinion

    a. Elite and Mass Opinion

    1332. Adler, Kenneth, and Bobrow, Davis. "Interest and Influence in
Foreign Affairs." 20 Public Opinion Quarterly (1956), 89-101.

Case study in the suburbs of a Midwestern city. In socio-economic status, communications exposure, and communications activity, the "influential" differ from the "interested" but not influential. The "influentials" were concentrated in the legal profession and among business and industry executives. They were highly educated, with many having annual incomes over $25,000 and had more exposure to political means of communication, particularly newspapers, magazines, and books. Influence was generally exerted through personal channels.

1333. Adorno, T.W., Brunswick, Else Frankel, Levinson, Daniel J., and Sanford, R. Nevitt. The Authoritarian Personality. New York: Harper, 1950, pp. xxxiii, 990.
Path-breaking work on personality, cognitive structure, and political attitudes that employed questionnaire data in part. Subsequent studies have indicated some difficulties with the method but it does help to explain relationships between authoritarianism, nationalism, and fears for national security that generate in some segments of a population a reliance on power rather than, e.g., the trust on which an uninspected nuclear test ban must rest.

1334. Alger, Chadwick F. "The External Bureaucracy in United States Foreign Affairs." 7 Administrative Science Quarterly (1962), 50-78.
On the creation of special study groups, commissions, and similar bodies as a means of providing the executive with new perspectives and of legitimating views of elite opinion groups.

1334-A. Angell, Robert C. Peace on the March: Transnational Participation. New York: Van Nostrand Reinhold, 1969, pp. ix, 205.
Analysis of an hypothesis that elites tend to influence policy-makers toward international accommodation, the analysis including a determination of changes through time in the number of each type of transnational participant, positive or negative effects on participants, and the social status of participants. Stress is on the impact of the individual on the host country and on his own decision-makers.

1335. Angell, Robert C., and Dunham, Vera Sandomirsky. A Study of the Values of Soviet and of American Elites. Studies in Deterrence, V, U.S. Naval Ordnance Test Station, China Lake, California. NOTS TP 3168, November 1963, pp. vi, 148.
Use of content analysis of Soviet and United States periodicals to compare the values of six Soviet and American elites.

1336. Arévalo, Juan José. The Shark and the Sardines. Translated by June Cobb and Raul Osegueda. New York: Lyle Stuart, 1961, pp. 256.
Attack on US foreign policy and "Yankee imperialism," of symptomatic interest, by the former President of Guatemala.

1337. Buchanan, William, and Cantril, Hadley. How Nations See Each Other: A Study in Public Opinion. Urbana: University of Illinois Press, 1953, pp. ix, 220.

Example of a survey in nine countries of attitudes toward an interviewee's own and other countries--a pilot study.

1338. Carnero Checa, Genaro. El aguila rampante: El imperialismo yanqui sobre América Latina. Mexico City: Ediciones Semanario Peruano, 1956, pp. 336.

Emotional condemnation of the United States and its actions in Latin America.

1339. Chavarri Porpeta, R. "Vecindad y enimistad de los Estados Unidos e Iberoamerica." 116 Revista de estudios políticos (1961), 149-172.

Attributes anti-Yankee sentiment in Latin America to mistakes in United States policy which lacks uniformity and which suffers from the opposition between the interests of many large companies and those of the Department of State.

1340. Cooper, Joseph B. "Psychological Literature on the Prevention of War." 3 Bulletin of the Research Exchange on the Prevention of War (No 3, January 1955), 2-15.

Analytical review of psychological abstracts between 1941 and 1953 that shows 68 articles dealing explicitly with peace as compared to 1,048 dealing with war.

1341. Cory, Robert H. "The Role of Public Opinion in the United States Policies toward the United Nations." 11 International Organization (1957), 220-227.

Support for the United Nations is constant, with satisfaction a function of the degree of international tension. Executives make policies according to their own decisions rather than by using public opinion as a basis for decision. Executives feel that the public does not fully understand the facts and that opinion is consistent in the desire to retain the UN, even though understanding of the functions of that body is shallow.

1342. Crespi, Irving. "Public Reaction to the Eichmann Trial." 28 Public Opinion Quarterly (1964), 91-103.

Examination of the Eichmann trial's impact on public opinion as indicated by two Gallup Poll questions.

1343. Cutler, Neal E. The Alternative Effects of Generations and Aging upon Political Behavior: A Cohort Analysis of American Attitudes Toward Foreign Policy, 1946-1966. ONRL-4321, UC-2-General, Miscellaneous, and Progress Reports. Contract No. W-7405-eng-26. Oak Ridge, Tennessee: Oak Ridge National Laboratory, December 1968, pp. xvii, 440.

In a secondary analysis of public opinion polls, eight question-sets, representing cognitions, evaluations, and policy preferences, were subjected to cohort analysis as conceived by demographers. It was found that the historically more recent the generational cohort, the greater the salience of foreign policy, the greater the expectation of war, and the greater the support for various foreign policy alternatives. In the light of such phenomena as the self-fulfilling prophecy and the mirror image, particularly as the latter may influence interpretations of another's intent, the rise in expectation of war among those who in the future will be in decision-making and policy-influencing positions is a matter that should give concern.

1344. Dawson, Raymond H. The Decision to Aid Russia, 1941: Foreign Policy and Domestic Politics. Chapel Hill: University of North Carolina Press, 1959, pp. 315.

A study of the interrelation of foreign policy and domestic politics that shows the Roosevelt Administration bound to a reading of public opinion that was in error according to survey data.

1345. Deutsch, Karl W., and Merritt, Richard L. "Effects of Events of National and International Images." In Herbert C. Kelman (ed.), International Behavior: A Social-Psychological Approach. New York: Holt, Rinehart and Winston, 1965, pp. 132-188.

Employs data related to the impact of events on images to reach a number of conclusions, among them that almost nothing can shift the images of 40% of the populations of most countries, that a combination of cumulative events, spectacular events, and governmental effort can on extremely rare occasions shift the remainders of the populations, and that most spectacular political changes involve a change of attitudes of one-fifth to one-third of the population in consequence of a combination of spectacular and cumulative events. Much more important than the findings is the example set of the effective integration of data from various sources to deal with the complexities of impacts of events.

1346. Díez Nicolas, J. "Grado de información y opioniones sobre política internacional." 6 Revista del Instituto de Ciencias sociales (1965), 123-138.

Report of an inquiry of November 1964 by the Spanish Institute of Public Opinion that sought to determine the extent of public information concerning international affairs. Responses to the eight questions posed indicate that 6% were well informed, 71% poorly or only fairly informed, and 23% were not informed at all. There appeared to be significant differences in the opinions of these groups, with the ill-informed hesitant to express opinions.

1347. Driver, Michael J., assisted by Gordon Russell, Thomas Cafferty, and Richard Allen. American College Elite Opinion and International Assurance. Technical Report #4.1. Studies of the Social and Psychological Aspects of Verification, Inspection and International Assurance. ACDA/E-104. Prepared for the U.S. Arms Control and Disarmament Agency. West Lafayette, Indiana: Herman C. Krannert Graduate School of Industrial Administration, October 1968, pp. vi, 79.

Analysis of public opinion poll data in an undertaking to trace the perceived level of trust and perceptions of relative Soviet-American power in 1961-1963, with evidence that the college educated take account of trust and its components and hold a complex notion of the elements of power.

1348. Driver, Michael J., assisted by Gordon Russell, Thomas Cafferty and Richard Allen. American Mass Opinion and International Assurance. Technical Report No. 4.2. Studies of the Social and Psychological Aspects of Verification, Inspection and International Assurance. ACDA/E-104. Prepared for the U.S. Arms Control and Disarmament Agency. West Lafayette, Indiana: Purdue University, Herman C. Krannert Graduate School of Industrial Administration, November 1968, pp. v, 57.

An analysis of public opinion poll data that shows the non-college-educated mass to take no account of trust and trustworthiness but to rest assurance in respect to an adversary and estimates of the probability of war solely on the perception of relative power, with power so simplistically conceived that, for example, no account is taken of science as an element of power.

1349. Driver, Michael J., with the assistance of Gordon Russell, Thomas Cafferty, and Richard Allen. Effects of Education on American Public Opinion: Effects of College Education on the Complexity and Content of Opinions Concerning International Assurance. Technical Report No. 4.3. Studies of the Social and Psychological Effects of Verification, Inspection and International Assurance. ACDA/E-104. Prepared for the U.S. Arms Control and Disarmament Agency. West Lafayette, Indiana: Herman C. Krannert Graduate School of Industrial Administration, December 1968, pp. vi, 49.

A comparison of college educated and mass opinion on international assurance, as elaborated in Technical Reports Nos. 4.1 and 4.2, that highlights the effects of college education in producing more complex cognitive structures and resultant inclusion of trust as an element in international assurance and production of a complex notion of power. It is noticeable that between summer 1961 and spring 1962 mass assurance toward the Soviet Union began to rise as soon as a perceived power disparity in favor of the Soviet Union began to change favorably to the United States but that elite assurance did not begin to rise until the level of trust began to rise about four months later.

1350. Elder, R.E. "The Public Studies Division of the Department of State: Public Opinion Analysts in the Formulation and Conduct of American Foreign Policy." 10 Western Political Quarterly (1957), 783-792.

Description of activities designed to keep foreign policy makers informed of expressed opinions.

1351. Feld, M.D. "Political Policy and Persuasion: The Role of Communications from Political Leaders." 2 Journal of Conflict Resolution (1958), 78-89.

Treats political communications as of two types, instruction and persuasion. Instruction is treated as objective and rational with the audience subordinate to the communicator. Persuasion is regarded as subjective and emotional with audience and communicator in a relationship of equality. Persuasion being the heart of the relationship between the political personality and his public, the politicians must treat the political environment, i.e., those groups or individuals on whom office-holding depends as composed of equals. Decisions represent changes in the political environment for which acceptance is sought, while policy

statements must indicate consideration of the opposition's views
and the taking of measures in the direct interest of the opposition.

1352. Galtung, Ingrid Eide. "Technical Assistance and Public Opinion."
1 Journal of Peace Research (1964), 19-35.
    Attitude surveys in Norway and India related to the Indo-
Norwegian project to develop fisheries in Kerala State, show
the following: (a) a change in the basis of evaluation by Nor-
wegians from moral to technical merits (a similar shift in the
tenor of Norwegian parliamentary debates is reported by Mari
Holmboe Ruge, "Technical Assistance and Parliamentary Debates,"
1 Journal of Peace Research (1964), 77-94); (b) negative attitudes strong in a small Norwegian fishing community which had
direct contacts with the project area and more positive attitudes, with less judgment on a technical basis, in a town lacking direct contacts with India; (c) a favorable view in the Indian villages, in contact with the project but no reaction in
the form of interest in Norway or in international relations in
general.

1353. Galtung, Johann. "Foreign Policy Opinion as a Function of Social Position." Peace Research Society (International), Papers. Ghent
Conference, 1964. Vol. II (1965), pp. 206-231. Also in 1 Journal of Peace
Research (1964), 206-231.
    Treating society as divided into a center or favored part
and a periphery or rejected part, the author finds the periphery
to suffer from insufficient communication and to be more absolutist, whether favoring sudden change or the status quo, in regard
to foreign affairs than is the revisionist center. Survey data
from Norway in 1959-1963 confirmed a number of points of the
theory. The author suggests means of stabilizing foreign policy
opinions in favor of peaceful policies.

1354. Glock, Charles Y., Selznick, Gertrude J., and Spaeth, Joe L.
The Apathetic Majority: A Study Based on Public Response to the Eichmann
Trial. New York: Harper & Row, 1967, pp. xii, 222.
    Based on a sampling of public opinion in Oakland, California,
in 1961 that sought opinions on the Eichmann case then in progress, this study provides, among other things, evidence of how
little international legal issues and principles penetrate the
public mind even in the rare instance of extensive press coverage. For example, it was found that only 13% of the individuals
interviewed were able to answer four elementary questions about
the Eichmann trial and its background. Even so, most respondents
were ready to express opinions.

1355. Halle, Nils H. "Social Position and Foreign Policy Attitudes."
3 Journal of Peace Research (1966), 46-74.
    Application to France, Poland, and Norway of a special in-
dex for social position, based on the "don't know" answers in a
survey in each country. The findings tend, with some qualifications, to uphold Johan Galtung's position that there is a variance

between the center and the periphery of a society in opinion-
holding (supra, no. 1353).

1356. Hero, Alfred O., Jr. "The American Public and the UN, 1954-
1966." 10 Journal of Conflict Resolution (1966), 436-475.
    Review of public opinion polls concerning American opinion
toward the United Nations and such related matters as the presence of the Soviet Union, the admission of Red China, the United
Nations Emergency Force, and developmental aid. Demographic
analysis is included, as well as some comparisons with polls
taken in other countries.

1357. Hickey, G.C. Village in Vietnam. New Haven: Yale University
Press, 1964, pp. 314.
    A comprehensive field study of a Vietnamese village that
finds the village to be self-contained and homogeneous, "a little
world that is autonomous and disregards the outside world."

1358. Hirabayashi, Gordon K., and Rhatib, M. Fathalla El. "Communication and Political Awareness in the Villages of Egypt." 22 Public Opinion Quarterly (1958), 357-363.
    This was a study of five contiguous villages in densely
populated Lower Egypt. A two-stage random sample design of
households and individuals within households was developed.
The province of Menoufia was chosen for it is characteristic of
the factors at work in an economically developing nation. The
study posed a question of the extent to which Egyptian villagers
are becoming aware of the political affairs of their local, national, and international environment. Political awareness was
strongest at the local affairs level. Foreign news was still
considered rather remote and irrelevant in comparison with local
and national affairs.

1359. Kelley, Harold H., and Woodruff, Christine L. "Members' Reactions to Apparent Group Approval of a Counternorm Communication." 52
Journal of Abnormal and Social Psychology (1956), 67-75.
    Report of an attempt to use a one-way communication to
change perceptions of norms by a small and tightly knit audience. The data indicate that listeners to a recorded speech
incompatible with their norms tended to accept the content to a
greater extent when afforded evidence that other members of their
group had approved the speech than when given evidence that an
irrelevant group of outsiders had done so. This article complements a report by Milgram (infra, no. 1717) on acceptance of a
directive to do injury and so is relevant to the problems of aggression, war crimes, and crimes against humanity.

1360. Kerstiens, Thom. The New Elite in Asia and Africa: A Comparative Study of Indonesia and Ghana. New York: Praeger, 1966, pp. vi, 282.
    On the concept, structure, and position of elites in Ghana
and Indonesia, with special reference to international concepts
such as Christianity, Communism, and international politics.

1361. Key, V.O., Jr. Public Opinion and American Democracy. New York: Knopf, 1961, pp. xxxiv, 566.

Includes sections on noncongruence between opinions on domestic and foreign policies as indicated by survey research data gathered in the United States in 1952 and 1956.

1362. Konz, Stephan, and Redding, Stephen. "The Effect of Social Pressure on Decision Making." 16 Journal of the American Institute of Industrial Engineers (November-December 1965), 381.

Employing the simple task of judging the relative length of lines, the experimenters found differences in the percentage of correct selections when there was no influence from others, incorrect choices by others, and correct choices by others. These differences suggest that social pressure affects the quality of decisions.

1363. Kristjanson, Leo. "Attitude Study in Saskatchewan." Research Review (Centre of Community Studies). Abstracted in 1 Peace Research Abstracts Journal (1964), 1072-1073.

Report on a random sample of 200 urban and 300 rural households in and around a Saskatchewan trade center. Both groups were aware of international dangers but had few suggestions for possible courses of action. In the case of the rural sample, 45% felt that nothing could be done while 15% thought that voluntary organizations might help. The author concludes that the general attitude of frustration and helplessness is unhealthy in a democracy. But it may be questioned whether the findings do not invite a probe both in respect to environmental differences affecting judgment as to probable effectiveness of work through voluntary organizations. In another direction, questions might be asked about the effect of the shield of state authority against the policy-influencing activities undertaken by international voluntary organizations and directed toward national governments.

1364. Kuroda, Yasumasa. "Peace-War Orientation in a Japanese Community." 3 Journal of Peace Research (1966), 380-388.

Survey of a community located close to Tokyo indicates Liberals as a whole to be more peace-oriented than Conservatives and that Conservatives involved in community life and politics tend to be peace-oriented while Conservatives least involved in community life tend to be war-oriented.

1365. Laulicht, Jerome. "An Analysis of Canadian Foreign Policy Attitudes." Peace Research Society (International), Papers. Chicago Conference, 1964. Vol. III (1965), pp. 121-136.

More thorough analysis of the data of Paul and Laulicht, In Your Opinion (supra, no. 1315) employing scale analysis, factor analysis, and multiple regression to produce the findings reported.

1366. Lerner, Daniel. The Passing of Traditional Society: Modernizing the Middle East. Glencoe: Free Press, 1958, pp. xiii, 466.

Includes a discussion of the inability of tradition-bound
persons to form opinions on world affairs.

1367. Martini, W. "Die Emotionalisierung der Aussenpolitik." 5 Aussenpolitik (1954), 428-487.
    Critique of popular influences on foreign policy, calling
attention to the incapacity of the masses to resolve the antinomy between morality and raison d'etat and to conceive of long
range policy. Emotionalization is seen as compelling mistakes
by national leaders.

1368. Meehan, Eugene J. The British Left Wing and Foreign Policy.
New Brunswick: Rutgers University Press, 1960, pp. 201.
    Theoretically oriented study of the influence of ideology
on foreign policy.

1369. Mendel, Douglas Heusted. The Japanese People and Foreign Policy: A Study of Public Opinion in Post-Treaty Japan. Berkeley: Universit
of California Press, 1961, pp. xv, 269.
    Employs the author's surveys and Japanese polls to study
Japanese opinion on foreign policy. The study requires use in
conjunction with more process-oriented research on Japan.

1370. Merritt, Richard L., and Puchala, Donald J. (eds.). Western
European Perspectives on International Affairs: Public Opinion Studies
and Evaluations. New York: Praeger, 1967, pp. xx, 552.
    Part I contains eight analytical and methodological arti-
cles in which the authors examine data presented in Part II to
identify patterns and trends in Western European views of international affairs. The data in Part II consists of USIA material on 53 survey topics covering eight major subjects.

1371. Oskamp, S., and Hartry, A. A Factor-Analytic Study of Attitudes Toward U.S. and Russian Actions in World Affairs. Mimeo. Claremont,
California: Claremont Graduate School, 1965.
    Finds that American college students project very different
interpretations of nearly identical actions by the United States
and the Soviet Union, with the projections tending to rate United
States actions as good and Soviet actions as bad.

1372. Peristiany, J.G. (ed.). Honour and Shame: The Values of Mediterranean Society. Chicago: University of Chicago Press, 1966, pp. 265.
    Although four of the six anthropologists who contribute to
the volume are concerned with an essentially domestic problem
among four peoples, two contributors attempt to define a general
theory of honor and so present provocative theses that could be
of help in explaining certain psychological dimensions of politicians' actions on the international scene in terms of their
relations as individuals, as well as of role holders, to their
societies.

1373. Ramírez Novoa, Ezequiel. La farsa del panamericanismo y la
unidad indoamericana. Buenos Aires: Indoamérica, 1955, pp. 215.

Critical view of United States policies by a Peruvian
Aprista.

1374. Rokeach, Milton. "Attitude Change and Behavioral Change." 30
Public Opinion Quarterly (1966-67), 529-550.
Treats attitude change as a function both of attitude toward an object and of attitude toward a situation and suggests
new methods of assessing attitude change in place of contemporary approaches that deal with changes in single and isolated
expressions of opinion.

1375. Rosenau, James N. The Attentive Public and Foreign Policy:
A Theory of Growth and Some New Evidence. Research Monograph No. 31.
Princeton: Center of International Studies, Princeton University, March
1968, pp. iii, 48.
Presents a theory and some evidence that the attentive
American public is growing slowly and steadily as a result of
increased objective political competence (derived from expanded
educational opportunities) and mounting subjective political
competence (stemming from the successes of the civil rights
movement).

1376. Rosenburg, Morris. "Misanthropy and Attitudes Toward International Affairs." 1 Journal of Conflict Resolution (1957), 340-345.
Subjects were rated on a "faith-in-people" scale. They
were questioned about the belief that power is the best method
of solving international problems, the belief in the inevitability of war, and on whether the UN or the atomic bomb was the
more successful deterrent of war. The results suggest a link
between an individual's view of human nature and his outlook on
international affairs.

1377. Rosi, Eugene J. "Mass and Attentive Opinion on Nuclear Weapons Tests and Fallout, 1954-63." 29 Public Opinion Quarterly (1965),
280-297.
Analysis of 18 national opinion surveys, in 15 of which the
attentive public seemed less in favor of test suspension and
more concerned about security than did the inattentive or mass
public. In respect to the health effect of fallout, security
considerations outweighed humanitarian concerns. Cleavages between the two publics were often considerable but not, in the
author's interpretation, drastic. The attentive public apparently responded positively and rapidly to firm policy determinations by the Administration. Whether the policy was to resume
or to halt nuclear tests, the Administration succeeded in mobilizing supportive opinion.

1378. Sáenz, Vicente. Nuestra América en la cruz: Site prólogos,
varias apologías y otros apruntes. Mexico City: Editorial América Nueva,
1960, pp. 370.
Indictment of US policies related to Latin America, symptomatic of feelings prior to the Kennedy Administration that produced the Alliance for Progress.

1379. Sampson, D., and Smith, Howard P. "A Scale to Measure World-Minded Attitudes." 45 _Journal of Social Psychology_ (1957), 99-106.

Defining world-mindedness as concern with the problems of humanity in which the primary reference group is mankind rather than nationals of a particular country and defining international mindedness as an interest in or knowledge about international affairs, the authors undertake to devise a Likert type scale of 32 items pertaining to eight dimensions of world-mindedness.

1380. Scott, William A. "Rationality and Non-Rationality of International Attitudes." 2 _Journal of Conflict Resolution_ (1958), 8-16.

Treating nonrational forces as likely to dominate when a cognitive attitude structure is weak in relation to other systems influencing an individual's response patterns, the author finds that the average citizen's attitudes toward international events are strongly nonrational. Consistent attitude structures are not developed to permit rationality. Remoteness of foreign affairs and availability only of second-hand information inhibit development of consistent attitude structures.

1381. Shuval, J.T. "The Role of Class in Structuring Inter-Group Hostility." 10 _Human Relations_ (1957), 61-75.

Responses of a large group of native Israeli and recent immigrants indicate that in a situation of generalized frustration the lowest groups in the hierarchy of classes are likely to be the most vulnerable to expressions of hostility. The conclusion is not unexpected, for it confirms the historical record of demagogic activities.

1382. Smith, P.A. "Opinions, Publics and World Affairs in the United States." 14 _Western Political Quarterly_ (1961), 698-714.

Public opinion surveys related to four international events reveal the existence of three "international publics," the most serious hindrance to internationalism, when articulate, being the low-educated who react to crisis events by seeking overt, aggressive, and decisive national policies and leadership.

1383. Unger, A.L. "The Public Opinion Reports of the Nazi Party." 29 _Public Opinion Quarterly_ (1965-66), 565-582.

On periodic "morale reports" submitted by the local party organizations in one totalitarian system. Much of the information concerning opinion critical of the regime that reached local party leaders suffered significant distortion in its progress through different levels of the Nazi hierarchy. The tendency to present a favorable picture of popular feelings was built into the system. In contrast, similar reports by the Nazi security services show greater access to critical opinion and no indication of a vested interest in its concealment.

1384. Walton, C.C. "The Hague Congress of Europe: A Case Study of Public Opinion." 12 _Western Political Quarterly_ (1959), 738-752.

A reminder of the brief Congress of Europe held at The Hague in 1948 that, despite inadequate preparation and extremely limited

working time, was able to supply imaginative spark and, in some
cases, the basic format for European institutions that have subsequently emerged. The 800 delegates represented the several
elements of the European political spectrum except the Communist.

1385. Walton, Richard E., assisted by G. Russell, T. Cafferty, and R.
Allen. A System of Attitudes Related to International Assurance: Theo-
retical Framework and Review. Technical Report No. 1. Studies of the So-
cial and Psychological Aspects of Verification, Inspection and International
Assurance. ACDA/E-104. Prepared for the U.S. Arms Control and Disarmament
Agency. West Lafayette, Indiana: Purdue University, Herman C. Krannert
Graduate School of Industrial Administration, September 1968, pp. vii, 65.
　　　　Presents a model of trust and its components with particu-
　　　lar reference to trust between adversary nations such as the
　　　United States and the Soviet Union.

1386. Whitaker, Urban, and Davis, Bruce E. The World and Ridgeway,
South Carolina. Columbia: University of South Carolina Press, 1968, pp.
xiv, 94.
　　　　The authors have employed extensive interviews with all seg-
　　　ments of the population of a rural South Carolina community to
　　　produce a case study of changing perspectives on international
　　　affairs.

1386-A. Willick, Daniel H. "Public Interest in International Affairs:
A Cross-National Study." 50 Social Science Quarterly (1969), 272-285.
　　　　Uses survey data to attempt to depict the relative sizes of
　　　the attentive publics for foreign affairs in West Germany, Great
　　　Britain, France, Japan, and Italy.

See also nos. 265, 1172, 1237, 1238, 1434, 1628, 1753, 1773, 1778,
1855, 2065, 2108, 2109, 2144, 2842.

b. Influence of Organized Interests

1387. Aspaturian, Vernon V. "Internal Politics and Foreign Policy in
the Soviet System." In R. Barry Farrell (ed.), Approaches to Comparative
and International Politics. Evanston: Northwestern University Press, 1966,
pp. 212-287.
　　　　Deals with the interplay of domestic interests and foreign
　　　policy in the Soviet political process, seeking to identify in-
　　　ternal and external forces shaping policy. Several generaliz-
　　　able factors, characteristic of all large states and not just of
　　　the Soviet Union, are identified, as well as factors either
　　　unique to the Soviet system or not generalizable even though not
　　　historically unique. Some developments blunting the ideological
　　　factor in Soviet foreign policy are identified. An effort is
　　　made to identify the beneficiaries of raised international ten-
　　　sions and the beneficiaries of relaxation of tensions.

1388. Bauer, Raymond A., Pool, Ithiel de Sola, and Dexter, Lewis A.
American Business and Public Policy. New York: Atherton, 1963, pp. 499.
      With reference to the Reciprocal Trade Acts of 1953, 1954,
and 1955 and the Trade Expansion Act of 1962, the book examines
public opinion, business executive opinion, local community opinion and action, communications with Congress, interest group performance, and congressional events and perceptions. The study,
which took 10 years, required not only three senior authors and
a research center but also a public opinion poll, a NORC survey
of 900 business executives, interviews with 500 Congressmen and
others associated with the legislation, and research in eight
communities.

1389. Blaisdell, D.C. "Pressure Groups, Foreign Policies, and International Politics." 319 Annals of the American Academy of Political and
Social Science (1958), 149-157.
      Discusses some reasons why American pressure groups have
become increasingly influential in international affairs, raises
the question of the universality of such activity, notes the inconsistency in the compromise outcomes of pressure group activity
in international affairs, and calls attention to the extension of
pressure group activity from foreign office to intergovernmental
organization decision processes, particularly through activities
of international nongovernmental organizations.

1390. Chambers, F.P. "Interest Groups and Foreign Affairs." 8 Year
Book of World Affairs (1954), 220-241.
      Certain instances of interest group influence upon American
foreign policy legislation are presented, along with an account
of the operation of British interest groups during the Japanese
bond settlement of 1952. The author concludes that the grand
transactions of foreign affairs may be a function of power politics, but the rest lies in the area of interest group activity.

1391. Ehrmann, Henry W. "The French Trade Associations and the Ratification of the Schuman Plan." 6 World Politics (1954), 453-481.
      Description of the effort of almost all French trade asso-
ciations, under the leadership of the National Steel Association, to oppose the Schuman Plan, particularly its restrictions
on cartel and concentration agreements. Despite the support
gathered within and outside parliament, the effort failed because the associations were outmaneuvered by the supporters of
the plan and because they were unable to arouse public support
for their position. Although the case is one in which the trade
associations failed to prevent an alteration of the European
legal and economic structures, it is illustrative of the importance to the content of international law of the domestic struggle
between interest groups seeking to control aspects of foreign
policy and of international law-making procedures.

1392. Feld, Werner. "National Economic Interest Groups and Policy
Formation in the EEC." 81 Political Science Quarterly (1966), 362-411.

On the strategies and techniques of national economic interest groups seeking favorable decisions and policies from Community institutions, with particular attention to reliance of
such groups on the governmental route to Community-level objectives, to the adverse attitudes of many national civil servants
to transferring power to Community officials, and to the unfavorable perceptions of European regional organizations entertained
by national interest group officials.

1393. Friedrich, Carl J. American Policy Toward Palestine. Washington: Public Affairs Press, 1944, pp. vi, 106.
    Shows the workings of a pressure group in respect to a par-
ticular foreign policy issue.

1394. Friedrich, Carl J. "The Agricultural Basis of Emotional Nationalism." 1 Public Opinion Quarterly (1937), 50-61.
    Agriculturalists have been thought to be especially nation-
alistic because they have a sense of love for their own country
or region derived from the farmers' existence in the fatherland.
The German referendum on the Weimar Constitution is treated as a
test case, and it is found that the agricultural regions were
most nationalistic. The author suggests that this may have occurred for the rather specific reason that the rural population
felt more keenly than the urban population the distress of the
economic crisis.

1395. Hardy, Margaret. The Influence of Organized Labor on the Foreign Policy of the United States. Liége: H. Vaillant-Carmanne, 1936, pp.
viii, 270.
    Includes labor's role and attitudes in respect to formula-
tion of policies on such matters as recognition of Russia, American adherence to the World Court, tariff, immigration, and the
treatment of seamen.

1396. Lerner, Daniel. "French Business Leaders Look at EDC: A Preliminary Report." 20 Public Opinion Quarterly (1956), 212-221.
    A survey of business leaders of France, to test the valid-
ity of current explanations for the defeat of EDC, showed that
the hypotheses suggested were all false. It was found that the
world situation affected their decisions and that they responded
largely in a pro-European manner. This shows French business
not to be opposed to European economic integration and casts
doubt on anti-supranationalism, anti-Germanism, and anti-Ameri-
canism as reasons for rejection of EDC.

1397. Manuel, Frank. The Realities of American-Palestine Relations.
Washington: Public Affairs Press, 1949, pp. viii, 378.
    Illustrates the workings of a pressure group in respect to
a particular area of foreign policy.

1398. McLellan, David S., and Woodhouse, Charles E. "Businessmen in
Foreign Policy." 39 Southwestern Social Science Quarterly (1959), 283-290.

Statistical analysis of the business community's access to the US government decision-making apparatus.

1399. McLellan, David S., and Woodhouse, Charles E. "The Business Elite and Foreign Policy." 13 <u>Western Political Quarterly</u> (1960), 172-190.
Analysis of positions taken by businessmen before Congressional committees and in recommendations submitted to the government concerning six major postwar international economic programs. Businessmen are found to fall into two groups, "fundamentalists" who appraise foreign economic policy in terms of rigid adherence to traditional American economic positions and "progressives" who accept innovations without abandoning belief in traditional principles.

1400. Meynaud, Jean. <u>La revolte paysanne</u>. Paris: Payot, 1963, pp. 308.
Dealing with a matter that is related to the development of EEC, particularly in the realm of agricultural policy, this book analyzes the agricultural crisis in economically developed lands where the peasant rebels either by leaving the land or, on occasion, by violent demonstrations. Economic bases of the unrest are dealt with and some suggestions are made for remedying the insecurities and other basic problems of peasant life. Particular attention is accorded the problems of French peasants.

1401. Mishler, Elliot G. "The Peace Movement and the Foreign Policy Process." In Roger Fisher (ed.), <u>International Conflict and Behavioral Science: The Craigville Papers</u>. New York: Basic Books, 1964, pp. 257-265.
Emphasizes obstacles and limitations that peace groups encounter in their attempts to influence foreign policy.

1402. Pye, Lucian W. "The Non-Western Political Process." 20 <u>Journal of Politics</u> (1958), 468-486.
Attempts to set forth the chief characteristics of non-Western politics, noting, among other things, a tendency of opposition parties to appear as revolutionary movements, relatively little relationship of the intensity and breadth of political discussion to political decision-making, and a paucity of explicitly organized interest groups with functionally specific roles. The last is viewed as requiring a national leadership to appeal to an undifferentiated public, a circumstance regarded as encouraging more clearly defined positions on international issues than on domestic issues.

1403. Reynaud, R. "Les syndicats et la construction européenne." 150 <u>Revue de l'action populaire</u> (1961), 787-806.
Labor unions have not hesitated to express their views during negotiations on integration. The World Federation of Trade Unions (Féderation Syndicale Mondiale) has been hostile to integration and has developed a tactic for the situation in which certain member unions have considered integration to work in their favor. In response, the free unions supported at once and

have continued to support the European project as providing ideal grounds for the international development of trade unionism. But treaty revision is wanted on a number of points as well as progressive establishment of community power based on flexible and evolving institutions. The author sees the hopes of unions in danger of frustration if they do not organize on the European level.

1404. Rifflet, R. "Les syndicats belges et la CECA." Revue de l'Institut de Sociolgie (1958), 139-230.
   Examination of the role of Belgian trade unions in regard to such matters as the establishment of ECSC, Community social and financial policy, and the problem of cartels. The author finds the unions to be lacking a supranationational policy. This lack is attributed to the extremely technical nature of Community problems, latent nationalism, and fear of assuming responsibilities. The mass of workers are uninterested but might be if an extremely simple and general issue, such as election of a European parliament, were presented.

1405. Robinson, Alan D. Dutch Organised Agriculture in International Politics, 1945-1960. The Hague: Nijhoff, 1961, pp. vii, 192.
   Dutch organized agriculture can claim some of the credit for the inclusion of agriculture in the final draft of the EEC treaty as an integral part of the plan for economic integration in Europe. The political activities of Dutch agriculture, particularly but not exclusively in relation to the negotiation and implementation of the EEC treaty, are set forth and channels of influence well defined in this study.

1406. Van Wagenen, Richard. "American Defense Officials' View of the United Nations." 14 Western Political Quarterly (1961), 104-119.
   An interview of 25 Department of Defense officials and their feelings and views toward the UN. Most felt that no present UN function should be abandoned and all agreed that there was very little left of the UN to support. All agreed that US military power was keeping the peace and not the UN. The UN was seen as useful for settling small differences and dealing with problems that are not between the US and the USSR.

1407. Yanaga, Chitoshi. Big Business in Japanese Politics. New Haven and London: Yale University Press, 1968, pp. xi, 365.
   Analyzing the nature, function, and role of the Japanese bureaucracy and finding the governing process to be essentially a joint undertaking of party government and big business, the author provides penetrating discussions of decision-making in such matters as the San Francisco Peace Treaty, the development of atomic energy, Southeast Asia reparations settlements, and the Treaty of Mutual Security and Cooperation between Japan and the United States.

See also nos. 801, 809, 819, 820, 1224, 1315, 1654, 1722, 1729, 1867, 2081, 2239, 2311, 2398, 2405, 2422, 2476, 2670, 2693, 2697, 2703, 2764, 2812.

c. The Role of Experts and Expert Opinion

1408. Bauer, Raymond. "Problems of Perception and the Relations Between the United States and the Soviet Union." 5 Journal of Conflict Resolution (1961), 223-229.
Warns that experts attempting to understand another country are misled by three factors: (1) their intentions shape their perceptions; (2) they tend to overrationalize the other society's position and thereby to treat nothing as an isolated accident; (3) their models are usually out of date yet are protected against evidence calling for changes and are employed to differentiate between societies that may be quite similar.

1409. Bonilla, Frank. "A National Ideology for Development: Brazil. In Kalman H. Silvert, Expectant Peoples. New York: Random House, 1963, pp 232-260.
Unlike most studies of Latin American countries, this volume gives some attention to the técnicos, government economists whose acceptance of the "ECLA doctrine" made possible the negotiation of the Treaty of Montevideo establishing LAFTA.

1410. Crawford, Elisabeth T., and Biderman, Albert D. (eds.). Social Scientists and International Affairs: A Case for a Sociology of Social Science. New York: Wiley, 1968, pp. xviii, 334.
Includes articles by such writers as Leonard W. Doob, Harold D. Lasswell, Irving L. Horowitz, and Philip M. Hauser that provide insight into the work of social scientists who are professional government employees and the utilization of social science research by government.

1411. Frías, P.J.H. "El papel de los expertos en la vida política de América latina." 128 Revista de estudios políticos (1963), 193-199.
A brief report presented to the International Political Science Association in September 1961 on the role of experts and their relations with politicians in Latin American administrations.

1412. Galtung, Ingrid Eide. "The Status of the Technical Assistance Expert: A Study of UN Experts in Latin America." 3 Journal of Peace Research (1966), 359-379.
Report on the analysis of the responses of 173 technical experts in Latin American countries in 1963 to a 40-page questionnaire on their perception of their status and roles. An hypothesis that the situation was so unstructured as to produce little consensus was confirmed. The role model seems to be a mixture of civil servant, diplomat, and other elements.

1413. Hourani, Benjamin Tamer. Lawyers and Politics. Ph.D. Dissertation. East Lansing: Michigan State University, 1966; Ann Arbor: University Microfilms, Inc., Order No. 66-8463, pp. 225.
A study of 144 lawyers from Ingham County, Michigan, that shows no significant differences in the overall degree of

political involvement but important differences in the kinds of activities undertaken by low-status and high-status lawyers. Low-status lawyers tended to participate in the politics of hierarchy as active party workers and office holders, while high-status lawyers were active in the politics of bargaining and discussion, made monetary contributions to political candidates, and influenced legislators and administrators by letter, word-of-mouth, and face-to-face communications. Low-status lawyers were more liberal, more likely to hold Machiavellian-like beliefs, seek state and local office, evaluate highly the rewards of political life, and treat political office as a means of advancing a legal career rather than a political career. High-status lawyers looked more to the national level and thought of public office virtually exclusively at that level.

1414. Jacobson, Harold Karan, and Stein, Eric. Diplomats, Scientists, and Politicians: The United States and the Nuclear Test Ban Negotiations. Ann Arbor: University of Michigan Press, 1966, pp. ix, 538.
Thorough account of the negotiations leading to the 1963 Moscow test ban treaty.

1415. Jouvenel, Bertrand de. "The Political Consequences of the Rise of Science." 19 Bulletin of Atomic Scientists (December 1963), 2-8.
Noting that scientists are replacing lawyers who previously replaced clerics in the domination of intellectual life, a distinction is drawn between government in the legal period on the basis of principles and precedents and in the present scientific period on the basis of aiming at a particular outcome. Although regarding the rule of a scientist as less likely than that of a science administrator, the author notes that the public, no longer able to participate in decisions, must now believe scientific conceptions of the universe in the same manner in which peasants of the Middle Ages believed superstitions.

1416. Kash, Don E. "Is Good Science Good Politics?" 27 Bulletin of Atomic Scientists (March 1965), 34-36.
Holds that scientists should not make political decisions and that, although international scientific enterprise may be good science, it is not necessarily good politics.

1417. Kelly, George A. "The Expert as Historical Actor." 92 Daedalus (1963), 529-548.
Deals, among other things, with the expert as a mediator between systems of knowledge and systems of power and with the expert's right to trespass on politics.

1418. Lakoff, Sanford A. (ed.). Knowledge and Power: Essays on Science and Government. New York: Free Press, 1966, pp. x, 502.
Fifteen essays on science and government that take account of the scientist's influence on American policy and the role of government in supporting scientific research. Of particular interest to international lawyers are the essay by Cecil H. Uyehara on scientific advice and the nuclear test ban treaty and that by Roger A. Kvam on Comsat.

1419. Marschak, Jacob. "Efficient and Viable Organizational Forms." In Mason Haire (ed.), _Modern Organization Theory_. New York: Wiley, 1959, pp. 307-320.

On the cost of additional pre-decisional information and the price that it would be rational to pay for such information.

1420. Merillat, H.C.L. (ed.). _Legal Advisers and Foreign Affairs_. New York: Oceana Publications, 1964, pp. x, 162.

Summary report and background papers of the conference of legal advisers and scholars, sponsored by the American Society of International Law, and held at Princeton in September 1963. The papers suggest that the role of legal advice in foreign policy decision-making should be approached through organization behavior as well as in terms of legal and political processes.

1421. Moore, Joan W., and Moore, Burton M. "The Role of the Scientific Elite in the Decision to Use the Atomic Bomb." 6 _Social Problems_ (Summer 1958), 78-85.

The authors assert C. Wright Mills to be inaccurate in making power elite explanation of the decision to drop the atomic bomb. A review of events indicates that before the decision there were complex political decisions made by men who were not of Mills' power elite. Scientists' key decisions, effective in the US but not in Germany, resulted from the kind of communication made, a modified academic seminar that maximized dissent and provided opportunity to develop consensus, influential upon the military and politicians, on policy issues.

1421-A. Mosher, Frederick C. _Programming Systems and Foreign Affairs Leadership: An Attempted Innovation_. New York: Oxford, 1970, pp. 288.

An examination of the origins and attempted operation of a PPB-type system in the foreign policy field, together with an explanation of why it did not work.

1422. Nitze, Paul. "The Role of the Learned Man in Government." 20 _Review of Politics_ (1958), 275-288.

Includes analysis of the problem of the scientist active in the realm of government who finds himself caught between the demand of political effectiveness and the need for approval by other scientists.

1423. Price, Don K. _The Scientific Estate_. Cambridge: The Belknap Press of Harvard University Press, 1965, pp. xi, 323.

A statement of contemporary political philosophy that, among other things, seeks to identify the place of the scientific estate in the governmental process and in relation to the professional, administrative, and political estates.

1424. Schilling, W.R. "Science, Technology and Foreign Policy." 13 _Journal of International Affairs_ (1959), 7-18.

Reviews general characteristics of the relationship between technological developments and international political changes over two centuries, including the consequences of the direct mobilization of science in support of foreign policy begun during World War II.

1425. Skolnikoff, Eugene B. <u>Science, Technology, and American Foreign Policy</u>. Cambridge: MIT Press, 1967, pp. xvi, 330.
　　Although restricted to problems of American foreign policy making, this book, based upon experiences while working for the Special Assistant to the President for Science and Technology, deals, among other things, with the need for policy experts to ask the types of questions which are likely to elicit technical plans enhancing the range of policy choices since, in the absence of such questions, technical agencies are unlikely to offer alternative plans. In the course of the discussion the author presents a useful five-fold classification of foreign policy issues in terms of their interaction with science: (1) issues in which technical objectives are dominant; (2) issues primarily political but depending heavily upon scientific technology; (3) issues resulting from application of scientific methods to science and technology; (4) issues altered in a general way by science and technology; (5) issues arising in anticipation of probably or possible developments in science and technology. Reference is made to the manner in which national prestige can give rise to scientific enterprises that in turn become policy issues and to the manner in which quantitative techniques and simulation to resolve one issue generates questions both about the future character of foreign relations and about the limitations of scientific methods in the foreign policy process.

1426. Strickland, Donald A. "Physicists' Views of Space Politics." 29 <u>Public Opinion Quarterly</u> (1965), 223-235.
　　Report on a random sampling of the American Physical Society with 78% response. Asked to attribute motives to and predict outcomes of the space race, the respondents saw prestige and military advantage as the primary motives, viewed both countries as aggressive and self-aggrandizing (the USSR somewhat more so than the US) and foresaw continued competition and possible intervening disaster. Both write-in comments and other evidence indicated reluctance to expose political opinions, took economic determinism quite seriously, and displayed cynicism about politics and policy-making.

1427. Strickland, Donald A. <u>Scientists in Politics: The Atomic Scientists Movement, 1945-46</u>. (West Lafayette, Indiana): Purdue University Studies, 1968, pp. xi, 149.
　　A study of the organization of American scientists and their efforts to influence policy in the immediate post-World War II period when political activity took the form of public display of partisanship, something of little advantage since the development of the scientific advisory culture gave comparatively easy access to public authorities, thereby making it more advantageous to indulge the customary scientific posture of political distance.

1428. Tarr, David W. "Military Technology and the Policy Process." 18 Western Political Quarterly (1965), 135-148.

Views military technology as limiting the circle of effective participants in the American policy-making process. Policies are more likely to be bargains struck between contending forces rather than basic resolutions of underlying strategic issues. The momentum of military programs, influence of military scientists, and incremental character of the decision process tend to undermine the authority of top-level policy-makers.

See also nos. 342, 815, 828, 1117, 1166, 1286, 1489, 2136-2138.

d. Bureaucratic Influences and Interests

1429. Davis, Vincent. The Admirals Lobby: Policymaking on the Sea and in Congress. Chapel Hill: University of North Carolina Press, 1967, pp. 392.

An exploration of the political activity of the officer corps of the United States Navy since 1900, with emphasis on the officers' political behavior during World War II and the ensuing 20 years and upon the political techniques employed.

1430. Dorn, W.L. "The Debate over American Occupation Policy in Germany in 1944-1945." 72 Political Science Quarterly (1957), 481-501.

Review of the conflict among the US State, War, and Treasury Departments over postwar occupation policy for Germany.

1431. Downs, Anthony. Bureaucratic Structure and Decision Making. RAND Report RM-4646-PR. Santa Monica: RAND Corporation, March 1966, pp. xii, 150.

Employing the three central axioms that (1) all social agents pursue their goals rationally and efficiently, (2) the nature of its social functions influence a bureau's internal structure and operations, and (3) bureau officials are at least in part motivated by self-interest, the study examines the behavior of bureaus in the conditions of uncertainty and of high cost for information and produces several testable hypotheses.

1432. Hammond, Paul. "Foreign Policy-Making and Administrative Politics." 17 World Politics (1965), 656-671.

On the problem of policy analysis in the national security sphere and the need to find ways of dealing with political as well as material resources. Holds that in foreign policy making cognitive requirements are met more from government sources and responsive capabilities are necessarily more unified than in domestic affairs.

1433. Huntington, Samuel P. The Soldier and the State: The Theory and Politics of Civil-Military Relations. Cambridge: Harvard University Press, 1957; Vintage ed., New York: Random House, 1964, pp. xiii, 534.

Holding that "America can learn more from West Point than West Point from America" and that "If the civilians permit soldiers to adhere to the military standard, the nations themselves may eventually find redemption and security in making that standard their own," the author presents a general treatment of theoretical and historical perspectives of military institutions and the state followed by an analytical narrative of American civil-military relations. Pages 263-266, 307-309, and Chapter 14 deal with military thought on foreign policy since the 1880s. Commenting on the static nature of the military's foreign policy thinking, the author remarks that in 1930 the military man saw international politics in the same way as did his predecessor in 1880, "not because the world was the same, but because he was the same." Treating self-interest as the only motivator of states and judging arbitration treaties, international law in general, and the League of Nations to be unable to guarantee peace, the military man regarded the balance of power, coupled with military strength based on calculations of enemy capabilities rather than enemy intentions, as the delayer of inevitable war. After World War II the military returned to balance-of-power thinking as expressed in a Joint Board memorandum of 1941. The author notes that the position was expressed by Secretary of State Marshall on November 7, 1947, and also in the containment policy. He regards the State Department under Marshall and Acheson as being often far more power-oriented than the military.

1434. Jensen, Lloyd. United States Elites and Their Perceptions of the Determinants of Foreign Policy Behavior. Paper presented to the Midwest Conference of Political Scientists. Chicago: April 29, 1966, pp. 39.

Report on an Events Analysis Study sponsored by the Simulated International Processes project at Northwestern University. Four groups were interviewed: State and Defense Department officials, academicians, and correspondents. Respondents rated such determinants of Soviet and American policy as power, the internal situation, behavior of other states, personality, and ideology. The correspondents were farthest from the mean response. State and Defense respondents were closer to each other than to the academicians but the latter difference was slight. Real differences were found between the responses of the intelligence and geographical desk officers in the Department of State and between the civilian and military officers in the Department of Defense. Still greater differences appeared when State Department personnel was divided between foreign service officers and nonforeign service officers.

1435. Kolkowicz, Roman. Conflicts in Soviet Party-Military Relations: 1962-1963. Memorandum RM-3760-PR. Santa Monica: RAND Corporation, August 1963, pp. ix, 49.

On possible uncertainties and sharp controversy among political and military elite groups in the Soviet Union during the Cuban missile crisis.

1436. Lowi, Theodore J. "Making Democracy Safe for the World: National Politics and Foreign Policy." In James N. Rosenau (ed.), <u>Domestic Sources of Foreign Policy</u>. New York: Free Press, 1967, pp. 295-331.
On the conflict in foreign policy politics that arises, among other things, from the existence of separate agencies with constitutional or legal rights of access and participation, and on the presidential efforts to propagandize both his colleagues and his several publics by resort, with attendant risks, to overselling the crisis or threat and overselling the remedy.

1437. Maxon, Yale Candee. <u>Control of Japanese Foreign Policy: A Study of Civil-Military Rivalry, 1930-1945</u>. Berkeley: University of California Press, 1957, pp. vi, 286.
The pre-World War II problem of civil-military rivalry in foreign policy decision-making and the system of coordination is studied through use of Japanese sources and Tokyo Trial materials.

1438. Sanderson, G.N. <u>England, Europe and the Upper Nile, 1882-1899: A Study in the Partition of Africa</u>. Edinburgh: University Press, 1965, pp. xiv, 456.
Excellent synthesis from documentary sources and a large literature that constitutes the best study of the Upper Nile developments in the last quarter of the 19th century. The volume is particularly valuable as a study of prolonged and often futile negotiations, of situations in which adventurous officers in the field often took control of events and so of policy away from governments, of interdepartmental conflicts in London, and of instances of permanent civil servants victimizing French ministers.

1439. Snyder, William P. <u>The Politics of British Defense Policy, 1945-1962</u>. Columbus: Ohio State University Press, 1964, pp. xii, 284.
Analysis of the manner in which British defense policies are formulated, the pressures affecting policies, sources and types of influence, processes for reconciling competing demands for resources, and the effect of the decision-making organization and process on policy.

1439-A. Tuite, Matthew F., Chisholm, Roger K., and Radnor, Michael (eds.). <u>Interorganizational Decision Making</u>. Chicago: Aldine-Atherton, 1972, pp. 384.
Multidisciplinary studies of interorganizational decision-making at various levels of organization including the national and international levels.

See also nos. 777, 834, 1035, 1260, 1272, 1669, 2063, 2081, 2143.

e. Mass Communication of News and Information

1440. Boorstin, Daniel J. <u>The Image: A Guide to Pseudo-Events in America</u>. New York: Harper & Row, 1964, pp. iv, 315.

On the creation of the illusion of news by reporters, including television news reporting. Help to public officials through interviews, press conferences, etc., is discussed along with such techniques of news-making as inciting inflammatory statements from interviewees, staged events for television, and the news leak.

1441. Breed, Warren. "Newspaper 'Opinion Leaders' and Processes of Standardization." 32 Journalism Quarterly (1955), 277-284.
An attempt to analyze the uniformity or standardization of the content of American newspapers. Attention is called to the wire services and syndicates, publicity handouts, chain ownership, and a tendency on the part of most publishers to maintain a conservative political policy.

1442. Brouwer, Marten. "Prolegomena to a Theory of Mass Communication." In Lee Thayer (ed.), Communication Concepts and Perspectives. London: Macmillan; Washington: Spartan Books, 1967, pp. 227-239.
The author would replace the stimulus-response model of mass communications with a mycelium model that concentrates on (a) communication-units conceived as all belonging to the same system, (b) specialized units that are offshoots from the rest of the system and would be replaced by others if they were removed, and (c) a dependence of specialized units on nonspecialized units. In regard to content, not a survey of opinions and attitudes but a "folklore" approach is preferred and ideas, opinions, thought patterns, stereotypes, and expressions are seen as exchanged between individuals and between groups, each group having its own specific folklore. In regard to the unit to be studied, the author questions the suitability of the individual and prefers the "item" (e.g., TV-program, question, rumor) and would study how items fare and fade away.

1443. Buzek, Anthony. How the Communist Press Works. New York: Praeger, 1964, pp. 287.
Important contribution to our knowledge of the East European Communist press, now depending more upon their own reporters for foreign news than formerly.

1444. Christoph, J.B. "The Press and Politics in Britain and America." 34 Political Quarterly (1963), 137-150.
A brief review of the problem of communication of political news, including the problem of packaged services. What is here dealt with may be used to aid analysis of the problem of developing consensus in support of international legal standards in the two countries that have produced the most important precedents and guides to the substance of international law.

1445. Cohen, Bernard C. The Press and Foreign Policy. Princeton: Princeton University Press, 1963, pp. xi, 288.
A study of foreign policy news-gathering, writing, and publishing practices in the circular process from news to newspaper to news. Particular attention is called to the small proportion

of foreign affairs news, the average published daily being about one-fifth or one-sixth of the foreign news supplied daily by the Associated Press alone (pp. 115-119). Reasons for the low proportion published are analyzed, along with uses made of newspapers by government, influences on policy, selection of items for publication, and the function of the newspaper as sources of information for government officials that is in general more rapid than diplomatic reporting.

1446. Conrad, Richard. "Social Images in East and West Germany: A Comparative Study of Matched Newspapers in Two Social Systems." 33 Social Forces (1955), 281-285.
    Employing two non-Communist and one Communist newspaper from German-speaking Switzerland as a check, East Berlin, West Berlin, and Swiss newspapers are matched in terms of party affiliation, labor orientation, religious orientation, and occupation power. The Western newspapers focused on news from the West to a greater extent than the East focused on its own social system. Military topics get the greater attention in the West as compared with Eastern papers' greater attention to labor matters. Social image structure differences are noted and also the contrast between the unified view of past, present, and future in the Eastern press and the lack of a Western unified image of these periods.

1447. Deutsch, Karl W. "Mass Communication and the Loss of Freedom in National Decision-Making: A Possible Research Approach to Interstate Conflicts." 1 Journal of Conflict Resolution (1957), 200-211.
    Sets forth the proposition that through their propaganda pronouncements, with intent to manipulate their own populations, governments may inhibit their alternatives, perhaps even leaving themselves no choice but war. A number of research approaches are then suggested, including legal studies, e.g., (1) on the feasibility of controlling the prominence given particular matters and (2) on the possibility of sanctions against national media of communication, together with United Nations supervision of communication media in recognized conflict situations.

1448. Dunn, Delmer D. Public Officials and the Press. Boston: Beacon Press, 1969, pp. xi, 208.
    An effort to ascertain the impact of the political reporter on the political decision-making process.

1449. Fisher, Margaret Welpley, and Bondurant, Joan Valérie. Indian Views of Sino-Indian Relations. Berkeley: University of California, Indian Press Digests Project, 1956, pp. 193, xxix.
    Summaries of press opinion and discussion on various aspects of Sino-Indian relations, the study being limited to the English-language press.

1450. Gerbner, George. "Press Perspectives in World Communication: A Pilot Study." 38 Journalism Quarterly (1961), 313-322.

A headline analysis of the New York Times and the Hungarian Socialist Workers' (Communist) party central daily, Nepszabadsag, for their treatment of the 1960 General Assembly session. Among the findings was that Nepszabadsag gave less attention to procedural matters than did the Times and greater attention to substantive issues generally accepted as of major daily concern and hope to most peoples, highlighting Communist initiative in these matters.

1451. Gould, Wesley L., assisted by William Klecka and Charles Weyant. The New York Times and the Development of Assurance Between Adversary Nations: Six Case Studies, 1961-1963. Technical Report No. 2. Studies of the Social and Psychological Aspects of Verification, Inspection and International Assurance. ACDA/E-104. Prepared for the U.S. Arms Control and Disarmament Agency. West Lafayette, Indiana: Purdue University, Purdue Research Foundation, December 1968, pp. iv, 309.

An analysis of the New York Times news reports in 1961-1963 that develops over 100 propositions about changes in the levels of trust and perceived relative power and the influence of the press as intermediary between a government and the reading public. Some of the hypotheses derived from the six cases are similar to some of those derived by Paige, The Korean Decision (supra, no. 1284).

1452. Greenwald, A.G. "Behavior Change Following a Persuasive Communication: The Role of Commitment Prior to the Influence Attempt." 29 Public Opinion Quarterly (1965-1966), 595-601.

Finds that persuasive communications produced a pattern of belief change but no behavior change in subjects who, before a communication, had committed themselves to an opposing position.

1452-A. Harik, Iliya F. "Opinion Leaders and the Mass Media in Rural Egypt: A Reconsideration of the Two-Step Flow of Communications Hypothesis." 65 American Political Science Review (1971), 731-740.

A study of Shubra, an Egyptian delta village, which includes some comparison with a study of five Colombian villages and a study of Quito, Ecuador, finds a positive but not commanding relationship between access to mass media and political awareness. But the study does not confirm the role of oral dissemination of information that is posited by the two-step-flow theory except in relation to a smaller group, mostly with less access to the mass media, who receive information and ideas as mediated by opinion leaders.

1453. Hoed, J. "De l'information des quotidiens belges de langue française en matière de politique étrangère." 6 Res publica (1964), 269-279.

Examination of French-language dailies in Belgium for a period of 10 days in August 1961 to ascertain the utilization of dispatches from abroad sent by three press agencies, Belga, AP, and UPS. The study attempts to ascertain the attitude of the dailies in respect to information concerning international politics, reasons for delays in utilization of certain press agency dispatches, and the objectivity of the newspapers in handling the dispatches.

1454. Hohenberg, John. <u>Between Two Worlds: Policy, Press, and Public Opinion in Asian-American Relations</u>. New York: Praeger, 1967, pp. xvi, 507.

   Based on extensive interviews with heads of states, ambassadors, foreign correspondents, editors, bureau chiefs, military strategists, information officers, university professors, and students, this study deals with the problems of communication between the United States and South and Southeast Asia, the extent of information the people of each region has about the other, of getting the news, and of "public diplomacy" and resultant dangers when American policy does not long remain a secret.

1455. Houghton, Neal D. "The Cuban Invasion of 1961 and the U.S. Press, in Retrospect." 42 <u>Journalism Quarterly</u> (1965), 422-432.

   This unrevised article, written in 1962, deals with a number of issues raised in the press, e.g., by James Reston, and includes the question of whether, given advance knowledge by newsmen of what was to happen, the American press exercised a proper self-restraint when it failed to protest the violation of treaties by the Bay of Pigs preparations and operation, even though it had been quite ready to protest British and French violations at Suez.

1456. Janowitz, Morris. "Mass Persuasion and International Relations 25 <u>Public Opinion Quarterly</u> (1961), 560-570.

   Review of recent literature dealing with the manipulation of attitudes in international relations.

1457. Katz, Elihu. "The Two-Step Flow of Communication: An Up-To-Date Report on an Hypothesis." 31 <u>Public Opinion Quarterly</u> (1957), 61-78.

   Exposition of the hypothesis of a "two-step flow" of communication via mass media and face-to-face channels.

1458. Kayser, J. "La presse de province en France et l'évolution de la situation internationale." 20 <u>Politique étrangère</u> (1955), 41-50.

   Analysis of the treatment of selected issues by 78 provincial newspapers in France, with particular attention to differing presentations of the news by journalists of similar opinions.

1459. Klapper, Joseph T. <u>The Effects of Mass Communication</u>. Glencoe Free Press, 1960, pp. 302.

   A review and synthesis of about a thousand communications studies. The book includes a section on persuasive communication as a general process, followed by a section on the specific content characteristics of mass media. The section on persuasive communication includes discussion of the following: reenforcement; minor attitude change; conversion; and the five mediating forces of predispositions (selective exposure, perception, retention), groups and group norms, interpersonal dissemination, opinion leadership, and the nature of media in a free society.

1460. Kruglak, Theodore E. "'Crash' Coverage of U.S. Media in Hungary and Middle East." 35 Journalism Quarterly (1958), 15-25.
The article tells of the difficulties of getting news coverage during a political crisis in a foreign country. So far, our newspapers have had fairly good coverage due to individual ingenuity. But the readers have few facts, if any, telling of the preceding events or events following the crisis. The article supports findings reported by Bernard Cohen (supra, no. 1445).

1461. Kruglak, Theodore Edward. The Foreign Correspondents. Geneva: Droz, 1955, pp. 163.
Critical appraisal of American correspondents and news agencies in Western Europe--a useful study if employed with care.

1462. Kruglak, Theodore Edward. The Two Faces of TASS. Minneapolis: University of Minnesota Press, 1962, pp. 263.
Study of Soviet newsgathering abroad and of other functions performed by TASS.

1463. Lee, John (ed.). Diplomatic Persuaders: New Role of the Mass Media in International Relations. New York: Wiley, 1968, pp. 205.
Selections on current trends and practices in the effort to employ the mass media to form world opinion.

1464. Meijers, Clara C. "The Public Relations Story Behind the European Common Market." 42 Journalism Quarterly (1965), 397-402.
An EEC information staff member presents an analysis of the strengths and weaknesses, successes and failures of the Common Market public relations program.

1465. Newland, Chester A. "Press Coverage of the United States Supreme Court." 17 Western Political Quarterly (1964), 15-36.
On the coverage of the Supreme Court by popular periodicals and newspapers and on distortions introduced by publishers' biases, reporting of public speeches which may often be attacks on the Court, and selective wire service reporting that prefers more sensational to more significant cases or inserts sensationalism into stories.

1466. Nixon, Raymond B. "Freedom in the World's Press: A Fresh Appraisal with New Data." 42 Journalism Quarterly (1965), 3-14, 118-119.
Making use of the Banks-Textor data, the author relates freedom of the press to several variables and finds that 25 characteristics emerge, among them the characteristic that freedom of the press is more closely associated with the Common Law system than with the Civil Law system, with particularly striking differences between former French and former British colonies.

1467. Pool, Ithiel de Sola, et al. The "Prestige Papers": A Survey of Their Editorials. Stanford: Stanford University Press, 1952, pp. vii, 146.

A study that finds that in each major country one newspaper stands out as an organ of elite opinion and enjoys a semiofficial status of intimacy with the government. Although seldom having large circulation, these papers are read by public officials, journalists, scholars, and business leaders, and so are read abroad by those whose business requires them to keep track of world affairs. A biographical analysis shows that prestige paper editors tend to come from the same social circles as do members of the elite and to share their education and attitude-forming experiences. What this means in terms of feedback loops, group self-reinforcement, influence on the substance of policy, and normative evolution are matters that warrant examination in terms of their impact on international law and its prestige as the level of policy influencers and policy decision-makers.

1468. Rose, E.J.B. "The Press and International Tensions." 38 International Affairs (1962), 52-62.
Description of the undertaking of the International Press Institute in Zurich to call together editors of papers in countries between which there are tensions. Such meetings are chaired by an editor from a neutral country and discussion is upon technical, not political, difficulties of the journalists of each country in covering the news in the other.

1469. Salinger, Pierre. With Kennedy. Garden City: Doubleday, 1966, pp. xvi, 391.
Particularly useful for its discussion and defense of news management and for the light it sheds on the use of informal routes of communication for bargaining purposes.

1470. Schramm, Wilbur L. Mass Media and National Development: The Role of Information in the Developing Countries. Stanford: Stanford University Press; Paris: UNESCO, 1964, pp. xiv, 333.
The function of information in economic and social development is discussed. Mass media effects, information flow, world distribution of communication facilities, finances and needs of mass media systems data are assessed. The relationship between mass media and institutional and legal problems in new countries is also discussed.

1471. Strickland, Donald A., assisted by G. Russell, T. Cafferty, W. Klecka, and S. Silver. Content Analysis. Technical Report No. 3. Studies of the Social and Psychological Aspects of Verification, Inspection and International Assurance. ACDA/E-104. Prepared for the U.S. Arms Control and Disarmament Agency. West Lafayette, Indiana: Herman C. Krannert Graduate School of Industrial Administration, September 1968, pp. iii, 40.
Content analysis of New York Times editorials and news items in 1961-1963 to ascertain, among other things, the different terms and concepts used in crisis and noncrisis situations and their probable impact on the level of trust.

1472. Thistlewaite, Donald L., de Hann, Henry, and Kamenetzky, Joseph "The Effects of 'Directive' and 'Non-Directive' Communication Procedures on

Attitude." 51 <u>Journal of Abnormal and Social Psychology</u> (1955), 107-113.

In a test of the hypothesis that among subjects who comprehend the intended conclusion of a persuasive communication equally well, conclusion drawing by the communicator will be less effective in changing attitudes than not drawing a conclusion, the experimenters used a matched-group design. Questionnaires were administered one week prior to communication, immediately after, and three weeks after the communication. It was found that unaided conclusion drawing is <u>not</u> associated with greater attitude change than conclusion drawing which follows an explicit suggestion by the communicator.

1473. Troldahl, Verling C., and Van Dam, Robert. "Face-to-Face Communication About Major Topics in the News." 29 <u>Public Opinion Quarterly</u> (1965-1966), 626-634.

A study of face-to-face communications in Detroit that bears implications for the theory of a two-step flow of communication. It appears that there was less opinion-giving on public affairs topics than opinion-sharing. Opinion givers and askers were more similar than earlier studies of opinion leadership have suggested. Similarity was observed in exposure to mass media content, information on national news, occupational prestige, and gregariousness.

1474. Van den Ban, A.W. "A Revision of the Two-Step Flow of Communications Hypothesis." 10 <u>Gazette: International Journal for Mass Communications Studies</u> (1964), 237-249.

Holds that the actual communications flow is too complex to be accounted for by the two-step model of Elihu Katz and Paul Lazarsfeld and argues that an appropriate model would consider the communication flow as multi-step.

1475. Vas Diaz, A. Arnold. "The World Press and the United Nations." 9 <u>Gazette: International Journal for Mass Communications Studies</u> (1963), 217-226.

On the problem of getting adequate press coverage of the UN in the world's newspapers, with some additional reference to radio and TV.

1476. Walton, Richard E., Gould, Wesley L., Strickland, Donald A., and Driver, Michael J. <u>Social and Psychological Aspects of Verification, Inspection and International Assurance: Final Report</u>. ACDA/E-104. Prepared for the U.S. Arms Control and Disarmament Agency. West Lafayette, Indiana: Purdue University, Purdue Research Foundation, January 1969, pp. 51.

Overall report of studies of the level of American trust of the Soviet Union during the Kennedy Administration that combines the results of events analysis, content analysis of the <u>New York Times</u>, and analysis of public opinion poll data. It is noticeable that all analyses concur in arriving independently at the same dates as crucial in Soviet-American relations. The <u>Studies</u> represent a mixture of collaboration (concurrent, not sequential) and independent work by four specialists in the different fields of bargaining and organization behavior, social psychology, group politics, and international affairs. The technical reports are separately annotated.

1476-A. Welch, Susan K. "The Press and Foreign Policy: The Definition of the Situation." Paper presented at the 66th Annual Meeting of the American Political Science Association, Los Angeles, September 8-12, 1970, pp. 39.

Based on a survey of the New York Times treatment of the Indochina issue in 1950-1956 and of the Chicago Tribune, Washington Post, and San Francisco Chronicle for selected intervals during the same time span, this article finds that the press accepted the Administration's definition of the situation and thereby reinforced the Administration's terms of debate and helped to constrain the search for alternative policies.

1477. Wilhelm, John. "The Re-Appearing Foreign Correspondent: A World Survey." 40 Journalism Quarterly (1963), 147-169.

Presents the results of a census of American foreign correspondents that provides evidence not only of an increase in their numbers by the early 1960s but also of their distribution which shows a concentration on major metropolises while leaving smaller countries uncovered.

See also nos. 265, 273, 771, 878, 1117, 1351, 1354, 1358, 1541, 1729, 1745, 1785, 1855, 1871, 2144, 2376, 2452.

6. Organizational Factors

1478. Brodie, Bernard. The Intractability of States: A Distinctive Problem. Mimeo. P-2970. Santa Monica: RAND Corporation, September 1964, pp. 13.

Governmental and individual responses to stimuli, that is, their particular responses to hostile acts, are distinguished essentially on the grounds of differences in entities and of time elapsing between stimulus and response.

1479. Chapin, F. Stuart, and Tsouderos, John E. "Formalization Observed in Ten Voluntary Associations: Concepts, Morphology, Process." 33 Social Forces (1955), 306-309.

Ten associations were intensively studied by the case history method to test the hypothesis that the extension of the organizational structure starts its common process from an amorphous, informal structure and develops into a formal or regimented structure. It was found that the rank-and-file membership becomes passive, that executive functions do not develop as though by "blue-print," and that problems of communication arise.

1480. Cohen, Arthur R. "Upward Communication in Experimentally Creat Hierarchies." 11 Human Relations (1958), 41-53.

This article attempts to clarify the differences between two groups of low rank and to highlight a more instrumental view of upward hierarchical communication by adding the concept of power to that of status. Status is defined as the amount of desirability and satisfaction inherent in a given position, while power is the relative ability to control one's own and others' need satisfaction. The findings showed that when rank in a hierarchy is defined in terms of power or control over need satisfaction as well as general status, those with low rank who can move upward communicate in a way guaranteed to protect and enhance their relations with the high rankers who exercise that control. Those for whom mobility upward is impossible have less need to communicate to the upper level in such a friendly, pro-motive, and task-oriented manner.

1481. Connell, John, pseud. (John Henry Robertson). The "Office": The Story of the British Foreign Office, 1919-1951. New York: St. Martin's Press, 1958, pp. 367.
Useful study of the Foreign Office, its policy-makers, and of changes in diplomatic life.

1482. Dayal, H. "The Genesis and Organization of the Indian Foreign Service." 1 Indian Year Book of International Affairs (1952), 26-34.
Indicative of a problem faced by new states is this descrip-tion of the need, not found in other branches of the civil serv-ice, to build up the foreign service from virtually nothing. In 1947 scarcely a score of Indian officials had any experience re-motely connected with foreign affairs. The service had to be developed under very frugal financial conditions that served as one limitation upon officer strength.

1483. Falk, S.L. "Organization and Military Power: The Japanese High Command in World War II." 76 Political Science Quarterly (1961), 503-518.
On the strengths and weaknesses of the Japanese High Com-mand as, in effect, the wartime government. Attention is given to the constitutional power over Cabinets, the domination of the Chiefs of Staff by their staff organizations, the power that lay in the bureaus of the War and Navy Ministries, military dic-tation to civilians in the Liaison Committee linking Imperial Headquarters and the Cabinet, and inter-service rivalries hamper-ing the efficiency of wartime government.

1484. Gauché, Général. Le Deuxième Bureau au travail (1935-1940). Paris: Amiot-Dumont, 1954, pp. 239.
Although a defense against the charge that French military intelligence failed to provide adequate information, the book provides some insights into the function of information, its communication, and its reception in the foreign policy and treaty-making processes--a study essentially of information flow as it occurred in a particular organizational structure.

1485. Heinlein, J.C. <u>Presidential Staff and National Security Polic</u> Occasional Papers--No. 2. Center for the Study of U.S. Foreign Policy of the Department of Political Science, University of Cincinnati, 1963, pp. 6.

An examination of the staffs of Presidents Truman, Eisenhower, and Kennedy, with some comparison with earlier presidential staffs, that gives particular attention to the uses of staff assistance in foreign affairs affecting national security. One case during the administration of each of the first three postwar Presidents is examined in the effort to ascertain the extent of each President's reliance upon formal organizations for advice and information as against informal groups. The three incidents examined are the outbreak of the Korean War, the Lebanon intervention, and the Cuban missile crisis--the last lacking an effective reconstruction of events and so rather speculative in nature.

1486. Hermann, Charles F. "Some Consequences of Crisis Which Limit the Viability of Organizations." 8 <u>Administrative Science Quarterly</u> (1963 61-82.

A model of the effects of crisis on an organizational structure that seeks to account for an organization's inability to respond to crisis as error increases and feedback is blocked.

1487. Janowitz, Morris, and Delaney, William. "The Bureaucrat and the Public: A Study of Informational Perspectives." 2 <u>Administrative Science Quarterly</u> (1957), 141-162.

A report on the information perspectives of higher and lower administrators in three agencies in metropolitan Detroit. The findings in respect to all three agencies supported the hypothesis that the higher the bureaucratic position, the less well informed is the bureaucrat about the agency's clients. The data for two agencies, but not that for the third, supported the hypothesis that the higher the bureaucratic position, the better informed is the bureaucrat about the perspectives of the general citizenry toward his agency.

1488. Jeffries, Sir Charles Joseph. <u>The Colonial Office</u>. New York: Oxford, 1956, pp. 222.

Review by a Colonial Office official of the work of the major departments of a branch of government that straddled the areas of internal policy and foreign policy.

1489. King, Jere Clemens. <u>Foch Versus Clemenceau: France and Germar Dismemberment, 1918-1919</u>. Cambridge: Harvard University Press, 1960, pp. 137.

A study of how peace-making can mix international and domestic issues, in this case involving the question of civil-military relations in France.

1490. McCamy, James L. <u>Conduct of the New Diplomacy</u>. New York: Harper and Row, 1964, pp. x, 303.

Analysis of the way in which the American executive is organized for the conduct of contemporary diplomacy. Included

is a case study of the U-2 affair with concern for the relationships of staffing and organization to results.

1490-A. Oettinger, Anthony G. "Compunications (sic) in the National
Decision-Making Process." Prepared for presentation in the lecture series,
Computers, Communications and the Public Interest, organized by Johns Hopkins and the Brookings Institution, May 14, 1970. Cambridge: Harvard University, Program on Science and Technology, n.d., pp. 34.
      On the problems of communication and computer retrieval as
aids to decision-making, with attention to the needs of executives at all hierarchical levels, the problems imposed by hierarchical structure in terms of the extremes of information overload and excessive filtering, and of institutional changes desirable if old ways are not to be frozen by computer technology
to the detriment of flexibility suitable to both routine situations and sudden crises.

1491. Ollé-Laprune, Jacques. La stabilité des ministres sous la Troi-
sième République, 1879-1940. Paris: Librairie Générale de Droit et de
Jurisprudence, 1962, pp. 376.
      Confirmation of the aphorism that French ministers may change
but the ministries remain. Important data is provided in respect
to the influence of bureaucracy and bureaucratic organization and
procedures upon the decision-making process.

1492. Rome, Beatrice K., and Rome, Sydney C. Leviathan: An Experimental Study of Large Organizations with the Aid of Computers. Technical
Memorandum TM-744. Santa Monica: System Development Corporation, August 17,
1962, pp. 87.
      Description of and rationale for a simulation, with the aid
of computers, of large organizations with reference to communications routes and to control by middle management and policy formation by top management, in an effort to explore the effect of
various actions and decisions by top and middle management on the
work of the technological or product-producing subsystem.

1493. Rosenbaum, H.J. "A Critique of the Brazilian Foreign Service,"
2 Journal of Developing Areas (1968), 377-392.
      Deals with the history, recruitment, selection, training,
performance, internal controversies, and public image of Brazil's foreign service and notes such defects affecting quality
as virtual lack of recruitment, overly legalistic training, controversy between economic specialists and political generalists,
and advancement through family connections and political contacts.

1494. Runge, William A. "Analysis of the Department of State Communications Traffic during a Politico-Military Crisis." Research Memorandum
OAD RM 109. Stanford Research Institute, 1963.
      A study of telegraphic traffic between the Department of
State and its embassies and consulates general in ten South
American countries during October-November 1962. Traffic volume for October, the month of the missile crisis, was 85% higher
than for November. More importantly for analytical purposes,

the data presented on traffic volume is susceptible of correlation with the size of diplomatic missions, whether or not one includes the deviant case of Bolivia with a small mission but large number of messages.

1495. Simon, Herbert A. "On the Concept of Organizational Goal," 9 Administrative Science Quarterly (1964), 1-22.
"Organizational goal" is defined so that the dilemma of "reification" of an organization in terms of its goals may not preclude the use of the concept of goal in organization theory. "Organizational goal" is employed to refer to constraints, or sets of constraints, imposed by the organizational role that have only an indirect relationship with the personal motive of the individual who fills the role. More narrowly, "organizational goal" may be used to refer particularly to the constraint sets that define roles at the upper administrative levels.

1496. Strang, William Strang, 1st Baron, et al. The Foreign Office. New York: Oxford, 1955, pp. 226.
Description of the work of the major departments of the Foreign Office, prepared by the former Permanent Under-Secretary of State for Foreign Affairs.

See also nos. 320, 1128, 1267, and sec. I, C, 24.

7. Values and Decision-Making--Traditional Values

1497. Jacob, Philip E., and Flink, James J., with the collaboration of Hedvah L. Shuchman. "Values and Their Function in Decision-Making: Toward an Operational Definition for Use in Public Affairs Research." 5 American Behavioral Scientist (supplement, May 1962), 38.
Includes among the topics covered: criteria of definition; values as normative standards of human action; some alternative conceptions of value; function of values as a determinant of action; properties of value in phylogenetic perspective; function of values in the policy process.

1498. Kerlinger, Fred N. "Decision-Making in Japan." 30 Social Force (1951), 36-41.
An attempt to describe decision-making in Japan and to show the interaction between Japanese thinking and the Japanese manner of reaching group decisions.

1498-A. Lovell, John P. Foreign Policy in Perspective: Strategy-Adaptation-Decision Making. New York: Holt, Rinehart and Winston, 1970, pp. 416.
Includes a consideration of the problem of applying criteria of legality, as well as those of morality and "realism" to the evaluation of the objectives and means of foreign policy.

1499. McClelland, David C., and Winter, David G. <u>Motivating Economic Achievement</u>. New York: Free Press, 1969, pp. xxii, 409.
Reports on a test of a new theory of individual personality change whereby a 10-day exposure to psychological inputs apparently increased the achievement motivation of businessmen and entrepreneurs in India, Oklahoma, and Washington, D.C. One may be skeptical both about the outcome of a 10-day experimental exposure and the validity for groups and nations of what may be accomplished with individuals. Even so, attention should be given to the authors' argument that traditional values are not so important in blocking change as is generally believed and that thought be given to the type of psychological education that might be conducive to change in various cultures and circumstances.

See also nos. 1187, 1288, 1975.

8. Armed Forces and Bases Abroad

1500. Brennan, Donald G., and Halperin, Morton. "Policy Considerations of a Nuclear Test Ban." In Brennan (ed.), <u>Arms Control, Disarmament and National Security</u>. New York: George Braziller, 1961, pp. 234-266.
Collaboration between a physicist and a political scientist that treats a test ban as service of notice that nuclear weapons are too dangerous and that they entail undue risks to warrant use in limited wars.

1501. Stambuk, George. <u>American Armed Forces Abroad: Their Impact on the Western State System</u>. Columbus: Ohio State University Press, 1963, pp. ix, 252.
An excellent blend of some analytical techniques of law and political science, particularly valuable for its exposition of the slowness of realization that armed forces could be in foreign territory for friendly rather than predatory purposes. Also valuable is a comparison of the speed of legal evolution, particularly with the aid of judicial decisions recognizing newer situations and possibilities given a recognition of friendly presence, as that evolution took place first before and then after the law was cast in treaty form. The pace slowed after the status-of-forces agreements were concluded.

See also nos. 2108, 2109, 2298.

9. Warships with Multinational Trainees

1502. Kestner, Jack. "The U.S.S. Ricketts Begins Big Test." 7 <u>Navy</u> (August 1964), 32-35.
On preparations for an 18-month period of training on the guided missile destroyer U.S.S. <u>Claude V. Ricketts</u> for a mixed crew of Americans, British, Turks, Germans, Greeks, Italians,

and Dutch, anticipation of probable troubles aboard ship including disputes between crew members' countries, and the applicability of the Status-of-Forces agreement in respect to discipline.

D. CENTRIPETAL TENDENCIES--CENTRALIZATION

1. Collective Security and Collective Intervention

1503. Deutsch, Morton. "Psychological Alternatives to War." 18
Journal of Social Issues (1962), 97-119.
    Assuming that the East-West conflict can be resolved peace-
fully, the author gives attention to some of the sources of misperception in international relations, e.g., the self-fulfilling
prophecy, conformity to perceptions of others, pressure for consistency, the mote-beam mechanism (perceiving certain characteristics in others that we do not perceive in ourselves). He then
suggests some psychological alternatives such as aiming for mutual security rather than national security, recognizing similarities rather than emphasizing differences, and peaceful international competition for prestige and influences through sports,
the arts, science, etc.

1504. Haas, Ernst B. "Types of Collective Security: An Examination
of Operational Concepts." 49 American Political Science Review (1955),
40-62.
    An historical approach is used to discuss the success and
failure of the "concert" principle vis-à-vis the Security Council that implies maximization of enforcement despite absence of
a concert. A case study of the Korean crisis is used to show
the essential feature of permissive enforcement to be growth of
the balancing concept to which it gives rise. Balancing is said
to be the concept most relevant to a theoretical formulation of
collective security in operational terms that implies a non-
normative approach to the issue of peace.

1505. Haight, J. McV., Jr. "France and the Aftermath of Roosevelt's
'Quarantine' Speech." 14 World Politics (1962), 283-306.
    Narrative of an abortive effort to bring about collective
action against aggression.

1506. Hogan, Willard N. International Conflict and Collective Security: The Principle of Concern in International Organization. Lexington: University of Kentucky Press, 1955, pp. 202.
    An appraisal of collective security that, among other things,
treats past failures as due less to refusal to subordinate national interests to collective security than to mistaken beliefs
concerning what would protect national interests.

1507. Johnson, Howard C., and Niemeyer, Gerhart. "Collective Securit
The Validity of an Ideal." 8 International Organization (1954), 19-35.

Examines the idea of universal collective security in the
light of manifest national policies that appear to inhibit the
development of habit-forming effects of invocations of collective security. The authors regard approaches through universalistic principles such as collective security to be a mistake and
treat collective security as workable only when, as in certain
historical instances, it coincides with the concrete action requirements of a number of states.

1508. Leiss, Amelia C. (ed.). Apartheid and United Nations Collective Measures: An Analysis. New York: Carnegie Endowment for International Peace, 1965, pp. xii, 170.
    A discussion of collective measures that might be taken to
bring abandonment of apartheid in the Republic of South Africa,
conditions of effectiveness of the several measures discussed,
and uncertainties and complications potentially involved in collective undertaking to overturn the domestic status quo and replace it with one more in harmony with international standards.

1509. Miller, Linda B. World Order and Local Disorder. Princeton:
Princeton University Press, 1967, pp. 235.
    Employs selected cases to examine the roles played by the
United Nations when civil strife in modernizing societies creates threats to the peace. Attention is given to legal and political limitations on the effectiveness of UN efforts to contain internal violence and to promote peaceful change.

1510. Slater, Jerome. A Reevaluation of Collective Security: The
OAS in Action. The Social Science Program of the Mershon Center for Education in National Security. Pamphlet No. 1. Columbus: Ohio State University Press, 1965, pp. 56.
    Evaluation of the OAS as a collective security system with
reference to the theories of collective security elaborated by
a number of leading political scientists. The study represents
a brief but effective effort to blend political theory in one
of its aspects with treaty interpretation based upon action under
the treaty, the latter bringing into play actors' perceptions, to
deal with law in a politically relevant manner that warrants
elaboration and extended use.

1511. Stromberg, Roland N. Collective Security and American Foreign
Policy From the League of Nations to NATO. New York: Praeger, 1963, pp.
301.
    Historical review of American policies toward collective
security.

1512. Stromberg, Roland N. "The Idea of Collective Security." 17
Journal of the History of Ideas (1956), 250-263.
    Deals with definitions of collective security, assumptions
underlying ideas of collective security, and the relations between collective security and liberal traditions, particularly
the idea that law derives from consent rather than from force.

1513. van Langenhove, Fernand. <u>La crise du système de sécurité col-</u>
<u>lective des Nations Unies</u>. The Hague: Nijhoff, 1958, pp. 272.
      Lucidly written examination of the diversion of the hope of
peace through collective security resting on agreement among the
Great Powers and the emergence of peace based on a balance of
terror.

1514. Wolfers, Arnold. <u>Discord and Collaboration: Essays on Inter-</u>
<u>national Politics</u>. Baltimore: Johns Hopkins Press, 1962, pp. xvii, 283.
      Collection of the author's writings, chiefly on postwar
matters but including an essay on the interwar period, that are
essentially interpretations of foreign policies. Particularly
relevant to international law are the chapters on collective
security and the chapter on "Statesmanship and Moral Choice,"
dealing with the so-called double standard. Also useful is an
examination of the contributions and limitations of the state-
as-actor and decision-making models and a consideration of the
relevance of political theory to analysis of international relations.

See also nos. 527, 926, 931, 992, 1004, 1018, 1034, 1284, 1829, 1971,
2236, 2489.

2. <u>International Control over Execution of Treaties</u>

1515. Berthoud, Paul. <u>Le contrôle international de l'éxécution des</u>
<u>conventions collectives</u>. Geneva: Imprimerie de Saint-Gervais, 1946, pp.
359.
      Detailed examination of efforts at international control
until World War II that seeks to draw general conclusions from
the fields of minorities, mandates, labor, narcotics, and disarmament.

1516. Fisher, Roger. "Responding to Disarmament Violations." 18
<u>Bulletin of Atomic Scientists</u> (September 1962), 22-27.
      Seeking rules for what to do in the event of violations of
disarmament agreements, the author sees the main principle to be
that of minimizing the damage to the agreement rather than punishment. The whole agreement should not be abrogated in response
to a small violation. Nor should governments be treated as criminals. Hence, violations should be regarded as disputes. Judicial machinery should be used for the interpretation of all questions of interpretation and obligation and should be used to re-
strain individuals, e.g., to enjoin an officer from continuing
the violation and thereby place the onus on the government to
comply with the injunction or to take on the responsibility of
disrupting the whole agreement.

1517. Freymond, Jacques. "Supervising Agreements: The Korean Experience." 38 <u>Foreign Affairs</u> (1959), 496-503.

Case study pointing up the shortcomings of the arrangements
for supervising the execution of the Korean Armistice Agreement
and offering suggestions for improvement of international supervision.

1518. Landy, E.A. The Effectiveness of International Supervision:
Thirty Years of I.L.O. Experience. London: Stevens, 1966, pp. xiv, 268.
Detailed attempt to determine whether systematic supervision can help to produce compliance with international obligations and to ascertain the role that can be played by nongovernmental groups in international supervision. Both quantitative
and qualitative analysis of about 1,000 cases in which breaches
of treaty obligations were discovered by ILO supervision, aid in
focusing attention on problems, implications, and prospects of
international supervision.

See also nos. 1561, 1562, 1793.

3. Disarmament and Arms Control

1519. Barnett, Richard J. "The Soviet Attitude on Disarmament." 10
Problems of Communism (1961), 32-37.
An argument that the Kremlin's confidence that the Communist
system can win the struggle in a world of near total disarmament,
with resort to violence at lower levels of force, leads it to
favor disarmament. But the question is raised whether their
faith in the inevitability of ultimate Soviet success is great
enough to permit them to accept the kind of restraints on their
international conduct that a system of effective controls over
disarmament would require.

1520. Batten, James K. Arms Control and the Problem of Evasion.
Research Monograph No. 14. Princeton: Center of International Studies,
Princeton University, June 30, 1962, pp. 28.
Deals with the important concern of evasion of commitments
that might be made under arms control agreements and so with the
problem of risk.

1521. Bloomfield, Lincoln P., Clemens, Walter C., and Griffiths,
Franklyn. Soviet Interests in Arms Control and Disarmament: The Decade
Under Khrushchev, 1954-1964. Prepared for the U.S. Arms Control and Disarmament Agency. Cambridge: Massachusetts Institute of Technology, Center
for International Studies, February 1, 1965, pp. vii, 249.
A review of manifest Soviet policies toward arms control
that seeks to relate those policies to such conditioning factors
as the military-strategic outlook, economic factors, and the external political situation. An annex volume by Clemens and Griffiths, The Soviet Position on Arms Control: Negotiations and
Propaganda, 1954-1964, adds details.

1522. Bobrow, Davis B. "Chinese and American Interests in Arms Control." 9 <u>Background</u> (1965), 91-110.

Concentrating primarily upon Communist Chinese capabilities and objectives, the article deals with forms of arms control which the Chinese appear to find objectionable and those which they prefer, the latter giving them the opportunity to present a good image and manipulate the United States into presenting a poor one, while also providing China with opportunities to conduct sublimited war under favorable conditions. A final section looks into American objectives and the demands imposed should the United States attempt to realize those objectives after accepting Chinese arms control preferences. The article is presented essentially in terms of a direct two-party bargaining situation, but with the recognition that both the policies of other countries and Chinese and American objectives affecting each other indirectly limit the conclusions.

1523. Brennan, Donald G. (ed.). <u>Arms Control, Disarmament and National Security</u>. New York: Braziller, 1961, pp. 475.

Special issue of <u>Daedelus</u> (Fall 1960) containing articles on the several facets of arms control and disarmament, useful as a summary of various points of view and of interest.

1524. Dallin, Alexander, <u>et al</u>. <u>The Soviet Union and Disarmament: An Appraisal of Soviet Attitudes and Intentions</u>. New York: Praeger for the School of International Affairs, Columbia University, 1964, pp. xi, 282.

Report compiled from working papers drafted after a meeting at Airlie House in 1963 at which an attempt was made to assess Soviet attitudes toward disarmament.

1525. Dean, Arthur H. <u>Test Ban and Disarmament: The Path of Negotiation.</u> New York: Harper & Row for the Council on Foreign Relations, 1966, pp. xiii, 153.

Description of the diplomatic maneuvering that led up to the test ban treaty and discussion of the issues involved, with emphasis on the continuing urgency to curtail nuclear proliferation.

1526. Deutsch, Karl W. "Integration and Arms Control in the European Political Environment: A Summary Report." 60 <u>American Political Science Review</u> (1966), 354-365.

Report on the employment of elite interviews in West Germany and France, analysis of mass opinion polls, survey of arms control and disarmament proposals, two content analyses of French, German, British, and American newspapers, and aggregate data about actual behavior, that produced significant findings on integration and arms control: (1) integration has been at a plateau since 1957-1958; (2) the <u>New York Times</u> treats integration quite differently from <u>Le Monde</u>, the <u>Frankfurter Allgemeine Zeitung</u>, and <u>The Times</u> of London; (3) there are marked differences of opinion between German and French and much more trust in the US and Britain than in each other; (4) nationalism has blunted the cutting edge of supranationalism; (5) arms control

and disarmament is acceptable on a global but not on a regional
scale. The report goes into much greater detail and requires
careful uses of its specific findings.

1527. Dougherty, James E., and Lehman, J.F., Jr. Arms Control for the
Late Sixties. Princeton: Van Nostrand, 1967, pp. xlvii, 265.
Among other things, emphasizes the antiproliferation issue
and its implications for NATO, the debate about ballistic missile defense, and the possible effects of the Chinese threat and
continuing war in Vietnam on the arms control détente with the
Soviet Union.

1528. Eayrs, James. "Arms Control on the Great Lakes." 2 Disarmament
and Arms Control (1964), 372-404.
An historical account of the manner in which Great Britain,
Canada, and the United States have maintained the Rush-Bagot
agreement despite infringements and flexible interpretations,
sometimes mutual, departing as during World War II from maintenance of absolute disarmament on the Great Lakes.

1529. Finkelstein, Lawrence S. "The United Nations and Organizations
for the Control of Armaments." 16 International Organization (1962), 1-19.
Discussion of the UN as the player of a principally exhor-
tatory role in respect to arms control. The author sees arms
control as an extremely divisive issue that could strain or destroy the organization administering disarmament arrangements.

1530. Galtung, Johan. "Two Approaches to Disarmament: The Legalist
and the Structuralist." 4 Journal of Peace Research (1967), 161-195.
This article is a diatribe against legalism and the legal
community. The legal community is treated as being in an en-
trenched power position from which it must be ousted by struc-
turalists if disarmament is to be realized. For the legalistic
characterization of behavior as true or false according to norms
the author would substitute, or at least establish as dominant,
the structuralist characterization of behavior as true or false
according to certain hypotheses. Prediction would replace or
delimit prescription. Dissonant behavior is a signal to the
legalist to change behavior and to the structuralist to change
standards. The author prefers an eclectic approach that would
have the legalist locate his standards within the structuralist's
range of choice of actions tending toward disarmament, proscribe
what has already been impeded, and subject to negative sanctions
only that which is false according to the structuralist's prediction.

1531. Glick, Edward Bernard. "The Feasibility of Arms Control and
Disarmament in Latin America." 9 Orbis (1965), 743-759.
Evaluation of the practicability of reducing and controlling
conventional and nuclear weapons systems in Latin America that
presents the problem of the impracticality of arms control in
areas where military systems play an integral part in maintaining order, engaging in nonmilitary activities for social and

economic good, providing administrative abilities for governments, and according prestige to individuals.

1532. Halperin, Morton H. China and Nuclear Proliferation. Chicago:
University of Chicago Center for Policy Study, 1966, pp. 48.
    A concise review of Communist China's position on nuclear
proliferation.

1533. Halperin, Morton H., and Perkins, Dwight, H. Communist China
and Arms Control. New York: Praeger, 1965, pp. xi, 191.
    Examines Communist China's policies toward arms control and
disarmament, and their implications for US security and arms control objectives. A projection is made of the probable influence
on China of any international arms control agreement.

1534. Hoagland, J.H. "Arms in the Developing World." 12 Orbis (1968
167-184.
    Among other things, this article gives attention to the
channels of diffusion of hardware and technology, especially
in the cases of small arms, jet aircraft, and ballistic missiles.
Attention is given to motives underlying the traffic and to potential impacts on global and regional security.

1535. Huntington, Samuel P. The Common Defense. New York: Columbia
University Press, 1961, pp. 500.
    Excellent history of the political struggle over American
defense policy that bears upon the issue of whether the United
States orientation is toward arms control or toward disarmament.

1536. Iklé, Fred C., et al. Alternative Approaches to the International Organization of Disarmament. R-391-ARPA. Santa Monica: RAND
Corporation, February 1962, pp. 44.
    A brief review of some proposed arrangements for disarma-
ment and arms control, with particular attention to suggested
types of control organizations.

1537. Katz, Amrom H. African Disarmament: A Proposal Seconded. P-
2868. Santa Monica: RAND Corporation, 1964, pp. 15.
    Exposition of a proposal by J.H. Mensah, an economic officer
of the Planning Commission of Ghana, at the June 1962 Accra Assembly and calling for an Inter-African Disarmament and Nonaggression Pact underwritten by all UN members. The argument is
that Africa could be both a laboratory providing experience in
the mechanisms of inspection, peacekeeping, adjudication, and
internal security and a pilot plant for East-West cooperation
on projects of mutual advantage. Obstacles to such a plan, such
as the interest of some African states in continuing continental
instability, presumed aid benefits dependent on East-West rivalry,
and Egypt's attitude on the Israeli presence, are discussed.

1538. Katz, Amrom H. "Hiders and Finders." 17 Bulletin of Atomic
Scientists (1961), 423-424.

To check out disarmament inspection procedures, the author proposes an actual, not simulated, game in which one team tries to build a secret missile site while another team tries to find it. After a US-only game, the activity could be expanded to joint NATO-Warsaw Pact exercises.

1538-A. Kemp, Geoffrey. "Arms Traffic and Third World Conflicts." International Conciliation. No. 577. March 1970, pp. 80.
    Deals with the magnitude of the arms supply, military, technical, and political criteria for the determination of weapons effectiveness in the third world, and, in terms of costs and benefits and of region-by-region analysis, the probability of greater arms control.

1539. Kolkowicz, Roman. "The Role of Disarmament in Soviet Policy: A Means or an End?" P-2952. Santa Monica: RAND Corporation, August 1964, pp. 15.
    An assessment of Soviet uses of the proclaimed disarmament objective.

1540. Melman, Seymour. "The Political Implications of Inspection for Disarmament." 13 Journal of International Affairs (1955), 34-36.
    Among other things, expresses the position of advocates of a nuclear test ban that a break would be made in traditional thought patterns and that a ban would be a first step toward a new political atmosphere in which the use of highly destructive weapons would be unthinkable.

1541. Merritt, Richard L., and Pirro, Ellen B. Press Attitudes to Arms Control in Four Countries, 1946-1963. Appendix 4. Arms Control in the European Political Environment. New Haven: Yale University, Political Science Research Library, January 1966.
    A systematic analysis of editorials concerning 10 disarmament events as found in 16 French, 17 West German, 29 British, and 35 American newspapers and periodicals. The American publications emerge as (1) least inclined to evaluate operationality, that is, the probability of acceptance and long-range effect of proposals, when promoting arms control and disarmament objectives, (2) generally strongly favorable to arms control and disarmament, (3) most strongly partisan toward Western proposals, (4) least likely to use emotional language, and (5) making the greatest shift over time (1946-1957 as contrasted with 1959-1963) toward a pro-arms control view of Eastern proposals.

1542. Pilisuk, Marc, and Rapoport, Anatol. "A Non-Zero-Sum Game Model of Some Disarmament Problems." Peace Research Society (International), Papers. Chicago Conference, 1963. Vol. I (1964), pp. 57-78.
    A description of an extension of the Prisoner's Dilemma game which barely touches upon simulations of the disarmament problem. The authors object to attempting to extract many variables on the grounds that only sporadic readings could be taken, relating the variables to each other, and producing no more than descriptions and anecdotal accounts. An optimal balance between

verisimilitude and theoretical tractability should be sought in
the effort to learn about the psychological aspects of structurally similar situations. The authors think that problems of
arms control and disarmament have psychological components at
least as crucial as the hardware and strategic components.

1543. Rapacki, Adam. "The Polish Plans for a Nuclear-Free Zone Today." 39 International Affairs (1963), 1-12.
     On the applicability of the Polish plan for a denuclearized
Central European zone and its relation to general disarmament
plans.

1544. Roa, R. "La América latina y la no proliferación de armas nu-
cleares." 27 Cuadernos americanos (No. 4, 1968), 47-66.
     An expression of Cuban opposition to the treaty on nonpro-
liferation of nuclear weapons.

1545. Ross, Anthony Clunies, and King, Peter. Australia and Nuclear
Weapons: The Case for a Non-Nuclear Region in South-East Asia. Sydney:
Sydney University Press, 1966.
     On the dangers of nuclear proliferation and efforts to pre-
vent further spread of nuclear arms, together with an outline of
a regional approach to nuclear disarmament.

1546. Rubinstein, Alvin Z. "Political Barriers to Disarmament." 9
Orbis (1965), 140-154.
     Classifies political barriers to disarmament in three cate-
gories: (1) substantive problems, including opposition or reluctance on the part of Soviet political, industrial, and military elites, of Red China, and of France; (2) rapid obsolescence
of political positions due to rapid technological change; (3)
Soviet perceptions of US motivations, policies, and objectives.
The article is one-sided in that it concentrates upon Soviet perceptions and distortions. The result is an incomplete picture
of political barriers to disarmament.

1547. Saaty, Thomas L. Mathematical Models of Arms Control and Disarmament: Application of Mathematical Structures in Politics. New York:
Wiley, 1968, pp. 190.
     Examines arms control and disarmament problems within the
framework of such mathematical models as the concept of equilibrium and the theory of games.

1548. Schelling, Thomas C. The Stability of Total Disarmament.
Study Memorandum I, Special Studies Group. Washington: Institute for Defense Analyses, October 1961, pp. 51.
     On the problem of disarmament and the potential for rearma-
ment, including the possibility of being panicked into rearma-
ment. Disarmament is treated as making military problems more
manageable but not as making them disappear.

1548-A. "Sino-Soviet Relations and Arms Control: Japanese Attitudes."
ACDA/E-77 III. Mimeo. Prepared for the U.S. Arms Control and Disarmament

Agency by the President and Fellows of Harvard University. May 1, 1969, pp. 30.

Based upon an earlier report by Abraham M. Halpern, this report of an April 1966 meeting in Japan with Japanese foreign affairs specialists takes account of subsequent developments in respect to Japanese attitudes on such matters as security problems, Communist China, Japan's potential as a nuclear power, defense as a domestic issue, Japanese-American relations, and arms control issues such as the nonproliferation treaty.

1549. Van Atta, Lester C. "Arms Control: Human Control." 18 American Psychologist (1963), 37-46.

Expounds the thesis that control of the arms race is not a problem of technology but one of human understanding and human control.

1550. Van Cleave, W.R. "The Nonproliferation Treaty and Fission-free Explosive Research." 11 Orbis (1968), 1055-1066.

Asserts that, in the negotiation of the nonproliferation treaty, too little attention was paid to relevant scientific research, particularly that in pure-fusion explosive technology, and that technological progress changes the conditions upon which treaties and arms control concepts rest.

1551. Wainhouse, David W., et al. Arms Control Agreements: Designs for Verification and Organization. Baltimore: Johns Hopkins Press, 1969, pp. ix, 179.

Seven political scientists present three case studies on the control of nuclear arms and a fourth on general and complete disarmament. The case studies are followed by a conceptual section analyzing the kinds of verification problems that might arise. The authors formulate some general principles for the type of international organization that might deal effectively with those problems. A single verification organization is recommended.

1552. Wainstein, Leonard. "Nations Without Arms--Part 2: Altered Patterns of War." 2 S.R.I. Journal (1962), 31-39.

Review of potential evasions of arms control measures, of the remaining capacity to produce nuclear weapons after disarmament, and of remaining potential forms of war. The article derives its conceptual base from the absence in military history of a universal rejection of any technological development.

1553. Young, W. (ed.). Existing Mechanisms of Arms Control. Oxford: Pergamon, 1966, pp. xiv, 150.

A useful introduction to arms control mechanisms that includes short articles on Western European Union, United States bilateral safeguards, Euratom, the European Nuclear Energy Agency, and the International Atomic Energy Agency.

See also nos. 677, 1146, 1172, 1211, 1451, 1568, 1570, 1793, 1802, 1837, 2102, 2136-2138, 2143, 2155, 2157, 2165, 2245, 2252, 2262, 2860.

4. Management of Power

1554. Claude, Inis L., Jr. "The Management of Power in the Changing United Nations." 15 International Organization (1961), 219-235.
Treats the balance of power, collective security, and world government, although ill-defined concepts, as systems related to each other along a continuum and differing particularly in the degree of centralization of power and authority which they imply. The degree of centralization is related to the degree to which states are deprived of the legal right to use violence at their own discretion.

1555. Gaudemet, J. "Esquisse d'une sociologie historique du pouvoir. 19-20 Politique (1962), 195-234.
Power, conceived as both a social and a juridical phenomenon, is treated as implying a reciprocity in the form of command and obedience. Authority is distinguished from power, but the most useful segments of the discourse are those on the foundations of obedience, on juridical, economic, and social constraints, and on the organization of power.

See also no. 527.

5. Authority of International Organizations

1556. Buehrig, Edward H. "The International System of Authority." 17 World Politics (1965), 369-385.
On domination of the current patterns of authority by territorial rule among equals that coexists with remnants of older religious systems. Communism is seen as having succumbed to the pattern of the Western state system. International organizations have not structured authority vertically but have expanded laterally with the formation of numerous organizations that become new independent variables in international relations.

1557. Economidès, Constantin P. Le pouvoir de décision des organisations internationales européennes. Leiden: Sijthoff, 1964, pp. 167.
Comparative study of the decision-making powers of 10 European and North Atlantic organizations both with regard to impact on member states and to impact on the internal systems of the organizations.

1557-A. Schwebel, Stephen M. (ed.). The Effectiveness of International Decisions. New York: Oceana, 1971, pp. 528.
Papers and proceedings of a 1967 conference of legal advisers, convened by the American Society of International Law, on the effectiveness of the decisions of international organizations, as embodied in treaties and other outputs, within member states.

1558. Sievers, Bruce. _A Decision-Making Approach to the Study of the Communist System_. Research Paper No. 2. Stanford Studies of the Communist System. Stanford University, September 1964, pp. 92.

Application of the Snyder-Bruck-Sapin theory of decision-making to analyze the functions of the Executive Council of COMECON in the Communist international system. Among the conclusions is an assertion that the Executive Council, holding a position of "quasi-legitimacy" stemming from the elements of its vertical authority structure, has since 1956 become more of a "tension management" or deliberative body than an administrative organ. Change of COMECON goals from an achievement orientation to determination of common purposes is regarded as, among other things, converting COMECON into an arbitration council, the first major conflict mediating body in Communist system history (cf. no. 2202-A).

1559. Singer, J. David. "Weapons Technology and International Stability." 5 _Centennial Review_ (1961), 415-435.

Nuclear weapons being primarily first-strike weapons, reciprocal fears are generated that will remain as incentive toward preemption. The proposal is made that fears be reduced by phased, multilateral transfer of strategic weapons to UN stockpiles and by transfer of conventional weapons to an international police force. The suggestion is, in effect, that the process of consolidation of power be that followed by national states, namely, virtually concurrent disarmament of regional or local powers and establishment of a virtual monopoly of force in a central authority. The proposal differs from the historic process in that national power centers usually had to win struggles for the virtual monopoly of force, not have the monopoly granted by the regions even by phases.

See also nos. 664, 992, 1004, 1054, 1067, 1099, 1101, 1112, 1406, 1719, 1769, 1846, 1926, 2202-A, 2832.

6. Peacekeeping; International Police; Inspection Verification; and Surveillance

1560. Boyd, J.M. "Cyprus--Episode in Peacekeeping." 20 _International Organization_ (1966), 1-17.

An evaluation of the UN effort to stabilize the security situation and to establish law and order on Cyprus.

1561. Brook, David. _Preface to Peace: The United Nations and the Arab-Israel Armistice System_. Washington: Public Affairs Press (1964), pp. 151.

Study of the operations of the machinery established to implement the Arab-Israeli armistice, its accomplishments, and its inadequacies. The tension-reducing function of keeping open lines of communications receives emphasis.

1562. Burns, E.L.M. <u>Between Arab and Israeli</u>. Toronto: Clarke, Irwin, 1962, pp. 336.

History of the Arab-Israeli dispute from 1948, including an account of the work of the Truce Supervision Commission and the UNEF, in which the author took part.

1563. Citrin, Jack. <u>United Nations Peacekeeping Activities: A Case Study in Organizational Task Expansion</u>. Monograph Series in World Affairs. Vol. III, No. 1. The Social Science Foundation and Graduate School of International Affairs, University of Denver, 1965, pp. 83.

Application of Ernst B. Haas' model of international integration to review and analyze the peacekeeping activities of the United Nations in Lebanon, the Congo, West Irian, and Cyprus, with particular attention to the impact of each intervention upon task expansion and resultant strengthening of the UN. The Congo intervention is seen as dysfunctional in its consequences.

1564. Curtis, G.L. "The United Nations' Observation Group in Lebanon." 18 <u>International Organization</u> (1964), 738-765.

A review of the observation group in Lebanon from June to September 1958 that concludes that UNOGIL had its greatest efficiency when its services were largely unnecessary, did not prevent United States intervention, but was of help in maintaining international peace.

1565. Dicks, H.V. "National Loyalty, Identity, and the International Soldier." 17 <u>International Organization</u> (1963), 425-443.

Brief examination of such problems as social integration of a military force, the relative advantages of homogeneous and heterogeneous forces, conflicts of ideology, identity, and loyalty, and deracination.

1566. Gilinsky, V., and Smith, B.L.R. <u>Civilian Nuclear Power and Foreign Policy</u>. P-3592-1. Santa Monica: RAND Corporation, February 1968, pp. 22.

On problems that have arisen in respect to civilian nuclear power, the Non-Proliferation Treaty, and IAEA, together with suggestions for IAEA certification of regional inspection systems conducted by regional associations of nonnuclear states and for US support of foreign construction of enrichment facilities.

1567. Haekkerup, Per. "Scandinavia's Peace-Keeping Forces for the United Nations." 42 <u>Foreign Affairs</u> (1964), 675-681.

Outline of the fundamentals of the plan of the Scandinavian states for a specially trained 4,000-man military force in a permanent state of readiness for service with the United Nations at short notice.

1568. Huddle, Franklin P. "Political Acceptability of a Disarmament Inspection System: Its Influence on System Design Criteria and Operation." 8 <u>Background</u> (1964), 175-186.

A somewhat speculative undertaking designed to anticipate political aspects, in terms of acceptability, of technical and legal aspects of arms control system design.

1568-A. James, Alan M. The Politics of Peacekeeping. London: Chatto
and Windus for the Institute of Strategic Studies, 1969, pp. 452.
　　　Employing a typology that excludes collective security because entailing overt war, the author discusses and describes
in detail the case histories of UN peacekeeping efforts. Peacekeeping efforts are classified as conciliatory "patching up" of
conflict situations (Palestine, Suez), preventive or "prophylac-
tic" (Cyprus, Kashmir, Perim), and vigorous "Proselytism" (Congo,
southern Africa).

1569. Kotani, Hidejiro. "Peace-Keeping: Problems for Smaller Countries." 19 International Journal (1964), 308-325.
　　　Discussion of some peacekeeping problems as revealed by the
Congo operation. Among the problems considered are national
legal impediments to the use of national armed forces for peacekeeping operations and the quite different methods of dealing
with legal impediments that were employed by Sweden and by Ireland.

1570. Latter, A.L., Le Levier, R.E., Martinelli, E.A., and McMillan,
W.G. A Method of Concealing Underground Nuclear Explosions. Santa Monica:
RAND Corporation, March 30, 1959.
　　　Important theoretical study on decoupling rejected by the
Soviet members of Technical Working Group II in November-Decem-
ber 1959 to continue basic East-West disagreements on several
critical technical points related to banning nuclear tests.

1571. Lentner, Howard. "The Political Responsibility and Accountability of the United Nations Secretary-General." 27 Journal of Politics
(1965), 839-860.
　　　Examination of the Secretary-General's accountability and,
conversely, extent of his freedom of decision with respect to
peacekeeping operations. The author sees the advisory committee
as perhaps a more effective instrument of control than might
have been viewed as the reality after the 1967 withdrawal of
UNEF at UAR request and without opportunity for opposition in
the advisory committee to have effect.

1572. Ljungqvist, Sten. "Scandinavia and U.N. Contingency Forces."
3 Disarmament (1964), 15-20.
　　　Description of the Scandinavian undertaking to establish a
permanent peacekeeping force, its organization, its control, its
recruitment, and its training.

1573. Lourie, S. "The United Nations Military Observer Group in India
and Pakistan." 9 International Organization (1955), 19-31.
　　　Discussion of some of the technical matters arising in the
use of UN observers to report on observance of a cease-fire
agreement and to aid local military leaders when incidents occur.

1574. Marshall, Charles Burton. "Character and Mission of a United
Nations Peace Force, under Conditions of General and Complete Disarmament."
59 American Political Science Review (1965), 350-364.

Essentially a commentary on a United States proposal of 1962 to the Eighteen Nation Disarmament Conference, the article deals with a number of basic problems that would be likely to arise in an effort to establish and administer a global peace force while at the same time retaining adequate national forces for internal security purposes. The author finds many suppositions and propositions, among them those of Clark and Sohn, to embrace the "typical civilian fallacy" of regarding military organizations in technical terms only.

1575. McNeil, Elton B. "Psychological Inspection." 1 Journal of Arms Control (1963), 124-138.

Regards disarmament inspection as inspection of men, machines, and man-machine systems and so as requiring guilty-knowledge detection by psychological means. Twelve techniques, divided into two basic categories of "psychological intrusion" and "physiological intrusion," are outlined. Most of these techniques are abhorrent to most cultures and, therefore, are unacceptable for disarmament inspection. Effectiveness and applicability of each method may differ from culture to culture and inspectees can be trained to resist most methods or adopt countermeasures. A practical minimum of psychological inspection is a training program to improve inspectors' common sense ability to judge people in face-to-face contact.

1576. Michalak, Stanley J., Jr. "Peacekeeping and the United Nations: The Problem of Responsibility." 11 International Studies Quarterly (1967), 301-319.

On the problem of balancing power and responsibility in the United Nations as a result of the Secretary-General's emergence as administrator of peacekeeping operations. The device of an advisory committee is seen as having served to provide support and legitimacy for the Secretary-General's freedom of decision in the UNEF and ONUC operations. But it is viewed as having failed in its "watchdog" functions, especially in the 1967 Middle East crisis when the Secretary-General ordered withdrawal of UNEF at UAR request despite disagreement on the advisory committee, which issued no call for a General Assembly meeting in accordance with the General Assembly resolution establishing the advisory committee for UNEF.

1577. Orear, J. "A New Approach to Inspection." 17 Bulletin of Atomic Scientists (1961), 107-110.

Advocates nonphysical methods of disarmament inspection, including the right to question citizens and a system of "inspection by the people" in which citizens are required to report violations.

1578. Osgood, Robert E. An International Military Force in A Disarming and Disarmed World. Washington: Institute for Defense Analyses, 1963, pp. viii, 374.

On military and political requirements of an effective UN Force, including the need to establish a UN authority that can prevent conversion of a Peace Force into an instrument of one coalition of states against other states.

1579. Pearson, Lester, "Keeping the Peace." 6 <u>Survival</u> (1964), 150-158.
Explanation by the then Canadian Prime Minister of his proposal for a standby peacekeeping force which would include Canadian units.

1580. Pederson, O.K. "Scandinavia and the UN Stand-by Forces." <u>Coop-</u>
<u>eration and Conflict</u> (No. 1, 1967), 37-46.
Employs chiefly Danish statements to analyze the initiative
taken by the Scandinavian Governments to set up standby peacekeeping forces in order to attend to Scandinavian interests, to
contribute to preservation of a balance of power favorable to
the West, and to influence the new states' concepts of international law and its application through the United Nations.

1581. Poirier, Pierre. <u>La force internationale d'urgence</u>. Paris:
Librairie Générale de Droit et de Jurisprudence, 1962, pp. 385.
A scholarly study of the United Nations Emergency Force
from a French point of view.

1581-A. Quester, George H. "The Nuclear Nonproliferation Treaty and
the International Atomic Energy Agency." 24 <u>International Organization</u>
(1970), 163-182.
On the IAEA's role and potential problems as the agency responsible for applying inspection safeguards under the Nonproliferation Treaty sponsored by the United States and the USSR.

1582. Rikhye, Indar J. "United Nations Peacekeeping Forces." 200
<u>Australian Army Journal</u> (January 1966), 29-42.
On peacekeeping forces, the role of the Military Adviser,
the need for a Senior Political Officer in the field as a result of the Congo complexities, and such problems as restraint
of force, national character of contingents, logistics, financing, standardization of weapons, procedures for contributing
national forces, and understanding of the United Nations role.

1583. Saeland, Einar. "Existing Arrangements for International Control of Warlike Material--4: The European Nuclear Energy Agency." 2 <u>Dis-</u>
<u>armament and Arms Control</u> (1964), 250-261.
Description of security regulations, on-the-spot verification by an international inspectorate, and other facets of surveillance of nuclear fuel in the charge of the joint enterprises
by the Control Bureau acting under the ENEA Steering Committee and
subject to judicial review by the European Nuclear Energy Tribunal.

1584. Stegenga, James A. <u>The United Nations Force in Cyprus</u>. Columbus: Ohio State University Press, 1968, pp. xiv, 227.
Examines the operations of the Cyprus force and its varied
contributions to the restoration of order and draws conclusions
on the limits of a military operation's capacity to manage a
civil conflict.

1585. Stenquist, Col. Nils. <u>The Swedish U.N. Stand-by Force and Ex-</u>
<u>perience</u>. Monograph Series No. 4. Paris: International Information Cen-
tre on Peacekeeping Operations, 1967, pp. 18.

A report by the Chief of the Swedish Army's U.N. Department on the status of the Swedish standby commitment for UN use and on the experience and lessons derived from Swedish participation in peacekeeping.

1586. Stokke, O. "United Nations Emergency Force--et politisk instru ment." Internasjonal Politikk (Bergen, No. 3, 1961), 250-265.
UNEF is viewed as a political instrument to be employed by the power most influential in the General Assembly, but is a limited force in that it cannot act in the sphere of vital interests of the Great Powers. The article, although implying that the limits of effectiveness are determined less by power itself than by that which stimulates the use of power, does not provide empirical tests of hypotheses related to determination of limits. Reference to the Hungarian and Suez cases provides at most a basis for a broad-stroke portrayal of vital interests.

1587. Wainhouse, David W., et al. International Peace Observation: A History and Forecast. Baltimore: Johns Hopkins Press, 1966, pp. xviii, 663.
Examines 70 successes and failures in peace-observation and peacekeeping by the League of Nations, the OAS, and the UN.

1588. Young, Oran R. Trends in International Peacekeeping. Research Monograph No. 22. Princeton: Center of International Studies, Princeton University, January 1966, pp. 45.
Identifies several approaches to peacekeeping that are being developed simultaneously at the UN and discusses the loss of dominance of the Hammarskjold approach as the Great Powers attempt to make use of the Security Council mechanism to exercise some control over peacekeeping. The essay, giving due attention to the structure of the international system in general and of the United Nations in particular, discusses peacekeeping in regard both to situations not involving the superpowers and those, such as Berlin and Cuba, in which they are·directly involved.

See also nos. 1146, 1228, 1540, 2203, 2423, 2435, 2833, 2874.

7. Collective International Political Decision-Making

1589. Burke, William T. "Aspects of Internation Decision-Making Processes in Intergovernmental Fishery Commissions." 43 Washington Law Review (1967), 115-178.
A legal scholar deals with intergovernmental decision-making in regard to a resource that has been very difficult to bring under effective regulation, among other reasons, because of the private economic interests affected.

1590. Coleman, James S. "Collective Decisions." 34 Social Inquiry (1964), 166-181.

Collective decisions can be made, without hostilities erupt-
ing violently, by rational self-interested actors. Although
decision-making structures may vary depending on organization and
social structure, some collective decisions can be made without
recourse to external power.

1591. Coleman, James S. Control of Collectivities and the Power of
a Collectivity to Act. P-3902. Santa Monica: RAND Corporation, August
1968, pp. 39.
  Mathematical analyses, based on possible voting subsets
analyzed by some of the Shapley-Shubik measures of power, of
the power of the US to enact legislation and of the UN Security
Council structure.

1592. Fernández-Shaw, F.G. "Reuniones de consulta de Ministros de
Relaciones Exteriores de América." 52 Política internacional (1960), 95-
116.
  A review of the fifth, sixth, and seventh meetings of the
OAS Council of Foreign Ministers dealing with the Caribbean
problems of Castro and, at the sixth meeting, of the Trujillo
regime.

1593. Hawden, John G., and Kaufmann, Johann. How United Nations Decisions Are Made. Leiden: Sijthoff, 1960, pp. 179.
  Analysis of United Nations machinery for considering economic questions and of forces and procedures determining how
the machinery works.

1594. Kohlhase, N. "Zum politischen Charakter der Europäischen Wirtschaftsgemeinschaft." 16 Europa-Archiv (1961), 339-346.
  Treats the taking of common decisions as manifestations of
political community and insists that the difference between economics and politics in the strict sense is fiction. British
hesitance over joining the Common Market is employed as evidence
for the argument.

1595. Manger, William. Pan America in Crisis: The Future of the OAS.
Washington: Public Affairs Press, 1961, pp. 104.
  Pessimistic conclusions follow an analysis that finds the
main difficulty to lie in US abjurance of collective action in
favor of bilateral dealings, occasional reversion to intervention, and failure to provide positive economic action either in
stabilizing commodity markets or giving aid, at least up to the
start of the Kennedy Administration.

See also nos. 722, 725, 726, 761, 770, 777, 778, 790, 845, 929, 1294,
1770, 2083.

IV. CONFLICT, OBLIGATIONS, RECIPROCITY, AND AGREEMENT

A. THE NATURE AND FUNCTIONS OF CONFLICT

1596. "Approaches to the Study of Social Conflict." 1 Journal of Conflict Resolution (June 1957), entire issue, pp. 105-240.
This symposium includes among the topics covered: parties and issues in conflict; organization and conflict; principles of intrapersonal conflict; interethnic conflict as one type of interest group conflict; mass communications and the loss of freedom in national decision-making; a possible research approach to interstate conflicts. Some of the articles are separately annotated.

1597. Archibald, Kathleen (ed.). Strategic Interaction and Conflict: Original Papers and Discussion. Berkeley: Institute of International Studies, University of California (1966), pp. viii, 277.
Contains papers by John C. Harsanyi, Morton Deutsch, Harold H. Kelley, Thomas C. Schelling, and Anatol Rapoport on strategic interaction and analytical problems in the theory of conflict.

1598. Bailey, N.A. "Toward a Praxeological Theory of Conflict." 11 Orbis (1968), 1081-1112.
Noting that in Eastern Europe some thinkers have been attempting to develop a science of "praxeology" (effective action) made up, among other things, of microeconomic analysis, cybernetics, and operations research, the author surveys conflict theories in the light of their operational content and concludes that an attempt should be made to develop political theory in the mode of economic analysis.

1599. Beaufre, Général d'Armeé André. Strategy of Action. Translated by Major-General R.H. Barry. New York: Praeger, 1967, pp. 136.
In his third volume on the subject, the author of An Introduction to Strategy and Deterrence and Deterrence and Strategy extends his theme to argue that coercion is no longer a function of the military alone, that all forms of pressure must be combined into one coordinated action, and that this requires the application of strategic thought to foreign policy in its broader meaning.

1600. Bernard, Jessie. "The Sociological Study of Conflict." In International Sociological Association, The Nature of Conflict: Studies on the Sociological Aspects of International Tensions. Paris: UNESCO, 1958, pp. 33-117.
A fairly general essay, but accompanied by an unusually extensive and wide-ranging bibliography.

1601. Boulding, Kenneth E. Conflict and Defense: A General Theory. New York: Harper, 1962. Torchbook ed., New York and Evanston: Harper & Row, 1963, pp. ix, 349.

This well-known book takes account of both static models and the dynamics of conflict. Besides an examination of pertinent theories, it examines conflicts between various parties such as individuals and groups and in such different settings as the industrial and the international. Consideration is also given to ideological and ethical conflict and to conflict resolution and control. Except for brief statements about the threat of punishment of a nation, on the difference between a nation's legal boundary and its critical boundary (with particular reference to the range of the projectile, and law equated with legal procedure as a means of conflict resolution), there is little in the book that deals directly with the substance of most international law studies. Indeed, the chapter on conflict resolution is a rather standard catalogue of methods, not a probe in depth. At the same time, the author's clear systematic articulation of the various facets of conflict are invaluable to the international lawyer's comprehension of conflict phenomena with which he must deal.

1602. Calvert, Peter. Latin America: Internal Conflict and International Peace. New York: St. Martin's, 1969, pp. 232.
A useful study of the forms of internal conflict in Latin America and their impact on international affairs.

1603. Coleman, James S. Community Conflict. Glencoe: Free Press, 1957, pp. 32.
Monograph that examines studies of communities in conflict and other sociological and psychological research in an effort to identify the processes underlying community controversy. Particularly useful is a conceptual framework that portrays the inner dynamics of controversy in terms of a chain of reciprocal causation or of mutually reinforcing relations.

1604. Coleman, James S. "Social Cleavage and Religious Conflict." 12 Journal of Social Issues (1956), 44-56.
Relationship between cross-pressures (i.e., societal integration) and the intensity and frequency of conflict.

1605. Coser, Lewis. The Functions of Social Conflict. Glencoe: Free Press, 1956; Free Press Paperback, 1964, pp. 188.
Built around 16 propositions derived from Georg Simmel's Conflict, the author examines social conflict in relation to such matters as group-binding and group-preserving functions, closeness and stability of relationships, intensity, internal group cohesion, definition of group structure, attitudes toward the antagonist, establishment and maintenance of a balance of power, and the creation of associations and coalitions.

1606. Dasgupta, Sugala. Peacelessness and Maldevelopment: A New Theme for Peace Research in Developing Nations. Paper presented to the International Peace Research Association, Tällberg, Sweden. June 17-19, 1967.

Holds that Western-type peace research, sharply distinguishing the horrors of war and the benefits of peace and emphasizing
that international conflict is unsuitable for developing nations.
Those nations exist in a peaceless state, restless, ready for
violence, and maldeveloped as a result of development projects
concerned with physical and material conditions rather than human
and social consequences.

1607. Fink, Clinton F. "Some Conceptual Difficulties in the Theory
of Social Conflict." 12 Journal of Conflict Resolution (1968), 412-460.
    Making use of a review of much of the literature on con-
flict, the author presents an argument for a generalist approach
to the study of conflict, examines the ambiguity of the term "social conflict," and proposes to define social conflict as "any
social situation or process in which two or more social entities
are linked by at least one form of antagonistic psychological relation or at least one form of antagonistic interaction."

1608. Jersild, Arthur T., and Markey, Frances V. Conflicts Between
Pre-School Children. New York: Teachers College, Columbia University,
1935, pp. ix, 181.
    In respect to initial aggressive acts producing conflict,
it was found that most were either actions intruding upon or
verbal attacks threatening a child's materials, space, or activities while a minority entailed injury of or threat to injure
the person. It may be that studies of children, when combined
with such findings as those concerning territoriality among animals, those concerning human defense of psychic space, and those
on the outbreak of intergroup and international violence may
lead to the identification either of common elements in the outbreak of violence or else of a level at which one set of stimuli
ceases to be operative and another set comes into play.

1609. Kautsky, John H. "Self-fulfilling Prophecy and Symbolic Reassurance in the East-West Conflict." 9 Journal of Conflict Resolution
(1965), 1-17.
    Discussion of how the expectation of inevitable capitalist-
communist conflict produced reactions in both groups that made
the myth come true. More recent lack of emphasis upon world
revolution, even though not repudiating the symbol, permits Soviet leaders to pursue policies incompatible with World Communism while reassuring people attached to Communist symbols. Anti-
communist symbols function in similar manner for the West. It
remains to be seen whether irrelevance of the myth of world revolution will break the circle of self-fulfilling prophecy in
Soviet-Western relations.

1610. Luard, Evan. Conflict and Peace in the Modern International
System. Boston: Little, Brown, 1968, pp. vii, 343.
    A general introduction to international relations, based
on what the author calls "a purely empirical approach," that
includes useful chapters on frontiers, colonies, civil wars,
coups d'état, and conflict resolution procedures.

1611. Mack, Raymond W. "The Components of Social Conflict." 12 Social Problems (1965), 388-397.
      Sets forth a number of the components of conflict, treats
social conflicts as related to ethnocentric behavior, group
boundaries, and sanctions to maintain boundaries, attempts to
distinguish between conflict and competition, and finds the most
serious defect of conflict theory to be the inability to determine where competition becomes conflict and the circumstances
existing when a group abandons the rules of competition.

1612. Mack, Raymond W., and Snyder, Richard C. "The Analysis of Social Conflict--Toward an Overview and Synthesis." 1 Journal of Conflict
Resolution (1957), 212-248.
      An effort to order the topics, concepts, and propositions
included within the study of social conflict. Amounts to a
propositional inventory of the literature.

1613. Mazur, Allan. "A Nonrational Approach to Theories of Conflict
and Coalitions." 12 Journal of Conflict Resolution (1968), 196-205.
      Suggesting that conflict theorists should reorient them-
selves from rational to nonrational (emotional) models, the author gives attention to the possibility of basing a nonrational
theory on the social-psychological notions of balance and dissonance, employs interpersonal conflict examples, and applies
the theory to the complex conflict-coalition system found in
tribal segmentary lineage systems.

1614. McClelland, Charles A., and Hoggard, Gary D. "Conflict Patterns in the Interactions Among Nations." In James N. Rosenau (ed.), International Politics and Foreign Policy: A Reader in Research and Theory.
Rev. ed. New York: Free Press, 1969, pp. 711-724.
      On the basis of reports in the New York Times in 1966, the
authors find that 20 participants account for almost 70% of the
reported international acts, that the United States and the Soviet Union are the most prominent originators and recipients of
the reported interactions, and that the 5 most active countries
(USA, USSR, China, United Kingdom, France) account for 40% of
the acts. Conflict behavior is not shown to dominate. Rather,
acts fall into three roughly balanced categories: cooperation
(33%), conflict (31.5%), and participation, i.e., meeting, con-
ferring, making arrangements for exchanges and communications,
etc. (35.5%). Excluded from the data, which was restricted to
single-action, nonroutine items, were reports of specific military events and acts of the Vietnam War.

1615. North, Robert C., Koch, Howard E., Jr., and Zinnes, Dina A.
"The Integrative Functions of Conflict." 4 Journal of Conflict Resolution
(1960), 355-374.
      Conflict is treated as existing whenever policy conditions,
viz., organizational goals or purposes with a time specification,
are incompatible. In overt conflict, four types of action are
possible: a nonviolent bid; a nonviolent commission; a bid of
violence; a commission of violence. Discussion of the integrative

effect of conflict focuses on nonviolent relationships that give rise to rules, procedures, or institutions for regulating, containing, or controlling conflicts. Consideration is given to both internal and external conflicts and to the contrast between the proliferation of loyalties in pluralistic systems and the demand for a single loyalty in monolithic systems. The processes of compromise and of integration are discussed in an effort to ascertain the durability of outcomes produced by these two processes. Integration is seen as the more durable because it involves no surrender, even though partial, of goals but a merging of purposes.

1616. Penrose, L.S. "Problems of International Co-Operation." Conference on the Pathogenesis of War, Cambridge, England, July 14-16, 1961. Medical Association for the Prevention of War, Bulletin No. 24 (September 1961).
   Views the essential primary factor in war, including civil war, as being the isolation of organized groups. Such isolation is seen as conducive to tension and mutual paranoia.

1617. Porsholt, Lars. "On Methods of Conflict Prevention." 3 Journal of Peace Research (1966), 178-193.
   Deals with military methods of conflict prevention on the basis of perceptions of probabilities of success in aggression and of the value of a goal compared with the values lost in the struggle to attain it. A distinction is made between aggressiveness by fear and nonexpansive attitudes, with attention given to the situation in which neither party is expansive and each perceives the other as nonexpansive--a situation in which peace is independent of military methods. A survey is made of nonmilitary conflict prevention measures, essentially in terms of expectations.

1618. Rapoport, Anatol. Fights, Games, and Debates. Ann Arbor, Michigan: University of Michigan Press, 1960, pp. xiv, 400.
   Threefold typology of conflict: fights (violence), games (interdependence of strategic moves), and debates (persuasion).

1619. Richman, Alvin. A Scale of Events Along the Conflict-Cooperation Continuum. Research Monograph Series, No. 10. Philadelphia: University of Pennsylvania, Foreign Policy Research Institute, March 1967, pp. iii, 39.
   Indicates a type of interval scale that can be used to obtain various groups' perceptions of both general and specific events of a cooperative and a conflict nature and possibilities for comparisons between groups, resources permitting.

1619-A. Richman, Alvin. "Curve of Conflict-Cooperation Events in Soviet-American Relations: August 1945-November 1950." Occasional Papers in Political Science, No. 17. Kingston: University of Rhode Island, 1969, pp. 38.
   Although confined to data for the first five years after World War II, this paper seeks to provide a technique for the

analysis of publicly known events in the form of an equal-
appearing interval scale that would provide a monthly indicator
of dyadic conflict and cooperation.

1620. Rummel, Rudolph J. Dimensions of Conflict Behavior Within and
Between Nations. Prepared in connection with research supported by the
National Science Foundation, Contract NSF-G24827. Mimeo. Evanston: June
1963, pp. viii, 108.
    A study based on 22 measures of foreign and domestic con-
flict behavior for 77 nations for 1955-1957. Data was inter-
correlated and factor analyzed, with factor scores being used
to determine the position of each nation along the foreign and
conflict dimensions that were found (war, diplomatic, and belligerent dimensions and, for domestic conflict, turmoil, revolutionary, and subversive dimensions) and to make a multiple
regression analysis of the relationship between domestic and
foreign conflict behavior. Correlation with the data of Richardson, Eckstein, and Cattell, indicated that the 1955-1957 data
may reflect long-range conflict behavior within and between nations. The three dimensions found for internal and the three
for foreign conflict behavior were uncorrelated. The war dimension emerged as the most important in accounting for variance of
conflict behavior between nations. Variation in acts or occurrences of foreign conflict behavior appear generally highly related to each other, as do also those of domestic conflict behavior to each other. But foreign conflict behavior was found
to be generally unrelated to domestic conflict behavior and did
not emerge as a necessary and sufficient condition for domestic
peace.

1621. Rummel, Rudolph J. "Testing Some Possible Predictors of Conflict Behavior Within and Between Nations." Peace Research Society (International), Papers. Chicago Conference, 1963. Vol. I (1964), pp. 79-111.
    A review of the study of 1955-1957 conflict situations and
of some of the findings and possible explanations of the findings. The most important predictor class of variables turned
out to be the demographic, perhaps because it is closely bound
to the personal lives and basic needs of a people. Technological development ranked last among the seven predictors in the
domestic conflict analysis and fifth in the foreign conflict
behavior analysis. In regard to foreign conflict behavior, the
subversion dimension is the most important predictor for the
partial and the product moment correlations, but with a uniformly negative direction of signs. In other words, the indication is that countries with less subversion have more foreign
conflict. Moreover, countries faced with the threat of both
subversion and revolution make few protests against other countries.

1622. Rummel, Rudolph J. "The Relationship Between National Attributes
and Foreign Conflict Behavior." In J. David Singer (ed.), Quantitative International Politics: Insight and Evidence. New York: Free Press, 1968,
pp. 187-214.

Employing data from the Dimensions of Nations Project and also taking note of findings of other studies, the author finds foreign conflict behavior to have an ambiguous relationship to the number of a nation's borders and to have little relationship to the following national attributes: (1) economic development or level of technology; (2) international communications and economic transactions; (3) amount of cooperation with the possible exception of signing treaties; (4) degree of totalitarianism; (5) national power; (6) domestic instability; (7) military capabilities; (8) psychological motivation; (9) values of a nation; (10) interaction of combinations of national characteristics. The author suggests (a) that this lack of correlation stems from formulation of the question as one of a relationship of magnitudes in the attribute and behavioral systems and (b) that distances between nations in the attribute system and directed behavior between nations in the behavioral system are what should be examined and related to each other.

1623. Scheffler, Harold W. "The Genesis and Repression of Conflict: Choiseul Island." 66 American Anthropologist (1964), 789-804.
On the theory of warfare and the function of the "state" as maintaining order or structuring change. Concludes that the broader social order is not the result of action either explicitly or implicitly principled. Multiple factions sort themselves out differently in the pursuit of interests and "this is all the 'order' there is or all that can usefully be meant by order in the context of the broader range of relations."

1624. Scheffler, Harold W. "The Social Consequences of Peace on Choiseul Island." 3 Ethnology (1964), 398-403.
This short article examines the consequences of European takeover not in terms of culture contact but of ending the rather constant wars among over 100 factions, primarily cognatic descent groups often allied to fight other coalitions. Forcible imposition of peace by the British destroyed much of the indigenous culture. Political and social leadership had been dependent on conflict. Elimination of conflict left a vacuum for political power. Early efforts to substitute competitive feasting and gift exchange were diverted by subsequent generations to acquisition of European material goods. Cooperation and solidarity within kin groups broke down; in the absence of external conflict and of the vengeance system, kinsmen lost compelling reasons for trusting one another. Self-interest took precedence over kinship obligations. The societies are leaderless. Only a few men of recognized importance have a measure of political power and that power is neither of such nature nor rests on cultural foundations to promote unity. Insofar as social relations have been reordered, it has been on the foundation of contact with European institutions, not on that of Choiseulese culture, now deprived of most of its meaning.

1625. Siegal, Bernard J., and Beals, Alan R. "Pervasive Factionalis 62 American Anthropologist (1960), 394-417.

Includes the finding that all types of conflict are prede-
fined by the social system in which they occur--a finding that
one might interpret to mean that what society finds to be abhorrent is not war but impropriety in war or other conflict.

1626. Simmel, Georg. Conflict and the Web of Group-Affiliations.
Translated by Kurt H. Wolff and Reinhard Bendix. Glencoe: Free Press,
1956; Free Press Paperback, 1964, pp. 195.
"Conflict" is a translation of chapter 4 of Soziologie
(1908, 3rd ed. 1923) and "The Web of Group-Affiliation" is a
translation of another chapter, "Die Kreuzung sozialer Kreise,"
of the same book. Of the two essays, "Conflict" is probably
the more important because its insights, e.g., on the integrative effects of conflict, have provided the basis for more recent sociological and political science investigations of and
theories about conflict.

1627. Singer, Kurt. The Idea of Conflict. New York: Cambridge University Press, 1950, pp. 181.
Employment of history and mythology to probe for the cultural roots of human conflict.

1628. Stagner, Ross. "Personality Dynamics and Social Conflict." 17
Journal of Social Issues (1961), 28-44.
Both personalizing nations and dealing with them as heroes
and villains produce conversations between cultures in which
there is talking but not hearing. Valuing his nation as an essential part of his environment, man tends to mobilize his energy to keep his image of it inviolate. Hence, he distorts
information and thereby contributes to the intensity and bit-
terness of international conflicts.

1629. Stagner, Ross. Psychological Aspects of International Conflict.
Belmont, California: Brooks/Cole Publishing Co., 1967, pp. xi, 234.
An overview of the nature of misperceptions, particularly
those of nationalism, that impede progress toward reduced international violence, effective negotiations, pacific settlement
of disputes, and the development of loyalty to international
organizations.

1630. Strausz-Hupé, Robert, et al. Protracted Conflict. New York:
Harper for the Foreign Policy Research Institute, University of Pennsylvania, 1959, pp. 203.
Study of Communist strategy and tactics in maintaining the
initiative in a conflict viewed as being of very long duration.

1631. Tanter, Raymond. "Dimensions of Conflict Behavior Within and
Between Nations, 1958-60." 10 Journal of Conflict Resolution (1966), 41-
64.
A replication for the period 1958-1960 of Rudolph Rummel's
study of conflict behavior in order to obtain additional evidence on dimensions of conflict behavior and the relationship
between foreign and domestic conflict behavior. Data from 83

nations on nine domestic and thirteen foreign measures of conflict was factor analyzed. Three foreign dimensions, war, diplomatic, and belligerency dimensions, and two foreign dimensions,
turmoil and internal war (the latter subsuming the revolutionary
and subversive dimensions of Rummel's study) emerged. From
factor analysis of domestic and foreign conflict behavior, the
domestic measures separated themselves from the foreign variables to imply a lack of relationship. A further investigation
through multiple regression yielded only a small relationship
between foreign and domestic conflict. Tabulations of raw data
are included in an appendix.

1632. Wilkenfeld, Jonathan. "Domestic and Foreign Conflict Behavior
of Nations." 5 Journal of Peace Research (1968), 56-69.
    Employing data from 1955-1960 to perform a correlation
analysis of 74 nations divided into three groups, personalist,
centrist, and polyarchic, the paper examines all pairs along the
Rummel dimensions for domestic and foreign conflict behavior.
It was postulated that type of nation and nature of conflict
would determine the nature of the relationship between a nation's domestic and foreign conflict behavior, but the results
indicate that the key variable may be type of nation rather
than the nature of the conflict.

1633. Wright, Quincy. "The Nature of Conflict." 4 Western Politica
Quarterly (1951), 193-209.
    In what is essentially an updated condensation of ideas set
forth in A Study of War, Professor Wright discusses the types,
tendency, methods, and solution of conflicts. The tendency of
conflict is traced essentially in terms of a psychological version of the arms race thesis, and a corresponding alliance policy
leading to the bipolarization conducive to absolute war. International law is portrayed as having, along with other devices,
the function of segregating the aspects of conflict (physical,
political, ideological, and legal) to prevent their becoming
united as in war in the legal sense.

1634. Yates, Aubrey J. Frustration and Conflict. London: Methuen;
New York: Wiley, 1962, pp. x, 236.
    Presents a fairly detailed exposition and evaluation of
general theories of frustration and conflict with reference to
experiments that have been carried out over the past 40 years.

1635. Yates, Aubrey J. (ed.). Frustration and Conflict: Enduring
Problems in Psychology--Selected Readings. Paperback. Princeton: Van
Nostrand, 1965, pp. x, 246.
    Selection of papers presenting a sample of the vast quan-
tity of experimental research on frustration and conflict, with
particular attention to studies of three dependent variables,
namely, aggression, fixation, and regression. Papers included
are representative examples of both theory and methodology in
this particular area of behavior.

See also nos. 80, 219, 426, 503, 560, 603, 1075, 1206, 1250, 1800, 1813, 1888, 1895, 1902, 2340, 2367, 2381.

1. Misunderstandings, Disputes, and Nonviolent Conflicts

1636. Billington, Ray Allen, et al. The Historian's Contribution to Anglo-American Misunderstanding: Report of a Committee on National Bias in Anglo-American History Textbooks. New York: Hobbs, Dorman, 1966, pp. xv, 118.
    An important study in the creation and/or perpetuation of misunderstandings, heightening the conflict potential, through the presentation of bias in the guise of scholarly discourse and exposition. Examining textbooks for secondary schools for their treatment of the American Revolution, the War of 1812, and World War I, three American and two British historians find that national pride, combined with ignorance of the latest scholarship, lead to sins of omission (unconscious falsification, bias by inertia, overcondensation) and sins of commission (fighting words, linguistic nuances, patriotic prose, cumulative implication, bias in reverse).

1637. Blake, Robert R., Shepard, H.A., and Mouton, Jane S. Managing Intergroup Conflict in Industry. Prepared for the Foundation for Research on Political Behavior. Houston: Gulf Publishing Co., 1964, pp. xiii, 210.
    Essentially a manual of cases of industrial conflicts that demonstrate nine approaches to conflict. Eight of the approaches have side-effects which do not promote an organization's objectives. The most common is the intergroup win-lose power struggle. The authors suggest a potentially creative method of problem solving by maximizing innovation and recognition of potential problem areas.

1638. Cooper, Peter. "Towards a Model of Politico-Moral Development." Peace Research Society (International), Papers. Cracow Conference, 1965. Vol. IV (1966), pp. 192-203.
    Compares the logic of samples of children and of British politicians in regard to war and finds each to produce three general and apparently irreconcilable types of logic that may in part be explainable in terms of training. The author suggests that disputes due to differences in reasoning (unlikely to be changed as the logics employed limit "channel capacity") may be distinguished from disputes due either to misunderstanding information or to differing interests. He also suggests that all three types of logic are probably represented on both sides of a conflict and that there may be optimum combinations of logic for purposes of negotiation.

1639. Hammond, K.R. "New Directions in Research on Conflict Resolution." 21 Journal of Social Issues (1965), 44-66.
    Treating the conflicts of the next 20 years as likely to be derived from cognitive differences about the means for

managing problems, a research paradigm is developed for studying cognitive conflict and its resolution in respect to problems not susceptible to perfect solutions.

1640. Ichheiser, Gustav. "Misunderstandings in International Relations." 16 American Sociological Review (1951), 311-316.
    Addressing himself to the question of why people of differ-
ent cultural and national backgrounds view the social world differently, the author calls attention to (1) the interdependence
between culture and emotions and that between perception and
emotions, (2) limits of insight that restrict understanding of
one's language, and (3) similar limits upon understanding various
religious and prestige symbols. Differences between conscious
and unconscious nationalism are noted. Some suggestions are made
concerning means that might be tried in an effort to overcome
misunderstandings.

1641. Russett, Bruce M. "Toward a Model of Competitive Internationa
Politics." 25 Journal of Politics (1963), 226-247.
    Exploratory attempt to apply propositions derived from the
study of intra-national politics--party systems, voting, issues--
to the international system.

1642. Todd, Frederick J., Hammond, Kenneth R., and Wilkins, Marilyn
M. "Differential Effects of Ambiguous and Exact Feedback on Two-Person
Conflict and Compromise." 10 Journal of Conflict Resolution (1966), 88-
97.
    Report of an experiment purporting to show that in con-
flicts entailing cognitive differences rather than differential gain the receipt of full information as feedback leads to
resolution by compromise while partial or ambiguous information leads to capitulation.

1643. Waskow, Arthur I. "Nonlethal Equivalents of War." In Roger
Fisher (ed.), International Conflict and Behavioral Science: The Craigville Papers. New York: Basic Books, 1964, pp. 123-141.
    Although the author's prescriptions are highly question-
able, a useful review of some nonlethal conflicts such as the
exploration race of the 15th and 16th centuries is included.

See also nos. 1704, 1705, 1761, 1813, 2175, 2404, 2708.

2. War; Limited War

1644. Abel, T. "The Element of Decisions in the Pattern of War." 6
American Sociological Review (1941), 853-859.
    A sample study of the history of 25 major wars suggests the
following conclusions concerning the nature of the decisions to
go to war: (1) the decision to fight is not reached on the spur
of the moment; (2) the rational, calculating decision to fight
is reached far in advance of the actual outbreak of hostilities,

preceding the outbreak by one to five years. The author holds
that the nature and role of decision are relevant to the problem of preventing war.

1645. Allport, Gordon W. "The Role of Expectancy." In Hadley Cantril
(ed.), Tensions That Cause Wars. Urbana: University of Illinois Press,
1950, pp. 43-78.
Holds that personal aggressiveness does not render war inevitable but is at most a contributing cause when people expect
war as a means of solving problems. Popular expectation of war
and preparation for war is regarded as a prerequisite for making
war under war-minded leadership. Peaceful relations are viewed
as breeding expectancy of peace. The article asserts that the
frequency of external turmoil is directly related to the frequency of internal turmoil.

1646. Aron, Raymond. La société industrielle et la guerre, suivi d'un
tableau de la diplomatie mondiale en 1958. Paris: Plon, 1959, pp. 179.
Most important is the first essay that examines the theory
that increasing industrialization will lead to the abolition of
war between industrial nations in the light of the present situation in which ideology rather than economics is the motive force
in international relations.

1647. Ash, Maurice A. "An Analysis of Power, with Special Reference
to International Politics." In James N. Rosenau (ed.), International Politics and Foreign Policy: A Reader in Research and Theory. New York:
Free Press, 1961, pp. 334-342.
Treats power as a result of relationships, not as means or
ends of foreign policy, and develops an analysis of increases in
levels of armaments in efforts to retain a power position, in
the face of another state's forces, that seeks to identify the
point at which further increase of armaments produces a decline
of power. The framework for the paper is built from the concepts of committee forces and general reserves and the ratio between them under differing circumstances of commitment and level
of armaments.

1648. Baldwin, John. "The Economics of Peace and War: A Simulation."
11 Journal of Conflict Resolution (1967), 383-397.
Description of a simulation that permitted players to win
either by peacefully trading goods or by war and plunder of each
other's resources. A feature of interest was that a situation
similar to Hobbes' war of every man against every man developed
and lasted until the players developed strategies and norms to
control wars. Both the norms and a strategy of trust were analyzed as resting on long-range self-interest.

1649. Below, Fritz. Armee und Soldat im Atomzeitalter. Karlsruhe:
Stahlberg, 1957, pp. 144.
The author makes an attempt to ascertain the place and
function of armies and citizen soldiers in the face of recent
scientific and technological developments.

1650. Benoit, Emile, and Lubell, Harold. "World Defense Expenditures." 3 _Journal of Peace Research_ (1966), 97-113.

Data are supplied providing a rough measure of the volume of resources going into national defense programs of 36 countries. Note is taken of the concentration of defense expenditures in the US and the USSR, giving a bipolar structure to the arms race despite loosening of alliances. Noting that over $1 billion is spent annually on weapons procurement by less developed countries, it is suggested that a weapons freeze in such countries would facilitate industrial development. The problem of burdens on the civilian economy is dealt with more fully in a volume edited by Benoit, _Disarmament and World Economic Interdependence_ (Oslo: Universitetsforlaget, 1966).

1651. Boulding, Kenneth E., and Gleason, Alan. "War as an Investment: The Case of Japan." _Peace Research Society (International), Papers_ Chicago Conference, 1964. Vol. III (1965), pp. 1-18.

Interim report on a research project that is part of a more comprehensive study of the international economics of arms control and disarmament, directed by Emile Benoit, Columbia University. The authors find that, although in earlier days war industries contributed to Japan's economic growth, the war industry of the 1930s and 1940s impeded economic development and produced losses, especially after 1937.

1652. Bramson, Leon, and Goethals, George W. (eds.). _War: Studies from Psychology, Sociology, Anthropology_. New York: Basic Books, 1964, pp. 407.

Selections from such writers as William McDougall, Gordon W. Allport, D.O. Hebb, and W.R. Thompson, Robert E. Park, Margaret Mead, Harold D. Lasswell, Morris Janowitz, and Raymond Aron on such subjects as pugnacity, expectancy, the authoritarian personality, the social function of war, the garrison state, and military elites.

1653. Calvocoressi, Peter. _Suez: Ten Years Later--Broadcasts from the B.B.C. Third Programme_. Edited by Anthony Moncrieff. London: British Broadcasting Corporation, 1967, pp. xvi, 160.

Reviews the Arab-Israeli War of 1956 in the perspective of ten years and with the benefit of materials from interviews with Nasser, Ben-Gurion, Abba Eban, Pineau, and Dayan.

1654. Crouzet, François. "Wars, Blockade, and Economic Change in Europe, 1792-1815." 24 _Journal of Economic History_ (1964), 567-588.

Examination of economic dislocations on the Continent resulting from the British maritime blockade, the "self-blockade" imposed by the French, and the changing of frontiers, customs barriers, and markets during the war. Besides noting that the blockade was in part retaliation and in part an act to placate West Indian shipping interests, the author concludes that the dislocations had a retardative effect on Continental industries, displaced industry from the seaboard to interior centers which, in the Hamburg-Paris-Milan triangle, are today the core of the

Common Market economy, and also turned Continental commerce inward, away from overseas and international markets to Continental
and especially national markets, to produce a sharp contrast with
England.

1655. Denton, F.H., and Phillips, W. Some Patterns in the History of
Violence. P-3609. Santa Monica: RAND Corporation, June 1967, pp. 32.
An empirical analysis purporting to demonstrate the existence of a short-term (15-30 years) and a long-term (80-120 years)
periodic fluctuation in violence, the former being attributed to
a generation effect in decision-making or a fading of remembrance
of past war experience and the latter to changes in political
philosophy, particularly in light of the association of long-term
fluctuations with social change or domestic turmoil.

1656. Fried, Morton, Harris, Marvin, and Murphy, Robert. War: The
Anthropology of Armed Conflict and Aggression. Garden City: Natural History Press for the American Museum of Natural History, 1968, pp. xxii, 262.
Eight anthropological papers and subsequent discussion of
various aspects of war including its functions, biological effects, diseases, and psychological preparations for war.

1657. Friedell, Morris F. "A Laboratory Experiment in Retaliation."
12 Journal of Conflict Resolution (1968), 357-373.
An experiment in retaliation that, among other things,
showed some tendency to retaliate in the belief that the experimenter wanted retaliation, that authoritarian personalities
tended to retaliate, and that introducing the possibility of
accident as the cause of a first strike, did not inhibit retaliation. The implications relevant to the problem of accidental war are discussed.

1658. Gabbay, Rony E. A Political Study of the Arab-Jewish Conflict:
The Arab Refugee Problem (A Case Study). Geneva: Droz, 1959, pp. xvi, 611.
Detailed study of the various aspects of the Arab-Jewish
conflict that includes a careful study of the Arab refugee
problem.

1659. Gladstone, Arthur. "Relationship Orientation and the Processes
Leading Toward War." 6 Background (1962), 13-25.
Effort must be made to understand what goes on in the period
of preparation for war. Processes bringing about conditions conducive to war are (1) an arms race, (2) changes in interactions
between two nations, and (3) mutually antagonistic behavior. Discussion of the concept of relationship orientation includes an
outline of the effects on behavior of the following orientations:
undifferentiated, egoistic, altruistic, balancing, and integrative. Three factors affect national orientation: (1) individual
predisposition to personal orientation, (2) behavior of the other
nations, and (3) social pressure. These three factors, along
with the previously mentioned processes, are considered in terms
of their influence upon development of the Cold War.

1660. Gross, Feliks. <u>World Politics and Tension Areas</u>. New York: New York University Press, 1966, pp. xvii, 377.

A study employing sociological, political science, and anthropological tools to examine why and how limited tensions do or do not lead to war. Case studies are included.

1661. Haas, Michael. <u>Social Change and International Aggression:</u> <u>A</u> <u>Correlational Study</u>. Paper presented to the Conference on Mathematical Applications in Political Science. Dallas, July 1965.

Employs regression techniques to correlate the frequency of participation in war by 10 countries since 1900 with unemployment, homicides, suicides, and death rates due to alcoholism.

1662. Haas, Michael. "Societal Approaches to the Study of War." 2 <u>Journal of Peace Research</u> (1965), 307-323.

Reviews some theories on the reasons for war and its social utility and then attempts a "prerequisites" approach employing the author's own correlations between frequency of war and unemployment, homicides, suicides, and death rates due to alcoholism, the factor analysis of cultural variables by Cattell and associates, the Rummel-Tanter data on foreign and domestic conflict, and the Banks-Textor and Gregg-Banks data on political variables. Banks-Textor and Rummel-Tanter data are correlated for the first time.

1663. Halperin, Morton H. <u>Limited War in the Nuclear Age</u>. New York: Wiley, 1963, pp. ix, 194.

Analysis of the limiting factors, including motives for expansion and limitation in interaction between adversaries, in such limited actions as the Korean War, Taiwan Strait (1955 and 1958), Laos, Vietnam, and Cuba (1962).

1664. Halperin, Morton H. "Nuclear Weapons and Limited War." 5 <u>Journal of Conflict Resolution</u> (1961), 146-166.

Penetrating examination of the problems of limited war and of the utility of nuclear weapons in limited war situations.

1665. Halperin, Morton H. "The Limiting Process in the Korean War." 78 <u>Political Science Quarterly</u> (1963), 13-39.

An attempt to fuse the approach of the military strategist and that of the political scientist and the historian and to test the military strategist's hypotheses against the historical event of the Korean War. Limitations in terms of geography, types of weapons, targets, and participation of certain countries are dealt with in terms of perceptions of decision-makers, the risk of retaliation, and especially the domestic and international context of the war rather than the dynamics of the war itself.

1666. Hartigan, R.S. "Noncombatant Immunity: Reflections on Its Origins and Present Status." 29 <u>Review of Politics</u> (1967), 204-220.

Includes the argument that the present norm of noncombatant immunity does not necessarily represent an ethically obligatory prescription and that the rule might be abandoned or radically changed without serious impact on efforts to define restrictions on nuclear war.

1667. Holsti, Ole R., Brody, Richard A., and North, Robert C. The Management of International Crisis: Affect and Action in American-Soviet Relations, October, 1962. Studies in Conflict and Integration. Stanford University, Mimeo, n.d.
    Revision of a paper delivered at the International Peace Research Society Conference at Ghent in 1964 and published in the Proceedings of the Society (Volume II). The paper compares the management of the 1914 and 1962 crises to ascertain reasons why one crisis escalated beyond control of the participants while the other did not. Failures of communication and failures to leave alternatives open to other parties in 1914 and contrasted with the better management on both grounds in 1962. Misperceptions of the other parties' intentions in 1914 and tying one's own policy to that of a weaker and less responsible ally are also compared with the 1962 events and situations.

1668. Huntington, Samuel P. (ed.). Changing Patterns of Military Politics. New York: Free Press, 1962, pp. 272.
    Papers on the role and control of violence in international affairs and on the military role in domestic politics.

1669. Kissinger, Henry. The Necessity for Choice: Prospects of American Foreign Policy. New York: Harper, 1961, pp. xii, 387.
    Includes an excellent chapter on the limited war challenge to the US that makes clear the political liabilities of reliance on nuclear weapons.

1670. Knorr, Klaus. Military Power and Potential. Lexington, Massachusetts: D.C. Heath, 1970, pp. 160.
    A new conceptual analysis of the dynamics of military potential and military power in world politics that uses a series of models to identify the determinants of both putative and actualized military power. Economic and technological capacity, administrative expertise, and political commitment and culture are related to the requirements of different types of war.

1671. Knorr, Klaus, and Read, Thornton (eds.). Limited Strategic War. New York: Praeger, 1962, pp. xi, 258.
    Collection of papers dealing with the nature of limited war and problems associated therewith.

1672. Kotzsch, Lothar. The Concept of War in Contemporary and International Law. Geneva: Droz, 1956, pp. 310.
    Covers a wide range of topics and contains much information, particularly concerning recent conflicts, and has been suggestive of ways of viewing war under current conditions.

1673. LeVine, Robert A. "Anthropology and the Study of Conflict: Introduction." 5 Journal of Conflict Resolution (1961), 3-15.

Survey of the anthropological literature with an attempt
to draw generalizations from it that bear on questions of war
and peace.

1674. McClintock, Robert. The Meaning of Limited War. Boston:
Houghton Mifflin, 1967, pp. xiv, 239.
A career diplomat employs the case method to examine six
types of limited war and to find some characteristics common
to all limited wars.

1675. McConnell, Richard M. "War Words and Tired Symbols." 12 ETC.:
A Review of General Semantics (1955), 103-108.
"War words" of a bygone age characterize our descriptions
of business activities and other events. They are one species
of tired symbols that becloud our rational processes in an age
when their use is entirely anachronistic. The task of general
semantics is to understand why we use such terms and to dispel
tired symbols and war words.

1676. Murphy, Robert F. "Intergroup Hostility and Social Cohesion."
59 American Anthropologist (1957), 1018-1035.
Study of the function of warfare in the 19th century society of the Mundurucu, an extremely warlike matrilocal tribe
of the Amazon basin. The explanation, possibly generalizable
to all matrilocal societies, is that social organization was
such as to render male solidarity on the village and tribal
levels a functional necessity lest the pitting of patrilineal
kin against each other destroy the fabric of the kinship structure through strife within villages and households. Open show
of aggression among men being prohibited, hostility could only
be unleashed against the outside world, a feature symbolized
by the use of the word for "enemy" to refer to any group that
was not Mundurucu. The mere existence of any non-Mundurucu
group was sufficient cause for war.

1677. Naroll, Raoul. Theoretical Results: Northridge Deterrence
Project, Report No. 33. Report to Project Michelson, U.S. Naval Ordnance
Test Station, China Lake, California. Mimeo. Northwestern University,
February 1, 1964, pp. ii, 62.
Report summarizing the theoretical results of a study of
deterrence in certain historical periods making up the sample.
Among the findings are a relationship between diplomatic activ-
ity and the frequency of war and, as with an earlier study of
primitive wars, a correlation between the size and quality of
armed forces and territorial growth.

1678. Naroll, Raoul. Warfare, Peaceful Intercourse and Territorial
Change: A Cross-Cultural Survey. Research for Project Michelson, U.S.
Naval Ordnance Test Station, China Lake, California. Mimeo. Northwestern
University, n.d., pp. ii, 68, x.
Examines 50 societies, usually for the century preceding
colonial conquest, to examine the influence of military factors

on cultural evolution. The study centers on the spread of culture by expansion and evolution. Two measures of territorial
change, territorial growth and territorial stability, are used,
both considering the ratio of territory gained or lost during
the period to the territory at the beginning of the period but
only territorial growth taking account of the direction of change.
A table on military expectations shows a Guttman scale, as Quincy
Wright suggested, but of different order from Wright's postulate.
Naroll's order is: revenge and defense (only one society shows
revenge only), plunder or subsistence wealth, prestige, and political control. Wright's postulate reversed prestige and plunder.
Between the theory that arms deter aggression and the theory that
they promote it, the correlations give only mild support to the
latter and none to the former theory. The remainder of the article, relating military action to territorial change and attempting to explain the frequency of war produces no significant
results, but its discussions of methods and of "causal influence" analysis and its brief comments on quality control of anthropological data are useful.

1679. Norbeck, E. "African Rituals of Conflict." 65 American Anthropologist (1963), 1254-1279.
The author presents a description of rites expressing social conflict among various African societies and offers suggestions concerning their functional significance. All the
customs discussed are institutionalized departures from everyday practice. Ritualized expressions of interpersonal and intergroup hostility may be seen as a part of a larger scheme of
the temporary suspension of ordinary restraints applying to almost any sphere of life.

1680. Osgood, Robert E., and Tucker, Robert W. Force, Order, and
Justice. Baltimore: Johns Hopkins Press, 1967, pp. viii, 374.
Interpretation of the role of force in international relations before and after the introduction of nuclear weapons, with
attention to the difficulties of managing and limiting the use
of force, particularly in the circumstance of technological innovation that deprives planners of the benefit of wartime experience with their weapons. Attempts to control force, including arms control and disarmament efforts, the rationale of force,
and the bellum justum theory are discussed. Force is seen as
both an upholder and potential disrupter of international order,
and the assessment is related to the structural aspects of the
international community before the coming of nuclear power,
under conditions of bipolarity, and in the possible circumstance
of nuclear proliferation.

1681. Otterbein, Keith F. Cross-Cultural Studies of Armed Combat.
Research Monograph No. 1 (edited by Glenn H. Snyder). Buffalo Studies.
State University of New York at Buffalo. (Vol. IV, No. 1, April 1968),
pp. 91-109.

Employs a sample of 50 primitive societies to study feuding and another 50 to study internal war. Armed combat between fraternal interest groups in the same political community is feuding; armed combat between political communities in the same cultural unit is internal war; armed combat between political communities belonging to different cultural units is external war. Societies with fraternal interest groups are more likely to have both feuding and internal war than societies without them. In a centralized political system (having at least one jurisdiction above the local, a government with legitimate use of force, or an official with economic redistributive functions) feuding occurs if war is absent and fraternal groups are present; feuding does not occur if wars are frequent even if fraternal groups are present. In a centralized political system, internal war occurs whether or not fraternal groups are present.

1682. Otterbein, Keith F., and Charlotte S. "An Eye for an Eye, A Tooth for a Tooth: A Cross-Cultural Study of Feuding." 67 American Anthropologist (1965), 1470-1482.
    A study of 50 societies drawn from the Human Relations Area Files indicates, among other things, a strong relationship between war and the absence of feuding in high level societies as contrasted with a positive correlation between war and feuding in low-level societies.

1683. Papadakis, Vasileios P. Histoire diplomatique de la question Nord-Épirote 1912-1957. Athens: Alevropoulos, 1958, pp. 195.
    Greek view of the Northern Epirus affair in which the Greek Government, like the Arabs later in respect to Israel, asserted the existence of a continuing state of war with Albania.

1683-A. Payne, James L. The American Threat: The Fear of War as an Instrument of Foreign Policy. Chicago: Markham, 1970, pp. xiv, 241.
    An argument for acknowledgement and intelligent use of the threat of war present in most international political conflict situations, with stress on the difference between the citizen's perception of an international conflict and the statesman's responsibility to confront the realities of such situations.

1684. Pruitt, Dean G., and Snyder, Richard C. (eds.). Theory and Research on the Causes of War. Englewood Cliffs: Prentice-Hall, 1969, pp. xvi, 314.
    Twenty readings and seven introductory essays on research into the causes of war.

1685. Ropp, Theodore. War in the Modern World. Durham: Duke University Press, 1959, pp. xv, 400.
    A history of warfare from the condottieri through the Korean War.

1686. Russett, Bruce M. "Case, Surprise and No Escape." 24 Journal of Politics (1962), 3-22.

Development of a rigorous conceptual framework for studying
the causes of war. The framework is adapted from one used for
the study of automobile accidents. The utilization of a standardized framework of analysis would permit the meaningful comparative study of various international conflicts.

1686-A. Sharabi, Hisham. Palestine and Israel: The Lethal Dilemma.
New York: Pegasus, 1969, pp. 224.
Besides a critique of American policy and an analysis of
Arab behavior, this book provides information about two Arab
commando organizations.

1687. Singer, J. David, Small, Melvin, and Kraft, George L., Jr.
The Frequency, Magnitude, and Severity of International War, 1815-1945.
Preprint 159. Ann Arbor: Mental Health Research Institute, University
of Michigan, July 1965.
This report provides basic data on the wars since the Napoleonic. It provides an excellent guide to what has happened in
the realm of international violence as science, technology, and
industry have grown and basic changes have occurred in the international society of states since the Vienna settlement.

1688. Sorbets, Jacques. "L'Est et l'Ouest et l'essence de leur an-
tagonisme." 25 Rivista di studi politici internazionali (1958), 220-228.
Theory on shifting the East-West struggle from the military
to the ideological plane, based on the premise that wars are not
fought to defeat the enemy forces but to make them change ideas.

1689. Sorokin, Pitirim A. Social and Cultural Dynamics. Vol. III:
Fluctuation of Social Relationships, War, and Revolution. New York: American Book Co., 1937.
A pioneering attempt, based on information in historical
accounts, to develop measures of the duration, scale, and intensity of wars and of fluctuations in internal disturbances of
European nations since 600 B.C.

1690. Stevenson, G.H. "The Psychiatric Public Health Aspects of War."
98 American Journal of Psychiatry (1941), 1-10.
The important psychiatric public health aspect of war considered by Stevenson is the elimination of war psychosis during
peacetime. The psychiatrist should take an active part in this
because of his special insight of psychopathological factors,
etc. He suggests the establishment of a permanent commission
of psychiatrists to act in an advisory capacity on international
problems during peacetime.

1691. Wittner, Lawrence S. Rebels Against War: The American Peace
Movement, 1941-1960. New York: Columbia University Press, 1969, pp. xi, 339.
The first book to carry the history of the American peace
movement beyond the 1930s, this study makes extensive use of
personal interviews and the largely untapped files of pacifist
groups.

1692. Wright, Quincy. "The Psychological Approach to War and Peace." 10 <u>India Quarterly</u> (1954), 23-31.

Suggests that the growth of societies tends to increase the probability of conflict between groups in proportion to reduction of conflict within the group--a proposition expressed by other writers besides Wright and stimulated the efforts of Rummel and Tanter to correlate internal and external conflict. Super-groups have widened the area of peace but have not accomplished the necessary psychological reconditioning to make peace possible.

1693. Yaryan, Ruby B., and Festinger, Leon. "Preparatory Action and Belief in the Probable Occurrence of Future Events." 63 <u>Journal of Abnormal and Social Psychology</u> (1961), 603-606.

An experiment was conducted to test the following hypothesis derived from Festinger's theory of cognitive dissonance: If people exert a great deal of effort in preparation for a possible future event, they should believe more strongly in the likelihood of occurrence of the event than people who do not have to engage in preparatory effort. The results of the experiment provide strong support for the hypothesis.

1694. Ziferstein, Isidore. "Psychological Habituation to War: A Socio-Psychological Case Study." 37 <u>American Journal of Orthopsychiatry</u> (1967), 457-468.

A discussion of habituation to war by gradual involvement in which each new step is presented as a logical, unavoidable result of a prior commitment, thereby producing acquiescence without an accompanying feeling that the right to disagree is being suppressed.

See also nos. 80, 132, 219, 390, 442, 483, 518, 689, 695, 704, 1273, 1284, 1293, 1340, 1343, 1364, 1500, 1503, 1620-1622, 1728, 1784, 1992, 2150, 2168, 2169, 2194, 2197, 2211, 2214, 2230, 2232, 2256, 2266, 2378, 2570.

3. <u>Aggression</u>

1695. Bandura, A., Ross, Dorothea, and Ross, Sheila A. "Transmission of Aggression Through Imitation of Aggressive Models." 63 <u>Journal of Abnormal and Social Psychology</u> (1961), 575-582.

Preschool children were assigned to observe either aggressive or nonaggressive adult models, while a third, control group had no such exposure. Tests for imitative and nonimitative aggression in a new situation showed a good deal of reproduction of aggression in the subjects that had observed aggressive adults. Those subjects exhibited significantly more partially imitative and partially nonimitative aggressive behavior and less inhibition than the other two groups. The experiment suggests that the opportunity to imitate may have at least a reinforcing effect not conducive to international order.

1696. Berkowitz, Leonard. <u>Aggression: A Social Psychological Analy-</u><u>sis</u>. New York: McGraw-Hill, 1962, pp. 361.

Supplements political, economic, and historical analyses of the causes of war, treating the "death wish" theory as greatly exaggerated and discarding the "instinct" theory of aggression on the ground that war is a social rather than a biological phenomenon. Fear of punishment and the urge to follow moral standards serve to inhibit aggression. But the author sees the latter as operative to date only within national boundaries, thereby leaving fear of punishment as the only available method in international affairs. Either the author lacks data providing evidence of an urge to follow moral standards that transcends national boundaries or what has been presumed to be an essential foundation of law has yet to be seeded on the international level. Whatever the proper assessment of the assertion of a national containment of the moral urge, the author's recommendations for remedies hold that providing equal-status contacts between nations will reduce the severity and frequency of tensions and frustrations. The recommendation is provocative in that in an international law context the doctrine of equality may have performed a function not yet clearly identified for lack of analysis in terms of social psychology.

1697. Berkowitz, Leonard. "The Expression and Reduction of Hostility." 55 <u>Psychological Bulletin</u> (1958), 257-283.

On the monotonic nature of frustration-aggression and interference-aggression relationships, the strength of instigation to aggression increasing with either the amount of frustration or the degree of interference.

1698. Broch, Tom, and Galtung, Johan. "Belligerence Among the Primitives: A Reanalysis of Quincy Wright's Data." 3 <u>Journal of Peace Research</u> (1966), 33-45.

Analyzes the data presented by Wright in <u>A Study of War</u>, dealing with primitive warfare, by means of multivariate analysis and index-construction. One-third of the societies are found to have been aggressive in that they are reputed to have engaged in aggressive war for economic or political objectives. The level of belligerence was found to be highest in the cases of the least primitive and the least isolated societies, with pastoral cultures showing high (100%) belligerency.

1699. Driver, Michael J. <u>A Structural Analysis of Aggression, Stress,</u> <u>and Personality in an Inter-Nation Simulation</u>. Institute for Research in the Behavioral, Economic, and Management Sciences. Institute Paper No. 97. Lafayette, Indiana: Herman C. Krannert Graduate School of Industrial Administration, Purdue University, January 1965, pp. xiii, 100.

In 16 replications of an Inter-Nation Simulation stress emerged as a critical factor, its role as a reducer of cognitive complexity in decision-makers being found to be related to aggression. Among other things, individuals with different levels of complexity of cognitive structure were found to differ in both frequency and determinants of their aggression, the latter

including differences in degrees of frustration-tolerance, threat
sensitivity, deterrence-awareness, and rigid adherence to general
attitudes. The principal finding was that in the simulation a
lower degree of integrative complexity in cognitive structures,
whether due to stress or to personality organization, led to a
lower threshold for aggression.

1700. Farber, Maurice L. "Psychoanalytic Hypotheses in the Study of
War." 11 Journal of Social Issues (1955), 29-35.
   An attempt to bring some psychoanalytic hypotheses to bear
upon the problem of war that leads, among other things, to the
assertion that democracies are more prone than totalitarian
states to be pushed toward war by those of their people who are
inclined toward war.

1701. Galtung, Johan. "A Structural Theory of Aggression." 2 Journal of Peace Research (1964), 95-119.
   Concerned that much research has dealt with how to control
aggression but relatively little has dealt with the origins of
aggression, the author, attempting no empirical verification,
develops a structural theory of aggression between individuals,
groups, and nations. Viewing a social system as units in interaction and multidimensionally stratified according to a number
of rank dimensions, the theory tries to locate the point of
maximum probability of aggression. Rank disequilibrium is proposed as a nearly sufficient condition of aggression, which is
defined as "drives toward change, even against the will of others."

1701-A. Green, R.T., and Santori, G. "A Cross-Cultural Study of Hostility and Aggression." 6 Journal of Peace Research (1969), 13-22.
   A comparative study of the structure of hostile attitudes
and aggressive behavior of Italians and Englishmen that finds
little difference in the overall level and general pattern of
response to the questionnaire, reveals divergences that reflect
differing social norms, and concludes that comparisons of ways
of handling and expressing hostility-aggression do not permit
a description of one culture pattern as being more or less hostile or aggressive than another.

1702. Hamblin, Robert L., Bridger, David A., Day, Robert C., and
Yancey, William L. "The Interference-Aggression Law?" 26 Sociometry
(1963), 190-216.
   Derived from the work of John Dollard and associates on
frustration and aggression and making use of Fechner's and
Stevens' psychological laws about perception, the research design included computer simulation experiments and laboratory
investigations to test three alternative hypotheses. The data
suggest that aggression is not a linear or a logarithmic but a
power function of interference, the power exponent being evi-
dently a function of the strength of instigation to goal response that suffers interference. Despite still unanswered
questions, the authors express a temptation to think in terms
of an interference-aggression law. The limitation of the study

is to individual psychology and does not carry over into interference with and aggression by groups. However, the undertaking may be considered as a step in such a direction.

1703. Hokanson, J.E. "The Effects of Frustration and Anxiety on Overt
Aggression." 62 Journal of Abnormal and Social Psychology (1961), 346-351.
    Experiment with retaliation by electric shock against frus-
trators that showed highly frustrated subjects to react more aggressively than subjects under low frustration.

1704. Klineberg, Otto. The Human Dimension in International Relations. New York: Holt, Rinehart and Winston, 1964, pp. ix, 173.
    Issues related to war and peace form the focus for this re-
view, evaluation, and some suggested modifications of psychological theories that have been applied to international affairs.
For example, the frustration-aggression theory requires modification to account for the facts that not all frustration produces aggression and that aggression need not take violent forms.
It also is necessary to find the relationships between individual
drives and group action to account for the need of all states to
employ the draft rather than rely on individual aggressiveness to
produce mass armies by enlistment and to account for the possibility that in a third World War more machines than men would
have the opportunity to meet frustration by undertaking aggression. Other subjects discussed include racism, hostility toward
minorities, stereotypes of nations, leadership and the use by
some countries of physicians' reports of physical fitness of
candidates but not of evaluation of their psychological condition, similarities in adjustments to change on the part of refugees, migrants, and people in developing countries, the applicability of mechanisms defined by Freudian theory, and questions
of multiple loyalties.

1705. Lieberman, E. James. Non-Violent Aggression. Paper presented
to the Fortieth Annual Meeting, American Orthopsychiatric Association.
Washington, D.C., March 1963.
    Contemporary nonviolence is treated as an application of
socially constructive aggression. The paper thus extends the
concept of aggression in two directions: (1) toward a more inclusive view that would account for all forms of aggression including aggression without violence, and (2) toward a concept
of shades of aggression in terms of its ratio of constructive
and destructive effects.

1706. McNeil, Elton B. "Personal Hostility and International Aggression." 5 Journal of Conflict Resolution (1961), 279-290.
    Analogy between the behavior of a group of aggressive, anti-
social boys toward one another and the behavior of hostile nations toward one another.

1707. McNeil, Elton B. "Psychology and Aggression." 3 Journal of
Conflict Resolution (1959), 195-293.

Review of various theories of aggression. Includes 400 references.

1708. Montagu, Ashley. The Human Revolution. Cleveland: World Publishing Co., 1965, pp. 224.
Exploration of implications of recent discoveries about animal behavior and the behavior of early man, particularly Australopithecines, which treats all lines of action, including extreme aggressiveness, as learned.

1708-A. Nye, N.J.J. Homo-Insapiens (Man the Fool). Brisbane: W.R. Smith & Patterson Pty. Ltd., 1968, pp. 79.
After an historical sketch of human blundering, the Australian author turns his attention to aggression and the alleged inevitability of war, concluding that on the basis of the instinctive and so unavoidable nature of aggression, effort must be devoted to change of the institutions and laws that affect human behavior.

1709. Osgood, Charles E. "An Analysis of the Cold War Mentality." 17 Journal of Social Issues (1961), 12-19.
Concepts of psycho-logic and cognitive stereotype are employed to describe human reactions to antagonism and stress. Acceptance of a bogey-man stereotype justifies aggressive behavior by the holder and nullifies nonaggressive ploys by the opponent. Such psychological mechanisms have their greatest social impact when they occur among the leaders of a culture. The GRIT plan is then outlined.

1710. Queener, Llewellyn. "The Development of International Attitudes." 29 Journal of Social Psychology (1949), 221-235.
A test of hypotheses that attitudes are positive imitations of prestigious individuals and groups, negative imitation of nonprestigious individuals and groups, and a form of aggression against the nonprestigious and against frustrating individuals and groups.

1711. Reiwald, Paul. Eroberung des Friedens. Zürich: Europa Verlag, 1944, pp. 218.
Eclectic use of psychoanalysis, social psychology, history, political science, law, criminology, and world literature to deal with the problem of state aggression by reference to the individual. Social forces, including a penal code, are regarded as having essentially repressed individual aggressive drives, established an identification with others, and channeled aggression into constructive uses including a collective, justified, and lawful unleashing of aggression against criminals and nonconformists. The state not having similarly repressed and channeled its aggressiveness but, instead, having employed insistence upon sovereignty as a demand to do that which it punishes among its citizens, the author recommends that the processes that brought the individual's aggressive tendencies under control be employed as guides for undertakings of international organizations.

1712. Rosen, Sidney. "An Approach to the Study of Aggression." 46 Journal of Social Psychology (1957), 259-267.

Proposes a theoretical model of aggression that includes the following dimensions: (1) aggressive motivation; (2) anticipation of consequences; (3) an attributed power motive; (4) one's own power motive; and (5) an action readiness. In terms of location along these five dimensions, three power patterns were distinguished on the basis of data on sixty 10-14 year old boys of lower socioeconomic class.

1713. Scott, John Paul. Aggression. Chicago: University of Chicago Press, 1958, pp. 148.

Contrasts some important results from current animal research with and relates others to human behavior, the book ranging from the physiology of aggression to the social causes and control of aggression.

1713-A. Scott, John Paul. "Biology and Human Aggression." 40 American Journal of Orthopsychiatry (1970), 568-576.

Dissatisfied with popularized accounts of human aggression that ignore much data, the author summarizes the major principles that have been developed through the study of nonhuman animals and indicates their relevance and limitations in regard to human affairs.

1714. Skinner, B.F. "Contingencies of Reinforcement in the Design of a Culture." 11 Behavioral Science (1966), 159-166.

On reinforcement patterns that once had survival value but have become a threat in a day of abundance, overpopulation, and war. A proposal is made for dealing with overindulgence in aggression, food, sex, etc., not by traditional methods but by a method based on "contingency reinforcement" but reversing the process by minimizing the effect of reinforcement. The author suggests that the concepts of drive and need are irrelevant and would seek to make aggression, food, and sex contingent on useful forms of behavior to which they are not naturally related. Governments are said to be doing a poor, uncoordinated job in this respect and to be too indulgent of puritanical solutions.

1715. Streufert, Siegfried. "Attitude Generalization in Social Triads as a Function of Personality Structure and Availability of Social Support." Mimeo. ONR Technical Report No. 10, Department of Psychology, Princeton University, 1963.

Includes the finding that, in the stress of disagreement, individuals with more simple, concrete cognitive structures develop more generally negative attitudes toward others, a finding which relates to other research outcomes indicating partial explanations of crisis situations that display higher levels of hostility and even the initiation of war.

1716. Tinbergen, N. "On War and Peace in Animals and Man." 160 Science (1968), 1411-1418.

An Oxford ethologist suggests that his field can offer method and discipline to the behavioral sciences but not substantive evidence from animal behavior that can explain human behavior. Using aggression as an example, he notes that while many species fight, only man fights to the death. To attribute this to the animal heritage of group territoriality is to omit the study of man in his own right and, for example, the impact of men like Hitler who have instinctive knowledge of and exploit the aggressive urges in man. With attention to man's unique ability to pass his experiences to subsequent generations, Tinbergen sees cultural evolution as the root of such troubles as the population explosion. Cultural evolution, proceeding at a faster rate than genetic evolution which has left man little changed since Cro-Magnon man, has made man a misfit in his own society. It has made possible long-distance communications to increase contacts to the point of continuous threat behavior, brainwashed the warrior into treating fleeing, originally an adaptive behavior, as cowardly, and long-range weapons that prevent both seeing the results of killing and receiving the victim's signals of appeasement, reassurance, and distress. Tinbergen agrees with Lorenz that re-education to eliminate aggression will be very difficult, if not impossible, and, at the least, requires first a massive research effort. In the meanwhile, in the hope that awareness of nuclear dangers provides for limiting resort to war, the most that he sees as possible is to employ the animal tactic of the redirected attack, e.g., sports, attack on problems, etc.

See also nos. 1645, 1732, 1782, 1794, 1796, 1798, 1810, 1811, 1855, 2005, 2494.

a. Obedience to an Order to Injure

1717. Milgram, Stanley. "Some Conditions of Obedience and Disobedience to Authority." 18 Human Relations (1965), 56-76.

A laboratory experiment at Yale was designed to examine the question of the acceptance of orders to injure a third party. Employing the authority-executant-victim triad, the experimenter's orders to subjects to administer electric shocks to third parties in a simulation of a learning experiment resulted in administration of the highest level of shocks by almost all subjects when no verbal protests were made despite such designations on the control panel as "Extreme Shock" and "Danger: Severe Shock." While protest and other conditions reduced the number who administered the highest level of shock, no condition --verbal protest by the accomplice victim, invisibility or visibility of the victim, physically forcing the victim to place his hand on the shockplate--produced a situation in which at least one-fourth of the subjects did not administer the highest possible shock level. The author regards the experiment as one that should raise concern about what governments can command their

subjects to do, since an anonymous experimenter could command
adults to subdue a 50-year-old man and inflict pain upon him.
This article should be compared with the complementary findings
of Kelley and Woodruff (supra, no. 1359) on group members' reactions to apparent group approval of a counternorm directive,
both articles being relevant not only to the problem of aggression but also to that of war crimes and crimes against humanity.

See also nos. 1359, 1755, 1855.

4. Disputes--Case Studies

1718. Abbas, Mekki. The Sudan Question. New York: Praeger, 1952,
pp. xix, 201.
A Sudanese Moslem's account of the dispute over the former
Anglo-Egyptian condominium prior to Nasser's assumption of power.

1719. Carroll, Faye. South West Africa and the United Nations. Lexington: University of Kentucky Press, 1967, pp. xii, 123.
Traces the 20-year course of the conflict between the
United Nations and South Africa over South West Africa, with
attention to the legal, political, and moral issues.

1719-A. Chayes, Abram, Ehrlich, Thomas, and Lowenfeld, Andreas F.
International Legal Process: Materials for an Introductory Course. 2
vols. and Documents Supplement. Boston: Little, Brown, 1968, 1969, pp.
xxiii, 704; vi, 705-1402; vi, 635.
Essentially narrative accounts of 17 cases on the limits
of adjudication, such economic affairs as ocean cargo rates,
coffee regulation, communications satellites, and devaluation
of the pound, and such political matters as the Moscow test ban
treaty, the Cuban missile crisis, the Dominican intervention,
and sanctions against Rhodesia. The narratives, which are interrupted with questions for students, throw light upon the relations between law, politics, and economics, the role of lawyers, and the functions of law in establishing parameters for
foreign policy decision-making and international communications.

1720. Fischer, Per. Die Saar zwischen Deutschland und Frankreich.
Berlin and Frankfurt: Metzner, 1959, pp. 308.
Detailed study of the Saar conflict and of the events that
followed the referendum of 1955.

1721. Fisher, Margaret W., Rose, Leo E., and Huttenback, Robert A.
Himalayan Battleground: Sino-Indian Rivalry in Ladakh. New York: Prae-
ger, 1963, pp. 176.
Historical perspective on the Sino-Indian border dispute.

1722. Freymond, Jacques. The Saar Conflict, 1945-1955. London:
Stevens; New York: Praeger, 1960, pp. xxviii, 395.

Excellent analysis, focused on decision-makers, public opinion, and interest groups, which, despite loose inference from historical but not from quantitative data, suggests ways of relating a larger international context to minor disputes to show how the former may affect the outcome of the latter.

1723. Gil Benumeya, R. "La cuestión de Omán y los problemas del 'Canal de Suez del aire'." 33 Política internacional (1957), 189-198.
    Examination of the position of Oman in terms of its function in respect to air routes and its strategic importance to England. The article also reviews the rivalry since 1915 between the Imam and the Sultan of Muscat and the related territorial issue that in 1955 upset a period of relative coexistence and led to an attempt to bring the issue before the Security Council and then to an effort of three Arab states to mediate.

1724. Guetzkow, Harold. "The Potential of Case Study in Analyzing International Conflict." 14 World Politics (1962), 548-552.
    Review of Freymond's The Saar Conflict, 1945-1955. Discusses the utility of a detailed case study for an understanding of the interdependence of small disputes and their larger international contexts.

1725. Lamb, Alastair. The China-India Border: The Origins of the Disputed Boundaries. New York: Oxford, 1964, pp. xi, 192.
    Examination of the background of a dispute that goes back to 17th century agreements between Indian rulers and Tibet and of issues between China and India and the strengths of the claims of each side.

1726. "Les Conflits entre états et compagnies privées." 17 Revue française de science politique (1967), 286-338.
    A short introductory note by J.-B. Duroselle on the international nature of conflicts between states and foreign companies is followed by five case studies: Egypt and the Suez Canal Company; Syria and the Iraq Petroleum Company; Colombia and the United Fruit Company; Bolivia and the tin mining companies; Zambia and the British South Africa Company.

1727. Manigat, L.F. "La crise haitiano-dominicaine de 1963-1964." 15 Revue française de science politique (1965), 288-296.
    Analysis of the conflict between Haiti and the Dominican Republic that treats the conflict as essentially political, although in an economic context, and treats such juridical aspects as territorial rights and rights of diplomatic asylum as essentially a public presentation of the political contest.

1727-A. Novak, Bogdan C. Trieste 1941-1954: The Ethnic, Political, and Ideological Struggle. Chicago: University of Chicago Press, 1970, pp. 512.
    On the Italian-Yugoslav border dispute over Trieste where the collision of Italian nationalism with Croat and Slovenian nationalism was aggravated by the clash of Western and Communist

ideologies. Attention is given to the impact of ethnic and ideological conflict on the lives and political activities of the people of the Trieste region.

1728. Palmer, Norman D. "Trans-Himalayan Confrontation." 6 <u>Orbis</u> (1963), 513-527.
A narrative and analytical account of the Sino-Indian armed conflict.

1729. Schmidt, Robert H. <u>Saarpolitik 1945-1957</u>. 3 vols. Berlin: Duncker & Humblot, 1959-1962.
Monumental work on the Saar from the end of World War II to reunification with Germany. Volume I deals with party organization, interest groups, lobbies, and the press, among other elements of the political. The last two volumes deal with political developments.

1730. Starner, Frances L. "Malaysia and the North Borneo Territories." 3 <u>Asian Survey</u> (1963), 519-534.
A discussion of the problems resulting from the British decision to relinquish North Borneo and Sarawak to the new Federation of Malaysia, including the indigenous conflicts of national and ethnic interests to increase the risks for Malaysia as a somewhat unnatural entity based on reconciliation of conflicting national interests.

See also nos. 872, 1110, 1231, 1233, 1799, 2193, 2201, 2210, 2211, 2214, 2347, 2350-2352, 2356, 2359, 2364, 2374, 2375, 2380, 2383, 2384, 2390, 2394, 2410-2412, 2421, 2483, 2499.

B. CRIMES

1. International Criminal Law; International Delicts

1731. Eliot, Thomas D. "A Criminological Approach to the Social Control of International Relations." 58 <u>American Journal of Sociology</u> (1953), 513-518.
If aggressive war is to be defined as crime, then its treatment, if it is to be effective, should follow the principles of intelligent criminology and the goals of international welfare rather than those of sentimental "patriotic" revenge. The popular crime theory of war does not view war objectively as a total situation in which all participants share causal accountability. War is defined rather as an unprovoked injury by an outlaw outgroup. The author suggests that if an aggressor government, as defined by a supra-national tribunal, is subjected to drastic but rehabilitative and probationary treatment consistent with modern criminological theory and practice, the vicious circles of cumulative international hatred and revenge may be broken.

1732. Turk, Austin T. "Conflict and Criminality." 31 American Socio
logical Review (1966), 338-352.
    This paper summarizes the conceptualizations of criminality
to be found in the literature and suggests possible resolutions
of basic conceptual issues. The author presents a partially developed theoretical scheme in the form of propositions about the
conditions under which the probability of conflict between legal
authorities and subjects varies and those under which criminal-
ization of the subject varies. Propositions include the following: (a) authorities will tend to appeal to legal norms or to
announce new ones in contradistinction to cultural norms taken
to be characteristic of the opposition, while the opposition, by
definition more or less excluded from lawmaking positions, will
appeal to more abstract principles; (b) the greater the behavioral significance of the legal norms for authorities both in
regard to congruence of cultural and social norms and in regard
to the priority of the norm over other norms, the greater the
probability that violators will be assigned criminal status.
With appropriate modifications to fit the international scene,
these and others of the author's propositions could be investi-
gated and tested in a manner aiding understanding of the workings of international law in the international political arena
in terms both of the emergence of a consensus that certain actions are international crimes and the evolution of other definitions of acceptable and unwanted behavior.

2. Piracy

1733. Belgrave, Sir Charles. The Pirate Coast. London: Bell, 1966,
pp. xii, 200.
    On the rise to power of Arab pirates in the Persian Gulf
and the efforts of the British, with help from the Sultan of
Muscat, to suppress them.

1734. Tarling, Nicholas. Piracy and Politics in the Malay World: A
Study of British Imperialism in Nineteenth-Century South-East Asia. Vancouver: Pacific Affairs, University of British Columbia, 1963, pp. 273.
    While concentration on British policy relative to piracy
limits the study to a single aspect of a complex matter and
omits, for example, the Dutch and Spanish roles, the study is
valuable in that it provides much new information derived from
over seven hundred references, including three categories of
Foreign Office and two of Colonial Office records, nine of the
East India Company Board, political dispatches of the India Office, and extensive private manuscript collections and printed
sources. Piracy from Sumatra to Borneo, including that practiced
by Chinese operating from the South China coast after the Opium
War and by the pirates of Sulu and Mindanao, was more a consequence of political disorganization than of lawlessness and moral
laxity. The semipiracy of Sumatran Acheh was connected with in-
terport warfare and the sultan's policy of levying tolls on ships.

The author discusses Calcutta courts' reluctance to convict, British Indian authorities' hesitance to deal with the nuisance of petty violence that seldom involved British vessels, the ease with which Chinese pirates could obtain clearance papers in Singapore, and the gradual abatement of piracy after 1860 in consequence of European use of armed steamers and concomitant extension of colonial administrative control. The study provides data for the comparison of Southeast Asian piracy with the classical European manifestation and also for comparison of the suitability and application of the international law of piracy in two culturally different parts of the world.

3. War Crimes; Crimes Against Humanity; Genocide

1735. Arendt, Hannah. Eichmann in Jerusalem: A Report on the Banality of Evil. Rev. and enlarged ed. New York: Viking, 1964, pp. 312.
A critical, controversial evaluation of the Eichmann case.

1736. Davidson, Eugene. The Trial of the Germans. New York: Macmillan, 1967, pp. vii, 636.
Regarding the Nürnberg Trials as the "catharsis of the pent-up emotions of millions of people," the author not only re-examines the legal and moral questions related to the Trials and the behavior of the defendants when in power and when on trial but also gives attention to the struggle of the defense lawyers to obtain evidence, the ideological orientations of the judges, and the indications of pettiness, zealousness, and political overeagerness of Tribunal, Prosecutors, and Defense.

1737. Fritzsche, Hans. The Sword in the Scales. As told to Hildegard Springer. Translated by Diana Pyke and H. Fraenkel. London: Wingate, 1953, pp. 335.
Personal report by an acquitted defendant, substituted for Goebbels, at the main Nürnberg Trial. The report reveals facets of the impact of the trial upon the defendants, their feelings about the comparative fairness of the Western and the Soviet judges, the somewhat bewildered reactions of the defendants to the adversary process and cross-examination, and the author's personal reaction to the criminality of liquidation of peoples compared with the criminality of aggression.

1738. Garfinkels, B. Les Belges face à la persécution raciale 1940-1944. Brussels: Éditions de l'Institut de Sociologie de l'Université Libre de Bruxelles, 1965, pp. 110.
A study of persecution of Belgian Jews during the German occupation of World War II.

1738-A. Hammer, Richard. One Morning in the War: The Tragedy at Son My. New York: Coward McCann, 1970, pp. 207.
A report on the Son My massacre that attempts not only to deal with the details of the massacre but also to present what

happened against the background of Vietnamese history and an account of the people of Quang Ngai.

1738-B. Hersh, Seymour M. My Lai 4: A Report on the Massacre and Its Aftermath. New York: Random House, 1970, pp. 210.
An account of the attack on My Lai 4 that rests on available documentation and on a tenacious journalistic effort that enabled the massacre to become known to the public.

1739. Mason, Henry L. The Purge of the Dutch Quislings: Emergency Justice in the Netherlands. The Hague: Nijhoff, 1952, pp. xii, 199.
While more in the domestic area of treason than in the international area, this volume deals with an important phase of the termination of war and the attempt to complete the exaction of justice by punishing not merely the occupiers but the collaborators among the citizenry of an occupied country whose offenses were often not just treason but also crimes against humanity.

1740. Meyrowitz, Henri. La Repression par les tribunaux allemands des crimes contre l'humanité et de l'appartenance à une organisation criminelle, en application de la loi no. 10 due Conseil de contrôle allié. Paris: Librairie Générale de Droit et de Jurisprudence, 1960, pp. 514.
A detailed analysis of about 300 German decisions on crimes against humanity and membership in criminal organizations.

1740-A. Minear, Richard H. Victors' Justice: The Tokyo War Crimes Trial. Princeton: Princeton University Press, 1971.
The first comprehensive account in English of the Tokyo Trial which raised some interesting questions about what constitutes aggression that were, in part, dealt with in Gould, An Introduction to International Law (1957) on the basis of mimeographed versions of the Judgment and trial proceedings and documents and in Justice Pal's published dissenting opinion. Some of the court's statements on what constitutes aggression are relevant to the Vietnam War.

1741. Naumann, Bernd. Auschwitz: A Report on the Proceedings Against Robert Karl Ludwig Mulka and Others Before the Court at Frankfurt. Translated by Jean Steinberg. New York: Praeger, 1966, pp. xxx, 423.
German journalist's account of Germany's first Auschwitz trial in which 20 men were convicted of individual and mass murder. Hannah Arendt's introduction concerns itself with relevant political, psychological, and legal problems.

1741-A. Nef, John U. Cultural Foundations of Industrial Civilization. Cambridge, England: The University Press, 1958; Torchbook ed., New York: Harper & Brothers, 1960, pp. xv, 164.
An historian's account of limitations on violence, chiefly technological and logistic, before modern times and of the apparent development of a new conscience that brought the concept of atrocity into being in the late 18th century as contrasted with its virtual absence in the 16th century.

1742. Papadatos, Pierre Achille. Le procès Eichmann. Geneva: Droz, 1964, pp. 125. The Eichmann Trial. London: Stevens, 1964, pp. x, 129.
Scholarly study of the Eichmann trial as a step toward strengthening the effort to curtail genocide and to produce a more effective international criminal law.

1743. Poltorak, Arkady, and Zaitsev, Y. Remember Nuremberg. Moscow: Foreign Languages Publishing House, (1961?), pp. 295.
An example of Soviet political literature on war crimes trials, this publication attempting to link the West German Federal Republic to Nazi crimes.

1744. Procopé, Hjalmar Johan Fredrik. Sowjetjustiz Über Finnland-- Prozessakten aus dem Verfahren gegen die Kriegsverantwortlichen in Finnland. Zürich: Thomas, 1947, pp. 325.
A defense attorney's account of the Finnish War Crimes Trials that involved a finding of guilt for continuing war after the first Soviet peace offer and, under Soviet pressure on the Finnish Court, increasing penalties or substituting guilty verdicts for what would have been acquittals.

1745. Sharf, Andrew. The British Press and Jews under Nazi Rule. New York: Oxford, 1964, pp. vi, 228.
Abundantly documented analysis of the British press that presents evidence of the capacity to manipulate foreign news in accordance with perceptions of reality. For example, until 1938 there was disproportionate stress on persecutions of Jews at the expense of other groups, while between 1938 and 1942, despite a shortage of newsprint, all major incidents of Nazi persecution, regardless of the identity of the victims, were printed. The issue of the treatment of war criminals and the attitude of the British press toward the Nürnberg trials is dealt with in depth to provide a most useful exposition of a part of the atmosphere that must be taken into account in assessing and explaining the trials.

1746. Tanner, Väino. The Winter War: Finland against Russia, 1939-1940. Stanford: Stanford University Press, 1957, pp. 274.
The Foreign Minister of Finland during the Winter War presents his account of Finland's foreign relations from the time of the Soviet Union's first suggestions (April 1938) for Finnish cooperation in the event of a German attack to the conclusion of the war. Perhaps the most significant feature of Finnish diplomacy at that time was a clear sense of objectives and of possibilities of their attainment. From the point of view of the misuse of the idea of war crimes, the volume warrants study as a companion to Procopé's account of the Finnish War Crimes Trials at which Tanner was a defendant who was found guilty and sentenced but only after an apparent verdict was withheld and revised in consequence of evident Soviet intervention.

1746-A. Wormser-Migot, Olga. Le système concentrationnaire nazi (1933-1945). Paris: Presses Universitaires de France, 1968, pp. 660, vii.

More of an encyclopedic than an analytic or interpretative
study, this historical survey of the Nazi concentration camp
system distinguishes the 1933-1939 period, when the camps were
"national" and used chiefly for incarceration, from the 1939-
1945 period, when the camps were "internationalized" and used
for such purposes as cheap wartime labor, medical experimentation, and extermination. The study complements Joseph Billig's
L'Hitlerisme et le système concentrationnaire (1967) but does
not provide as effective a portrayal of the dynamics of the SS
as does Martin Broszat's essay, "The Concentration Camps, 1933-
1945," in Hans Buchheim et al., Anatomie des SS Staates (1965).

See also nos. 1342, 1354, 1359, 1717, 1850, 1910, 2266, 2305, 2638.

C. COMMITMENT, OBLIGATION, AND CONFORMITY

1. Obligation (Binding Force)

1747. Austin, John Langshaw. Philosophical Papers. Oxford: Claren
don Press, 1960, pp. 242.
Chapters 3, 6, and 10 are particularly important for their
probe into the nature of promises.

1748. Beilenson, Laurence W. The Treaty Trap: A History of the Per
formance of Political Treaties by the United States and European Nations.
Washington: Public Affairs Press, 1969, pp. xiii, 344.
This volume includes an introduction by William R. Kintner,
Deputy Director of the University of Pennsylvania's Foreign Policy Research Institute, that asserts that "the effort to fix international relations within the legal strait jacket of treaties
could jeopardize the survival of nations" and that "treaties are
too inflexible to deal with a world in flux." The volume gives
particular attention to alliances, subsidy treaties, antisubver-
sion treaties, peace treaties, nonaggression pacts, treaties for
economic sanctions, guarantee treaties, and disarmament treaties.
With a look at ancient times and at treaties since 1661, the
author argues that the norm is unreliability and that, therefore,
the United States should be particularly careful about entering
into treaties, particularly disarmament treaties. Political
treaties are treated as paper; "iron" and interest are said to
be decisive in international affairs. A warning is issued
against the "disease of reliance." In reaching the conclusion
that "a nation should give little or no weight to the expectation of performance of a political treaty," the author presents
over 325 instances of violations, most of them involving actions
in time of war. The sampling is highly selective, omitting many
types of treaties, giving much weight to violations in defeat of
agreements not to make a separate peace, and only occasionally
mentioning instances of fidelity to agreements. The sole merit
of the book is that it does attempt to examine the record over

time and suggests a type of study that could be undertaken usefully if done thoroughly, with proper attention to "nonbreaches," and without inhibiting assumptions.

1749. Bishop, Donald G. The Roosevelt-Litvinov Agreements: The American View. Syracuse: Syracuse University Press, 1965, pp. viii, 297.
Analysis of the Soviet record of fulfillment of its commitments as set forth in the Roosevelt-Litvinov Agreements of 1933.

1750. Cavell, S.L. "Must We Mean What We Say?" In V.C. Chappell, Ordinary Language. Englewood Cliffs: Prentice-Hall, 1964, pp. 75-112.
Argument against a social utilitarian concept of the social practice of promising. The author holds that promising is not merely useful but, in addition, is indispensable to the concept of society and human life.

1751. Forman, Robert E. "Resignation as a Collective Behavior Response." 69 American Journal of Sociology (1963), 285-290.
This article investigates different models of behavior in crises including a panic model of mass behavior, a rational action model, and a resignation attitude as related to modern conditions. Particular attention is given to resignation which is also considered in relation to rational behavior and rational action. Both concepts of consensus and explanations of obedience to a rule of international law should give more attention to resignation and to explanation of why the attitude of resignation should develop both in respect to particular situations and in general.

1751-A. Gerstein, Robert S. "The Practice of Fidelity to Law." 4 Law and Society Review (1970), 479-493.
Deals with the problems of obligation and of whether there can be a system of law in the absence of fidelity to law in terms of a critique of H.L.A. Hart's attempt to correct Kelsen's analysis of official coercion.

1752. Herberichs, G. "On Theories of Public Opinion and International Organization." 30 Public Opinion Quarterly (1966-1967), 624-636.
Noting that, except in the case of the Council of Europe, history does not support the optimistic views of pacifists and internationalists that public opinion is a constructive driving force, the author suggests that public opinion has the function of rendering institutions durable by accepting them even if only passively.

1753. Lerner, Daniel, and Kramer, Marguerite N. "French Elite Perspectives on the United Nations." 17 International Organization (1963), 54-75.
A survey of the opinions of 2,000 leading Frenchmen, taken over a seven-year period and entailing five groups of interviews on an array of issues related to France's international position, provided the data for this article dealing with one of the issues. One finding is that enthusiasm for the UN appears to decline as national involvement rises.

1754. Lutzker, Daniel R. "Internationalism as a Predictor of Co-operative Behavior." 4 Journal of Conflict Resolution (1960), 426-430.

Report of an experiment that showed internationalist subjects to be more cooperative than highly isolationist subjects. Internationalists did not decrease their cooperation as the game progressed as did isolationists and the control group. Isolationists made more real choices than either the internationalists or the control group. The experimenter suggests that perhaps a syndrome, in form similar to that for authoritarianism, is associated with internationalism.

1755. Milgram, Stanley. "Behavioral Study of Obedience." 67 Journal of Abnormal and Social Psychology (1963), 371-378.

This experiment is a study of obedience to one who is perceived to be a legitimate authority. Forty subjects, in turn, respond to an experimenter's command to administer shocks to a "learner" which increase in intensity upon each incorrect answer. Shocks are administered by the test subject on a simulated shock generator which is believed to be authentic. Results show extreme conflict between the values of not harming others and obedience to legitimate authority. Twenty-six out of the forty subjects obeyed to the final and highest shock designation, although extreme stress was observed.

1756. Pitkin, Hanna. "Obligation and Consent." 59-60 American Political Science Review (1965, 1966), 990-999, 39-52.

Examines the relation of consent to obligation in its multiple complexity, raising questions concerning the limits of obligation, the locus of sovereignty, the difference between legitimacy and mere coercion, and the justification of obligation.

1757. Radlow, Robert, and Weidner, Marianna Fry. "Unenforced Commitments in 'Cooperative' and 'Noncooperative' Non-Constant-Sum Games." 10 Journal of Conflict Resolution (1966), 497-505.

Description of a Prisoner's Dilemma experiment with results that indicate that negotiations with unenforceable commitments provide almost as much security as negotiations with enforceable commitments.

1758. Rawls, John. "Two Concepts of Rules." 64 Philosophical Review (1955), 3-32.

Important for an examination of promises and their obligation that notes the irrelevance of utilitarianism as a criterion for keeping particular promises and its relevance at the level of the social practice of promising.

1759. Singer, J. David, and Small, Melvin. "Formal Alliances, 1815-1939: A Quantitative Description." 3 Journal of Peace Research (1966), 1-32.

An examination of defense pacts, neutrality and nonaggression pacts, and ententes to ascertain patterns of alliance distribution and annual alliance aggregation, with attention to distinctions among the central (European) system, the major powers, and the total international system. War performance is employed as a test of fulfillment of alliance obligations. In terms of percent aiding, remaining neutral, or opposing alliance partners the central system performed slightly better and the major powers markedly better than the total system. In terms of alliance class, war performance showed that fulfillment of obligation was best for defense pacts. Further refinements of the analysis provide additional information about the strength of the obligation of the three types of alliances and about the nature and map of the international system between 1815 and 1939.

1760. Stimson, Henry. "The Decision to Use the Bomb." 194 Harper's Magazine (February 1947), 97-107.
　　Important both in what it has to say about government decision processes and also for what it reveals about the action-oriented official's view of what can be done as represented in the phrase that the new explosive was "as legitimate as any other" explosive weapon of modern war. What Stimson says about the use of the atomic bomb may be compared with Acheson's statement to the American Society of International Law (Proceedings, 1963, p. 14) that law does not deal with questions of ultimate power.

1761. Weinstein, Franklin B. "The Concept of a Commitment in International Relations." 13 Journal of Conflict Resolution (1969), 39-56.
　　Focusing on alliance commitments and especially on France and the United States, this article suggests that alliances suffer in that the members do not share the same understanding of what it means to be committed and that in the case of France and the United States the former holds a "situational" view of commitment and the latter, a "nonsituational" view. The article includes a brief discussion of the relationship of rebus sic stantibus to the situational view.

See also nos. 683, 715, 919, 1333, 1455, 1518, 1763, 1764, 1766, 1831, 1833, 1847, 1864, 1866, 2043, 2081, 2131, 2161, 2313, 2357, 2366, 2380, 2381, 2441, 2499, 2726.

a. Model, Myth, Masque, and Mystique

1762. Chroust, Anton-Hermann. "Law: Reason, Legalism, and the Legal Process." 74 Ethics (1963), 1-18.
　　Deals with the relationship of law to the real world. The law is seen as a manipulable symbolic system, but a system not making a perfect fit with reality, for the law is unable to contain all "rules of the game" for all possible games and variations thereon and is unable to avoid ambiguities. Legal rules are treated as working hypotheses subject to testing or, more

broadly, as abstractions or fictions simplifying understanding
of social and political history.

1763. Manning, C.A.W. The Nature of International Society. London:
London School of Economics and Political Science, G. Bell and Sons Ltd.,
1962, pp. xi, 220.
Thought-provoking effort to distinguish the notional and
factual realms of international affairs, with particular attention to the notional. Chapter IX, "The Mystique of the Law,"
deals with the law as a set of ideas that derives its binding
force from the act of thinking that binding force is implied in
the notion of law. The following chapter deals with some problems of the relation of behavior to norms. Distinctions are
drawn between the areas of "Diplomatics" and of "Government,"
and the author proceeds to his suggestions for the study of international relations by means of a social cosmology that, where
fitting, would seek to be scientific and, where appropriate,
would be frankly philosophical.

1764. Taylor, John F.A. The Masks of Society: An Inquiry into the
Covenants of Civilization. New York: Appleton-Century-Crofts, 1966, pp.
xiii, 273.
A provocative exposition probing the foundations of consent in an effort to understand the fact of human society not
just as data but as moral achievement. Holding that juristic
philosophy is the path to a new science and that the principles
that men live by are more stably secured by habit than by
thought, the author prefers the historian's mode of encounter
based on empathy--the actor's ways of relating himself to
things and to others--as more relevant than the observer's
point of view. Behavioral scientists are taken to task for
concentrating upon externals, e.g., the written instrument, the
legal formality, and the handshake which a court of law will
accept as evidence but not mistake for the objective social reality of the engagement, the invisible moral bond or obligation
that is the ratio essendi, not the ratio cognoscendi, of the
contract. Holding civilization to be a juristic phenomenon,
the author suggests that the notion of a community under covenant is both general and recurrent and that beneath politics
and law, science and religion, art and economy, education and
the moral life, lie operative covenants that should be studied
in the effort to understand society. The key chapter deals with
the law as a mask and employs the concept of legal personality
to make certain comparisons between an individual's role in society, something not determined by nature, with the actor's role
within the dimensions established by the playwright. In this
chapter, which leads into discussions of the ethical foundation
of the market, science and the covenant of inquiry, the covenants of art, and problems in reconstruction of the human covenant, a distinction between the de jure and the de facto in society is introduced by an argument for a constitutive view of
de jure recognition.

See also no. 1950.

2. Congruity of Behavior Patterns, Rules for
System Maintenance, and Legal Norms

1765. Musulin, Janko. Degen und Waage--Schicksal und Gesetz europäischer Politik. München: Oldenbourg, 1954, pp. 300.
 A journalist's analysis of efforts toward European unification since the Reformation. A typology of three political systems is established: hegemony (the monarchy of Charles V), balance of power (English history in the early 18th century), and alliance (Holy Alliance, League of Nations, United Nations). Alliance systems are regarded as having failed because neither comprehensive nor effective nor evolutionary (giving expression to all contemporary movements). More important and going to the problem of the nature of treaties, the author holds that collapse of earlier alliances occurred because of ignorance of the laws of alliances and because such ignorance led members to be untrue to their treaty commitments.

See also nos. 684, 2357, 2366.

3. Conformity and Compliance; Pressures to Conform

1766. Asch, S.E. "Effects of Group Pressure upon the Modification and Distortion of Judgments." In Harold Guetzkow (ed.), Groups, Leadership, and Men. Pittsburgh: Carnegie Press, 1951, pp. 177-190.
 An examination of the social and personal conditions that induce individuals to resist or to yield to group pressures when the pressures are perceived to be contrary to fact. The method employed was to produce a radical divergence between a majority and a minority and to observe the ways in which individuals reacted to the situation. Independence and yielding were found to be a joint function of the character of the stimulus situation, the group forces, and the individual himself. Character differences, especially those pertaining to the person's social relations, seemed most relevant.

1767. Deutsch, Karl W. "Power and Communication in International Society." In Anthony de Reuck and Julie Knight (eds.), Conflict in Society. London: Churchill, 1966, pp. 300-316.
 Treats conflict and integration as two variants of interdependence, the former entailing negative co-variance and the latter positive co-variance measured by transactions. Power is dealt with as a resultant of the habit of obedience. Political change is viewed as the result of changes outside the compliance-enforcement feedback system that change the compliance habits.

1768. Etzioni, Amitai. <u>A Comparative Analysis of Complex Organiza-</u>
<u>tions</u>. New York: Free Press, 1961, pp. 366.

As important as this work is for its analysis of other
facets of complex organizations, for purposes of legal studies
it is particularly important for its conceptualization of the
organizational compliance structure as being composed of three
analytical types: (1) coercive power, resting on the threat of
physical sanctions; (2) remunerative power, resting on the ability to apply economic sanctions; (3) normative power, resting on
the manipulation of symbolic rewards. Those regulated by coercive power have an alienative involvement, by remunerative power
a calculative involvement, and by normative power a moral involvement with the organization. Any mixture is possible but
congruent cases, matching power and involvement, are most frequent because most effective. Political compliance structures
are depicted as employing a greater mixture of the three types
of power than do organizational compliance structures.

1769. Lande, Gabriella Rosner. "The Effect of the Resolutions of the
United Nations General Assembly." 19 <u>World Politics</u> (1966), 83-105.

Outline of the conceptual framework for a study in progress
of the General Assembly. Resolutions of the General Assembly
are susceptible of examination on the basis of two focal points:
(1) compliance of Member States and the effectiveness of resolutions in achieving their objectives; (2) ancillary and secondary
outcomes of resolutions concerning both political disputes and
general principles of international political cooperation. The
former can be dealt with in terms of seven specified variables
including the legal status of a resolution. The influence and
legitimacy of the General Assembly are to be sought not only in
specific implementation of decisions but also in more extensive
generic, or indirect effect on Member States, the UN, and the
international system.

1769-A. Lee, Luke T. <u>China and International Agreements: A Study</u>
<u>of Compliance</u>. Leiden: Sijthoff; Durham: Rule of Law Press, 1969, pp.
231.

A study that attempts to estimate, on the basis of available materials and Chinese concepts of law and treaties, the
extent and probability of Communist China's compliance with
international agreements on various subjects. Much of the research was done in Japan and included a number of off-the-record
interviews with diplomatic personnel and journalists, among
others.

1770. Manno, Catherine Self. "Majority Decisions and Minority Responses in the UN General Assembly." 10 <u>Journal of Conflict Resolution</u>
(1966), 1-20.

In respect to the 9th, 14th, and 17th General Assembly
Sessions, the article indicates the pattern of voting responses
to resolutions proposed in both plenary sessions and committees.
Interesting data about the Sixth Committee are included. A section is devoted to compliance with recommendations and its

correlation with the direction of the message, that is, to states
in general, to a particular subgroup, or to a particular state.

1771. Pruitt, Dean G. "National Power and International Responsiveness." 7 Background (1964), 165-178.
    Employing data on responsiveness obtained in interviews
with members of a State Department agency responsible for policies toward another country, first steps are taken toward a
theory of compliance based upon the four variables of resources,
needs, credibility, and good will.

1772. Raven, Bertram H., and French, John R.P., Jr. "Legitimate Power,
Coercive Power, and Observability in Social Influence." 21 Sociometry
(1958), 83-97.
    Employing an experiment in which one set of supervisors
were apparently chosen with group support and a second set apparently took over the job without group support, it was found
that the influence of the legitimate supervisor was privately
accepted but not that of the supervisor dependent on coercion.
Coercion by the legitimate supervisor was accepted but the expected increase in public conformity under legitimacy and coercion did not occur.

1773. Ruys, P. "Opinion publique et relations internationales." 20
Bulletin de l'Institut de Recherches économiques et sociales (1954), 637-
659.
    With reference to the discomfort of jurists and sociologists
in efforts to ascertain the place of public opinion in the elaboration of norms of the law of nations, the author sees little
gain in this approach, particularly in view of evidence that Belgian opinion shows but minimal concern for international questions. Public opinion is treated as presupposing a social organization that includes generators, transformers, and distributors
of opinion. In respect to international problems, public opinion
requires a structure of opinion groups within each land. In
their absence, comparisons of national public opinions lose all
significance and the expression "world opinion" has no scientific
content.

1773-A. Tedeschi, James T., Bonoma, Thomas V., Schlenker, Barry R.,
and Lindskold, Svenn. "Power, Influence, and Behavioral Compliance." 4
Law and Society Review (1970), 521-544.
    A social psychological examination of concepts of power and
an attempt to integrate them into a more comprehensive theory of
influence within dyads. Attention is given to reward and punishment power, attraction power, legitimate power, prestige power,
counterinfluence, and expert power, respect, and esteem. Note is
taken that the decisions of Germany in 1914 and Japan in 1941 to
go to war resemble laboratory findings that defiance of threats
may occur when punishment for noncompliance is perceived as no
worse than the costs of compliance. The possibility of applying
Charles Osgood's GRIT (graduated reciprocation in tension reduction) scheme for international relations to black-white relations

in the United States is considered, with attention to the probability that speedy change has been obviated by rendering blacks uninfluenceable by white threats and promises until blacks have gained self-respect. The last point may be relevant to the international behavior of revolutionary states.

See also nos. 684, 715, 1167, 1197, 1359, 1749, 1751, 1752, 1793, 1866, 1887, 1912, 2131.

a. Precedent and Imitation

1774. Becker, Theodore L. "A Survey Study of Hawaiian Judges: The Effect on Decisions of Judicial Role Situations." 60 American Political Science Review (1966), 677-680.
Report on responses to a questionnaire sent to 26 Hawaii judges in an effort to produce a systematic and rigorous collection of role-portraits of judges. In addition, the judges decided a hypothetical case presenting precedential guidelines contrary to the personal attitudes of 22 of the judges. Fifteen of the 22 decided against the precedent and seven in accordance with the precedent to at least raise some questions concerning attitude structure and attitude priority in relation to the function of precedent in judicial decision-making, due account being taken of type of case and the social setting at the time of decision.

1775. Luchins, A.S., and Luchins, E.H. "Einstellung Effect in Social Learning." 55 Journal of Social Psychology (1961), 59-66.
Report on a maze experiment with 30 Canadian students, including a pre-instructed student whose task was to respond first and orally on each trial to see whether uninstructed students would imitate his solution. Subjects were found to rigidly adhere to one principle, even though they could not verbalize it, that had proved successful even though on subsequent trials that principle did not work. Most students were reluctant to admit imitation, but some conceded that they had imitated in order to be sure of being regarded as right in their approach to the problem. The authors express concern that what is learned when social influence is a cue to correct responses may produce a mechanization preventing solution of subsequent similar-appearing social situations. While additional experimental evidence may be desirable, it would appear that the evidence from this particular experiment may be correlated (a) with historical evidence of resort to established and socially acceptable techniques for dealing with political, legal, and socioeconomic problems similar to past situations and (b) with the frequent paucity of results of searches for new approaches to such problems.

See also no. 1695.

D. RECIPROCITY, COMPULSION, AND EFFECTIVENESS

1. Effectiveness

1776. Carbonnier, Jean. "Effectivité et ineffectivité de la règle de droit." L'Année sociologique (3e série, 1957-1958), 3-17.

Noting that both the ineffectiveness and the effectiveness of the rule of law are sociological phenomena and merit equal attention, the author places his emphasis on the phenomenon of ineffectiveness. Total ineffectiveness is his point of departure. He makes two classifications: (1) the powerlessness of laws and (2) the disuse of laws. In regard to the former, he notes that the original nonapplication of a law is not always an abnormal situation, for many laws are purely discretionary and, indeed, most rules of law allow an appreciable degree of ineffectiveness. A preponderance of intermediate states is seen between total effectiveness and ineffectiveness and a gray zone of partial ineffectiveness as dominating. The author holds that people too quickly forget that a rule even of ineffective law can have its use in creating a climate of legal insecurity, of responsibility, and of "bad conscience." Ineffective in the eyes of the jurist, the legal rule remains at least partially effective for the sociologist.

1777. First, Ruth. South West Africa. Baltimore: Penguin, 1963, pp. 269.

Exposition of the history of South West Africa before and since it was established as a mandate under the League of Nations. The book helps to place the legal problems of South West Africa, dealt with by the International Court of Justice, in their historical and political settings and to illuminate some of the limits to effectiveness of international law at the present stage of world organization. The author is a member of the White opposition in South Africa.

See also nos. 1101, 1110, 1793, 2401.

2. Reciprocity and Responsiveness

1778. Canning, Ray R., and Baker, James M. "Effect of the Group on Authoritarian and Non-Authoritarian Persons." 64 American Journal of Sociology (1959), 578-581.

Subjects with authoritarian and with nonauthoritarian personalities were subjected to three laboratory experiments in autokinesis. First tested alone to establish individual norms, they were then exposed to small-group situations designed to exert social pressures toward extreme judgments, after which they were again tested individually. Differential effects of group pressure were marked. The mean estimate of light movement increased over 100% among nonauthoritarian and over 500% among the authoritarian personalities. Although the effect of group pressure apparently did not mount with successive trials, it did remain relatively effective even in the final individual tests.

1779. Deutsch, Morton. "Producing Change in an Adversary." In Roger Fisher (ed.), International Conflict and Behavioral Science: The Craigville Papers. New York: Basic Books, 1964, pp. 145-160.
    Assuming that the Communists seek to dominate the world, the author considers the question of Communist incorrigibility and lists the policy alternatives to this conception. The Communist orientation, one of unyielding resistance toward the West, is then reviewed and the question is raised of how this hostile orientation can be changed.

1780. Dupreel, Eugene. Sociologie générale. Paris: Presses Universitaires de France, 1948, pp. 397.
    Includes a chapter on the "Evolution of Extended Conflicts" that deals, among other things, with intermingling of the characters of aggressor and defender as the opposing forces tend to take the same forms in order to meet and neutralize each other. Resort to use of the same means to balance the other side's actions because balance or imbalance is decisive renders the moral issue of defender versus aggressor irrelevant to the outcome. The point is relevant to the concept of bellum justum in which an originally just cause might not maintain itself in view of improper conduct of hostilities, for it is conceivable that war measures could include innovations shocking the conscience and reversing the locus of justice.

1781. Gouldner, Alvin W. "The Norm of Reciprocity: A Preliminary Statement." 23 American Sociological Review (1960), 161-178.
    Discussion of the functions of the norm of reciprocity and its contribution to the stability of social systems. Earlier treatments of the concept are criticized for neglecting the class of unequal exchanges. Reciprocity connotes that each party has rights and duties, while complementarity connotes that one has rights and another has obligations and vice versa. The author hypothesizes that a norm of reciprocity is universal and that it makes two interrelated demands: people should help those who have helped them. The functions of the norm include stabilizing human relations both in the absence and presence of a well-developed system of specific status duties. It also provides a further source of motivations and an additional moral sanction for conforming, as well as being a "starting mechanism," by helping to initiate social interaction.

1782. Holsti, Ole R. "The 1914 Case." 59 American Political Science Review (1965), 365-378.
    One of the several papers of the Stanford Conflict Studies program that dealt with the outbreak of World War I. In discussing several hypotheses tested through content analysis of the messages of June 27-August 4, 1914, significant messages

and perceptions are presented as illustration of what is otherwise demonstrated with the aid of statistical tools.

1783. Liska, George. International Equilibrium. Cambridge: Harvard
University Press, 1957, pp. 221.
    Posits a decentralized legal system in which rules are re-
ciprocally followed in order to restore a disturbed social
equilibrium.

1784. North, Robert C., Brody, Richard A., and Holsti, Ole R. "Some
Empirical Data on the Conflict Spiral." Peace Research Society (International), Papers. Chicago Conference, 1963. Vol. I (1964), pp. 1-14.
    A study of the six weeks prior to the outbreak of World War
I to test a conflict model of perceptions and expressions and
the relation of perceptions of hostility to mobilization measures.
Mobilizations accounted for some but not all variance in hostility
--a not unexpected result since there was a steady rise in hostility prior to mobilization. The study employs content analysis to
code expressions and perceptions of hostility, the Q-sort technique for the scaling of intensity, and statistical correlation
techniques for the analysis of escalation.

1785. Pool, Ithiel de Sola. Symbols of Internationalism. Stanford:
Stanford University Press, 1951, pp. 73.
    Content analysis of leading newspapers of the United States,
Great Britain, France, Germany, and Russia over a period of
nearly 50 years. Attitudes of these powers seemed to reflect
each other in that hostility expressed in the editorial opinion
of one state toward another state was virtually matched by the
counterhostility of the editorials in the second state. Another
finding was that the greater the feeling of security, the less
the hostility toward other states.

1786. Pruitt, Dean G. Problem Solving in the Department of State.
Monograph Series in World Affairs. Monograph No. 2, 1964-1965. The Social Science Foundation and Department of International Relations, University of Denver (1964), pp. 56.
    A study of a geographic office in the Department of State
as an agency tending to be responsive to the states with which
it deals. Techniques of consultation and persuasion of other
officers and agencies are set forth. One instance related to
a treaty negotiation is dealt with, the agency concerned supporting a version of a military base agreement submitted by the
foreign country but encountering a Department of Defense proposal to alter the claims and jurisdiction proposed. Compromise took the form of an Under Secretary's oral reservation at
signature, expressing concern over possible abuse of the claims
and jurisdiction clause.

1787. Pruitt, Dean G. Reaction Systems and Instability in Interpersonal and International Affairs. Research Monograph No. 1 (edited by
Glenn H. Snyder). Buffalo Studies. State University of New York at Buffalo, Vol. IV, April 1968, pp. 3-25.

Deals with the effect of one party's behavior on another's, with concern for changes in one party's level of output on one dimension and the other party's level of output on the same or another dimension. Reciprocal changes are seen as sequenced in various ways, e.g., vicious or benevolent circles, and a geometrical formulation for interpreting the various sequences is suggested.

1788. Pruitt, Dean G. "Reciprocity and Credit Building in a Laboratory Dyad." 8 Journal of Personality and Social Psychology (1968), 143-147.

In a test of four hypotheses based on Alvin W. Gouldner's theory of reciprocity, it was found that a greater reward was provided the other person in three circumstances: (a) the more the other had given in the past, (b) the larger his future resources, and (c) the smaller his past resources. However, there was no interaction between past experience with the other person and the size of his future resources.

1789. Pruitt, Dean G. Two Factors in International Agreement. Report of a Research Project for the Naval Ordnance Test Station. China Lake, California, Contract No. N123(60530)25875A. Mimeo. Northwestern Universit 1961, pp. 119.

Focusing on trust and responsiveness as two factors determining the likelihood that two nations will reach agreement in negotiation, an analysis is made of the effects of these variables and the influence of their interaction on the outcome of negotiations.

1790. Reigrotski, E., and Anderson, N. "National Stereotypes and Foreign Contacts." 23 Public Opinion Quarterly (1960), 515-528.

A follow-up of a 1948 UNESCO study. Questionnaires were given to Belgian, Dutch, French, and German samples to probe their stereotypes of and attitudes toward each other and Italians. Responses of the French and German subjects supported the idea that stereotypes tend to be modified through education but even more so through foreign contact and acquaintance. Amount of schooling was of less importance than contact. Data is also presented on stereotypes of fellow-citizens and on the relationship between contact and sympathy-antipathy.

1791. Roland, Alan. "Persuasibility in Young Children as a Function of Aggressive Motivation and Aggression Conflict." 66 Journal of Abnormal and Social Psychology (1963), 454-461.

Example of a study producing empirical support for a hypothesis that might have been regarded as confirmed intuitively on the basis of an observer's own experiences and so left without systematic investigation. The hypothesis asserts a positive relationship between (1) little persuasibility and open aggressive orientation, (2) easy persuasibility and a need to control strong aggressive motivation, and (3) medium persuasibility and relative absence of aggressive motives.

1792. Russett, Bruce M. "International Communication and Legislative Behavior: The Senate and the House of Commons." 6 <u>Journal of Conflict Resolution</u> (1962), 291-307.
    A study of Senators and M.P.'s for the years 1890 and 1954 seeking to correlate Anglo-American "ties" with attitude (responsive, neutral, or unresponsive) toward the other country. Voting record was used to judge Senators' responsiveness, while speeches and statements were employed to judge that of M.P.'s. Guttman scale analysis was used for analysis in an effort to minimize the effects of differing importance of topics rendering estimation of weighting factors very difficult. Personal and economic ties were found to increase responsiveness, but party was found to be even more significant. Having more than one tie did not increase responsiveness. Economic ties may be more significant than personal ties but the evidence is not conclusive. Constituency ties are influential in proportion to the weight of the economic interest of the constituency.

1793. Schelling, Thomas C., and Halperin, Morton H. <u>Strategy and Arms Control</u>. New York: Twentieth Century Fund, 1961, pp. 148.
    A study of "arms control" rather than "disarmament" that concentrates on possibilities for reciprocal self-enforcement and likens enforcement problems to the problems of government regulatory agencies rather than to police problems.

1794. Smoker, Paul. "Sino-Indian Relations: A Study of Trade, Communication and Defense." 2 <u>Journal of Peace Research</u> (1964), 65-76.
    Without access to a computer, the author attempts a crude measure of the relationship over time of three variables for one dyad of nations. The variables are value of trade, communications between decision-makers, and defense expenditure. He finds inverse relationships between communication rate and defense ratio and between Sino-Indian trade and Indian defense expenditure. In an extension beyond the Sino-Indian dyad, the author finds that trading relationships of other dyads produce patterns making it easy to identify alliances and that since 1958 China's trading relations with the non-Communist world have deteriorated while Russia's have increased markedly. He also finds that an increase in Sino-Indian communications preceded the outbreak of hostilities in 1962, a pattern similar to the Stanford findings about the days preceding World War I. Noting that massive attempts at conflict resolution failed to prevent hostilities-- although it is possible that an arms race might have failed sooner and more disastrously--the author suggests that in view of the possibility of a breaking point at which the volume of communication precipitates crisis, decision-makers might be wise to avoid communication if their own or the other party's decision-making machinery is having difficulty evaluating communications quickly.

1795. Tennant, Ernest William Dalrymple. <u>True Account</u>. London: Max Parrish, 1957, pp. 256.

A British-born specialist on Germany tells of his efforts
to produce understanding between Britain and Germany in the
1930s.

1796. Thibault, John W., and Coules, John. "The Role of Communication
in the Reduction of Interpersonal Hostility." 47 Journal of Abnormal and
Social Psychology (1952), 770-777.
    This experiment tested the hypothesis that overt acts of
aggression in response to instigation to hostility will reduce
the level of hostile tension in the aggressor. Twenty-one subjects were permitted to communicate back to an instigator immediately after instigation to hostility while another 20 subjects
were not permitted this final communication. The first group
showed more post-experimental friendliness toward the instigator,
thus giving qualified confirmation to the hypothesis.

1797. Triska, Jan F., and Finley, David D. "Soviet-American Relations: A Multiple Symmetry Model." 9 Journal of Conflict Resolution (1965)
37-53.
    Application of the concept of response-in-kind to Soviet-
American diplomatic relations in terms of responses disrupting
the existing system. The model, based on a theorem of Eugene
Dupréel, does not rest on historical necessity but takes account
of failure to respond to disruptive innovation, escalation, and
misperceptions including those that lead to response in another
sector that may set off a new challenge-response chain. The
article notes that in the area of conventional diplomacy the
Soviets in most countries gained diplomatic privileges and immunities for their permanent trade delegations without providing significant similar arrangements for other states.

1798. Zinnes, Dina A. "Hostility in International Decision-Making."
6 Journal of Conflict Resolution (1962), 236-243.
    The article relates to the 1914 Austro-Hungarian decision
to send an ultimatum to Serbia and Russia's decision for complete mobilization and is based on a content analysis of written
communications in terms of hostile perceptions and hostile
actions.

See also nos. 256, 348, 492, 1126, 1347-1349, 1385, 1445, 1451, 1471,
1478, 1771, 1823, 1824, 1837, 1847, 2078, 2087, 2173, 2461.

3. Force Short of War: Retaliation,
   Reprisal, and Retorsion

1799. Barros, James. The Corfu Incident of 1923: Mussolini and the
League of Nations. Princeton: Princeton University Press, 1965, pp. xxi,
339.
    Employs previously unavailable source materials, both govern-
ment and private, in a careful reexamination of an incident crucial in the history of the League of Nations.

1800. Bohannan, Paul (ed.). Law and Warfare: Studies in the Anthropology of Conflict. Garden City: Natural History Press for the American Museum of Natural History, 1967, pp. xiv, 441.

The selections, chiefly from anthropologists, that are included in this collection deal with such topics as primitive judicial procedures, justice in Moscow, law and change, the medieval and the Liberian ordeal, song duels, vengeance, the blood feud, and primitive warfare.

1801. Davison, Walter Phillips. The Berlin Blockade: A Study in Cold War Politics. Princeton: Princeton University Press, 1958, pp. 423.

Combines diplomatic history with an examination of public attitudes in dealing with the maneuvers by which the blockade was brought about and countered, the whole constituting a part of East-West bargaining through a process that was essentially the use of force short of war.

1802. Gomer, Robert. "Some Thoughts on Arms Control." 17 Bulletin of Atomic Scientists (April 1961), 133-137.

Includes a proposal, even though deemed by the author to be unlikely of acceptance, that retaliation weapons be placed in the hands of a third country, perhaps the Scandinavian countries or Switzerland. The proposal illustrates the type of thinking that regards third parties as doing more than just arbitrating or otherwise pronouncing judgment and may be illustrative of a recurrent feature of societal development in its institutional and legal aspects.

1803. Hasluck, Margaret Masson (Hardy). The Unwritten Law in Albania. New York: Cambridge University Press, 1954, pp. xv, 285.

Posthumously published study in Albanian ethnography and the customary law of the highland tribes, including the institution of vengeance.

1804. Kelsen, Hans. Society and Nature: A Sociological Inquiry. Chicago: University of Chicago Press, 1943, pp. viii, 391.

Review of anthropological findings on the nature of primitive law and of retribution, with reference to the development of the idea of causation. The footnotes provide an excellent guide to and summary of the literature on retribution, together with an assembling of pertinent practices identified or observed.

1805. Lambert, Jacques. La vengeance privée et les fondements du droit international public. Paris: Sirey, 1936, pp. 136.

Description of and inferences from the institutions of private vengeance and of clan and intertribal vengeance, together with conclusions on probable means of diverting international vengeance into nonviolent channels.

1806. Lewis, William H. "Feuding and Social Change in Morocco." 5 Journal of Conflict Resolution (1961), 43-54.

Notes that feuding may have destroyed weaker clans but that it maintained the system and so played a constructive role, providing a social stability not otherwise present since the French broke old Moroccan community ties.

1807. Teger, Allan I. The Effect of Past Cooperation on the Escalation of Conflict. Technical Report No. 5. Studies of the Dynamics of Cooperation and Conflict. ONR Contract N00014-67-C-0190. Buffalo: State University of New York, Department of Psychology, August 30, 1968, pp. 45.
Report of an experimental game in which the subjects received hostile acts of varying magnitudes either at the start of interaction or after a period of cooperation. The latter produced greater retaliation, and conflict of greater magnitude and longer duration, although there was somewhat less retaliation when, after cooperation, the hostile act was mild. In terms of expectancy disconfirmation, contrast seems a better explanation than frustration for retaliation after prior cooperation that seemed to establish a norm concerning what was fair and just.

See also nos. 1254, 1255, 1478, 1654, 1657, 1681, 1682, 1735, 1742, 1851, 1875, 2214.

4. Theory of the Just War

1808. Kardelj, Edvard. Socialism and War: A Survey of Chinese Criticism of the Policy of Coexistence. London: Methuen, 1960, pp. 209.
A version of bellum justum that limits such wars to defensive wars and to "people's liberation and internal revolutionary wars," such wars being labelled "progressive" as well as justified. The same thesis was expressed by Khrushchev.

1809. Tucker, Robert W. The Just War: A Study in Contemporary American Doctrine. Baltimore: Johns Hopkins, 1960, pp. 207.
An inquiry into the justification that constitutes part of the American response to employment of force in the nuclear age.

See also nos. 1680, 1780.

a. Preventive War

1810. Galtung, Johan. "Balance of Power and the Problem of Perception: A Logical Analysis." 7 Inquiry (1964), 277-294.
Relevant to the concept of preventive war and to disarmament, the article is an analysis of the ways in which structural and psychological determinants of perception will operate in power systems and will change in time of crisis.

1811. Jeismann, Karl Ernst. Das Problem des Präventivkrieges im europäischen Staatensystem, mit besonderem Blick auf die Bismarckzeit. Freiburg and Munich: Karl Alber (1957), pp. 200.
Examination of the problem of preventive war in the light of German history and the functioning of the European state system.

See also nos. 1617, 1645.

5. Deterrence, Threats, and Threat Perception

1812. Boulding, Kenneth E. "Toward a Pure Theory of Threat Systems." 53 American Economic Review (1963), 424-434.
Boulding looks at threat as an abstract human relationship, as an economist might look at exchange, and considers how this might be used as an organizer of society. He discusses four responses to a threat: submission, defiance, counterthreat, and the integrative response. Regarding the most important single feature of systems of deterrence to be long-run instability, he relates this to credibility. The integrative response is defined as that which establishes community between the threatener and the threatened, i.e., produces common values and a common interest.

1813. Boulding, Kenneth E. "Toward a Theory of Peace." In Roger Fisher (ed.), International Conflict and Behavioral Science: The Craigville Papers. New York: Basic Books, 1964, pp. 73-87.
Peace is identified as a property of the conflict system and as a system boundary. The three major subsystems are said to be the threat, exchange, and integrative systems. The significance of threat lies in the image it evokes in the mind of the threatened. The author asserts that the web of reinforcing relationships involved in the combination of threat and integrative systems is worthy of careful study and that there is a need for models of the learning process as it operates in society as a whole.

1814. Deutsch, Morton. "Some Considerations Relevant to National Policy." 17 Journal of Social Issues (1961), 57-68.
Doubts the value, in the effort to move from mutual terror to mutual trust, of the policy of military superiority and of the policy of stable deterrence, the latter based, among other things, upon rationality of the decision to use weapons, the credibility and nonprovocativeness of the threat, and the assumption that the problem is a two-country instead of an N-country problem.

1815. Hoag, Malcolm W. "On Stability in Deterrent Races." In Morton A. Kaplan (ed.), The Revolution in World Politics. New York: Wiley, 1962, pp. 388-410.

Regarding deterrence as resting on a state of mind, the article manipulates models to illustrate some arms fundamentals related to deterrence in a decentralized peacekeeping structure.

1816. Holsti, Ole R. "East-West Conflict and Sino-Soviet Relations." 1 Journal of Applied Behavioral Science (1965), 115-130.

Employs the General Inquirer to analyze systematically the contents of 36 Russian and 42 Chinese documents to measure Sino-Soviet consensus in terms of their perceptions of American policy. The analysis indicates that in periods of heavy inter-bloc tension Soviet and Chinese attitudes converge and that in times of lessening tension they diverge. It is suggested that East-West tension is a necessary but not a sufficient condition for Sino-Soviet cohesion.

1817. Janis, Irving L., and Terwilliger, R.F. "An Experimental Study of Psychological Resistance to Fear Arousing Communications." 65 Journal of Abnormal and Social Psychology (1962), 403-410.

Report that recipients tended to reject messages based upon a high degree of fear and unpleasantness and to close their minds to all arguments in the messages in a manner that might be expected of simpler cognitive structures.

1818. Lieberman, E. James. "Threat and Assurance in the Conduct of Conflict." In Roger Fisher (ed.), International Conflict and Behavioral Science: The Craigville Papers. New York: Basic Books, 1964, pp. 110-122.

The author is concerned with the need to extend the range of policy alternatives in conflict situations and with the strategy of deterrence through threat and assurance by interpreting the reaction to threats on the level of the individual. The author generalizes to the level of nations and the role that threat and assurance play in the strategy of deterrence. Lieberman urges the use of the term challenge rather than threat, for challenge connotes a desirable stimulus, while threat does not. Since challenge is primarily concerned with the offense rather than the defense, it puts its emphasis on maximizing gain for all.

1819. Milburn, Thomas W. "The Concept of Deterrence: Some Logical and Psychological Considerations." 17 Journal of Social Issues (1961), 3-11.

Deterrence is defined as a policy that influences the behavior of another and so as a topic within the realm of psychology. Loose hypotheses are stated. A taxonomy of deterrence is suggested. Goals, means, and processes would be distinguished. A concept of an optimum level of deterrence is called for because certain kinds of acts of opponents are not subject to any kind of violent deterrent counteraction.

1820. North, Robert C., Koch, Howard E., Jr., and Zinnes, Dina A. "Capability, Threat and the Outbreak of War." In James N. Rosenau (ed.), International Politics and Foreign Policy. New York: Free Press, 1961, pp. 469-482.

Report of an empirical investigation of a set of hypotheses derived from a study of the outbreak of World War I. The authors studied 3,000 documents drawn from German, Russian, Austrian, French, and British sources to find statements pertaining to perceptions of capability, hostility, coalition, and the significance of a conflict. The two hypotheses tested were: (1) a state will not go to war if it perceives its capabilities to be significantly less than those of the enemy; (2) a state's perception of injury or hostility will offset the importance of its perception of capability.

1821. Pool, Ithiel de Sola. Human Communication and Deterrence. Studies in Deterrence, VI. U.S. Naval Ordnance Test Station, China Lake, California. NOTS TP 2841. September 1963, pp. 58.
Concise study of escalation, deterrence, disarmament probabilities and strategies, that includes some comparison of international organizations to the Fourth French Republic as issue-perpetuating, peacekeeping organizations usable to impose solutions. The author sees a trend toward toleration of international intervention and of brief, invited interventions such as that of the British in Kuwait. In regard to deterrence, a threat revealed, organized, or mobilized in time of crisis is treated as less effective than a deterrent threat made quietly, long in advance, and always there and ready, a sort of trip-mechanism--a threat much like the legal threat particularly when backed by effective organization.

1822. Pool, Ithiel de Sola, with the collaboration of Barton Whaley. Deterrence as an Influence Process. Mimeo. Cambridge: Center for International Studies, Massachusetts Institute of Technology, May 1963, pp. 60.
A study of deterrence as a special case of the psychology of influence. The study provides a point of entry into further research on influence processes for those who may choose to examine its relevance to military deterrence. While not dealing with law as a deterrent or with law-enforcing processes, sections of the study, particularly that on the generation of fear, are adaptable to the problem of the deterrent effect of law with reference to international affairs. Hypotheses concerning the influence of fear include suggestions (1) that fear may be effective when a danger is certain to be faced within a finite time period but that the mechanism of denial may be used if the danger is only a possibility and (2) that fear will be effective upon those whose role is to concern themselves with the danger but may activate denial in persons lacking responsibility. If these and related hypotheses are valid, the message conveyed by a strong force-in-being to diplomats, soldiers, and statesmen may be effective provided force is not verbally brandished.

1823. Pruitt, Dean G. "Definition of the Situation as a Determinant of International Action." In Herbert C. Kelman (ed.), International Behavior: A Social-Psychological Analysis. New York: Holt, Rinehart and Winston, 1965, pp. 393-432.

Deals with threat perception, trust, and responsiveness, with the development of each, and with stability and change in images of other nations.

1824. Pruitt, Dean G. Threat Perception, Trust and Responsiveness to International Behavior. Technical Report No. 11 to the Office of Naval Research, Washington, D.C. for Contract Number Nonr-2285(02). Newark, Delaware: January 9, 1964.

Reducing international behavior to the behavior of individuals, the author draws upon principles of psychology to derive a number of hypotheses. With reliance upon the results and suggestions of a number of psychological experimenters and theorists, the relations between threat perception, distrust, and responsiveness are explored, as are the relations of threat perception, trust, and responsiveness to predisposition, past experience, reduction of dimensionality of thinking during stress, contingency planning, institutions for coping with threat, capabilities, actions, and positive and negative fate control. Examples from recent international events are presented. The study concludes with an adaptation of the Richardson equations to provide equilibrium models of vicious circles of threat perception and of benevolent circles of responsiveness.

1825. Russett, Bruce M. "The Calculus of Deterrence." 7 Journal of Conflict Resolution (1963), 97-109.

Seventeen cases of "deterrence" (1935-1961) in which an "attacker" threatened a "pawn" while the "defender" tried to prevent the attack were examined in an effort to identify factors that correlated with the success or failure of deterrence. In general, it appeared that to increase credibility, the defender should increase his stake in the country defended.

1826. Singer, J. David. "Inter-Nation Influence: A Formal Model." 57 American Political Science Review (1963), 420-430.

Regards the key variables in inter-nation influence to be the influencer's preference, prediction, and perception, which, combined, produce four persuasion situations and four dissuasion situations. The influencee responds to influence attempts by combining his subjective probabilities for some possible outcomes with his preferences for each. There are four main influence techniques, namely, threat, promise, punishment, and reward. Threat apparently produces the stress needed for rational response but can also produce inadequate decision processes and either irrational responses or contracted repertoires.

1827. Törnudd, K. "Konflikt inom en organisation." Politiikka (1964) 246-261. With English summary.

Application of Schelling's model of conflict to a conflict of the type represented by the UN financial crisis in which one state employs the threat of application of the Charter to deprive the other state of loss of vote while the second state employs the counterthreat of aggravation of international relations. This renders the credibility of the two threats dependent upon the attitudes of other members.

See also nos. 264, 423, 683, 1255, 1273, 1274, 1283, 1289, 1376, 1408, 1522, 1810, 1889, 2077, 2150, 2169, 2214, 2461, 2764.

6. Sanctions

1828. Arens, Richard, and Lasswell, Harold D. In Defense of Public Order: The Emerging Field of Sanction Law. New York: Columbia University Press, 1961, pp. x, 314.

The authors' concern is primarily with the system of sanction law in the United States, and references to international law is only occasional and suggestive. The first part of the book identifies types of sanctions in terms of relationship to skill, wealth, etc., and classifies them, in accordance with the sociological approach, as positive or negative. The second part of the book deals with the possible scope and method of sanction law and includes discussion of the stages, the process, and the strategy of sanctions. It may be noted that the discussion is based upon rejection of the civil-criminal sanction distinction and retains the core of the criminal sanction, viz., the corrective code. It is in relation to strategic objectives that deterrence is included as one of five objectives, the others being prevention, restoration, rehabilitation, and reconstruction.

1829. Aron, Raymond. "Suez, Budapest e l'ONU." 2 Tempo presente (1957), 7-12.

Commentary on the Hungarian and Suez affairs, the solutions in each being seen as morally objectionable but easily understood. The solutions result from the simultaneous operation of the UN principle of collective security and the principle of the division of the world into spheres of influence. Because the zone in which the French and English operated was neutral in respect to the two superpowers, they incurred the sanction of the UN system which could not function within the Soviet sphere of influence.

1830. Aubert, Vilhelm. Am Straffens sosiale funksjon. Oslo: Akademisk Forlag, 1954, pp. 241.

A penetrating effort seeking to ascertain the social function of punishment and thereby to find guidelines for appropriate uses of one form of sanction.

1831. Ball, Harry. "Social Structure and Rent-Control Violations." 65 American Journal of Sociology (1960), 598-604.

An investigation of rent control violations that found different procedures employed in the development of rent ceilings elicited varying feelings of unfairness and opposition to controls. The degree of violation correlated with procedures for arriving at control and not with severity of sanction alone. These findings are pertinent for international law in that they are analogues to the new states' insistence that they are not

bound by rules to which they did not consent during the age of
imperialism.

1832. Bronfenbrenner, Urie. "Allowing for Soviet Perceptions." In
Roger Fisher (ed.), <u>International Conflict and Behavioral Science: The
Craigville Papers</u>. New York: Basic Books, 1964, pp. 161-178.
    The Soviet image of American acts and intentions includes
fear of Western attack, fear of West Germany as Nazi-dominated,
and disbelief of the American strategy of deterrence. The author
notes the necessity of treating Russian perceptions as if they
were real. He argues that we need to obtain and analyze data
which can inform us as to the nature of Soviet perceptions,
fears, and motives.

1832-A. Curtin, T.R.C. "Total Sanctions and Economic Development in
Rhodesia." 7 <u>Journal of Commonwealth Political Studies</u> (1969), 126-131.
    An examination, based on the assumption that a closed econ-
omy results if one abstracts from evasion, of whether the total
sanctions imposed on Rhodesia by the United Nations in 1968 are
more likely than previous actions to produce economic collapse
and political change. Attention is given to how a closed economy provides release from balance-of-payments constraints on the
use of deficit finance and how a minimum wage policy for African
workers becomes feasible to build a market for home manufactured
goods.

1833. Edel, May, and Edel, Abraham. <u>Anthropology and Ethics</u>. Spring
field, Illinois: Charles C. Thomas, 1959, pp. 250.
    Review of anthropological findings as they pertain to the
genesis, evolution, and impact of values in primitive societies.
Of particular importance to understanding the function of values
in law and the sociological basis of changes in legal values are
Chapter VI on control of in-group aggression and Chapter XIII on
sanctions and moral feelings, the latter including some discussion of the nature of obligation. A useful bibliography is included. One author is an anthropologist; the other, a philosopher.

1834. Esgain, Albert J., and Hammerman, Gay M. "Patterns of Response
to Treaty Violations." In Historical Evaluation and Research Organization,
<u>Study "Riposte": Responses to Violations of Arms Control and Disarmament
Agreements</u>. Report for the United States Arms Control and Disarmament
Agency, 3 vols. Washington: April 12, 1964, Vol. III, Annex 3-D.
    Charts patterns of responses to violations of treaties in
1919-1941 and 1942-1963, the last incident reported being the
1963 dispute between Haiti and the Dominican Republic. Responses
are classified according to agent responding, technique employed,
and purpose (preventive, deterrent, corrective, or punitive).

1834-A. Feeley, Malcolm. "Coercion and Compliance: A New Look at an
Old Problem." 4 <u>Law and Society Review</u> (1970), 505-519.
    An economic approach is used to try to deal with the prob-
lem of the function of coercive sanctions. Consensus on goals
and individual behavior not emerging as necessarily interdependent;

the function of coercion is seen not just as curbing those who
do not accept the goal of a legal rule but as curbing all who
do not want to pay the costs, whether or not they accept the
goal.

1835. Firth, Raymond. Human Types: An Introduction to Social Anthropology. Rev. ed. Edinburgh: Thomas Nelson, 1957; Mentor Book ed., New
York: New American Library of World Literature, 1958, pp. 173.
    Although introductory in nature, this short volume provides
a useful guide to approaches and problems of anthropological research, as well as glimpses of facets of life in a number of
primitive communities. Chapter V deals with the rules of conduct, notes differences in anthropologists' concepts of sanctions, identifies as the anthropologist's objective in regard to
law and sanctions the general conditions of community life supporting rules of conduct, and makes some pertinent comparisons
with European life. Some attention is given to the impact of
European contacts upon primitive rules of behavior. Particularly valuable are the references to situations in which the European and native laws conflict either in definition of offense or
in severity of sanction. The author also contrasts the dishar-
mony and conflict situations of European societies in which ethics, law, and religion are at variance with the harmony and lack
of variance of ethics, law, and religion in primitive societies.

1836. French, John R.P., and Raven, Bertram. "The Bases of Social
Power." In Dorwin Cartwright (ed.), Studies in Social Power. Ann Arbor:
University of Michigan, Institute for Social Research, 1959, pp. 150-167.
Reprinted in part in J. David Singer (ed.), Human Behavior and International Politics: Contributions from the Social-Psychological Sciences.
Chicago: Rand McNally, 1965, pp. 136-144.
    Distinguishes and outlines the bases of five forms of
power: referent power, expert power, reward power, coercive
power, and legitimate power. The discussion of reward power
and coercive power is relevant to some basic problems of
sanctions.

1837. Historical Evaluation and Research Organization. Study "Riposte":
Responses to Violations of Arms Control and Disarmament Agreements. Report
for the United States Arms Control and Disarmament Agency, 3 vols. Washington: April 12, 1964.
    A first volume of narrative pointed toward the problem of
violations of disarmament and arms control agreements that is
based upon the papers collected in two annex volumes that deal
more generally with the problems of sanctions and responses to
violations of treaties, largely through case studies. Particularly valuable are articles by Possony and by Esgain and Hammerman that indicate that rather prompt response of Great Powers
before World War I and after World War II to disturbances around
the globe has been a more effective peacekeeping device than the
interwar hesitance to respond in a manner bringing an appropriate amount of force or the threat thereof into play.

1838. Hoffmann, Fredrik. "The Functions of Economic Sanctions: A Comparative Analysis." 4 Journal of Peace Research (1967), 140-160.

Compares the economic sanctions against Italy in 1935 and against Rhodesia and finds the former to have been primarily a product of the constitutional system of the League of Nations having little to do with basic realities of European power politics and the latter essentially a decision of British politics to meet political cross-pressures, national and international. Economic sanctions are seen as well suited to the alleviation of tension in a cross-pressure situation--a device of procrastination, as a politician's substitute for the withdrawal that he cannot make--and very unlikely to be efficient. One hypothesis put forward is that sanctions will not be used if the sanctioning country is extremely motivated toward destroying its political opponent. Another hypothesis is that when a country's political leadership feels strongly a need to do something "but not much" and is also influenced by legalistic models of thought characteristic of such organizations as the League and the UN, sanctions will appear as a good solution. The author concludes that since sanctions are not likely to attain the desired goal, a decision to apply sanctions indicates a political motivation insufficiently strong to cope with the difficulties involved. Some attention is given to the effects of sanctions upon the sanctioning country.

1839. Hosoya, C. "Miscalculations in Deterrent Policy: Japanese-U.S. Relations, 1938-1941." 5 Journal of Peace Research (1968), 97-115.

An effort to ascertain the reasons for the failure of US economic sanctions against Japan to have a deterrent effect.

1840. Kecskemeti, Paul. Punishment as Conflict Resolution. P-2290. Santa Monica: RAND Corporation, 1961, pp. 35.

Argues that punishment should be seen not as retribution or therapy as a simple treatment of an offender but as resolution of conflict in which the crucial question is the post-punitive relationship between society and offender. Meaningful punitive practices require either full reinstatement in society or the offender's banishment or elimination. Attention is called to primitive purificatory rights that, along with elimination of the offender, focused upon the conflict-generating aspect of offenses rather than, as in modern "autonomous" morality, upon personal guilt and responsibility. A published version of this paper appeared in the Archives of Criminal Psychodynamics (Fall 1961).

1841. Medler, Jerry Francis. Negative Sanctions: Their Perception and Effect in the Political System. Ph.D. Dissertation. Eugene: University of Oregon, 1966; Ann Arbor: University Microfilms, Inc., Order No. 67-1867, pp. 158.

This dissertation deals with informal sanctions (e.g., social ostracism and loss of economic opportunity) that are imposed by members of a political system other than role incumbents. Although based on a factor analysis of data limited to that obtained by interviews conducted in Portland, Oregon, and of Negro residents of Albina District, the findings may be suggestive of behavior that might be found in examinations both of international affairs and of rebellion. Low-status individuals and activists appeared to be more perceptive of negative sanctions than others interviewed. At the same time sanctions were the least effective deterrents of political activity when low-status people perceived what could be called "anti-sanction support." In the absence of such support, they were most vulnerable to control by negative sanctions, a circumstance that the author thinks might be related to feelings of political impotence.

1842. Nieburg, H.L. "Uses of Violence." 7 <u>Journal of Conflict Resolution</u> (1963), 43-54.
The threat of violence and its occasional outbreak, which gives the threat credibility, are treated as essential to conflict resolution at subnational, national, and international levels. Law is treated as based on violence and the attempted monopoly thereof by states. Hence, the author regards the idea of substituting "world law" for violence as a contradiction. Democratic and totalitarian regimes are discussed in terms of their stability as indicated by their attempts to control violence. Violence is also treated as a mechanism of social change and the task of control is treated as a task of preventing escalation. Nieburg further develops his concepts in relation to national law in "Violence, Law, and the Informal Polity," 13 <u>Journal of Conflict Resolution</u> (1969), 192-211.

1843. Osgood, Charles E. "Questioning Some Unquestioned Assumptions about National Security." 11 <u>Social Problems</u> (1963), 6-12.
Another expression of the argument for GRIT, the article questions some assumptions about the nature of political man, about the nature of deterrence, and about the nature of nonviolent alternatives. One assumption questioned is that the credibility of our deterrent requires a hostile image of ourselves in the eyes of the opponent--the remarks being relevant also to sanctions and perception thereof.

1844. Parsons, Talcott. "Some Reflections on the Place of Force in Social Process." In Harry Eckstein (ed.), <u>Internal War: Problems and Approaches</u>. New York: Free Press, 1964, pp. 33-70.
Starting with a discussion of force and systems of normative order, the essay then distinguishes four types of attempted control over situations and control over the intentions of other parties, namely inducement, coercion, persuasion, and activation of commitments. The article then develops an analogy between power systems and credit creation in the sense that both require extension of the range of effective organization and both are vulnerable in that they cannot meet all their obligations at once. Parsons suggests that the analogy is helpful in relation to the problem of internal war in that vulnerability to vicious circles of power-deflation, accentuated by the tendency of governments to polarize, gives rise to a tendency to use force as threat, as

counterthreat, and as warning. In this conceptualization, threat is defined as "a direct expression of intention to impose a specific negative sanction, contingent on performance of a forbidden or disapproved act," while warning is "a demonstration of the capacity and readiness to act should alter perform any of a much wider range of actions undesired by ego."

1845. Reisman, William M. "The Role of the Economic Agencies in the Enforcement of International Judgments and Awards: A Functional Approach." 19 Internationa1 Organization (1966), 929-947.

The international community being dependent on organic enforcement by a variety of functional enforcers employing a variety of controls. The author calls attention to three specialized financial agencies (IMF, IBRD, and the Inter-American Development Bank), the developed enforcement system of each, and the direct control of each over assets of its members. The author finds that the three agencies have not probed such questions as possible adverse effects of enforcement on the activities of the organization and so recommends an enforcement policy.

1846. Schermerhorn, Richard A. Society and Power. New York: Random House, 1961, pp. 114.

Employs a range of possible organizational authority structures that extend along a continuum, graphically illustrated by a dual-axis diagram to portray four dimensions of power: legitimate, illegitimate, noncoercive, and coercive.

1847. Schwartz, M. "The Reciprocities Multiplier: An Empirical Evaluation." 9 Administrative Science Quarterly (1964), 264-277.

A test of the concept of style of rule enforcement as a function of Alvin W. Gouldner's reciprocities multiplier, an analogy being drawn between the multiplier and partial reinforcement. Lack of enforcement of bureaucratic rules is treated as a reward for conformity that should elicit reciprocity from subordinates. In a laboratory experiment establishing the conditions of constant enforcement, partial enforcement, no enforcement, and laissez-faire, group effectiveness was found to be highest under constant and partial enforcement. The experimenter's interpretation is that superiors' actions tend to be best reciprocated under partial enforcement and that the experiment seems to support Gouldner's hypothesis.

1848. Schwartz, Richard D., and Skolnick, Jerome H. "Televised Communication and Income Tax Compliance." In Leon Arons and Mark A. May (eds. Television and Human Behavior: Tomorrow's Research in Mass Communication. New York: Appleton-Century-Crofts, 1963, pp. 155-165.

An effort to test which sanctions are most effective in achieving compliance with income tax laws.

1849. Segal, Ronald (ed.). Sanctions against South Africa. Baltimore Penguin, 1964, pp. 272.

Papers presented to the International Conference on Economic
Sanctions against South Africa held at London in April 1964,
which was attended by governmental delegations from 30 countries,
among others. The papers deal with economic, racial, political,
legal, and strategic aspects of sanctions that might be applied
against South Africa in an effort to defeat apartheid.

1850. Sherwood, John J. "Authoritarianism, Moral Realism, and President Kennedy's Death." 5 British Journal of Social and Clinical Psychology
(1966), 264-269.
This article reports on the responses of 49 past and present officers of midwestern man's organizations concerned with
realism and those of 65 liberal arts undergraduates scoring low
on the F scale. Questionnaires were designed to probe the characteristics of those most interested in "justice being served"
when a strongly held common value is violated. High authoritarian adults had great concern for affixing blame and meting
out punishment after President Kennedy's death, their responses
being quite similar to nine statements that Piaget (The Moral
Development of the Child, London: Kegan Paul, 1932) found to
characterize the young child's conceptions of morality and justice. A second study showed that high authoritarians tended to
recommend punishment as a problem-solving technique in dealing
with workers who violate management's expectations about worker
behavior and tended to recommend expiatory punishment more than
punishment by reciprocity.

1851. Skilling, H. Gordon. Communism, National and International:
Eastern Europe after Stalin. Toronto: University of Toronto Press in association with the Canadian Institute of International Affairs, 1964, pp.
xi, 168.
A narrative account of events in Communist Europe that,
among other things, calls attention to efforts to employ ideological and diplomatic sanctions against deviant satellites in
East Europe and, in the case of Hungary, the resort to armed
force as police action and ouster of the deviant government as
sanction.

1852. Spence, J.E. Republic under Pressure: A Study of South African
Foreign Policy. London: Oxford, 1965, pp. vi, 132.
Deals with the impact of internal politics on South Africa's
foreign policy and includes discussion of two considerations that
bear upon the willingness of other states to apply sanctions in
an effort to end apartheid: (1) economic dependence of neighboring African states on the Republic; (2) the investments of Western states in the Republic that at the least may have been perceived by the Nationalists as a guarantee of Western hesitation
to take coercive action.

1853. Tanner, R.E.S. "Law Enforcement by Communal Action in Sukumaland, Tanganyika Territory." 7 Journal of African Administration (1955),
159-165.

Short description of community action, particularly ostracism, as punishment for acts considered to be public offenses
endangering corporate unity. The article treats anonymity of
community action as a means of avoiding personal feuds, thereby
raising a question that, transferred to the international realm,
might suggest that a partial explanation of the weakness of law
enforcement through self-help might be made in terms of revan-
chism against an identifiable agent of enforcement, even assuming no excessive aggrandizement by the enforcer in a self-help
system.

1854. Wallenstein, Peter. "Characteristics of Economic Sanctions."
5 Journal of Peace Research (1968), 248-267.
Examining ten cases of economic sanctions over the preceding 35 years, the author finds economic sanctions to have been
generally unsuccessful and often intended to be only acts of
protest and condemnation. Sanctions oriented toward a resolution of a conflict are seen to have been instrumental and attempts to compromise are noted. Economic sanctions aimed at a
particular political structure and the demand for more or less
complete change are shown to have been part of a polarization
process that had led to the breaking off of other types of
interaction.

1855. Weiss, Walter, and Fine, Bernard J. "The Effect of Induced Aggressiveness on Opinion Change." 52 Journal of Abnormal and Social Psychology (1956), 109-114.
Investigation of the hypothesis that aggressively aroused
people are more influenced by punitively oriented communications and less influenced by leniency-oriented communications
than are nonaggressively aroused people. One group of students
was placed in a failure-insult situation and a second group in
an ego-satisfying situation. Half of each group read a communication advocating punishment of juvenile delinquents and the
other half of each group read a communication urging leniency
in US relations with Red China. The degree and direction of
opinion change supported the hypothesis. This study is relevant not to an aggressor who could be threatened with punitive
action but to populations and segments thereof whose opinions
concerning international events might have an impact supportive
of war crime charges, demands for satisfaction, punitive peace
settlements, and the like.

See also nos. 715, 857, 1254, 1255, 1315, 1508, 1768, 1772, 1793, 182
1856, 1858, 1886, 2094, 2231, 2691.

7. Rewards

1855-A. Baldwin, David A. "The Power of Positive Sanctions." 24
World Politics (1971), 19-38.

A deductive approach that suggests that 14 behavioral differences related to the choice of whether to employ positive or
negative sanctions ought to be carefully studied. The author is
concerned about a bias in the political science literature in
favor of negative sanctions and notes some conceptual problems
arising from efforts to subsume positive sanctions under rubrics
derived from the institution of negative sanctions.

1856. Bornstein, Morris. "Economic Sanctions and Rewards in Support
of Disarmament Treaties." Papers and Proceedings of the Eightieth Annual
Meeting of the American Economic Association (1967): 58 American Economic
Review (May 1968), 417-427.
　　　　Deals with both rewards (positive sanctions) and negative
sanctions in relation to the specific problem of disarmament,
with an economic emphasis in harmony with the panel topic of
the economic consequences of disarmament.

1857. Hodges, Donald Clark. "Reward." 19 Philosophy and Phenomeno-
logical Research (1958), 198-211.
　　　　On retributive and nonretributive meanings of reward and
on the juridical concept thereof that proportions reward to
desert but limits the application thereof by regard for the
general welfare.

1858. Mulder, Mauk, van Dijk, Rob, Stelwagen, Tilly, Verhagen, Jan,
Soutendijk, Sibe, and Zwezerijnen, Jan. "Illegitimacy of Power and Posi-
tivity of Attitudes toward the Power Person." 19 Human Relations (1966),
21-37.
　　　　Manipulates three conditions of reward and punishment power
of one person over another and measures the attitudes of the
second person to find that, whether the power was legitimate or
illegitimate, the greater the first person's power the more negative the attitudes of the second person toward him. The authors
regard it as a particularly significant behavioral phenomenon
that their experiments show a consistency in that in precisely
the conditions in which it is most dangerous to do so (when the
other's power is large compared with the subjects power) resistance to power is manifest.

1859. Stennett, R.G. "The Relationship of Performance Level to Level
of Arousal." 54 Journal of Experimental Psychology (1957), 54-61.
　　　　An analysis of auditory tracking helpful to the understanding of the impact of reward. Performances in a relatively simple
task were compared to note the effects of varied instructions,
some promising more reward in the task than others, that found
that optimal performance occurred when an extreme of inducement
was avoided.

1860. Zipf, Sheila G. "Resistance and Conformity under Reward and
Punishment." 61 Journal of Abnormal Psychology (1960), 102-109.
　　　　Report on an experiment in which rewards and punishments
were employed in an effort to induce conformity in the form of
speeding up performance of a manual task. Among other things

it was found that influence by punishment produced greater resistance than influence by reward if there was, along with reward for conformity, no probability of punishment for nonconformity. It was noted that individuals with strong needs for
independence from control figures were aroused to resist when
repeated attempts were made to influence them by punishment.

See also nos. 320, 1826, 1828, 1836, 1847, 1885.

E. AGREEMENT

1. Treaties and Other International Agreements

1861. Boulding, Kenneth E. "National Images and International Systems." 3 Journal of Conflict Resolution (1959), 120-131.
Based upon the theory which the author set forth in The
Image (1956), the paper sets forth uses and limitations of the
matrix for measurement of the friendliness-hostility variable.
Within its limitations such a matrix appears susceptible of refinement to provide one predictor of potential durability of
international agreements and, perhaps also, of propensity to
enter into agreements by treating the friendliness-hostility
dimension at a given time as constant and agreements, grouped
by types on the basis of essential content, as variables. Comments on the persistence of the image produced by territorial
demarcations can be related to Mamadou Dia's remarks on the effects of territorialism on the Mali Federation (supra, no. 1214)
and to Thomas Walker's definition of international law as the
science of territorial sovereignty.

1862. Leites, Nathan. A Study of Bolshevism. Glencoe: Free Press,
1954, pp. 639.
An analysis of the Bolshevik character, based on psychoanalytic examination of the imagery, fantasy, and characteristic
literary metaphors of Bolshevik leaders and of fictional models
in Russian literature with which the leaders identify or which
they assail. In regard to international agreements the conclusion is that a settlement sharply and indefinitely reducing the
existing mutual threat is inconceivable but agreements codifying
momentary force relationships, subject to being broken at strategic moments in the continuing basic struggle, are possible.
The volume is a more thorough version of Leites' The Operational
Code of the Politburo (1951) which was used by American negotiators in Korea as a tactical manual.

1863. Patterson, Stewart Marshall. The Use of International Executive Agreements in the Foreign Assistance and Mutual Security Programs,
1940-1956. Ph.D. Dissertation. Washington: American University, 1957;
Ann Arbor: University Microfilms, Inc., Publication No. 21,662, Mic. 57-
4296, pp. 347.

Detailed study of two uses of executive agreements, suggestive of a more comprehensive study that could be made to ascertain preferred instruments in an international environment in
which the older, slower treaty process may not be appropriate
in as large a proportion of situations as in the past. This
particular study is in part shackled to the Bricker Amendment
controversy, and its more valuable parts are those not constricted thereby.

1864. Toscano, Mario. Lezioni di storia dei trattati e politica internazionale. I. Parte generale. Torino: Giapichelli, 1958, pp. iv, 518.
The History of Treaties and International Politics. Part I: An Introduction to the History of Treaties and International Politics; The Documentary
and Memoir Sources. Baltimore: Johns Hopkins Press, 1966, pp. xv, 685.
On the ground that there is a lack of correspondence between
the present-day situation and certain institutions that arose and
were developed in other centuries, the author tries to define the
salient characteristics of the international situation in an effort to identify the necessary process of bringing institutions
up to date or replacing them. Solemn, formal agreements between
the capitalist and communist worlds are said to be impossible and,
therefore, satisfaction must be had with what the author regards
as de facto agreements. In regard to treaties in general, the
author prefers to examine them from the point of view of international politics not for the purpose of ascertaining their value
as legal instruments but as crystallizations or mirrors of situations involving two or more states. He regards such situations
as a balance, or at least a measure of balance, for which treaties are the evidence. Part III of the lectures is an excellent
analysis, from the political rather than the legal viewpoint, of
the characteristics and evidentiary value of diaries, memoirs,
etc., of statesmen, diplomats, and other makers of international
events. This analysis of primary sources is followed by a discussion of the more interesting materials from the Congress of
Vienna to the end of World War I in terms of their historical
value within the context of the events to which they are related.

1865. Triska, Jan F. "Soviet Treaty Law: A Quantitative Analysis."
29 Law and Contemporary Problems (1964), 896-909.
Analysis of Soviet agreements in 1958-1961 that notes the
change in treaty partnerships in terms of volume as compared
with the period 1917-1957. Change in types of treaties is also
noted. The author finds distrust and suspicion of Soviet treaty
performance to be unrelated to economic and trade agreements,
functional, cultural or technical agreements, or with agreements
on consular and diplomatic affairs, but rather to "solemn" political treaties, a type not concluded in 1958-1961. Bilateral
agreements remained dominant as in the earlier period.

1866. Triska, Jan F., and Slusser, Robert M. The Theory, Law, and
Policy of Soviet Treaties. Stanford: Stanford University Press, 1962,
pp. xi, 593.

Exhaustive analysis of Soviet treaties seeking to ascertain, among other things, the types of Soviet treaties that can be considered to have value, as well as the grounds, intrinsic or extrinsic, on which the USSR is likely to conform to treaties. Treaty form, interpretation, termination, and treaty partners are discussed, in addition to nonaggression, neutrality, mutual assistance, peace, peaceful solution of disputes, and state trading.

See also nos. 219, 539, 678, 695, 1084, 1501, 1749, 1759, 1761, 1896, 2081, 2357, 2380, and sec. VI, A, 5.

2. Ratification; Reservations

1867. Cook, A.H. "The International Labor Organization and Japanese Politics." 19 Industrial and Labor Relations Review (1965), 41-57.
On the reception of ILO Convention No. 87 in Japan, the problem of modification of three sets of labor relations laws to produce conformity with the Convention, the opposition of the Socialist Party to change of the legislation and its impact upon parliamentary procedure in the effort to revise the pertinent legislation, and the eventual ratification of the Convention in 1965 together with a victory for the unions in the form of the repeal of the paragraphs of domestic legislation concerning the Public Corporation Labor Relations Law.

1868. Lerner, Daniel, and Aron, Raymond (eds.). France Defeats the E.D.C. New York: Praeger, 1957, pp. 225.
Deals with the politics of the interesting parallel to United States rejection of its own proposal for a League of Nations, in this case the French defeat in 1954 of the European Defense Community that France had proposed.

1869. Packard, George R., III. Protest in Tokyo: The Security Treaty Crisis of 1960. Princeton: Princeton University Press, 1966, pp. xiv, 42?
A study of the political struggle of May-June 1960 with its riots that delayed ratification of the revised treaty until later in the year.

1870. Scalapino, Robert Anthony, and Masumi, Junnosuke. Parties and Politics in Contemporary Japan. Berkeley: University of California Press 1962, pp. ix, 190.
Japanese political organizations and procedures are studied with a focus upon the May-June 1960 events in reaction to the effort to gain speedy approval of the security treaty with the United States.

1871. Whittemore, Edward P. The Press in Japan Today--A Case Study. Columbia: University of South Carolina Press, 1961, pp. vii, 91.
A study of the activities and statements of Asahi, Mainichi, and Yomiuri, accounting for over half the daily sale of newspapers in Japan, at the time of the Kishi's Government's effort

to obtain approval of the United States-Japanese security treaty
that led to demonstrations and the cancellation of President
Eisenhower's visit. An appendix presents in parallel columns
the stories published by the three newspapers on the session of
May 19 in which a rump Lower House approved the Treaty.

See also nos. 1310, 1311, 1320, 1391, 1786.

3. Interpretation of Agreements

1872. Guggenheim, Paul. Survey on the Ways in Which States Interpret
Their International Obligations: General Report of the International Committee on Comparative Law. UNESCO Reports and Papers in the Social Sciences.
No. 1. Paris: 1955, pp. 21.
Survey of ways of interpretation that draws its importance
from its attention to political interpretation and, in consequence, to compliance.

1873. Lochner, N. "Was bedeuten die Begriffe Harmonisierung, Koord-
inierung und gemeinsame Politik in den europäischen Verträgen?" 118 Zeitschrift für die gesamte Staatswissenschaft (1962), 35-61.
A study in the problem of treaty interpretation in the face
of a need to avoid straitjackets if transformation, in this case
from customs union to economic community, is to be afforded opportunity to take place.

1874. Luard, Evan. Peace and Opinion. London: Oxford University
Press, 1962, pp. 170.
A former member of the British foreign service presents his
evaluation of such problems as those of authority and of the development of an international order resting on public opinion.
A chapter is specifically devoted to international law, although
consideration of the law runs throughout the book. The author
makes a case for flexibility of interpretation, for interpretation in terms of the needs of the day in a changing system rather
than in terms of the intent of framers of agreements and for interpretation by authoritative international political, rather
than judicial, entities to facilitate the adaptation of the law
to political changes. The views expressed are not unusual, but
the mode of expression sometimes facilitates insight and on other
occasions helps to identify hypotheses requiring testing.

See also nos. 1501, 1510, 1864, 1866, 1939, 2161.

4. Revision and Termination of Agreements

1875. Hammond, Paul Y., and Masters, Roger D. "Interchange." 7
Journal of Conflict Resolution (1963), 91-95.

In a discussion of an article by Hammond, Masters proposes limited, not total, abrogation of self-enforcing arms agreements as a response to limited violations. Under this concept of "limited agreements" escalation to total abrogation would be avoidable. For example, the United States could respond to a Soviet underground testing by itself testing only underground and thus maintaining a ban on atmospheric tests. Masters' concept thus runs counter to the international law principle, at least as traditionally expressed, that violation by one party renders a treaty voidable at the option of the other. This particular interchange deals with another aspect in that, in answer to a question by Hammond, Masters views it as advisable that the United States cheat first or even enter into an agreement with the intention to cheat first. Hammond accepts this position but feels that the United States would not act first, nor even necessarily respond to a Soviet violation, and so would place itself at a disadvantage by entering into a self-enforcing arms agreement.

1876. Wurfel, David. "Okinawa: Irredenta on the Pacific." 35 Pacific Affairs (1962-1963), 353-374.
A study of political and military obstacles to the revision of the Japanese peace treaty that would give effect to the desire of Okinawans to return their island to Japan, as was finally arranged for 1972.

See also nos. 669, 1866.

V. GENESIS, FUNCTIONS, DYNAMICS AND EVOLUTION
OF INTERNATIONAL LAW

A. LAW IN INTERNATIONAL RELATIONS

1. Communication, Socialization, and Other Functions

1877. Boasson, Charles. "The Place of International Law in Peace Research." 5 Journal of Peace Research (1968), 28-43.
The author rejects the idea that international law is a "primitive" law that will evolve into something mature and more effective. He critically appraises the suggestion that international law must first absorb and reflect the cultural patterns and legal systems of the world's peoples. Complaints that the desires and demands of dissatisfied nations are not met are seen as tensions normal in any legal order and as the product of defective adjustments to ideal demands. Arguing that the experience and theoretical categories of municipal law are inapplicable to international relations, the author suggests that there is a need for functional adaptations to basic differences between municipal and international situations.

1878. Bredemeier, Harry C. "Law as an Integrative Mechanism." In William M. Evan (ed.), Law and Sociology. New York: Free Press, 1962, pp. 73-90.

Provocative suggestion for an approach to law that treats law as contributing coordination to a society by providing certain outputs to other sectors of society in exchange for certain inputs. Six strategic areas for sociological research are suggested: (1) possible sources of extra-legislative conceptions of collective goals; (2) mechanism of reinforcement of and support for legal ideals within the profession; (3) channels for communicating scientific information to lawmen; (4) public perceptions of the legal system and their foundations; (5) reactions of individuals to the use of law to impose new liabilities; (6) alternatives to the legal system as a device for conflict resolution.

1879. Catton, William R., Jr. "Origin and Establishment of Lend-Lease Policy: A Study in Symbolic Paralysis." 7 ETC: A Review of General Semantics (1956), 180-188.

Investigates the origin and establishment of Lend-Lease as an example of misunderstanding of the symbolic process of a money economy, with the result that symbols disrupt rather than facilitate the distribution of goods and services. The concept of symbolic paralysis that underlies this study could be brought to bear in case studies focusing upon the communication function of law.

1880. Chavez, Antonio. Os suditos inimigos e o direito de guerra brasileiro. São Paulo: Gráfica Editora "Lex," 1945, pp. 426.

Study of the attitudes toward and treatment of enemy subjects in Brazil during World War II. A torrent of decree-laws, ordinances, resolutions, instructions, and circulars from the Vargas regime prevented the growth of a system. It is an example of a communications overload in legal form that produced such chaos that anti-enemy measures were sometimes taken against Brazilian citizens. Jewish refugees were treated as enemy subjects but Austrians were not. Among the examples of chaos was a levy against bank deposits of enemy subjects in order to create an Indemnity Fund for relatives of sailors on torpedoed Brazilian ships, but no distribution plan was established and the relatives were unable to collect for several years.

1880-A. Cherry, Colin. World Communication: Threat or Compromise?-- A Socio-technical Approach. New York: Wiley, 1971, pp. 268.

An examination of the nature of human communication, various aspects of the communication explosion and its implications for the future, leading to the conclusion that rapidly expanding global communication systems have great organizing powers through which to operate new, practical institutions to develop trade, exchange, and international law.

1881. Coplin, William D. Functions of International Law. Chicago: Rand McNally, 1966, pp. xi, 294.

A broad stroke effort to integrate traditionalist studies
of international law with some recent writings in the social
sciences in an effort to assess the position of international
law in today's world. Four functions are attributed to international law: (1) the allocation of legal competences; (2) the
limitations of the principle of territorial supremacy; (3) the
limitation of international violence; (4) the development of
international social and welfare legislation. A final chapter,
making the greatest effort to employ social science studies and
the concepts expressed therein is concerned with international
law as a technique for communicating and developing a climate
of opinion about the nature of the international system, with
the limited audience reached by international law, with problems
of consensus, and with the development of an international political culture. An important basic concept of the book equates,
or at least treats as similar, legal procedures and bargaining.

1882. Coplin, William D. "International Law and Assumptions About
the State System." 17 World Politics (1965), 615-634.
An approach to the relationships between international law
and politics in terms of a system of quasi-authoritative communications (e.g., concerning the reasons for state actions)
that reflects common attitudes about the nature of the state
system and the assumptions that have structured these attitudes.

1883. Dechert, Charles R. "A Pluralistic World Order." Proceedings
of the American Catholic Philosophical Association. Washington: The
Catholic University of America, 1963, pp. 167-186.
Law is treated as a substitute for continuing communications flows among components of a system. It is a manageable
method of lending predictability to the actions of others. It
permits decentralization of decision-making, that is, subsystem
autonomy, to cope with limitations of the communications process. On a world scale, the rule of law would reduce the ability
of organized groups, including states, to act coercively or to
obtain supereminent power in a world characterized by a multi-
tude of dimensions and by a cluster of organizations with degrees of competition and cooperation between groupings and
clusters of groupings. Government itself should be conceived
as a multiplicity of organizational loci of power, not as a
sovereign possessed of a specific locus of decision.

1884. Evan, William M., and Schwartz, Mildred A. "Law and the Emergence of Formal Organization." 48 Sociology and Social Research (1964),
270-280.
This article examines some aspects of the latent function
of law, particularly the emergence of private formal organizations following the enactment of a law. They may be either
functional or dysfunctional relative to the law that brings
them about. The attributes of a law that generate an organization response are (a) the values embedded in it, (b) the efficiency of its enforcement provisions, and (c) the social units
it affects. Law is treated as an intervening variable in the

process of social change, not as a mere consequence of other institutional structures of society. Organizations with dysfunctional consequences for a law (i.e., those dedicated to opposing,
repealing, or subverting a law) face the problem of establishing
their legitimacy in the local community.

1885. Koebner, Richard. "Semantics and Historiography." 7 Cambridge
Journal (1953), 131-144.
      Notes that the semantic approach to history reveals a close
interconnection between political and juridical expressions, with
the juridical transformed more slowly than the political. This
general observation may require modification to fit differences
in forms of law to adjust to the differentiation and time lag
noted, respectively, by Max Huber and Maxwell Cohen.

1886. Merelman, Richard M. "Learning and Legitimacy." 60 American
Political Science Review (1966), 548-561.
      An examination of the theory of political legitimacy in
terms of psychological learning theory and the theory of cognitive dissonance. Sanctions, both positive and negative, are
treated as reinforcements of policy in the form of policy payoffs. What is known about four stages of animal learning is
transferred to the learning behavior of human populations. To
this is added a stage of reduction of cognitive dissonance to
convert positive affect toward government into a grant of legitimacy. This stage is then regarded as followed by the regime's
elaborating a set of "condensation symbols" standing for governmental processes which, in the fourth lower animal analogy stage
of secondary reinforcement, has seen processes established as
symbols of unconditional reinforcement stimuli such as food, security, and shelter. Some attention is accorded decentralized
political structures and it is suggested that the decentralized
situation may be characterized by a higher proportion of reward
than punitive sanctions and, accordingly, by greater resort to
bargaining to assure that many groups get something.

1887. Walker, Edward L., and Heyns, Roger W. An Anatomy for Conformity. Englewood Cliffs: Prentice-Hall, 1962, pp. 103.
      Report on psychological experiments manipulated to produce
conformity or nonconformity. Familiarity with the reference
group to which a norm is attributed ("own group" or "other people" being one reference employed for purposes of manipulation)
added effectiveness to the norm as a producer of conformity.
However, the more familiar the subject was with the object of
the attitude or behavior to be influenced by a norm, the less
effective was the pressure toward conformity. In experiments
with the norm as a source of information it was found that effectiveness of a norm depended on (1) the attribution of high
or low value to it, (2) the degree of confidence a subject has
in his own solution to a problem in an area with which he is not
completely familiar, (3) the extent of agreement (or disagreement) between the norm and the subject's own experience, and (4)
the extent of disagreement between the norms and another source

of information designated as "official" or "correct." In regard
to information concerning a problem, it was observed that providing much information, even though simple, in a very short period
of time produced confusion and lack of confidence in a subject's
own solution to a problem and consequent reliance upon a norm
(even though, in the experiment, attributed to "other people").
Other experiments reported relate conformity to degree of stimulus ambiguity, number of alternatives and the degree of their
appropriateness, needs, goals, and the instrumental character of
the norm in relation to the goals.

See also nos. 129, 130, 261, 264, 275, 304, 336, 518, 1121, 1237, 1285
1762.

a. Law and Adjudication as Bargaining

See nos. 1236, 1881, 2043, 2220.

B. DYNAMICS OF INTERNATIONAL LEGAL EVOLUTION

1. Sources; Norm-Generating Forces

1888. Aubert, Vilhelm. Elements of Sociology. New York: Scribner's
1967, pp. viii, 247.
    Particularly useful for its chapters on expecations and
norms and on conflict and deviance.

1889. Averch, H., and Levin, M.M. Simulation of Decision-making in
Crisis: Three Manual Gaming Experiments. RM-4202-PR. Santa Monica: RANI
Corporation, August 1964, pp. 42.
    A simulation that throws some light on the role of ad hoc
rules of behavior in escalation situations and upon threat patterns. Inadequacies of the game included lack of opportunity to
explore the meanings of diplomatic notes (which, without accompanying military moves, were taken to mean weakness).

1890. Becker, Howard Paul. "Normative Reactions to Normlessness." 2
American Sociological Review (1960), 803-810.
    Including a preface by the author's son, Christopher Bennett
Becker, this posthumously published Presidential Address to the
August 1960 meeting of the American Sociological Association relates primarily to anomie rather than to deviance and deals with
the normative reaction, as reaction, to be found whenever a subject defines an action situation, i.e., the societal context, as
"normless"--a reaction itself generative of norms.

1891. Bendix, Reinhard. <u>Max Weber: An Intellectual Portrait</u>. Garden City: Doubleday, 1960, pp. 480.
Summarizes Weber's theories on the historical development of law and the legal profession.

1892. Calvert, Peter. "The Typical Latin-American Revolution." 43 <u>International Affairs</u> (1967), 85-95.
Treating force rather than unconstitutionality as characteristic of Latin American revolts, the author sees the process of violent governmental change as relatively easy in Latin America due to the vesting of vital executive functions in one man. Not economic distress but disaffection in a presidential system is seen as accounting for the military character of Latin American revolutions. The author stresses the Latin American revolution as a contributor to international jurisprudence by stimulating rules regarding the behavior of foreign states, particularly in regard to intervention.

1893. Colby, Benjamin N. "Behavioral Redundancy." 3 <u>Behavioral Science</u> (1958), 317-322.
Provocative examination of redundancy, based upon the assumption that life, like languages, seeks an equilibrium of about 50% redundancy, between the unexpected and the predictable, between disorganization and organization. Attention is given to values, particularly to the 13-fold arrangement of Charles Morris, the values being treated as a kind of programming for individual behavior. Value structures are treated as susceptible of intermeshing with redundancy patterns either as psychologically peripheral "traits" or as more central "motives". While the article presents no evidence of what it asserts except for reference to experiments by Lilly and by Hebb on the bearing that relative presence or absence of physical stimulation has upon the image-producing processes within the brain, it does include suggestions that might prove fruitful in explanation of the development and maintenance of customs.

1894. Cowan, Thomas A., and Strickland, Donald A. <u>The Legal Structure of a Confined Microsociety (A Report on the Cases of Penthouse II and III)</u>. With the collaboration of Martin Stow, Suellen Lanstein, and John Bosley. Internal Working Paper #34, Space Sciences Laboratory, Social Sciences Project, University of California, Berkeley, August 1965, pp. xi, 325.
Report by a lawyer and a political scientist on experiments conducted under a NASA grant in the Penthouse of the Department of Nutritional Sciences at the University of California. Narratives of happenings during the 89-day confinement of Penthouse II--the log is appended--and of the 43 days of Penthouse III are followed by chapters on decision and persuasion in each confined microsociety, a chapter on the sociological and psychological structure of such a society, a cluster analysis of a legal attitudes questionnaire, and, in an appendix, an essay on ecology, law, and anti-law. The narrative presents interesting accounts of decision processes relative to the development of operating rules by the subjects themselves, adherence to the experimenters' requirements, certain cases at law presented to the subjects, and

certain simulated space flight occurrences including a prior
landing and territorial claim by the Russians. Among the findings were the presence of sufficient solidarity and incentive to
permit conflict resolution, a reluctance of the two groups to
formulate rules for their own governance, a need for a concept
of "anti-law" to contain resistance to "legal" exactions, persistent challenge and testing of externally imposed rules, definite efforts to retain "psychic space" against individual and
group intrusions, development of negative attitudes toward overt
conflict resolution, and avoidance of decision-making tasks. A
most important conclusion by the authors is that man does not
want to know how he governs himself, expends forethought on physical gear, and the like, and that the problem of government is
assumed to be taken care of if there has been opportunity to select congenial and competent companions.

1895. Etzioni, Amitai. "On Self-Encapsulating Conflicts." 8 Journal
of Conflict Resolution (1964), 242-255.
       Encapsulation is a process whereby conflicts become curbed
or limited by rules (capsules) imposing dependence on the en-
capsulated parties. Encapsulation must be self-propelling. The
process of conflict itself, without neutral third parties, can
produce its own curbs in the form of self-imposed limitations on
the means of conflict. The Soviet Union and the United States
have been engaging in such a process. A containment-deterrence
strategy would extinguish expansionism by frustration while encapsulation tends to sublimate expansionist drives and allow
legitimate outlets for ambition. Peaceful competition and ending of psychological states of war can result from encapsulation,
as well as strengthening the line separating armed from unarmed
conflict.

1896. Faucheux, C., and Thibault, J. "L'Approche clinique et expérimentale de la genèse des normes contractuelles dans différentes conditions
de conflit et de menace." 13 Bulletin du C.E.R.P. (1964), 225-243.
       Two threats appear in groups in which there is inequality
of power, one internal and the other external, both threatening
the survival of the group. The internal threat entails a conflict of interest which raises among the group members lacking
power a fear that members possessing power will not effect an
equitable distribution of common revenues. The exterior threat
provides interesting alternatives that may result in abandonment
of the powerless by the powerful. In such a situation the powerful make an appeal to norms of good faith while the powerless appeal to norms of equity. But this occurs only when the two
threats appear simultaneously so that contractual activity becomes possible to guarantee the survival of the group. An experiment, manipulating the two threats to produce the four combinations of high and low level that are possible, was conducted
in a manner permitting the powerful-powerless dyads to negotiate.
The results were a confirmation of the hypotheses set forth concerning cohesion, power, and negotiation.

1897. Goffman, Erving. Behavior in Public Places: Notes on the Social Organization of Gatherings. New York: Free Press, 1963, pp. 248.
    While primarily concerned with mental health, Goffman sheds
unexpected light on the way in which norms and customs arise in
minimally structured social contexts.

1898. Jones, Joseph Marion. The Fifteen Weeks (February 21-June 5,
1947). New York: Viking, 1955; Harbinger ed., New York: Harcourt, Brace
& World, 1964, pp. viii, 296.
    Example of a case study, employing conventional methods,
covering a concentrated period entailing the genesis of a policy (the Marshall Plan) that entailed a normative, although not
necessarily legal, element in the sense of establishing a standard of responsibility for the well-being of other nations.

1899. Kahn, Herman. "The Arms Race and World Order." In Morton A.
Kaplan (ed.), The Revolution in World Politics. New York: Wiley, 1962,
pp. 332-351.
    A brief statement of some of the author's views that in-
cludes his view of the possibility of producing technical agreements with little or no political effects and, more importantly,
of measures negotiable on an informal basis and lacking the
binding effect of treaties but which are susceptible to legiti-
mation through aging and transformation into custom.

1900. Kaplan, Morton A. (ed.). The Revolution in World Politics. New
York: Wiley, 1962, pp. xxii, 477.
    A collection of 14 papers presented at the 1961 interna-
tional relations panels of the American Political Science Association, plus one paper published in World Politics and five
papers added to provide more adequate coverage. The papers,
some of which are separately annotated, deal with the general
movement of protest against Western societies, protest movements
in developed areas, revolutionary protest movements in underdeveloped areas, the Communist challenge to the status quo, problems of international order, and problems of policy in a revolutionary age.

1901. Sherif, Muzafer, et al. Intergroup Conflict and Cooperation:
The Robber's Cave Experiment. Norman: University of Oklahoma Press, 1961,
pp. 212.
    Experiment on conflict and cooperation in a boys' camp that
develops some findings on the generation of norms that may be
related to what historical studies have uncovered. For example,
the hypothesis that groups in a condition of interdependence and
sharing common goals will generate standardized norms may be
compared with Adda Bozeman's suggestion that nations facing the
same hazards or the same environmental uncertainties will produce common norms. The finding that the introduction of superordinate goals reduced intergroup enmity is in the same direction as the Romes' findings that taking the system point of
view improved performance in experimental organizations and also
suggests a less costly way of reducing hostility than the "common

enemy" approach that served to reduce hostility in an earlier
Sherif and Sherif experiment.

1902. Strickland, Donald A. A Note on Proto-Political Behaviors.
Working Paper No. 24. Space Sciences Laboratory, Social Sciences Project,
University of California, Berkeley, February 1965, pp. 15.
    Holds that the politics of the public realm are continuous
with other human dynamics and that the basic arts of persuasion
and influence are learned before entering public office. Some
examination is made of sociological and anthropological literature prior to analyzing conflict behavior in a closed environment as revealed in the logs and diaries under study at the Naval
Medical Neuropsychiatric Research Unit at San Diego which deal
with interactions in the mixed naval-scientific teams wintering
in the Antarctic. From this data a number of conflict categories
are developed and also a list of proto-political activities such
as protesting, conspiring, demanding, adjudicating, etc. A four-
part hypothesis is then suggested as susceptible of being tested
by laboratory simulation of such small group situations as space
flight.

1903. Strickland, Donald A. Preliminary Thoughts on the Politics of
Closed Environments. Internal Working Paper No. 16. Space Sciences Laboratory, Social Sciences Project, University of California, Berkeley,
August 1964, pp. 34.
    Reviews literature on such closed environments as Antarctic
expeditions, concentration camps and prisons, surrounded armies,
mutinies at sea, etc., calls attention to conflicts and to uses
of political symbols from the outside world, notes the impact of
the approach of escape or disaster, gives attention to possible
effects of size and of partial contact with the outside upon behavior in the closed environment, and suggests hypotheses and
research to test them. The author holds that the substantive
contents of political conflicts in closed societies are trans-
latable into the substantive contents of the political debates
of the great societies. What is suggested by this paper, when
read in conjunction with other reports on the NASA project on
which the author worked, is that there are ways of studying the
emergence of the political and the legal and their changes over
time that permit direct observation to supplement memoirs and
other historical data, assuming that the problem of translation
is faced and adequately dealt with.

1904. van der Wee, H. The Growth of the Antwerp Market and the Euro
pean Economy, Fourteenth-Sixteenth Centuries. 3 vols. The Hague: Nijhof:
1963, v. 1: pp. lix, 562; v. 2: pp. xi, 436; v. 3: pp. 168.
    Painstaking, well-organized study of the growth of Antwerp
during the formative period of international law. The study
provides much fundamental data on maritime commerce, transcon-
tinental trade, and the industrial boom of the 16th century,
including much statistical data essential to comprehension of
the socio-economic foundations of early modern international
law.

1905. Weyrauch, Walter O. "Law in Isolation: The Penthouse Astro-
nauts." 5 Trans-Action (June 1968), 39-46.
   Report on observations of a NASA isolation experiment, attention being given to the impact of isolation on the norms operative on the subjects, the breakdown of some rules, and the
development of new, unwritten norms. One interesting finding
is that a norm would develop and be followed until the experimenter articulated it but, once articulated, disobedience became
common.

See also nos. 603, 644, 647, 749, 1118, 1134, 1136, 1143, 1154-1156,
1167, 1216, 1221, 1223, 1297, 1499, 1501, 1615, 2763.

2. Scientific and Technological Influences

1906. Burke, William T. Ocean Sciences, Technology, and the Future
International Law of the Sea. Social Science Program of the Mershon Center
for Education in National Security, The Ohio State University. Pamphlet
Series, No. 2. Columbus: Ohio State University Press, January 1966, pp.
91.
   A study by a professor of law, employing Myres McDougal's
framework, that is distinguished for its use of the most recent
scientific and technological works on the animate and inanimate
resources of the sea and for its attention to the problems
raised by the devices employed for research and for exploration
for and exploitation of the ocean's resources.

1907. Estep, Samuel D. "International Lawmakers in a Technological
World: Space Communications and Nuclear Energy." 33 George Washington
Law Review (1964), 162-180.
   On the possible extent to which important foreign and economic policy questions coming before the International Telecommunications Union and the International Atomic Energy Agency may
be producing international law.

1908. Gouldner, Alvin W., and Peterson, Richard A. Notes of Technology and the Moral Order. Indianapolis: Bobbs-Merrill, 1962, pp. 96.
   A statistical study of primitive societies which endeavors
to establish relationships between technological complexity and
the system of social control. Also of interest for its discussion of factor analysis as a means of investigating causality in
social research.

See also nos. 129, 130, 136, 138, 151, 1136, 1159-1162, 2136-2138,
2586, 2805, 2810, 2815, 2820, 2821, and sec. III, A, 2, a.

3. Claims and Demands

1909. Scott, Andrew M. "Challenge and Response: A Tool for the Analysis of International Affairs." 18 <u>Review of Politics</u> (1956), 207-226.
Advocates a challenge and response approach to the study of the balance-of-power concept rather than preoccupation with equilibrium. The author argues that (a) challenge and response is the durable element while equilibria, even if achieved, are only temporary, (b) from the prescriptive viewpoint, statesmen do not always seek an equilibrium, and (c) as a prescription, equilibrium is today irrelevant. Challenge and response is actually relevant to all systems, hence not a criterion for distinguishing the balance of power from other international systems. From the point of view of utility for international law studies, the article's emphasis suggests a bridge drawing together a theory of international relations and McDougal's emphasis upon claims and demands in international law.

See also no. 1224, and secs. IV, A, 4; VII, A, 1, 4.

4. Impact of Deviants

1910. Eban, Abba. <u>The Final Solution: Reflections on the Tragedy of European Jewry</u>. Robert Waley Cohen Lecture. London: Council of Christians and Jews, 1961.
Urges that a need exists to deny the shelter of the law to ideas, such as Nazism, fatal to social morality.

1911. Katz, E., Libby, W.L., Jr., and Strodtbeck, F.L. "Status Mobility and Reaction to Deviance and Subsequent Conformity." 27 <u>Sociometry</u> (1964), 245-260.
In an experiment with store employees, the investigators found that group members hesitate to reward the increased conformity of lower status members. The group appears to need these deviant members and roles. In addition, increased conformity threatens the rank of the higher status positions. The need for deviant members may also be a feature of international affairs more basic to the growth of a rule of law than may appear at first glance.

1912. Spitzer, Stephen T. "Consensual States and Communicative Behavior." 27 <u>Sociometry</u> (1964), 510-515.
Report of tests of two hypotheses concerning pressures to communicate with deviant group members. Support was found for the hypothesis that a low degree of imagined reference group consensus in the definition of a norm decreases the tendency to initiate communication with a deviant group member and for the hypothesis that pressures to communicate are attributable to individual cognitive states of perceived nonconsensus.

1913. Streufert, Siegfried. "Communicator Importance and Interpersonal Attitudes toward Conforming and Deviant Group Members." 2 <u>Journal of Personality and Social Psychology</u> (1965), 242-246.

This experiment deals with the effect of the importance of group members to the subjects' evaluation of the other members, importance being varied in terms of the interaction distance between subjects and conforming and deviant group members. It was found that as interaction distance was decreased, attitudes toward deviant members became increasingly unfavorable while those toward conforming members became increasingly favorable.

See also nos. 1154-1156, 1776, 1778, 1841, 1884, 1888, 2312.

5. Private Lawyers' Attitudes and Influences

1914. Carlin, Jerome E. _Lawyers on Their Own_. New Brunswick: Rutgers University Press, 1962, pp. 234.
    A study of Chicago lawyers practicing individually or in nonpartnership association with others that helps to identify some differences among lawyers that renders it difficult to make generalizations about them as a professional group. The volume is useful also in that it may help to locate the points in the legal profession at which dubious competence and dubious ethics enter into the legal process and its related social processes.

1915. Hazard, Geoffrey C., Jr. "Reflections on Four Studies of the Legal Profession." In _Law and Society_, a supplement to the Summer issue of _Social Problems_ (1965), 46-54.
    Reviewing O'Gorman, _Lawyers and Matrimonial Cases_, the author (p. 51) remarks that it is hard to believe that sociological studies of law would have proceeded in the form and direction they have taken "in the hand of someone reasonably well versed in the history and contemporary legal and social literature concerning divorce and divorce procedure. More generally, sociologists' discussions of law and legal processes sometimes sound as though they were born yesterday. What, for example, is to be inferred about one who makes the carefully measured statement that 'it is unlikely that many people can experience the dissolution of their marriages without some sense of personal disorganization'? A less easily recognizable form of the same naïvety is a sophomoric worldliness that seeks to explain highly complicated interest-value problems in terms of some simple conceptual models."

1916. "Lawyers in Developing Societies with Particular Reference to India." 3 _Law and Society Review_ (1968-1969). Entire issue, pp. 191-468.
    Papers on lawyers and judges in India, together with abstracts on the role of lawyers in Egypt, types and roles in the Japanese legal profession, and the impact of tradition upon Chinese Communist criminal procedure. A bibliography of 167 items relevant to the study of Indian lawyers is included.

1917. O'Gorman, Hubert J. _Lawyers and Matrimonial Cases_. New York: Free Press, 1963, pp. xviii, 206.

A study of attitudes toward divorce practice of a sample of
New York City lawyers handling such cases. The study relies
heavily on the concepts of Merton and of Parsons. It suffers
from a misconception of what lawyers are and apparently from un-
familiarity with the legal literature concerning divorce and
divorce procedure.

1918. Smigel, Erwin O. The Wall Street Lawyer: Professional Organization Man? New York: Free Press, 1964, pp. ix, 369.
A study of Wall Street lawyers based on interviews. While
much of what is reported is useful, the full value of the study
may, perhaps, only come to the fore through comparison with lawyers located elsewhere and/or otherwise engaged. A limit upon
the value of the interview procedure, or at least a need for improved structuring of interview questions, is indicated by the
failure of the study to ascertain what Wall Street lawyers do as
professionals in respect to the private sector of the world economy. Other methods may be required in view of the incapacity of
survey research techniques to penetrate the confidence between
lawyer and client.

See also nos. 238, 1413, 1948, 2703, 2763, 2799.

6. Activities of Private Persons

1919. Marx, Daniel, Jr. International Shipping Cartels: A Study of
Industrial Self-Regulation by Shipping Conferences. Princeton: Princeton
University Press, 1953, pp. xiii, 323.
A study of private international arrangements, organizations,
and conferences in respect to shipping that deals with the matter
in terms of whether such conference procedures establish an un-
regulated monopoly control.

See also nos. 1092, 1893, 2135, 2401, 2482, 2686, 2999.

7. Impact of Systemic Change

1920. Bernstein, Basil. "Elaborated and Restricted Codes: Their Social Origins and Some Consequences." In J.J. Gumperz and D. Hymes (eds.),
"The Ethnology of Communication." 66 American Anthropologist (No. 2, Special Publication, 1966), 55-69.
An attempt to show how two general linguistic coding systems, a restricted and an elaborated system, and their variants
are elicited by the structures of social systems.

1921. Deutsch, Karl W. "The Probability of International Law." In
Deutsch and Stanley Hoffmann (eds.), The Relevance of International Law--
Essays in Honor of Leo Gross. Cambridge: Schenkman, 1968, pp. 57-84.

This discussion of international law is based upon the persistence of the nation-state and upon the power differentials of
states. International law and organization are seen as forming
the pattern of coordination when power differential and social
and political compatibility are both low and reliance on formal
rules and institutions is high. International law is regarded
as a law _of_ behavior, arising from pragmatic experience, consent,
and the leadership of the most powerful and the most respected.
It is viewed as being enforced not by authority but by the costs
of noncoordination that follow long or frequent noncompliance.
International law is not seen as a law _for_ behavior, that is a
law prescribing what ought to be done and influencing behavior
rather than codifying what is usually done. One reason given
for taking this perspective is the insufficient power differential between a would-be enforcer and potential violators--a differential seen as presently declining. A period of quasi-law
and proto-law is suggested as a likely future during which the
conditions for true law, i.e., strict law, might be established.
Two basic rules are suggested as necessary for survival to a
possible future of true law and attention is called to two tacit
agreements that seem to have come into being to limit conflict.

See also nos. 1143, 1161, 1501, 1654, 2344, and sec. III, A, 2, 3.

8. Impact of Change Within Units on International Systems of Norms

1922. Davis, Kingsley. "Social Changes Affecting International Relations." In James N. Rosenau (ed.), _International Politics and Foreign Pol-
icy_. New York: Free Press, 1961, pp. 130-140.
Review of the impact on international relations of (1) a
rise of _per capita_ income moving an economy away from subsistence, (2) the motivation of individuals to limit consumption,
(3) the need for such ideologies as nationalism and communism
in order to induce motivation, (4) population increase, (5)
threats to national unity, and (6) the slow change of underdeveloped states with enlarging aspirations. The last is seen as
creating an ever greater disparity between underdeveloped and
developed countries and a resultant irresistible political
vacuum that gives rise to satellitism that in turn could lead
to the disappearance of the nation-state into either monism or
polarization.

See also no. 1162, and sec. II, E, 7.

9. Impact of New States

1923. Andrus, J. Russell, and Mohammed, Azizali F. _The Economy of
Pakistan_. Stanford: Stanford University Press, 1958, pp. xviii, 517.

Includes chapters and sections on such problems as ports
and shipping, civil aviation and telecommunications, foreign
trade, the canal waters dispute with India, the impact of International Labor Conventions, and the refugee problem in India and
Pakistan, as well as other subjects, some related to problems of
succession, generally covered in surveys of national economies.
A generous amount of statistical material helps to present the
picture to 1955 of the economic status and international economic
relations of an underdeveloped state and to provide bridges between economic and legal matters of international concern.

1924. Andrus, J. Russell, and Mohammed, Azizali F. Trade, Finance,
and Development in Pakistan. Stanford: Stanford University Press, 1965,
pp. xii, 289.
Detailed study of the development of Pakistan in finance
and commerce that produced changes in the South Asian international subsystem by reversing several key aspects of Pakistan's
foreign trade pattern, e.g., by changing the country since 1958
from an importer to an exporter of textiles and from an exporter
to an importer of grain.

1925. Brecher, Michael. The New States of Asia: A Political Analysis. New York: Oxford, 1963, pp. xiv, 226.
An analysis of political instability in Southeast Asia that
includes a chapter reproducing the concepts of a World Politics
article and also a chapter on the new states in world politics.
The analysis of neutralism is sharp. Somewhat out of place but
useful is a chapter on "Israel and Afro-Asia." An effort is
made to explain South Asian politics by analogy with Central
Europe between the two wars, an analogy the validity of which
may be better determined by more empirically grounded comparative study but which warrants consideration as a possible route
to the understanding of new states and their impact, negative
or positive, on international law and politics.

1926. Haas, Ernst B. "Dynamic Environment and Static System: Revolutionary Regimes in the United Nations." In Morton A. Kaplan (ed.), The
Revolution in World Politics. New York: Wiley, 1962, pp. 267-309.
Analysis of the development of the United Nations as a mul-
tiphase organization, the latest phase at the time of writing
being that of increase in the number of new and revolutionary
states able to establish both a consensus on the colonial issue
and their own version of human rights. Particular concern is
with (1) the development of UN authority more than with its legitimacy, (2) changes in the environment attributable to the
United Nations system, and (3) the significance of such task
expansion as occurred after the participation of revolutionary
regimes became significant.

1927. Padelford, Norman J., and Emerson, Rupert (eds.). Africa and
World Order. New York and London: Praeger, 1963, pp. 152.
Deals with such matters as African unification movements,
the African presence at the United Nations, the Congo problem

and the African impact on the Commonwealth. A helpful 16-page
bibliography is included.

1928. Phillips, Claude S., Jr. The Development of Nigerian Foreign
Policy. Evanston: Northwestern University Press, 1964, pp. xii, 154.
Against the background of domestic political conditions,
this study traces the evolution of the foreign policy of Nigeria
from the first efforts to formulate it in 1959 in anticipation
of independence through 1962. It includes reference to issues
of consequence to the maintenance and evolution of an international rule of law. The study is based on public pronouncements
and thus is expressive of attitudes in part related to domestic
political objectives. Issues of interest to Nigerian decision-
makers and those provoking little or no interest and activity
are identified. Some material descriptive of the Nigerian foreign policy decision-making process is included.

1929. Rapisardi-Mirabelli, M. Andréa. La Guerre Italo-Turque et le
droit des gens. Reprint from Revue de droit international et de législation comparée. Brussels: Bureau de la Revue, 1913, pp. 206.
History of Italy's appropriation of Turkish Tripoli that
warrants attention as the effort to justify Italy's action reveals psychological factors akin to those affecting new states
of today but reinforced, as also for Bismarck's Reich, by the
perception of a potential for Great Power--a perception more
recently indulged by the Soviet Union and Red China.

1930. Rivkin, Arnold. The African Presence in World Affairs: National Development and Its Role in Foreign Policy. New York: Free Press,
1963, pp. xvi, 304.
A contribution to the understanding of the international
behavior of new states, important for the understanding of potential courses of development of international law. Discussion
of the nature of African neutralism follows consideration of the
operation of the complex of economic and political forces that
shape the African states' foreign policies, the feedback of international events on internal situations, and the conflicting
appeals of nationalism, Pan-Africanism, and Eurafricanism. Attention is given to the impact of African blocs on African
development.

See also nos. 189, 552, 713, 1036, 1165, 1251, 1275, 1297, 1831, 1964,
2381, 2439.

10. International Legislation

1930-A. Baehr, Peter R. The Role of a National Delegation in the
General Assembly. Occasional Paper No. 9. New York: Carnegie Endowment
for International Peace, December 1970, pp. 90.
A study of the Netherlands delegation to the General Assembly that deals with such matters as the relations between a

delegation and its Government, consultations within a delegation, the relationship of the Permanent Mission to the auxiliary nonprofessional members of a delegation, decision-making within a delegation, participation in Western group meetings at the Committee level, the subjects of regional group meetings, interregional group meetings, and decision-making in geographical consultation groups.

1931. Briggs, Herbert W. The International Law Commission. Ithaca: Cornell University Press, 1965, pp. xvi, 380.
 The first comprehensive legal and political study of the International Law Commission, including a description of the Commission's methods, procedures, and achievements. Special attention is given to the Commission's relations with the General Assembly and its Legal Committee.

1932. Friedheim, Robert Lyle. The Politics of the Sea: A Study of Law-Making by Conference. Ph.D. Dissertation. Seattle: University of Washington, 1962; Ann Arbor: University Microfilms, Inc., Order No. 62-6590, pp. 322.
 Study of the 1958 and 1960 Geneva Conferences on the Law of the Sea that seeks to ascertain the influence of the conference process on the legal subject matter being negotiated, with particular reference to parliamentary diplomacy as a negotiating technique and to the attitudes of the state-actors toward international law and toward negotiations concerning that law. A measure of quantitative analysis is employed to aid assessment of the influence of states, blocs, and individuals on the substantive results of the Conferences. The author finds that the new states made no distinction between legal and political thought and were unconcerned with doctrinal inconsistencies, that the Soviet bloc position was ambivalent in attempting simultaneously to negotiate for legal doctrines protecting its growing economic interests and to use the negotiations for political purposes, and that the West declined to think in political terms and sought doctrinal consistency. In the analysis of ten blocs shown by the data to have existed and of four artificially constructed groups representing common economic or political interests, it was found that blocs composed primarily of new states and Latin American states were relatively ineffective in efforts to display solidarity.

1933. Simon, Sheldon W. "The Asian States and the ILO: New Problems in International Consensus." 10 Journal of Conflict Resolution (1966), 21-40.
 Examines the position of the Asian states and the apparent conflicting answers of those states and the ILO Office on the question of whether there can be uniform global labor standards in a nonuniform world. The author regards the steps taken in producing paper norms as a useful step, if developed states provide means for fulfillment of the norms, on the road to creating international law on the subject.

1934. Skubiszewski, Krzysztof. "Forms of Participation of International Organizations in the Lawmaking Processes." 18 International Organization (1964), 790-805.
A review of the actions of international organizations, ranging from preparatory and subsidiary actions to enactment of regulations, in international legislative processes.

1934-A. Todd, James E. "The 'Law-Making' Behavior of States in the United Nations as a Function of Their Location within Formal World Regions." 15 International Studies Quarterly (1971), 297-315.
A study of the voting behavior of members of the Sixth Committee from 1952 through 1966, focusing on "major" issues (those with a roll-call vote) and "controversial" issues (those with 20 or more votes cast differently from the majority). The findings, based upon classifications by caliber of state and correlations between "legal behavior" and national attributes as of 1955, suggest that attention to formal world regions, as defined by shared attributes of political alliance, economic development, and political development, has considerable predictive potential when applied to the legal dimension of international behavior.

1935. Yakemtchouk, Romain. "Le droit africain du travail dans ses incidences internationales." 6 Cahiers économiques et sociaux (No. 2, 1968), 157-176.
Discusses the position of Africa in the ILO, adhesion of African states to multilateral agreements on the right to work, international repercussions of the freedom to form trade unions, and the condition of foreign workers in Africa, and of African workers outside that continent, especially in France.

See also nos. 715, 2586, 2811.

11. Codification

1936. Castañeda, Jorge. "The Underdeveloped Nations and the Development of International Law." 15 International Organization (1961), 38-48.
Examination of the possibilities and the limitations of purely declarative codes of customary rules adopted by the United Nations General Assembly and their use as a means of discharging the various organs' responsibilities. A discussion of the method of creating international law, whom the law favors, and who has an interest in the modification of the law is set in terms of the interests of the underdeveloped countries and the permanent interests of the various small non-European countries. The final conclusions deal with the contribution of the General Assembly and its quasi-legislative functions.

See also nos. 1931, 2100.

12. Diplomatic Protest

1937. McKenna, Joseph C., S.J. Diplomatic Protest in Foreign Policy: Analysis and Case Studies. Chicago: Loyola University Press, 1962, pp. xiii, 222.
Selection of cases of protest by the United States in various situations and involving both large and small nations in differing sets of circumstances. Analysis of the cases includes an effort to evaluate the effectiveness of protest essentially in political terms.

1938. Pfluger, Franz. Die einseitigen Rechtsgeschäfte im Völkerrecht. Zürich: Schulthess, 1936, pp. 347.
A study of the role of diplomatic protest in relation to international law.

13. Judicial Lawmaking

1939. Budner, Stanley. "Intolerance of Ambiguity as a Personality Variable." 30 Journal of Personality (1960), 29-50.
Includes a distinction of three types of situational ambiguities that could be usefully applied to the "agreement in principle," to problems of judicial lawmaking and interpretation, and to the decision ex aequae et bono.

1940. Jarvad, Ib Martin. Power versus Equality: An Attempt at a Systematic Analysis of the Role and Function of the International Court of Justice, 1945 to 1966. Paper presented at the Second General Conference of the International Peace Research Association (IPRA). Rev. version. Mimeo. Copenhagen: Institute for Peace and Conflict Research, 1967, pp. i, 15, 15.
A preliminary report on an analysis of the international system as it functions within the framework of the ICJ, this paper finds that the function of the Court has been primarily a norm-creating function rather than settlement of disputes by resort to established norms. A general rank model is employed to analyze background variables on the nations and on the judges' home states. Testing a set of hypotheses against standardized data on the 38 cases submitted to the Court in the period under consideration, it was found that, among other things, involvement in violent international conflict and in cases before the ICJ are positively correlated with rank along a power dimension. Some light is also cast upon the relations between differing perceptions of the role of the ICJ and differing behaviors of disputing parties and of the Court itself in respect to references to different classes of sources of law and different types of argumentation.

1941. Shapiro, Martin. Law and Politics in the Supreme Court: New Approaches to Political Jurisprudence. New York: Free Press, 1964, pp. xi, 364.

Attention is concentrated on the evaluation of political considerations in the Supreme Court's decision process, with attention to the ways in which the court acts as political scientist, economist, and labor and tax lawyer.

See also nos. 130, 168, 238, 715, 1501, 1874.

C. CULTURAL FACTORS; VALUE SIMILARITIES
   AND DIFFERENCES

1. General Principles of Law and Morality;
   Intercultural Norms

1942. Binder, Leonard. "Pakistan and Modern Islamic-Nationalist Theory." 11-12 Middle East Journal (1957, 1958), 382-396, 45-56.
    Dealing with the period from 1924 to Nehru's ascendancy in India, this article is concerned with the causes and consequences of the formation of Pakistan, including the unacceptability of democratically produced Indian laws. Attention is given to the legislative, legalistic, nationalistic, and partially democratic nature of Islamic political theory and to its traditionalist flavor.

1943. Bondurant, Joan. "Traditional Polity and Dynamics of Change in India." 22 Human Organization (1963), 5-10.
    Deals with Sanskrit tradition, especially with the concept of dharma defined as a culture that decomposes into rules that each man must follow--a norm of action that entails the observance of precepts aimed at upholding the given order of things.

1944. Chu, Yu-kuang. "Interplay between Language and Thought in Chinese." 22 ETC.: A Review of General Semantics (1965), 307-329.
    Reviews the relation between language structure and thought processes in Chinese and problems resulting when the Western impact required the representation of new ideas in the Chinese language and, later, the transmission of messages over such communications systems as the telegraph. Questions are raised concerning the extent of future modification of Western and Marxist ideas by Chinese linguistic peculiarities.

1945. Heaps, D. "Union Participation in Foreign Aid Programs." 9 Industrial and Labor Relations Review (1955), 100-108.
    Review of efforts of American unions to participate in the European aid programs after 1948, the reasons why American unionists were suspect in France and Italy, and the inapplicability of American "solutions" where European union objectives differed greatly from those of American unions.

1946. Nakamura, Hajime. Ways of Thinking of Eastern Peoples: India, China, Tibet, Japan. Rev. English translation edited by Philip P. Wiener. Honolulu: East-West Center Press, 1964, pp. xx, 712.

Study of differences in ways of thinking in Asia that includes a demonstration of the ways in which linguistic differences have subjected Buddhism to differences in interpretation
by the four peoples studied.

1947. Swartz, Marc J. "Negative Ethnocentrism." 5 _Journal of Conflict Resolution_ (1961), 75-81.
Provides examples of negative ethnocentrism among the Trukese, that is, of a group's use of itself as a standard and viewing another group as superior in particular traits. However,
since, in general, the Trukese do not generalize the superiority
of Americans that they may perceive in the particular, the author
concludes that the basic perception of Americans is that held by
rich Trukese who have by chance done better. He also concludes
that ethnocentrism leads to seeing other groups as having the
same values.

1948. Weyrauch, Walter O. _The Personality of Lawyers_. New Haven:
Yale University Press, 1964, pp. 316.
Results of an American lawyer's interviews of German lawyers in an effort to ascertain whether lawyers' perspectives
are similar from country to country, regardless of differences
in the written law, and to determine whether a unifying impact
on law appears in practice.

See also nos. 218, 219, 555, 556, 1960, 1965-A, 1971, 2224, 2338, 2717.

a. Cultural Symbols; Beliefs

1949. Jaeger, G., and Selznick, P. "A Normative Theory of Culture."
29 _American Sociological Review_ (1964), 653-669.
The authors desire a _rapprochement_ between the humanist and
the social science concepts of culture. Such a _rapprochement_ is
needed, not only to overcome one version of the "two-cultures"
split, but also to provide a better theoretical foundation for
the sociology of culture. It is argued that this outcome may
be achieved in a theory that stresses (a) the psychic source of
culture in the quest for person-centered meanings and authentic
experience; (b) symbolic elaboration as a major resource for,
and product of, this quest for meaning; and (c) the aesthetic
potential in symbolization as well as in consummatory experience. Thus, culture is viewed as expressive symbolism and any
social product, including language, contributes to culture insofar as it sustains symbolic experience. A proper theory of culture is normative in the sense that it permits diagnostic evaluation of both symbolism and symbolic experience. The authors'
approach might well be adapted to law as a symbol and a normative expression and related to the problem of development of an
international culture.

1950. Malinowski, Bronislaw. <u>Magic, Science and Religion and Other Essays</u>. Boston: Beacon Press, 1948, pp. xiii, 327; Anchor edn., Garden City: Doubleday, 1954, pp. 274.

Includes the long unavailable <u>Myth in Primitive Society</u> (1926) that emphasizes myth as a cultural force and as a narrative containing the germs of future literature. Among other things, the order-facilitating function of myths, the relation of myths of origin and primitive legal ideas, and the adjustment of myth and mythological principle to cases in which the foundation of myth is frequently violated receive attention. In regard to magic, Malinowski notes that it is not employed by Trobriand Islanders in situations where knowledge and skill suffice or, as in war, as a substitute for strength, courage, and agility but in efforts to master the elements of change and luck in situations of danger and uncertainty of results.

1951. Wheeler, Harvey. "The Role of the Myth Systems in American-Soviet Relations." 4 <u>Journal of Conflict Resolution</u> (1960), 179-184.

On the problem of struggle to maintain fundamental forms or myths, in this case those called "capitalism" and "communism," to keep peoples apart and make coexistence difficult even though diametric demands, stemming from change, tend to negate the original substantive purpose of one of the forms.

See also nos. 136, 575, 1178, 1498, 1499, 2404.

2. Cultural Divergence and the Genesis
    of International Norms

1952. Kotenev, A.M. <u>Shanghai: Its Mixed Court and Council.</u> Shanghai: North China Daily News and Herald, 1925, pp. xxvi, 588.

Study of one of the institutions that came into being to deal with problems arising from contacts between Chinese and Occidentals. The Shanghai court is of particular interest because the role that it played was more often that of a mediator or that type of arbitrator that is more inclined to seek compromise than to decide according to strict law.

1953. Raestad, Arnold. <u>Europe and the Atlantic World.</u> Oslo: I Kommisjon Hos H. Aschehoug and Co. (W. Nygaard), 1958, pp. 114.

Posthumous publication of a manuscript completed in August 1942 by the wartime counselor of the Norwegian Government-in-Exile. The most important part of the book is Chapter II which is an attempt to define the meaning and role of culture in international political life. Western civilization is sharply distinguished from culture. The former is regarded as a technical and methodological apparatus, organized by the Greeks and today finding its highest expression in mathematical representation of the universe, the canons of modern harmonized music, the general theory and technique of the figurative arts, the principles of law, and the common elements of universal religions.

Culture is defined as the stage "in which the world or a nation finds itself in the process of drawing values from the use and application of such technical and methodological means and central irreductible ideas as civilisation puts at our disposal." The criterion of an advanced culture is the degree of its eclecticism. In promotion of this end, cultural cooperation should first be sought between closely linked groups of national cultures. It may be suggested that attention to Raestad's criterion of eclecticism, along with the problem of receptivity permitting eclecticism to develop, warrants examination in relation to the development of international law, with some attention given to his incomplete effort to put forth his ideas concerning international law in his posthumously published La philosophie du droit international public (Oslo, 1949).

1954. Zürcher, E. "Dialogue of Misunderstandings." 7 Higher Education and Research in the Netherlands (No. 2, 1963), 17-25.
    On gross misperceptions of China by the West in the 17th and 19th centuries and the dangers of continuing misperceptions as one tries to judge how much of the traditional survives and permeates the changes brought by Marxism.

See also nos. 176, 1127, 1157, 1185, 1187, 1965-A, 2460.

3. Chemical and Bacteriological Weapons
   and Value Conflicts

1954-A. "Benefits of CBR Research." 24 Army Digest (August 1969), 6-13.
    A review of health, economic, and social benefits said to result from research in chemical and biological warfare, including antidotes for heavy metal poisoning, the use of mustard gas to treat cancer and certain types of nerve gas to relieve glaucoma, fire-extinguishing chemicals, and improved methods for detecting minute quantities of cyanide in industry.

1955. Brown, Frederic J. Chemical Warfare: A Study in Restraints. Princeton: Princeton University Press, 1968, pp. xix, 355.
    Examines the political, military, economic, and psychological restraints operative between 1915 and 1945 in an effort to ascertain why chemical weapons were not used during World War II and what implications may be drawn about the future of the Cold War.

1955-A. Cookson, J., and Nottingham, J. A Survey of Chemical and Biological Warfare. London: Sheed and Ward, 1969, pp. xii, 272.
    A comprehensive collection and critical analysis of available evidence on possible uses and effects of chemical and biological weapons.

1956. Fuller, J.W. "The Application of International Law to Chemical and Biological Warfare." 10 Orbis (1966), 247-273.

On the ground that relevant treaties and declarations do not present a clearcut prohibition of the use of chemical and biological weapons, the author argues that lethal, toxic chemical weapons should be absolutely condemned but that nontoxic types, ideal for an international peacekeeping force, should be allowed. The author regards it as irrational to prohibit nontoxic chemical weapons while permitting the use of more horrible devices.

1957. Krickus, Richard J. "On the Morality of Chemical Biological Warfare." 9 Journal of Conflict Resolution (1965), 200-210.

Suggests that the "chemical/biological taboo" may be preventing discussion and research on control of these types of weapons even though an agreement concerning them would not be destabilizing. The alleged immorality of such weapons is said to arise in part from the just war theory in that they have no use in counterforce warfare.

1958. Larson, Carl A. "Biological Warfare: Model 1967." 46 Military Review (1966), 31-39.

Discusses such directions of biological warfare research as isolation of infectious microbes, modification of toxic agents to counter existing defenses, production of artificial mutations, transfer of genetic information from another strain by union of two bacteria, transformation of the DNA molecule from one microbe for recombination with the DNA of another, and the use of cryptanalysis to examine DNA and ribonucleic acid structures to devise methods for artificial production.

1958-A. Meselson, Matthew S. "Chemical and Biological Weapons." 222 Scientific American (May 1970), 15-25.

A Harvard biologist's discussion of chemical and biological weapons in the light of President Nixon's November 25, 1969, announcement that the United States will not be the first to resort to lethal or incapacitating chemical weapons, that under no circumstances would the United States use biological weapons, and that the 1925 Geneva Protocol would be submitted to the Senate. Among other things, attention is given to harassing agents and defoliants used in Southeast Asia.

1959. Miller, Walter L. "Chemicals vs. Guerrillas." 48 Marine Corps Gazette (July 1964), 37-39.

An argument for the use of chemical agents, particularly nonlethal agents, to be employed along with close infantry support to restrict the movement of guerrilla forces and to gain control of large areas without subjecting the local peoples to permanent injury. The author also states his argument in 49 Ordnance (November-December 1964), 298-299.

1960. Oldendorf, W.H. "On the Acceptability of a Device as a Weapon." 18 Bulletin of Atomic Scientists (January 1962), 35-37.

Only weapons which are extensions of the fang and the claw are acceptable. Such weapons bludgeon, cut, penetrate, and dismember. Weapons which act not violently but quietly like toxins are not acceptable in war. Explosion, fire, and possibly nuclear heat and blast seem to be more acceptable than fallout and it may be that "clean" bombs will make nuclear war psychologically more likely. The article is thus suggestive as to the type of study of values as applied to weapons, which may parallel values concerning proper and improper (e.g., espionage) ways of fighting, that may help to provide depth to studies of efforts to outlaw weapons and weapons tests and to generate stronger demands for disarmament than in days of more primitive and perhaps conceptually more manly confrontation.

1960-A. Perazić, Gavro. "Impermissibility of the Use of Chemical and Bacteriological Weapons." 20 Review of International Affairs (Belgrade) (October 20, 1969), 28-29.
A Yugoslav view of the desirability of a convention prohibiting biological means of warfare, with some consideration of existing treaty prohibitions on chemical warfare.

1961. Rose, Steven, and Pavett, David (eds.). CBW--Chemical and Biological Warfare: A Conference, London, 1968. Boston: Beacon, 1969, pp. 214.
Papers on developments in research on instruments of chemical and biological warfare and problems that lie in their potential utilization.

1962. Rosebury, Theodore. "Some Historical Considerations." 16 Bulletin of Atomic Scientists (June 1960), 227-236.
Discussion of the development and alleged use of bacteriological warfare since 1915, noting that no accusation of employment of bacteriological warfare has been fully authenticated. Reference is made to the allegations that the United States employed bacteriological warfare during the Korean War and to the efforts of the International Scientific Commission to prove the allegations. About half the article deals with efforts to prohibit or condemn bacteriological warfare, and an appendix of declarations since 1947 is included.

1963. Thimann, Kenneth W. "The Role of Biologists in Warfare." 3 Bulletin of Atomic Scientists (August 1947), 11-12.
On the role of biologists during World War II, with less stress on defensive than on offensive warfare tasks, the latter being divided into attack on man and attack on food. An outline is given of the strategy of adopting pathogenic bacteria for military uses with attention to the usable types of bacteria, defensive measures available, variations available to hinder recognition of an attack, and the destructive power of various toxins. Difficulties inherent in inspection of biological research are noted.

See also no. 2247.

4. Intercultural Law, Relations, and Adjustments

1964. Agrawal, Kedar Nath. "The Indian Judiciary and Public International Law." 25 Indian Journal of Political Science (1964), 292-300.
Reviews cases decided by the Indian judiciary that show its preference for statutory law over customary international law. Similar preferences having been displayed by a number of Western courts, questions arise concerning the extent to which the preference stems from lack of knowledge, from socialization in respect to the extent of judicial authority, or from a sentimental judicial attachment to national law as a symbol comparable to the layman's attachment to the national flag.

1965. Banno, Masataka. China and the West, 1858-1961: The Origins of the Tsungli Yamen. Cambridge: Harvard University Press, 1964, pp. x, 367, xlv.
Employing both published and unpublished documentary sources of the British, French, American, and Imperial Chinese governments, the volume helps to explain the behavior of most Chinese officials and literati toward foreigners in the first decades of contact with the West that were to provide China with a role in the family of nations but also a long struggle for full membership, respect, and participation. Thus, it helps to make clear some of the problems of culture contact and of the establishment of working relations facilitating the growth of effective norms having international status.

1965-A. Bozeman, Adda B. The Future of Law in a Multicultural World. Princeton: Princeton University Press, 1971, pp. xvii, 229.
An excellent study of the differences between Western rationalism and modes of thought in China, the Middle East, India and Indianized Asia, and Africa South of the Sahara, that gives attention to the process of reception of foreign ideas and their conversion from their original meanings. The book questions the optimism of the "rule of law" concept that assumes that Western concepts of constitutionalism and international law are readily transplantable to other cultures and that attempts to transplant do not undermine the basic concepts even in their culture of origin.

1966. Callis, Helmut G. "The Sociology of International Relations." 12 American Sociological Review (1947), 323-334.
The author states that the study of nations in their cultural context seems to constitute a profounder and more systematic approach to the problem of international relations and adjustment than any other so far attempted. The sociology of international relations is defined as the study of institutional structure characteristic of contemporary nations, with special regard to their problems of mutual assimilation and adjustment and to possibilities of their integration into socio-cultural regions and the international society as a whole. Suggestions are made for a three-step plan of research: (1) examination of

the ideology and social structure of individual nations; (2)
comparative study of nations in the context and as subspecies
of their respective culture areas; (3) comparative study of
world culture regions and of the problem of their integration
and mutual accommodation.

1967. Corpuz, O.D. "The Cultural Foundations of Filipino Politics."
4 Philippine Journal of Public Administration (1960), 297-310.
    Example of a nationalistic view of politics that employs as
whipping boy the position that Filipino political and social institutions are essentially adulterated foreign imports and not
manifestations of Filipino culture. Conceding the influence of
culture contacts with Hindu, Moslem, Spaniard, and American, particularly the last two, the author then identifies three other
determinants of the Filipino political system: (1) the structure
of Filipino society; (2) Filipino social psychology; (3) economic
conditions. His analysis of the interplay of the four factors
leads to the conclusion that Filipino politics reflect both the
national past and contemporary circumstances that can be compared
with but not judged by alien systems and standards.

1968. Fisher, Charles A. Southeast Asia: A Social, Economic and Political Geography. London: Methuen, 1964, pp. xix, 831.
    Excellent examination of Southeast Asia and the conflict of
cultures, particularly the India-based culture of Cambodia and
the China-based culture of Vietnam, that relates such clashes to
economic, geographical, and political factors affecting the international politics of the region.

1969. French, J.R.P., Jr., and Zajonc, R.B. "An Experimental Study
of Cross-Cultural Norm Conflict." 54 Journal of Abnormal and Social Psychology (1957), 218-224.
    Report of an experiment examining normative conflict in 44
Indian students. Norms were treated as force-fields and predictions were made about the resolution of intergroup norm conflict
under two conditions. The basic hypothesis was that resolution
of intergroup norm conflict favors the norm of the group whose
situational potency is increased. However, although all results
presented a consistent pattern in harmony with the theoretical
formulation, the hypothesis was not regarded as definitively validated. The results were lacking in clarity, with acceptable
levels of significance being reached in only about half of the
tests made.

1970. Hall, Edward T., and Whyte, William Foote. "Intercultural Communication: A Guide to Men of Action." 19 Human Organization (1960), 5-12
    With reference chiefly but not exclusively to Latin America,
the authors discuss some of the problems of communication between
cultures, particularly with reference to the time-space aspects
of communication.

1971. Harari, Maurice. The Turco-Persian Boundary Question: A Case
Study in the Politics of Boundary-Making in the Near and Middle East. Ph.D

Dissertation. New York: Columbia University, 1958; Ann Arbor: University Microfilms, Inc., L.C. Card No. Mic. 58-3226, pp. 274.

Examination of boundary-making as affected by geographical factors, the nomadic habits of frontier tribes, conflict between European and Oriental ideas and methods, religious incompatibilities (Shi'i-Sunni), European intervention over seven decades during most of which the European Powers involved did not present a united front, and in varying conditions and degrees of intermittent pressure on Turkey--Persia being at all times subject to pressure--to arbitrate, no thought of such pressure coming to the fore prior to the Crimean War.

1972. Hunold, Albert (ed.). Europa--Besinnung und Hoffnung. Erlenbach, Zürich, and Stuttgart: Eugen Rentsch, 1957.

Collection of articles on various subjects on the history of thought, current political events, economics, and social psychology that have something of a common meeting ground in the Suez and Hungarian events of 1956. The most interesting contribution is by Helmut Schoek on "Der Masochismus des Abendlandes," dealing with the self-accusation of Europeans when they desire to develop relations with the world's colored peoples. Schoek analyzes the East-West cleavage between sympathy, "admission of guilt," and desire to help on the one hand, and, on the other, sober, nonsentimental, appraisal of the political situation and of trends and warns the West to beware of "sympathizing" journalists and intellectuals, particularly those of socialist persuasion.

1973. Mössner, Jörg Manfred. Die Völkerrechtspersönlichkeit und die Völkerrechtspraxis der Barbareskenstaaten (Algier, Tripolis, Tunis 1518-1830). Neue Kölner Rechtswissenschaftliche Abhandlungen, No. 58. Berlin: De Gruyter, 1968, pp. xxxii, 170.

A scrutiny of the treaty relationships between the Barbary States and the European powers that finds that a kind of intercultural law existed that differed in substance from intra-European law. The author goes beyond his material to make some unsupported assertions about the modern world to the effect that only the general law of treaties is applicable interculturally. Excluding such assertions, the author's work represents a fine descriptive beginning of the intercultural law once in force between the Barbary states and Europe.

1974. Mundy-Castle, Alastaire. "The Development of Nations: Some Psychological Considerations." 24 Journal of Social Issues (1968), 45-54.

Addressing itself to the problem of how technological information can best be communicated so that it will be properly absorbed, this article suggests that the acquisition of knowledge about neuro-psychological processes by which information is received and processed requires studies of sensory discrimination, perceptual-verbal and perceptual-motor responses, remembering, thinking, attitudes, values, and norms about receiving and using information. Attention is called to research that indicates the presence of important cognitive and perceptual

differences between the developed countries and some African
nations. This article is of consequence to any who are concerned with the development of international norms and procedures that would elicit positive responses from peoples of diverse cultures.

1975. Proctor, J. Harris (ed.). <u>Islam and International Relations</u>.
New York: Praeger, 1965, pp. ix, 221.
Collection of papers on the Islamic religion and its relation to politics, foreign policy, neutralism, solidarity and
conflict among Muslim countries, the appeal of Communism, and
relations with new African states.

1976. Sissons, Jack. <u>Judge of the Far North: The Memoirs of Jack
Sissons</u>. Toronto and Montreal: McClelland and Stewart, 1968.
Memoirs of a Canadian judge among Eskimos and Indians that
is particularly valuable for the attention it gives in Chapter
24 to bureaucratic misuses of law and the legislative process,
especially to infringe upon Eskimo and Indian hunting rights.
Infringement occurred by taking a bureaucratic posture favoring
equality of rights and by restricting Eskimo and Indian rights
only in the case of species declared by Order-in-Council to be
in danger of extinction, which was immediately done in respect
to caribou, muskox, and polar bear. Also valuable is Chapter 25
which calls attention to something not understood by many bureaucrats, namely, the Eskimo's lack of a Scotch-Presbyterian concept
of guilt and of being guilty, with the result that a habit exists
among the Justices of the Peace and the bureaucrats of treating
an Eskimo's admission that he had done something as an admission
of guilt.

1976-A. <u>Stimulating Intercultural Communication through Role-Playing</u>.
Technical Report 69-7. HumRRO Division No. 7. Prepared for the Office of
Research and Development, Department of the Army. Alexandria, Virginia:
George Washington University, 1969, pp. 57.
Report on the training of army advisors for work with peo-
ple of another culture. The training program entails exercises
that simulate various interpersonal interactions between indi-
viduals of different cultures.

See also nos. 186, 559, 586, 644, 1127, 1157, 1952, 1993, 2379, 2797.

5. <u>Impact of the West on Non-Western Cultures;</u>
   <u>Reception of Western Law</u>

1977. Ali, Muhammad Mohar. <u>The Bengali Reaction to Christian Mis-
sionary Activities, 1833-1857</u>. Chittagong: Mehrub Publications, 1965,
pp. xii, 243.
Valuable antidote to oversimplifications of indigenous responses to the West that takes account not only of the differing
responses of the several segments of Bengali society but also of

the complexity whereby a particular group would respond in one
way to certain stimuli and in other ways to other stimuli.

1978. Allen, George Cyril, and Donnithorne, Audrey G. Western Enterprise in Indonesia and Malaya: A Study in Economic Development. New York:
Macmillan in cooperation with the Institute of Pacific Relations, 1957, pp.
321.
    Analysis of the role of Western enterprise in the economic
development of two Southeast Asian countries.

1979. Ashby, Sir Eric. African Universities and Western Tradition.
Cambridge: Harvard University Press, 1964, pp. vi, 113.
    On the problem of the impact of the West as it takes form
in the problem of how to combine creatively African nationalism
and the British academic heritage in West Africa.

1980. Cohn, B.S. "From Indian Status to British Contract." 21 Journal of Economic History (1961), 613-628.
    In this paper the development of the legal system in India
is discussed. The British came and followed what was there but
improved it and established a legal society. At first the court
system failed because the British failed to understand or even
consider Indian customs, traditions, and their way of life.
Failure to understand the nature of Indian society, assumptions
based on British practice, mistakes, and short-term practical
considerations, rather than the unfolding of a social law, lay
behind the movement in Indian society from "Status to Contract."

1981. Davran, Bulent. "Die Rechtsstellung der Pflegekinder und die
Rezeption des Schweizerischen Zivilgesetzbuches." 3 Annales de la Faculté
de droit d'Istanbul (1954), 405-424.
    A discussion of the use of the Swiss Civil Code as one phase
of Turkey's replacement of Islamic law by Western law in order to
employ the law as a basic instrument of modernization and Westernization of the nation.

1982. Elias, T. Olawale. Government and Politics in Africa. 2nd ed.
Bombay: Asia Publishing House, 1963, pp. 288.
    A short survey by the Federal Attorney-General and Minister
of Justice of Nigeria, including a chapter on the impact of
English law on African law.

1983. Fletcher, Arnold. Afghanistan: Highway of Conquest. Ithaca:
Cornell University Press, 1965, pp. ix, 325.
    Survey of Afghan history with particular attention to such
matters as recent relations with the United States and the USSR
and influences upon Afghan internal development, especially the
influences of British India and Tsarist Russia.

1984. Galanter, Marc. "The Displacement of Traditional Law in Modern
India." 24 Journal of Social Issues (1968), 65-91.
    Deals with the transformation of Indian law through the im-
pact of British law, courts and recorded judgments, and a highly

trained legal profession and with the fact that not even national independence has revived past legal procedures.

1985. Gann, L.H., and Duignan, Peter. Burden of Empire: An Appraisa of Western Colonialism in Africa South of the Sahara. New York: Praeger for the Hoover Institution on War, Revolution and Peace, 1967, pp. 435.
  Attempts to delineate the several patterns of imperialism and to evaluate the resultant cultural diffusion, its achievements, and its ills.

1986. Hamon, L. "Les sciences administratives et la diffusion de la pensée française à l'étranger." 7 Revue administrative (1954), 243-246.
  Development of administration, international and domestic, is treated as the most distinctive mark of our times. On the international level there are two forms: international organization and aid to underdeveloped countries. Two traditions dominate the latter type, the Anglo-Saxon, preoccupied with techniques applicable to both public agencies and private enterprise, and the French, emphasizing administration properly so-called and the spirit of the civil service. A subjective view in its reflection of concern for the apparent disadvantages faced by France in the provision of personnel to influence development in overseas regions, the article has value in its focus upon administration as the agency for the extension of cultural values, including legal values.

1986-A. Hazard, John N. "Law and Social Change in Marxist Africa." 13 American Behavioral Scientist (1970), 575-584.
  On the impact of Marxism on the legal, political, and economic systems of Guinea, Mali, and Senegal, and on the persistence of various French and indigenous institutions and models. This article is part of a special issue on "Law and Social Change" edited by Stuart S. Nagel.

1987. Jäschke, Gotthard. Der Islam in der neuen Turkei. Leiden: Brill, 1951, pp. 174.
  Includes an examination of Atatürk's undertaking to secularize and modernize Turkish law and administration and to use them as instruments to produce a modern and secular society.

1988. Jaspan, M.A. "In Quest of New Law: The Perplexity of Legal Syncretism in Indonesia." 7 Comparative Studies in Society and History (1965), 252-266.
  Discussion of the influence of "Western positive" law, adat (customary) law, Islamic law, and "Indonesian socialist" law, with stress upon the problems of developing a syncretic philosophy of law in the face of a widening gap between the ideas and ideals of legal theorists and the actual needs of ordinary people for a simple, cheap, effective system of law.

1989. Léger, François. Les influences occidentales dans la révolution de l'Orient: Inde, Malaisie, Chine, 1850-1950. 2 vols. Paris: Plon, 1955.

An important study of Western influences in generating and channeling social and political change in India, Southeast Asia, and China that can be helpful in clarifying the background of attitudes and policies of recent years and is suggestive as to problems and techniques for fostering the amalgamation of procedures and values essential to the broadening of the base of intercultural law.

1990. Liebesny, Herbert J. "Legal Processes: Stability and Change --Islamic Law." Paper delivered at the Annual Meeting of the American Political Science Association. September 1964, pp. 20.
Chronological review of modernization and secularization of Islamic law, with emphasis upon law as an instrument of modernization and identification of parts of the law of the more advanced Moslem countries that remain based upon the shari'a, upon Shi'ite (Iran), or upon Malekite law (Pakistan).

1991. Luchaire, F. "L'Apport européen dans l'élaboration des droits nationaux des pays en voie de développement." 102-103 Revue administrative (1964, 1965), 565-581, 11-19.
A review of the impact of French law on African communities, resistance to that law, and the undertaking of the African states to retain in force the legislation valid at the time of independence. Attention is also given to the impact of political processes, of socialism, and of the necessity that development build upon the inherited juridical situation.

1992. Malinowski, Bronislaw. The Dynamics of Culture Change: An Inquiry into Race Relations in Africa. Paperback ed. by Phyllis M. Kaberry, 1945. New Haven: Yale University Press, 1961, pp. xvii, 171.
Deals with the impact of Europe on Africa and includes a chapter on African warfare, treated as having had its old causes removed and new ones introduced. An outline for the study of African warfare, including the place of intertribal law in war and peace, is set forth with the intention of permitting identification of forms of tradition that survive the European impact.

1993. Maunier, René. The Sociology of Colonies: An Introduction to the Study of Race Contact. Edited and translated by E.O. Lorimer, 2 vols. London: Routledge & Kegan Paul, 1949.
English translation of Sociologie coloniale (1932, 1942), the second volume of which is devoted to legal evolution in colonies. The relevance of the study to research on international law is that the product that emerged from contact and conflict between European and indigenous law is a form of intercultural law as international law is becoming now that it is no longer bound exclusively to European cultures. Account is taken of the differing techniques whereby particularly French, British, and Dutch laws were introduced into or displaced local law--a process continuing as, since independence, official law continues to displace local law. Some attention is given to mechanisms of reception and adoption, to attitudes of recognition, condescension, and intolerance, and to methods

of abrogation, confirmation, degradation, and alteration as they operated in the transformation process.

1994. Phillips, A. "The Future of Customary African Law." 7 Journal of African Administration (1955), 151-159.

On the need for an additional "reception" of European criminal and commercial law and a further restriction of the sphere of customary law if Africa is to adjust to modern conditions.

1995. Pye, Lucian W. Aspects of Political Development. Boston: Little, Brown, 1966, pp. xiii, 205.

Among other things, this book deals with law as a source of both rigidity and instability, the enduring consequences of the Westernization of legal systems, the commencement of rebellions, and the art of controlling rebels.

1996. Qadri, Anwar Ahmad. Islamic Jurisprudence in the Modern World. (A Reflection upon Comparative Study of the Law). Bombay: N.M. Tripathi, 1963, pp. xi, 366.

A study of modern Islamic law by a Lecturer at the Aligarh Muslim University in India. Chapter XV deals with the problem of social change and with the impact of the West on Islamic law. Occasional effort is made to find influences of Islamic law upon European law, e.g., the capacity to transfer a debt being held to be a shari'a principle received into the European civil law.

1997. Sarkisyanz, Emanuel. Russland und der Messianismus des Orients --Sendungsbewusstsein und politischer Chiliasmus des Ostens. Tübingen: J.C.B. Mohr, 1955, pp. xii, 419.

A study of Bolshevism that, by treating Russia as a superficially westernized state, and by comparing theocratic and messianic features of Russian thought with eastern, particularly Moslem thought, raises questions as to whether a sufficiently deep interpenetration of values can occur to provide a support for a stable world system.

1998. Schacht, Joseph. An Introduction to Islamic Law. Oxford: Clarendon, 1964, pp. viii, 304.

An excellent concise survey of Islamic law in which Chapter 14 on "Anglo-Muhammadan Law and Droit Musulman Algérien" deals briefly with differing English and French impacts, while Chapter 15 deals with the impact of modernist legislation. Three important points illustrative of differences between Western and Islamic law are brought to attention: (1) Islamic law does not recognize juristic persons, not even the public treasury; (2) the concept of the corporation does not exist; (3) the concept of responsibility is subsumed under that of legal capacity, the latter including the capacity of obligation (of acquiring rights and duties) and the capacity of execution (of contracting, disposing, and validly fulfilling obligations).

1999. Těng, Ssú-yü, and Fairbank, John King. China's Response to the West. Cambridge, Mass.: Harvard University Press, 1954, pp. vi, 296.

Employs excerpts from essays, diaries, speeches, and other sources to set forth the reactions of the Chinese scholar-official class to the impingement of the West upon their society in the period from 1839 to 1923.

2000. Von Grunebaum, Gustave Edmund. Modern Islam: The Search for Cultural Identity. Berkeley: University of California Press, 1962, pp. viii, 303.

Analysis of the Islamic community, its cohesiveness, its ability to adapt and expand, Muslim nationalism's uniqueness, the role of the university in politics in the Near East, the theme of acculturation in present Arab literature, and cultural influences. Bearing on this analysis is the author's concern with the reaction of the Islamic community to the West's direction of its development for the past hundred years.

See also nos. 586, 1126, 1129, 1624, 1835, 1965-A, 1972, 2460.

6. Imperialism, Colonialism, and Anti-Colonialism

2001. Bennett, George. Kenya: A Political History--The Colonial Period. London: Oxford, 1963, pp. v, 190.

About two-thirds of the volume deal with the actions of the British and Kenya governments and of the settlers while the remainder deals with African reactions that led to independence.

2002. Bronfenbrenner, Martin. "Burdens and Benefits of Empire: American Style." In Leland Hazard (ed.), Empire Revisited. Homewood, Illinois: Irwin, 1965, pp. 45-66.

One of a series of lectures that formed part of an executive development program at Carnegie Tech in the spring of 1964, the lecture deals primarily with American aid and alternatives thereto, with brief reference in its last section to the Korean student riots against the "normalization" treaty with Japan. Perhaps the most useful part of the article is its first section which sets forth four economic and four political-military criteria of neo-imperialism and one criterion covering both categories. A brief attempt is made to identify neo-colonialism, followed by a use of the Berle-Means thesis about the separation of ownership and control of corporations to neo-imperialism and neo-colonialism in the absence of exercise of sovereignty (ownership) in the traditional colonial style.

2003. Charles, Raymond. L'Étoile rouge contre le croissant. Paris: Calmann-Lévy, 1962, pp. 243.

Account of an assimilation policy, in this case assimilation of Soviet Moslems, which might warrant comparison with the French effort at certain periods to apply an assimilation policy to their overseas territories.

2004. Chilcote, Ronald H. Portuguese Africa. Englewood Cliffs: Prentice-Hall, 1967, pp. x, 149.
Survey of Portuguese colonialism in Angola, Mozambique, Guinea, the Capte Verde Island, São Tome, and Principe.

2005. Doob, Leonard W. "Introduction to the Psychology of Acculturation." 45 Journal of Social Psychology (1957), 143-160.
A report on a pilot study in Africa that found that persons having greater contact with Europeans showed greater antagonisms toward both traditional authorities and Europeans, deviated from traditional beliefs and practices concerning the family, were frustrated and aggressive, possessed readily verbalized opinions on controversial issues, and displayed greater sensitivity toward other human beings.

2006. Hayit, Baymirza. Turkestan im XX. Jahrhundert. Darmstadt: Leske, 1956, pp. 406.
Comprehensive history of Uzbekistan, Turkmenistan, Kirgizia, and Tajikistan in the present century that provides one of the best pictures of the area to be found in a Western language. The author has used a great number of Russian and Turkic sources.

2007. Kahin, George McTurnan. Nationalism and Revolution in Indonesia. Ithaca: Cornell University Press, 1952, pp. xii, 490.
Coherent, well-documented study of independence movements and Dutch reactions.

2008. Lijphart, Arend. The Trauma of Decolonization: The Dutch and West New Guinea. New Haven: Yale University Press, 1966, pp. xi, 303.
A synthesis of a great deal of material to describe and interpret the events and pressures leading to withdrawal of the Netherlands from West New Guinea.

2009. Matossian, Mary Allerton Kilbourne. The Impact of Soviet Policies in Armenia. Leiden: Brill, 1962, pp. x, 239.
Account of Soviet methods to secure control over Armenians.

2010. Myint, H. "The Gains from International Trade and the Backward Countries." 22 Review of Economic Studies (1954-55), 129-142.
The existing theory of the distribution of the gains from international trade is examined in relation to the process by which some of the backward countries were opened up to international trade and foreign investment. The broad features of the process are also examined in terms of their effect on the internal terms of cooperation between the "domestic" factors and "foreign" factors of production of these countries. Finally, the "indirect" or "dynamic" gains of international trade are examined and here it is seen that the backward countries got the larger share of these gains in the form of secondary rounds of economic activity and a general stimulus to economic growth.

2011. Neres, Philip. French-Speaking West Africa. London and New York: Oxford for the London Institute of Race Relations, 1962, pp. 101.

A short narrative account of the rejection of colonialism
in former French West Africa, chiefly in regard to relations of
the former territories with France and with each other, and with
some attention to the backgrounds of the political elite.

2012. Panikkar, Kavalam Madhava. Asia and Western Dominance. New
York: John Day, 1954, pp. 530.

Perhaps the most important feature of this view of the
"Vasco da Gama epoch" recently ended is the author's perspective
on the First World War as the "European Civil War," thereby making a point of some consequence in the evolution of international
law in that one basic feature has been the split in its social
foundation with the shattering of the 19th century system and ineffective reconstruction and innovation in the interwar years.

2013. Pelissier, R. "Spain's Discreet Decolonization." 43 Foreign
Affairs (1965), 519-527.

Disclaiming any parallel between Madrid and Lisbon in respect to colonial policy, the article indicates the objectives
of policies toward Spanish colonies. The author expects that
the Spanish Sahara will probably see a transfer of Spanish power
to one or more neighboring countries, notes that assimilation
efforts in Guinea were not successful, and hopes that, despite
the autonomy voted in 1963 as a step toward independence, a His-
pano-Guinean state can be created that will represent Spanish
culture in black Africa.

2014. Pierce, Richard A. Russian Central Asia, 1867-1917: A Study
in Colonial Rule. Berkeley: University of California Press, 1960, pp.
viii, 359.

Scholarly account of imperialism and colonization in contiguous territory that is a reminder that 19th century imperialism was not limited to overseas ventures. Moreover, it raises
the question, as do similar policies of other countries, as to
the precise nature of the value distinction between overseas and
contiguous imperialism and colonization and, in light of the
rise of the demand for self-determination by inhabitants of territories acquired by adjacent alien authorities, of the value
distinction concerning the propriety of contiguous empire.

2015. Plamenatz, John Petrov. On Alien Rule and Self-Government.
New York: Longmans, 1960, pp. 224.

An attempt to clarify some of the confusion in arguments
about "self-government" and "alien rule" that, although primarily in the context of European rule over non-Europeans, can be
of assistance in efforts to develop generalized concepts of
imperialism.

2016. Thornton, A.P. Doctrines of Imperialism. New York: Wiley,
1965, pp. ix, 246.

Treats imperialism as an integral facet of history and international affairs that is animated by emotional overtones. An
attempt is made to identify common factors in contrasting eras
and places.

2017. Vardys, V.S. "The Colonial Nature of Soviet Nationality Policy." 1 <u>International Review of History and Political Science</u> (1964), 1-19
On the Soviet use of political, cultural, and economic institutions, as well as colonization by Russians, to bind the Baltic Republics to the Soviet Union.

2018. Wieschhoff, H.A. <u>Colonial Policies in Africa</u>. African Handbooks: 5. Philadelphia: University of Pennsylvania Press, The University Museum, 1944, pp. vii, 138.
Concise exposition of the land problem and other features of Africa under colonialism that makes clear the many grievances that Africans could feel against whites, particularly against settlers, and could carry over into independence.

2019. Wingenroth, Carl Gustav. <u>Das weissen Mannes Bürde: 2000 Jahre Kolonialismus</u>. Cologne: Kiepenheuer, 1961, pp. 408.
Survey of colonialism and imperialism since the days of Rome and Carthage that should aid in counteracting the narrow view of imperialism as primarily a modern phenomenon or of no older vintage than the Age of Discovery.

See also nos. 303, 644, 1624, 1993.

7. <u>Non-Western Attitudes, Feelings, Opinions, and Influences</u>

2020. Ahmed Khan, Bashir. "Development of Nationalism in South East Asia." In <u>Proceedings of the Third All Pakistan Political Science Conference, 1962</u>. Edited by Muhammad Aziz Ahmad. Karachi: International Press for the All Pakistan Political Science Association (1965), pp. 239-244.
A Pakistani's concise analysis of the differences in the nationalisms of the several countries of Southeast Asia, the presence, absence, and differing degrees of anti-foreignism including anti-Indian and anti-Chinese feelings, and the differing degrees of territorial consciousness entering the thought of the various peoples.

2021. Anchieri, Ettore. "La costruzione della communità araba e l'Occidente." 9 <u>La Communità Internazionale</u> (1954), 221-236.
A useful analysis of reasons for Arab hatred of the West, of barriers to effective and integrating agreements between Arabs and the West, and of the vulnerability of Arabs to Soviet penetration which is seen as greater on the strategic level than on the level of social revolution.

2022. Ashford, Douglas E. <u>Perspectives of a Moroccan Nationalist</u>. Totowa, N.J.: Bedminster, 1964, pp. xiii, 171.
Case study of political development through examination of the careers and perspectives of the men who liberated Morocco and played influential parts in the first years of independence. The study includes analysis of the effect on party officials of participation in violence during the revolution.

2023. Ayub Khan, Mohammad. <u>Friends Not Masters: A Political Auto-</u><u>biography</u>. New York: Oxford University Press, 1967, pp. iv, 275.
Having the unusual quality of being written while still in office, the President of Pakistan's autobiography and description of events includes an expression of Pakistani attitudes not just toward India but also toward the world in general.

2024. Banerji, J.K. <u>The Middle East in World Politics</u>. Calcutta: World Press, 1960, pp. 390.
Useful chiefly for its recording of an Indian's perspective on the international affairs and crises of the Middle East.

2025. Dutt, Vidya Prakash. <u>China and the World: An Analysis of Com-</u><u>munist China's Foreign Policy</u>. New York: Praeger, 1966, pp. x, 356.
Analysis of Communist China's foreign policy by the Head of the Department of East Asian Studies at the Indian School of International Studies, New Delhi.

2026. Elwell-Sutton, L.P. "Nationalism and Neutralism in Iran." 12 <u>Middle East Journal</u> (1958), 20-32.
On distrust of the West and of any foreign nation and feelings of national pride.

2027. Falk, Richard A. "Revolutionary Regimes and the Quality of International Legal Order." In Morton A. Kaplan (ed.), <u>The Revolution in</u> <u>World Politics</u>. New York and London: Wiley, 1962, pp. 310-331.
Examination of some aspects of the impact of revolutionary states upon international law, particularly in relation to the problem of intervention, and the equally norm-disturbing response of <u>status quo</u> nations with its contribution to instability. The essay is particularly valuable for its efforts to place cultural differences in proper perspective distinguishable from other variables generating instability and for its recognition of the effects of politicization of legal norms.

2028. Hevi, Emmanuel John. <u>The Dragon's Embrace: The Chinese Com-</u><u>munists and Africa</u>. New York: Praeger, 1966, pp. 152.
A Ghanaian, leader of the mass exodus of African students from Peking University in 1960 and subsequently a member of the faculty of Olu-Iwa College in Western Nigeria, examines Chou En-lai's promise, during his 1963-1964 tour of Africa, to maintain the principles of <u>panchsheela</u> and sees the Chinese record as one of betrayal of the five principles both in Africa and in India.

2029. Hovet, Thomas, Jr. <u>Africa in the United Nations</u>. Evanston: Northwestern University Press, 1963, pp. xii, 336.
A more narrowly focused continuation of the author's analysis of United Nations bloc politics. The 1958 Accra Conference is treated as marking the emergence of an African voice and personality in diplomacy and of an African role in the United Nations. Attention is called to the permanent body set up in New York by decision of the Accra Conference, an illustration of the

use of UN representatives for non-UN business and saving the African states the financial burden of maintaining embassies in
the several African capitals. In regard to voting data, the
author notes the association of the Soviet Union with the Africans on issues which the latter regard as in their vital interests, while in most instances of African-United States voting
opposition the United States had opposed the African position
rather than vice-versa.

2030. McKay, Vernon (ed.). African Diplomacy: Studies in the Determinants of Foreign Policy. New York: Praeger, 1966, pp. xiii, 210.
        Contributions attempting to explain why the African states
have taken an independent policy position and why some African
states have sought to promote moderation, stability, and orderly
progress while others have favored radical, revolutionary, and
racist policies.

2031. Shihata, Ibrahim F.I. "The Attitude of New States Toward the
International Court of Justice." 19 International Organization (1965), 203-
222.
        Sees the new nations at least as favorably inclined to use
of the ICJ as the older nations but declining to use the Court
for different reasons, particularly revolutionary or military
governments' lack of orientation toward judicial action. The
author also suggests that disproportionate influence in the General Assembly may make political settlement appear to be more
favorable than legal settlement. The author feels that, in the
long run, court action should be favored as aiding new states
to enhance their reputations for meeting obligations and as permitting compliance to law that is less embarrassing politically
than compliance with a solution imposed by outside pressure.

2032. Singh, A.K.P., and Upahyaya, O.P. "Eleven Ethnic Groups on a
Social Distance Scale." 57 Journal of Social Psychology (1962), 49-54.
        Test of social preferences of 500 Indian university students
employing a modified Bogardus scale to score responses. Decreas-
ingly favorable attitudes toward marriage were indicated toward
Indians, French, Americans, and English. Antipathy was greatest
toward Chinese, decreased toward Pakistanis and Negroes, and was
considerably less toward Americans, English, and Russians.

See also nos. 647, 1081, 1258, 1290, 1297, 1357, 1358, 1360, 1366, 1402,
1932, 1936, 1943, 1944, 1946, 2460, 2717, 2753.

8. Communist Impact on International Law

2033. Jacobson, Harold Karan. The USSR and the UN's Economic and Social Activities. Notre Dame: University of Notre Dame Press, 1963, pp.
xviii, 309.
        Useful study of a mix of politics, economics, and ideology,
with repercussions upon the process of negotiation of international

economic and social agreements. The study deals also with the
impact of conservatism in international affairs, including Soviet
support of conservative legal principles, upon economic and social attitudes in respect to such matters of international concern as control of narcotics.

2034. Nordenstam, Gunnar. "Destalinization in Soviet Political Science." 7 Acta Sociologica (Scandinavian Review of Sociology) (1964), 131-
150.
Analysis of changes in the nature and content of articles
in Soviet State and Law since 1953 and quantitative tests of
frequency of use of sources. Relating of changes to political
and official ideological changes aids in tracing the course of
Soviet jurisprudence, including doctrine concerning international law, since 1953.

2035. Pachter, Henry M. "The Meaning of Peaceful Coexistence." 9-10
Problems of Communism (1961), 1-8.
Treats peaceful coexistence as a form of conflict which, in
the eyes of the Kremlin, includes violence in the form of "wars
of liberation."

2036. Welch, William. "The Sources of Soviet Conduct: A Note on
Method." 6 Background (1963), 17-27.
In view of inconsistency in data on whether Soviet conduct
is primarily nationalist or Communist and in view of defects in
methods employed to reconcile the inconsistencies, the author
attempts to develop his own method for reconciliation by defining problems and actions and looking at Soviet history. His
method leads him to conclude that Soviet conduct is more nationalist than communist.

See also nos. 503, 855, 965, 1865, 1866, 2027, 2265, 2366.

VI.   INTERNATIONAL PROCEDURES AND AGENTS

A. NONVIOLENT PROCEDURES

1. Law, Politics, and Diplomacy

2037. Henkin, Louis. How Nations Behave: Law and Foreign Policy.
New York: Praeger for the Council on Foreign Relations, 1968, pp. xii, 317.
Impressionistic attempt to bridge the conceptual gap between the champions and detractors of international law by
tracing the response of the law to scientific and technological
developments, the Cold War, the multiplication of new states,
the transformation of old states, and the influence of the
United Nations. Four cases are employed to examine both the
short run and the long-range influence of international law

upon diplomacy and of diplomacy on international law (Suez Canal nationalization, the 1956 attack on Sinai and Suez, the Eichmann abduction, and the Cuban missile crisis). The basic argument is that legal and political analyses of international affairs are complementary, mutually dependent, and mutually supporting.

2038. Hoyt, Edwin C. National Policy and International Law: Case Studies from American Canal Policy. Monograph Series in World Affairs. Vol. 4, No. 1, 1966-1967. The Social Science Foundation and Graduate School of International Studies, University of Denver, 1966, pp. 80.

Historical review of the Clayton-Bulwer Treaty issue (1850-1901), treaty relations with Colombia and Panama (1902-1964), and the Panama Tolls controversy (1912-1914) in an effort to ascertain ways in which international law affects national policy-making.

2039. Kahng, Tae Jin. Law, Politics and the Security Council. The Hague: Nijhoff, 1964, pp. xiv, 252.

Deals with the ways in which the Security Council handles legal questions related to international disputes and situations coming before it.

2040. Kozolchyk, B. Law and the Credit Structure in Latin America. RM-4918-RC. Santa Monica: RAND Corporation, March 1966, pp. 102.

Analysis of how law and legal institutions affect business behavior and economic development in Latin America, particularly important because its undertaking to establish general relationships between legal and quasi-legal institutions and credit or financing operations involving hard or durable goods is something of an antidote to the one-way relationships propounded by some students of international and domestic politics who treat law as a response to but not as a producer of social relations. In the Latin American credit structure example, a number of problems are traceable to statutory formulations and to the processes and attitudes affecting enactment, implementation, application, enforcement, and obedience.

2041. Ronning, C. Neale. Law and Politics in Inter-American Diplomacy. New York: Wiley, 1963, pp. 167.

A study of inter-American diplomacy that takes excellent account of the blend of law and politics and of the consequences of particular blends in regard to such questions as recognition of governments, treatment of aliens, intervention, the breadth of the territorial sea, European colonies, Antarctic claims, the Panama Canal, and expropriation. Attention is also accorded to sociological factors and the activities of private groups and their influence on policy, e.g., the oil companies and the disagreement between the Departments of State and Interior on the value of expropriated oil properties in Mexico.

2042. Scheinman, Lawrence, and Wilkinson, David (eds.). International Law and Political Crisis: An Analytic Casebook. Boston: Little, Brown, 1968, pp. xix, 273.

Seven case studies attempting to assess the role of international law in crisis decision processes. The case studies are based upon a minimum of data--much data not being available--and so include a great deal of conjecture concerning what decision-makers may have been thinking, as well as prejudgment of the role of international law that tends to downgrade that role by requiring an effectiveness that domestic law does not attain. With the exception of the case studies by Richard A. Falk and that by Wolfgang Friedmann and Lawrence A. Collins, the cases set up expectations of what international law should do that betray lack of understanding of legal history and of the role of law in societies in process of change. Despite these defects, this casebook should be seen as a pioneering attempt to assess the role of international law in governmental decision-making and should suggest possibilities for further attempts based upon cases for which more complete information is obtainable.

2043. Schmitt, David R. "The Invocation of Moral Obligation." 27 Sociometry (1964), 299-310.
The study investigates the conditions under which moral obligation will be used as a persuasive technique. Hypotheses were tested using the subjects' statements of another's response to a number of hypothetical situations. A moral appeal was most frequently used when a person perceived another to be unwilling, able, and the only one who could provide his wants. With greater power, the person tended to prefer a threat of force to a moral appeal only after the appeal had proved ineffective. The results demonstrate the importance of morals not only as guidelines for behavior but also as statements which serve as a means of social control.

See also nos. 1051, 1062, 1121, 1222, 1510, 1797, 1932, 2079, 2081.

2. Diplomatic Institutions

2044. Barnett, Vincent M., Jr. "Changing Problems of U.S. Representation Abroad." 17 Public Administration Review (1957), 20-31.
The author contends that in the 1950s the functioning and machinery of our overseas representation were not adequate to the tasks involved in execution of American foreign policy. He notes a number of changes in the magnitude and character of US overseas activities. Every phase of a country's political and economic life, as well as its military, commercial, scientific, technical, and cultural activities, are to be taken into account in the organization and concept of the Foreign Service. Particular attention is given to the position of leadership assumed by the US since World War II that fundamentally changed the role of economic representatives overseas. Problems of staffing delegations with persons having the necessary skills and experiences are discussed.

2045. Cadieux, Marcel. Le Diplomate canadien: Éléments d'une défini tion. Montreal: Bibliothèque Économique et Sociale, Éditions Fides, 1962, pp. 125.

Provides insights into the Canadian diplomatic system, the author being a civil servant who has exercised functions comparable to those of the Legal Adviser in the United States. His Premières armes (Montreal, Le Cercle du Livre de France, 1961) is also of use for Canadian foreign policy studies.

2046. Cardozo, Michael H. Diplomats in International Cooperation: Stepchildren of the Foreign Service. Ithaca: Cornell University Press, 1962, pp. 142.

Examines the problem of agents performing functions other than those of traditional diplomacy but inescapably a part of the diplomatic scene. A plea is made for adequate recognition of the new types of personnel as an integral part of an increasingly unified international community.

2047. Cardozo, Michael H. "Immunities, Protocol and the Public." 17 Journal of International Affairs (1963), 61-69.

This article deals with the concepts of diplomatic immunities, protocol, and the ranking of State Department officials and shows the need for and the uses of protocol and diplomatic ranking.

2048. Cordier, Andrew W. "Diplomacy To-day." 17 Journal of International Affairs (1963), 1-8.

Explores the successful and the not-so-successful ways of carrying on diplomatic relations in today's different situations. The author investigates the uses of bilateral diplomacy, multilateral diplomacy, summit conferences, and parliamentary diplomacy and compares them with the older diplomatic processes.

2049. "Diplomacy in Transition." 17 Journal of International Affairs (1963). Entire issue, pp. 92.

Among the topics considered in this symposium are: diplomacy today; the Golden Age in perspective; the decline of classical diplomacy; United Nations diplomacy; dialectics and duplicity in Soviet diplomacy; diplomatic immunities, protocol and the public. Some of the articles are separately annotated.

2050. Fiszman, Joseph R. "The Development of Administrative Roles: The Labor Attaché of the U.S. Foreign Service." 25 Public Administration Review (1965), 203-212.

Discusses a relatively little known undertaking, the labor attaché program designed both to influence foreign labor publics and to make the aspirations of international labor known to US policy makers, and the status of that program as caught between conflicting organizational demands and conflicting attitudes of the Administration toward labor in general. Although the focus is not essentially upon international interactions, the article does call attention to an essentially postwar penetration of the field operations of diplomatic missions.

2051. Forbes, William H. "The Role of Science Attachés." 19 <u>Bulletin of Atomic Scientists</u> (October 1957), 274-276.
On the tasks of science attachés, including giving advice on the scientific aspects of political problems and reporting information about science as it affects foreign policy.

2052. Forgac, Albert A. <u>Essai sur la diplomatie nouvelle</u>. 2nd ed. Paris: Pedone, 1952.
Review of changes in diplomatic methods since the world wars that raises questions concerning the increasing passivity of diplomats, their potential loss of role, and the impact upon disputes of democratization with its tendency to air extreme views, thereby tending to undermine the composure, the continuity, and, above all, the moderation which is the climate of diplomacy.

2053. Fraga Iribarne, M. "La diplomacia en el sistema actual de las relaciones internacionales." 52 <u>Política internacional</u> (1960), 9-33.
An impressionistic and speculative article suggesting that the decline of traditional diplomacy is an accompaniment of (1) the decline in the importance of the state, (2) the increased importance of economic and ideological groups, (3) the greater influence of legislatures, the press, and public opinion, and (4) resort to conferences of heads of state. Restricted as the article is, particularly in not taking full account of the growth of international organizational channels for diplomacy, the article at least suggests some possibilities for research into the channels for international interaction and the groups actively using them and, in the process, producing an evolution toward an international system quite different from that based on traditional diplomatic activity.

2054. Gerbore, Pietro. <u>Il vero diplomatico</u>. Milan: Longanesi, 1956, pp. 424.
Guide to the diplomatic art written by an Italian diplomat.

2055. Kaznacheev, Aleksandr Iur'evich. <u>Inside a Soviet Embassy</u>. Philadelphia: Lippincott, 1962, pp. 250.
Story of training and diplomatic career of a young Soviet official who defected from the Embassy in Rangoon in 1959. The story sheds some light upon the espionage facets of Soviet embassy work as well as upon other facets of contemporary diplomatic activities.

2056. Mattingly, Garrett. <u>Renaissance Diplomacy</u>. London: Cape; Boston: Houghton Mifflin, 1955, pp. 323; Baltimore: Penguin, 1964, pp. 284.
Concentrating upon the uses of embassies and the duties of diplomatic agents, this descriptive-historical study emphasizes identifiable lines of development of diplomatic institutions in the Italian state system and in its spread to Transalpine Europe. Particularly valuable are the first four chapters on diplomatic institutions and law prior to the establishment of permanent embassies and chapters V-IX on the emergence of permanent embassies

as a tactic for coordinating the actions of allies and later for
securing and maintaining alliances in the precarious Italian
balance-of-power system. The study is based upon materials in
various Italian archives as well as numerous monographs, particularly M.A.R. Maulde-la-Clavière's three-volume La diplomatie au
temps de Machiavel (Paris, 1892-1893). For the institutions and
law of the period before permanent embassies, particular attention is given to Bernard du Rosier's treatise on ambassadors of
1436. The notes form an excellent guide to the literature for
and about the period.

2057. Mejan, F. "Le rôle des nonces apostoliques." 7 Revue administrative (1954), 14-33.
　　　The intervention of Monseigneur Marsella in the matter of
the French worker-priests gave rise to a controversy as to the
role of papal nuncios. Although the canon law, like international law, restricts their tasks to those of an ambassador,
after Liberation the successive governments tolerated involvement of papal nuncios in purely internal French affairs and
their becoming progressively the real heads of the Church in
France.

2058. Merillat, H.C.L. (ed.). Legal Advisers and International Organizations. Dobbs Ferry: Oceana for the American Society of International
Law, 1966, pp. xviii, 124.
　　　A report of the proceedings of a conference at Bellagio in
August 1965 that dealt with such topics as the structure and
role of legal services at international organizations, the capacity and personality of international organizations, the
formation of consensus, compliance with decisions of international organizations (methods of assuring compliance, sanctions),
and the structures and procedures of legal services in 10 international organizations.

2059. Numelin, Ragnar. The Beginnings of Diplomacy. London:　Oxford,
1950, pp. 372.
　　　Discusses correspondence between international and primitive diplomatic practice, but suffers from lack of an explicit
methodology or a theoretical framework.

2060. Pederson, Richard F. "National Representation in the United Nations." 15 International Organization (1961), 256-266.
　　　Deals primarily with the tasks of United Nations missions
and delegations, in addition to the traditional diplomatic mission of furthering the national interest. Functions listed are
(1) negotiation and parliamentary action, (2) formulation of
policy and tactics, (3) influencing opinion, (4) information
gathering and exchange, (5) representation, and (6) public
relations.

2061. Pool, Ithiel de Sola. "Behavioral Technology." In Foreign Policy Association, Toward the Year 2018. New York:　Cowles Education Corporation, 1968, pp. 87-96.

Indicating that within 50 years all documents, news reports, and other materials will be available on demand at a Department of State desk officer's console, the author suggests that the scientifically trained technician will gradually take over from the generalist of the foreign service, for the user of scientific methods will have gained the speed formerly monopolized by the man of intuition.

2062. Regala, Roberto. The Trends in Modern Diplomatic Practice. Milan: Giuffre, 1959, pp. 209.
A Philippine ambassador's views of diplomacy and diplomatic practice in the postwar world.

2063. Vagts, Alfred. The Military Attaché. Princeton: Princeton University Press, 1967, pp. xiv, 408.
Narrative in form, with an abundance of illustrative detail but often analytically superficial, this volume traces the development of the institution of military attaché in Europe and the United States since 1800, with attention to the encroachment on political territory and even duplication of the work of diplomats. Attention is given to the variety of functions performed by military attachés, including diplomacy, espionage, an instrument in the military's struggle with the civilian government for supremacy in foreign affairs, and a pre-1914 European channel whereby monarchs could circumvent ministers.

2064. Waters, Maurice. The Ad-Hoc Diplomat: A Study in Municipal and International Law. The Hague: Nijhoff, 1963, pp. xii, 233.
A study of the law relating to the ad hoc diplomat, this book aids in understanding the position in current diplomacy of a functionary not often a focus of study.

2065. Wildner, Heinrich. Die Technik der Diplomatie. Vienna: Springer, 1959, pp. x, 342.
Manuscript, finished in 1943, by an author who was Secretary General of the Austrian Foreign Office and containing essays on several aspects of diplomacy including, among other things, negotiating techniques and public control of foreign policy.

2066. Wilson, Clifton E. Cold War Diplomacy: The Impact of International Conflicts on Diplomatic Communications and Travel. International Studies, No. 1. Institute of Government Research, University of Arizona. Tucson: University of Arizona Press, 1966, pp. 67.
On deviations from traditional freedom of movement, communications, and freedom of diplomats.

2067. Wilson, Clifton E. "The Information Agent Abroad: New Dimension in International Law." 42 Journalism Quarterly (1965), 243-252.
This article deals with the problems posed for traditional diplomats when information agents hold diplomatic status. In 1962 the 8,000 USIA personnel amounted to double the number of State Department employees at the outbreak of World War II, and

not quite half of the 1,300 American citizens stationed abroad
with USIA enjoyed a status traditionally entitling them to diplomatic or consular immunities. The author examines the resultant impact upon diplomatic privileges and immunities in general, the unevenness of the status of information agents in receiving states as national regulations vary in stringency, and
the vulnerability of information agency buildings and personnel
to hostile action based on assumptions of propaganda activity
and espionage. Attention is given to the problem of the diplomatic pouch and its use in transporting propaganda materials.

See also nos. 1126, 1165, 1221, 1232, 1236, 1260, 1290, 1480.

3. Consular Institutions

2068. Candioti, Alberto M. Historia de la institución consular en la
antigüedad y en la edad media. Buenos Aires: Editoria Internacional, 1925,
pp. 801.
    Excellent history of the consular institution in its ancient
and medieval forms that helps to make clear how mercantile activity gives rise to public institutions having an international
character.

2069. Ravndal, Gabriel Brie. The Origin of the Capitulations and of
the Consular Institution. 67th Cong., 1st sess., Senate Doc. 34. Washington: Government Printing Office, 1921, pp. 112.
    Outstanding English-language historical examination of the
consular institution and the capitulations as they grew out of
the needs of merchants in the Mediterranean and of the generos-
ity of Moslem rulers to permit non-Moslems to find a way of
settling disputes other than that of a law from which they were
excluded.

See also no. 2482.

4. International Agents, Offices, and Headquarters; International Civil Service

2070. Bedjaoui, Mohammed. Fonction publique internationale et influences nationales (International Civil Service). New York: Praeger, 1958,
pp. xviii, 674.
    Systematic and comprehensive study of the status, rights,
and obligations of international officials and employees. Careful attention is paid to the problem of national influences upon
international civil servants.

2071. Bloch, Roger, and Lefèvre, Jacqueline. La fonction publique
internationale et européenne. Paris: Librairie Générale de Droit et de
Jurisprudence, 1963, pp. 219.

General treatise that includes consideration of the functions and recruitment of international civil servants including
the staffs of European regional organizations.

2072. Langrod, Georges. <u>The International Civil Service: Its Origins,
Its Nature, Its Evolution</u>. Leyden: Sijthoff; Dobbs Ferry: Oceana, 1963,
pp. 358.
     Study of the origins, nature, and evolution of the interna-
tional civil service from the League of Nations to the Congo
crisis.

2073. Loveday, Alexander. <u>Reflections on International Administration</u>.
New York: Oxford, 1956, pp. 334.
     Provides insights into many problems that have to be dealt
with through the internal law and regulations of international
organizations.

2074. Saarlandes, Universitat des. <u>Der europäische öffentliche Dienst
--Internationales Kolloquium, Nov. 1955</u>. Stuttgart: Kohlhammer: Brussels:
Librairie Encyclopédique, 1957, pp. 203, 208, 15.
     Symposium on the training and status of international offi-
cials and employees in Europe.

See also nos. 721, 724, 868, 1228.

5. <u>Negotiation and Bargaining</u>

   a. <u>Negotiation</u>

2075. Bell, Coral. <u>Negotiation from Strength</u>. London: Chatto and
Windus, 1962, pp. 223.
     Cites extensive uses of the concept by Western statesmen.

2076. D'Andea, Ugo. "Un negoziato difficile." 9 <u>Esteri</u> (1958), 13-15.
     A brief note on the problems of negotiation between a static
bloc and a dynamic bloc and the risk of deception or delusion of
the former as long as the latter remains in a dynamic phase in
regard to its sphere of action.

2077. Deutsch, Morton, and Krauss, Robert M. "Studies of Interpersonal Bargaining." 6 <u>Journal of Conflict Resolution</u> (1962), 52-76. Reprinted in part in Martin Shubik (ed.), <u>Game Theory and Related Approaches
to Social Behavior: Selections</u>. New York: Wiley, 1964, pp. 324-337.
     Report on a two-person experimental bargaining game in
which agreement was most easily reached in a No Threat condition, more difficult in a Unilateral Threat condition, and extremely difficult or impossible in a Bilateral Threat condition.
In Bilateral Threat no amount of communication seems to have had
an ameliorating effect. The mere existence of channels of communication provided no guarantee that they would be used, with

likelihood of use decreasing as competitive orientation increased. An "affront-offense-punitive behavior" pattern emerged, a possibility predicted by Siegel and Fouraker (Bargaining and Group Decision-Making (1960)). Deutsch and Krauss speculate that threat is most likely to occur when the threatener has no positive interest in the other person's welfare, when the threatener believes that the other has no interest in his welfare, and when the threatener anticipates this, his threat will be effective or, if ineffective, will not worsen his situation.

2078. Dodd, Stuart C. "Ten Semantic Tangles and the Threat of War." 35 Journalism Quarterly (1958), 170-176.
     International misbehavior in speech can add its bit to endangering the world's peace. The article gives examples of how speech can be misinterpreted. It also suggests 10 rules or "straighteners" on how to get the correct interpretation.

2079. Gould, Wesley L. "Laboratory, Law, and Anecdote: Negotiations and the Integration of Data." 18 World Politics (1965), 92-104.
     An article reviewing Iklé, How Nations Negotiate, that points to the need to bring a knowledge of the law and of legal data to bear upon the study of negotiations as well as to make use of documentary sources, memoirs, and laboratory findings.

2080. Gripenberg, G.A. Finland and the Great Powers: Memoirs of a Diplomat. Translated by Albin T. Anderson. Lincoln: University of Nebraska Press, 1965, pp. xx, 380.
     Written by the first Permanent Representative of Finland to the United Nations who from 1939 to 1944 was stationed at London, the Vatican, and Stockholm, these memoirs present an excellent example of how not to conduct foreign policy and how not to negotiate in a nation's interest. For example, in 1939 the Foreign Minister, confident that there would be neither a general war nor a Soviet attack on Finland, instructed Gripenberg not to bother to obtain information on whether Finland was being discussed in Great Power negotiations, made no effort to purchase large quantities of war materials abroad, and showed little interest in putting Finland's case before the British public. Moreover, the Minister was seldom issued instructions and those issued were usually incomplete and late.

2081. Iklé, Fred Charles. How Nations Negotiate. New York: Harper & Row, 1964, pp. xii, 272.
     Styles, techniques, objectives and rules of negotiating behavior, particularly between the Cold War opponents, are analyzed by means of skillful organization of chiefly anecdotal evidence derived from memoirs, reports, and monographs. The theoretical foundation owes much to Thomas Schelling's work on bargaining. The consequence is a development of some bargaining rules that may be and are compared with various recommendations by earlier writers. While the entire work is of consequence to the study of international law, to the genesis of international treaty norms, and to the potential legal, as well as political, consequences

of particular bargaining tactics, the express concern is primarily political. The one direct reference to legal consequences judicially expressed relates to the issue of whether amplifications spelling out the details of offers are binding. A section of a chapter entitled "Negotiating for Side-Effects" deals with the impact of negotiations on third parties in terms of political concerns and objectives. Attention is also given to problems of intra-governmental coordination and of pressure politics. Resort to the approach of this volume should strengthen the political dimension of studies of treaties. At the same time, politically oriented studies such as this one could give greater express attention to the legal consequences of treaties and the weight such consequences may bear in the eyes of negotiators. It may be noted that the one direct reference to a judicially expressed opinion cites two secondary sources. No other legal texts and no primary legal sources are cited either in footnotes or in the appended bibliographical note. The volume, along with overly legalistic studies of treaties, illustrates the need for appropriate synthesis of legal and political data and approaches.

2082. Kaufmann, Johann. Conference Diplomacy: An Introductory Analysis. Leiden: Sijthoff; Dobbs Ferry: Oceana, 1968, pp. 222.
A useful survey of debating and voting procedures, preparation and organization, conflicts, leadership, publicity, presiding officers' roles, secretariats, delegation composition and working methods, delegate characteristics, nature and functions of groups, tactics, and case studies related to conference diplomacy since World War II.

2083. Keller, Paul W. "The Study of Face-to-Face International Decision-Making." 13 Journal of Communication (1963), 67-76.
Survey of some of the work done on international decision-making, its inadequacies to date, and its limitations in that, until more is or can be done to study directly the dynamics of decision-making in international meetings, most findings are applicable only by inference.

2084. Lall, Arthur. Modern International Negotiation: Principles and Practice. New York: Columbia University Press, 1966, pp. xii, 404.
With reference to negotiations in which he participated, to other problems before the United Nations, and to India's conflicts with her neighbors, the author derives 20 principles of international negotiations.

2085. Muench, George A. "A Clinical Psychologist's Treatment of Labor-Management Conflicts: A Four-Year Study." 3 Journal of Humanistic Psychology (1963), 92-97.
On difficulties in labor-management negotiations through refusal to listen and to understand the opponent's proposals that seemed to have merit and an apparently successful approach by requiring repetition of the opponent's point, a procedure often revealing misperceptions, before attacking it.

2086. Paulin, Charles Oscar. <u>Diplomatic Negotiations of American Naval Officers, 1778-1883</u>. Baltimore: Johns Hopkins Press, 1912, pp. 380.
　　An historical review of a relatively little known subject, confined to "negotiations" and thus illuminating but one of the many aspects of naval duties related to diplomacy. Other sources must be consulted for the latter, e.g., for such incidents as the Kotzka affair that had a causal effect in crystallizing rules regarding the status of foreigners naturalized in the United States which, in turn, had its impact in regard to the function of determinations of nationality in matters pertaining to international law and relations.

2087. Pruitt, Dean G. <u>Negotiation as a Form of Social Behavior</u>. Technical Report No. 6. <u>Studies of the Dynamics of Cooperation and Conflict</u>. ONR Contract N00014-67-0190. Buffalo: State University of New York, Department of Psychology, October 28, 1968, pp. 31.
　　Based upon the literature on bargaining and negotiation, this study treats two methods or decision rules as determining the nature of the agreement reached through negotiation. These are (1) pure bargaining in which each party makes concessions only as the other displays the capacity and the willingness to delay agreement and to carry out threats and (2) mutual responsiveness in which each makes concessions as the other demonstrates a need for them. Stable relationships are treated as a mix of the two. Mutual responsiveness is seen as the long-run solution to the conflict between two pairs of motives (a) moving the other party toward one's own position and impressing constituents, and (b) reaching agreement and generating new solutions. Adoption and sustaining of mutual responsiveness is seen as dependent on the capacity to do future favors, friendliness, and shared understanding of relative bargaining strength. Pure bargaining is seen as characteristic of periods in which the relative bargaining strength of two parties is changing.

2088. Sawyer, Jack, and Guetzkow, Harold. "Bargaining and Negotiation in International Relations." In Herbert C. Kelman (ed.), <u>International Behavior: A Social-Psychological Approach</u>. New York: Holt, Rinehart and Winston, 1965, pp. 466-520.
　　Employs the findings of experimenters to describe the several stages of negotiating processes, points to various needs for more research, and reviews prospects and methods that may be employed for further social-psychological research on negotiation that might lead to an integrated theory of negotiation.

2089. Sharp, Walter R. "A Check List of Subjects for Systematic Study of International Conferences." 5 <u>International Social Science Bulletin</u> (1953), 311-339.
　　In an effort to assist researchers to formulate working hypotheses and to develop a conceptual framework for research on conferences, the author lists and discusses 25 problems warranting study.

2090. Verbit, Gilbert P. Trade Agreements for Developing Countries. New York: Columbia University Press, 1969, pp. xi, 249.

Analyzes problems and procedures of negotiation that come into play when trade agreements are being worked out between industrialized and underdeveloped countries.

2091. Walton, Richard E. "Two Strategies of Social Change and Their Dilemmas." 1 Journal of Applied Behavioral Science (1965), 167-179.

Consideration of the dilemmas faced by leaders of groups, whether in international affairs, civil rights, or labor relations, seeking concessions while also seeking improvements in relations with other groups. The one requires power strategies; the other, attitude change strategies. The author calls attention to methods of employing both strategies sequentially or simultaneously and the implications for social science if it is to make itself relevant to practitioners who must deal with the total reality, not just selected realities, in a complex situation.

2092. Walton, Richard E., and McKersie, Robert B. A Behavioral Theory of Labor Negotiations: An Analysis of a Social Interaction System. New York: McGraw-Hill, 1965, pp. xiv, 437.

Develops an integrated theory of bargaining composed of four models: (1) distributive bargaining, (2) integrative bargaining, (3) attitudinal structuring, and (4) intraorganizational bargaining. Related strategies and tactics are discussed, and a final chapter applies the theory in sketchy fashion to international negotiation and to civil rights negotiation. The theory builds on the work of Schelling and others and, although the exposition is overwhelmingly in terms of labor negotiations, develops the problem-solving feature of integrative bargaining with an emphasis not found in Iklé's discussion of international negotiations. Laboratory experimentation occupies a prominent place in the exposition, whereas it is not brought explicitly into Iklé's discussion. But the same requirement of a conflict of interest is present as a requisite for bargaining, although with greater emphasis on its secondary role in certain bargaining situations.

2093. Walton, Richard E., and McKersie, Robert B. "Behavioral Dilemmas in Mixed-Motive Decision Making." 11 Behavior Science (1966), 370-384.

Analysis, at the level of process behavior and negotiating tactics, of dilemmas in a mixed-motive situation entailing problem-solving (cooperative) and bargaining for advantage in a competitive situation. Two dilemmas, that of choosing between hard bargaining and low risk and that of sharing information or maintaining future bargaining strength, arise. The second type of dilemma presents difficulties in implementing a complex strategy, and these difficulties and the tactical dilemmas related thereto are analyzed in detail. Certain ways of attempting to minimize process dilemmas are discussed including the development of norms about appropriate shares as a substitute for bargaining and developing norms about appropriate bargaining tactics.

2094. Webster, Sir Charles. <u>The Art and Practice of Diplomacy</u>. New York: Barnes and Noble, 1962, pp. 245.

Selection of papers and articles produced over a 30-year period. Most pertinent to international law matters are "The Art and Practice of Diplomacy" providing useful anecdotal evidence on treaty-making, "The Council of Europe in the Nineteenth Century" on the role of Great Powers in 19th century conferences, and "Sanctions: The Use of Force in an International Organization."

2095. Zartman, I. William. <u>The Politics of Trade Negotiations Between Africa and the European Economic Community; The Weak Confront the Strong</u>. Princeton: Princeton University Press, 1971, pp. xi, 243.

A study of negotiations between some underdeveloped countries and the industrialized states able to negotiate as a semi-integrated unit.

See also nos. 336, 390, 1294, 1789, 1965, 2033, 2043, 2065, 2199, 2202, 2340, 2366, 2671.

b. Negotiation--Case Studies

2096. Bader, William B. <u>Austria Between East and West, 1945-1955</u>. Stanford: Stanford University Press, 1966, pp. ix, 250.

Makes use of the unpublished John Foster Dulles Papers at Princeton to review the East-West struggle over Austria and thereby trace the evolution of competing objectives to a point at which a "half a loaf" settlement at least temporarily served the interests of both contending parties.

2097. Beckhoefer, Bernard. "Negotiating the Statute of the International Atomic Energy Agency." 13 <u>International Organization</u> (1959), 38-59.

Noting the steps from bilateral US-USSR exchanges to informal eight-state discussions, a twelve-state meeting, and, finally, the International Conference of 1956, the author attributes success of the negotiations to the quality of the negotiators, procedures followed, coincidence of US and USSR interests to exclude basic Cold War tactics, and a broad, well-conceived US policy.

2098. Fifield, Russell H. <u>The Diplomacy of Southeast Asia: 1945-1958</u>. New York: Harper, 1958, pp. xv, 584.

Useful review of diplomatic problems and crises in Southeast Asia, particularly the diplomacy related to independence movements.

2099. Friedheim, Robert L. "The 'Satisfied' and 'Dissatisfied' States Negotiate International Law: A Case Study." 18 <u>World Politics</u> (1965), 20-41.

Critical appraisal of the attitudes expressed in the records of the two Law of the Sea Conferences that highlights the differences between the legalistic orientation of the spokesmen for the satisfied states and the political orientation of the dissatisfied states. The article takes note of the tendency of the dissatisfied states to include men with recent General Assembly experience on their delegations in contrast with the satisfied states' tendency to rely on lawyers and other technical experts. Attention is also given to the expressed distaste of dissatisfied states for expertise and detailed regulation and to the Western spokesmen's failure to communicate in terms understood by the dissatisfied spokesmen.

2099-A. Hopmann, P. **Terry.** "Some Effects of International Conflict on Arms Control Negotiations: The Partial Test Ban Case." Paper presented at the 66th Annual Meeting of the American Political Science Association, Los Angeles, September 8-12, 1970, pp. 26.
　　Making use of an "events interaction analysis" as a basis for scaling and of a categorical content analysis, this paper finds a positive relationship between the degree of conflict or cooperation in the external interactions of negotiating adversaries and their negotiating behavior and undertakes to characterize the negotiating behaviors of the United States, Great Britain, and the Soviet Union.

2100. Horowitz, David. State in the Making. Translated from the Hebrew by Julian Meltzer. New York: Knopf, 1953, pp. 349.
　　Diplomatic negotiations from 1946 to 1948 on the Palestine issue as seen by a Zionist negotiator who subsequently became Director General of Israel's Ministry of Finance.

2101. Lall, Arthur S. Negotiating Disarmament--The Eighteen Nation Disarmament Conference: The First Two Years, 1962-64. Cornell Research Papers in International Studies--II. Ithaca: Center for International Studies, Cornell University, 1964, pp. 83.
　　Exposition and analysis of the Geneva disarmament negotiations by the former Indian Permanent Representative and Ambassador to the United Nations, a governor of the International Atomic Energy Agency, and representative of India during the first year of the Eighteen Nation Disarmament Conference. Three chapters deal with the issues and problems of disarmament, including UN peacekeeping forces, while another chapter is devoted to conference organization, procedures, and the delegations. The most important chapter is probably Chapter III which sets forth the negotiating tactics and strategies observed by the author, with particular emphasis upon the tactics and strategies of the nonaligned states with which the author was most closely associated. He does not hesitate to identify, in phrasing suggestive of Georges Scelle's concept of the obligations of national officials and organs, "one crucial error" in the spring of 1963 when the contending states became informed of a nonaligned proposal before the nonaligned governments had approved and to characterize the yielding to Soviet and United States

representations to suppress the proposal as a "failure on the part of the nonaligned to fulfill their duty" to help to bring the nuclear powers closer to agreement on inspection.

2102. Moussa, Farag. Les négociations anglo-egyptiennes de 1950-1951 sur Suez et le Soudan--Essai de critique historique. Geneva: Droz, 1955, pp. 261.
Careful account by an Egyptian historian of the 1950-1951 negotiations between England and Egypt on Suez, the Sudan, and the Anglo-Egyptian alliance.

2103. Phillips, L.H. "Multilateral Constitution-Making: The International Atomic Energy Agency." 12 Western Political Quarterly (1959), 727-737.
Treats the success of the negotiations for IAEA as due to the utilization of several forums of negotiation and to the interplay of proposals of a small group of sponsors, the suggestions of many interested governments that were transmitted to the sponsors, General Assembly debates and concluding amendments at a large conference.

2104. Preeg, Ernest H. Traders and Diplomats: The Kennedy Round of Trade Negotiations. Washington: Brookings Institution, 1969, pp. xiv, 320.
A member of the American delegation for the Kennedy Round presents the background of the negotiations and a chronological account of the negotiations that treats separately the industrial sector groups and agriculture.

2105. Prescott, J.R.V. "The Evolution of the Anglo-French Inter-Cameroons Boundary." 4 Nigerian Geographical Journal (1963), 103-120.
Includes discussion of the consequences of an incorrect decoding of a British telegram in 1916 in regard to the position of the boundary of German Bornu, including French refusal to rectify the error which then enabled Britain to press successfully for some areas to the south to reunify the Holma, Zummu, and Higi peoples.

2106. Rios Gallardo, Conrado. Chile y Perú: Los pactos de le 1929. Santiago de Chile: Editorial Nascimento, 1959, pp. 405.
Detailed and well-documented account of the Tacna-Arica boundary controversy and the negotiations that led to its settlement in 1929.

2106-A. Rout, Leslie B., Jr. Politics of the Chaco Peace Conference, 1935-1939. Latin American Monographs, No. 19. Austin: University of Texas Press for the Institute of Latin American Studies, 1970, pp. xviii, 268.
An historian's account of third party activities in the settlement of the Chaco dispute, including the mediators' development of the face-saving procedure whereby the boundary was settled by a secret agreement and a sham arbitration was employed to make the agreement public in the form of an arbitral award.

2107. Wohlstetter, Albert, and Wohlstetter, Roberta. "Controlling the Risks in Cuba." <u>Adelphi Papers</u>. No. 17. Institute for Strategic Studies, London, April 1965.

Careful analysis, based upon available sources, of the Cuban crisis of 1962 that includes reference to the problems of effective communication of intent, of exploitation of trust, and of differing national behavior patterns, the last including reference to the tendency to project one's own behavior on the adversary.

2108. Zartman, I. William. <u>Morocco: Problems of New Power</u>. New York: Atherton, 1964, pp. ix, 276.

Chapter 2 is a case study of the negotiations and the Moroccan decision process concerning American bases established by an agreement with France that Moroccans considered not to be binding on their country. Attention is given to the manner in which, during the sporadic negotiations from May 11, 1957, to agreement in December 1959, the Moroccan elite acted without a foreign policy and then, by allowing the issue to arise before the National Consultative Assembly, became committed to "nondependence" and American evacuation of the bases. The elite is then portrayed as the prisoner of its own perception of public pressure and partisan politics. The resultant difficulties for American negotiators and some tactical failures are noted, as is also the American tactic that took advantage of the November 1959 political commitment of the Moroccan Government to reach agreement by the end of the year. A final chapter sets this case study and four studies of Moroccan domestic matters in the context of recurrent decision procedures in emergent states.

2109. Zartman, I. William. "The Moroccan-American Base Negotiations." 18 <u>Middle East Journal</u> (1964), 27-40.

Narrative of the negotiations between Morocco and the United States in 1956-1963 concerning military bases, with attention to the impact of internal Moroccan politics upon the negotiations.

See also nos. 1438, 1784, 1794, 1798, 2311, 2314, 2317, 2381, 2393, 2646.

c. Metropolitan Negotiations

2110. Holden, Matthew, Jr. "The Governance of the Metropolis as a Problem in Diplomacy." 26 <u>Journal of Politics</u> (1964), 627-647.

Treats metropolitics and international politics as having a common place within diplomatic systems, the latter being defined in terms of (1) ecological rather than political communities, (2) governmental primary actors, (3) communications structures dominated by a mythology of legitimacy that inhibits nongovernmental actors, and (4) procedures of intergovernmental relations. The author proposes testing the models of Haas, Kaplan, and Deutsch by application to strategies of metropolitan consensus formation.

d. International Business Negotiations

2111. Robinson, Richard D. Cases in International Business. New
York: Holt, Rinehart and Winston, 1962, pp. x, 146.
      Ten case studies of problems faced, procedures in dealing
with them, advice given, negotiating strategy and tactics, and
the impact of the Cold War and other political variables, as
American business firms seek to establish themselves in underdeveloped countries. The studies are particularly useful in
that the approach from the direction of private business permits
insights into routes to agreement, factors affecting the keeping
of agreements, and the interplay of economic, ideological, political, and socio-psychological variables that are more difficult to attain by an approach from the sensitive area of public
affairs. Particularly valuable is the study of Merck and Company's negotiations with India for a joint Merck-Indian Government venture for the manufacture of certain drugs and for private production of other drugs. The negotiations occurred at a
time when the Soviets were offering assistance that might have
precluded agreement with Merck and so raises questions about
the complexity of roles of private concerns that, in the pursuit of their own objectives, are also unavoidably engaged in
functions as informal representatives of their states. The
Merck and Company case permits a closer look at problems and
strategies of negotiations than would be possible in most contemporary face-to-face bargaining between governments and, even
bearing in mind the limitations of analogy, suggests an approach
to throw light upon problems faced in the negotiation of agreements between governments.

See also nos. 2842.

e. Laboratory Experiments

2112. Bartos, Otomar J. "Concession-Making in Experimental Conditions
10 General Systems Yearbook (1965), 145-156.
      Report on experimental findings that the less time that
negotiators have, the greater the probability that making concessions will be a profitable strategy, while the availability
of a great deal of time renders concession-making an unprofitable strategy. Another version of the paper, under the title,
"Concession Making in Experimental Negotiations," appears in J.
Berger, M. Zelditch, and B. Anderson (eds.), Sociological Theories in Progress (Boston: Houghton Mifflin, 1965).

2113. Bartos, Otomar J. Concession-Making in Experimental Negotiations. Mimeo. Scientific Report prepared for Air Force Office of Scientific Research as part of the project Predictive Model for Intra-Group
Negotiation. University of Hawaii, November 16, 1964.

Report of an undertaking to test the Osgood hypothesis, embodied in the GRIT proposal, that concessions are usually reciprocated. The experiments described included an effort to distinguish "natural allies" from "natural opponents." Although there were some inconclusive aspects of the experiments, there was confirmation of another hypothesis also tested, namely, that of Siegel and Fouraker that concessions are made when the situation of failure exists in the form of low offers by an opponent but not when the opponent makes a high offer. On the basis of the results obtained, it is suggested that concession-making is an unprofitable policy, subject to the qualification that, had the subjects had much less time in which to reach an agreement, concession-making might have been a profitable strategy.

2114. Berkowitz, Leonard. "Repeated Frustrations and Expectations in Hostility Arousal." 60 Journal of Abnormal and Social Psychology (1960), 422-429.
Unexpected frustrations produce more hostility than expected frustrations, while subjects who expect hostility and receive friendliness demonstrate a greater trend toward friendliness than those who have a reason to expect friendliness.

2115. Berkowitz, Leonard. "Some Factors Affecting the Reduction of Overt Hostility." 60 Journal of Abnormal and Social Psychology (1960), 14-21.
Report of an experiment in which the subjects rated each other three times in a 50-minute session. The first rating was right after seeing each other. The second was after communications, supposedly written by the partners, to half the subjects and designed to induce dislike. Then half the subjects were informed that they had been rated unfavorably and the other half that they had been rated favorably on the second questionnaire. When inconsistent with earlier behavior, this apparent evaluation had the greatest effect in changing attitudes toward partners. It is suggested that, in conflict resolution efforts, the probabilities of success are greater when negotiators expect less yielding by the other side than actually occurs.

2116. Contini, Bruno. "The Value of Time in Bargaining Negotiations: Some Experimental Evidence." 58 American Economic Review (1968), 374-393.
Report on an experiment to test hypotheses about time as a variable in the utility function of each bargainer, particularly the assertion that the lower the evaluation of time by one bargainer, the better the outcome of negotiations for him.

2117. Fouraker, Lawrence E., and Siegel, Sidney. Bargaining Behavior. New York: McGraw-Hill, 1963, pp. ix, 309.
An extension of controlled experiments through laboratory situations reported in Bargaining and Group Decision Making (New York: McGraw-Hill, 1960), which dealt with bilateral monopoly situations. This study reports on another type of bilateral monopoly experiment and on oligopoly experiments. The experiments showed a dominance of the maximizing tendency. They also

showed that variations in the amount of information regarding profit payoffs led to diversified behavior by permitting the emergence of different bargaining types. Experiments of this type may be suggestive of explanations of the bargaining procedure indulged in barter and other commercial agreements with more apparent, more readily calculable, and more immediate payoffs, but may be less useful in respect to long-range and less readily discernible payoffs as in the case of lawmaking and constitutive agreements.

2118. Hermann, Margaret G., and Kogan, Nathan. "Negotiation in Leade and Delegate Groups." 12 Journal of Conflict Resolution (1968), 332-344.
Report of an experiment on negotiations that seeks to identify differences between the negotiating behavior of leaders and that of delegates. Little research having been done in this area, the report breaks some ground and provides suggestions for further experimentation.

2119. Joseph, M. L., and Willis, R. H. "An Experimental Analog to Two-Party Bargaining." 8 Behavioral Sciences (1963), 117-127.
Experimental representation of the fait accompli in bargaining by contrasting "simultaneous choice," with neither party knowing the other's choice at the time of making hiw own choice, with "sequential choice," in which the second party could only accept or reject the first party's choice, rejection causing both to receive nothing. Sequential choice produced greater inequality of rewards.

2120. Kelley, Harold H. "A Classroom Study of the Dilemmas in Interpersonal Negotiations." In Kathleen Archibald (ed.), Strategic Interaction and Conflict: Papers and Discussion. Berkeley: Institute of Internationa Studies, University of California, 1966, pp. 49-73.
Report of negotiations between members of a university class in group behavior, 50% of each student's grade depending on his performance in negotiating with classmates. The article deals with the dilemmas of goals, trust, honesty and openness, and co-operation. The article discusses the patterns of exploratory offers, negotiating an entire contract as against one issue at a time, high demand beginnings, use of available time, inducing the other party to make concessions, making economical concessions, and assembling information concerning reasonable outcomes.

2121. Liebert, Robert L., Smith, William P., Hill, J.H., and Keiffer, Miriam. "The Effects of Information and Magnitude of Initial Offer on Interpersonal Negotiations." 4 Journal of Experimental Social Psychology (1968), 431-441.
Report of an interpersonal bargaining experiment with the group divided in terms of knowledge of the other party's range of profit and favorable or unfavorable initial offer by the other party. The evidence is treated as supporting the hypothesis that uninformed bargainers use opponents' bids to set their own goals, while informed bargainers use them to assess the reasonableness of the opponent's goals.

2122. Pilisuk, Marc, Winter, J. Alan, Chapman, Reuben, and Hass, Neil. "Honesty, Deceit, and Timing in the Display of Intentions." 12 <u>Behavioral Science</u> (1967), 205-215.

Study of the performance of players in four variations of a non-zero-sum game that simulates an arms race. Opportunity to communicate tended to retard the development of stable groups that would polarize as either mutually cooperative or mutually competitive. Due to frequent use of communication for deceptive purposes, gross rates of cooperative behavior were not automatically augmented. But a condition of late inspection tended eventually to produce near total cooperation in most pairs. A theoretical explanation is offered and suggests that binding commitments are significant in reversing deadlocks of distrust.

2123. Pruitt, Dean G., and Drews, Julie Latané. "The Effect of Time Pressure, Time Elapsed, and the Opponent's Concession Rate on Behavior in Negotiation." 5 <u>Journal of Experimental Social Psychology</u> (1969), 43-60.

Report of a negotiating experiment that showed that on the first trial increased time pressure lowered goals, levels of demand and bluffing, that subsequent trials reduced demand and bluffing but not goals, that after the first trial neither time pressure nor the adversary's rate of concession affected the rate of change of demand or bluffing, and that wishful thinking about the adversary's goals appeared to take place.

2124. Schelling, Thomas C. "An Experimental Game for the Study of Bargaining." 14 <u>World Politics</u> (1961), 47-68.

Experiment on the bargaining process in such conflict situations as limited war entailing bargaining by both maneuver and words, poor communications, lack of legal enforcement, the making of irreversible moves by participants, uncertainty concerning the other party's values, and a capacity of each party to inflict damage. In this exploration of tacit bargaining, the experimenter's hypothesis is that limits have to be qualitative and discrete rather than quantitative and continuous.

2125. Shure, Gerald H., Meeker, Robert J., and Hansford, Earle A. "The Effectiveness of Pacifist Strategies in Bargaining Games." 9 <u>Journal of Conflict Resolution</u> (1965), 106-117.

Report of experiments at System Development Corporation on the bargaining behavior of pacifist personalities. Of particular interest is the conflict between the dominating personality and the pacifist personality, the latter sticking to his attempt to be cooperative despite continued injury and rising demands in response to his cooperative effort. Although defections did occur, that is, some cooperators were induced by teammates to switch to dominating behavior and some dominators made a sustained effort to avoid administering shocks to their bargaining opponents, the experiment indicates that on the whole the pacifist strategy of cooperation appeared to be unsuccessful, for it also seemed to invite exploitation and aggression even by those who did not originally intend so to act.

2125-A. Vidmar, Neil, and McGrath, Joseph E. "Forces Affecting Success in Negotiation Groups." 15 Behavioral Science (1970), 154-163.
Report on two experimental studies designed to test the predictive power of a tri-forces model of negotiations by obtaining a number of measures of the three role forces and combining them in a multiple regression equation. The three role forces, acting on the individual negotiator, are (1) forces toward a solution in accord with the reference group's position, (2) forces toward agreement with representatives of the contending reference group, and (3) forces toward creative, constructive solutions in harmony with the values and interests of the surrounding social system.

See also nos. 176, 683, 2208.

f. Bargaining Models

2126. Bartos, Otomar J. "A Model of Negotiation and the Recency Effect." 27 Sociometry (1964), 311-326.
The article describes a mathematical model of negotiation based on the von Neumann-Morgenstern theory of utility and the Bush-Mosteller stochastic model of learning. The author believes that much is to be gained by formulating models that lie in the gray area between the purely normative and the purely descriptive models. Both are intended to be incorporated in the model presented. The model includes a "recency effect" in accord with which the later in a negotiating session a proposal is introduced, the more it influences the final decision. The implication was tested and the data gathered from 35 experimental sessions showed the "mediator" behaving as predicted, that is, likely to endorse the most recent proposal.

2127. Borah, L.A. "The Effects of Threat in Bargaining." 66 Journal of Abnormal and Social Psychology (1963), 37-44.
Finds interpersonal bargaining to be poorer under stress, with apparent diminished ability to perceive the other person's ideas, plans, or wishes.

2128. Coddington, A. Theories of the Bargaining Process. London: Allen & Unwin; Chicago: Aldine, 1968, pp. xx, 106.
Presents a framework focused on the dynamics of bargaining, makes suggestions for the treatment of expectations in formal bargaining models, and compares the elaborated framework with that offered by game theory.

2129. Iklé, Fred Charles, and Leites, Nathan. "Political Negotiation as a Process of Modifying Utilities." 6 Journal of Conflict Resolution (1962), 12-28. Reprinted in Martin Shubik (ed.), Game Theory and Related Approaches to Social Behavior: Selections. New York: Wiley, 1964, pp. 243-258.

Develops a bargaining model for two parties or two alliances
in respect to a single issue. The model accounts for bargaining
ranges in terms of minimum dispositions and estimates of opponents' minimum dispositions, estimated probable outcomes, and sham
bargaining ranges. Differences from reality and from multi-issue
situations are recognized and from time to time indicated. The
impact of negotiation mores, particularly important in the West,
and disadvantages that can accrue to defensive status quo bargainers are noted. The most important emphasis is the changing
nature of utilities in real life situations, so that initial
minimum dispositions related to payoff and changes in negotiators'
expectations and estimates not due to factual changes in payoffs
have a profound effect upon the negotiatory process. The problem
of a sham bargaining position in relation to East-West negotiations is dealt with briefly and, still more briefly, that of third
party perception (possibly mistaken) of the bargaining range and
the resultant deduction of a "fair" outcome.

2130. Kuhn, Alfred. "Bargaining Power in Transactions: A Basic
Model of Interpersonal Relationships." 23 American Journal of Economics
and Sociology (1964), 49-63.
    The model, treated as applicable to transactions between
heads of states as well as other individuals and illustrated by
reference to international trade, sets forth four factors, i.e.,
the value of each of two things to each of two parties, as determining the terms or limits of all transactions. The dichotomy, market vs. bargaining power forces, is rejected in favor of
another dichotomy, bargaining power forces (the ingredients determining the terms on which a transaction will take place) vs.
strategy and tactics. Transactions, which often come in sets,
are treated as a type of subsystem. In turn, subsidiary transactions are subsystems within the larger transaction. The parameters of the transaction, determined by the environment of
the system, constitute independent variables. Motives of the
parties are located in the environment. Strategic maneuvers
constitute manipulation of the environment, not operations within the system. Tactics constitute an information subsystem
within the main system and either do not come into being or are
quickly eliminated by negotiations when perfect consensus makes
the transaction determinate. Although confined to selfish,
unique, and voluntary transactions, one of the objectives of the
paper is to demonstrate a conceptual identity between separate
models of bargaining power that appear in economic, power-
political, and psycho-sociological analyses.

2131. Randolph, Lillian. "A Suggested Model of International Negotiation." 10 Journal of Conflict Resolution (1966), 344-353.
    Seeks to present a more complete model of international
negotiations by taking into account the relationships among
elements in bargaining phases that are conducive to reaching
an enforceable agreement and the elements in bargaining that
are of help in enforcing an agreement. A series of hypotheses,
e.g., "that which encourages a willingness to negotiate hinders

efforts to conclude an agreement and to enforce it," are presented but not supporting data. Nevertheless, the propositions should be provocative of more precise investigation not merely into the bargaining process but also into the nature of obligation and of enforceability.

g. Informal Bargaining Channels

See nos. 1272, 1451, 1469.

h. Summit Negotiations

2132. Eubank, Keith. The Summit Conferences, 1919-1960. Norman: University of Oklahoma Press, 1966, pp. xii, 225.
        Reviews the 1919 Peace Conference, the 1938 Munich Conference, the 1943 Teheran Conference, the 1945 Yalta and Potsdam Conferences, the 1955 Geneva Conference, and the 1960 Eisenhower-Khrushchev "Conference" in an attempt to assess the impact of summit conferences on the course of subsequent events and to ascertain when other forces proved more potent.

2133. Plischke, Elmer. "Eisenhower's 'Correspondence Diplomacy' with the Kremlin--Case Study in Summit Diplomatics." 30 Journal of Politics (1968), 137-159.
        On the 72 communications between Eisenhower and the Kremlin, their detailed nature, their early publication, and their failure to produce accommodation or significant negotiated results.

2134. Plischke, Elmer. Summit Diplomacy--Personal Diplomacy of the President of the United States. College Park, Maryland: Bureau of Government Research, 1958, pp. viii, 125.
        Treating summit diplomacy as entailing summit conferences, the use of personal communications, of personal diplomatic representatives, and ceremonial state visits--and therefore an older device than is generally believed--the author presents an informative and evaluative work that suggests lines for more thorough investigation and analysis.

i. Treaty-Making Through International
   Negotiations by Private Parties

2135. McFadyean, Sir Andrew (ed.). The History of Rubber Regulation, 1934-1943. London: Allen & Unwin for the International Rubber Regulation Committee, 1944, pp. 244.
        Official account, prepared for the International Rubber Regulation Committee, of the formulation and implementation of

international rubber control schemes to World War II. Chapter
III provides some indication of the interplay of governmental
and private groups in the negotiations leading to the International Rubber Regulation Agreement, signed May 7, 1934, and of
the extent of international nongovernmental negotiation required
to reconcile conflicting economic interests before an agreement
among governments could come into being. The problems requiring
resort to intergovernmental agreement, particularly the application of agreed-on measures to native rubber in the Netherlands
East Indies, are identified. The case is particularly useful as
a narrative of private group activity that so prepared the ground
and worked out the compromises as to make governmental negotiation essentially a ratification of agreement previously reached
by the interest groups concerned.

See also nos. 801, 2699, 2703.

j. Negotiation by Specialists

2136. Gilpin, Robert. American Scientists and Nuclear Weapons Policy.
Princeton: Princeton University Press, 1962, pp. viii, 352.
        Includes analysis of the 1958 Geneva Conference of Experts
that dealt with arms control and nuclear test-ban problems.
The conclusion is that the American scientists "undertook a
task beyond their political experience and competence" while
the Soviet experts gave a political tone to the meeting. An
article by Donald A. Strickland casts doubt upon Gilpin's
conclusions.

2137. Strickland, Donald A. "Scientists as Negotiators: The 1958
Geneva Conference of Experts." 8 Midwest Journal of Political Science
(1964), 372-384.
        Examination of the negotiations conducted by Soviet and
American scientists at Geneva, with particular attention to the
lack of agreement between the two countries concerning what the
scientists were to accomplish. The author's conclusion is that,
contrary to Gilpin's assertion, no special method of negotiation
could be attributed to the scientists and that the failure of
negotiations was due to initial differences of purpose of the
two countries that even professional diplomats could not have
overcome.

2138. Zoppo, Ciro E. Technical and Political Aspects of Arms Control
Negotiations: The 1958 Experts' Conference. RAND Report RM-3286-ARPA.
Santa Monica: RAND Corporation, September 1962, pp. 114.
        Analysis of the 1958 Experts' Conference that finds it to
be unrealistic to expect to separate political and technical
questions. The author's opinion is that the scientists could
have profited from more explicit and more detailed guidance before tackling the political problems that entered the negotiations.

See also no. 1414.

k. Third-Party Influence

2139. Ahmed, Samir. "The Role of Neutrals in the Geneva Negotiations
1 Disarmament and Arms Control (1963), 20-32.
Discussion of the tactics of eight neutralist delegations,
acting not as a bloc but as a third party, sometimes in the form
of a loose diplomatic group and sometimes differing or acting
separately, in an effort to produce concessions and lucid proposals and explanations by the two contending sides during the
first year's negotiations of the Eighteen Nation Disarmament
Conference (Geneva).

2140. Boissier, L. "Le Comité international de la Croix-Rouge et ses
interventions dans les conflits politiques." 5 Annuaire, Association suisse
de science politique (1965), 7-14.
On the activities of the Red Cross in regard to such matters
as the repatriation of North Koreans in Japan, together with a
discussion of the success of the Red Cross in matters related to
human rights as contrasted with the adaptation of the law of war
to modern conditions.

2141. Caplow, Theodore. Two Against One: Coalitions in Triads.
Englewood Cliffs: Prentice-Hall, 1968, pp. vii, 183.
An exploration of the idea that social interaction is fundamentally not linear, but triangular, because always influenced by
a present or nearby audience.

2142. O'Connor, Raymond G. Perilous Equilibrium: The United States
and the London Naval Conference of 1930. Lawrence: University of Kansas
Press, 1962, pp. 188.
A useful contribution to the literature on the Naval Conference of 1930 and the impact of a political desire for a treaty
upon the agreement-making process and a consequent impetus toward
resting faith upon the unenforceable. The tortuous course leading to Anglo-American compromise and the interaction of naval and
diplomatic developments are clearly traced, as is also the process
of interdepartmental accommodation in the United States and the
ultimate subordination of the influence of the Navy, divided within itself, so that of the politicians at Washington.

2143. Thompson, James D., and McEwen, William J. "Organizational
Goals and Environment: Goal Setting as an Interaction Process." 23 American Sociological Review (1958), 23-31.
Deals with competition as a form of rivalry mediated by a
third party, e.g., the customer, and with three types of cooperative strategy, namely, bargaining, co-optation, and coalition, in each instance with reference to the potential power of
an outsider in the decision process of an organization.

See also nos. 1802, 1827, 2081, 2101, 2126, 2129, 2191.

1. Interdepartmental Accommodations and
   Negotiations

See no. 2081.

m. Domestic Influences; Opposition to
   Concessions

2144. Fagen, Richard R. "Some Assessments and Uses of Public Opinion in Diplomacy." 24 Public Opinion Quarterly (1960), 448-457.
    Public opinion is dealt with as "hard goods." Opinion is expressed through the press, personal contacts, and public demonstrations. It is used to add a national dimension to a governmental position, to define the national threshold of tolerance, to excuse the other's actions, and to excuse one's own actions. A concept of public opinion as a raw force is said to permeate the thinking and writing of decision-makers during a crisis period.

2145. Haas, Ernst B., and Whiting, Allen S. Dynamics of International Relations. New York: McGraw-Hill, 1956, pp. xx, 557.
    Particularly useful is the section on United States policy toward the recognition of the Soviet Union in 1917-1933, which provides identification of the American groups engaged in conflict over the issue and of their political, economic, military, and humanitarian ends. The exposition is a penetration beyond the terms generally employed to describe the international issue in terms of national policy. It attempts to reach to the conflict within the nation that had an impact upon the law of recognition. Intra-nation conflicts, not outward manifestations and effects of foreign policies, are treated as the essential object of study in efforts to determine whether a specific policy is directed toward self-extension or self-preservation. The volume deals with international law (pp. 385-427) in a highly critical manner and portrays it as incapable of growth in areas subject to basically conflicting values and aspirations--a view based upon traditional approaches to international law and not charting routes for probing such questions as the survival of the law, rather than of particular rules or sets of rules, even through times of basic conflict. More useful is the last chapter on conflict among regional systems that suggests a method of approaching some basic law-affecting conflicts, whether the cleavages be economic, political, or of another nature.

2146. Rintala, M. "The Two Faces of Compromise." 22 Western Political Quarterly (1969), 326-332.

On the differences among political systems of prevalent
attitudes toward compromise, e.g., the British view that compromise means adjustment to the views of others to get common action and the German view of Kompromiss as betrayal of one's
principles. Treating the differences as flowing from divergent
concepts of the purpose of politics and from contradictory concepts of human nature, the author regards differences in attitudes toward compromise to be basic to explanations of both domestic and international political behavior.

See nos. 1266, 1310, 1321, 1347-1349, 1385, 1451, 1471, 1778, 2075,
2081, 2405, 2422, 2786, 2798, 2855.

(1) Influence of Constituent Units of Federal States

See nos. 2411, 2785, 2788.

n. Conflict and Bargaining

2147. Diesing, Paul. "Bargaining Strategy and Union-Management Relations." 5 Journal of Conflict Resolution (1961), 369-378.
      Sets forth four principles for good working relations among
negotiators: (1) the weaker side must be able to inflict damage
on the stronger; (2) both sides must signal their intention not
to destroy the basic power resources of the other; (3) sharable
principles and goals must be found; (4) honesty to the proper
degree is required. Three kinds of bargaining are distinguished:
(1) power bargaining, where bluffing within limits is advantageous
and an agreement is "the best we could do" under the circumstances;
(2) working harmony, requiring honesty in concessions and productive of "fair" agreements; (3) cooperation, requiring honesty
to know what will help the other side since agreement is designed
to help one side as much as the other. The author believes "armed
truce" to be necessary under certain political circumstances,
e.g., low inner cohesiveness, existence of an opposition faction
that forces an effort to secure immediate results, or lack of opportunity for joint problem-solving.

2148. Kahn, Herman. "Some Comments on Controlled War." In Klaus Knorr
and Thornton Read (eds.), Limited Strategic War. New York: Praeger for the
Center of International Studies, Princeton University, 1962, pp. 32-66.
      Simplified models are used to indicate potential dependence
of bargaining power upon the relations between opposing strategic
forces.

2149. Kaplan, Morton A. "Limited Retaliation as a Bargaining Process."
In Klaus Knorr and Thornton Read (eds.), Limited Strategic War. New York:

Praeger for the Center of International Studies, Princeton University, 1962, pp. 142-162.

A view of the Soviet-Western conflict as a struggle to legitimatize favorable rules. Agreement to terminate a limited strategic war is seen as more promising when based upon the more universalistic or less one-sided interpretation of the rules in contention.

2150. Schelling, Thomas C. The Strategy of Conflict. Cambridge, Massachusetts: Harvard University Press, 1960; Galaxy ed., New York: Oxford, 1963, pp. ix, 309.

Develops a model of conflict strategy with particular emphasis upon bargaining, communication, randomization of promises and threats, and surprise attack. Particularly noteworthy is the development of the concept of tacit bargaining. The study draws upon game theory. Its strength lies in its treatment of the conflict aspect of bargaining. Problem-solving, entailing a more cooperative approach to other states, is not a major focus of this study.

2150-A. Sullivan, Michael P. "International Bargaining Behavior." 15 International Studies Quarterly (1971), 359-382.

Starting with Schelling's notion of "interdependent decision-making," the author notes that the use of static rather than dynamic models and the difficulty in systematically collecting data on dynamic situations impedes follow-up of Schelling's ideas. He also notes that practitioners seem to be more concerned with the action-reaction phenomenon in the decisional aspects of international relations than do scholars. The author then looks at some suggested approaches to the problem, the possible lack of adequate conceptual tools, and asks whether we are fated to study interdependent decision-making only in the large, with second-step inferences to the small, or whether we can examine changes in smaller social systems of which the international system is comprised.

2151. Young, Oran R. The Politics of Force: Bargaining During International Crises. Princeton: Princeton University Press, 1969, pp. xii, 438.

A part of the author's continuing exploration of the nature of conflict and the role of coercion in international politics, this volume focuses on the bargaining that takes place during international crises.

See also nos. 1385, 1451, 2081, 2092.

o. Negotiations Between Enemies During War

2152. Mourin, Maxime. Les tentatives de paix dans la Seconde Guerre Mondiale (1939-1945). Paris: Payot, 1949, pp. 221.

Makes use of the Nürnberg documents to reconstruct portions of the negotiations between enemies during the course of World War II.

See also nos. 2308, 2317.

p. National Negotiating Styles

2153. Aspaturian, Vernon V. "Dialectics and Duplicity in Soviet Diplomacy." 27 Journal of International Affairs (1963), 42-60.
Duplicity is treated as inherent in Soviet diplomacy because its base is a double standard depending on whether relations are with capitalist or communist countries. Norms are, therefore, relative, nonintervention and sovereignty, for example, having meanings varying with the parties involved in a situation. Diplomacy requiring a lack of dispute over ideological and social questions, "non-consensus" diplomacy is possible under enumerated objective conditions that must be imposed through deterrence and capability for retaliation, since the Soviets will never recognize objective conditions except through acceptance of them as necessary to their own survival.

2154. Avon, Anthony Eden, 1st Earl of. Full Circle: The Memoirs of Anthony Eden. Boston: Houghton Mifflin, 1960, pp. 676.
First volume published of Eden's memoirs and perhaps the most important in that it helps to reveal differences in British and American styles of diplomacy in the postwar period.

q. Communist Bargaining with the West

2155. Beckhoefer, Bernard. Postwar Negotiations for Arms Control. Washington: Brookings Institution, 1961, pp. xiv, 641.
Reviews the bargaining behavior that took place during the first 15 years of post-World War II arms control negotiations.

2156. Fedder, Edwin H. "Communication and American-Soviet Negotiating Behavior." 8 Background (1964), 105-120.
Findings are that (1) American officials relate success in negotiations to military posture, (2) the language barrier poses only trivial problems, (3) negotiators lack self-awareness and fail to examine their own attitudes, motivations, perceptions, preconceptions, etc., and (4) negotiators tend to project the low credibility that they have attached to counterparts upon the subject of negotiations.

2157. Jensen, Lloyd. Postwar Disarmament Negotiations: A Study in American-Soviet Bargaining Behavior. Ph.D. Dissertation. Ann Arbor: University of Michigan, Center for Research on Conflict Resolution, Preprint, November 1962, pp. 266.

Content analysis of verbatim records of disarmament negotiations from 1946 to 1960, employing an index based on substantive concessions and retractions made by the United States and
the USSR and a second index based on calculations of the level
of agreement reached at various points in time. Separate indices
are developed for nuclear test ban negotiations. Attention is
accorded the obstacles of political tension, confidence in deterrence, and sense of insecurity about the risks of disarmament. In regard to tension, the author concludes that neither
extreme highs or lows but a moderate level of tension is accompanied by greater propensity to negotiate on disarmament. An
operational code of five rules for disarmament negotiation is
developed. The thesis also includes a bit of interesting data
on responses to concessions and on US and Soviet response times.

2158. Joy, Charles Turner. *How Communists Negotiate*. New York: Macmillan, 1955, pp. 178.
Well-known assessment of Communist negotiating practices
as displayed during the Korean armistice negotiations.

2159. Kissinger, Henry A. *American Foreign Policy: Three Essays*.
New York: Norton, 1969, pp. 143.
Includes five short chapters on the Vietnam negotiations.

2160. Lall, Arthur. *How Communist China Negotiates*. New York: Co-
lumbia University Press, 1968, pp. ix, 291.
Analysis of the Laos negotiations in the context of the
Chinese Communist theory of international relations.

2161. Mosely, Philip E. *The Kremlin and World Politics*. New York:
Vintage, 1960, pp. 567.
Includes a discussion of Communist negotiating tactics and
strategies, the dangers of ambiguous agreements and agreements
in principle, and the erosion of ambiguous agreements and agreements in principle in the course of working out details.

2162. North, Robert C., Triska, Jan F., and Brody, Richard A. *Progress Report*. Studies in International Conflict and Integration. Stanford
University, May 27, 1963.
Includes a report on Harold Stevens' study, employing the
Hoover Institution's documents on the theory and practice of international communism, of theoretical writings on negotiations
with the West. These writings are correlated with the history
of Soviet-Western negotiations from Brest-Litovsk to the early
1960s. Arousal of emotions, tensions, conflicts, and hopes, associated with alternation of warlike motives and utterances with
overtures for peace, appear to be a calculated technique drawn
from Soviet social science and designed to permit calculation
of what Western responses are likely to be.

2163. Spanier, John W., and Nogee, Joseph L. *The Politics of Disarmament: A Study in Soviet-American Gamesmanship*. New York: Praeger, 1962,
pp. ix, 226.

Objectives and tactics of disarmament negotiations are treated as a complex part of the overall US-USSR struggle for power.

2164. Speier, Hans. Divided Berlin: The Anatomy of Soviet Blackmail New York: Praeger, 1961, pp. 201.
Review of the development of the Berlin crisis to the end of July 1961.

2165. Wedge, Bryant, and Muromcew, Cyril. "Psychological Factors in Soviet Disarmament." 9 Journal of Conflict Resolution (1965), 18-36.
Systematic review of the record of the Eighteen Nation Disarmament Conference that finds Soviet negotiators following distinctive and consistent negotiation patterns. These patterns are based upon commitment to state sovereignty, the right of the state to secrecy, and preoccupation with possible German revanche and foreign bases. Soviet representatives were thoroughly instructed, preferred to barter dissimilar values, and tended to include the full range of political relations in negotiation on any subject. The market-place tactics of threat, bluster, and deceit were prominent.

2166. Young, Kenneth. Negotiating with the Chinese Communists: The United States Experience, 1953-1967. New York: McGraw-Hill, 1968, pp. xvii, 461.
An account of bilateral negotiations between Red China and the United States that attempts to delineate the style more as Marxist and Maoist than Chinese. The book suffers from concentration on a particular bilateral, adversary situation and so throws no light on how Communist China negotiates with friendly nations.

See also nos. 919, 1298, 1408, 1779, 1801, 2081.

r. Force, Threat, and Bargaining; War
    as Bargaining

2167. Jensen, Lloyd. "Military Capabilities and Bargaining Behavior. 9 Journal of Conflict Resolution (1965), 155-163.
Presents empirical and quantitative evidence relating to the validity of the belief that nations negotiate more effectively from positions of military superiority. The hypothesis that the greater the confidence in deterrent capabilities, the less the propensity to negotiate was tested by developing indices of the US and USSR propensities to compromise and indices of their confidence in deterrent capabilities. The tests confirm the hypothesis.

2168. Read, Thornton. "Limited Strategic War and Tactical Nuclear War." In Klaus Knorr and Thornton Read (eds.), Limited Strategic War.

New York: Praeger for the Center of International Studies, Princeton University, 1962, pp. 67-116.

Both types of war are treated as examples of bargaining behavior entailing a conflict of wills in which the capacity to withstand punishment rather than to inflict it is decisive.

2169. Schelling, Thomas C. Arms and Influence. New Haven: Yale University Press, 1966, pp. ix, 293.

A continuation of the author's earlier works in the form of a theoretical investigation of the role of armed forces in affecting other nations' behavior. The emphasis is upon war, threat of war, alliances, the arms race, and constraints imposed by military technology.

2170. Schelling, Thomas C. "Experimental Games and Bargaining Theory." 14 World Politics (1961), 47-68. Reprinted in Martin Shubik (ed.), Game Theory and Related Approaches to Social Behavior--Selections. New York: Wiley, 1964, pp. 311-323.

An argument for the use of games as experimentation in regard to international affairs and a description of a game employed in an experimental study of the bargaining process in limited war--war being treated as a bargaining situation.

See also nos. 1451, 1801.

s. Individual Behavior and Negotiations

2171. Block, Jack, and Bennett, Lillian. "The Assessment of Communication: Perception and Transmission as a Function of the Social Situation." 8 Human Relations (1955), 317-325.

A report on the "consensual accuracy" of an individual's social perceptions and communications and how this accuracy varies as a function of the interpersonal situation. Consensual accuracy is defined as the extent to which an individual's appraisal of his various two-person social situations coincides with the evaluation of the same situation by the other participating individuals. The authors note the possibility of classifying individuals into four categories: effective receiver and sender; effective receiver, ineffective sender; ineffective receiver, effective sender; ineffective receiver and sender.

2172. Mellinger, Glen D. "Interpersonal Trust as a Factor in Communication." 52 Journal of Abnormal and Social Psychology (1956), 304-309.

A study of communication among scientists in a large government research laboratory provided general support for the proposition that an individual will distort his own opinions in communicating them to persons he distrusts with the result that the recipient's accuracy of perception is impaired. Overstatement or understatement of agreement results. Also affecting accuracy of perception of opinions are the relative status of communicator and recipient and the nature of the issue.

2173. Torre, Mottram. Health and Diplomacy. Unpublished manuscript.
1962.

Since diplomats rarely are trained in anthropology and psychology and so face difficulties in ascertaining whether behavior of statesmen and politicians of receiving countries, found
to be incomprehensible in terms of standards familiar to the diplomat, is due to cultural differences or to neurotic or psy-
chotic condition, the author has prepared a list of symptoms
that may have cross-cultural applicability. The list of symptoms is not intended to provide an automatic evaluation of the
actual situation in any particular case nor does it assume that
all symptoms will be readily evident to facilitate diagnosis.
It is intended to provide guidance, enhancing awareness of the
possible range of abnormal behaviors, as a first step in aiding
the diplomat to handle and to report with greater accuracy to
his government on delicate situations.

See also nos. 1263, 1287, 1289, 2081, 2125.

t. Perception and Bargaining

2174. Blake, Robert R. "Psychology and the Crisis of Statesmanship."
14 American Psychologist (1959), 87-94.

On the decline in the capacity of statesmanship to resolve
intergroup conflict due to failure to use psychological theory
when confronting dilemmas. Among four ways to handle group conflicts, one is selected as best, namely, resolution through interaction, discussion, and decision. Stress is placed on intergroup therapy that brings groups qua groups together to work out
stereotypes and "invalid perceptions" of each other and, once
animosities have been worked out, reach agreements for cooperation toward attainment of superordinate goals.

2175. Blake, Robert R., and Mouton, Jane S. "Comprehension of Own
and of Outgroup Positions under Intergroup Competition." 5 Journal of Conflict Resolution (1961), 304-309.

Suggestive experiment on the differences in understanding
of one's own solution to a problem and of that of a competitive
group, the latter not being fully understood even by those who
think they understand it.

See also nos. 1165, 1283, 1289, 1408, 1810, 1832, 2085.

u. Tacit Bargaining

2176. Duroselle, J.-B. "Le 'marchandage tacite' et la solution des
conflits." 14 Revue française de science politique (1964), 738-754.

Analysis of the concept, "resolution of international conflicts," that finds the basic feature to lie in the preference

of each adversary for one of two objectives: (1) attainment of
all stakes sought or (2) reestablishment of normal relations
with the other party. After examining the nature of mistrust
and its foundations, the author considers the situation in which
neither extreme solution, full reconciliation, nor victory of
one party, obtains and then examines Schelling's concept of
tacit bargaining, seeks historical examples especially from the
Franco-Algerian conflict, and deals with the relevance of tacit
bargaining to the East-West conflict.

2177. McClelland, Charles A. "Action Structures and Communication in
Two International Crises: Quemoy and Berlin." 7 Background (1964), 201-
215.
     Analysis of the nonverbal aspects of the Berlin and Quemoy
situations in an effort to ascertain the nature and extent of
tacit bargaining during the two crises.

2178. Quester, George H. "Bargaining and Bombing during World War II
in Europe." 15 World Politics (1963), 417-437.
     Treats the early stages of World War II as an example of
restraint and tacit bargaining about resort to aerial bombard-
ment. Tacit bargaining failed with the gradual breakdown of
communications, of command and control, and of joint interest
in restraints. Collapse of tacit bargaining rendered all-out
bombing the rule. The author contends that the German Government consistently but ineptly sought to limit the air war while
the British Government sought to expand it, employing the first
RAF bombing of Berlin to achieve expansion in order to expose
London but protest the RAF fighter strength.

See also nos. 1451, 2081, 2124, 2150.

v. Information, Credibility and
    Diplomatic Language

2179. Hovland, I., and Weiss, W. "The Influence of Source Credibility
on Communication Effectiveness." 15 Public Opinion Quarterly (1952), 635-
650.
     The credibility of a source was found to influence opinion
in favor of the trustworthy communicator immediately after communication. However, after a period of time it was found that
often the communicator's name was forgotten and the influence
of the communication of the less worthy communicator increased.

2180. Keller, Suzanne. "Diplomacy and Communications." 20 Public
Opinion Quarterly (1956), 176-182.
     This article examines those aspects of diplomatic communi-
cation derived not from conscious operational codes but from
social factors of which the diplomat is unaware or over which
he has no control. It is a study of the social group from which
he comes and whose values he represents. Two aspects of

communication are dealt with: (1) the technical side of knowing
the symbols used by others to establish cognitive contact, and
(2) the emotional reaction to what has been said or written and
to agreement not on the symbols but on what feelings they evoke.

2181. Ostrower, Alexander. Language, Law, and Diplomacy: A Study of
Linguistic Diversity in Official International Relations and International
Law. 2 vols. Philadelphia: University of Pennsylvania Press, 1965, pp.
963.
    Part I deals with national, international, and diplomatic
languages, past and present, and with linguistic practices.
Part II focuses on linguistic provisions in constitutions, treaties, and resolutions and recommendations of the League of Nations and the United Nations. Part III deals with diplomatic
languages in relation to such matters of international law as
general principles, sources, usage, custom, comity, treaties,
desuetude, termination of international engagements, the claus-
ula rebus sic stantibus, and judicial decisions.

w. Embarrassment, Surprise, and Negotiations

2182. Gross, E., and Stone, G.P. "Embarrassment and the Analysis of
Role Requirements." 70 American Journal of Sociology (1964), 1-15.
    This article is based on an analysis of 1,000 recalled in-
stances. Embarrassment is found to occur whenever a central
assumption in a transaction is unexpectedly and unqualifiedly
discredited for at least one participant. The results are two-
fold: (1) the embarrassed individual is incapacitated for role
performance, (2) embarrassment is infectious and may spread out
to incapacitate others not previously embarrassed.

2183. Shackle, G.L.S. Decision, Order, and Time in Human Affairs.
Cambridge, England: Cambridge University Press, 1961, pp. xiv, 302.
    The founder of the "focus element" school of expectational
economics reports on the state of development of his enterprise
by systematically restating and elaborating his basic concepts.
He views decision-makers as arraying possible outcomes on a line
according to the degree of gain or loss as compared with the
present "viewpoint" situation. To each point along the line a
degree of "potential surprise," representing the extent to which
he would be surprised by occurrence of the indicated gain or
loss, is assigned by the decision-maker. The decision-maker
does not pay equal attention to all logically possible outcomes.
His attention varies directly with the positive or negative distance from the "viewpoint and inversely with the potential surprise. Only focus gain and focus loss, occurring where potential surprise is on the upgrade but not so high as to make the
outcome appear unreal, are considered in choosing from among a
set of possible actions. The pairs are referred to a two-
dimensional "gambler's indifference map," the action selected

being the one with focus elements ranking highest with respect
to the particular indifference curve. The potential of Shackle's
framework lies in the possibility of its yielding prescriptions
for decision-making through a simpler scheme than statistical
probability theory or game theory. Indeed, in Shackle's view
decision-makers are already conforming to his model.

x. Commitment as a Bargaining Technique

2184. Becker, Howard S. "Notes on the Concept of Commitment." 66
American Journal of Sociology (1960), 32-40.
    Commitment is treated as coming into being when a "side
bet," often a consequence of participation in social organizations, links extraneous interests with a consistent line of activity. Understanding commitments requires analysis of the
value system in which side bets are made. The author holds
that the limited conception of commitment as side bet avoids
the tautology involved in most concepts of commitment. Among
illustrative examples are Schelling's notion of commitment in
bargaining and Goffman's discussion of commitment to a front or
"face" in interaction. The author's concept may be helpful in
understanding commitment in treaty-making negotiations and in
relation to obligation.

See also nos. 2043, 2081, 2150.

y. Concession, Compromise, and Other
Settlement Techniques

2185. Alger, Chadwick F. "Non-Resolution Consequences of the United
Nations and Their Effect on International Conflict." 5 Journal of Conflict
Resolution (1961), 128-145.
    Delegate conflict and decision-making in UN organs and com-
mittees, with an analysis of the cross-pressures that result
from multiple group affiliations.

2186. Andrews, E.M. "The Australian Government and Appeasement." 13
Australian Journal of Politics and History (1967), 34-46.
    Besides discussion of the internal struggles in Australia
in 1938-1939 over appeasement, the article tries to distinguish
between the circumstances in which appeasement is not immoral
and those, e.g., the sacrifice of others, in which appeasement
is immoral. Attention is given to the Australian Government's
expectation that the Czechs would back down before Hitler and
to Australia's refusal to consider the return of Papua to Germany.

2187. Bohannan, Laura. "A Genealogical Charter." 4 Africa (1952),
301-315.

Important attempt to relate primitive conflict resolution procedures to society's major symbols, by showing how mediators solve disputes by "adjusting" ambiguous lineage formulations.

2188. Braithewaite, R. Theory of Games as a Tool for the Moral Philosopher. New York: Cambridge University Press, 1955, pp. 75.

Utilizes game theory to investigate the problem of what constitutes an equitable solution for two or more conflicting parties.

2189. Fisher, Roger. "Fractionating Conflict." In Roger Fisher (ed.) International Conflict and Behavioral Science: The Craigville Papers. New York: Basic Books, 1964, pp. 91-109.

The author treats the conscious formulation of issues in conflict and considers the advantages and disadvantages of breaking up big issues into little ones (i.e., fractionation). He notes that little study has been devoted to the criteria and methods by which a country should formulate and expand or contract issues in controversy. Suggestions include: downgrading a dispute and treating it as one between individuals rather than between governments; expanding the subject of conflict until it is large enough for a bargain which benefits both parties; coupling issues, i.e., recognizing that two matters are shared in common by the two parties.

2190. Holsti, Kalevi J. "Resolving International Conflicts: A Taxonomy of Behavior and Some Figures on Procedures." 10 Journal of Conflict Resolution (1966), 272-296.

Discussion of six modes of behavior available when states seek to achieve or defend incompatible goals, values, interests, or positions: (1) avoidance; (2) violent conquest; (3) forced submission or withdrawal; (4) compromise; (5) award by a third party; (6) passive settlement. Figures are given on the methods of settling 77 conflicts involving the threat or use of force that have occurred and have been ended since 1919.

2191. Kopytoff, Igor. "Extension of Conflict as a Method of Conflict Resolution among the Sukir of the Congo." 5 Journal of Conflict Resolution (1961), 61-69.

When, for example, the case of the theft of a pig is not resolved by direct confrontation or by judicial action, the injured party may steal the pig of a third party who then confronts the original thief to try to obtain a settlement. Irreconcilability of the original conflict stems from the need to judge one party right and the other wrong. Involvement of a third party tends to stop a direct feud and to lead to mutual readjustment of opposing versions. Extension of conflict does not work so well in certain types of cases.

See also nos. 1451, 2081, 2084, 2087, 2092, 2112, 2113, 2120, 2123, 2125.

6. Third-Party Settlement (Nonjudicial)

2192. Aubert, Vilhelm. "Competition and Dissensus: Two Types of Conflict and of Conflict Resolution." 7 Journal of Conflict Resolution (1963), 26-42.

Outline of a general and cross-cultural theory of law and bargaining, based on the distinction between conflicts of interest and conflicts of value. Includes an analysis of the role of third parties in conflict resolution.

2193. Barros, James. The Aaland Islands Question: Its Settlement by the League of Nations. New Haven: Yale University Press, 1968, pp. xiii, 362.

A study in third-party settlement of a dispute that also demonstrates how the members of an international organization can use the organization in pursuit of their own interests.

2194. Bourne, K., and Watt, D.C. Studies in International History: Essays Presented to W. Norton Medlicott, Stevenson Professor of International History in the University of London. Hamden, Connecticut: Archon Books, 1967, pp. xiii, 446.

This exceptionally high quality Festschrift contains 18 articles among which are: Donald Watt, "South Africa's Attempts to Mediate between Britain and Germany"; Alan S. Milward, "German Economic Policy towards France, 1942-1944"; and Duncan Hall, "The British Commonwealth and the Founding of the League Mandate System."

2195. Brecher, Michael. The Struggle for Kashmir. New York: Oxford, 1953, pp. xii, 211.

Study of the Kashmir mediation effort, somewhat critical of Pakistani attitudes and proposing that the mediators would have done better to get to the roots of the dispute than to employ the fringe approach of attempting to solve the technical details of a plebiscite.

2196. Burton, John W. Conflict Resolution: The Use of Controlled Communication in International Relations. New York: Free Press, 1969, pp. xvii, 246.

Reporting on research done at the Centre for the Analysis of Conflict at University College, London, this volume critically examines traditional methods of mediation that have been applied in international conflicts and describes experiments in face-to-face techniques employed in situations involving social conflict.

2197. Ekvall, Robert B. "Peace and War Among the Tibetan Nomads." 66 American Anthropologist (1964), 1119-1148.

Reviews, among other things, the causes and forms of war, mediators and the mediation process, and peacemaking among Tibetan nomads.

2197-A. Frei, Daniel. "Conditions Affecting the Effectiveness of Small State Mediative Functions." Paper presented at the International Peace Research Association meeting, Karlovy Vary, Czechoslovakia, September 20-23, 1969, pp. 4.

The author describes a research project at the University of Zürich that seeks to identify the independent variables of successful mediation and to formulate hypotheses on the probable correlations between these variables and success in mediation. The research strategy is to examine a few cases in which Switzerland served as mediator and, after developing hypotheses, testing by means of less detailed examination of a large number of cases. A tentative list of variables is provided.

2198. Kahn-Freund, Otto. "Intergroup Conflicts and Their Settlement." 5 British Journal of Sociology (1954), 193-227.

This article, which concentrates on settlement of labor conflict chiefly in Britain, deals with analogues of international institutions and processes. It treats standards of conduct and norms as a product of collective bargaining. These standards and norms may or may not have the force of contractual legal obligations. If a code results, it strengthens ties between parties and gives each an interest in the other's well-being. The law may affect both the normative and the contractual function of the established standards. More importantly, it may give normative force to agreements by investing the bargaining groups with legislative power in place of merely social power. Social power may be as effective as legal power where both sides are well integrated and strongly organized. Negotiation, mediation, arbitration, and inquiry are the main means of settlement. Mediation (conciliation) and arbitration pose the problem of how to select mediators and arbitrators. Prior to institutionalization, which in Britain results in staffing by administrators, selection tended to be on the basis of personal qualities. The quality of a judicial process is still a feature of arbitration.

2199. Keltner, John W. "Communication and the Labor-Management Mediation Process: Some Aspects and Hypotheses." 15 Journal of Communication (1965), 64-80.

A former mediator with the Federal Mediation and Conciliation Service draws distinctions between the kinds of pressure and power used in dealing with differences arising from day-to-day work negotiations and contract interpretations and those used in contract negotiations. The tenor of the situation becomes more nearly comparable to formal contract table bargaining when grievances are not solved at lower-level, informal, face-to-face interaction. Attention is accorded the six stages of the contract bargaining process, the communication objectives of the parties, the techniques with which objectives are approached including persuasion, coercion, bluffing, rationalization, and deception (a highly refined technique expected as part of the game), and the mediation role. Several explorable hypotheses

about the mediator and his communication role are set forth.
Among them is the hypothesis, based on experience as to what is
becoming increasingly evident, that "the greater the control
that a mediator exerts over the communication system, the
greater the facility of persuasion of the parties," a control
that, among other things, "may enable the mediator to maneuver
through stratagems and feints in order to develop movement."

2200. Kerr, Clark. "Industrial Conflict and Its Mediation." 60 _American Journal of Sociology_ (1954), 230-245.
Useful for its description and classification of mediation
and mediation disputes, with attention to the possibility that
mediation may prolong a dispute when employed merely to indicate
that "something is being done."

2201. Korbel, Josef. _Danger in Kashmir_. Princeton: Princeton University Press, 1954, pp. 351.
Analysis of the Kashmir dispute based on observation as
Czechoslovakian member and chairman of the United Nations Commission sent in 1948 for the purpose of mediating.

2202. Pruitt, Dean G., and Johnson, Douglas F. "Mediation as an Aid to Face Saving in Negotiations." 14 _Journal of Personality and Social Psychology_ (1970), 239-246.
Report of a negotiating experiment that found a mediator's
suggestion of a halfway point of settlement to produce substantial concessions, that high time pressures increased the concession rate, and that concessions were made when the other negotiator moved rapidly toward agreement. Intervention by a mediator was found to remove the sense of personal weakness that accompanies the making of concessions.

2202-A. Rao, G.R. "The Concept of a Third Force in Conflict Resolution." 48 _Gandhi Marg_ (1968), 421-430.
Discusses possible roles of third forces in terms of goals,
gives attention to methods of conflict resolution, and makes
suggestions about the limits to the functional effectiveness of
third forces. The author recommends that case studies be made
of the United Nations, the Shanti Sena (Peace Army) of the Sarva
Sena, and the Nagaland Peace Mission.

2202-B. Remington, Robin Alison. _The Warsaw Pact: Case Studies in Communist Conflict Resolution_. Cambridge: MIT Press, 1971, pp. 288.
A study of the role of the Warsaw Pact as an instrument for
containing intrabloc conflicts and as a device that legitimizes
the application of the Brezhnev Doctrine (cf. no. 1558).

2203. SarDesai, D.R. _Indian Foreign Policy in Cambodia, Laos and Vietnam, 1947-1964_. Berkeley: University of California Press, 1968, pp. xiii, 336.
Aside from insights into Nehru's Southeast Asian policy,
the most important segment of this book deals with India's

position as Chairman of the International Control Commission for
the area.

2204. Steinberg, B.S. "The Korean War: A Case Study in Indian Neutralism." 8 Orbis (1965), 937-954.
Examination of India's role as mediator in an effort to determine whether neutralist states can judge a conflict on its merits. No conclusion is reached on the basis of India's participation on the Neutral Nations Repatriation Committee, although India's actions as a balancing agent between the two groups of participants (Polish/Czech and Swiss/Swedish), including her striking alternation of support, seem to invite the conclusion that India's decisions were based on the broader aspects of the issues, i.e., world peace, rather than on narrower foreign policy objectives.

2205. Stjernquist, P. "Paralleller mellan medling i internationella tvister och medling i arbetsvister (Parallel between Mediation in International Disputes and Mediation in Wage Disputes)." 56 Statsvetenskaplig Tidskrift (Lund, 1953), 442-454.
Compares mediation in labor disputes as an arena for airing grievances with the United Nations system in which the positions of the parties are asserted before international organizations. Considerations of prestige and tendencies of mediation to formalize even to the point of selection from a panel are discussed.

2206. Taylor, Alastair M. Indonesian Independence and the United Nations. Ithaca: Cornell University Press, 1960, pp. xxix, 503.
Deals with the part played by the United Nations in settling disputes between the Dutch and the Indonesians.

2207. "Techniques of Mediation and Conciliation." 10 International Social Science Bulletin (1958), 507-630.
The first article in this symposium of descriptive articles on mediation and conciliation deals with the settlement of international disputes.

2208. van den Hove, Didier. Étude de deux modes d'influence sociale dans la resolution d'un conflit d'intérêt: Médiation et observation--Recherche expérimentale exploratoire. 2 vols. Louvain: Université Catholique de Louvain: Faculté de Philosophie et Lettres, Institut de Psychologie et des Sciences de l'Éducation, 1968.
Report of a laboratory experiment on third-party impact on interpersonal negotiations that finds differences in third-party impact to be related to differences in the situation and differences in the level of cognitive complexity of the subjects. Whether the third party acted as mediator or as observer also made a difference, and it appears that in some situations observation produces a deterioration in the parties' performance as negotiators. Mediation was found to have little effect on bilateral negotiations, serving chiefly to bring about a mild amelioration in performance of cognitively simple subjects only.

2209. Walton, Richard E. Legal Justice, Power-Bargaining, and Social Science Intervention: Mechanisms for Settling Disputes. Paper No. 194. Institute for Research in the Behavioral, Economic, and Management Sciences. Herman C. Krannert Graduate School of Industrial Administration. Lafayette, Indiana: Purdue University, March 1968, pp. 63.

The three approaches of legal justice, power-bargaining, and social science intervention are distinguished, social science analysis and intervention being treated as taking account of many facets of the social system and seeking to resolve the dispute in a manner consistent with the objective of preserving or changing the social system or certain of its characteristics. The paper argues (1) that the three mechanisms are fundamentally different in that they assume very different solution criteria, (2) that they are operationally distinguishable in their use of different types of data, different methods of gathering and processing data, different types of influence tactics, etc., (3) that both the principals and third parties can influence which mechanism will be used in a given dispute, and (4) both distinctions among mechanisms and propositions governing their use are applicable to many social settings including the interpersonal, intergroup, and international.

2210. Wild, Patricia Berko. "The Organization of African Unity and the Algerian-Moroccan Border Conflict." 20 International Organization (1966), 18-36.

An account of the background of the border dispute, the unsuccessful effort to get United Nations help due to Western fears of escalation into an East-West conflict, the personal efforts of the Emperor of Ethiopia and the President of Mali to facilitate a settlement, and the approach to the Organization of African Unity. The last led to an agreement showing a preference for direct negotiations apparently prompted by the mediation and conciliation activities of a committee appointed by the OAU Council of Ministers.

2211. Wood, Bryce. The United States and Latin American Wars, 1932-1942. New York: Columbia University Press, 1966, pp. x, 519.

Thorough, well-documented study of the Chaco War, the Leticia dispute, and the Maranon conflict, that provides much information on third-party processes, successful and unsuccessful, in conflict resolution efforts, with particular attention to the role of the United States in relation to these three Western Hemisphere conflicts.

2212. Young, Oran R. The Intermediaries: Third Parties in International Crises. Princeton: Princeton University Press, 1967, pp. x, 427.

Generates hypotheses about the management of conflict. Attention is given to actions available to third parties, types of third parties, three images of the United Nations system, United Nations intervention in Soviet-American crises, several hypothetical superpower crises, intervention by the Secretary-General and Secretariat, and prospects for the future.

2213. Zacher, Mark W. "The Secretary-General and the United Nations' Function of Peaceful Settlement." 22 International Organization (1966), 724-749.

Analyzes the changing role of the Secretary-General, notes that the Secretary-General was designated to implement a Security Council or General Assembly recommendation in 7% of the instances occurring in 1946-1954 and in 61% of the 1955-1965 cases, and includes an appendix describing the 40 cases in which the Secretary-General or others have had delegated tasks and 32 independent attempts by the Secretary-General to obtain peaceful settlements.

2214. Zook, David H., Jr. The Conduct of the Chaco War. New York: Bookman Associates, 1960, pp. 280.

History of the Chaco War and of preceding and attendant diplomatic negotiations, particularly useful in respect to the light thrown upon the use of negotiation by both Bolivia and Paraguay to obtain a favorable basis for arbitration, the ultimate use of arbitration for public consumption after the outcome had already been agreed upon by each party separately with the mediators, the problems of third parties attempting mediation, misperception by each of the contending governments of the other's policy as threatening, and, prior to the outbreak of war, attempted reprisals by both sides that broke down into what amounted to a feud. Basic to the entire matter was the ambiguity concerning boundaries not clarified when independence came to Bolivia and Paraguay.

See also nos. 381, 905, 909, 1236, 1558, 1561, 1592, 1719-1799, 1952, 1971, 2081, 2126, 2174, 2378.

7. Law as Implicit Third Party

2215. Barkun, Michael. "Conflict Resolution Through Implicit Mediation." 8 Journal of Conflict Resolution (1964), 121-130.

Interrelating the studies of anthropologists and international lawyers, the article identifies similarities between the primitive and the international decentralized legal systems. Emphasizing the change from diadic to triadic systems characterized by a third party as mediator, the author makes an important contribution to understanding of the nature of the international legal system by demonstrating how the system itself can, in effect, become the third party.

See also no. 145.

8. International Arbitration

2216. Chaudhri, Mohammed Ahsen (ed.), The Prospects of International
Arbitration. Karachi: Pakistan Publishing House, 1966, pp. 131.
  Examination of arbitration by scholars and officials of
Egypt, Pakistan, and Poland. Chaudhri surveys arbitration since
1945 with particular attention to the attitudes of the new states.
Tadeusz Szurski discusses the significance of commercial arbitra-
tion in East-West relations. Mohammed Tewfik Hussanein's essay
concentrates on the Permanent Court of Arbitration.

2217. Hackett, Frank Warren. Reminiscences of the Geneva Tribunal of
Arbitration, 1872--The Alabama Claims. Boston: Houghton Mifflin, 1911, pp.
xvi, 450.
  Reminiscences by the secretary to Caleb Cushing, senior
American counsel, that throw light both upon techniques of argument and upon the relation of diplomacy to the actual course of
arbitration.

2218. Scelle, Georges. "Intergovernmental Arbitration Today." 1 International Relations (1954), 3-9.
  Diplomatic and jurisdictional arbitration are distinguished,
the former being entrusted to outstanding political personalities
whose word is final and the latter to jurist-arbitrators whose
decisions may give ground for voidability. The ILC favored the
jurisdictional concept based on the idea that the undertaking to
resort to arbitration is irrevocable.

See also nos. 1971, 2198, 2211, 2214.

9. International Courts and Adjudication

2219. Aubert, Vilhelm. "Courts and Conflict Resolution." 11 Journal
of Conflict Resolution (1967), 40-51.
  On the judge as decision-maker and on reasons why parties
may go into court instead of settling out of court. A section
on implications for international law suggests that states have
motivational structures entirely different from human organisms.
Thus, while individual self-righteousness may lead the parties
into courts to furnish the judiciary with the cases needed to
reassert the authority of law, national self-righteousness di-
minishes the chance of going to court because doing so may be
perceived by compatriots as admission of weakness rather than,
as for the individual, a display of a firm attitude and a fighting spirit. Moreover, in comparison with, e.g., an insurance
company, states are less willing to buy predictability by loss
of a case in court. The author suggests that today legal models
appear less relevant than models built upon scientific and technical competences, e.g., the technical knowledge of a physician
or air transport personnel or predictions about the development
of the market that are derived from economics.

2220. Brigman, William Edward. <u>The Office of the Solicitor General of the United States</u>. Ph.D. Dissertation. Chapel Hill: University of North Carolina, 1966; Ann Arbor: University Microfilms, Inc., Order No. 67-969, pp. 160.

A section on the strategy of litigation indicates that a strategy of docket management is employed in the effort to present the most favorable position to the Supreme Court, that no appeal that could be won in the Court of Appeals is taken if it seems likely that the case would be lost in the Supreme Court, and that conflicts between lower courts are developed when it is deemed desirable to assure review by the Supreme Court. Attention is given to the effect on public policy of control of appeals by the Executive Departments and by regulatory commissions other than the Interstate Commerce Commission. Similar study of strategies of selecting tribunals and cases, as well as of choices of legal or political arenas, and of negotiations when states' preferences in these matters conflict, would do much to elucidate the nature of international dispute settlement, the pertinent processes, and the relations between law and bargaining.

2221. Hensley, Thomas R. "National Bias and the International Court of Justice." 12 <u>Midwest Journal of Political Science</u> (1968), 568-586.

The author examines the Judges' voting behavior and finds that, despite a general disposition to favor their own countries in decisions of greater national importance, the Judges display no statistically significant tendency toward such favoritism. The conclusion is that such national bias as is present does not violate the criterion of independence.

2222. Holden, Matthew, Jr. "Litigation and the Political Order." 16 <u>Western Political Quarterly</u> (1963), 771-781.

Holds that the concern of the political scientist is served by making the litigant the center of action with special attention to three points: (1) What stakes do litigants seek? (2) How do they become involved in the litigation process? (3) How do they evaluate the moral legitimacy of tribunals? Within this context, litigation is seen as fundamental to comprehension of the political order, i.e., the distribution of power plus the rules and practices governing the order of precedence among potential participants in the system. Depending upon the answers to the three questions, litigation may be either a form of struggle or a form of bargaining, with the extent to which one or the other predominates in a given society being a sensitive indicator of faction in Madison's sense.

2223. Moe, Henry A. "A Lawyer's History Lesson." 15 <u>Physics Today</u> (April 1962), 30-34.

Relates the history of the development of the trial, in which the hardest step appears to have been to establish that the malefactor had to submit to a court's jurisdiction, to the problem of gradually developing among states the habit of submitting to the jurisdiction of international tribunals.

2224. Scott, William A. "International Ideology and Interpersonal Ideology." 24 Public Opinion Quarterly (1960), 419-435.
Survey data shows that people's notions of ideal international relations correspond to their conceptions of ideal interpersonal relations. If the findings are indicative, it would appear that one factor mitigating against resort to international judicial procedures is the ideal which hardly can be expected to portray interpersonal relations as litigation. It should be noted that the findings of this survey do not go to the questions of perception of the reality of international relations and of the gap between the ideal and the reality, nor do they indicate whether litigous personalities hold a different view of international judicial processes than personalities preferring to avoid litigation.

See also nos. 662, 1315, 1881, 2031.

10. Regional Courts and Special Tribunals

2225. Scheingold, Stuart A. The Rule of Law in European Integration. New Haven: Yale University Press, 1965, pp. xiv, 331.
A systematic legal history, written by a political scientist, that deals with the bulk of the activities of the Court of Justice of the European Communities in 1954-1964. Functionalism, visualizing the law as prescribing rules of behavior necessary for achieving agreed-on objectives and presuming agreement on ends and common values, is the concept used to organize the history and to evaluate the Court's jurisprudence.

11. The Problem of Blame and Stigma

2226. Schwartz, Richard D., and Skolnick, Jerome H. "Two Studies of Legal Stigma." 10 Social Problems (1962), 133-142.
Study of the impact of such criminal law labels as "accused," "acquitted," and "certified innocent" upon an applicant's ability to get a job requiring menial work, with results indicating that an accusation is virtually as stigmatizing as a conviction.

2227. Wright, T.P., Jr. "National Integration and Modern Judicial Procedure in India: The Dar-us-Salam Case." 6 Asian Survey (1966), 675-682.
Focusing on the problem of Muslims torn between the protection of the shari'a and integration with the Hindu majority under a secular common civil code, the author gives attention to the impact of legal procedures borrowed from Britain on the minority's traditional mediation procedures, the possibility that integration can sharpen the definition of nationality to exclude some minorities, and the danger that a minority community's resort to modern courts may be dysfunctional to integration by

compelling contestants to parade animosities. Although the article is oriented to national integration, its warnings are relevant to integrative efforts among nations.

See also no. 1840.

12. Choice of Legal or Political Methods

2228. Barkun, Michael, and Levine, James. Social Change Through Direct
Action: A Case Study of a Civil Rights Movement. Mimeo. Prepared for
presentation to the 1965-1966 meeting of the Advisory Committee to the Program in Law and the Social Sciences, Northwestern University, Evanston, Illinois, February 19-20, 1966, pp. ii, 97.
     Report on the North Shore Summer Project of 1965, directed
with little success against the failure of realtors to show
houses in most parts of certain Chicago suburbs to Negroes. A
chapter on the Project and the law finds the lawyers' role to
have been small with those in charge declaring that even information was not wanted from lawyers unless requested, that the
lawyers' role should be strictly the technical one of keeping
the Project from breaking the law, and that not legalistic but
rhetorical responses to the realtors were wanted. The possibility of bringing an action at law was consistently tabled. Lawyers' efforts to mediate--in effect, to seek a pre-trial settle-
ment--were rejected and the legal advisor to the Steering Committee had his attempt to preserve communications with the real
estate board lead to his dismissal. The authors suggest that
among the reasons for the minimal role played by lawyers were
the fact that legal action would not produce results during the
single summer's life of the Project, that resort to the law
would be technical and involve only a few people with specific
skills in a cloistered setting and so a violation of the norm
of mass participation, and that the leaders, lacking knowledge
of law and legal issues, hesitated to initiate activities which
they could not themselves control and which would subject the
leaders to the lawyers' judgment.

2229. Claude, Inis L., Jr. "Problems of Inter-American Neighborliness:
A Review of Bryce Wood: The Making of the Good Neighbor Policy, and William
Manger: Pan America in Crisis: The Future of the OAS." 6 Journal of Conflict Resolution (1962), 355-358.
     In reference to Wood's book, the reviewer points out (1)
that emphasis on a national point of view does not inevitably
lead to conflict and may be an advance over emphasis on a subnational viewpoint, and that (2) legal settlement, besides being
neither necessarily the only alternative to violence nor always
preferable to political settlement, may represent a "hard" rather
than a "soft" policy.

See also no. 891.

B. HOSTILITIES

1. Types of Violence

2230. Nieburg, H.L. Political Violence: The Behavioral Process.
New York: St. Martin's, 1969, pp. 192.
An attempt to explain all types of violence in politics
that includes an analytical matrix of extreme forms of social
action in a single continuum of political behavior connecting
stability and disorder. Individual violence, group violence,
and war are related in the behavioral continuum. An assumption
of a relatively rational choice between violent and nonviolent
means serves as a basis for treating violence as symptomatic of
an urge for greater integration and more equitable distribution
of values.

2231. Walter, E.V. "Violence and the Process of Terror." 29 American Sociological Review (1964), 248-257.
Treats terror as composed of (a) violence, (b) fear, and
(c) reactive behavior. Distinctions are made between the siege
of terror and the reign of terror, between social uses of violence to change the conditions of control. Among other things,
terrorism, war, and legal punishment are differentiated. A
typology of power systems based on the use of violence is advocated.

2232. Wolin, Sheldon S. "Violence and the Western Political Tradition." 33 American Journal of Ortho-Psychiatry (No. 1), 15-28.
Cultural-anthropological analysis of violence in terms of
its quality, its explosive character, and its excessive destruction relative to its purpose.

See also nos. 1842.

2. Economic Warfare

2233. Albinski, Henry S. "Australia and the Chinese Strategic Embargo." 19 Australian Outlook (August 1965), 117-128.
Treats the Australian embargo on the sale of strategic materials for China as a successful exercise in Realpolitik in
that little is lost while also permitting continued high sales
of primary products to China. The author regards the embargo
as revealing a good deal about the interplay of commerce, politics, and diplomacy.

2234. Armytage, Frances. The Free Port System in the British West
Indies: A Study in Commercial Policy, 1766-1822. London: Longmans for
the Royal Empire Society (1953), pp. 176.

History of the free ports in the West Indies that were
originally established to capture trade from neighboring Spanish colonies and which worked well until Latin American independence.

2235. Vaudaux, Adolphe. Blockade und Gegenblockade. Zürich: Polygraphischer Verlag, 1948, pp. 128.
     Problems of a landlocked state in the formulation and exe-
cution of export and import policies.

See also nos. 1216, 1217, 1654.

3. Maritime Warfare

     2236. Lieuwen, Edwin. The United States and the Challenge to Security
in Latin America. Social Science Program of the Mershon Center for Education in National Security, The Ohio State University, Pamphlet Series, No.
4. Columbus: Ohio State University Press, April 1966, pp. 98.
     Deals with United States bases in Latin America and reviews
current training and coordination of antisubmarine preparations
and of antisubversive and counterinsurgency efforts, including
the hemisphere-wide program of the Inter-American Security Committee to curtail the travel of subversives and guerrillas to
and from Cuba as well as the flow of arms and propaganda from
Cuba. Attention is given to Soviet attempts to wean Latin America from the US orbit, Red China's efforts in Latin America, and
the Castroite undertaking to train revolutionaries to initiate
revolution in other Latin American countries and to dispense
propaganda and arms. Internal threats antedating Castroite support and local efforts to outlaw Communist parties are discussed
and also instances of insurgency and its potential in the several Latin American countries. A section is devoted to deficiencies in OAS efforts to apply sanctions, to engage in peacekeeping, and to establish a permanent force to safeguard Western
Hemisphere countries against Communist takeovers, the absolutist
principle of nonintervention, together with underlying supportive
Latin American attitudes, being treated as the root of the deficiencies.

     2237. "Oceans Hold Challenge Market of the Sixties." 9 Data (July
1964), 9-13.
     On the uses of submarines in nuclear, strategic economic,
and conventional warfare, on developments in antisubmarine warfare, and on improvement of countermeasures for submarines.

     2238. Siney, Marion Celestia. The Allied Blockade of Germany, 1914-
1916. Ann Arbor: University of Michigan Press, 1957, pp. x, 339.
     First of two volumes on legal, political, and diplomatic
aspects of the Allied blockade.

2239. Smith, Gaddis. _Britain's Clandestine Submarines, 1914-1915_. New Haven: Yale University Press, 1964, pp. vi, 155.
    Deals with a significant episode early in World War I that involved President Wilson and American neutrality, Charles Schwab and Bethlehem Steel, and the North Atlantic Triangle.

See also nos. 1654.

4. Aerial Warfare

2240. Brodie, Bernard. _Strategy in the Missile Age._ Princeton: Princeton University Press, 1959, pp. 423.
    Describes strategic thinking at the beginning of the air era, analyzes the role of strategic airpower in World War II, and discusses the strategic issues posed by nuclear weapons.

2241. Quester, George H. _Deterrence before Hiroshima_. New York: Wiley, 1966, pp. xii, 196.
    Study of air strategy issues before and after August 1945 that traces a pattern of breakdowns in restraints on aerial bombardment in World Wars I and II that raises serious doubts about man's capacity for self-restraint even with today's weapons.

5. Nuclear Weapons

2242. Badurina, Berislav. "Quasi-Tactical Nuclear Weapons." 16 _Review of International Affairs_ (1965), 12-14.
    Treats weapons of payload up to 100 kilotons as "tactical" when part of the arsenal of a large nation that also possesses long-range and large payload weapons and as "strategic" when in the hands of states with average-sized populations and less extensive arsenals.

2243. Batchelder, Robert C. _The Irreversible Decision, 1939-1950_. New York: Macmillan, 1961, pp. 306.
    An analysis of the interplay of moral principles and historical events in the decision to make the first use of atomic weapons. The moral dilemma is the main theme of the volume in the discussion of consequences as well as the decision itself.

2244. Batten, E.S. _The Effects of Nuclear War on the Weather and Climate_. RM-4989-TAB. Santa Monica: RAND Corporation, August 1966, pp. 66.
    On possible effects of nuclear debris and extensive fires on weather and climate.

2245. Birnbaum, Karl. "Sweden's Nuclear Policy." 20 _International Journal_ (1965), 297-311.

An explanation of factors conditioning Sweden's policy toward nuclear armaments that views the possibility of a Swedish decision "to go nuclear" as a danger signal for the international community in terms of the probability of proliferation.

2246. Blackett, P.M.S. "Nuclear Weapons and Defense: Comments on Kissinger, Kennan and King-Hall." 34 International Affairs (1958), 421-434.
Includes the hypothesis that technological superiority compensated not for a deficiency of Western manpower but for a disinclination of Western peoples to serve as soldiers.

2247. Brode, H.L. A Survey of the Weapons and Hazards which May Face the People of the United States in Wartime. P-3170. Santa Monica: RAND Corporation, June 1965, pp. 24.
Dealing primarily with nuclear weapons but also giving attention to conventional explosives and to biological and chemical weapons, the report provides information on various forms of damage to be anticipated and suggests some precautions.

2248. Chiu, H. "Communist China's Attitude towards Nuclear Tests." 21 China Quarterly (1965), 96-107.
Review of China's official policy before and after the negotiations for the test ban treaty of 1963.

2249. Dyson, Freeman. "The Future Development of Nuclear Weapons." 38 Foreign Affairs (1960), 457-464.
First statement in US literature on the "neutron" bomb as a fission-free weapon by a scientist acquainted with the US nuclear weapons program. The article also deals with other matters including the 1958 Geneva meeting of scientists.

2250. Frank, Jerome D. "Breaking the Thought Barrier: Psychological Challenges of the Nuclear Age." 23 Psychiatry (1960), 245-266.
Nations are seen as responding maladaptively to the threat of nuclear war. Responses of apathy, habituation, and denial are common to psychiatric patients. Denial is facilitated by representation of earlier weapons as having limited destructive capabilities, by "insensitivity to the remote, and by the use of reassuring terms like defense." Anxiety paralyzes initiative and facilitates stereotyped perception. Correction of mutual distortions is hindered by mutual distrust that disrupts communications. The author sees abolition of war as only solution and finds hope in a presumed increase of nonviolent settlement of personal and group conflicts, in a plasticity of human nature, and in the molding of individual behavior by group standards such as those of Ghandi and Martin Luther King.

2251. Frank, Jerome D. "Emotional and Motivational Aspects of the Disarmament Problem." 17 Journal of Social Issues (1961), 20-27.
Responses to nuclear threat have either been maladaptive or apparently adaptive because attempts to achieve destructive superiority, sacrifice one's life for ideals in war, and demonstrate courage by threatening violence, have been adaptive in

the past. Martin Luther King and Ghandi have created group
standards that make refusal to use violence a demonstration of
courage and thus remove the main psychological barrier to disarmament, namely, its association with cowardice and surrender.

2252. Hansen, Erland Brun, and Ulrich, J.W. "Some Problems of Nuclear
Power Dynamics." 1 Journal of Peace Research (1964), 137-149.
　　The authors of this article are, respectively, a physicist
and a chemist at the University of Copenhagen. Nuclear power
in a binary system can be split into actual nuclear power and
potential nuclear power, their relative importance differing
for high and low levels of actual nuclear power. Lowering the
actual nuclear power level without devising simultaneous stabilizing systemic constructions will probably not result in decisive, if any, security gains. Dealing with potential nuclear
power requires such extensive encroachments into existing systems that these encroachments are unlikely to occur within any
possible disarmament schedule. As may be inferred from equations setting forth the relationships of states A and B in a
binary system, controlled disarmament does not appear to represent even a provisional solution to the disarmament problem.

2253. Hanunian, N. Dimensions of Survival: Post-Attack Survival
Disparities and National Viability. RM-5140-TAB. Santa Monica: RAND
Corporation, December 1966, pp. 228.
　　An attempt to foresee possible changes in the American societal structure as a result of nuclear attack. Among other
things, the author suggests that the impact of nuclear war seems
much more oppressive when a substantial number of well-chosen
indicators are employed rather than a single measure such as
mortalities.

2254. Heer, David M. After Nuclear Attack: A Demographic Inquiry.
New York: Praeger, 1965, pp. xxxiii, 405.
　　A study of the demographic effects of large-scale nuclear
attack on the United States. Starting from two given geographical distributions of fatalities, the study calculates the characteristics of the population surviving each of the two hypothetical attacks.

2255. Intriligator, Michael D. Some Simple Models of Arms Races.
RM-3903-PR. Santa Monica: RAND Corporation, April 1964, pp. 28.
　　An attempt to adapt classical models of arms races to a
world of nuclear weapons. Limitation of focus to the single
policy variable of the level of weapon stocks restricts the
utility of the analysis to suggestion only.

2256. Kahn, Herman. On Thermonuclear War. Princeton: Princeton
University Press, 1960, pp. xx, 652.
　　Lengthy analyses of war, strategies, objectives, and the
concepts of deterrence, together with a series of hypothetico-
deductive deterrence models.

2257. Lowry, I.S. The Post-Attack Population of the United States. RM-5115-TAB. Santa Monica: RAND Corporation, December 1966, pp. 153.
Analyzes potential demographic consequences of a nuclear attack upon the United States. A related paper by B.F. Goeller, The Sensitivity of Mortality Estimates to Variations in Aggregate Population Representations (RAND Report RM-5141-TAB, December 1966), indicates the dependence of mortality estimates on the manner of representing the geographical distribution of the population.

2258. Mitchell, H.H. Survey of the Infectious Disease Problem as It Relates to the Post-Attack Environment. RM-5090-TAB. Santa Monica: RAND Corporation, August 1966, pp. 92.
On the probable incidence of infectious disease after nuclear attack, possible countermeasures, and needed studies.

2259. Nogee, Joseph L. Soviet Policy Toward International Control of Atomic Energy. Notre Dame, Indiana: Notre Dame University Press, 1961, pp. xiv, 306.
Summarizes negotiations on control of atomic energy, disarmament, and banning nuclear bomb tests, focusing on Soviet policy particularly in 1945-1948 prior to the first Soviet atomic explosion.

2260. Pogrund, R.S. Nutrition in the Postattack Environment. RM-5052-TAB. Santa Monica: RAND Corporation, December 1966, pp. 71.
Investigates the dietary problems, including that of adaptation to unfamiliar foods, that would follow a nuclear attack upon the United States.

2260-A. Tanaka, Yasumasu. "Japanese Attitudes Toward Nuclear Arms." 34 Public Opinion Quarterly (1970), 26-42.
A Japanese scholar's survey of students' expectations about nuclear development in their country and a semantic analysis of their changing evaluations of this development. Nuclear arms are regarded as undesirable but, if nuclear proliferation continues, necessary for survival.

2261. Tate, Merze, and Hull, Doris M. "Effects of Nuclear Explosions on Pacific Islanders." 33 Pacific Historical Review (1964), 379-393.
On the observable consequences of testing in the Marshall Islands, including the international and domestic political consequences.

2262. Younger, Kenneth. "The Spectre of Nuclear Proliferation." 42 International Affairs (January 1966), 14-23.
Elaboration of the views and interests of nuclear superpowers, nuclear powers, and nonnuclear powers in concluding a nonproliferation treaty and the difficulties encountered in attaining a treaty "void of loop-holes" which the United Nations Resolution advocated.

See also nos. 518, 1216, 1217, 1377, 1421, 1451, 1559, 1665, 1670, 1760, 2101, 2150, 2602, 2869.

6. Neutrality

2263. Divine, Robert A. The Illusion of Neutrality. Chicago: University of Chicago Press; Toronto: University of Toronto Press, 1962, pp. xi, 370.
A comprehensive treatment of the evolution of United States neutrality enactments from 1927 to 1939. No serious challenge is presented to conventional interpretations of New Deal foreign policy. The author seldom conceals his conviction that the policy of neutrality led to uniformly bad results.

2264. Dutoit, Bernard. La neutralité suisse à l'heure européenne. Paris: Librairie Générale de Droit et de Jurisprudence, 1962, pp. 138.
A reappraisal of the validity and role of Swiss neutrality in the light of European Community developments.

2265. Fiedler, Heinz. Der sowjetische Neutralitätsbegriff in Theorie und Praxis. Cologne: Verlag für Politik und Wirtschaft, 1959, pp. 301.
Extended analysis of Soviet theory and practice in regard to neutrality and of the theme as it appears in the coexistence doctrine.

2266. Goodrich, Austin. Study in SISU. New York: Ballantine, 1960, pp. 144.
Deals with the Winter War and with Finland's follow-up war against the Soviet Union, the resettlement of Karelians, the Russo-Finnish Armistice of 1944 and the Helsinki war crimes trial, the 1947 Russo-Finnish mutual assistance agreement, and the course of imposed neutrality in the postwar period as it affects Finland's relations with European and North Atlantic associations and also in respect to avoidance of a Communist regime despite a Communist-staffed State Police (VALPO) until after the 1948 elections.

2267. Haug, Hans. Neutralität und Völkergemeinschaft. Zürich: Polygraphischer Verlag, 1962, pp. viii, 191.
Problem of neutrality and its function amid the growth of international organizations.

2267-A. Jakobson, Max. Finnish Neutrality: A Study of Finnish Foreign Policy since the Second World War. New York: Praeger, 1969, pp. 116.
The Finnish Ambassador to the United Nations deals with the problem of a Western democracy's being neutral while maintaining a mutual assistance pact with the Soviet Union.

2268. Leifer, Michael. Cambodia: The Search for Security. New York: Praeger, 1967, pp. ix, 209.

Review of an important aspect of Southeast Asian development that identifies the clashes of claims and demands that embroil Cambodia with Vietnam and Thailand. These claims and demands include such succession problems as the position of Vietnamese who were in the French civil service in Cambodia, as well as boundary disputes. This study brings somewhat more up to date the author's earlier Cambodia and Neutrality (Canberra: Australian National University, 1963).

2269. Soldati, Agostino. "Considérations sur la neutralité." Revue militaire générale (No. 9, 1965), 534-550.
Historical background of neutrality and discussion of its role in this era, with projections as to its future status.

2270. Stranner, Henri. Neutralité suisse et solidarité européene. Lausanne: Éditions Vie, 1959, pp. 284.
Analysis of the political and economic implications for Switzerland of the growth of European integration.

See also nos. 1115, 1312, 2275, 2342.

7. Partisans and Resistance Movements

2271. Battaglia, Roberto. Storia della resistenza italiana--8 settembre 1943--25 aprile 1945. Turin: Einaudi, 1953, pp. 621.
Extensive history of the Italian resistance movement, appearing also in an abridged English edition under the title The Story of the Italian Resistance (London: Oldhams, 1958).

2272. Baudoin, Madeleine. Histoire des groupes francs (M.U.R.) des Bouches-du-Rhone de septembre 1943 à la libération. Paris: Presses Universitaires, 1962, pp. 284.
Account of the activities of the Mouvements Unis de Resistance in southern France.

2273. Catalano, Franco. Storia del C.L.N.A.I. Bari: Laterza, 1956, pp. 456.
Well-documented account of the resistance movement in Milan and northern Italy.

2274. Gérard, Ivan. Armée secrète: Souvenirs de commandement. Brussels: La Renaissance du Livre, 1962, pp. 266.
Account of wartime resistance in Belgium by one of the generals of that period.

2275. Lampe, David. The Danish Resistance. New York: Ballantine, 1960.
First published in England in 1957 under the title, The Savage Canary, this book presents a narrative account of the resistance of Danes to the German occupation of their neutral country and of Danish assistance to the Allies. Some references

are also made to the help provided by Swedes to the Danes and to the Allied war effort.

2276. Luther, Hans. Der französische Widerstand gegen die deutsche Besatzungsmacht und seine Bekämpfung. Tübingen: Institut fur Besatzungs-fragen, 1957, pp. 297.
    Study of French resistance to the German occupation and of countermeasures taken by the Germans.

2276-A. Mastny, Vojtech. The Czechs under Nazi Rule: The Failure of National Resistance, 1939-1942. New York: Columbia University Press, 1971, pp. 274.
    Making use of previously unknown captured German documents, this book deals with the question of the possibilities and lim-its of defiance of a powerful occupation force and the extent to which failure was due to failure of Czech leadership, support of the people, and Nazi occupation policies.

2277. Michel, Henri. Les courants de pensée de la résistance. Paris: Presses Universitaires, 1962, pp. 844.
    An attempt to identify and to analyze the main currents that fed into the French resistance movement.

2278. Molden, Otto. Der Ruf des Gewissens: Der österreichische Frei-heitskampf 1938-1945. Vienna: Herold, 1958, pp. 370.
    Detailed account of the Austrian resistance movement from Anschluss to the unsuccessful revolt of July 20, 1944.

2279. Redelis, Valdis. Partisanenkrieg: Entstehung und Bekämpfung der Partisanen--und Untergrundbewegung im Mittelabschnitt der Ostfront 1941 bis 1943. Heidelberg: Vowinckel, 1958, pp. 152.
    Account of Soviet partisan activities by an officer who fought against them.

2280. Schroers, Rolf. Der Partisan: Ein Beitrag zur politischen Anthropologie. Cologne: Kiepenheuer & Witsch, 1961, pp. 344.
    An attempt to probe motivations and characteristics under-lying modern guerrilla warfare.

2281. Secchia, Pietro, and Moscatelli, Cino. Il Monte Rosa è Sceso a Milano: La resistenza nel Biellese, nella Valsesia e nella Valdossola. Turin: Einaudi, 1958, pp. 655.
    Detailed account of a resistance movement in a section of Piedmont.

2282. Valeriano, Napoleon D., and Bohannan, Charles T.R. Counterguer-rilla Operations: The Philippine Experience. New York: Praeger, 1962, pp. 275.
    Consideration of counterguerrilla operations based on the Philippine experience over a period of 65 years.

2283. Vo-Nguyen-Giap. People's War, People's Army: The Viet Cong Insurrection Manual for Underdeveloped Countries. New York: Praeger, 1962, pp. 217.
Papers on guerrilla war and insurrection by the conqueror of the French.

See also no. 2550.

8. Belligerent Occupation; Postwar Occupation

2284. Amouroux, Henri. La vie des français sous l'occupation. Paris: Fayard, 1961, pp. 577.
Description of life in the various zones of France during the German occupation.

2285. Bader, William B. Austria between East and West, 1945-1955. Stanford: Stanford University Press, 1966, pp. ix, 250.
Examines the four-power occupation of Austria with emphasis on the complexities of East-West competition over Austria and with an effort to explain the Soviet withdrawal in 1955.

2286. Baerwald, Hans H. The Purge of Japanese Leaders under the Occupation. Berkeley: University of California Press, 1959, pp. 111.
Study of a feature of postwar occupation, particularly as it has developed in the 20th century, that should be taken into greater account as a feature of termination of wars, and of the law related thereto, that differs from past practices.

2287. Balabkins, Nicholas. Germany under Direct Controls: Economic Aspects of Industrial Disarmament, 1945-1948. New Brunswick: Rutgers University Press, 1964, pp. xi, 265.
Based on a great deal of material, this book sets forth the US and British economic policies in their occupation zones of Germany, including the manner in which, until 1948, these two occupying powers attempted to intervene through direct controls.

2288. Baudot, Marcel. L'Opinion publique sous l'occupation: L'Exemple d'un département français (1939-1945). Paris: Presses Universitaires, 1960, pp. 268.
Well-documented study of the German occupation that concentrates upon the single département of Eure.

2289. Brunvand, Olav. "The Underground Press in Norway." 9 Gazette: International Journal for Mass Communications Studies (1963), 125-132.
Reviews the activities of the underground press in Norway during World War II, with some reference to German retaliatory action.

2290. Buschhardt, Leo, and Tønnesen, Helge. "The Illegal Press in Denmark During the German Occupation, 1940-1945." 9 Gazette: International Journal for Mass Communications Studies (1963), 133-142.

Reviews the activities of the underground press in Denmark in the struggle against the German forces in a nonbelligerent country.

2291. Ebsworth, Raymond. Restoring Democracy in Germany: The British Contribution. New York: Praeger, 1961, pp. 222.
An account, based in part upon the author's experience, of the British occupation of Germany after World War II.

2292. Friend, Theodore. Between Two Empires: The Ordeal of the Philippines, 1929-1946. New Haven: Yale University Press, 1965, pp. xviii, 312.
Includes a study in depth of the Philippines relations with Japan during the years of wartime occupation.

2293. Garthoff, Raymond L. "Soviet Intervention in Manchuria, 1945-1946." 10 Orbis (1966), 520-547.
Actually covering the period 1939 to 1965, with emphasis on the two years, 1945-1946, makes the article essentially a study of a postwar occupation.

2294. Gimbel, John. A German Community under American Occupation. Stanford: Stanford University Press, 1961, pp. vi, 259.
A study of postwar occupation that concentrates upon Marburg.

2295. Gordenker, Leon. "The U.N., U.S. Occupation, and the 1948 Election in Korea." 73 Political Science Quarterly (1958), 426-450.
Story of the UN attempt to set up free and representative elections in Korea but omitting the Soviet objections to UN participation in the area.

2296. Grayson, Cary Travers, Jr. Austria's International Position, 1938-1953: The Re-establishment of an Independent Austria. Geneva: Droz, 1953, pp. xvi, 317.
Substantial study of Austria's international role particularly in the period of Four-Power control after 1945.

2297. Hayes, Paul M. "Quisling's Political Ideas." 1 Journal of Contemporary History (1966), 145-157.
On the career of Vidkun Quisling, his reaction to his experiences under Fridjof Nansen in the League of Nations Relief Commission, his vision of a "Greater Nordic Peace Union," and his effort to revive the dispute with Denmark over Greenland which was also one of three territorial claims which he presented at his first meeting with Hitler.

2298. Higa, Mikio. Politics and Parties in Postwar Okinawa. Vancouver: Publications Center, University of British Columbia, 1963, pp. x, 128.
Survey of the Okinawan side of a knotty foreign policy problem. The history of sovereignty over the islands is reviewed and the climate of opinion on such issues as reversion to Japanese sovereignty and American military bases is discussed. Particularly important is the description of liaison

between Japanese and Okinawan political parties with reference
to the popular desire to convert residual to actual Japanese
sovereignty. The volume, although short, provides data on nonlegal foundations for the later emergence of a legal determination of status.

2299. Lee, Chong-sik. Counterinsurgency in Manchuria: The Japanese
Experience, 1931-1940. RM-5012-ARPA. Santa Monica: RAND Corporation,
January 1967, pp. 368.
    Provides useful information on Japanese activities in the
puppet state of Manchukuo, with the text being essentially a
commentary on translated documents selected for their relevance
to more recent problems of counterinsurgency similar to those
faced by the Japanese occupiers of Manchuria.

2300. Lewe van Aduard, E.J. Baron. Japan from Surrender to Peace.
The Hague: Nijhoff, 1953, pp. xv, 351.
    A Dutch diplomat's review of the occupation of Japan.

2301. Peretz, Don. "The Arab-Israeli War: Israel's Administration
and Arab Refugees." 46 Foreign Affairs (1968), 336-346.
    On the problem of Arabs in Israeli-administered territories
after the 1967 war, efforts to restore local Arab administration,
incorporation of services into the Israeli system, and resettlement plans that caused friction with UNWRA.

2302. Petrov, Vladimir. Occupation Currencies in Europe in the
Second World War: A Political Analysis with Emphasis on American Experience. Ph.D. Dissertation. New Haven: Yale University, 1965; Ann Arbor:
University Microfilms, Order No. 65-9708, pp. 416.
    On occupation currency policies as reflections of the vic-
tors' policies toward the defeated. Relinquishment of the power
to control monetary circulation to the local administration is
treated as the crucial event in liberalization of the economic
features of occupation.

2303. Rennell of Rodd, Lord. British Military Administration of Occupied Territories in Africa during the Years 1941-1947. London: His
Majesty's Stationery Office, 1948, pp. viii, 637.
    Survey of military occupation of African territories and
the Dodecanese during World War II and the first two years
thereafter.

2304. Rundell, Walter, Jr. Black Market Money: The Collapse of U.S.
Military Currency Control in World War II. (Baton Rouge): Louisiana State
University Press, 1964, pp. xiii, 125.
    Examination of a facet of military occupation documenting
a seriously unsatisfactory situation that can arise from control
by military decision-makers of an area of activity with which
they are little acquainted. That it took pressure from the Treasury Department to produce a rectification raises the question of
whether the traditional rules regarding military occupation and

the forms thereof are suited to the complexities of contemporary socioeconomic affairs.

2305. Schaeffer, Eugene. L'Alsace et la Lorraine (1940-1945): Leur occupation en droit et en fait. Paris: Librairie Generale de Droit et de Jurisprudence, 1953, pp. 158.
An Alsatian's examination of the German occupation that gives particular attention to the controversy surrounding the Oradour war crimes trial.

2306. Willis, Frank Roy. The French in Germany, 1945-1949. Stanford: Stanford University Press, 1962, pp. viii, 308.
Account of the French Zone of Occupation and an assessment of the occupation as an instrument for improved understanding between nations.

2307. Zink, Harold. The United States in Germany, 1944-1955. Princeton: Van Nostrand, 1957, pp. x, 374.
An account of United States administration and relations with West Germany during the period of occupation.

See also nos. 666, 669, 1119, 1222, 1738, 2276-A, 2550.

C. RESTORATION OF PEACE

1. Termination of War--Armistices, Peace Treaties, and Cessation of Hostilities

2308. Abt, Clark C. The Termination of General War. Ph.D. Dissertation. Cambridge: MIT (1965), pp. 324.
With concern for the problem of the termination of general nuclear war, case studies are made of the termination of World War I by Germany, of the Russo-German aspect of that war, and of the termination of World War II in Europe and in the Pacific. Attention is given to such matters as strategies available to victors and losers, communication between belligerents, domestic conflict in the losing countries, methods of termination, and the aftermath of partial or complete occupation, disarmament, and annexation. In terms of data presented, questions raised, and conclusions reached this study is essential to understanding the procedures for terminating wars and the environment in which relevant rules of international law must be applied and for which they require a flexibility to meet specific situations.

2309. Butow, Robert J.C. Japan's Decision to Surrender. Stanford: Stanford University Press, 1954, pp. xi, 259.
A case study of the decision to terminate World War II in the Pacific.

2310. Catoire, Maurice. <u>La Direction des Services de l'Armistice</u>.
Paris: Berger-Levrault, 1955, pp. 102.
Brief study of the agency created to deal with problems
arising from the armistice of 1940 between France on the one
hand and Germany and Italy on the other.

2311. Cohen, Bernard C. <u>The Political Process and Foreign Policy:</u>
<u>The Making of the Japanese Peace Settlement</u>. Princeton: Princeton University Press, 1957, pp. x, 293.
Although the Japanese peace settlement was an atypical in-
stance of treaty-making, particularly because Secretary of State
Dulles bypassed normal Department channels, the study is particularly useful in that it accords attention to the activities of
specific interest groups, to press coverage, to the interaction
between public opinion and government, and to legislative-execu-
tive relations. Generalization from this particular negotiation,
as well as from the related negotiation of the North Pacific
Fisheries Convention dealt with in Chapter 12, would have to be
confined to situations in which both public and Congressional
interest are, as in this case, low.

2312. Coser, Lewis A. <u>Continuities in the Study of Social Conflict</u>.
New York: Free Press, 1967, pp. x, 272.
A collection of the author's essays including essays on the
termination of conflict in terms of the importance of communica-
ble symbols, on interval violence as a mechanism for conflict
resolution, and on some functions of deviant behavior.

2313. Coser, Lewis A. "The Termination of Conflict." 27 <u>American</u>
<u>Sociological Review</u> (1962), 5-19.
Application of some of Schelling's principles to the termination of conflict, with emphasis upon the need for a visible
event symbolizing to both sides that one has reached an objective that can be acquiesced in by the other. The author stresses
the desirability of research on symbols which move men to accept
compromise or defeat.

2314. Dunn, Frederick S. <u>Peace-Making and the Settlement with Japan</u>.
Princeton: Princeton University Press, 1963, pp. xviii, 210.
Descriptive account of the making of the peace treaty with
Japan, with particular attention to the American draft of Octo-
ber 13, 1949, Dulles' negotiations in 1950 and 1951, and the
San Francisco Conference.

2314-A. Fox, William T.R. (ed.). "How Wars End." 392 <u>Annals of the</u>
American Academy of Political and Social Science (November 1970), entire
issue, pp. 262.
Essays on problems of war termination efforts, successful
and unsuccessful, that given attention to such matters as misunderstood signals, peace treaties and alternatives, domestic
politics and the decisions to seek peace, the calculus of peace-
making, and problems of nuclear war termination.

2315. Hentig, Hans von. <u>Der Friedensschluss</u>. Stuttgart: Deutsche Verlags-Anstalt, 1952, pp. 319.

Comparison of peace treaties over a century and a half that leads the author to ask what has become of the capacity to conclude a tactful and magnanimous peace.

2316. Hutchinson, Elmo H. <u>Violent Truce</u>. New York: Devin-Adair, 1956, pp. xxvi, 199.

Experiences of an American observer with the UN Truce Supervision Organization in Palestine.

2317. Kecskemeti, Paul. <u>Strategic Surrender: The Politics of Victory and Defeat</u>. Stanford: Stanford University Press, 1958, paperback ed., New York: Atheneum, 1964, pp. ix, 287.

Perceptive inquiry into surrender as a political concept, tactical and strategic uses of surrender and the related bargaining processes, the consequences of an objective of unconditional surrender, and the potential role of surrender in the strategy of nuclear war. The case study method is employed, the four cases examined being the French, Italian, German, and Japanese surrenders during World War II.

2317-A. Randle, Robert F. <u>Geneva 1954: The Settlement of the Indochinese War</u>. Princeton: Princeton University Press, 1969, pp. xviii, 639.

Detailed, comprehensive analysis of the Eisenhower-Dulles policies, the effects of the Dulles-Eden antipathy, Mendes-France's policies, and the day-by-day bargaining that produced the Geneva Accords of 1954. Consideration is also given to the defects of the Accords and their implementation in Cambodia, Laos, and Vietnam.

See also nos. 1561, 1562, 1573, 1850. 2149, 2266.

2. <u>War Damages and Reparations</u>

2318. Bukovics, Wilhelm. <u>Das deutsche Eigentum in Österreich und seine rechtliche Behandlung auf Grund des ersten Staatsvertragsdurchführungsgesetzes</u>. Vienna: Manzsche Verlags-und Universitäts-Buchhandlung, 1956, pp. 122.

Concise discussion of the seizure by the Russians of German property in Austria and of arrangements for its disposition by the Austrian Government.

See also no. 1407.

VII. INTERNATIONAL REGULATORY PROBLEMS

A. THE REGULATION OF SPACE

1. Territory: Title, Claims, Acquisition, Loss

2319. Alvarado Garaicoa, Teodoro. *Sinopsis del derecho territorial ecuatoriano*. Guayaquil: Editorial Cervantes, 1952, pp. 396.
Historical review of the law, politics, and diplomacy of Ecuador's boundary problems. Two months after publication of this volume, the author was appointed Foreign Minister of Ecuador.

2320. Doolin, Dennis J. *Territorial Claims in the Sino-Soviet Conflict*. Stanford University: Hoover Institution, 1965, pp. 77.
Soviet and Chinese documents and articles on the border dispute.

2321. Frenzke, Dietrich. "Die Gebietsforderungen der Volksrepublik China gegenüber der Sowjetunion." 20 *Europa-Archiv* (1965), 812-821.
Treats the Chinese territorial demands, vague concerning the size of territorial claims but employing the unfair treaty argument, as essentially propaganda designed to discredit the Soviet Union.

2322. Gulliver, P.H. "Land Shortage, Social Change, and Social Conflict in East Africa." 5 *Journal of Conflict Resolution* (1961), 16-26.
A study of the differing reactions of the Nyakyusa and the Arusha to land shortage, that includes an example of the *Lebensraum* concept at the tribal level, as well as of the circumstance of thinking that a problem can be solved by an action not actually to the point. The example is the Arusha belief that a claim to a particular land region will solve their land shortage.

2323. Kelly, J.B. *Eastern Arabian Frontiers*. New York: Praeger, 1964, pp. 319.
Detailed and well-documented study of the struggle over the status of Qatar, Muscat and Oman, and the Trucial sheikdoms, centering after 1949 on Buraimi oasis and the British eviction of the Saudis who had seized the area in 1952.

2324. Kelly, J.B. "Sovereignty and Jurisdiction in Eastern Arabia." 34 *International Affairs* (1958), 16-24.
Review of Eastern Arabian frontier difficulties chiefly in terms of Arab society's lack of a concept of territorial sovereignty and its failure to grasp a concept of political sovereignty in the European sense. Complications stemming from nomadic tribal life are noted as well as the relation of rulers' claims to jurisdiction to claims to authority over inhabitants, settled or nomad.

2325. Mariam, Mesfin Wolde. "Background to the Ethio-Somalian Boundary Dispute." 2 *Journal of Modern African Studies* (1964), 189-220.
Historical review of the ties between Ethiopians and Somalis and of the events productive of the current situation entailing a boundary dispute.

2326. Michel, A.A. "Foreign Trade and Foreign Policy in Afghanistan."
12 Middle Eastern Affairs (1961), 7-15.
On the dispute between Pakistan and Afghanistan over the
Pathan area, Kabul's contention that the area should be granted
independence, and the effect of Pakistan's closing its border,
thereby compelling Afghanistan to turn to the USSR for goods and
transit facilities.

2327. Paladin, L. "Il territorio degli enti autonomi." 11 Rivista
trimestrale di diritto pubblico (1961), 607-690.
Although dealing with entities within Italy, the article is
a contribution to the theory of territory and to its legal, as
contrasted with military, protection that is susceptible of adaptation to the international scene.

2328. Parker, R.H. "The French and Portuguese Settlements in India."
26 Political Quarterly (1955), 389-398.
Surveys the differing postwar policies of France and Portugal with respect to enclaves in India and traces the main steps
of the peaceable French transfer of title to the enclaves to
India under the agreement of June 1948.

2329. Rahul, R. "Russia's Other Boundaries." 11 Australian Journal
of Politics and History (1965), 23-40.
Examines the Soviet Union's boundaries with China and Chinese accusation and questioning of Soviet title to Central Asian
and Siberian possessions.

2330. Spain, J.W. "Pakistan's North-West Frontier." 8 Middle East
Journal (1954), 27-40.
On the frontier as almost a separate entity from the rest
of Pakistan, its dual system of administration, Afghanistan's
challenge to Pakistan's title, the lands important to Southeast
Asia, and the effects of its integration with the rest of
Pakistan.

2331. Spain, J.W. "The Pathan Borderlands." 15 Middle East Journal
(1961), 165-177.
Descriptive narration of the Pathan territorial problem and
of the lack of resources and population pressures that render
statehood, as suggested by Afghanistan, a solution of doubtful
merit, despite the demonstrated inadequacies of both Pakistani
and Afghan administration in the border areas.

2332. Tashjean, John E. Where China Meets Russia: An Analysis of
Dr. Starlinger's Theory. Central Asian Collecteana, No. 2. Washington:
1959, pp. 67.
Analysis of the theory of Wilhelm Starlinger, a German
doctor who spent five years in a Soviet concentration camp and
emerged convinced that China would be compelled to solve its
population problem by moving into Trans-Baikalia, the Soviet
Far East, Outer Mongolia, and Southeast Asia. Starlinger's

conclusions had an impact on French and West German geopolitical thinking.

2333. Wiegend, G.G. "Effects of Boundary Changes in the South Tyrol."
40 Geographical Review (1950), 364-375.
　　　Examination of the economic and population changes resulting from transfer of the South Tyrol to Italy in 1919.

2334. Wright, Leigh R. "Historical Notes on the North Borneo Dispute.
25 Journal of Asian Studies (1966), 471-484.
　　　An historian's analysis of the status of North Borneo with
reference to the Philippine claim.

See also nos. 583, 1244, 1678, 1718, 1719, 1721, 1723, 1729, 1730, 2297
2298, 2417, 2499.

2. Hegemony; Spheres of Influence

2335. Conil Paz, Alberto, and Ferrari, Gustavo. Argentina's Foreign
Policy, 1930-1962. Translated by John J. Kennedy. Notre Dame: University
of Notre Dame Press, 1966, pp. xi, 240.
　　　An Argentinian view of inter-American affairs and institutions with attention to United States' efforts to exercise hegemony in the Western Hemisphere and the Argentine responses
thereto.

2336. Shepherd, Gordon. Russia's Danubian Empire. London: Heine-
mann, 1954, pp. 262.
　　　General review of the means by which the Soviet Union gained
hegemony over the Danubian countries.

2337. Whiting, Allen A., and General Sheng Shih-ts'ai. Sinkiang:
Pawn or Pivot? East Lansing: Michigan State University Press, 1958, pp.
xxii, 314.
　　　A political scientist and a former governor of Sinkiang
deal with Sino-Soviet relations in Sinkiang and with past and
potential clashes of interest that have produced boundary problems and problems of hegemony over Turkic peoples. Whiting reviews Soviet strategy in Sinkiang in 1933-1949, while General
Sheng's contribution is in the form of memoirs of the ten years
during which he ruled the province.

See also nos. 1127, 1829, 1965, 2689.

3. Peacetime Reconnaissance, Espionage, and the Need to Know

2338. Blanchard, William H. "National Myth, National Character, and
National Policy: A Psychological Study of the U-2 Incident." 6 Journal of
Conflict Resolution (1961), 143-148.

An attempt to demonstrate a method whereby, as suggested by
S. Rudin in 1959, psychological techniques might be used in
studying national decisions and policies. The U-2 incident and
the decision to confess are discussed in terms of the cherry
tree morality embodied in the Parson Weems story which is treated
as coming to the fore in the hectic days following the downing
of the U-2 by the Russians and Khrushchev's exposure of the fal-
sity of the detailed NASA story about weather reconnaissance.
The article ends with a warning of the potential conflict embodied in projections of the national ethos as though it were a
part of an acknowledged international morality, particularly
when carrying the implication that another nation is misbehaving.

2339. Bourcart, J.R.D. L'Espionnage soviétique. Paris: Fayard,
1962, pp. 316.
    History of Soviet espionage in several areas.

2340. Coser, Lewis A. "The Dysfunctions of Military Secrecy." 11
Social Problems (1963), 13-22.
    The author notes that in contentions for national or inter-
national power as distinct from, e.g., economic competition, no
clearcut index of strength is readily available. Not only must
multidimensional factors be dealt with but also motivations and
attitudes that are difficult to assess before they have been converted into actions. Coser claims that indeterminacy in the assessment of the strength of the opponents increases the likelihood that violence rather than other means of resolution will be
resorted to by the opponents. A high measure of pluralistic ignorance is built into any conflict situation in which there are
no single indices of strength. Since the joint utility of searching for the means of restraining from struggle should take primacy
over the pursuit of unattainable individual utilities, a strategy
of disclosure would allow the adversary to better assess relative
strength and increase the chances that adjustments can be made
through bargaining rather than through violence. Accumulation
of reliable information about relative strength is the precondition for rational bargaining. The author concludes that the
atomic age maximizes the chances that bargaining rather than
violent conflict will be the mode of adjustment engaged in by
both adversaries.

2341. Dallin, David J. Soviet Espionage. New Haven: Yale University
Press, 1955, pp. xiv, 558.
    Well-documented account of Soviet espionage activities.

2342. Kimche, Jon. Spying for Peace: General Guisan and Swiss Neutrality. London: Weidenfeld, 1961, pp. 168.
    Journalistic account of General Henri Guisan's efforts to
maintain Switzerland free of Nazi conquest during World War II.

2343. Wise, David, and Ross, Thomas B. The U-2 Affair. New York:
Random House, 1962, pp. 269.

Journalistic account of the affair of May 1, 1960, and its immediate aftermath.

See also nos. 1211, 1216, 1217, 1451, 1484, 1490, 2055, 2063, 2067, 2423, 2435.

4. Frontier Zones and Boundaries

2344. Alexander, Lewis M. World Political Patterns. 2nd ed. Chicago: Rand McNally, 1963, pp. xii, 628.
An exposition of present concepts of political geography that includes an important chapter on the changing nature and functions of international boundaries.

2345. Ancel, Jacques. Géographie des frontières. Paris: Gallimard (1938), pp. xi, 209.
Amplification of lectures given at the Hague Academy of International Law in 1936, the book deals with boundaries as reflections of relationships between neighboring groups and stresses types of states, not types of boundaries. Amorphous states are classified as molecular societies, nomadic states, and maritime empires, with consideration of the first two types centering on the economy and the way of life of citizens. In dealing with frontières plastiques (moulded boundaries) and frontières mouvantes, Ancel develops a concept of boundaries as consequences of pressure from two sides establishing a line of equilibrium. Unfortunately, this led him to employ the metaphor, "political isobars," for which he has been attacked. The final part of Ancel's book examines the ways in which boundaries develop, the means employed to maintain them, and factors influencing their advance or retreat.

2346. Anene, J.C. The International Boundaries of Nigeria 1885-1960: The Framework of an Emergent African Nation. London: Longmans, 1968, pp. xi, 300.
An examination of Nigeria's boundaries and the consequences thereof for the peoples separated thereby.

2347. Ashford, Douglas E. "The Irredentist Appeal in Morocco and Mauretania." 15 Western Political Quarterly (1962), 641-651.
On the claim of Morocco to historic, precolonial boundaries and about Mauretanian attitudes related to the Moroccan claim.

2348. Austin, Dennis. "The Ghana-Togo Frontier." 1 Journal of Modern African Studies (1963), 139-145.
On the problem of the Ghana-Togo frontier that inhibits Ewe unification and on efforts to establish functional unification across the frontier.

2349. Beaucourt, Chantal, et al. Les frontières européennes de l'U.R.S.S., 1917-1941. Paris: Colin, 1957.

Symposium, under the direction of Jean-Baptiste Duroselle, on the frontier disputes between the Soviet Union and its western neighbors down to June 1941. Aside from providing additional data on frontier problems, the study deals with issues that under the present system could be termed dormant rather than dead issues in light of the habit of reviving boundary issues and nationality questions long after presumed settlement.

2350. Castagno, A.A. "The Somali-Kenyan Controversy: Implications for the Future." 2 Journal of Modern African Studies (1964), 165-188.
A review of and effort to perceive the consequences of the border dispute over the northern territories embraced in Kenya.

2351. Charlier, T. "À propos des conflits de frontière entre la Somalie, l'Ethiopie et le Kenya." 16 Revue française de science politique (1966), 316-319.
On the differences between the Ethiopia-Somalia and Kenya-Somalia border disputes, the former being somewhat like some European "nationalities" experiences while the latter entails risk to the existence of Kenya as a state and also the risk of setting off throughout Africa a series of insoluble conflicts.

2352. Clifford, E.H.M. "The British Somaliland-Ethiopian Boundary." 51 Geographic Journal (1936), 289-307.
An important study of the boundary issue that today disturbs the relations between Ethiopia and Somalia. Before Mussolini's invasion of Ethiopia attempts were made to find a line that would serve the needs of nomadic groups on both sides. The article deals with the failure of Ethiopia and then Italy to solve this problem in concert with British Somaliland authorities. Attention is given to such occurrences as the destruction, within 24 hours after erection, of boundary monuments by nomadic tribes in the belief that the land belonged to the people.

2353. Coleman, James S. "Togoland." International Conciliation, No. 509, September 1956, pp. 91.
Contains probably the most complete discussion to date of the Ewe unification problem stemming from the location of the Ghana-Togo frontier.

2354. Cordero Torres, José Maria. Fronteras hispánicas: Geografía e historia, diplomacia y administración. Madrid: Instituto de Estudios Políticos, 1960, pp. 470.
Study of the historical, geographical, administrative, and diplomatic aspects of frontier regions in the Spanish-speaking world in Europe, Latin America, and Africa.

2355. Cornish, Vaughan. Borderlands of Language in Europe and Their Relation to the Historic Frontiers of Christendom. London: Sifton, Praed, 1936, pp. vii, 105.
Traces the evolution of such language borderlands as Flanders, Lorraine, Friuli, Istria, and Macedonia and finds that in each case the language frontier coincides with an earlier political

frontier between Christendom and heathen states. Polyglot languages grew only where the frontier did not coincide with a divisive physical feature. Such regions are called "link-lands"
by the author who finds that only during the 19th century, due
to improved mass communications between state-areas and link-
lands, did language bonds become more important than the regional
ties of the link-lands.

2356. Curzon of Kedelston, Lord. Frontiers. Oxford: Clarendon
Press, 1907, pp. 58.
    Introduces the important concepts of frontiers of separa-
tion and frontiers of contact.

2357. Daveau, Suzanne. Les régions frontalières de la montagne Juras-
sienne--Étude de géographie humaine. (Trévoux): Imp. de Trévoux, Patissier
1959, pp. 571.
    Excellent study of the Franco-Swiss frontier in the Jura in
modern times and of population movements and of land lease and
purchase in respect to agriculture and forestry, as well as the
relationship of the frontier to the watchmaking industry. The
study reveals an economic boundary related to such things as
customs regulations and the value of the French franc as compared with that of the Swiss franc. The economic boundary lies
to the west of the political boundary. Although reciprocity
was written into the boundary conventions of 1882 and 1938, the
written guarantees proved meaningless and the unfavorable rate
of the French franc assured an economic boundary favorable to
Switzerland, particularly after World War I.

2358. Dion, Roger. Les frontières de la France. Paris: Hachette,
1947, pp. 110.
    Analysis of such types of frontiers as the natural, the
ethnic, the political, etc.

2359. Drysdale, John. The Somali Dispute. London: Pall Mall Press,
1964, pp. 183.
    Examination of the intricacies of the border disputes be-
tween Somalia and its neighbors.

2360. East, W.G. "The Nature of Political Geography." 2 Politica
(1937), 259-286.
    Fullest development of the concepts of frontiers of separa-
tion and frontiers of contact introduced by Curzon (Frontiers
(1907)). East holds that states have always sought frontiers of
separation rather than of assimilation with neighbors. However,
some frontiers, whether because of the attraction of their resources or the ease with which they can be crossed, are viewed
as allowing contact between separated groups. But, whatever the
physical barriers to contact, East holds that in no case does the
geography of the frontier determine the degree of intercourse.
This determination is attributed to the attitudes and policies
of the separated states.

2361. Fischer, Eric. "On Boundaries." 1 World Politics (1949), 196-222.

An attempt to recognize factors working for boundary stability and to identify ways of reducing functions applied at boundaries to render them obsolete or, conversely, to increase them to entrench the boundary in the landscape. The study appears to ignore such historical realities as the relative permanence of some boundaries that were drawn with little regard to physical or human factors and includes statements not documented. Some generalizations appear to be drawn from the special example of the boundaries separating the constituent units of the United States.

2362. Fischer, Eric. "The Nature and Function of Boundaries" and "The Impact of Boundaries." In Hans W. Weigert, et al., Principles of Political Geography. New York: Appleton-Century-Crofts, 1957, Chaps. 4, 5.

Includes an attempt to redefine "frontier" as the part of the state extending inward from the boundary and merging imperceptibly with the interior. Fischer's definition is criticized by Prescott (infra, no. 2381) as ill-timed in that it came when there was reason to hope that the distinction between boundary and frontier and that between frontier and borderland had been leading to careful usage. Fischer's effort to classify boundaries on the basis of extent of their recognition by other states has been criticized as the employment of a criterion of no consequence either geographically or in terms of state functions applied.

2363. Gottmann, Jean. "La politique des états et leur géographie. Paris: Colin, 1952, pp. 228.

An effort to relate geography to politics and to historical change, the fundamental point of view being that the earth is a closed area although lacking uniformity and homogeneity. Against this background the author sets his views of frontier areas and boundaries and their functions.

2364. Hubert, Kurt. Drohte dem Tessin Gefahr? Der italienische Irredentismus gegen die Schweiz, 1912-1943. Aarau: Keller, 1955, pp. 335.

Study of Italian claims against the Swiss canton of Ticino.

2365. Hunter, James M. "The Extent of the Legal Confines, the State-Idea, and the Zone of Function of France and Germany in the Saarland." 11 International Studies Quarterly (1967), 237-243.

Application of Ratzel's concepts of peripheral areas to take account of the extension of the state-idea of Germany beyond its legal boundary, the penetration of the authority and operations of France beyond its boundary between October 23, 1955, and July 5, 1959, and their influence on German state measures since the latter date in respect to social security for Saarlanders, shipment of French goods to the Saarland, and sale of Saar coal to France.

2366. Jackson, W.A. Douglas. Russo-Chinese Borderlands: Zone of Peaceful Contact or Potential Conflict? Searchlight Books. Princeton: Van Nostrand, 1962, pp. vii, 126.

A survey of the geographical features of the borderlands, of their ethnic composition, of Sino-Russian political history related to the borderlands, and of economic developments in the 1950s. An appendix summarizes boundary treaty provisions. Besides providing a view of the roots of Sino-Soviet conflict over boundaries and hegemony, the volume touches upon the attitudes of China and Russia about the relationship between power and consent in treaty-making and about the obligation of treaties.

2367. Kapil, Ravi L. "On the Conflict Potential of Inherited Boundaries in Africa." 18 World Politics (1966), 656-673.

Reviews the nature of African boundaries and finds that, except in the cases of Morocco and Somalia where issues of pre-European history or ethnic self-determination come to the fore, the conflict potential is low. Conflict potential is regarded as high when boundaries are superimposed across valued continuities of interaction. Although African boundaries disrupt traditional aspects of the time-space milieu, the decline of the traditional and the rise of the modern political community relegate boundary matters to nonconflict status, particularly in light of the lack of cultural homogeneity that imposes on political leaders a need to concentrate on internal integration.

2368. Kristoff, L.A.D. "The Nature of Frontiers and Boundaries." 49 Annals, Association of American Geographers (1959), 269-282.

Theoretical study that uses Fischer's concept of the frontier as a zone extending inward from the boundary and merging with the interior rather than as a zonal division between states in which a boundary is located.

2369. Kuhn, Delia and Ferdinand. Borderlands. New York: Knopf, 1962, pp. xxi, 335.

Excellent for its portrayal of the ethnic complexities of six Asian borderlands.

2370. Lamb, Alastair. Asian Frontiers: Studies in a Continuing Problem. New York: Praeger, 1968, pp. ix, 246.

A judicious blend of political history and geography that, with sensitivity to Asian ethnic and linguistic consciousness, deals with the policy implications for Great Powers that have struggled with problems arising chiefly from the borders around China.

2371. Lapradelle, Paul de Geouffre de. La frontière--Étude de droit international. Paris: Les Éditions Internationales, 1928, pp. 368.

Unlike most studies of frontiers, this study, in precise language, carefully documented, and of simple plan, is not tightly bound to the period in which it was written. It is an outstanding example of what can be produced by a judicious blending of the traditional methods of international law research and

legal data with the methods, concepts, and findings of other
disciplines relevant to the topic under study. Distinguishing
boundaries and frontiers, Lapradelle observes that frontiers
exist before and after boundary delimitation as zones having
special political, legal, and economic regulations. Treating
the frontier as a zone of transition (un milieu de transformation), he divides the total area (le voisinage) into three
zones: territoire limitrophe, the central zone of mingling and
fusion where international law may apply; two frontières, the
peripheral areas subject to the internal laws of the possessing
states. Boundary-making is dealt with as entailing three stages:
preparation, decision, and execution. Legal aspects of the organization of the three areas are dealt with, including state collaboration in regard to police, health, and trade regulations.
Strong objection is raised to failure to study the legal realities of border areas and to the corresponding treatment of the
entire state area as subject to the uniform application of internal laws. Lapradelle's work might well be used in combination and comparison with what Judge Charles de Visscher says
about land confins in his Problèmes de Confins en Droit International Public (Paris: Pedone, 1969).

2372. Lewis, I.M. "Force and Fission in a Northern Somali Clan." 63
American Anthropologist (1961), 94-112.
    On segmentary lineage as the dominant feature of Somali so-
cial organization and the genealogical system, reinforced by a
common language and religion, that provides Somalia with a homogeneity not found elsewhere in Africa, renders Somalia the only
African political unit to approach the European nation-state
model, and produces a sensitivity among Somali decision-makers
to demands originating in the traditional culture, e.g., those
reflected in the boundary disputes with Ethiopia and Kenya.

2373. Logan, W.S. The Evolution and Significance of Selected Intra-
National Boundaries in South-Western Victoria. Unpublished dissertation
for the degree of B.A., University of Melbourne, 1963.
    Analysis of sales statistics of two newspapers in the area
of the Victoria-South Australia border, with full recognition
that preference is affected by such factors as newspaper style
and differing delivery times, shows that the boundary is not a
rigid barrier. The Adelaide Advertiser does not penetrate Victoria to any considerable extent except in municipalities adjacent to the border, particularly the Wimmera which has close
historic, economic, and environmental ties with South Australian
regions, while the Melbourne Sun penetrates the whole south-
eastern region of South Australia, another symptom of the area's
isolation from its capital and of its association with Victoria.

2374. Marín, Rufino. Las tres bombas de tiempo en América Latina.
Guatemala: Tip. Nacional, 1959, pp. 265.
    Study of three boundary conflicts: Guatemala and Belize,
Equador and her former eastern territories; and Bolivia's quest
for a port on the Pacific.

2374-A. Mayer, Peter. "Why the Ussuri? Reflections on the Latest Sino-Soviet Fracas." Monograph No. 1. Waltham, Massachusetts: Westinghouse Electric Corporation, Advanced Studies Group, December 1969, pp. 21.

On the Chinese attack on Damanskiy Island on March 2, 1969, and after, a possible relationship to the ending of the Soviet-East German effort to prevent the use of West Berlin as the place for the election of a West German President, and the subsequent undertakings to negotiate about navigation on the Amur and the Ussuri and on boundary disputes in general.

2375. Méric, E. "Le conflit algéro-marocain." 15 Revue française de science politique (1965), 743-752.

Reviews the course of the frontier dispute between Algeria and Morocco beginning with the occupation of certain posts by the Algerians in October 1962.

2376. Minghi, J.V. "Television Preference and Nationality in a Boundary Region." 33 Sociological Enquiry (1963), 165-179.

Suggests that preference for competing television and radio stations in a border zone may be a clue to political attachments.

2377. Mitrany, David. "Evolution of the Middle Zone." 271 Annals of the American Academy of Political and Social Science (September 1950), 1-10.

Includes a consideration of the ribbon of territory forming the Iron Curtain as having been also a barrier to the Romans, to Western Protestantism, and to the industrial revolution.

2378. Plass, Jens, and Gehrke, Ulrich. Die Aden-Grenze in der Südarabienfrage (1900-1967)--Die Adener Grenzkommission (1901-1907); Überblick über die englisch-jemenitischen Beziehungen unter dem Gesichtspunkt des Süd-jemenanspruchs (1900-1967). Opladen: C.W. Leske, 1967, pp. x, 345.

Two separately authored monographs on the boundary problems of Aden and Yemen, the Aden Boundary Commission's attempt to delimit the frontier, the course of Anglo-Yemeni relations and the fate of the Commission's recommendations, protracted border skirmishing and abortive attempts to settle the frontier issue, and Yemeni irredentism and its potential impact upon Aden's successor state, the People's Republic of South Yemen, formed in November 1967.

2379. Platt, Robert S. assisted by Bücking-Spitta, Paula. A Geographical Study of the Dutch-German Border. In English and German. Münster: Geographische Kommission, 1958, pp. 88.

Examination of an agricultural, an industrial, and a mining area that finds no significant differences in field patterns, industrial forms, political organizations, methods of production, and output, with one exception related to differing physical circumstances of coal reserves. Even so, there appear to have been intangible differences because boundary shifts were found to have done damage to organizational units that seemed only slowly to be healing--the damage occurring despite the fact that, for example, only after World War I did the textile industry show some nationalistic tendencies affecting operations.

2380. Pommerening, Horst. Der chinesisch-sowjetische Grenzkonflikt: Das Erbe der ungleichen Verträge. Olten: Walter-Verlag, 1968, pp. 266.
The author traces the Sino-Soviet border dispute since the 16th and 17th centuries, with attention to traditional Chinese attitudes toward foreigners. A legalistic analysis is made of Western, Soviet, and Chinese views on unequal treaties and of the Chinese application of the unequal treaties argument to the boundary dispute with the Soviet Union. An important section is devoted to traditional and recent Chinese attitudes toward other states and to the very important difference between Western and Chinese thought, the latter lacking the concept of a border as a dividing line between separate states. The Soviet defense of its position is put in the largely power considerations of (1) reacquisition after Chinese seizure of the areas in the 17th century, (2) the more progressive nature of Russian than Chinese imperialism, (3) possession, and (4) the necessity of peaceful settlement of all border disputes in a nuclear age. The author notes that neither party is willing to apply the principles of proletarian internationalism to the dispute.

2381. Prescott, J.R.V. The Geography of Frontiers and Boundaries. London: Hutchinson University Library, 1965, pp. 190.
Excellent, concise review of leading concepts concerning frontiers and boundaries, together with a discussion of the zonal nature of frontiers, state activity at frontiers, the evolution of boundaries, border landscapes and cultural and organizational aspects thereof, and boundary disputes and their origins including the effects of technological change. Common criticisms of African boundaries are set in their proper light in terms of insufficient knowledge, European efforts to preserve the integrity of tribes and of recognizable indigenous states, and avoidance of an exercise of authority that would impede habitual movements, activity, and land possession of divided tribes and the movements of nomads across borders to pastures. The impact of independence has been to produce a much stricter control of boundaries than in the heyday of imperialism, thereby generating fears of political infiltration, raising previously irrelevant territorial issues, and provoking the abrogation of treaties giving nomads the right to cross boundaries. These matters are examined with the aid of condensations of several case studies. A number of illustrative case studies of boundary disputes, among them river boundary disputes, are included, as well as cases illustrating the differences between economic and political boundaries and cases indicating the effects of boundary changes and related population movements. A chapter is devoted to intranational boundaries. A number of essential research projects are suggested, including projects of consequence to international law and to treaty-making and related negotiations.

2382. Rao, G.N. The India-China Border Dispute: A Reappraisal. London: Asia Publishing House, 1968, pp. xv, 106.

A reexamination of China's claims in Northern Ladakh that makes use of previously unpublished documentary material.

2383. Reyner, Anthony S. "Morocco's International Boundaries: A Factual Background." 1 Journal of Modern African Studies (1963), 313-326.

On the Moroccan boundary which in the south has been in dispute with Algeria between Teniet as-Sassi and the western Tarfaya where a border war broke out in 1963. No Franco-Moroccan agreement on a border had been made by the date of Algeria's independence but only an agreement of 1958 to establish the Algerian-Moroccan confins as a no-man's-land.

2384. Reynolds, David R., and McNulty, Michael L. "On the Analysis of Political Boundaries as Barriers." 4 East Lakes Geographer (1968), 21-38.

With reference to studies of social scientists as well as geographers, the authors construct a conceptual model of a political boundary zone.

2385. Rouch, Jean. "Migration au Ghana." 36 Journal de la Société des Africanistes (1956), 1-95.

Includes a discussion of the counterproductive effects of the wartime closing of borders between French and British African territories owing to the nature of borders, border regimes, and tribal life.

2385-A. Schmitt, Hans O. "The National Boundary in Politics and Economics." Paper presented at the 66th Annual Meeting of the American Political Science Association, Los Angeles, September 8-12, 1970, pp. 28.

Distinguishing three types of boundaries--of the nation, the state, and the economy--and noting that each is affected both by its own set of principles and by interactions among them, the paper develops a logic of boundary formation within the economic sphere that takes account of capital flows, currency unification, and labor migration. In dealing with current trends, particular attention is paid to Western Europe and to such innovations as the multinational firm and the Euro-dollar market.

2386. Sevrin, R. "Les échanges de population à la frontière entre la France et la Tournaisis." 58 Annales de Géographie (1949), 237-244.

Traces trans-boundary movements in the Franco-Belgian borderland and finds a close relationship among the value of the French franc, measures to try to maintain its exchange value, and the number of Belgian workers in the French borderland, as well as between the level of textile production and the number of Belgian workers.

2386-A. Solomon, Robert L. "Boundary Concepts and Practices in Southeast Asia." RM-5936-1-ARPA. Santa Monica: RAND Corporation, December 1969, pp. 72.

On the insecurity and lack of "hardness" of Southeast Asian boundaries that were established by colonial administrations. Mobility across such boundaries, not designed to withstand international pressures, is general to render the elimination of enemy sanctuaries a matter of having an administrative, not a military presence.

2386-B. Trout, Frank E. Morocco's Saharan Frontiers. Geneva: Droz, 1969, pp. 561.
    A study of the need for boundaries once colonial regimes were extended into the Sahara, the conflicts between French leadership in Algeria and French officials in the Moroccan protectorate, and the development of Morocco's territorial appetite once independence was secured. Attention is given to the hazards to peace and the potential impact upon nomads of continuation of a situation of de facto borders without international boundary agreements.

2387. van der Veur, Paul W. "New Guinea Annexations and the Origin of the Irian Boundary." 18 Australian Outlook (1964), 313-339.
    One of two articles on the boundary between the Australian and Indonesian territories in New Guinea, this article deals with problems of boundary-making on the island, with the history of the boundary to 1885, and with the modification in 1895 of the southern part of the boundary.

2388. van der Veur, Paul W. Search for New Guinea's Boundaries: From Torres Strait to the Pacific. Canberra: Australian National University Press, 1966, pp. xii, 176.
    The task of delineating New Guinea's boundaries being still unfinished even though it was in 1848 that the Dutch began the task, the author presents the result of his examination of Dutch, German, British, Australian, and Indonesian sources to review a century of negotiations and the stakes involved in boundary demarcation.

2389. van der Veur, Paul W. "The Irian Boundary Slumber, 1905-1962." 19 Australian Outlook (1965), 73-96.
    Accords attention to the northern segment of the border originally separating German and Netherlands territories, the frontier as a whole, and three trouble spots. An account is given of the slow realization of a need for better demarcation and of frantic activity at the time that Netherlands New Guinea became West Irian.

2390. Van Eekelen, W.F. Indian Foreign Policy and the Border Dispute with China. The Hague: Nijhoff, 1964, pp. 220.
    A useful study of the Sino-Indian border dispute and of the Indian view that the water division was the proper border and the Chinese view of the reach of administrative authority as the basis for boundary determination.

2391. Watson, Francis. The Frontiers of China. New York: Praeger; London: Chatto & Windus, 1966, pp. 224.

Carefully documented survey of China's frontier policy during the first 16 years of the Communist regime.

2392. Wilkinson, H.R. "Jugoslav Kosmet." Transactions and Papers, Institute of British Geographers (1955), 171-193.

Excellent study of the Kosmet as a frontier between such different entities as the Eastern and Western parts of the Roman Empire, the Bulgar and Byzantine Empires, Christianity and Islam, and Yugoslavia and Albania, with resultant economic neglect and other hindrances to development.

2393. Yakemtchouck, Romain. La Ligne Curzon et la IIe Guerre Mondiale Louvain: Éditions Nauwelaerts; Paris: Béatrice-Nauwelaerts, 1957, pp. 135.

Chronological exposé of the stages of development of the effort, beginning with the Ribbentrop-Molotov Pact, to settle the question of Poland's eastern frontier, including the Soviet attempt to transform the Ribbentrop-Molotov frontier arrangement into an obligation in a form binding upon Germany's enemies. By making his primary effort that of placing a maze of confused evidence in a chronological structure, the author is able to set in order the wartime events leading to decisions reached, thereby establishing a basis for further investigation in terms of decision theory. Among other things, the volume represents an excellent use of the writings of actors whose personal decisions affected the outcome in the form of a decision carrying international legal consequences. The works consulted amount to a bibliography in six languages.

2394. Zartman, I. William. "A Disputed Frontier is Settled." 8 Africa Report (August 1963), 13-14, and correction, 9 Africa Report (March 1964), 31.

On the first settlement of a border dispute by newly independent African states, rectifying the border between Mauritania and Mali.

2395. Zartman, I. William. "The Politics of Boundaries." 3 Journal of Modern African Studies (1965), 155-173.

Deals with the political aspects of boundary disputes of West Africa, particularly the historically based claims of Morocco.

See also nos. 583, 596, 1216, 1217, 1244, 1610, 1654, 1683, 1722, 1725, 1728, 2105, 2268, 2561, 2564, 2744, 2806.

5. Territorial Waters and Contiguous Zones

2396. Boggs, S. Whittemore. "Problems of Water Boundary Definition: Median Lines and International Boundaries through Territorial Waters." 27 Geographical Review (1937), 445-456.

Concise examination by a geographer of the problems of defining water boundaries in both internal waters and territorial
waters with attention to the interests of the peoples and states
concerned.

2397. Collins, S.V., and Keeble, P. "Diamonds from the Sea Bed." In
J.G. Strykowski (ed.), Underwater Yearbook 1962. Chicago: Underwater So-
ciety of America, 1962, pp. 12-14.
Account of diamond mining on concessions obtained by S.V.
Collins of The Diamond Mining Corporation and extending from
the mouth of the Orange River to Diaz Point near Luderitz, South
West Africa, and from the low water line seaward a distance of
three miles.

2398. Davis, Morris. Iceland Extends Its Fisheries Limits: A Political Analysis. Oslo: Universitetsforlaget, 1963, pp. 136.
Study of the impact of political parties and pressure groups
on the Icelandic policy process in production of the decision to
extend the fishery limits from 4 to 12 miles. References are
made to the 1958 Geneva Conference on the Law of the Sea and to
matters of concern extending far beyond the locale of the case.

2399. Dionisopoulos, P. Allan. "Japanese-Korean Relations: A Dilemma in the Anti-Communist World." 1 Midwest Journal of Political Science
(1957), 60-76.
A narrative of Japanese-Korean relations to 1954, including
the dispute over the Rhee Line and over the island of Takeshima.

2400. Lee, Chong-sik. "Japanese-Korean Relations in Perspective."
35 Pacific Affairs (1962-63), 315-326.
Deals with such problems as questions arising out of Japanese occupation, territorial waters, title to an island,
treatment of Korean residents in Japan, and jurisdiction of the
Republic of Korea.

See also nos. 686, 2577, 2581, 2592, 2593.

6. Gulfs, Bays, and Bights

2401. Booth, Alan R. "American Whalers in South African Waters."
32 South African Journal of Economics (1964), 278-282.
A resumé of a series of events forming part of the history
of the law of the sea. American whalers' practices and habits
in South African bays led the Dutch and the British Governments
to prohibit Americans from whaling in the bays and to annex all
important bays on the southwestern coast. The proclamations
were not backed up by force and American sails continued to
dominate the waters until the 1870s.

See also no. 2820.

7. Islands and Archipeligoes

2402. Halkin-Destrée, L. "Le differend territorial nippo-soviétique: Les iles Kouriles et Sakhaline." 18 Chronique de politique etrangère (1965) 293-328.
Reviews the differences between Japan and Russia over the Kuriles and Sakhalin and the arguments related thereto, including the question of whether the USSR can rely upon the San Francisco Treaty to which she was not a party or the Yalta Agreement to which Japan was not a party.

2403. Wells, Tom Henderson. "The Swan Islands Dispute." 6 Journal of Inter-American Studies (1964), 57-68.
A review of the course of events related to the conflicting claims of the United States and Honduras. The Honduran claim, raised in 1923, is based essentially on discovery. The case, although susceptible of political exploitation, has to date been another example of continuing disagreement on a low-pressure issue without impairment of general friendship.

2404. Wertheim, W.F. East-West Parallels: Sociological Approaches to Modern Asia. Chicago: Quadrangle Books, 1965, pp. ix, 284.
Deals, among other things, with inter-island migration in Indonesia and the limits imposed by a shipping shortage that impedes other uses of the archipeligo's water routes, overpopulation and underpopulation in terms of relations of numbers to land cultivation and broader economic systems, society as a composite of conflicting value systems, and corruption in Southeast Asia.

See also nos. 2399, 2400.

8. International Rivers and Lakes

2405. Chevrier, Lionel. The St. Lawrence Seaway. New York: St. Martin's Press, 1959, pp. x, 174.
A study of the struggle between the United States and Canada and among conflicting private interests that preceded construction of the St. Lawrence Seaway.

2406. Chiesa, Pierre Albert. La régime international du Rhin et la participation de la Suisse. Fribourg: Librairie de l'Université, 1952, pp. 198.
An inquiry into the Rhine regime and the participation of Switzerland therein and the consequences of such participation.

2407. Croizat, V.J. The Mekong River Development Project: Some Geographical, Historical, and Political Considerations. P-3616. Santa Monica: RAND Corporation, June 1967, pp. 155.

A review of the Mekong project, its status, and its impact on attitudes toward the United Nations after 10 years' effort.

2408. Dees, Joseph L. "Jordan's East Ghor Canal Project." 13 Middle East Journal (1959), 357-371.
On the financing and construction, then under way, of the East Ghor Canal to divert the waters of the Yarmuk River, a tributary of the Jordan, for irrigation purposes in Jordan.

2409. Ferrier, Charles-Antoine. La liberté de navigation sur le Rhin de Bâle à la mer. Winterthur: P.G. Keller, 1955, pp. xii, 115.
Study of the freedom of navigation of the Rhine below Basle as related to such matters as taxes, exploitation for energy production, fishing, uses for domestic purposes, navigation in wartime, the competence of the Central Commission of the Rhine, police regulation, and Rhine courts.

2410. Hodges, R.C. "Indus Waters for Pakistan." 61 Canadian Geographical Journal (September 1960), 96-105.
On the canal water dispute between India and Pakistan.

2411. Hundley, Norris, Jr. Dividing the Waters: A Century of Controversy Between the United States and Mexico. Berkeley: University of California Press, 1966, pp. xii, 266.
Historical account of the controversies between the United States and Mexico concerning the allocation of the waters of the upper and lower Rio Grande valleys, of the Colorado River, and of the Tiajuana river system supplying the San Diego area. The controversies, particularly that over the Colorado River waters, demonstrate one form of influence over foreign relations that constituent units of federal states can exercise.

2412. Karan, Pradyumna P. "Dividing the Water: A Problem in Political Geography." 13 The Professional Geographer (No. 1, 1961), 6-10. Reprinted in W.A. Douglas Jackson (ed.), Politics and Geographic Relationships: Readings on the Nature of Political Geography. Englewood Cliffs: Prentice-Hall, 1964, pp. 274-280.
Surveys the problems of water division as illustrated by the Colorado River and the Indus River systems.

2413. Kojanec, G. "Le commissioni fluviali--Contributo allo studio dell'organizzazione internazionale." 16 Communità internazionale (1961), 745-771.
A study of river commissions and the problem of the refusal of states to renounce sovereignty, which leaves the commissions with an essentially technical competence.

2414. Lador-Lederer, J.J. "Vom Wasserweg zur internationalen Gemeinschaft." 53 Friedens-Warte (1956), 225-244.
Notes that waterway problems, once limited to assurance of freedom of navigation, have extended to the several uses of entire river basins, each being an economic unit requiring its own plan of development under an international financial scheme. Not

a law of nations based upon national sovereignty but the law of
a functional community is said to be required.

2415. Mayer, Harold M. "Great Lakes-Overseas: An Expanding Trade
Route." 30 Economic Geography (1954), 117-143.
        Examination of the Great Lakes in world trade in terms of
the potential of the St. Lawrence route, which should emphasize
the importance of the extension of maritime law by the Taney
court to areas above the tidewater.

2416. Michel, Aloys Arthur. The Indus River: A Study of the Effects
of Partition. New Haven: Yale University Press, 1967, pp. xxv, 595.
        An excellent exposition of the dynamics of the relations
between a river, man, human institutions, and politics that
covers much more ground than its misleading, restrictive subtitle suggests. The narrative extends back to century-old
British efforts to reconcile the interests of upstream and
downstream riparians.

2417. Naroll, Raoul. Waterways and Territorial Change. Final Report
on Contract No. 60530/1000Y4041-64. (Project Michelson, U.S. Naval Ordnance Test Station, China Lake, California). Mimeo. (Northwestern University), n.d., pp. 5.
        Addendum to Warfare, Peaceful Intercourse and Territorial
Change: A Cross-Cultural Survey that presents a brief summary
of the navigation data on the primitive tribes of that study.
The results are: (1) there is little, if any, relationship between water routes accessibility per se and territorial change;
(2) those tribes that use boats appear to be somewhat more
likely to expand territorially than those who do not; (3) there
appears to be a greater likelihood that tribes will contract
territorially when river currents flow from tribal frontiers
toward the center of the tribal territory than when they do not.

2418. Regan, Mark M. "Sharing Financial Responsibility of River Basin
Development." In Stephen C. Smith and Emery N. Castle (eds.), Economics and
Public Policy in Water Resource Development. Ames, Iowa: Iowa State University Press, 1964, pp. 209-221.
        Includes a section on cost-sharing in international rivers,
noting some differences from the cost-sharing problem for national rivers that are structural in nature to render a different entity the entity to be compensated for disassociations of
benefits and costs. Brief reference is made to the recommendations of the Dubrovnik meeting (1956) of the International Law
Association as imposing a restriction upon the alternatives from
which to choose when adjusting for disassociations.

2419. Schaaf, C. Hart, and Fifield, Russell H. The Lower Mekong:
Challenge and Cooperation in Southeast Asia. Princeton: Van Nostrand,
1963, pp. 136.
        A survey of the efforts of the United Nations Economic
Commission for Asia and the Far East in respect to the lower

Mekong basin, of the establishment by Cambodia, Laos, Thailand, and Vietnam of a Committee for Co-ordination of Investigations of the basin, and of projects begun or proposed by the early 1960s.

2420. Smith, R.H. "Great Lakes Water Levels: A Look at the Problem of Control." 72 Canadian Geographical Journal (1966), 112-123.
On the problem of Great Lakes water levels, control of diversions, and possible diversions of rivers of other drainage basins in view of the Reference of October 7, 1964, to the International Joint Commission that calls first for ascertainment of what can be done with waters already in the Great Lakes system.

2421. Stevens, Georgiana G. Jordan River Partition. Stanford University: Hoover Institution, 1965, pp. 90.
Deals with the plan for the division of the waters of the Jordan as developed by Eric Johnson, the status of the plan as a guide even though not formally accepted, and technological developments that have opened new perspectives since 1955.

2422. Willoughby, William R. The St. Lawrence Waterway: A Study in Politics and Diplomacy. Madison: University of Wisconsin Press, 1961, pp. xiv, 381.
A detailed examination of the politics, particularly in the United States, and the diplomacy of the long drawn-out process of bringing the St. Lawrence Seaway into being.

See also nos. 583, 585, 636, 1120, 1122, 1528, 1923, 2381, 2396, 2562, 2578, 2579, 2586-2588, 2744, 2758.

9. Air Space

See nos. 1211, 2338, 2343, 2432.

10. Outer Space

2423. Bloomfield, Lincoln P. "Outer Space and International Cooperation." 19 International Organization (1965), 603-621.
Reviews United Nations actions in respect to outer space, indicates the extent to which General Assembly actions represent some approximation to a common law for outer space, and suggests the possibility of bypassing inspection on the ground through inspection from outer space even in the absence of international agreements.

2423-A. Codding, George A., Jr., and Beheshti, Mohammed. An International Agency for Earth Resources Experiments. Boulder: Bureau of Governmental Research and Service, College of Arts and Sciences, University of Colorado, January 1972, pp. 39.

An argument, accompanied by a draft treaty proposal, for
the creation of a new international organization designed to
bring the benefits of the orbiting space laboratory, potentially
offering man a new look at the earth's resources, to the developing nations for whom the information obtained may be crucial
to survival.

2424. Coulter, John M., and Loret, Benjamin J. "Manned Orbiting
Space Stations." 16 Air University Review (May-June 1965), 33-41.
Discussion of the role of the space station in the overall
national space effort and a description of NASA and Department
of Defense activities in space station planning.

2425. Davies, M.E., and Murray, B.C. The Soviet Planetary Missions.
P-3364. Santa Monica: RAND Corporation, May 1966, pp. 27.
Examination, based on released materials concerning the
Venus 2 and 3 flights, of the Soviet approach to the exploration
of Venus and Mars that takes note of differences between Soviet
and American engineering, operations, and goals in regard to
planetary exploration.

2426. Fogel, Robert William. "Railroads as an Analogy to the Space
Effort: Some Economic Aspects." 76 Economic Journal (March 1966), 16-43.
Examines the space effort in terms of an investment of resources that might have been invested in other activities, and,
using the analogy of the railroad, attempts to estimate the impact of the space effort on economic life through the knowledge
potentially to be gained by the biological and physical sciences.

2427. Freeman, R.J., Moore, R.C., and Schilling, G.F. Logistic Implications of an Astronomical Observatory on the Moon. RM-4916-PR. Santa
Monica: RAND Corporation, February 1966, pp. 44.
Employment of a mathematical model developed in an earlier
study (RM-4520-PR, April 1965) to test the logistic feasibility
of a lunar astronomical research program that culminates in
construction of a lunar-based observatory.

2428. Friedman, Bruno. "Lunar International Laboratory." UNESCO
Courier (May 1966), 30-34.
On the conduct of studies on problems of establishing on
the moon a laboratory for lunar research, the studies being car-
ried on by the Lunar International Laboratory Committee of the
International Academy of Astronautics.

2429. Frutkin, Arnold. International Cooperation in Space. Englewood Cliffs: Prentice-Hall, 1965, pp. 186.
On the United States space program, efforts to cooperate
with the USSR, and the mechanisms provided by European regional
organizations, the UN, and other agencies.

2429-A. Frutkin, Arnold W. "International Cooperation in Space." 169
Science (1970), 333-339.

Reviews the various instances of international cooperation
in space projects that involve NASA's work with foreign agencies
and takes note of constraints on and gaps in space cooperation.

2430. Goldsen, Joseph M. (ed.). Outer Space in World Politics. New
York: Praeger, 1963, pp. vii, 180.
Articles on political and military uses of outer space, on
the prestige factor stemming from successful space flights, and
similar subjects. Most closely related to international law is
Klaus Knorr's essay on "The International Implications of Outer-
Space Activities" (pp. 114-138) which seeks for criteria broadly
indicating the likelihood of eventual agreement on outer space
and the probability of particular matters being included in such
an agreement.

2431. Haythorn, William N., and Altman, Irwin. "Together in Isolation." 4 Trans-Action (January-February 1967), 18-22.
Report on an experiment, relevant to space travel, that entailed isolation for 10-day periods of 18 pairs of men previously
tested for personality attributes. As compared with a control
group that could go out for meals and go home nights, the pairs
of isolates expressed territoriality early with respect to beds
with slight decline with time, while for chairs and place at
table territoriality developed slowly and became increasingly
definite. For controls, the opposite progressions occurred.
Isolates exchanged more personal information than controls and
experienced more stress, although performing work tasks better.
The tendency of isolates to show hostility was greatest for (a)
2 dominants and 2 dogmatics, and (b) a pair differing in need
for affiliation and 2 dogmatics, a pair differing in need for
achievement. For the first two combinations hostile interaction,
even fighting, occurred, while for the last two combinations
passivity and withdrawal took place.

2432. Kucherov, Samuel. "The USSR and Sovereignty in Outer Space."
12 Bulletin of the Institute for the Study of the USSR (February 1965),
25-33.
Description of the Soviet Union's policy on sovereignty of
"airspace" before and after the launching of Sputnik and discussion of its relevance to the intended meanings of the Paris
and Chicago Conventions on this subject.

2433. Levy, Lillian (ed.). Space: Its Impact on Man and Society.
New York: Norton, 1965, pp. xv, 228.
A series of contributions on the implications of space exploration and of its uses to date and to be anticipated. Among
the subjects covered, all in nontechnical language, are space
law (by Nicholas de B. Katzenbach), labor in the space age, the
military role (excluding espionage), disarmament (excluding inspection by satellite), career opportunities, the aerospace industry, weather satellites, communications, medical advances,
and the impact of space exploration on the English language.

2434. Murray, B.C., and Davies, M.E. A Comparison of U.S. and Soviet Efforts to Explore Mars. P-3285. Santa Monica: RAND Corporation, January 1966, pp. 41.
Comparative study of American and Soviet programs of planetary exploration that points out differences in objectives and styles and indicates some possible results.

2435. Ossenbeck, Frederick J., and Kroeck, Patricia C. (eds.). Open Space and Peace: A Symposium on Effects of Observation. Stanford University: Hoover Institution, 1964, pp. 227.
Contains papers on such problems as peaceful uses of photo-reconnaissance satellites, opening the Soviet system and obtaining information on Communist China's capabilities and intentions, the relation of neutral nations to space activities, unilateral observation, and United Nations surveillance. Allan N. Littman and James F. Kirkham contribute an article on space problems for lawyers.

2436. Schwartz, Leonard E. International Organizations and Space Co-operation. Durham: Duke University Press, 1962, pp. 108.
Deals with the structure and functions of governmental and nongovernmental organizations, including scientific organizations, active in the exploration of outer space and related activities.

2437. Singer, Lieutenant Colonel S.E. "The Military Potential of the Moon." 11 Air University Quarterly (1959), 31-53.
Necessarily speculative, this article attempts to assess possible military uses of the moon including the firing of thermonuclear warheads.

2438. Singer, S. Fred. "A Look at the Weather from Outer Space." In Lillian Levy (ed.), Space: Its Impact on Man and Society. New York: Norton, 1965, pp. 133-145.
Nontechnical discussion of weather satellites and their potential benefits and of international dissemination of weather information through the World Meteorological Organization and through direct communication to countries lying in the paths of hurricanes, typhoons, and tropical storms.

2439. Strickland, Donald A. New States, Prestige, and the Space Age: Some Probable Connections. Space Sciences Laboratory, University of California. Berkeley: May 1964, pp. ii, 48.
In an effort to ascertain the changes in the level of Soviet and of American prestige in the new states between Sputnik I (October 5, 1957) and the US Venus probe (December 15, 1962), trade, aid, and treaty statistics and also editorial comment in the new states' press are examined. It appears, although inconclusively, that the Soviet Union did gain a bit of prestige in non-Western viewpoints.

2440. Walsh, John. "ESRO: Space Sciences Research in Europe Suffers Growing Pains." 158 Science (1967), 242-244.

Although concentrating on the European Space Research Organization (ESRO), established by a convention of 1962 that entered into force in 1964, the article also accords attention to related activities of the European Launcher Development Organization (ELDO), the European Conference on Satellite Communication (CETS), and the European Space Conference, a ministerial organization recently given permanent status. Besides giving an indication of recent activities of the organizations, the article deals in part with interorganizational programs. It also displays a sensitivity to what national aerospace activities obtain in the form of contracts in relation to national contributions and to differences among member nations over what the organizations, particularly ESRO, should do.

2441. White, Irvin L. Decision-Making for Space: Law and Politics in Air, Sea, and Outer Space. Lafayette: Purdue University Studies, 1970, pp. xii, 277.
　　Employing quantitative methods and statistical analytical techniques as well as historical description and informed speculation, this study analyzes both space law literature and sea and air law rules in an effort to determine why national decision-makers accept or reject specific rules. Noting that decision-makers say that they accept rules about the air and the sea on the basis of their protection or furtherance of chiefly conservation, economic, and strategic interests, an exploratory analysis of variance, based on a computer reduction technique, is employed and supports the analysis of what decision-makers say. Finding that the same three interests are involved in space law issues but that when the space problem is not comparable with the other two areas it is due to differences in location, accessibility of resources, and the nature of threats, the author concludes that simply changing the environment does not change the basic reasons why decision-makers accept or reject rules and principles of international law--a conclusion that should be a starting point for examination in depth of the recurrent and its various foundations.

See also nos. 1158, 1894, 2450, 2454, 2456-2459.

11. Polar Regions

2442. Fletcher, J.O. The Heat Budget of the Arctic Basin and Its Relation to Climate. R-444-PR. Santa Monica: RAND Corporation, October 1965, pp. 194.
　　Relates what is known of the Arctic heat budget to what is known of the dynamics of climate, deals with the interaction of the Arctic Ocean with other oceans, and suggests needed research on the Arctic heat budget and some possible climatic experiments. The report should stimulate thought about the problems that it does not discuss, namely, global concern for the regulation of what may yet prove feasible in the control of climate.

2443. Grattan, C. Hartley. <u>The Southwest Pacific Since 1900: A Mod-</u><u>ern History--Australia, New Zealand, the Islands, Antarctica</u>. Ann Arbor: University of Michigan Press, 1963, pp. x, 759, xxviii.
> The section on Antarctica deals with such matters as modern-
> ization of whaling, the Nazi attempt to take the area claimed by
> Norway, and the Antarctic Treaty of 1959.

2444. Hatherton, Trevor (ed.). <u>Antarctica</u>. New York: Praeger, 1965, pp. xvi, 511.
> Contributions by 21 scientists on findings during a decade's
> exploration of Antarctica that includes an essay on national in-
> terests in the continent.

2445. Jones, Stephen B. <u>The Arctic: Problems and Possibilities</u>. Memorandum No. 29. New Haven: Yale Institute of International Studies, December 20, 1948, pp. 24.
> On economic development, diplomatic problems, and military
> aspects of the northern high latitudes.

2446. Macdonald, R. St. J. (ed.). <u>The Arctic Frontier</u>. Toronto: Uni versity of Toronto Press, 1966, pp. 311.
> Contributions from social scientists and governmental per-
> sonnel that attempt to assess the economic, population, scien-
> tific, and military significance of Canada's Arctic frontier.

2447. Priestley, Sir Raymond, Adie, Raymond J., and Robin, Geoffrey de Q. <u>Antarctic Research</u>. London: Butterworths, 1964, pp. xi, 360.
> Detailed account of the findings of the scientific explora-
> tion force in Antarctica during the International Geophysical
> Year, 1957-1958.

12. <u>International Communications, Propaganda,</u>
    <u>and International Information Flow</u>

2448. Browne, Don R. "Problems in International Television." 17 <u>Jour</u><u>nal of Communication</u> (1967), 198-210.
> On the possibilities of international television comparable
> to the Voice of America and Radio Moscow, problems to be dealt
> with, and directions research should take, e.g., whether "two
> dimensionality" of the visual image hinders communication with
> certain cultures.

2449. Browne, Don R. "The Limits of the Limitless Medium--Interna-tional Broadcasting." 42 <u>Journalism Quarterly</u> (1965), 82-86, 164.
> Raises questions concerning whether international broad-
> casting is in fact a system of mass communication given certain
> technical difficulties, listeners' lack of interest in short
> wave reception, the uncertainty of foreign-based medium wave
> operations dependent upon treaty relations vulnerable to polit-
> ical repercussions, and the limited group of listeners consist-
> ing primarily of students, educators, and government officials.

It is, therefore, questioned whether international broadcasting is really an instance, at least on a mass basis, of unimpeded communication between sender and receiver, especially when most listeners hear only the digest of monitored foreign broadcasts that are presented by domestic newscasters.

2450. Centre National de la Recherche Scientifique, Groupe de Travail sur le Droit de l'Espace. Les télécommunications par satellites: Aspects juridiques. Paris: Cujas, 1968, pp. xii, 456.
Useful study relevant to the law that is developing in respect to communications by satellite.

2451. Coyne, Michael John. A Study of the Participation of the Soviet Union in the International Telecommunication Union, 1946-1959. Ph.D. Dissertation. Washington: American University, 1965; Ann Arbor: University Microfilms, Order No. 65-10,140, pp. 559.
Narrative of the Soviet bloc's limited cooperation with the ITU, particularly in the matter of submitting frequency lists.

2452. Davison, W. Phillips. International Political Communication. New York: Praeger for the Council on Foreign Relations, 1965, pp. xii, 404.
Deals with the effects of mass communications on individuals and groups, the role of mass media in democracies, Communist states, and emerging states, and the chief propaganda activities of the United States and the Soviet Union.

2453. Emery, Walter E. National and International Systems of Broadcasting: Their History, Operation and Control. East Lansing: Michigan State University Press, 1969, pp. xxxi, 752.
An important and thorough study of problems of modern international mass communications, including problems of control.

2453-A. Ende, Asher H. "Satellite Communications: Domestic Regulation and International Cooperation." Paper presented at the Conference on International Telecommunications by Satellite. Stanford University: April 1970, pp. 19.
A paper by the Deputy Chief, Common Carrier Bureau, Federal Communications Commission, that includes discussion of some of the problems that result when an international undertaking such as the International Satellite Telecommunications Consortium is dependent upon approval given an agency such as Comsat by a national regulatory agency, as well as problems, so far avoided, that could result from the dual role of Comsat as manager for Intelsat and as United States signatory.

2453-B. Hopkins, Mark W. Mass Media in the Soviet Union. New York: Pegasus, 1970, pp. 384.
Includes chapters on radio and television programming for foreign consumption and on the handling of foreign news and propaganda by the press, together with reports of Soviet surveys of readers' and listeners' preferences.

2454. Johnson, Leland L. Some Implications of New Communications Technologies for National Security in the 1970's. P-3639. Santa Monica: RAND Corporation, September 1967, pp. 24.

Reviews technological developments in communications with emphasis on the contribution of communications satellites to national security, uses of satellites for communication during crises and for wartime command and control, and implications related to open and closed political societies, centralized and decentralized decision-making, and bargaining and negotiation.

2454-A. König, H. "Der sowjetisch-chinesische Rundfunkkrieg." 19 Osteuropa (1969), 560-574.

Analysis of the "radio war" between the Soviet Union and Communist China as a propaganda war restricted by the censorship of both countries to a single medium that may reach more people in other parts of the world than in the countries toward which the propaganda is directed.

2455. Koerner, Ralf Richard. So haben sie es damals gemacht: Die Propagandavorbereitungen zum Österreich-Anschluss durch das Hitler-regime 1933 bis 1938. Vienna: Gesellschaft zur Förderung Wissenschaftlicher Forschung, 1958, pp. 327.

Able study of Hitler's propaganda campaign against Austria in the years preceding Anschluss.

2455-A. Martin, L. John (ed.). "Propaganda in International Affairs." 398 Annals of the American Academy of Political and Social Science (November 1971), entire issue, pp. 234.

A series of articles on the role, techniques, instrumentalities, and agencies of international propaganda, with attention to legal, moral, sociological, and psychological aspects of international persuasion.

2456. Mitchell, Thompson H. "International Satellite Communications." In Lillian Levy (ed.), Space: Its Impact on Man and Society. New York: Norton, 1965, pp. 146-158.

Review by the President of RCA of developments and cooperation in international communication by satellite and some competing forms such as the transistorized submarine cable which has a capacity up to 720 voice-quality circuits and is capable of handling television.

2457. Nichols, R.T. Submarine Telephone Cables and International Telecommunications. RM-3472-RC. Santa Monica: RAND Corporation, February 1963, pp. 42.

On the development of the global network of submarine cables and the potential competition of communications satellites. This report is one of several RAND reports of various degrees of technicality that deal with telecommunication possibilities via satellite.

2458. Schwartz, M.L. Foreign Participation in Communication Satellite Systems: The Implications of the Federal Communications Act. RM-2971-NASA

Santa Monica: RAND Corporation, December 1961, pp. 58.
A supplement to RM-2934-NASA, Foreign Participation in a
U.S. Communication Satellite System, which discusses the problem in terms of policy formulation and of negotiation of agreements, this memorandum assesses legal eligibility of foreign
nations to share in ownership or control of US-licensed communication satellite operations.

2459. Sollfrey, W. Earth Coverage Patterns with High-Gain Antennas
on Stationary Satellites. RM-4894-NASA. Santa Monica: RAND Corporation,
February 1966, pp. 38.
Presents coverage patterns attainable through use of highly
directive antennas on stationary communications satellites, thus
providing a guide to one aspect of the international communications problem for which legal controls may be desirable. An
overlay Mercator map provides a flexible aid to visualization of
what the diagrams included would represent in terms of surface
area covered from various positions above the earth.

See also nos. 324, 363, 518, 731, 732, 735, 737, 864, 866, 870, 1445,
1447, 1461-1463, 1468, 1743, 2067, 2236, 2433, 2437.

VIII. HUMANITARIAN AND ECONOMIC AFFAIRS

A. ALIENS: WELFARE

1. Perceptions and Stereotypes; National
    Social Distance Studies

2460. Adenarayan, S.P. "A Study of Racial Attitudes in India." 45
Journal of Social Psychology (1957), 211-216.
A survey, employing Vetter's Attitude Scale and Bogardus'
Social Distance Scale, that showed that among the 485 Hinuds,
Muslims, and unclassified women who responded as generally sus-
picious of all foreigners, nearly 60% declared that a large influx of Europeans would endanger India. Moral danger was considered most likely. The survey was conducted by mail with the
usual difficulties limiting the reliability of that type of
survey.

2461. Diab, L.N. "National Stereotypes and the Reference Group Concept." 57 Journal of Social Psychology (1962), 339-351.
106 male Arab students at the American University of Beirut
were asked to select adjectives describing 13 national groups.
Indications were that stereotypes persist over 10 years with declining favor expressed toward French and Turks. Stereotypes
were not identical when the sample was subdivided according to
religious and to political affiliation.

2462. Kassof, Allen. "The Prejudiced Personality: A Cross Cultural Test." 6 Social Problems (1958), 59-67.

Former citizens of the Soviet Ukraine were questioned to test three generalizations of Gordon W. Allport: (1) that prejudice is a generalized attitude, (2) that the prejudiced person tends to have extreme nationalistic sentiments, and (3) that the prejudiced person tends to be extrapunitive. The results tended to support the generalizations and to suggest that, although societal factors may be important in explaining prejudice, a personality factor--a generalized pattern cutting across societies-- also exists.

2463. Rosenblatt, Paul C. "Origins and Effects of Group Ethnocentrism and Nationalism." 8 Journal of Conflict Resolution (1964), 131-146.

An inventory of testable propositions drawn from a wide sampling of the literature. The propositions are arranged topically within a conceptual framework wide enough to embrace contributions from several disciplines.

2464. Triandis, Harry C., Davis, Earl E., and Takezawa, Shin-Ichi. "Some Determinants of Social Distance among American, German and Japanese Students." 2 Journal of Personality and Social Psychology (1965), 540-551.

Results suggest that individuals in different cultures employ different weights for characteristics of race, religion, occupation, and nationality in determining the social distance that they experience toward other persons. The major emphasis in Greece was on religion, in Germany and Japan on occupation, and in the United States on race.

2465. Vaughn, G.M. "Social Distance Attitudes of New Zealand Students toward Maoris and 15 Other National Groups." 57 Journal of Social Psychology (1962), 85-92.

80 white native-born New Zealand psychology students were asked to indicate situations in which they would accept other national groups. Most acceptable were the Northwest European stocks, especially British and Protestants. Significantly less acceptable were, first, Maoris and Russians, and, second, Hindus, Chinese, and Japanese. There was a significant correlation with judgments on physical similarity.

2466. Weakland, John H. Chinese Political and Cultural Themes: A Study of Chinese Films. Studies in Deterrence XIV. Technical Paper TP 402, Naval Ordnance Test Station, China Lake, California, August 1966.

Explores, among other things, the themese to be found in Chinese films that relate to attitudes toward foreigners and to the status of minority groups.

2467. Zaidi, S.M. Hafeez. "National Stereotypes of University Students in Karachi." 63 Journal of Social Psychology (1964), 73-85.

Employment of adjectives to assign traits to 13 national groups, with less than one-fourth of the students questioned assigning traits to Russians, Chinese, Japanese, and Negroes. As in the earlier study in East Pakistan, Arabs were most favorably rated.

2468. Zaidi, S.M., and Ahmed, M. "National Stereotypes of University Students in East Pakistan." 47 Journal of Social Psychology (1958), 387-395.

Results of a questionnaire employing selection of adjectives as a means of determining stereotypes held concerning nine national groups.

See also nos. 181, 1965, 2005, 2032, 2594.

2. Migration

2469. Citroen, H.A. Les migrations internationales--Un probleme economique et social. Paris: Médicis, 1948, pp. 186.

Discussion of modern migrations with attention to various forms of restrictions inhibiting international movements and the doctrines underlying such restrictions.

2470. Goodrich, Carter. "Possibilities and Limits of International Control of Migration." In Milbank Memorial Fund, Postwar Problems of Migration: Papers Presented at the Round Table on Population Problems, October 29-30, 1946. New York: 1947, pp. 74-81.

On the possibilities of regulation of population movements by means of bilateral agreements such as that of 1945 between Mexico and the United States in contrast with multilateral agreements less amenable to policy changes and more in need of widespread consensus.

2471. Golay, Jean. "Italian Labor in Switzerland." 19 Journal of International Affairs (1965), 233-243.

On the economic, social, political, and religious aspects of the influx of Italian workers as a consequence of Swiss acceptance after 1945 of the principle of free movement of workers to the point of saturation.

2472. Kindleberger, C.P. "Mass Migration, Then and Now." 43 Foreign Affairs (1965), 647-658.

Compares the current mass migration from Southern to Northern Europe with that from South and East Europe to the US in 1880-1913, notes similarities such as the differential between capacity to absorb immigrants of different stock and capacity to absorbe people of similar stock, and calls attention to differences such as the active role of governments today to correct or prevent abuses of exploitation and the greater ease with which the immigrant could become an American citizen. The author suggests that today the mass immigrant is in danger of becoming a man without a country.

2473. Koenig, Samuel. "Immigration and Culture Conflict in Israel." 31 Social Forces (1952), 144-147.

Sketch of the effects of large-scale immigration on Israel's social structure, including the impact of non-European Jews entering the country.

2474. Mohan, R. "Immigration Policy of Burma in Relation to India--A Brief Survey." 16 Indian Journal of Political Science (1955), 165-170.

Reviews the history of Burmese immigration policy after the separation from India in 1937. This policy included implementation of the Indo-Burmese Immigration Agreement of 1941 that was delayed by war, a brief postwar policy of free immigration of Indians, and a resumption of restriction. The author justifies restriction on the ground of Burma's limited capacity to absorb aliens and on the basis of a state's constitutional right to determine the composition of its population.

2475. Röpke, William. "Barriers to Immigration." In Glenn Hoover (ed.), Twentieth Century Economic Thought. New York: Philosophical Library, 1950, pp. 607-645.

Examines the various barriers to immigration as they existed in mid-century.

2476. Tomasek, Robert D. "The Migrant Problem and Pressure Groups." 23 Journal of Politics (1961), 295-319.

Political parties show little interest in the movement of Mexican contract labor and "wetbacks" into the United States, an important reason for the lack of concern being that the migrants are voteless. Pressure groups seem to have exclusive roles in respect to the migrants with the result that solutions reached have been disturbing and, among other things, have relegated democratic processes to a secondary role. Government policies tend to reflect the disparities in strength and motives of pressure groups, their channels of access, and their influence upon governmental decision-making agencies.

See also nos. 745, 796, 1170, 1923, 2236, 2381, 2385, 2400, 2465, 2553, 2625.

3. Social Security Abroad; Internationalization
   of Social Security

2477. Howard, James. "Notes from Abroad." 10 Oasis (April 1964), 12-14, 21.

Description, in the Social Security employees' magazine, of some aspects of the disbursement of Social Security checks to payees in Bulgaria, Greece, Cyprus, and Jordan. Reference is made to the institution of a court proceeding and subsequent evidence gathering in Greece in the case of a presumed overpayment and to the problem of claims helpers and their fees in Cyprus and Jordan. The article, although in light style, calls attention to a relatively unknown aspect of relations among states.

2478. Marti Bufill, Carlos. "Legal Aspects of the Practical Application of International Social Security Conventions." 20 International
Social Security Review (1967), 313-359.
    The Secretary General of the National Social Insurance In-
stitute of Spain discusses the internationalization of social
security through general, multilateral, and bilateral agreements, principles of application of the conventions, and legal
and administrative problems for social security institutions
that arise from the application of international conventions.
Twenty-nine pages of informative tables are included.

See also nos. 796, 1170, 2033.

4. Asylum

    2479. Cavelier, German. La política internacional de Colombia.   2nd
ed., 4 vols. Bogotá: Editorial Iqueima, 1959.
    A history of Colombia's foreign policy that is of particu-
lar interest because of its well-documented examination of the
question of asylum.

    2480. Kimminich, O. "Asyl in Stützpunkten der UN-Truppe." 8 Zeit-
schrift für Politik (1961), 235-240.
    Raises the issue of whether the presence of United Nations
troops in the Congo provided Lumumba, at one stage of the proceedings, a right of asylum at a military post. Given the political situation and the circumstances producing the UN presence, the author does not regard the case as one to be treated
as a normal case of asylum because to so treat it would assure
individuals a better protection than the state provides and so
give a novel character to United Nations interventions. What
the article points up, at least by inference, are the potential
political consequences of legal determinations and conceptualizations.

    2481. Ronning, C. Neale. Diplomatic Asylum: Legal Norms and Politi-
cal Reality in Latin American Relations. The Hague: Nijhoff, 1965, pp.
vi, 242.
    Comparison and contrast of the Latin American practice of
diplomatic asylum and the legal arguments used by governments
to justify or deny the legality of the practice. Both practice
and legal argument are set against social, economic, and political backgrounds.

See also nos. 2483, 2549.

5. Extraterritoriality

    2482. Vedovoto, Giuseppe. L'Ordinamento capitolare in Oriente nei pri-
vilegi toscani dei secoli XII-XIV. Florence: Monnier, 1946, pp. 176.

Survey of privileges obtained by Tuscan cities in the Levant in the 12th to the 14th centuries that, in a focus upon one city, provides further information pertinent to the emergence of inter-governmental rules and institutions in consequence of nongovernmental activities.

See also no. 1965.

6. State Responsibility for Treatment of Aliens

See nos. 583, 1221.

B. HUMAN DIGNITY AND HEALTH

1. Human Rights

2483. Butler, Jeffrey. "South Africa and the High Commission Territories: The Ganyile Case, 1961." In Gwendolen M. Carter (ed.), Politics in Africa: 7 Cases. New York: Harcourt, Brace and World, 1966, pp. 245-283.
  Case study of a dispute between Great Britain and South Africa over Anderson Ganyile, a young nationalist leader who escaped a South African banishment farm, was granted asylum in Basutoland, and then was kidnapped by South African officials.

2484. Danelski, David J. "A Behavioral Conception of Human Rights." Paper presented at the Annual Meeting of the American Political Science Association, September 1964, pp. 9.
  A tentative step toward a jurisprudence anchored in human behavior and presenting hypotheses empirically verifiable. Human rights, distinguished from civil rights which amount to legal rights, are defined in terms of the probabilities (a) of perception of a man as fully human, (b) of acknowledgement that his humanity entitles him to certain treatment, and (c) action consistent with the acknowledgment.

2485. Eide, Asbjörn, and Schou, August (eds.). International Protection of Human Rights: Proceedings of the Seventh Nobel Symposium, Oslo, September 25-27, 1967. Stockholm: Almqvist & Wiksell; New York: Interscience Publishers, 1968, pp. 300.
  These Proceedings begin with a survey of the attitudes taken toward human rights yesterday and today and then deal with the law, the politics, and the system of protection of human rights. The legal approach dominates the papers and the appended discussion.

2486. Korey, W. "The Key to Human Rights--Implementation." Inter-national Conciliation. No. 570, November 1968, pp. 70.
A survey of international efforts since 1945 to implement human rights, with attention to the UN, ILO, Council of Europe, and OAS.

2487. Monconduit, François. La Commission Européenne des Droits de l'Homme. Leiden: Sijthoff, 1965, pp. 559.
Concentrates on the organization, internal structure, and roles and procedures of the Commission, but also deals with problems of substance and with much of the case law of the Commission.

2488. Mudge, George Alfred. "Domestic Policies and U.N. Activities: The Cases of Rhodesia and the Republic of South Africa." 21 International Organization (1967), 55-78.
Takes the position that United Nations oratory and resolutions have produced, along with other factors, more strongly racist regimes and policies in Rhodesia and South Africa than need necessarily have been chosen.

2488-A. Pollack, Ervin H. Human Rights--Amintaphil I. Buffalo: Jay Stewart Publications for the American Section of the International Association for Philosophy of Law and Social Philosophy, 1971, pp. xviii, 419.
Papers by a multidisciplinary group that examine such matters as the definition, justification, and identification of human rights, the relation of human rights to legal rights, and human rights in the light of contemporary conditions and problems.

2489. Schreiber, Anna P., and Schreiber, Philippe S.E. "The Inter-American Commission on Human Rights in the Dominican Crisis." 22 International Organization (1968), 508-528.
On the activity of the Inter-American Commission on Human Rights, with particular attention to its presence, effectiveness, and acceptance during the Dominican crisis when it employed liberal interpretations of its authority that in due course obtained OAS approval.

2489-A. Van Dyke, Vernon. Human Rights, the United States, and World Community. New York: Oxford, 1970, pp. 304.
A policy-oriented approach to issues faced by the United States in the UN, the OAS, and other international organizations, with attention to the identification of human rights in international discussions, controversies, and agreements, the problem of international obligation, and implementation of agreements.

See also nos. 715, 888, 2501, 2502.

a. Slavery, Forced Labor, and Peonage

2490. Barton, Paul, pseud. L'Institution concentrationnaire en Russie (1930-1957). Paris: Plon, 1959, pp. 519.
Well-documented study of Soviet forced labor camps that supplements an earlier study by Dallin and Nicolaevsky.

2491. Carlton, Richard K. (ed.). Forced Labor in the "People's Democracies." New York: Praeger for the Mid-European Studies Center of the Free Europe Committee, 1955, pp. iv, 248.
Papers on forced labor in Eastern Europe after World War II and on the liberalization of administration after 1952 in an attempt to achieve greater labor efficiency.

2492. Greenidge, Charles Wilton Wood. Slavery. New York: Macmillan, 1958, pp. 235.
Report on contemporary chattel slavery and peonage.

See also no. 897.

2. Minorities

2493. Arfa, Hassan. The Kurds. London: Oxford, 1966, pp. xi, 178.
Particularly useful for the information provided on Kurdish revolt since 1958, on the insurgents' organization, and on the Kurds' relations with the Soviet Union and with Iraqi Communists.

2494. Berkowitz, Leonard, and Green, James A. "The Stimulus Qualities of the Scapegoat." 64 Journal of Abnormal and Social Psychology (1962), 293-301. Reprinted in Aubrey J. Yates (ed.), Frustration and Conflict: Enduring Problems in Psychology--Selected Readings. Princeton: Van Nostrand, 1965, pp. 31-48.
The authors are dissatisfied with the one-sidedness of the "pure drive" scapegoat theory of prejudice that holds that frustration-generated aggression finds an outlet not against an invisible thwarting agent or an agent capable of severe punitive retaliation but against an innocent minority or weaker group, particularly in the light of the White-Lippitt findings of scapegoating against boys who could hold their own singly against any of the others. They are also dissatisfied with the "pure stimulus" theory that rests explanation on properties of the objects of aggression. Hence, they undertook to build on their earlier experimental work by testing the hypothesis that aggression will generalize from the anger-instigator to another person in direct proportion to the degree of dislike for the latter individual. Frustration was induced for some subjects and not for others in manners described in the paper. The generalization of hostility observed tended to support the hypothesis and thereby suggest a link between the "pure drive" and the "pure stimulus" theories. Although in the absence of further research, unable to account for an unexpected generalization of hostility to the confederate, the authors feel that their data is of value in that it does not require the postulate

of a stimulus induced generalization of aggressive tendencies from the immediate frustrator to the disliked individual. The Freudian view of the aggressive drive as energy continually seeking an outlet, could be accommodated, as well as, in light of apparent inhibition of aggression in evaluations of neutral confederates and the presumably like subjects, Newcomb's "balance" proposition and Festinger's "dissonance-avoiding" hypothesis. However, the authors suggest that perhaps only people who have inflicted injury--one might include those perceived or believed to have done so--will evoke generalized aggression and not every disliked person.

2495. Berkowitz, Leonard, Green, James A., and Macauley, Jacqueline R. "Hostility Catharsis as the Reduction of Emotional Tension." 25 Psychiatry (1962), 23-31.
The authors do not believe that tension-reduction accompanying aggressive acts necessarily means a reduction in drive, that is, in the desire to commit additional acts of aggression against the frustrating object. By taking this position they oppose an explanation advanced by the frustration-aggression hypothesis. Increased guilt feelings and fear of retaliation may be what actually decreases the desire to commit aggressive acts. Whatever catharsis exists--and there appears to be one-- it is not based on the hypothesis put forward as part of the frustration-aggression thesis. It is conceivable that pleasurable feelings stem from the completion of the previously inhibited act. If the authors' last conjecture is correct, then it may be that the route to control of aggression is to provide inhibitions other than, or in addition to, prohibitions that, if violated, provide a measure of satisfaction stemming from the doing of what would ordinarily be inhibited.

2496. Bharati, A. "Problems of the Asian Minorities in East Africa." 17 Pakistan Horizon (1964), 342-349.
On the East Africans' image of Indian and Pakistani Asians as money-grabbing, blood-sucking, unsmiling traders possessing 80% of East African wealth. Reference is made to Asian and African marriage restrictions hindering assimilation. The status that Asians once enjoyed is regarded as gone for good and the development of a modus vivendi, then still possible to hope for, is seen as requiring Asian caution, modification of the Asian value system, and alteration of the system of economic superiority by offering voluntary partnership to Africans.

2497. Bischoff, Ralph F. Nazi Conquest through German Culture. Cambridge: Harvard University Press, 1942, pp. x, 198.
On Nazi exploitation of German organizations abroad for political objectives of expansion and conquest.

2498. Blau, J. "Les relations inter-communautaires en Irak." 5-6 Correspondence d'Orient Études (1964), 87-102.

On the intercommunity relations of Arabs, Kurds, Turks, and eight other communities and their impact on basic domestic and foreign policy of Iraq.

2499. Burgueño Alvarez, G. "El Sud-Tirol o Alto Adige, en su proceso de problema europeo." 53 Política internacional (1961), 85-103.
On the status of the South Tyrol and conditions therein, on the Fascist effort to produce a systematic political integration, and the failure of Italy to observe the provisions of the Treaty of Paris of September 5, 1946, guaranteeing the existence and development of the South Tyrol. The conflict is viewed as one of the obstacles to European integration.

2500. Chang, Sen-dou. "The Distribution and Occupations of Overseas Chinese." 58 Geographical Review (1968), 89-107.
On the migration of Chinese, their concentration in Southeast Asia and coastal cities, and their occupations.

2501. Claude, Inis L., Jr. National Minorities: An International Problem. Cambridge, Massachusetts: Harvard University Press, 1955, pp. xii, 248.
Conceptualizations of political leaders are treated as restrictions upon explorations of alternative devices to deal with basic questions. World War I Allies treated the problem of minorities as part of the problem of securing rights of small nations. But the League system of protection failed because states protecting minorities resented the impediment to "nationalization" of their minorities, the qualification of their sovereignty, and discrimination in applying the system to but a few states, with the Great Powers among the exemptions. "Kin" states, dissatisfied with League protection, claimed a direct interest in protecting minorities of their own culture, thus opening the door to exploitation of the status of such minorities for irridentist and subversive purposes. The Allies of World War II approached the minorities problem with conceptual tools constrained by the ideology of human rights of a universalist nature, the "melting pot" assumption of the dominant member of the alliance, and a desire to protect states against subversion that, among other things, attempted to deal with specific minority situations by exchanges of populations and by bilateral arrangements between states with minorities and "kin" states.

2502. Condominas, G. "Minoritiés autochtones en Asie du Sud-Est." 28 Politique étrangère (1963), 44-57.
The article calls attention to the problem of the autochthonous minorities of Southeast Asia and the problems of divided peoples, of populated and unpopulated zones, and of varieties of cultural development. Particular attention is given to Burma, Thailand, Vietnam, and Laos, in the last the minorities covering three-quarters of the land. While the picture set forth is of particular importance to studies of nation-building, it is also useful for the identification of minorities and human rights problems, differing from those of Europe, that can be of consequence

for the development of, in McDougal's terminology, an international law of human dignity.

2503. Conquest, Robert. The Soviet Deportation of Nationalities. New York: St. Martin's, 1960, pp. 203.

Well-documented narrative of the mass deportation of seven of the national groups in the Soviet Union that helps to clarify the present limits upon the international capacity to employ normative means to protect individuals and other groups unable to assert international personality.

2504. Dekmejian, R.H. "Soviet-Turkish Relations and Politics in the Armenian SSR." 19 Soviet Studies (1968), 510-525.

On Armenian resentment of Soviet leadership, dissatisfaction with improved relations with Turkey, the April 1965 demonstration in Yerevan and subsequent Kremlin purge of the Armenian Communist Party and anti-nationalist propaganda, and Armenian territorial aspirations.

2505. Eisenstadt, S.N. "Communication Processes Among Immigrants in Israel." 16 Public Opinion Quarterly (1952), 42-58.

Deals with the problems of immigrants from Yugoslavia, Yemen, North Africa, and Eastern and Central Europe in terms of communication processes and networks and of old and new elites.

2506. Fishel, Wesley R. (ed.). Problems of Freedom: South Viet Nam since Independence. New York: Free Press for the Bureau of Social and Political Research, Michigan State University, 1961, pp. xvi, 233.

Includes a chapter on ethnic minorities in South Vietnam.

2507. Freyre, Gilberto. New World in the Tropics: The Culture of Modern Brazil. New York: Knopf, 1959; Vintage ed. 1963. Rev. ed. of Brazil: An Interpretation (1945), pp. 286, xii.

In the chapter on foreign policy the Brazilian author stresses the affinity between Russia and Brazil stemming from what he regards as their shared freedom from racial discrimination and this affinity as providing a basis for a common initiative to suggest important changes in international law.

2508. Friedrich-Ebert-Stiftung. Überwindung von Vorurteilen. 2nd ed. Hannover: Verlag für Literatur und Zeitgeschehen, 1960, pp. 97.

A short volume on topics debated at a 1959 conference dealing with such matters as prejudice against minorities, research on prejudice, and national bias as an obstacle to international understanding.

2509. Gantner, S. "Le mouvement national kurde." 32-33 Orient (1964-1965), 29-114.

Useful review of the problem of Kurdistan and of the national movement, particularly of the Kurds in Iraq.

2510. Ghai, Dharam P. (ed.). Portrait of a Minority: Asians in East Africa. New York: Oxford, 1966, pp. 154.
        Six studies by East African and Asian scholars that provide historical, political, social, economic, and educational surveys of the 360,000 Asians of Kenya, Uganda, and Tanzania.

2511. Ghai, Dharama P., and Ghai, Yash P. "Asians in East Africa: Problems and Prospects." 3 Journal of Modern African Studies (1965), 35-52.
        On the situation of Pakistani and Indians in East Africa, their prospects, and need to adapt to circumstances quite different from those of the past.

2512. Griffith, John Aneurin Grey, et al. Coloured Immigrants in Britain. New York: Oxford for the Institute of Race Relations, 1960, pp. xii, 225.
        A study of a minority problem of the postwar period.

2513. Hughes, Everett Cherrington, and Hughes, Helen MacGill. Where Peoples Meet: Racial and Ethnic Frontiers. Glencoe: Free Press, 1952, pp. 204.
        Concise discussion of situations produced by contact between diverse ethnic groups and their intermingling.

2514. Kunstadter, Peter (ed.). Southeast Asian Tribes, Minorities, and Nations. 2 vols. Princeton: Princeton University Press, 1967, pp. xviii, 902.
        Twenty anthropologists and other specialists report on the relationship between rural minorities and central governments in seven Southeast Asian countries and present evidence that the Communists have recognized more clearly than the non-Communists the strategic importance of rural minority and tribal groups both for military purposes and for the development of nation-states.

2515. Lang, C.L. "Les minorités arménienne et juive d'Iran." 26 Politique étrangère (1961), 460-471.
        Survey of the relatively autonomous situation of Armenians and Jews in Iran, their economically active existence, and the exodus of young Armenians to the USSR and of young Jews to Israel, the latter toward a more difficult but independent life. Economic stagnation of Iran is blamed for the exodus of the two groups and note is taken of the loss to Iran of two young elites that could make useful contributions to modernization.

2516. La Ponce, J.A. The Protection of Minorities. Berkeley: University of California Press, 1960, pp. 236.
        Comparative studies of the many aspects of minority rights and of the problems faced by minorities.

2517. Lettrich, Jozef. History of Modern Slovakia. New York: Praeger, 1955, pp. 329.

Recent history of Slovakia, including the development of separatism, the emergence of a state of Slovakia in 1939, and the uprising of 1944.

2518. Levin, M.G., and Potapov, L.P. (eds.). The Peoples of Siberia. Translated by Scripta Technica, Inc. Translation edited by Stephen P. Dunn. Chicago: University of Chicago Press, 1964, pp. viii, 948.
    An edited publication of works by many Soviet authorities on the Soviet people, customs, religion, social organization, Russian contracts, and their history during and after the Revolution. The articles reflect Soviet views of minorities in their nation.

2519. Mahajani, Usha. The Role of Indian Minorities in Burma and Malaya. Bombay: Vora, for the Institute of Pacific Relations, 1960, pp. xxx, 344.
    Deals with a major minorities problem in Southeast Asian countries.

2520. Maver, B. "Le Nazioni Unite e la protezione delle minoranze." 31 Rivista di studi politici internazionali (1964), 536-564.
    Examination of the status of minorities under the UN system that subsumed the matter under the concept of human rights and, by treating the problem of minorities as marginal, left them pretty much to the disposition of governments.

2521. Means, G.P. "Eastern Malaysia: The Politics of Federalism." 8 Asian Survey (1968), 289-308.
    On the problems and political demands for substantial autonomy on the part of the non-Malay peoples of Sabah and Sarawak.

2522. Mikus, Joseph A. La Slovaquie dans le drame de l'Europe: Histoire politique de 1918 à 1950. Paris: Les Îles d'Or, 1955, pp. 475.
    Study of Slovak efforts to attain independence that sheds light on the circumstances surrounding the 1939 secession and the 1944 uprising.

2523. Moseley, George. A Sino-Soviet Cultural Frontier: The Ili Kazakh Autonomous Chou. Harvard East Asian Monographs, No. 22. Cambridge: East Asian Research Center, Harvard University, 1966, pp. viii, 163.
    On the impact of Communist Chinese rule over the Kazakh minority and the sharpening of the Sino-Soviet controversy as it relates to this frontier region.

2524. Peretz, Don. "The Arab Minority of Israel." 8 Middle East Journal (1954), 139-154.
    Discussion of the position of the Arabs in Israel and the dichotomy between the legal matrix circumscribing daily life and improvement in material and social welfare. Irridentism has been fostered by Ministry of Defense rule over Arab areas, policy toward absentee property owners, and a discriminatory Nationality Law, all of which tended to counteract the planting

of seeds of loyalty by other ministries, e.g., Agriculture. The
problems of the impact of wider regional issues and of the inherent incompatibility of full Arab participation in a "Jewish
state" are discussed.

2525. Rondot, P. "La nation kurde en face des mouvements arabes."
2 Orient (No. 7, 1958), 55-69.
Contrasts the situation of the Kurds in Syria with that in
Iraq.

2526. Rose, Arnold M., and Rose, Caroline B. (eds.). Minority Prob-
lems: A Textbook of Readings in Intergroup Relations. New York: Harper
& Row, 1965, pp. x, 438.
Selections on intergroup relations, chiefly in the United
States but including eight essays on minority problems in other
parts of the world.

2527. Rothermund, Indira. Die politische und wirtschaftliche Rolle
der asiatischen Minderheit in Ostafrika--Kenya, Tanganyika/Sansibar, Uganda.
Berlin, Heidelberg, and New York: Springer, 1965, pp. xi, 75.
Study of the political, sociological, and other aspects of
the presence of Asian minorities in East Africa, together with
consideration of consequent problems of diplomatic relations between India and Pakistan on the one hand and the East African
states on the other, before the Kenya anti-Asiatic action of
1968 aggravated matters and raised racial issues in England.

2528. Stevenson, William. "Africa's Uneasy Asians." Globe Magazine:
Globe and Mail (Toronto), July 27, 1963.
On the problem of Asian minorities in Africa, their dis-
placement from jobs and unpopularity with both black and white.
The author sees their plight as comparable to that of Jews in
Europe and Chinese in Southeast Asia.

2529. Thompson, Virginia, and Adloff, Richard. Minority Problems in
Southeast Asia. Stanford: Stanford University Press, 1955, pp. viii, 295.
Study of minority problems, including those that are in
part a consequence of the period of association under the
French, of the now separate states of Cambodia, Laos, and
North and South Vietnam. Minority problems with other and
older roots form an important part of the study.

2530. Tomson, Edgar. Die Volkrepublik China und das Recht nationaler
Minderheiten. Frankfurt: Metzner, 1963, pp. 201.
Study of the rights of national minorities in Communist
China.

2531. Vali, Ferenc A. "Transylvania and the Hungarian Minority." 20
Journal of International Affairs (1966), 32-44.
Review of the situation of the Hungarians in Transylvania
since 1919, with attention to the 1952 inclusion in the second
Communist constitution of Rumania of special minorities provisions providing a preferential status that ended after the revolt
in Hungary in 1956.

2532. van der Kroef, J.M. "The Arabs in Indonesia." 7 <u>Middle East Journal</u> (1953), 300-323.
On a minority that held itself aloof from the Indonesian nationalist movement but which after 1949 tended to assimilate more than previously with Indonesians.

2533. van der Kroef, J.M. "The Eurasian Minority in Indonesia." 18 <u>American Sociological Review</u> (1953), 484-493.
On the problems of the Eurasian minority, of dual loyalty, of their colonization in New Guinea, and of the Indonesian government's preference for their assimilation into native society, a process more natural for the lower strata of Eurasians.

2534. van der Veur, P.W. "The Eurasians of Indonesia: Castaways of Colonialism." 27 <u>Pacific Affairs</u> (1954), 124-137.
Survey of a special minority problem, a legacy of colonialism in the form of a group who were not colonizers, immigrants, or invaders.

2534-A. Veiter, Theodor. <u>Das Recht der Volksgruppen und Sprachminderheiten in Österreich, mit einer ethnosoziologischen Grundlegung und einem Anhang (Materielen)</u>. Vienna and Stuttgart: Wilhelm Braumüller Universitäts-Verlagsbuchhandlung, 1970, pp. xxvii, 890.
Wealthy in resources, historical perspective, and range of inquiry, this book analyzes various proposed conceptual definitions of such component elements of the nationality question as "nation" and "ethnic group," examines such themes as borderland minorities and hinterland minorities, discusses the position of ethnic and linguistic minorities in Austria, considers the body of domestic and international legal principles applicable to Austria's minorities, and reviews the formal complaints lodged by minorities with various international organizations. A documentary appendix is included.

2535. Viefhaus, Erwin. <u>Die Minderheitenfrage und die Entstehung der Minderheitenschutzverträge auf der Pariser Friedenskonferenz 1919</u>. Würzburg: Holzner, 1960, pp. xv, 244.
Study of European minority problems in the 19th and 20th centuries and the origins of the minorities provisions in the 1919 peace treaties.

2536. Wagley, Charles, and Harris, Marvin. <u>Minorities in the New World: Six Case Studies</u>. New York: Columbia University Press, 1958, pp. xvi, 320.
Comparative study, sponsored by UNESCO, of minority groups in Latin America and the United States--Indians in Brazil and Mexico, Negroes in Martinique and the United States, French Canadians, and Jews in the United States.

2537. Wittram, Reinhard. <u>Das Nationale als europäisches Problem: Beiträge zur Geschichte des Nationalitätsprinzips vornehmlich im 19. Jahrhundert</u>. Göttingen: Vandenhoeck, 1954, pp. 244.
Essays on nationality conflicts in the Baltic area.

See also nos. 952, 1231, 1233, 1704, 2005, 2032, 2330, 2333, 2346, 2348, 2353, 2381, 2404, 2463, 2465, 2466, 2494, 2495.

3. Refugees and Displaced Persons; Population
   Exchanges; Forced Migrations

2538. Bouman, P.J., Beijer, G., and Oudegeest, J.J. The Refugee Problem in Western Germany. Translated by H.A. Marx. The Hague: Nijhoff, 1950.
   Survey of the events productive of migration of German refugees into Western Germany with consideration for the economic influence of the refugees in West Germany and the social and psychological consequences for both the refugees and the local population.

2539. Bruhns, Fred C. "A Study of Arab Refugee Attitudes." 9 Middle East Journal (1955), 130-138.
   Findings from an inquiry into the attitudes of Arab refugees from Palestine that indicated that the majority was willing to accept Israel's existence under certain compromise conditions and that objection to resettlement outside Israel stemmed from an incapacity to take clan, village elders, friends, and religious leaders with them. These findings suggest the need for international norms and institutions that are suitable to the situation of the refugee's need for his community.

2539-A. Buehrig, Edward H. The UN and the Palestinian Refugees: A Study in Nonterritorial Administration. Bloomington: Indiana University Press, 1971, pp. 254.
   A study of the United Nations Relief and Works Agency's efforts to help displaced Palestinians, the politics of relations with the Arab states, and the Agency's unintended contributions to Palestinian political solidarity even when failing to resettle displaced families.

2540. Frings, Paul. Das internationale Flüchtlingsproblem, 1919-1950. Frankfurt-am-Main: Frankfurter Hefte, 1951, pp. 295.
   Deals with national and international efforts since World War I to deal with the refugee problem.

2541. Gadolin, Axel de. The Solution of the Karelian Refugee Problem in Finland. The Hague: Nijhoff, 1952, pp. xi, 47.
   Deals with the problem of refugees from the areas on the Karelian Peninsula that Finland had to surrender to the Soviet Union.

2542. Gleisberg, A. À la recherche d'une patrie. Paris: 1946.
   Provides glimpses and criticisms of French practices in regard to refugees from Franco's armies in 1938-1939.

2543. Hernandez, Jesus. La Grande Trahison. Paris: Fraquelle, 1953, pp. 254.

Memoirs of a Spanish exile exposing in detail the highly selective Soviet practice concerning the admission of exiles.

2544. Holborn, Louise W. "International Organizations for Migration of European Nationals and Refugees." 20 International Journal (1965), 331-349.

Operations and achievements of organizations concerned with European migration and with refugees, with attention to partnerships among international, national, and voluntary organizations and interactions between international objectives and national policies.

2545. Holborn, Louise W. "The Palestine Arab Refugee Problem." 23 International Journal (1967-1968), 82-96.

On the more recent aspects of the Arab refugee problem and on the organization and coordinating activities of UNWRA.

2546. Kee, Robert. Refugee World. New York: Oxford, 1961, pp. 153.

Reminder based on observations in July 1960 that the refugee problem remains serious in Germany and Austria, a problem far from satisfactorily dealt with by international means.

2547. Kostanick, Huey L. "Turkish Resettlement of Refugees from Bulgaria, 1950-1953." 9 Middle East Journal (1955), 41-52.

On the Turkish program for resettlement of the 250,000 Turks who had been living in Bulgaria and who had been given, by a Bulgarian decree of August 1950, three months to return to Turkey and on the problem of absorption of the refugees into the Turkish economy.

2548. Kraus, Hertha. "Work Programs in International Aid: Employment of Arab Refugees, 1949-1952." In Howard M. Teaf, Jr., and Peter G. Franck (eds.), Hands Across Frontiers: Case Studies in Technical Cooperation. Ithaca: Cornell University Press, 1955, pp. 517-579.

Report on an effort of a United Nations agency to act constructively in regard to Arab refugees from Palestine by means of a work program for 100,000 men.

2549. Ludwig, Carl. La politique pratiquée par la Suisse à l'égard des réfugiés au cours des années 1933 à 1955--Rapport adressé au Conseil fédéral à l'intention des conseils législatifs. Bern: 1957, pp. 411.

Also in a German edition, this important compilation of documents deals with Swiss policy toward political refugees, including the policy of denying privileges of asylum for racial reasons.

2550. Luva, Radomir. The Transfer of the Sudeten Germans: A Study of Czech-German Relations, 1933-1962. New York: New York University Press, 1964.

An important study of national minorities, relocation of populations, and modern European history. The massive deportation of Germans from Czechoslovakia after the Second World War is detailed. The creation of the Czechoslovak Republic is outlined. Pan-Germanism, Nazi occupation, the Protectorate regime, and the Czech Resistance movement are also discussed.

2551. Pallis, A.A. "Racial Migrations in the Balkans During the Years 1912-24." 66 Geographic Journal (1925), 315-331.
Review of movements of Balkan peoples as a result of cessions after the Balkan Wars and World War I.

2552. Peretz, Don. "Problems of Arab Refugee Compensation." 8 Middle East Journal (1954), 403-416.
Review of the Arab refugee problem and of efforts to get Israel to consider payment for abandoned Arab property and to secure the release of funds from accounts frozen in Israeli banks.

2553. Petersen, William. The Politics of Population. Garden City: Doubleday, 1964, pp. x, 350.
Essentially a collection of previously published papers that deal with such subjects as forced migration and planned migration. A fair amount of attention is given to Dutch migration and the international relations related thereto as in the Dutch-Canadian case. The book is concerned with both domestic and international aspects of migration and population control.

2554. Poole, P.A. "Thailand's Vietnamese Refugees: Can They Be Assimilated?" 40 Pacific Affairs (1967-1968), 324-332.
On the Vietnamese refugees who settled in Northeast Thailand just after World War II, their vulnerability to social and economic pressures induced by Communists among them, and the extent to which their children have blended into Thai society.

2555. Proudfoot, Malcolm J. European Refugees, 1939-52: A Study in Forced Population Movement. Evanston: Northwestern University Press, 1956, pp. 542.
Deals with the handling of 60 million refugees in Europe during and after World War II, forced labor in wartime, escape routes from German areas, the work of UNNRA, SHAEF, and IRO, concentration camps, problems of mass repatriation, resettlement problems, and Jewish and German refugee movements. During World War II the author served in the Displaced Persons Branch of SHAEF.

2556. Report of the Zellerbach Commission on the European Refugee Situation. 2 vols. New York: Zellerbach Commission, 1958-1959, pp. ix, 164; 96.
Report on the refugee situation in Europe after the Hungarian uprising, together with some suggestions for long-range remedies.

2557. Ristelhueber, René. *Au secours des réfugiés*. Paris: Plon, 1951.

Description of the work of the International Refugee Organization.

2558. Schechtman, Joseph B. *Postwar Population Transfers in Europe, 1945-1955*. Philadelphia: University of Pennsylvania Press, 1962, pp. ix, 417.

Story of the postwar displacements and population shifts in East-Central Europe.

2559. Stoessinger, John George. *The Refugee and the World Community*. Minneapolis: University of Minnesota Press, 1956, pp. v, 239.

Consideration of League of Nations and IRO efforts to meet the refugee problem.

2560. Vernant, Jacques. *The Refugee in the Post-War World*. New Haven: Yale University Press, 1953, pp. xvi, 827. *Les réfugiés dans l'aprés-guerre*. Monaco: Éditions du Rocher, 1953, pp. 919.

Extensive survey of the refugee situation and the problems related to their positions in each nation and under national regulations down to the time of writing.

2561. Wiskemann, Elizabeth. *Germany's Eastern Neighbours: Problems Relating to the Oder-Neisse Line and the Czech Frontier Regions*. New York: Oxford for the Royal Institute of International Affairs, 1956, pp. x, 309.

Deals with German-Pole and German-Czech issues since Hitler's rise to power but especially from World War II to the mid-1950s. Attention is given to territorial changes, the movement of Germans from and of Poles into the area east of the Oder-Neisse line, and the impact of Polish agricultural activities and structures on the area.

See also nos. 304, 887, 940, 1230, 1658, 1923, 2266, 2297, 2381, 2501, 2503.

a. Resettlement Due to Flooding from Downstream River Development

2562. Shaw, D.J. "Resettlement from the Nile in Sudan." 21 *Middle East Journal* (1967), 463-487.

On the problems associated with and possible benefits from the resettlement of Sudanese made necessary by flooding behind the Aswan High Dam, the cost of which has been estimated at ₤S. 26.2 million, of which ₤S. 15 million were granted by the UAR to the Sudan Government.

4. Nomads

2563. Halpern, Manfred. The Politics of Social Change in the Middle East and North Africa. Princeton: Princeton University Press, 1963, pp. xxv, 431.

Includes discussion of the problem of nomads who have on a number of occasions proved a threat to a state's integrity by fighting for autonomy or entering into alliances with foreign powers.

See also nos. 1244, 2351, 2352, 2359, 2369, 2381.

5. International Medical and Sanitation Law

2564. Campos, E.G., Trevino, H.A., and Strom, L.G. "The Dispersal of Mosquitoes by Railroad Trains Involved in International Traffic." 21 Mosquito News (1961), 190-192.

Report on inspection of trains upon arrival at Matamoros from the interior of Mexico and the species of mosquitoes collected.

2565. Cassel, J. "Social Science Theory as a Source of Hypothesis in Epidemiological Research." 54 American Journal of Public Health (1964), 1482-1488.

Epidemiologists cannot rely exclusively on etiological models of the past. A new or modified model of disease causation is needed to handle problems of prevention of epidemics. Social science theory may be a source for such an endeavor.

2566. Finney, D.J. "An International Drug Safety Program." 3 Journal of New Drugs (1963), 262-265.

Advocates the drawing up of a detailed plan for the international flow of information on new drugs to avoid crystallization of national differences in observation and recording that may of themselves be of little importance but which may become obstacles to international analysis that are hard to remove.

2567. Foster, George McClelland. Problems in Intercultural Health Programs: Memorandum to the Committee on Preventive Medicine and Social Science Research. Pamphlet 12. New York: Social Science Research Council, 1958, pp. 49.

A most useful memorandum indicating the obstacles to the intercultural approach to health problems and to the establishment of international standards based on common values and objectives.

2568. Frederiksen, Harald. "Strategy and Tactics for Smallpox Eradication." 77 Public Health Reports (1962), 617-622.

On the possibility of eradication of smallpox through synchronized efforts such as mass vaccination, with reference to mechanisms for worldwide sharing and timing of national efforts that are provided by the World Health Organization and by the World Health Assembly.

2569. Jacchia, Enrico. Atome et sécurité: Le Risque des radiations à l'age nucléaire. Paris: Dalloz, 1965.
    An enlarged edition, the original appearing in Italian in 1963, that deals with the problem of protection of workers and populations from nuclear radiation and accords attention to legal arrangements for such purposes, particularly within the European Communities.

2570. Langer, Elinor. "The Court-Martial of Captain Levy: Medical Ethics v. Military Law." 156 Science (1967), 1346-1350.
    A review of the Levy trial that points up the dilemma of medicine in military service, the issue of the subordination of medicine to political and military objectives, and the problem of Special Forces that do not make the distinction between medical and military functions that is traditional both in international law and in the regular organization of the United States Army. Given the role of guerrilla warfare in internal uprisings, serious questions are suggested as to whether the traditional distinction can or should be maintained.

2571. McKinnon, Mildred L., and Smith, Louis C. Redmund. "Quarantine Inspection of International Air Travelers." 77 Public Health Reports (1962), 65-69.
    Report of a pilot study conducted by the Division of Foreign Quarantine, US Public Health Service, at 14 international airports in 1960. The quarantine station at Idlewild Airport sampled 10% of the incoming flights from October 24 to November 2, 1960, and found that in 17 of the countries visited quarantinable diseases had been reported to WHO, that 1% of the arriving passengers failed to present a valid smallpox vaccination certificate, and that 6.5% required surveillance as possible threats to the health of United States citizens.

2572. Moureau, Paul. "Le Problème du sang sur le plan international." Annales de droit international médical (No. 3, December 1958), 28-36.
    A member of the Medical Faculty at Liège calls attention to such problems concerning blood and its derivatives as free circulation during war, eliminating discrimination, elimination of pressures on physicians in regard to who shall receive a transfusion, and protection of zones of storage of reserves of blood, plasma, and other derivatives.

2573. Pfeffermann, H., and Wiebringhaus, H. "Les activités du Conseil de l'Europe dans le domaine de la santé publique." Annales de droit international médical (No. 11, December 1964), 46-62.
    Reviews what has been done by the Council of Europe in an effort to promote public health programs and takes note of agreements concluded that relate to the field. The article thus touches upon such various matters as identification of blood groups, pharmaceutical problems, camping hygiene, sanitary control of food products, and the rehabilitation and reemployment of invalids.

2574. Renborg, Bertil A. <u>International Drug Control</u>. Washington: Carnegie Endowment for International Peace, 1947, pp. xi, 276.

Discussion by the former Chief of the Drug Control Section of the League of Nations Secretariat of the system of drug control developed by the League and handed over to the United Nations.

2575. Shewan, J.M., and Liston, J. "A Review of Food Poisoning Caused by Fish and Fishery Products." 18 <u>Journal of Applied Bacteriology</u> (1955), 522-534.

This item refers to a problem which is presently subject to national regulation but which, given an international effort to deal with the world's food supply problem without becoming enmeshed in the complexities of differing national regulations based on differing tastes--e.g., the US blockage of the use of fish meal--may require the formulation of international standards dominated by health and nutrition considerations rather than by the imposition of particular peoples' preferences.

2576. Stamp, L. Dudley. <u>The Geography of Life and Death.</u> Ithaca: Cornell University Press, 1964, paperback ed. 1965, pp. 160.

Presents a concise overall view of the locations of major killing and debilitating diseases, their relation to population changes, and the spread, consolidation, and retreat of diseases. Some attention is given to diseases of animals. Mapping techniques to assist in the control of disease in general, as well as to deal with pandemics, is discussed.

2576-A. Taylor, Arnold H. <u>American Diplomacy and the Narcotics Problem, 1900-1939: A Study in International Humanitarian Reform</u>. Durham: Duke University Press, 1969, pp. x, 372.

Makes use of documents and personal papers to portray the role of the United States in attempts to establish international narcotics control in the years prior to World War II.

See also nos. 730, 1158, 2033.

a. <u>Pollution of Rivers, Lakes, Seas,</u>
   <u>and the Air</u>

2577. Callaghan, James. "International Aspects of Oil Pollution." <u>Transactions of the 26th North American Wildlife and Natural Resources Conference</u> (1961), 328-342.

Reports on efforts to deal with pollution of the sea under conditions of an increase in the number of oil-burning vessels and increased shipping of oil.

2578. Christ, Wolfgang, <u>et al</u>. <u>Aspects of Water Pollution Control: A Selection of Papers from the Conference on Water Pollution Problems in Europe, Geneva, 1961</u>. <u>Public Health Papers</u>, No. 13. Geneva: World Health Organization, 1962, pp. 115.

Papers on such subjects as water pollution control in Eastern Europe, water pollution in international law, liability in
national and international law for damage through water pollution, assessment of economic damage caused by water pollution,
and financial and economic aspects of water pollution prevention.

2579. Fair, G.M. "Pollution Abatement in the Ruhr District." 34
Journal (of the) Water Pollution Control Federation (1962), 749-766.
    Laudatory description of seven river basin authorities in
the Ruhr district, their responsibilities, budgets, organization
and activities which constitute an important aspect of pollution
abatement having effect upon an international waterway into
which a tributary flows. However, given the condition of the
Rhine as it reaches the Netherlands, the author seems to have
overpraised the Ruhr control system.

2580. Fischerhof, J. Hans. "Liability in National and International
Law for Damage through Water Pollution." Public Health Papers, No. 13.,
Aspects of Water Pollution Control. Geneva: World Health Organization,
1962, pp. 75-87.
    Legalistic analysis of the concept of liability and its
formulation for application to boundary and continuous rivers,
with particular reference to Europe.

2580-A. Gerber, William. "Coastal Conservation." Editorial Research
Reports. Vol. I, 1970, pp. 141-160.
    This report, published by Congressional Quarterly, Inc.,
provides a brief overview of the problem of pollution of American coasts, with reference also to the Torrey Canyon and Santa
Barbara Channel incidents, Lake Erie, the Everglades, European
experience in handling coastal abuses, and international agreement on the use of the marginal sea.

2581. Giles, Lester A., Jr., and Livingston, John. "Oil Pollution of
the Seas." Transactions of the 25th North American Wildlife Conference
(1960), 297-303.
    Reviews the problem of oil pollution, the areas affected,
international efforts to combat it, and the effect on wildlife.

2582. Hardin, Garrett. "The Tragedy of the Commons." 162 Science
(1968), 1243-1248.
    Points out that because optimum population density is below
the maximum that an area can support, no technical solution to
the problem of pollution by overpopulation exists and that,
therefore, resort must be had to legal and moral means of mutually agreed-on coercion.

2583. Hawkes, Alfred L. "A Review of the Nature and Extent of Damage
Caused by Oil Pollution at Sea." Transactions of the 26th North American
Wildlife and Natural Resources Conference (1961), 343-355.
    Discusses sources and effects of oil pollution, and esti-
mated direct and indirect financial losses.

2584. Katz, M., and Gaufin, A. "The Effects of Sewage Pollution on the Fish Population of a Midwestern Stream." 82 <u>Transactions of the American Fisheries Society, 1952</u> (1953), 156-165.

    An important study of the effects of pollution of a particular stream.

2585. Katz, M., Van Horn, W.M., and Anderson, J.B. "The Effect of Kraft Pulp Mill Wastes on Some Aquatic Organisms." 79 <u>Transactions of the American Fisheries Society, 1949</u> (1950), 55-63.

    A report on the effect of one form of pollution on marine life. One of the authors, Katz, has provided annual reviews of the biological and bacteriological literature on either the toxicity of industrial wastes or sewage treatment and water pollution control in <u>Sewage and Industrial Waste</u> from 1949 to 1959 and in the <u>Journal of the Water Pollution Control Federation</u> since 1960.

2586. Livingstone, Dennis. "Pollution Control: An International Perspective." 10 <u>Scientist and Citizen</u> (September 1968), 172-181.

    Takes note of what has already been done to produce international legislation concerning pollution of the high seas, the upper atmosphere, and the earth and gives attention to the problem of developing international regulations to deal with pollution of international rivers and other areas under national jurisdiction.

2587. MacCallum, J.L. "The International Joint Commission." 72 <u>Canadian Geographical Journal</u> (1966), 76-87.

    Reviews the work of the IJC and calls particular attention to its recent tasks of ascertaining the extent of pollution of the Red River and of the Great Lakes and suggesting remedies.

2588. Manner, E.J. "Water Pollution in International Law." <u>Public Health Papers</u>, No. 13., <u>Aspects of Water Pollution Control</u>. Geneva: World Health Organization, 1962, pp. 53-73.

    Review of some national legislation concerning pollution of inland waters, of pertinent treaties, pertinent literature, the views of international organizations, and custom concerning the asserted obligation to avoid pollution injurious to other states.

2589. Mörzer Bruyns, M.F. "Stookolievogels op de Nederlandse kust." 62 <u>Levende Natuur</u> (1959), 172-178.

    Report on sea birds, washed ashore in the Netherlands, that are victims of oil pollution, and a discussion of the probabilities of reduction in the number of victims through implementation of the convention on pollution of the sea.

2590. Murphy, Earl F. <u>Governing Nature</u>. Chicago: Quadrangle Books, 1967, pp. x, 333.

    Emphasizing the inadequacy of regulation alone to protect life-cycle resources from the effects of pollution, the author discusses complementary economic incentives such as permit systems, effluent charges, receptor levies, assessment, and cost-internalizing procedures.

2591. Pearson, Erman A. (ed.). Proceedings of the First International Conference on Waste Disposal in the Marine Environment, University of California, Berkeley, July 22-25, 1959. New York: Pergamon, 1960.
Papers on the use of the oceans as a receptacle for various wastes and the potential damage to some resources as a result of the practice.

2592. Sylvester, R.O. Report on the Reinspection of the Intertidal Zone in the Vicinity of the Ferndale Refinery. General Petroleum Corporation (Ferndale, Washington), 1956, pp. 10.
One of a series of similarly titled studies conducted by the author and published by the General Petroleum Corporation that deal with the biological and oceanographic characteristics of southeast Georgia Strait before and after building the Ferndale, Washington, refinery of the General Petroleum Corporation, with particular attention to the intertidal beach zone. An additional report on the pre-operational environment was published in the Proceedings of the Eleventh Industrial Waste Conference, Purdue University, Series 91.

2593. Sylvester, R.O., and Clogston, F.L. A Study of the Pre-Operational Environment in the Vicinity of the Texas Company Refinery, Puget Sound Works, Anacortes, Washington. The Texas Company, 1958, pp. vii, 157, 11.
Related to Sylvester's studies of the Ferndale, Washington, refinery's effect on water quality, this study of conditions prior to operations at Anacortes is, like those related to the Ferndale operations, of international interest both because of the international character of the Puget Sound-Georgia Strait waters and because of the refinement of crude oil that has been transported from Canada over an international pipeline network.

2594. United Nations. Conference on Water Pollution Problems in Europe: Documents Submitted to the Conference. 3 vols. Geneva: 1961.
Includes exploration of the problems requiring international control and of liability for damage in municipal and international law, as well as existing intergovernmental agreements for the protection of water resources.

See also nos. 129, 130.

b. Nuclear Radiation

2595. Asimov, Isaac, and Dobzhansky, Theodosius. The Genetic Effects of Radiation. Washington: U.S. Atomic Energy Commission, Division of Technical Information, 1966, pp. 49.
Traces the genetic effects of radiation with respect to the structure of genes and chromosomes, normal cellular sexual reproduction, spontaneous mutation, and the mutation rate.

2596. Brill, A.B., and Forgotson, E.H. "Radiation and Congenital Malformations." 90 <u>American Journal of Obstetrics and Gynecology</u> (1964), 1149-1168.

Provides information on radiation damage based on extensive studies of prenatal injury in animals and confirmations in less extensive human experience.

2597. Brown, Bernice B. <u>Long-Term Radiation Damage: Evaluation of Life-Span Studies</u>. RM-5083-TAB. Santa Monica: RAND Corporation, 1966, pp. 66.

On the basis of experiments with rats and mice, the effect of radiation on man was extrapolated to produce the hypothesis that a single acute exposure would shorten human life by 7 to 12 days per roentgen.

2598. Chadwick, Donald R., and Abrahams, Simon P. "Biological Effects of Radiation." 9 <u>Archives of Environmental Health</u> (1964), 642-648.

On the unsuccessful attempt to determine a threshold dose below which there would be no radiation damage, the constant downward revisions as more data became available, and the apparent lack of a threshold below which no individual would be harmed. The article thus presents a problem relevant to a standard setting, national or international.

2599. Conard, R.A., Rall, J.E., and Sutow, W.W. "Thyroid Nodules as a Late Sequela of Radioactive Fallout in a Marshall Island Population Exposed in 1954." 274 <u>New England Journal of Medicine</u> (1966), 1391-1399.

Report on a medical study of Rongelap Islanders, with special attention to pathological thyroid changes, that finds the hazard, particularly from radioiodine, to be more serious than expected.

2600. Donaldson, L.R. <u>A Radiological Study of Rongelap Atoll, Marshall Islands, during 1954-1955</u>. U.S. Atomic Energy Commission Report UWFL-42, 1955.

One of several reports on specific studies of radiation effects that were conducted for the Atomic Energy Commission by the author and his associates in conjunction with nuclear tests in the Pacific.

2601. Donaldson, L.R. <u>Program for Education and Research Needed in Radiation and Biology in the Expanded Federal Effort</u>. Statement on S.901, the Marine Sciences and Research Act of 1961, before the Committee on Interstate and Foreign Commerce, U.S. Senate, March 17, 1961.

Sets forth some of the needs that should be met if knowledge is to be furthered and information adequately disseminated about the effect of radiation on life in the seas.

2602. Donaldson, L.R., and Foster, R.F. "Effects of Radiation on Aquatic Organisms." In <u>The Effects of Atomic Radiation on Oceanography and Fisheries</u>. Publication No. 551. Washington: National Academy of Sciences--National Research Council, 1957, pp. 96-102.

Report of investigations on the effects of radiation on
various forms of sea life.

2603. Federal Radiation Council. Radiation Hazards in Uranium Mines.
Washington: Government Printing Office, 1967, pp. 60.
Examines the health hazards in uranium mining with particu-
lar attention to the dangers of lung cancer.

2604. Grüneberg, H. "Genetical Research in an Area of High Natural
Radioactivity in South India." 204 Nature (London, October 17, 1964), 222-
224.
On the investigation of mammals in an area on the Malabar
Coast in which radioactivity is 7.5 times that of inland control
areas. Lack of evidence of radiation-produced mutation was not
regarded as ruling out mutations lurking below the surface
evidence.

2605. International Commission on Radiological Protection. Radiation
Protection: Recommendations of the International Commission on Radiological Protection, as Amended 1959 and Revised 1962. New York: Macmillan for
the International Commission on Radiological Protection, 1964, pp. v, 70.
Recommendations concerning permissible levels of partial
and whole-body radiation doses received by individuals and populations from natural, medical, and occupational sources.

2606. Little, John B. "Environmental Hazards: Ionizing Radiation."
275 New England Journal of Medicine (1966), 929-938.
An examination of the effects of radiation that distinguishes between the carcinogenic risk that is of importance to
the exposed person and the genetic risk that is important to
entire populations.

2607. Mayneord, W.V. "Background Radiations and Their Origins." 21
Advancement of Science (1964), 127-131.
On the relative exposure of populations to radiation from
natural sources and from nuclear testing.

2608. Norman, Amos et al. "Chromosome Aberrations in Radiation Workers." 23 Radiation Research (1964), 282-289.
On the likely implications of chromosome aberrations among
33 radiation workers who were exposed for a number of years to
gamma ray dose rates about 10 times as high as normal background levels.

2609. Rapp, R.R. A Re-Examination of Fallout Models. RM-4910-TAB.
Santa Monica: RAND Corporation, February 1966, pp. 55.
Review of the steps necessary to produce a fallout model,
a comparison of recent fallout models, and a suggestion for the
development of a flexible computer model to predict fallout
hazards.

2610. Russell, R. Scott (ed.). Radioactivity and Human Diet. New
York: Pergamon, 1966, pp. 564.

Contains papers on food chains on dry land, aquatic food chains, and the problems of assessment and control of the effects of radioactivity on food supplies.

2611. Tomkins, Paul C. "A Consideration of Basic Radiation Protection Guides Applicable to the General Population." 9 Archives of Environmental Health (1964), 659-663.
On the genetic aspects of the abandonment of the threshold concept of radiation dosage and its replacement by the concept of a permissible dosage defined in terms of appreciable bodily injury during a person's lifetime. Attention is given to the risks involved, the genetic implication that the total imposition on society of a small mutation generation rate change is measured by the mean dose to populations rather than by the dose to any individual, and the need to measure potential health risks against the benefits derived from exposure.

2612. Welander, A.D., Lowman, F.G., Palumbo, R.F., and Weeks, D.R. Distribution of Radioactivity in Sea Water and Marine Organisms Following an Underwater Nuclear Detonation at the Eniwetok Test Site in 1958. U.S. Atomic Energy Commission Report UWFL-58, Technical Information Service. Oak Ridge, Tennessee: 1959.
One of several reports by Welander and associates on radiation distribution in the sea and among the organisms of the sea as a consequence of the testing of nuclear devices by means of underwater and other explosions.

2613. Wilson, Floyd W. "The Role of the Government and Private Enterprise in Radioactive Waste Disposal." 27 Journal of Environmental Health (1965), 818-823.
Review of the tasks of government agencies and private concerns in the disposal of radioactive waste and the virtual elimination of ocean disposal since ground burial of solid and liquid low level wastes has proved safe subject to maintenance and surveillance in perpetuity. Consideration is given to the high costs of sea burial and the limits on the quantities that can be buried on land.

6. Food

2614. Bartlett, B.R. "The International Shipment of Adult Entomorphagous Insects." 55 Annals of the Entomological Society of America (1962), 448-455.
On a method of shipping by air-mail transport adult entomorphagous insects, avoiding shipment of undesirable hyperparasitic species, that is safe and that assures the insects the necessary sustenance.

2615. President's Science Advisory Committee. The World Food Problem. 4 vols. Washington: Government Printing Office, 1967.

Prepared by a panel headed by Ivan L. Bennett, Jr., Deputy
Director of the Office of Science and Technology, this report
draws on more than 100 specialists from government, industry,
and universities. Its findings are contained in the first volume, with subpanel reports and technical and other special
papers contained in the other volumes. Concluding that no in-
surmountable biological, technical, or economic barriers prevent finding a solution to the world food problem during the
next 20 years, the report questions whether the world is up to
meeting the problem. The reports give attention to population
projections, with and without family planning, for 1985 and 2000,
to food requirements in 1985 and expectations of a doubled demand
even if the fertility rate is reduced by nearly one-third, to the
relationship between the food problem and economic growth rates
in developing countries, to possible projects to improve the food
supply, and to possible changes in the United States foreign aid
program including rejection of withdrawal or curtailment of assistance as a foreign policy sanction in anything less than the
gravest of crises.

2616. Revelle, Roger. "International Cooperation in Food and Population." 22 International Organization (1968), 362-391.
    Dealing more with the organization of aid in the production
of food than with family planning, the author notes that multilateral policies and programs require preponderant approval, the
lack of which accounts for WHO's disappointing role in family
planning. The author suggests that however theoretically desirable multilateral technical aid may be, in the circumstances bilateral aid is often more effective.

2617. Schultz, Theodore W. Economic Crisis in World Agriculture.
Ann Arbor: The University of Michigan Press, 1965, pp. viii, 114.
    Agriculture is discussed with regard to the farmer's profit,
and a means to change traditional to modern agriculture is suggested by a theory of dynamic imbalance. US overseas food shipments are discussed in regard to their long-range benefits. The
agricultural workers' relationship to the welfare state situation in the US is reviewed.

See also nos. 138, 748, 1135, 1158, 2575, 2629, 2823, 2826.

7. Water Supply

2618. Logan, John A. "The International Municipal Water Supply Problem: A Health and Economic Appraisal." 9 American Journal of Tropical
Medicine and Hygiene (1960), 469-476.
    With reference to WHO and ICA sponsorship of municipal
water supply programs, the article deals not just with the social benefit aspects of such programs but also with economic
aspects, particularly in terms of competition with other capital
requirements and of value as an investment in relation to commercial and industrial growth of developing countries.

2619. Sylvester, R.O. "Some Influences of Multi-Purpose Water Usage on Water Quality." Proceedings of the International Union for Conservation of Natural and Water Resources. Brussels: 1959.
    A useful paper on the problem of maintaining water of satisfactory quality in the face of the many uses to which the resources can be put in an era of industrialization.

2620. World Health Organization. International Standards for Drinking Water. 2nd ed. New York: Columbia University Press, 1963, pp. 206.
    An example of an attempt to assure the application of standards and analytical practices, in this case to assure improved treatment to bring potable water to all people, that will contribute to the attainment of satisfactory health levels.

8. Population Control

2621. Afriat, S.N. "People and Populations." 17 World Politics (1965), 431-439.
    Discussion of the population explosion that suggests that the principle presently emerging is that while self-replacement is the right of an individual, to exceed replacement is in effect an aggression against society and against mankind as a whole.

2622. Appleman, Philip. The Silent Explosion. Boston: Beacon, 1965 pp. xii, 161.
    A useful introduction to the problem of world population expansion and the various beliefs that impede efforts to deal with the problem.

2623. Beaujeu-Garnier, Jacqueline. The Geography of Population. Translated by S.H. Beaver. London: Longmans, 1965, pp. xiii, 386.
    Results of 15 years' research on problems of the population explosion.

2624. Bourgeois-Pichat, Jean. "Population Growth and Development." International Conciliation. No. 556, January 1966, pp. 81.
    Drawing upon material submitted to the United Nations World Population Conference held in Belgrade in August 1966, the author, among other things, deals with the present and prospective future roles of international organizations with respect to the population problem.

2625. Chandrasekhar, Sripati. Hungry People and Empty Lands: An Essay on Population Problems and International Tensions. London: Allen & Unwin; New York: Macmillan, 1955, pp. 306.
    An argument for the organized migration of people in overpopulated regions of Asia to more sparsely populated lands in Australia, Africa, and Latin America--an example of a point of view that has produced particularly African reaction against what has been treated as potential imperialism by India.

2626. Enke, Stephen. "The Economic Aspects of Slowing Population Growth." 76 Economic Journal (March 1966), 44-56.

Examines the relative growth rates of outputs and population and concludes that resources used to retard population growth can increase per capita income perhaps as much as a hundred times more than resources employed to accelerate growth of output.

2627. Freedman, R. (ed.). Population: The Vital Revolution. Garden City: Doubleday-Anchor, 1964, pp. vi, 274.

Essays on world population problems and the changing trends of population.

2628. Gourou, Pierre. Les pays tropicaux. Paris: Presses Universitaires, 1947, pp. viii, 196.

Concise treatise on human and economic geography expounding the thesis that tropical conditions require a sparse, agricultural population except where rice culture is feasible or where irrigation may be employed to produce crops that do not exhaust the soil.

2629. Leonard, Warren H. "World Population in Relation to Potential Food Supply." 85 Scientific Monthly (1957), 113-125.

An attempt to relate population growth to food supply that is particularly useful in that it provides several references to other studies and also provides detailed examples of potential supplies of specific foods.

2630. Ng, Larry K.Y., and Mudd, Stuart (eds.). The Population Crisis: Implications and Plans for Action. Bloomington: Indiana University Press, 1965, pp. xi, 364.

Papers by 28 scientists, humanists, and statesmen on the potential consequences of overpopulation and some possible ways of averting them.

2631. Notestein, Frank W. "The Population Crisis: Reasons for Hope." 46 Foreign Affairs (1967), 167-180.

Reviews the dangers in population growth over the remainder of the 20th century and suggests that hope lies in the rapidity with which developing countries are becoming aware of the dangers, the implementation of birth control programs in several countries, the interest of poor people in limiting families, improvements in contraceptive technology, and reductions of birth rates in some countries. A danger exists that programs for economic progress to meet the demands imposed by larger populations may be given priority over prerequisite development of social, educational, and medical services.

2632. Organski, Katherine, and Organski, A.F.K. Population and World Power. New York: Knopf, 1961, pp. ix, 263, ix.

Deals with such matters as international migrations, national population policies, the problem of colonial populations, relations between birth control and economic development,

relations between population and national power, and political
uses of the Lebensraum theory. The central theme of the book
is power and the consequences for international politics of
changes in the relative sizes of nations when industrialized.
The authors see Communist China's plan of modernization as an
appropriate means for nondemocratic states, suffering from rural
overpopulation, to modernize. They see world power passing from
the West to the East, with neither the US nor the USSR able to
match the India and the China of tomorrow. The book contains
some useful information but must be used with care in light of
speculations too narrowly tied to the population-power-industri-
alization relationship.

2633. Organski, A.F.K., Spengler, Joseph, and Hauser, Philip M. World
Population and International Relations. Washington: The National Institute
of Social and Behavior Science, 1960, pp. viii, 229.
Papers dealing with the population problem as it relates
to world economic development, to European politics, and to
world politics.

2634. Silberman, L. "Der Fall Mauritius." 26 Zeitschrift für Geopolitik (1955), 676-690.
Examination of Mauritius as an overpopulated area needing
family planning as advocated in a report of the first official
committee on population.

2634-A. Spengler, Joseph J. "Population Problem: In Search of a
Solution." 166 Science (1969), 1234-1238.
An economist's discussion of the population problem and
his suggestions for what would be essentially indirect uses of
law to provide a social security program and a compulsory insurance and interest-bearing fund that would entail financial
deprivation should family size be excessive.

2635. Taylor, Carl E., and Hall, Marie-Françoise. "Health, Population, and Economic Development." 157 Science (1967), 651-657.
Centering on the fertility problem, this article helps to
provide background for a comprehensive view of the population
problem by considering not only such aspects as improvement in
health and various norms and taboos but also the apparent effects
of agricultural development, improved transportation and communications, education, industrialization, and urbanization.

2636. Turner, F.C. "The Implications of Demographic Change for Nationalism and Internationalism." 27 Journal of Politics (1965), 87-108.
Raises questions concerning the impact of the population
explosion on the formation of national communities and about
the relationships between demographic changes and nationalism,
patterns of loyalty to a national group and changes in size,
and geographic distribution and group composition of the population. The suggestion is also made that changes in size and
composition of the world's population can serve both to provide

a challenge equivalent in unifying effect to the military-economic danger presented by nation-states and can stimulate technological breakthroughs in communications media and resource use while also promoting an ideological drive for equality that can be a foundation for internationalism.

2637. Vielrose, E. Elements of the Natural Movement of Population. Translated from the Polish by I. Dobosz. Translation edited by N. Infeld and P.F. Knightsfield. Oxford and New York: Pergamon, 1965, pp. 288.
 Study of demographic phenomena against their historical background that, among other things, takes account of the social and economic phenomena of war, migration, the state of various countries' development, and resulting shifts in structures of populations.

See also nos. 138, 2404.

9. Sick and Wounded; Prisoners of War;
 Civilian Populations; War Victims

2638. Hartendorp, A.V.H. The Santo Tomas Story. Edited by Frank H. Golay. New York: McGraw-Hill, 1964, pp. xvi, 446.
 History of the prison camp established by the Japanese on the premises of the University of Santo Tomas in Manila, reduced by the editor, a Cornell economist, from the detail of the original 4,000 typed pages to publishable length.

2639. Iklé, Fred Charles. The Social Impact of Bomb Destruction. Norman: University of Oklahoma Press, 1958, pp. xxii, 250.
 The concern of the author is with the primary and secondary repercussions of damage caused by bombing particularly in England, Germany, and Japan.

2640. Prisoners of War. Washington: Institute of World Polity, School of Foreign Service, Georgetown University, 1948, pp. vi, 98.
 An attempt to develop solutions to prisoner of war problems through revision of the rules of World War II. The effort centers around a two-year collective study by 30 former prisoners of war, the study group being under the direction of Professor Ernst H. Feilchenfeld.

2641. Schein, Edgar H. "The Chinese Indoctrination Program for Prisoners of War." 19 Psychiatry (1956), 149-172.
 On the Chinese Communist program during the Korean War for controlling and indoctrinating prisoners of war that employed as one method the small group as a medium for self-criticism.

2642. Vidalenc, Jean. L'Exode de Mai-Juin 1940. Paris: Presses Universitaires, 1957, pp. 439.
 A study of the movement of civilians, chiefly from the French border areas, during the blitzkrieg of 1940 and the

German tactics to harass and herd the civilians to impede French
military movements.

2643. Zawodny, Janusz Kazimierz. Death in the Forest: The Story of
the Katyn Forest Massacre. Notre Dame, Indiana: University of Notre Dame
Press, 1962, pp. 235.
     Careful study of the Katyn massacre.

See also nos. 1667, 2552, 2555.

C. INTERNATIONAL BUSINESS AND FINANCE

2644. Aubrey, Henry G. The Dollar in World Affairs: An Essay in International Financial Policy. New York: Praeger for the Council on Foreign Relations, 1964, pp. xii, 292.
     Deals with the role of the dollar in the international
monetary system. Attention is accorded to such matters as the
Eurodollar system, foreign loans, informal agreement among central banks to avoid untimely demands for gold that would upset
the Bank of England's stabilizing operations in the London gold
market in the 1960s and the additional cooperation in the form
of a "gold pool," currency swap arrangements, and the functions
of domestic political considerations and of the United States'
international political responsibilities in producing operational divergences in the equilibrating processes of economic models.
The discussion of existing problems is conducted under the intuitive feeling that there is an unmeasured relation between the
shift of trade and finance away from London toward New York and
the westward movement of the center of gravity in world politics.
Due attention is given to the impact of responsibility stemming
from international use of the dollar, to the consequent loss by
the United States (as by Britain at an earlier date) of unilateral control over monetary policy, and to the need of other
states to cooperate to defend the dollar.

2645. Bloch, Ernest. Eurodollars: An Emerging International Money
Market. New York University Institute of Finance. Bulletin No. 39. New
York: New York University Press, 1966, pp. 32.
     A useful exposition of the Eurodollar system and its impli-
cations for the international financial system.

2646. Curzon, Gerard. Multilateral Commercial Diplomacy: The Genera
Agreement on Tariffs and Trade and Its Impact on National Commercial Policies and Techniques. New York: Praeger, 1966, pp. xii, 367.
     Deals with trade negotiations under GATT and the relation
of trade to such matters as full employment, agricultural protectionism, economic regionalism, and economic development.

2647. Einzig, Paul. Foreign Dollar Loans in Europe. London: Macmillan; New York: St. Martin's, 1965, pp. xi, 160.

Lucid account of the practice of issuing loans in Europe in terms of US dollars or composite units of account, the relations between this practice and the Euro-dollar system, and the effects of the system in promoting internationalization of finance by permitting a bank to serve as entrepôt for transactions abroad.

2648. Einzig, Paul. The Euro-Dollar System--Practice and Theory of International Interest Rates. London: Macmillan; New York: St. Martin's, 1964, pp. ix, 162.

A study of the Euro-dollar market, still lacking definite form but a factor of importance in the integrative process in Western Europe and the North Atlantic. The author has published a short but important supplementary article, "Some Recent Changes in the Euro-dollar System," 19 The Journal of Finance (1964), 443-449. The focus is upon the European market in short-term dollar credits.

2649. Martyn, Howe. International Business. New York: Free Press, 1964, pp. xiv, 288.

An examination of the allocation of capital and human resources by international business, of economic and social factors leading to the establishment of overseas subsidiaries, and of problems encountered by international business organizations. Chapter 5 deals with the pattern of international investment, chapter 6 with the legal framework affecting international business, and chapter 14 with state trading.

2650. Mendershausen, Horst, and Meyer, Nancy. The Concept of Hostile Trade, and a Case Study of Seventeenth Century Japan. RM-4433-PR. Santa Monica: RAND Corporation, April 1965, pp. xvi, 116.

A general discussion of the concept of hostile trade, that is, of trade between hostile societies, and the interaction of political tensions and trade relations, followed by a study of the foreign trade of 17th century Japan. The discussion points toward a general concept relevant to international commercial law during a period of cold war.

2651. Morselli, Emanuale (ed.). Enquête sur l'imposition des revenus industriels commerciaux et professionnels. Paris: Librairie Générale de Droit et de Jurisprudence, 1954, pp. xxv, 519.

Survey of the imposition of taxes on business and professional men in 20 countries of Europe and North and South America.

2652. Roosa, Robert V. Monetary Reform for the World Economy. New York: Harper & Row for the Council on Foreign Relations, 1965, pp. 173.

A review of the different functions performed by currencies, that also posits standards to be met in order to have an effective international monetary system, is followed by an evaluation of proposals for monetary reform and by the author's proposals. Attention is accorded swap arrangements and their uses, although not in the detail given by Charles A. Coombs, Vice

President of the Federal Reserve Bank of New York, in the Bank's publications.

2653. Thorelli, Hans B., and Graves, Robert L. International Operations Simulation. New York: Free Press, 1964, pp. xix, 405.
A volume written for potential users and administrators of games. As the first game focused on problems of international operations and foreign competition, INTOP (International Operations Simulation) provides pointers useful in the development of simulations that would place more emphasis upon the legal aspects of international business.

2654. Thorelli, Hans B., Graves, Robert L., and Howells, Lloyd T. International Operations Simulation: Player's Manual. New York: Free Press, 1963, pp. 58.
Companion piece to the preceding entry, the manual sets up a model that has been used by such firms as IBM, General Electric, and Westinghouse as part of their management training programs.

See also nos. 538, 543, 826, 1162, 1201, 1923, 1924, 2723.

1. Some Problems of Diversity and Imbalance

2655. Angell, Robert C. "The Growth of Transnational Participation." 23 Journal of Social Issues (1967), 108-129.
On the trends of a decade on six measures of collaboration between peoples or of living in close contact, including sojourn abroad for business purposes.

2656. Basi, Raghbir S. "Role of the 'Free Enterprise' Ideology in Less-Developed Countries." 26 American Journal of Economics and Sociology (1967), 173-188.
On the inadequacy of some tenets of the "free enterprise" ideology that have been applied in analyses of less-developed countries.

2657. Bicaric, Rudolf. "Economics of Socialism in a Developed Country." 44 Foreign Affairs (1966), 633-650.
On the 1965 Yugoslav economic reform designed, among other things, to combat inflation, depoliticize economic decision-making, counteract the balance of payments deficit, replace the multiple exchange rate for the dinar with a uniform rate, and deal with the inadequacy of short-term commercial operations by integrating the Yugoslav economy fully into world markets.

2658. Cohen Orantes, I. "Los países pobres, la U.N.C.T.A.D. y los países ricos." 27 Cuadernos americanos (July-August 1968), 7-23.
A Latin American's view of the gap between the developed and the underdeveloped nations, the failure of international

agencies to do much about it, and the inadequacies of UNCTAD except as an open forum.

2659. Neuberger, E. The USSR and the West as Markets for Primary Products: Stability, Growth, and Size. RM-3341-PR. Santa Monica: RAND Corporation, March 1963, pp. 150.
An evaluation of the Soviet claim that the Communist countries provide superior markets for primary products than do the Western countries, with attention to the growth that was taking place in primary-products imports by Communist countries.

2660. Pfaltzgraff, Robert L. "The Future of Atlantic Economic Relationships." 10 Orbis (1966), 408-437.
On the imbalance inherent in the restriction of four-fifths of the world's economic exchanges to the North Atlantic area and the need for increased collaboration among the nations.

2661. Pincus, John. Trade and Development: The Rich and the Poor Nations. New York: McGraw-Hill for the Council on Foreign Relations, 1967, pp. 400.
A RAND Corporation economist examines the impact of the trade and aid policies of the Atlantic Community nations on the underdeveloped countries, the latter classified into economic types on the basis of differing interests, needs, and internal problems.

2662. Servan-Schreiber, Jean-Jacques. The American Challenge. New York: Atheneum, 1968, pp. 320.
Warrants attention particularly for its references to imbalances that lie in the organizational, managerial, and research and development realms.

2663. Stavropoulos, Constantin M. "The United Nations Commission on International Trade Law." 4 UN Monthly Chronicle (April 1967), 89-94.
On reasons for the establishment of a permanent commission to deal with international trade law, including the disparity of national laws and regulations.

2664. Subhan, Malcolm. "Manufactured Preferences." 51 Far Eastern Economic Review (1966), 357-375.
On roadblocks to developing countries' sales of processed and partly-processed products essential to bringing prosperity not possible in dependence on sales of raw materials that existing tariff and shipping regulations favor.

2. State Trading

See nos. 1749, 2649.

3. International and Multinational
   Corporations

2665. Adam, H.T. Les établissements publics internationaux. Paris:
Librairie Générale de Droit et de Jurisprudence, 1957, pp. ix, 323.
    Analysis of European public corporations or authorities.
The organizations are classified according to the following
scale of internationalization: (1) firms lacking international
organs; (2) firms with international organs, (3) full-fledged
international firms such as Eurofima.

2666. Adam, H.T. Societé Européenne pour le Financement du Materiel
Ferroviaire (Eurofima). The Hague: Nijhoff, 1957, pp. 21.
    Short analysis of the European Organization for finance of
railway equipment and of the special regime whereby, although a
Swiss corporation, Eurofima is relieved of some of the obligations of Swiss law by virtue of Statutes annexed to its constitutive convention.

2667. Blake, David H. Multinational Corporation, International Union,
and International Collective Bargaining: A Case Study of the Political, Social, and Economic Implications of the 1967 UAW-Chrysler Agreement. Presented at the International Institute for Labour Studies, Geneva, Spring
1969. Ditto. Detroit: Wayne State University, August 1969, pp. 54.
    An examination of the follow-ups of the Canadian-American
Automotive Products Agreement in the forms of rationalization
of production, the November 1967 acceptance by Chrysler of wage
parity for the January 1968 contract negotiation with the Canadian union, and the resort to international collective bargaining in 1970 between Chrysler and the UAW that represents the
first true international collective bargaining in a major industry. Attention is given to union, employer, and Canadian Government attitudes and to the circumstances that are propitious
for international collective bargaining. This paper will be
~ blished as a chapter in a book resulting from the Geneva
Symposium.

2668. Bonin, Bernard. Harmonies and Tensions Between the Multinational Firm and the Nation State. Paper presented to the Canadian Peace
Research and Education Association Meeting. University of Calgary, June
7-8, 1968.
    On the harmony and tensions between foreign companies and
host countries, including reference to the conflict that arises
when a sector is defined as a "key" sector, in which foreign
domination is viewed as entailing dangers, only after foreign
penetration has occurred.

2668-A. Feld, Werner J. "The Changing Impact and Incidence of Non-
Governmental Organizations: A Quantitative Approach." Paper presented at
the 66th Annual Meeting of the American Political Science Association, Los
Angeles, September 8-12, 1970, pp. 22, xxvii.

The first part of this paper deals with traditional international nongovernmental organizations and their impact on the
international system. More importantly, the heart of the paper
gives attention to the multinational corporation and to transnational business collaborations, e.g., the collaboration of
AGFA A.G. and Photo Produits Gevaerts to establish, with 50-50
ownership, Agfa-Gevaerts A.G. in Germany and Gevaerts-Agfa in
Belgium. A brief final section deals with political parties as
nongovernmental international actors. Twenty-seven pages of
appended tables provide a more detailed view of the growth of
nongovernmental organizations and multinational corporations.

2668-B. Hellmann, Rainier. The Challenge to U.S. Dominance of the
International Corporation. New York: Dunellen, 1970, pp. xix, 348.
A description of the extent of monopoly by American enterprise of direct foreign investment and control of ownership,
management, price determination, research, and policies of multinational corporations is followed by an analysis of the European counteroffensive.

2669. Hymer, Stephen. The Politics of the Multinational Corporation.
Paper presented to the Canadian Peace Research and Education Association
Meeting. University of Calgary, June 7-8, 1968.
This paper draws attention to the conflict between efforts
to render United States corporations instruments of government
policy and the development of functional centralization through
corporations having a cosmopolitan outlook and preferring to set
their own policies. The corporations are viewed as linking
countries but asymmetrically due to United States dominance.
Attention is also called to the short-range concerns of government with such matters as the balance of payments and the long-
range nature of foreign investments. Governmental concerns with
trade protection and protection of the state and of its internal
sectors from disruption by foreign penetration also receive attention, as do the EEC countries' continuing fears of each other
and doubts about the desirability and consequences of multinational (EEC-wide) firms.

2669-A. Litvak, A., and Maule, C.J. "The Multinational Corporation:
Some Perspectives." 13 Canadian Public Administration (1970), 129-139.
A discussion of the economic, political, and legal challenges to host countries that are presented by multinational
corporations, together with some suggested policy alternatives
that might be employed.

2670. Martyn, Howe. "Multinational Corporations in a Nationalistic
World." Challenge (November-December 1965), 13-16.
Treating as multinational corporations those chains of companies (e.g., IT&T, IBM, Massey-Ferguson, Volvo, Heinz, and Coca-
Cola) that conduct similar operations in several countries under
several government charters but the same management, the author
calls attention to nationalistic opposition attributed to the
limited promotion opportunities for the top men in subsidiaries,

inability of nationals of countries in which subsidiaries exist
to buy stock, the drain of scientists to the parent country, and
lack of encouragement of exports by subsidiaries.

2671. Modelski, George. "The Corporation in World Society." Year
Book of World Affairs (1968), 64-79.
   On business enterprises of such size and displaying such
dynamics of growth as to be components of world order of an importance that rivals that of states. Note is taken of the contradiction between corporative activities and their structure
that centers on one nation and entails subordination thereto.
Suggestions are made for maximizing corporate contributions to
world order by reducing the gaps between structure, activities,
responsibility, and responsiveness.

2671-A. Schiller, Herbert. "The Multinational Corporation as International Communicator." Paper presented at the 66th Annual Meeting of the
American Political Science Association, Los Angeles, September 8-12, 1970,
pp. 36.
   On the impacts of American advertising agencies abroad,
public relations firms, opinion survey organizations, market
research companies, management consulting firms, and brokerage
offices on the international flow of communications.

2671-B. Vernon, Raymond. Sovereignty at Bay: The Multinational
Spread of U.S. Enterprises. New York: Basic Books, 1971, pp. x, 326.
   On the organizational forms, adaptations to technological
changes, and efficiency of American multinational enterprises.

See also nos. 597, 598, 1726.

4. Investments

2672. Johnson, Leland L. U.S. Private Investment in Latin America:
Some Questions of National Policy. RM-4092-ISA. Santa Monica: RAND Corporation, July 1964, pp. xi, 86.
   In part a chronology and in part an attempt to identify
potential sources of conflict between United States enterprises
and host countries, the study raises some useful questions
about the impact of private investments upon the United States
bargaining position.

2673. Lindeman, John, and Armstrong, Donald. Policies and Practices
of United States Subsidiaries in Canada. Washington and Montreal: Canadian
American Committee, 1961, pp. xi, 82.
   A study of the problem of United States investment in Canada, particularly the control of about two-thirds of Canadian
mining and petroleum development, and Canadian reactions.

2674. May, Stacy, and Plaza, Galo. The United Fruit Company in Latin
America. Washington: National Planning Association, 1958, pp. xv, 263.

Treats of the role of a major enterprise in domestic affairs of other countries and in international affairs.

2675. Taylor, W.C., and Lindeman, J. The Creole Petroleum Corporation in Venezuela. Fourth Case Study of United States Business Performance
Abroad. Washington: National Planning Association, 1955, pp. x, 105.
     A useful study of the relations of Creole Petroleum Corpo-
ration, and so of Jersey Standard, with the Venezuelan Government and public.

2676. Vernon, Raymond (ed.). How Latin America Views the U.S. Investor. New York: Praeger, 1966, pp. x, 117.
     Essays on attitudes toward US investors as found in Argen-
tina, Brazil, and Mexico and from the point of view of LAFTA
proponents.

See also nos. 826, 1034, 1062, 1089, 1852, 2010, 2649, 2670, 2671,
2709, 2724, 2783.

5. Concession Agreements

2677. Cattan, Henry. The Evolution of Oil Concessions in the Middle
East and North Africa. New York: Oceana, 1967, pp. xvi, 173.
     On the major features of oil concessions and the changes
in such agreements since the oil industry first began to develop
Middle Eastern and North African resources.

2678. Finnie, David Haldeman. Desert Enterprise: The Middle East
Oil Industry in Its Local Environment. Cambridge, Massachusetts: Harvard University Press, 1958, pp. x, 224.
     Consideration of the problems involved as the oil companies
endeavor to get along with Arab authorities and to maintain themselves as enterprises.

2679. Lenczowski, George. Oil and State in the Middle East. Ithaca:
Cornell University Press, 1960, pp. 379.
     Significance of the Middle East in the world economy and
consideration of the relations between oil companies, government, populace, and employees in host countries.

2680. Longrigg, Stephen Hemsley. Oil in the Middle East. 2nd ed.
New York: Oxford for the Royal Institute of International Affairs, 1961,
pp. 401.
     Story, by a former executive of the Iraq Petroleum Company,
of Middle Eastern oil exploitation and of the rivalries between
companies that have involved governments.

2681. Longrigg, Stephen H. "The Economics and Politics of Oil in the
Middle East." 19 Journal of International Affairs (1965), 111-122.
     Discussion of arrangements between governments and exploit-
ing countries, channels through which revenues are diffused,

uses and misuses of revenues, and some impediments to political
stability.

2682. Mikdashi, Zuhayr. A Financial Analysis of Middle Eastern Oil
Concessions, 1901-65. New York: Praeger, 1966, pp. xv, 340.
A consultant for the Organization of Petroleum Exporting
Countries presents a financial history of major oil concessions
in Iran, Iraq, Saudi Arabia, and Kuwait and analyzes reasons
for the establishment of various methods of payment by the con-
cessionary countries to the host countries.

6. Nationalization (Expropriation and
   Confiscation)

2683. Bronfenbrenner, Martin. "The Appeal of Confiscation in Economic
Development." 3 Journal of Economic Development and Cultural Change (1955),
201-218.
Confiscation is viewed as a pragmatically effective method
of shifting income from consumption, transfer abroad, and such
investments as luxury housing to developmental investment. The
author does not expect underdeveloped countries, whose modernization is lagging, to eschew confiscation indefinitely. A succession of models are employed to illustrate the attractiveness
of nationalization. Eight factors relating to the development
of advanced countries are noted. Among them is a lack of confiscation of capitalist property as an essential factor in development. But it is noted that resources were confiscated from
aboriginal tribes, the English peasantry during the enclosure
movement, French feudal baronies, and English ecclesiastical
properties, while the rice subventions of the Japanese samurai
were an Oriental manifestation of confiscatory activity for development purposes.

2684. Einaudi, Mario, Byé, Maurice, and Rossi, Ernesto. Nationalization in France and Italy. Ithaca: Cornell University Press, 1955, pp. 260.
Provides data on problems arising from nationalization
policies in France and Italy.

2685. Katzarov, K. Théorie de la nationalisation. Neuchâtel: La
Baconnière, 1960, pp. xiv, 515. Theory of Nationalization. Revised English ed., prepared with the assistance of A.W. Bradley. The Hague: Nijhoff, 1964, pp. viii, 392.
Bulgarian professor's exposition of a theory of nationalization with reference, among other things, to the international
political aspects of nationalization.

2686. Klein, Herbert S. "The Creation of the Patiño Tin Empire." 19
Inter-American Economic Affairs (1965, Autumn), 63-74.
Narrative of the establishment of the Bolivian tin and
tungsten enterprise that, under the international control
scheme, had a quota averaging 50-55% of the market allocation.

International aspects of the empire are noted. This survey of
the Patiño organization is a helpful guide to the implications
of nationalization of Bolivian tin enterprises. The article
also gives some attention to the Patiño position on the Tin
Council after 1929.

2687. Muñoz Ledo, P. "La nationalisation du pétrole au Mexique." 11
Revue française de science politique (1965), 1145-1153.
     Treats as the decisive factor productive of the 1938 expro-
priation of the oil companies in Mexico the conflict which developed in 1936 between the companies and the trade union. Thus,
the article emphasizes the potential of domestic conflict and domestic pressure group activity for influencing the course of international relations and that of international law.

2688. Thomas, K.D., and Glassburner, B. "Abrogation, Take-Over and
Nationalization: The Elimination of Dutch Economic Dominance from the Republic of Indonesia." 19 Australian Outlook (1965), 158-179.
     Concentrating on three events, namely, Indonesia's unilat-
eral abrogation of the "Round-Table Agreement" in 1956, take-
over of Dutch enterprises in 1957, and nationalization of the
enterprises beginning in 1958, the article seeks to demonstrate
the separateness of each event and to attempt an explanation of
an apparent lack of meaningful Indonesian policy orientation.

See also nos. 891, 1215, 2724, 2852.

7. International Transactions

2689. Collis, Maurice. Wayfoong: The Hongkong and Shanghai Banking
Corporation. London: Faber and Faber, 1965, pp. xii, 269.
     A study of East Asia's political, financial, and economic
transformation during the last 100 years.

2690. Crombie, Sir James. Her Majesty's Customs and Exise. London:
Allen & Unwin; New York: Oxford University Press, 1962, pp. 224.
     On the organization and work of the Department of Customs
and Exise, patterns of customs control, administration and enforcement, and international cooperation in customs matters,
with reference to such international and European organizations
as the Customs Co-operation Council.

2691. Macauley, Stewart. "Non-Contractual Relations in Business: A
Preliminary Study." 28 American Sociological Review (1963), 55-67.
     Preliminary findings indicate that businessmen often fail
to plan exchange relationships completely, and seldom use legal
sanctions to adjust these relationships or to settle disputes.
Planning and legal sanctions are often unnecessary and may have
undesirable consequences. Transactions are planned and legal
sanctions are used when the gains are thought to outweigh the

costs. The power to decide whether the gains from using the contract method outweigh the costs will be held by individuals having different occupational roles. The occupational role influences the decision that is made. The lack of legal sanctions is made up by the use of nonlegal sanctions: (1) all commitments are to be honored; (2) a firm must stand behind its work; (3) to be successful one must keep a favorable reputation. Absence of a legal sanction may also result from not knowing "what the risk is" that one is taking by not employing legal contracts.

2692. Nehrt, Lee C. International Marketing of Nuclear Power Plants. Indiana University Social Science Series No. 22. Bloomington: Indiana University Press, 1966, pp. xiv, 405.
On US legislation, development of nuclear power plants in the US, the Atoms for Peace Plan, IAEA, the European Nuclear Energy Agency, Euratom, the UK nuclear power framework and its foreign sales activities, and the atomic energy frameworks in Japan, Belgium, Germany, and Italy. Case studies are included: (1) American and foreign power company projects; (2) Atomics International (North American Aviation, Inc.); (3) American Machine and Foundry Co.; (4) the SENN project (Società Elettronucleare Nazionale) that saw the first competitive international bidding for a nuclear power plant; (5) Westinghouse Electric International Co.; (6) the sale of a large-scale plant by Westinghouse International to SELNI (Società Elettronucleare Italiana); (7) the La Spezia project that involved a sale to Edisonvolta.

See also nos. 2130, 2653, 2654.

8. Commercial and Trade Agreements; Most-
Favored-Nation   Clause

2693. Cheng, Tao. The Treatment of Aliens and British Commercial Treaties. Ph.D. Dissertation. New York: Columbia University, 1961; Ann Arbor: University Microfilms, Inc., Order No. 62-1915, pp. ii, 278.
An example of what might be accomplished by a carefully structured analysis of treaty provisions, in this case of British treaty provisions relating to aliens and their right to engage in economic activities. The analysis reveals that at the indicated periods the following groups have dominated the demand for treaty protection against aliens: (1) in the 17th and 18th centuries, the traders; (2) in the 19th century, the shipping interests; (3) at present, the investors. Of related interest are the stipulations concerning the types of property that aliens could hold. Early treaties assured only the right to dispose of personal property in the event of death. Most 19th century treaties permitted disposal of all types of property but limited acquisition to personal property. In the present century aliens may acquire, hold, and dispose of property of all types subject to specified restrictions.

2694. Hawkins, Harry Calvin, et al. Commercial Treaties and Agreements: Principles and Practice. New York: Rinehart, 1951, pp. vii, 254.
Exposition of principles of international trade and of problems to be faced in efforts to negotiate commercial agreements.

2695. Johnson, Harry G. "An Economic Theory of Protectionism, Tariff Bargaining, and the Formation of Customs Unions." 73 Journal of Political Economy (1965), 256-283.
Deals with the difficulties of tariff-reduction based on the most-favored-nation clause particularly as generalized through GATT, the possibility of preferential or discriminatory tariff reductions and the possibility of mutual advantage through mutual protection of industrial production by picking and choosing commodities on which to reduce tariffs, and the limitation on the scope of customs unions to countries with a similar degree of preference for industrial production and having a similar degree of comparative advantage. Note is taken of the Treaty of Rome provisions designed to assure each member of the Common Market a fair share of industrial production and of the LAFTA provisions envisioning the Treaty as concerned chiefly with new industries and the allocation of a fair share.

2696. Viner, Jacob. The Customs Union Issue. New York: Carnegie Endowment for International Peace, 1950, pp. viii, 221.
A primarily economic analysis of customs unions that accords attention to such matters as the compatibility of customs unions with the most-favored-nation clause and exemptions of arrangements other than customs unions from the operation of that clause.

2697. Watson, Richard A. "The Tariff Revolution: A Study of Shifting Party Attitudes." 18 Journal of Politics (1956), 678-701.
An article useful in relating international and domestic issues because of its identification of some major American interest groups' stands on reciprocal trade agreements in the mid-fifties.

See also no. 2090.

9. Commodity Agreements

2697-A. Geer, Thomas. An Oligopoly: The World Coffee Economy and Stabilization Schemes. New York: Dunellen, 1971, pp. 315.
Application of an industrial organization theory and the theory of imperfect competition to the study of the world coffee market.

2698. Hanson, Simon G. "The Experience with the International Coffee Agreement." 19 Inter-American Economic Affairs (Winter 1965), 27-66.

The negotiation of the International Coffee Agreement and its goals are compared with what followed in the coffee market in the form of rise in prices and decrease in consumption. The author blames the State Department's "deceitful" procedures and actions for the results.

2699. Knorr, K.E. World Rubber and Its Regulation. Stanford: Stanford University Press, 1945, pp. x, 265.
A study of an international commodity agreement, its negotiation, and the nature and effect of the agreed-upon regulations. The study both points out the role of private associations in the development of the International Rubber Regulation Agreement, signed on May 7, 1934, and takes note of the growth in the 1930s of an elite of commodity controllers with interlocking memberships in different control bodies.

2700. Pincus, John A. Commodity Policy and Economic Development. RM-3887-ISA. Santa Monica: RAND Corporation, 1963, pp. vii, 81.
Deals with commodity policy from the point of view of the economic development process and includes estimates by commodity and by country of the contribution of commodity agreements to the foreign exchange needs of the less developed countries.

2701. Pincus, John. "Commodity Agreements: Bonanza or Illusion?" 2 Columbia Journal of World Business (1967), 43-50.
An assessment of the effectiveness of commodity agreements as a means to the realization of the objectives of the parties thereto.

2702. Rowe, J.W.F. Primary Commodities in International Trade. New York: Cambridge University Press, 1965, pp. xi, 223.
Includes excellent descriptions of the commodity restriction schemes of the 1930s and examination of the significance of the post-World War II commodity control arrangements embracing both producing and consuming countries.

2703. Wickizer, Vernon Dale. Tea under International Regulation. 2nd rev. ed. Stanford: Stanford University, Food Research Institute, 1951, pp. vi, 222.
Study of international arrangements in regard to tea and the role of private persons in developing intergovernmental agreements.

See also no. 2686.

10. International Loans

2704. Baldwin, David A. "The International Bank in Political Perspective." 18 World Politics (1965), 68-81.
Analysis of the political aspects of the work of the International Bank for Reconstruction and Development in terms of (a)

taking political considerations into account in assessing willingness and ability to repay, (b) effect upon the distribution
of power within and among nations, and (c) efforts to influence
the behavior of governments, e.g., through strategic withhold-
ing of loans.

2705. De Laume, G.R. International Loans. New York: Oceana, 1967,
pp. xxiii, 371.
    A comprehensive study of international loans that covers
such topics as the validity and administration of international
loans, guaranteed loans, secured loans, arbitration agreements,
and the effects of war.

See also nos. 839, 1034, 1390, 2644, 2647.

11. Monetary and Payments Systems

2706. Dave, Surendra. "India's Trade Relations with East European
Countries; 1952-53 -- 1959-60: A Study in Bilateralism." 9 Indian Economic Journal (1961-1962), 48-68.
    A study of the effects of the payments agreements of 1958
with East European countries that entailed a step toward strict
bilateralism by requiring payments in nonconvertible Indian
Rupees instead of retaining a choice between Rupees and Pounds
Sterling.

2707. Schmitt, Hans O. "Political Conditions for International Currency Reforms." 18 International Organization (1964), 543-557.
    Inquiry into the political aspects of reform of the patch-
work system of international currency with particular reference
to three possible currency relationships among economic regions,
namely, integration, autonomy, and dominance.

See also nos. 534, 546, 571, 573, 1307, 2644, 2764.

D. ECONOMIC DEVELOPMENT

1. Foreign Aid

2708. Beim, David. "The Communist Bloc and the Foreign Aid Game."
17 Western Political Quarterly (1964), 784-799.
    Essentially an expression in game theoretic terms, employ-
ing a non-zero-sum game orientation, of some commonly expressed
views of Soviet, American, and recipient countries' strategies
and tactics, with indications of possible outcomes that could
be predicted with the aid of game theory.

2709. Benham, Frederic. <u>Economic Aid to Underdeveloped Countries</u>. London: Oxford for the Royal Institute of International Affairs, 1962, pp. 121.

Includes discussion of a need for a World Investment Code establishing safeguards for both investing and receiving countries. Perhaps the most important feature of the book is a redefinition of economic aid to exclude not only private loans but also loans made by governments and international organizations at commercial rates, while counting only the differential as "aid" in the case of low interest loans. The redefinition suggests the possibility of sharper identification and analysis of systems of relations between states and so of the compatibility of economic with legal relations.

2710. Friedmann, Wolfgang G., Kalmanoff, George, and Meagher, Robert F. <u>International Financial Aid</u>. New York: Columbia University Press, 1966, pp. xiv, 498.

Excellent study of policies and institutions of the major donor nations, the relationships of those nations to international and regional agencies, the uses of aid by recipient countries, the impact on development, and possible future aid policies.

2711. Goldman, Marshall I. <u>Soviet Foreign Aid</u>. New York: Praeger, 1966, pp. xiv, 265.

Review of the benefits and burdens of Soviet aid in both satellite and nonaligned countries, useful for the examination of the possible growth in a situation of Cold War rivalry of an international obligation to assist developing countries.

2712. Hoffherr, René. "L'Aide de la France aux pays en voie de développement." 21 <u>Revue de défense nationale</u> (1965), 730-740.

Discussion of the development of the French aid program, especially to its dependencies, and the benefits of not only financial aid but cultural and technical assistance for political development.

2713. Kirdar, Üner. <u>The Structure of United Nations Economic Aid to Underdeveloped Countries</u>. The Hague: Nijhoff, 1966, pp. xxiv, 361.

Besides a discussion of the various international financing and aid dispensing agencies, the book deals with the attitudes of UN member states toward assistance to developing nations, with international law and the problem of economic aid, and with economic aid as a legal obligation.

2714. Klausen, Arne Martin. "Technical Assistance and Social Conflict: A Case Study from the Indo-Norwegian Fishing Project in Kerala, South India." 1 <u>Journal of Peace Research</u> (1964), 5-18.

In view of the issues that have been raised about whether and what forms of intervention might be necessary, as well as their impact on the inter-American principle of nonintervention, the present article is pertinent. It provides data on five situations entailing conflict arising from the social impact of an

aid project and also indicating how the principle that assistance should be neutral may impede effective achievement of goals.
Some discussion of mechanisms that may make intervention acceptable is included within a context of intervention of a less crude
nature than that traditionally associated with inter-American
affairs.

2715. Kreinin, Mordechai E. Israel and Africa: A Study in Technical
Cooperation. New York: Praeger, 1964, pp. 206.
    Deals with Israel's aid to African states.

2716. Millikan, Max F., and Blackmer, Donald L.M. (eds.). The Emerging Nations: Their Growth and United States Policy. Boston and Toronto:
Little, Brown, 1961, pp. xiv, 168.
    Ten authors combine their efforts to discuss such matters
as the disruption of traditional societies, resistance and conflict in the modernization process, military and economic assistance, and reasons for aid. Some attention is given to the
international administration of aid but in terms of its probability and of obstacles to providing a sufficient quantity of
international aid. Obstacles are considered to be the demand
of granting parliaments for control over the use and administration of aid, the differing objectives of donor countries,
and the tendency to create new international agencies without
abolishing the old national institutions performing the same
functions.

2717. Montgomery, J.D. "Crossing the Culture Bars: An Approach to
the Training of American Technicians for Overseas Assignments." 13 World
Politics (1961), 544-560.
    Examination of cultural errors involved in technical as-
sistance reveals that donors may make two types of assumptions:
(1) "national" assumptions based on the donor's culture; (2)
"transfer" assumptions made by individual technicians, that is,
generalizations about the non-Western world based on one or two
experiences that need be neither typical nor relevant to the
immediate situation. The author recommends extending conventional area studies by employing "clusters of cases" to identify cultural obstacles affecting projects in a variety of
fields and in various communities.

2718. Owen, D. "The United Nations Expanded Program of Technical As-
sistance--A Multilateral Approach." 323 Annals of the American Academy of
Political and Social Science (1959), 25-32.
    Consideration of multilateral assistance as a fulfillment
by the UN of the Charter pledge to promote higher standards of
living, full employment, and conditions of social and economic
development that can be regarded as raising the question whether
a comparable duty can be assumed to rest upon the Members acting
in the exercise of their own capacities for decision-making.

2719. Pincus, John A. Economic Aid and International Cost Sharing.
Baltimore: Johns Hopkins Press, 1965, pp. xviii, 221.

Analysis of the demand for economic aid and of international economic assistance to underdeveloped countries. With
the addition of the subtitle, A Report Prepared for the Office
of the Assistant Secretary of Defense, International Security
Affairs, this study is also available as a 1965 RAND Corporation report, R-431-ISA.

2720. Rosenstein-Rodan, Paul N. "The Consortia Technique." 22 International Organization (1968), 223-230.
    The author suggests that, instead of a comprehensive inter-
national agency to integrate and fuse all sources of aid, a
"second-best" approach of "bilateral aid within a multilateral
framework" may be more likely. He then discusses the extent to
which the present consortia technique, in most cases developed
through the IBRD and with the United States promising to match
the other countries' total contributions, meets his criteria by
providing aid according to national development programs rather
than by projects.

2721. Tickner, Frederick J. Technical Cooperation. New York: Praeger, 1966, pp. vii, 206.
    Examines both UN programs and programs administered by in-
dividual nations, describing a number of typical projects and
defining the problems involved in planning allocation of manpower and of economic resources.

See also nos. 826, 1034, 1898, 2002, 2779.

2. Economic Development--Impact; Expectations;
   Emerging Duties

2722. Decoufle, A. "Sociologie politique du développement: problèmes et méthodes." 3 Tiers-Monde (1962), 17-26.
    Discussion of the need for a new typology to deal with the
deficiencies of the typologies of classical politics by embracing developing states' essential preoccupations in external as
well as internal affairs. The superiority of economics over
politics in these countries needs to be accounted for and also
the concepts to be found in the writings of responsible political personalities.

2723. Deutsch, Karl W., and Eckstein, Harry. "National Industrialization and the Declining Share of the International Economic Sector." 13
World Politics (1961), 267-299.
    In harmony with Werner Sombart's suggestion, the investiga-
tors find that, by comparison of the ratio of exports to national
net economy, in 1928-1957 there was a decline in the export ratio
for eight of the fourteen North Atlantic Area countries studied.
In strikingly parallel patterns the main non-Communist trading
countries show rises in the earlier stages of industrialization
and then decline. Only the Soviet bloc countries showed minor

contradictions requiring careful study. The authors hypothesize
that the decline may be accounted for by a rise of service components in advanced stages of industrialization, by the replacement of significant amounts of imported materials, by technology
allowing the use of local resources, and by a vulnerability of
advanced countries to economic instability.

2724. Gupta, Arun K. Datta. "Foreign Contribution in British Capital Market Development: A Note." 10 Indian Economic Journal (1962-1963),
454-457.
     Calls attention to Britain as the most important exception
to the circumstance in which economic development becomes dependent upon capital market finance long before financing economic
growth becomes a business proposition for the capital market.
Without government intervention and/or capital import, the economy finds itself in a trap. Growth is hindered by lack of a
well-organized capital market, and such a market cannot function
successfully in the absence of growth. Countries which have been
able to handle the catching-up problem did so through official
initiative in encouraging or quickly organizing credit institutions and by popularizing credit instruments. The article also
takes note of the increased proportion of home issues in Britain
after World War I that was hastened by, among other things, the
weakening of Britain's international position, government restriction of foreign lending, modern capital-intensive techniques,
and large-scale production. The importance of large foreign deposits in expanding banking and capital market facilities to enable Britain to meet the legitimate requirements of the public
and private sectors of the economy is noted.

2725. Rao, V.K.R.V., and Narain, Dharm. Foreign Aid and India's
Economic Development. Bombay: Asia Publishing House, 1963, pp. 111.
     Foreign aid as viewed by economists in a recipient country,
with an effort to deal with the problem of the growth of systems
of benevolence and dependence by distinguishing between spheres
of activity in which the potential for developing domestic capability exists and those in which such capabilities as domestic
production of replacement parts are unlikely to develop or to
develop relatively early. The study is suggestive of lines of
further inquiry into the relationship between acceptance of aid
and retention of independence in foreign policy decision-making
and related treaty-making.

2725-A. Stauffer, R.B. "The Biopolitics of Underdevelopment." 2
Comparative Political Studies (1969), 361-387.
     Noting that theories of political development do not make
explicit use of biological variables as possible limiting parameters and that these theories have rested on implicit biological assumptions appropriate to industrial societies, research was conducted in two bodies of biological literature for
possible contrary assumptions warranting inclusion in multi-
causal models of political development. Among the conclusions
were the following: (1) biological parameters in the Third

World affect attitudes in a direction opposite to that hypo-
thesized in the theoretical literature as necessary for political development; (2) the disease syndrome of underdevelopment
perpetuates damage through generations to contribute to rendering populations disadvantaged for "nation-building" tasks as
compared with populations in industrial societies.

2726. White, John. Pledged to Development: A Study of International
Consortia and the Strategy of Aid. London: Overseas Development Institute
1967, pp. 235.
    The use of consortia and consultative groups is explored
through case studies of Turkey and Pakistan. Finding these
cases to represent relatively successful attempts to translate
the idea of a common aid effort and commitment into an operational reality, the author then suggests that the greatest need
is to develop managing agencies, e.g., regional banks, to administer funds.

See also nos. 151, 189, 197, 548, 1059, 1061, 1062, 1123, 1132, 1922,
2010, 2407, 2418, 2419, 2779, and sec. II, D, 7.

E. TRANSPORTATION

1. Transportation as an Indicator of
    Inter-Nation Interaction

2727. Ullman, Edward L. "The Role of Transportation and the Bases of
Interaction." In William L. Thomas, Jr. (ed.), Man's Role in Changing the
Face of the Earth. Chicago: University of Chicago Press, 1956, pp. 862-
895.
    In the effort to explain interaction between two areas,
Ullman employs three basic concepts: (1) complementarity, with
an economic connotation rather than the communications connotation of Karl W. Deutsch; (2) intervening opportunity, borrowed
from the sociologist Samuel Stouffer, denoting the intrusion of
a third area more conveniently supplying a demand and thus inhibiting interaction between two otherwise complementary areas,
and (3) transferability, relating the possibility of interaction
to costs in time and effort to move goods from one area to another.

2. International Transportation--Rail;
    Pipeline; Electric Grids

2728. Aitken, Hugh G.J. "The Midwestern Case: Canadian Gas and the
Federal Power Commission." 25 Canadian Journal of Economics and Political
Science (1959), 129-143.
    Examination of the second application of Midwestern Gas
Transmission Company to import Canadian gas and the denial in

1958 of the application on grounds of Canadian abilities. This
case is one in the transition period in the last half of the
1950s during which the Federal Power Commission came to a position that in 1960 allowed approval of imports on the basis of
public interest, mutual confidence, and respect in the absence
of a treaty. It is a step toward what could become a pooling
of North American resources.

2729. Claval, Paul. Géographie générale des marchés. Paris: Les
Belles Lettres, 1962, pp. 359.
    Excellent study of markets with reference to transportation
including electric grids and pipelines, to agricultural commodities, international trade flows, international pricing systems,
etc.

2730. Clozier, René. Géographie de la circulation. Vol. I. L'Économie des transports terrestres (rail, route et eau). Paris: Génin, 1964, pp. 404.
    Review, relying chiefly on French sources, of the land
transportation systems of the world, with brief attention to
such auxiliary forms as high-tension wires, water supply, telecommunications, and pipelines.

2730-A. Connors, T.T. "An Examination of the International Flow of
Crude Oil with Special Reference to the Middle East." P-4209. Santa Monica: RAND Corporation, October 1969, pp. 85.
    On the changing patterns of transporting crude oil since
the 1967 closing of the Suez Canal and the discoveries of new
oilfields, with reference to larger tankers and improved pipeline technology that could open both new overland and submarine
routes.

2731. Hanson, Eric J. Dynamic Decade: The Evolution and Effects of
the Oil Industry in Alberta. Toronto: McClelland & Stewart, 1958, pp. 314.
    Includes chapters on natural gas and petroleum pipelines as
they were in 1957, together with what were then projects, since
realized, for their extension.

2732. Jensen, E.J., and Ellis, H.S. "Pipelines." 216 Scientific
American (January 1967), 62-72.
    Readable summary of basic developments of pipeline systems,
national and international, and of techniques for the transmission of liquids, gases, and molten sulfur and of transport of
soldis in slurry form or, as successful experiments suggest for
the future, in capsules and in cylindrical or spherical masses.
Small-scale maps of the oil and gas pipeline networks of North
America, South America, and of the European, North African, and
Western Asian complex are provided, as well as diagrams illustrating some pipelining techniques.

2733. Kamptner, H.K. "Das Erdol in seiner weltwirtschaftlichen und
teknischen Bedeutung." 63 (12) Umschau in Wissenschaft und Technik (1963),
361-363.
    Some reference to the problem of pipeline transport.

2734. Kopelmanas, L. "Internationale Rechtsfragen des Energietransports durch Pipelines." In Aktuelle Fragen des Energierechts. Cologne: Institut für Energierecht, 1960, pp. 65.
> One of the few undertakings to deal with the problem of the development of pipeline networks in Western Europe with reference to the legal problems to be faced.

2735. Krüger, W. "Fernleitungen für Gas und Öl in Europa." 63 (12) Umschau in Wissenschaft und Technik (1963), 363-366.
> Outline of development of gas and oil pipelines in Europe and of plant development in England, France, the Netherlands, West Germany, and the USSR.

2736. Leeston, Alfred M., and Crichton, John A. "The Natural Gas Industry in Foreign Countries." In Alfred M. Leeston, John A. Crichton, and John C. Jacobs, The Dynamic Natural Gas Industry: The Description of an American Industry from the Historical, Technical, Legal, Financial, and Economic Standpoints. Norman: University of Oklahoma Press, 1963, pp. 337-384.
> Includes a description of international transportation by pipeline to the United States from Canada and Mexico and then-planned pipeline transportation through Mexico from Texas to California, pipeline transportation from Rumania to Hungary, and planned transportation from Northern Argentina to Northern Chile and from Algeria to Europe. Possibilities of ocean transport from Algeria and Venezuela and the lack of a market for and resultant waste of Arabian gas are mentioned in a review of the world's natural gas reserves proven at the time of writing.

2737. Peyret, Henri. Histoire des chemins de fer en France et dans le monde. Paris: Société des Éditions Françaises et Internationales, 1949, pp. 350.
> Survey of railway systems in terms of their political, strategic, and economic functions.

2738. "Pipeline Network Expands in Europe." Europe and Oil (December 1964), 54-57.
> Review of pipeline development, accomplished, under construction, and planned, chiefly in Western Europe but also in East Europe with preparation to parallel the Druzhba (Friendship) pipeline.

2739. Reference Material on Canadian Oil and Gas. Prepared for the Ways and Means Committee of the Independent Petroleum Association of America. Mimeo. 1960, pp. ii, 37, vii.
> Review of the pipeline system established for transportation of Canadian crude oil through and to the United States and indicating in part the facilities for bringing Canadian natural gas to the United States.

2740. Vergnaud, Pierre. Les transports routiers internationaux. Paris: Librairie Générale de Droit et de Jurisprudence, 1960, pp. 262.

Study of international highway transportation in Europe with special reference to the needs resulting from integration.

2741. Wägenbaur, R. "Mineralölfernleitungen in der Europäischen Wirtschaftsgemeinschaft." 10 Aussenwirtschaftsdienst des Betriebs-Beraters (July 1964), 206ff.

Examines the problem of the development of oil pipelines in the EEC region.

2742. Wedensky, Georg. "Achievements of the Soviet Oil and Gas Industries in 1964: Review of the Year." Europe and Oil (December 1964), 12-17.

Review of Soviet developments including the commissioning of the Druzhba (Friendship) oil pipeline in September 1964, another step in the linking of East Germany, Hungary, Czechoslovakia, and Poland to the Soviet Union, oil having first reached these countries by pipeline at various times in 1962 and 1963.

2743. Wedgwood, Sir Ralph. International Rail Transport. London: Oxford, 1946, pp. xii, 162.

Useful survey, by a retired railroad executive, of problems of and attempts to regulate international rail transport.

2744. Wolfe, Roy I. Transportation and Politics. Princeton: Van Nostrand, 1963, pp. 129.

Deals with such problems as boundaries and other artificial barriers to political interaction, the disruption of economies by the selection of boundary sites, the influence of transportation on national integration, and some problems of land, river, and ocean transportation that have been amenable to international legal settlement. Attention is also given to the present imbalance between transportation for the military offense and transportation for defense, an aspect of the imbalance in what the author regards as the old regulatory system composed of the configuration of the earth's surface, political action, and the technology of transportation.

See also nos. 586, 751, 2564, 2788, and sec. VIII, F, 5.

3. High Seas--Jurisdiction; Freedom of Navigation; Resources

2745. Davies, D.W. A Primer of Dutch Seventeenth Century Overseas Trade. The Hague: Martinus Nijhoff, 1961, pp. xii, 160.

A very useful review of Dutch commercial activity at the time of the classic advocacy of freedom of the seas. A concluding bibliographical note provides a guide to additional data concerning the interests in the United Provinces that benefited from access to the sea lanes.

2746. Griel, J.V., and Robinson, R.J. "Titanium in Sea Water." 11 Journal of Marine Research (1952), 173-179.
On the presence of one metal in the sea water itself that entails recovery problems quite different from those of recovery from the ocean floor.

2747. Gullion, Edmund A. (ed.). Uses of the Sea. Englewood Cliffs: Prentice Hall (Spectrum Books), 1968, pp. xv, 202.
These essays, the panel papers presented to the Thirty-Third American Assembly, Columbia University, deal with ocean sciences and marine resources, the changing law of the sea, national and international organization of the seas, the strategic consequences of Britain's revised naval role, Soviet attention to the sea, and a suggested American strategy. Among the contributors are Louis Henkin, Eugene Skolnikoff, Marshall Shulman, and Hedley Bull.

2748. Laevastu, T., and Thompson, T.G. "The Determination and Occurrence of Nickel in Sea Water, Marine Organisms, and Sediments." 21 Journal du Conseil International pour l'Exploration de la Mer (No. 2, 1956), 125-143.
On a problem related to the mineral potential of the sea water, ocean sediments, and certain organisms.

2749. Lindberg, Folke. "Power Politics and the Baltic." 54 American-Scandinavian Review (1966), 158-168.
On Soviet claims and proposals since 1950 for a Baltic Sea regime, the strategic position of Denmark in NATO, and the historical evidence that the Baltic has not necessarily been regarded as an open sea.

2750. Nelson, K.H., and Thompson, T.G. "Deposition of Salts from Sea Water by Frigid Concentration." 13 Journal of Marine Research (1954), 166-182.
On a method for recovering certain of the sea's potential assets.

2751. Redfield, Alfred C. "The Biological Control of Chemical Factors in the Environment." 46 American Scientist (1958), 205-221.
This article treats the oceans as the governor of the biosphere, which, by slowing and controlling the rate of decomposition and nutrient regeneration, creates and maintains the highly aerobic terrestrial environment on which man depends. Since overenthusiastic attempts to feed human populations could result in eutrophication of the ocean with resultant adverse effect on the atmosphere's reservoir of oxygen, it could be inferred that, if Redfield is correct, the open oceans should be permanently retained as protective rather than productive territory.

See also nos. 2577, 2581, 2583, 2586, 2589, 2591.

4. Interoceanic Canals

2752. Klette, Immanuel J. From Atlantic to Pacific: A New Interocean Canal. New York: Harper & Row, 1967, pp. 156.
Deals with issues involved in replacing the Panama Canal with a new waterway, including the following: whether to employ nuclear or conventional excavation methods; tolls; management and operations; disposition of the present canal; political conflicts; international repercussions including those over use of nuclear excavation methods.

2753. Parihar, R.R. "National Sovereignty in Panama Canal Dispute." 25 Indian Journal of Political Science (1964), 60-66.
An Indian view of the Panama Canal dispute.

2754. Semidei, M. "Le conflit de Panama." 15 Revue française de science politique (1965), 752-766.
Review of the conflict over the Canal Zone and of the differing objectives of Panama and the United States.

2755. Stratton, J.H. "Sea-Level Canal: How and Where." 43 Foreign Affairs (1965), 513-518.
Review of problems and issues related to the construction of a replacement for the present Panama Canal, including consideration of the economic impact on Panama should a new route be adopted or a sea-level canal be built on the present site-- issues raising a question as to the extent of protection that can properly be accorded a state economically dependent on the location of an artificial international waterway.

2756. Tate, M.D. "The Panama Canal and Political Partnership." 25 Journal of Politics (1963), 119-138.
Surveys the historical background, recent political, economic, and legal issues, and those suggestions for dealing with the Panama Canal problem that were made prior to the agreement of 1965.

See also nos. 1050, 1326, 1653.

5. Ships and Shipping

2757. Brown, Robert T. Transport and the Economic Integration of South America. Washington: Brookings Institution, Transport Research Program, 1966, pp. xiii, 288.
Thorough analysis of the transportation problems of South America, particularly overdependence on ocean shipping, that present formidable obstacles to the achievement of LAFTA objectives.

2758. Colby, Charles C. North Atlantic Arena: Water Transport in the World Order. Carbondale: Southern Illinois University Press, 1965, pp. xiv, 253.

On the development and utilization of water transport in the Mediterranean, the North Atlantic, and the Rhine, the core region in the development of the law concerning ocean and river shipping.

2759. Gumpel, Werner. Die Seehafen--und Schiffahrtspolitik des COMECO Berlin and Munich: Duncker und Humblot, 1963, pp. 235.

Study of Communist bloc policy in regard to ports and shipping.

2760. Harbron, John D. Communist Ships and Shipping. London: Adlard Coles, 1962, pp. x, 262.

On such matters as the increase in Soviet shipping capacity, the use of former German ships to carry settlers from Vladivostok to new ports on the Soviet Pacific Coast, and Poland's desire for self-sufficiency in shipping and its relation to the Polish uprising of 1956.

2761. Hunold, Albert (ed.). Lateinamerika: Land der Sorge und der Zukunft. Erlenbach-Zürich: Rentsch, 1962, pp. 315.

Includes a contribution by Guillermo W. Klein, "Die Lateinamerikanische Integration und die Weltwirtschaft," that gives attention to the high costs of coastal shipping that hinder establishment of a more integrated regional community. Nationalistic shipping policies, highly protectionist in nature, are seen not only as impeding regional community development but also as depriving each protectionist country of the advantages of advanced transport technology.

2762. Leeston, Alfred M. "Ocean Shipment of Natural Gas." In Alfred M. Leeston, John A. Crichton, and John C. Jacobs, The Dynamic Natural Gas Industry: The Description of an American Industry from the Historical, Technical, Legal, Financial and Economic Standpoints. Norman: University of Oklahoma Press, 1963, pp. 254-259.

Brief description of arrangements for shipping liquified methane, butane, and propane by sea and of the type of ship employed.

2763. Sturmey, Stanley George. British Shipping and World Competition. London: Athlone Press, University of London; New York: Oxford, 1962, pp. 436.

Deals with the question of why British shipping, which accounted for over 45% of the world's tonnage in 1900, declined to about 16% of the total in 1960, and finds the reasons to lie in internal constraints. The data provided are important in assessing Britain's influence on the law of the sea in the 20th century as contrasted with her influence in the 19th century.

2764. Wionczek, Miguel S. "Latin American Free Trade Association." International Conciliation. No. 551, January 1965, pp. 80.

A concise review of LAFTA's limited results to date and of impediments to progress, including inadequate stipulations in the Treaty of Montevideo. Attention is accorded the virtual inaction in the field of monetary cooperation, the relationship of vested interests to the slowness of progress, and the relative inaction in dealing with the transport problem. In regard to the transport problem, note is taken of the hostility of international maritime conferences, supported by governments of major maritime powers, to every proposed draft of a convention designed to provide advantages to Latin American shipping, of the diplomatic protest of the United States that LAFTA proposals violated the 1846 navigation treaty with Colombia, and of the diplomatic protests by major European maritime states and open threats by international shipping conferences to suspend cargo service to Uruguayan ports when Uruguay attempted unilaterally to rescind some surcharges and deposits on imports carried by national flag vessels.

See also nos. 204, 1919, 1923.

6. Maritime Law and Politics

2765. Friedheim, Robert L. "Factor Analysis as a Tool in Studying the Law of the Sea." In Lewis M. Alexander (ed.), The Law of the Sea: Offshore Boundaries and Zones. Columbus: Ohio State University Press, 1967, pp. 47-70.
　　Factor analysis of the voting at the Geneva Law of the Sea Conferences of 1958 and 1960 makes clear the clustering of states by groups of issues that came to decision.

See also nos. 686, 1906, 1932, 2099, 2457, 2826.

7. Ports; Foreign Trade Zones

2766. Alexandersson, Gunnar, and Norstrom, Goran. World Shipping: An Economic Geography of Ports and Seaborne Trade. New York: Wiley, 1963, pp. 507.
　　Contains much important information about the geography of ports and about patterns and types of seaborne trade. The book is divided into two sections, the first being a general survey and the second a regional survey. Use is made of a trade distribution index similar to the coefficient of localization employed in industrial location problems. A valuable list of statistical sources by countries is appended. Attention is given to many small and/or recently opened ports and their seaborne trade.

2767. Fair, Marvin L. Port Administration in the United States. Cambridge, Maryland: Cornell Maritime Press, 1954, pp. xvi, 217.

Includes a brief review of the free port system in Europe, with reference to the French 19th century extension of national control to administration of ports under which France continued to require merchandise in transit to remain in bond. The French system is contrasted with the more general European system of well-established local port authorities. Discussion of the development of port administration in the United States includes a section on the operations of the free trade zones established at New York, New Orleans, San Francisco, Los Angeles, and Seattle, as well as a discussion of the value of the free zone to protectionist countries desiring to function as important world trade centers.

2768. <u>Foreign-Trade Zones</u>. Corps of Engineers, U.S. Army and U.S. Shipping Board. Miscellaneous Series No. 3, 1929.
Includes discussion of the nature of "free zones" or "foreign-trade zones," the applicability of regulations governing port dues, public health, postal service, and immigration, and a zone's freedom from tariff policy.

2769. Hesberg, Walter. <u>Die Freihandelszone als Mittel der Integrationspolitik</u>. Frankfurt-am-Main: F. Knapp (1960), pp. 190.
Examination of free trade zones of the 19th century and of the present time as instruments for integration.

2770. Kolff, B. <u>Rotterdam, Freer than a Free Port.</u> Rotterdam: "Stichting Havenbelangen," 1938.
Best description of the Rotterdam system which provides various arrangements which obviate all need for free port facilities while yet meeting transshipment and other needs by means of a variety of devices.

2770-A. Konstantinović, Velimir. "Duty-Free Zones in Yugoslavia." 20 <u>Review of International Affairs</u> (Belgrade) (October 20, 1969), 32-33.
A brief discussion of free warehouses, duty-free zones, and free ports, followed by exposition of the system established in the duty-free zones in Rijeka, Koper, Split, Ploče, Belgrade, and Novi Sad.

2771. Lomax, Alfred Lewis. <u>The Foreign-Trade Zone</u>. Eugene: Bureau of Business Research, School of Business Administration, University of Oregon, 1947, pp. 40.
An argument for the establishment of a "free zone" or "foreign-trade zone" in Portland, Oregon. After distinguishing the segregated foreign-trade zone from "free-trade ports" such as Hong Kong, where ships can come and go at will and cargoes move inland without payment of duties, and after noting the decline in number of free-trade ports and increase in the number of free zones (the free ports of Europe being really free zone ports), the history and functions of free zones are outlined from Frederick I's grant of a charter in 1189 that exempted Hamburg from the payment of customs duties on the lower Elbe. The history of efforts to establish foreign-trade zones in the United

States from 1894 to the passage of the Foreign-Trade Zones Act of 1934 and its amendment in 1945 are discussed in greater detail, as is the operation of the New York zone and the efforts up to 1946 of other cities to establish zones.

2772. Miller, Charles John. A Free-Trade Zone for Puget Sound: Its Economic Desirability and Feasibility. (Seattle): Port of Seattle and Division of Progress and Industry Development, 1947, pp. 173.
Distinguishes foreign-trade zones from free-trade ports, describes the modern European free port arrangements and operations, and deals with American foreign-trade zones since the passage of the Foreign-Trade Zones Act of 1934. Particular attention is given to the New York zone and to the shortlived Mobile zone of 1937 which foundered in Alabama political struggle. The author advocates forming a Puget Sound zone.

2773. Organization for European Economic Co-operation. Foreign Trade Zones in the U.S.A. Technical Assistance Mission No. 28. Paris: O.E.E.C., 1954, pp. 67.
A review of the United States effort to establish and maintain free zones that is dominated by an optimistic view of the zones as windows in a tariff wall.

2774. Redfield, A.C. "The Analysis of Tidal Phenomena in Narrow Emboyments." Papers in Physical Oceanography and Meteorology. Vols. XI, No. 4. Massachusetts Institute of Technology and Woods Hole Oceanographic Institution: July 1950.
An example of the type of research report that should be examined when dealing with such issues as the responsibility of state to other states for untoward consequences of its construction of waterfront structures. An example of works that could have raised the issue of responsibility and, indeed, did, although before damage was done, is the Netherlands' Delta-Plan which, besides suggesting a design accomplishing the objectives without cutting off the Scheldt and so also the port of Antwerp, might have had serious effects upon the water level at such other North Sea ports as London, Bremen, and Hamburg.

2775. Thoman, Richard S. "Foreign-Trade Zones of the United States." 42 Geographical Review (1952), 631-645.
Review of the operations of foreign-trade zones in the United States that raises the question of whether such zones are but a belated and not too successful form of competition with bonded warehouses rather than a promoter of international trade.

2776. Thoman, Richard S. Free Ports and Foreign-Trade Zones. Cambridge, Maryland: Cornell Maritime Press, 1956, pp. x, 203.
Best survey of the world's free ports, with particular emphasis upon Germany, Denmark, Sweden, and the United States, that presents the essentials of the history, facilities, organization and administration of the various free ports and foreign-trade zones. Attention is given to the extent of usage

and to the distribution of goods between imports and reexports, the latter, in industrialized countries, being a rather small portion of the goods brought to free port facilities. Alternative facilities for transit, among them bonded warehouses, are described with particular attention to the ports of Rotterdam, Antwerp, and London which have no free port device. The author questions whether the free port is needed in view of its declining use despite excellent facilities, but lacking cost accounting details, refrains from comment on the economic wisdom of shippers' preference for other facilities.

See also no. 2759.

8. Access to the Sea

2777. Pounds, Norman J.G. "A Free and Secure Access to the Sea." 49 Annals, Association of American Geographers (1959), 256-268. Reprinted in W.A. Douglas Jackson (ed.), Politics and Geographic Relationships: Readings on the Nature of Political Geography. Englewood Cliffs: Prentice-Hall, 1964, pp. 241-256.
 Deals with the problem of access to the sea by reference to various proposals and arrangements either for corridors or for establishing rights of transit.

9. Civil Aviation

2778. Gleditsch, Nils Petter. "Trends in World Airline Patterns." 4 Journal of Peace Research (1967), 366-408.
 Employing data for 125 countries for 1930, 1951, 1958, and 1965, the author finds that at each of these times affiliations with a colonial system, geographical distance, and the rank of nations in the international system had major impact on airline patterns. Over time, the latter two increased in importance, while colonial affiliation first increased but for the last time-period decreased. Three conflicts--the East-West, the new "cold war" with China, and the Arab-Israeli--were examined for their impacts on airline patterns.

2779. Heymann, Hans, Jr. Civil Aviation and U.S. Foreign Aid: Purposes, Pitfalls, and Problems for U.S. Policy. RAND Report R-424-RC. Santa Monica: RAND Corporation, January 1964, pp. xi, 87.
 Although related primarily to United States policies, the study has broader application. By focusing on the economic and political consequences of the growth, with foreign economic assistance, of prestige international airlines owned by the governments of new and underdeveloped states, the study reaches to newer structural features of potential effect upon the future development of international air law.

2779-A. O'Connor, William E. Economic Regulation of the World's Airlines: A Political Analysis. New York: Praeger, 1971, pp. 204.

An evaluation of the network of 2,500 bilateral commercial aviation agreements, a review of attempts between 1944 and 1969 to achieve a multilateral system, and a proposal for a new approach designed to lower fares, centralize economic planning, and improve the situation of the developing countries in the world airline picture.

2780. Raymond, A.E. Over the Horizon in Air Transportation. P-3396. Santa Monica: RAND Corporation, August 1966, pp. 16.

An attempt to foresee the nature of civil air transport in 1980 and after, with attention to the possible impacts of air traffic control problems and terminal congestion.

2781. Straszheim, Mahlon. The International Airline Industry. Washington: Brookings Institution, 1969, pp. viii, 297.

On the advances, setbacks, and losses of the international airline industry as a whole and of separate carriers, including new and inefficient carriers, with attention to government policies, management practices, and some aspects of collaboration through an international nongovernmental organization.

2782. Thayer, Frederick C., Jr. Air Transport Policy and National Security: A Political, Economic, and Military Analysis. Chapel Hill: University of North Carolina Press, 1966, pp. xxiii, 342.

Primarily concerned with American air policy, including the political development of aviation as a commercial enterprise and as a tool of military policy, this book gives attention to the nature of international operations before and after World War II, the postwar policy structure for the international airlines, the interrelations of US trunk airlines and international carriers, the 1960 breakthrough in military airlift, and the status of international airline regulation in the 1960s.

2782-A. Thornton, Robert L. International Airlines and Politics: A Study in Adaptation to Change. Michigan International Business Studies, No. 13. Ann Arbor: Program in International Business, Graduate School of Business Administration, University of Michigan, 1970, pp. xii, 268.

An attempt to find ways of reconciling the differing aims of governments and commercial enterprises in the light of technical and political changes, among them the possible expansion of Soviet air transport activities, a lessened importance of certain small states in terms of strategic location, larger aircraft, and a possible consortium of West European flag airlines.

See also nos. 738, 1923, 2571.

F. NATURAL RESOURCES

1. Control and Allocation of Natural Resources

2783. Aitken, Hugh G.J. "The Changing Structure of the Canadian Economy with Particular Reference to the Influence of the United States." In Hugh G.J. Aitken, et al., The American Economic Impact on Canada. Durham: Duke University Press, 1959, pp. 3-35.

Includes discussion of the political aspects of United States investment in Canada, including participation in the Trans-Canada Pipeline and Westcoast Transmission Company ventures that form part of the overall system for the international overland transportation of natural gas.

2784. Caldwell, Lynton K., and Fox, Irving K. Research on Policy and Administration in Environmental Quality Programs. In Lynton K. Caldwell (ed.), Environmental Studies: Papers on the Politics and Public Administration of Man-Environment Relationships. No. IV. Bloomington, Indiana: Institute of Public Administration, Indiana University, March 30, 1967, pp. 53.

Although focused at the national and subnational levels, these two papers, presented under a single cover, suggest lines of inquiry along such dimensions as the engineering-economic, the institutional, and the attitudinal that with appropriate adaptation could be employed at the international level in light of the failure of environments, natural resources, and even industrial processes to be contained within political boundaries.

2785. Davis, John. Natural Gas and Canada-United States Relations. (Washington and Montreal): Canadian-American Committee, 1959, pp. xii, 32.

Reviews the increasing use of natural gas, proven reserves and potential resources, prospective markets for Canadian gas, and problems of getting compatible regulations from autonomous national, state, and provincial authorities.

2786. Davis, John. Oil and Canada-United States Relations. (Washington and Montreal): Canadian-American Committee, 1959, pp. xii, 36.

Study of oil in Canadian-American relations and its relation to a struggle between pressure groups in the United States, that is, between the independents, often employing uneconomic exploration methods, who wanted to prohibit foreign oil from entering the United States and the international companies who favored entry of foreign oil. The study also deals with natural gas before several applications for export of Canadian gas to the United States were approved in 1960.

2787. Friedheim, Robert L. Understanding the Debate on Ocean Resources. Monograph Series in World Affairs, No. 3, 1968-69. The Social Science Foundation and Graduate School of International Studies, University of Denver, 1969, pp. 38.

Excellent review of the positions expressed on the directions that should be taken in developing the law on ocean resources. The monograph brings to the fore the main characteristics of the arguments and proposals that the author classifies as normative nationalist, functional nationalist, functional internationalist, and normative internationalist.

2788. Gould, Wesley L. "Metals, Oil, and Natural Gas: Some Problems of Canadian-American Co-operation." In David R. Deener (ed.), Canada-United States Treaty Relations. Durham: Duke University Press, 1963, pp. 151-184.

On the interdependence of Canada and the United States in investment, distribution, consumption, and employment in respect to uranium, nickel, copper, lead, zinc, oil, and natural gas, pipeline transportation, the growth of energy systems across national borders, and the reaching of complementary quasi-judicial decisions by regulatory agencies without violating the principles of sovereignty and judicial independence.

2789. Hunter, W.D.G. "The Development of the Canadian Uranium Industry: An Experiment in Public Enterprise." 28 Canadian Journal of Economics and Political Science (1962), 329-352.

Account of the development of an industry which relied heavily on the United States government's preemptive purchases only to have the government support exploration of domestic sources so heavily that discoveries of large American sources of uranium ore and production from those sources led to refusal to exercise options and consequent disruption of the Canadian industry. Since the article is primarily concerned with the nature of the Canadian uranium industry as at least partly public enterprise, the full picture of the effects of failure to exercise options is to be obtained by supplementary reading in Canadian newspapers in 1960 and after.

2790. Levin, Jonathan A. The Export Economies. Cambridge: Harvard University Press, 1960, pp. xiv, 347.

Careful study of reasons for the long stagnation of most raw material export economies and for their recent policies that have tended to give new dimensions to the international politics of raw materials as host countries and investor countries oppose each other. Included are case studies of such matters as Peru's 19th century guano boom and Burma's rice-marketing board.

2791. Marts, Marion E., and Sewell, W.R.D. "Fish and Power at the Crossroads in the Pacific Northwest." 19 University of Washington Business Review (April 1960), 3-8.

On an area of contention involving both values and interests. A similar article entitled "Fish and Power" appeared in 12 Water Power (April 1960), 129-134.

2792. Marts, Marion E., and Sewell, W.R.D. "The Conflict Between Fish and Power Resources in the Pacific Northwest." 50 Annals, Association of American Geographers (1960), 42-50. Japanese translation in 6 Americana (November 1960), 129-134.

Discussion of a conflict in resource utilization and of values that are of a type susceptible to settlement on the basis of the political effectiveness of the interest groups concerned.

2793. Masson, Francis, and Whitely, J.B. Barriers to Trade between Canada and the United States. (Washington and Montreal): Canadian-American Committee, 1960, pp. 97.
    Deals with some of the national barriers to continental utilization of North American resources.

2794. Rose, John. "Hong Kong's Water-Supply Problem and China's Contribution to Its Solution." 56 Geographical Review (1966), 432-437.
    On the development since 1960 of water supplies for Hong Kong from mainland China.

2795. Southworth, Constant, and Buchanan, W.W. Changes in Trade Restrictions between Canada and the United States. (Washington and Montreal): Canadian-American Committee, 1960, pp. 65.
    Deals with such restraints upon continental utilization of North American resources as the United States freight-rate structure which discriminates against certain Canadian lead and zinc producers.

2796. Sovani, N.V. The International Position of India's Raw Materials. New Delhi: Indian Council of World Affairs and Oxford University Press, 1948, pp. xi, 332.
    A review of India's raw materials position at the coming of independence and of the potential for change in India's competitive position in the role of supplier of raw materials in the world economy. The volume only touches upon other facets of India's economy and their relation to the world economy.

2797. Spoehr, Alexander. "Cultural Differences in the Interpretation of Natural Resources." In W.L. Thomas, Jr. (ed.), Man's Role in Changing the Face of the Earth. Chicago: University of Chicago Press, 1956, pp. 93-101.
    Discusses contrasts in attitudes toward natural resources, particularly differences affecting the exploitation and uses of resources and about whether man has or lacks control over his environment.

2798. Tugendhat, Georg. "The European Oil Industry at the Turn of 1964." Europe and Oil (December 1964), 8-10.
    Provides data on unilateral actions in pursuit of national objectives or in the effort to deal with national problems that add to the difficulties of realizing a rational distribution of energy fuels, including distribution of the market among fuels. For example, in Germany a boom in refinery construction led to a 30% cutback in coal production and then to attempts to prevent further dislocation. Attention is called to the oil revenue structure whereby British import duties provide revenue exceeding the total oil revenues of the producing Middle Eastern governments.

2799. Wolfe, Alvin W. "The African Mineral Industry: Evolution of a Supranational Level of Integration." 11 Social Problems (1963), 153-164.

Conceptualizes the industry as both a "stateless" society and an international system.

2800. Wolfe, Roy I. "Transportation and Politics: The Example of Canada." 52 Annals, Association of American Geographers (1962), 176-190.
On the Canadian-American rivalry stemming from the cession of the Ohio country to the United States that disrupted the unity of the St. Lawrence watershed on which the fur trade was based, the attempts of Canada to reconstruct the unity of the watershed, and the rivalry of interests seeking to maintain the supremacy of the Hudson river system.

See also nos. 129, 130, 136, 138, 266, 563, 583, 585, 589, 591, 1063, 2397, 2649, 2699, 2728, 2742, 2806, 2811, 2813, 2826, 2835.

2. Deep-Sea Floor Resources

2801. Brooks, David B. "Deep Sea Manganese Nodules: From Scientific Phenomenon to World Resource." 8 Natural Resources Journal (1968), 401-423.
An economic functionalist consideration of manganese resources on the ocean bottom that applies some of the concepts employed in discussion of fisheries and resting on the notion that ocean resources are common property resources.

2802. Commission on Marine Science, Engineering and Resources. Our Nation and the Sea: A Plan for National Action. Washington: Government Printing Office, 1969.
Report of a US Presidential Commission that calls for an International Registry Agency to register claims to explore or exploit deep-ocean resources, to exercise limited policing and dispute settling functions, and to collect a portion of the value of seabed raw materials to form an International Fund to assist developing nations and to finance marine science activities.

2803. Mero, John L. The Mineral Resources of the Sea. Amsterdam, London, and New York: Elsevier Publishing Company, 1965, pp. xiii, 312.
Provides important information on resources and the technical capacity for the extraction thereof from marine beaches, sea water, the continental shelves, strata underlying the soft sea-floor sediments, and the deep-sea floor. A final chapter deals with the economic and legal aspects of ocean mining, the final section being an abstract of Wilbert M. Chapman's paper on the law pertaining to deep-sea deposits that was presented before the American Chemical Society in 1963. A useful bibliography of the scientific and technical literature is included.

See also no. 2826.

3. Continental Shelf

2804. Alexander, Lewis M. Offshore Geography of Northwestern Europe: The Political and Economic Problems of Delimitation and Control. Chicago: Rand McNally, 1963, pp. xii, 162.

Examination by a political geographer of the physical, political, economic, legal, historical and other influences upon claims to offshore control in the North Sea basin and adjacent waters from Iceland to Denmark. The book gives considerable attention to fisheries; but the discovery of offshore gas deposits occurred after the text was written.

2805. Emery, K.O. "Submarine Phosphorite Deposits Off California and Mexico." 46 California Journal of Mines and Geology (1950), 7-15.

Report on phosphorite in samples of rock dredgings off the California coast and on phosphorite deposits off California and Mexico.

2806. Enright, Robert J. "The North Sea--Oil's Biggest Gamble to Date." 63 Oil and Gas Journal (May 10, 1965), 127-163.

Review of developments to May 1965 in oil and gas exploration on the North Sea continental shelf that includes: (1) the status of boundary negotiations in May 1965 and the stalemates in Dutch and Danish negotiations with West Germany; (2) the impact of the fall of the Dutch Government after it closed down a commercial television station erected on a platform outside the three-mile limit; (3) onshore gas finds to 1965 in the Netherlands; (4) arrangements made by three governments and planned by the fallen Dutch Government for offshore exploration and production; (5) problems encountered and actions taken in the British area in respect to communications with shore, customs and immigration, navigation, safety, and aircraft usage; and (6) anticipated rate of development of usage of natural gas in Western Europe. In regard to boundaries, the self-restraint of governments in not awarding blocks near anticipated boundaries is noted.

2807. Hobbs, Mel. "North Sea Drilling Effort Begins to Pick Up Speed." 161 World Oil (August 15, 1965), 65-67.

Report on North Sea drilling activities, the first article in the 1965 annual international outlook issue.

2808. Lee, C.O., Bartlett, Z.W., and Feierabend, R.H. "The Grand Isle Mine." 12 Mining Engineering (1960), 587-590.

Description of mining operations and techniques at the Freeport Sulphur Company's mine seven miles off the Louisiana shore.

2809. Palmer, P. "Sulphur Under the Sea." 6 Sea Frontiers (1960), 210-217.

Deals with the mining of sulphur by the Freeport Sulphur Company seven miles seaward of Grand Isle, Louisiana.

2810. "The North Sea: Europe's Major Hope for New Petroleum Reserves." 159 World Oil (August 15, 1964), 75-80.

Report on oil and gas exploration activities in offshore areas in the North Sea, one of a series of activity reports in the 19th annual international outlook issue. Reference is made to such boundary problems as that in the area claimed by Norway where there is a trench in excess of the 200-meter depth referred to in the Geneva convention on the continental shelf.

2811. Tugendhat, Georg. "Oil and Natural Gas in the North Sea." Europe and Oil (September 1964), 38-40.

Review of the first British steps to explore and develop the gas and oil potential of the North Sea under the Geneva regime of the continental shelf.

2811-A. Wenger, Alain. Pétrole et gaz naturel en Mer du Nord--droit et économie. Paris: Editions Technip, 1971, pp. viii, 255.

A study of the economics and the law related to exploration for and exploitation of the natural gas and crude oil found under the North Sea.

See also nos. 2397, 2826.

4. Fisheries

2812. Bidwell, R,G.S. "Decline of the Lobster." Letter in 158 Science (1967), 1136-1137.

This article (1) provides information on the decline of the lobster catch in Northumberland Strait, between Prince Edward Island and Nova Scotia, from an average catch per lobster boat of 16,000 pounds in 1964 to 2,000 pounds in 1967, (2) indicates the inefficient fishing practices and oversupply of lobster fishermen, (3) suggests the need for replacement of free enterprise by an effective system sponsored either by government or by a large concern possessed of sole fishing rights, and (4) notes the dependence of some types of fishery regulation on international agreement and on settlement of questions of sovereignty.

2813. Christy, Francis T., Jr., and Scott, Anthony. The Common Wealth in Ocean Fisheries. Baltimore: Johns Hopkins Press, 1965, pp. xiii, 281.

An economic functionalist approach to the problem of ocean resource management that deals thoroughly with the problems of fisheries and gives attention to the activities of fisheries commissions.

2814. Cooley, Richard A. The Decline of the Alaska Salmon. New York: Harper & Row, 1963, pp. xxi, 230.

Employing historical and economic tools of analysis, the author examines the pressure politics of salmon conservation. Management of the resource by controls upon the efficiency of

fishing gear rather than upon the number and location of fishermen is criticized. A case study of the formal record of the conflict which led to the passage of the White Act of 1924 and of
the continuing struggle over its administration serves as a vehicle for presentation of the struggle between conflicting pressure groups and their relationships with Congress and Executive.
Although the setting is restricted to domestic politics, the
portrayal, somewhat incomplete in paying little attention to informal party and legislative politics, is useful in providing a
view of one facet of the fisheries problem that also affects efforts directed toward international regulation.

2815. Crutchfield, James. "The Marine Fisheries: A Problem in International Cooperation." Papers and Proceedings of the Seventy-sixth
Annual Meeting of the American Economic Association (1963): 54 American
Economic Review (1964), 207-218.
        Measuring the performance of most of the world's fisheries
on the basis of physical relationships without regard for economic considerations is said to lead to inadequate approaches
to regulation. Optimal utilization of Northeast Pacific fisheries is hardly the same thing for Canadians and Americans, who
can market only certain species profitably, as for Japanese or
Russians who can market a wide variety of species and, therefore, are motivated to organize fisheries around highly efficient gear that can harvest at low cost. However, these considerations do not enter into official negotiations between Canada,
Japan, and the United States in which the problem has been
treated only in physical terms. The author argues that the international law of fisheries cannot be satisfactory in the absence of a break with tradition so that net economic maximization becomes an objective to be implemented by the treaty technique. Economic maximization is declared to require abandonment of the traditional concept of freedom of the seas and of
the concept that appropriation of marine resources is impossible.
Both restriction of total fishing effort when necessary and admission, for economic reasons and not just for political reasons,
of new entrants to managed fisheries must be possible, whether
the method of regulation be that of regional agreements on shared
fisheries or, as a more remote possibility, of a supranational
fishing authority having exclusive rights over a geographic area
encompassing an appropriate ecological unit.

2816. Crutchfield, James A. (ed.). The Fisheries: Problems in Resource Management. Seattle: University of Washington Press, 1965, pp. x,
136.
        Deals with the fisheries problem from the point of view of
economic management and utilization of a living resource.

2816-A. Crutchfield, James A., and Pontecorvo, Giulio. The Pacific
Salmon Fisheries: A Study of Irrational Conservation. Baltimore: Johns
Hopkins Press for Resources of the Future, 1969, pp. xii, 220.
        Argument against basing management of salmon fisheries on
biological considerations alone and a proposal for a program of

public regulation taking account of both biological and economic criteria.

2817. Gordon, H. Scott. "The Economic Theory of a Common Property Resource: The Fishery." 42 Journal of Political Economy (1954), 124-142.
Presents the economic theory of common property resources that is the basis of the economic functionalist argument concerning proper management of fisheries that would get at such problems as depletion for fear that a competitor will get the resource, overcapitalization, and inefficient use of labor.

2818. Hart, J.L. "Some Sociological Effects of Quota Control of Fisheries." 22 Canadian Fish Culturalist (1958), 17-19.
Quota control appears to discourage specialized full-time fishermen or those specializing in one fishery. A related effect is to encourage many fishermen to participate due to high productivity at the beginnings of quota periods but with resultant reduction of the potential of professional fishermen.

2819. Helin, Ronald A. "Soviet Fishing in the Barents Sea and the North Atlantic." 54 Geographical Review (1964), 386-408.
Survey of the Soviet effort to provide fishery products for 30-40% of the Soviet protein diet. About 3/4 of the 3.2 million tons annual catch is from marine fisheries, 1 million tons through Barents Sea ports, with the Barents Sea controlled under the North-east Atlantic Fisheries Convention. The article accords attention to Soviet medium-range fishing activities from Iceland to Norway, to long-range activities off North America where often grounds too deep for the equipment of other states are worked, and to plans for increased fishing off Western Greenland and North America, use of the Cuban base, and exploitation of the African Coast.

2820. Johnson, Ralph W. "Regulation of Commercial Salmon Fisheries: A Case of Confused Objectives." 55 Pacific Northwest Quarterly (1964), 141-145.
A popularly written article by a law professor on the problem of "featherbedding" in commercial salmon fishing. Laws and regulations of three states and of British Columbia require the use of inefficient methods that have increased the number of fishermen so that some 30,000 American, and Canadian fishermen hunt salmon in the North Pacific, about 27,000 of them being unnecessary to retain present levels of catches. Present methods do not permit proper selection for spawning purposes. The article describes more effective methods. However, with federal regulation covering only the few cases involving treaties, correction of the matter is left to state action and the political circumstance that boat fishermen have political strength, while since as a state Alaska banned the use of traps and weirs, formerly used detrimentally by cannery owners, trap and weir operators have been nonexistent. In brief and readable language the author has identified a feature of state and provincial politics that has a bearing upon the effort to regulate Northeast Pacific

fisheries by treaty, a problem dealt with more extensively in collaboration with R. Van Cleve in The Management of the High Seas Fisheries of the Northeastern Pacific (1963).

2821. Kasahara, Hiroshi. Fisheries of the North Pacific Ocean. H.R. MacMillan Lectures in Fisheries, 2 vols. Vancouver: University of British Columbia, 1961, 1964, pp. 202.

Excellent review of Japanese literature on North Pacific fisheries and fishing stocks, together with an explanation of the policy of the Japanese Government and fishing industry and their objection to the principle of abstention, their preference for the development of new resources, and their explanation for the steady decline in the catch of Hokkaido herring since 1960.

2822. Paulik, G.J. "Bristol Bay Salmon Fisheries." Abstract. 18 Biometrics (1962), 631-632.

Of interest in that it relates to a body of water over which the State of Alaska attempted to exert jurisdiction over Japanese vessels and their masters even though they were conducting operations beyond the territorial waters delimited in terms of miles off shore.

2823. Paulik, G.J., Royce, W.F., Bevan, D.E., Crutchfield, J.A., and Fletcher, R.L. Salmon Gear Limitation in Northern Washington Waters. University of Washington Publications in Fisheries. New Series. Vol. II, No. 1. Seattle: 1963.

On an aspect of fishing regulation that has been a subject of controversy on both the domestic and the international level, raising the issue of the propriety of modernizing fishing equipment.

2824. Peterson, C.E. "Financial Assistance to Fishing Industries in Various Countries." 23 Commercial Fisheries Review (No. 11, 1961), 8-13.

Compares the assistance given to operators of 22 foreign nations with that given the fishing industry in the United States.

2825. Scott, Anthony D. "Food and the World Fisheries Situation." In Marion Clawson (ed.), Natural Resources and International Development. Baltimore: Johns Hopkins Press for Resources for the Future, Inc., 1964, pp. 127-151.

Discusses the following topics: (1) projected growth of demand for fish as food, meal, or flour; (2) indicated productivity of the oceans; (3) incentives or lack thereof for the use of newer gear; (4) potential methods of increasing ocean productivity; (5) overfishing with reference to economic aspects and lack of incentive for fishermen to concern themselves with protection of fertility in high seas fisheries or with catching predators; (6) patterns of treaty cooperation in respect to fisheries; (7) limits on progress to date, including concern for fertility aspects of common-property fisheries but not for wastes of capital and labor. The essay takes the position that

fishing is still in the stage of hunting rather than husbandry
and that the first steps, except for improvements in intensive
farming of brackish waters, have yet to be taken to produce a
developmental stage preliminary to a true fisheries revolution.

2826. "The Ocean." 221 Scientific American (September 1969), Special
issue, pp. 54-234, 284-287.
An excellent collection of articles that deal in clear
language, with the aid of well-conceived diagrams and maps,
with such matters as the origins and movements of the deep-
ocean floor, the relationship between the atmosphere and the
ocean, the continental shelves, the nature of oceanic life,
physical and food resources, overfishing and inadequacies of
control systems, technological advances, and problems of study
and exploitation of the oceans in mutually beneficial manner.
Legal aspects are related to technological, economic, and nutritional factors. A useful bibliography is included.

2827. Turvey, Ralph. "Optimization and Suboptimization in Fishery
Regulation." 54 American Economic Review (1964), 64-76.
Mathematical construction of models of optimization and
suboptimization of mesh size and of fishing effort in a trawl
fishery with reference to fishery regulation as a sphere of economic policy.

2828. Van Cleve, Richard. "Problems of the Commercial Fisheries--
Conservation, Technology, Economics." 84 Transactions of the American
Fisheries Society, 1954 (1955), 299-313.
Reviews the fisheries problem from the point of view of the
commercial fisherman's needs.

2829. Van Cleve, Richard, and Johnson, Ralph W. Management of the
High Seas Fisheries of the Northeastern Pacific: A Preliminary Survey of
Current Issues. University of Washington Publications in Fisheries, Vol.
II (new series), No. 2. Seattle: 1963, pp. viii, 63.
Includes a review of the legal environment in which high
seas fisheries must operate but gives greater attention to the
biological and economic bases for fisheries management and to
the principles of abstention, maximum sustained yield, and optimum economic yield, with special reference to the salmon and
halibut fisheries of the northeastern Pacific. One of the
authors is a Professor of Law and the other is Dean of the
College of Fisheries, University of Washington.

2830. Yu Yu, Marti (ed.). Soviet Fisheries Investigations in the
Northwest Atlantic (translation). Office of Technical Services, U.S. Department of Commerce. Washington, D.C.: 1964.
This is a translation of reports of Soviet investigations
of the North Atlantic and its fishing prospects.

See also nos. 686, 1906, 2311, 2398, 2804.

a. Whaling

2831. Laws, Richard M. "Problems of Whale Conservation." 25 Trans-actions of the North American Wildlife Conference (1960), 304-319.
    Review of international conservation measures, their ef-fectiveness, technical difficulties of regulating quotas for individual species of whale, catching capacity and profit mar-gin, biological problems in regulation that make it difficult to obtain quantitative evidence of depletion, and the desira-bility of employing national quotas as a regulatory instrument.

2832. McVay, Scott. "The Last of the Great Whales." 215 Scientific American (August 1965), 13-21.
    On the overkill of several species of whales and current re-duced Antarctic yields, the inadequacies of attempted regulation by the International Whaling Commission, the predominant influ-ence impeding effective regulation of the then three major whal-ing states, Norway (now disengaged), Japan, and the USSR, viola-tion of treaty protection of right whales and Commission orders concerning sperm whales, and recent efforts to reduce Antarctic quotas.

2833. Walsh, John. "Whales: Decline Continues Despite Limitations on Catch." 157 Science (1967), 1024-1025.
    On the problem of restricting the catch of whales, despite the fact that at the time of writing only Japan, the Soviet Union, and Norway (now disengaged) were engaged in pelagic whal-ing. The article gives attention to the limited authority of the International Whaling Commission, its incapacity to seek or to apply legal sanctions, its lack of authority over nations maintaining land stations and not belonging to the Commission, the explicit barrier to the Commission's setting national quotas as well as a total catch limit, and the failure of the attempt to employ inspectors on ships other than those of the ship's nationality.

5. Energy Fuels and Electric Power

2834. Adelman, M.A. "The World Oil Outlook." In Marion Clawson (ed.), Natural Resources and International Development. Baltimore: Johns Hopkins Press for Resources for the Future, Inc., 1964, pp. 27-125.
    An examination of the world oil market, the impact of over-supply, and the price structure that tries to set in perspective certain myths such as those concerning price fixing and those concerning tending to exclude economic considerations when dis-cussing the Soviet "oil offensive." Particularly useful is a section examining the price structure of the 1950s that finds that not a cartel but an informal world commodity agreement--a commodity agreement in effect but not in form--existed as a result of government restraint of competition at home and virtual

inaction by the companies. Discussion of the deterioration of
the market after 1957 ascribes the change to the Japanese demonstration that entry into the Middle East could occur relatively
inexpensively, thereby encouraging newcomers, the cutting of
prices by the old international companies lest rejection of one
sale lead to other losses of sales, and the appearance of independent refiners whether private, government, or quasi-govern-
ment enterprises. The article includes some discussion of Western Europe's energy problems.

2834-A. "Boundaries Cloud E. China Sea Outlook." 68 Oil and Gas Journal (August 10, 1970), 83.
    On the offshore boundary wrangling involving Japan, Red
China, Taiwan, and South Korea as an impediment to exploration
for oil under the East China Sea, with particular attention to
Japanese and South Korean grants of exploration rights.

2834-B. Burch, William R., Jr. "Resources and Social Structure:
Some Conditions of Stability and Change." 389 Annals of the American
Academy of Political and Social Science (May 1970), 27-34.
    With particular attention to energy resources and the energy
surplus of the now-closed frontier on which Western industrialization depended, an Associate Professor of Forest Sociology constructs a model of the way in which social-structural forms and
cultural myths define materials as a resource to virtually compel
particular adaptive strategies.

2835. Cantor, Leonard M. "The Columbia River Power Project and the
Pacific Northwest-Southwest Intertie." 65 Journal of Geography (1966),
20-28.
    On the US-Canadian collaborative generation of electric
power under the Columbia River Treaty, the release of Canadian
power to California at times when it is surplus to the Northwest's needs, and on the Intertie in the US linking two dams
on the Columbia River with Hoover Dam and with Los Angeles and
Phoenix.

2836. Center for Strategic and International Studies. The Gulf: Implications of British Withdrawal. Special Report Series No. 8. Washington:
Georgetown University, February 1969, pp. ix, 110.
    Although designed to produce policy recommendations that
point to military solutions, this study contains useful data on
the Persian Gulf area, territorial disputes, and exploitation
of the area's oil reserves.

2837. "Common Market is Aim of Latin Americans in ARPEL." 160 World
Oil (May 1965), 176.
    This article, in a special issue devoted to international
offshore exploration, sets forth the objective of a petroleum
common market of ARPEL (Asistencia Reciproca Petrolera Estatal
Latino-americana), the organization of government oil companies
of South America (excluding Ecuador which had no government oil
company) and Mexico. Reference is made to the objective of

mutual assistance and to the making of arrangements for an exchange of Peruvian crude for Argentine fuel oil.

2838. Dechert, Charles R. Ente Nazionale Idrocarburi: Profile of a State Corporation. Leiden: Brill, 1963, pp. ix, 116.
On Italy's powerful agency for enforcement of a national energy policy, this volume is a careful study of the relations between foreign and domestic policy and of the impact of a corporation on the world oil economy and Italy's securing of a needed share of exploitable foreign oil sources and supplies.

2839. Frankel, P.H. Mattei: Oil and Power Politics. New York: Praeger, 1966, pp. 190.
Important both as a study of the role of a particular enterprise in the development of the international system and its law but also as a study of the efforts of a country to gain a favorable allocation of a needed fuel.

2839-A. "Gas Output Buoys Petroleum Industry in Communist Bloc." World Oil (August 15, 1970), 126-132.
A review of oil and gas developments in Eastern Europe and of arrangements for imports into some of these countries.

2840. Hanson, E.J. "Natural Gas in Canadian-American Relations." 12 International Journal (1957), 186-198.
On the development of pipeline systems that would serve to built a continental distribution system rendering otherwise useless gas resources useful.

2841. Hartshorne, Richard. "The Role of the State in Economic Growth: Contents of the State Area." In Hugh G.J. Aitken (ed.), The State and Economic Growth. New York: Social Science Research Council, 1959, pp. 287-324.
Presents data on economic development, and classifies factors making for economic growth, including power resources, particularly coal, and the importance of having such resources within reach given the entrepreneurship necessary for their effective exploitation.

2842. Hirst, David. Oil and Public Opinion in the Middle East. New York: Praeger, 1966, pp. 127.
On Arab distrust of the oil industry and the economic, political, and legal aspects of Arab oil opinion, with case studies of the negotiations between the Government of Iraq and the Iraqi Petroleum Company and of the origins and subsequent development of the Organization of Petroleum Exporting Countries.

2843. "How Dutch Gas is Affecting Western Europe." 159 World Oil (August 15, 1964), 81-84.
On companies drilling in the Netherlands, on completed or potential agreements for the distribution of Dutch gas from the Slochteren field, and on a projection of the share of Dutch gas in the West European energy market to 1975.

2844. Kish, Geo. "Eastern Europe's Power Grid." 58 Geographical Review (1968), 137-140.
　　On the power economies of the Eastern European countries and the Unified Electrical System, inaugurated in 1963, into which the Soviet Union supplies more power than it receives.

2845. Lubell, Harold. Middle East Oil Crises and Western Europe's Energy Supplies. Baltimore: Johns Hopkins Press for the RAND Corporation, 1963, pp. xx, 233.
　　A response to the Iranian oil stoppage of 1951-1954 and the Suez Canal stoppage of 1956-1957, this book tries to foresee future Middle East crises, the consequent oil transit problems, and the costs and consequences of replacement of Middle East supplies by Venezuelan, Mexican, Canadian, and United States oil. The study is one in which vision is impeded by the past, in this case by the substitutions made in 1956-1957, and consequent failure to foresee what shipbuilding technology could accomplish or what actually occurred after the stoppage of the Suez Canal in 1967.

2846. Mainguay, Y. L'Économie de l'énergie. Paris: Dumond, 1967, pp. 519.
　　Makes use of the approaches and findings of several disciplines to bring a global perspective to bear on the energy fuel economy and to take account of regional situations such as that of the European Communities.

2847. Marossi, Ruth. "Canada's Uranium Crisis." 17 Bulletin of Atomic Scientists (September 1961), 281-286.
　　On the difficulties created for Canada by the US Atomic Energy Commission's decision not to renew contracts that expired in 1962-1963.

2848. Marts, Marion E. "An American Viewpoint." On Resources of the Northern Cordillera. "Energy" Panel. Transactions of the Twelfth British Columbia Natural Resources Conference. Vancouver: 1959, pp. 82-85.
　　This and other statements made by members of the Energy Panel highlight some of the problems and potential of energy resource development on the national and international levels.

2849. McCaffree, K.M. "The Atom vs. Falling Water in the Far Northwest." 62 Pacific Builder and Engineer (July 1956), 73ff.
　　A comparison of two sources of energy in terms of their potential and economic feasibility in the Northwest.

2850. Melamid, Alexander. "Geographical Distribution of Petroleum Refining Capacity--A Study of the European Refining Program." 31 Economic Geography (1955), 168-178.
　　A study of the European oil refining system as it stood on the eve of the negotiation of the EEC Treaty.

2850-A. "North Sea Discoveries May Alter Import Plans." World Oil (August 15, 1970), 107-124.

Review of developments in oil and gas exploration in Western European countries and the North Sea to mid-1970.

2850-B. "North Sea Looking Better All the Time." 68 Oil and Gas Journal (July 20, 1970), 30-31.
On the latest developments in exploration for oil under the
North Sea after a finding of oil in the Echofish stepout, well
off Norway, by the Phillips-Agip-Fina-Petronord group.

2851. Odell, Peter R. An Economic Geography of Oil. New York:
Praeger, 1963, pp. xii, 219.
On world patterns of oil production, refining, and consump-
tion and on transportation problems.

2852. Rassmuss, J.E. "Politics Versus Oil in Latin America." 159
World Oil (August 15, 1964), 88-91.
Report on cancellation of contracts, threats of nationalization, tightening of government oil monopolies or strengthening government companies, and increased restrictions and taxes
on private oil companies operating in Latin America.

2853. Salin, Edgar. "Energie-politik europäischer Industrie-staaten
oder europäische Industriepolitik." 14 Kyklos (fasc. 4, 1961), 451-481.
Good survey of different national approaches to energy policy in Europe that indicates quite a number of the difficulties
in attempting to develop a common energy policy even for the
Inner Six.

2853-A. Sander, N.J. "What's Ahead for the International Offshore?"
World Oil (July 1970), 83-88.
Deals with technological, economic, political, and legal
problems of offshore oil and gas development in the non-
Communist world, with attention to the probable replacement of
current barter agreements for manufactured goods against supplies of oil by arrangements whereby the consuming country provides all or part of the capital to find and develop oil and
gas supplies and by guaranteeing a market.

2854. Swiss, M. "Gas at Sea." Europe and Oil (November 1964), 16-17.
Review of the growing energy gap in Britain and on the
Continent and of potential systems to meet the needs after
1969, including commercial shipment of refrigerated methane.

2855. Swiss, M. "The Supply of Natural Gas to Europe." Europe and
Oil (January 1965), 12-14.
Review of a speech by L. Corrandini on Europe's energy
needs, the growth of natural gas pipelines and of ocean transport of refrigerated gas, with particular reference to the
French need to reach decisions on the uses to be made of supplies from the Lacq fields and between Algerian and Dutch
sources of gas imports.

2856. Tanzer, Michael. The Political Economy of International Oil and the Underdeveloped Countries. Boston: Beacon, 1969, pp. x, 435.
A study of the dynamics of power in the world petroleum markets in terms of the countries that have, those that need, and those that distribute oil.

2857. Thirring, Hans. Energy for Man: From Windmills to Nuclear Power. Bloomington: Indiana University Press, 1958; Torchbook ed., New York: Harper & Row, 1962, pp. 409.
Second edition of a volume originally published under the title Power Production (London: Harrap, 1956). Provides basic information on the evolution of power production with attention to engines for power production and sources of energy. The latter deals with fossil fuels, fuels from vegetation, water power with a section on the international power trade, solar energy, and nuclear energy.

2858. van der Esch, B. "Legal Aspects of a European Energy Policy." 2 Common Market Law Review (1964-5), 139-167.
Deals with economic, fiscal and social, as well as legal, aspects of a Western European energy policy, including the un-foreseen competition that oil and gas would provide for coal, national regulations and policies that conflict with the effort to construct a Community energy system, and the need for Community jurisdiction if a pipeline network is to be developed and maintained free from obstacles that could be imposed by national policies. Some attention is given to the problem of the import of crude oil from the Sahara and of oil products from the Netherlands Antilles.

See also nos. 563, 583, 597, 598, 1158, 1159, 2670, 2675, 2785, 2786, 2788, 2798, 2805, 2807, 2810, 2811, 2867, and sec. VIII, E, 2.

6. Peaceful Uses of Nuclear Energy

2859. Beaton, Leonard. "Safeguards on Plutonium." 212 Nature (London) (1966), 1517-1519.
On the need, if nonproliferation is to be realized, to guard against acquisition of plutonium stocks by nations sup-plying reactors and subsequently acquiring the plutonium pro-duced by the reactors in recipient countries in the attempt to assure that recipient countries are restricted to peaceful uses of nuclear energy.

2860. Emelyanov, V. "Atomic Power and Disarmament." 19 Bulletin of Atomic Scientists (October 1963), 16-20.
Commentary on the slowness of development of atomic power for peaceful purposes that asserts that the amounts of plutonium required for fast breeder reactors is limited due to the tie-up of plutonium in nuclear warheads. The author then argues that

disarmament is a necessary precondition for nuclear power
development.

2861. Green, Harold P., and Rosenthal, Alan. The Government of the
Atom: The Integration of Powers. New York: Atherton, 1963, pp. ix, 281.
    A political history of the US atomic energy program with
particular attention to the influence of the Joint Committee on
Atomic Energy. Although dealing with but one country and particularly with a congressional institution, the volume is of
particular value for research aimed at finding the meeting point
of domestic and international interests, policies, and decision-
making and the outcomes in the form of international legal norms,
including those expressing the authority of international agencies.

2862. Hasson, J.A. The Economics of Nuclear Power. London: Longmans, 1965, pp. viii, 160.
    Includes a cost-benefit analysis by areas and countries and
consideration of transport costs and competition from other fuels.

2863. Hodgetts, J.E. Administering the Atom for Peace. New York:
Atherton, 1964, pp. xi, 193.
    Review of the problems of administration of research and
development essential to putting nuclear energy to work for
peaceful purposes. Attention is given to both national and international undertakings, the national administrations considered being those of the US, the UK, France, Canada, Japan, and
Italy.

2864. Hogerton, John F. "The Arrival of Nuclear Power." 218 Scientific American (February 1968), 21-31.
    On the market breakthrough of electric power obtained from
nuclear fission which by 1968 accounted for nearly half of all
new generating capacity being ordered by utilities in the United
States.

2865. Inglis, David R., and Sandler, Carl L. "Prospects and Problems: The Nonmilitary Uses of Nuclear Explosives." 23 Bulletin of the
Atomic Scientists (December 1967), 46-53.
    An evaluation of Project Plowshare that includes a review
of possible uses of nuclear explosives for excavation, unearth-
ing natural resources, and experiments in pure science. The
authors suggest that Plowshare and the peaceful uses of nuclear
energy with which it is concerned could be an inducement to
arms control or, if necessary, be set aside to achieve it.

2866. Kramish, Arnold. The Peaceful Atom in Foreign Policy. New
York: Harper and Row for the Council on Foreign Relations, 1963, pp. xi,
276.
    Examines international cooperation in developing peaceful
uses of atomic energy, probes what can and cannot be done
through international agencies, and reviews United States policy toward such agencies.

2867. McCaffree, K.M. "Atomic Energy in the Pacific Northwest." 14 Pacific Northwest Business (July 1955), 11-15, 18-23.
An attempt to foresee the potential contributions of atomic energy to the development of the Pacific Northwest.

2868. Mullenbach, Philip. Civilian Nuclear Power: Economic Issues and Policy Formation. New York: Twentieth Century Fund, 1963, pp. xiv, 406.
Includes consideration of world energy prospects and requirements and the consideration of nuclear power in relation to foreign policy in terms of peaceful uses, expansion of technical knowledge, and unification of energy policies.

2869. Murray, Thomas. Nuclear Policy for War and Peace. Cleveland: World Publishing Company, 1960, pp. 241.
Problems of peaceful uses of nuclear energy and of such wartime uses as anti-tank weapons that would give a small ground force a blast charge equivalent to that of 50 B-29s of World War II are discussed by the late author who had been a member of the Atomic Energy Commission. US policy on a nuclear test ban prior to 1948 is also discussed.

2870. Panel on the Impact of the Peaceful Uses of Atomic Energy, Robert McKinney, Chairman. Peaceful Uses of Atomic Energy. 2 vols. Washington: Government Printing Office, 1956.
An attempt to assess from various points of view the potential of nuclear energy in the future.

2871. Polach, Jaroslav G. "Nuclear Energy in Czechoslovakia: A Study in Frustration." 12 Orbis (1968), 831-851.
On Soviet reluctance to provide the East European bloc countries with access to advanced nuclear technology despite agreement to aid their nonmilitary nuclear power development, particularly with regard to rising Czech energy requirements and disappointments.

2872. Sahovic, Milan. "International Control of the Uses of Nuclear Energy." 4 Journal of Peace Research (1965), 297-306.
The author, on the staff of the Institute of International Politics and Economy in Belgrade, analyzes methods of control of the uses of nuclear energy provided for in bilateral treaties and in the framework of international organizations including the European Agency. He sees the development as one of mixed solutions representative of contemporary possibilities for cooperation and of the level of development of international law. Controls entrusted to national bodies are treated as expressive of the state of affairs and the necessity for its acceptance but inadequate for compliance with principles of equal cooperation.

2873. Seaborg, Glenn T. "Atomic Power: The Key to Supremacy in Space." In Lillian Levy (ed.), Space: Its Impact on Man and Society. New York: Norton, 1965, pp. 82-91.

Sets forth the need for and potential uses of nuclear power in the exploration of outer space.

2874. Seaborg, Glenn T. "The Promise of the International Atomic Energy Agency." 158 Science (1967), 226-230.
Laudatory review of IAEA activities that, among other things, identifies specific peaceful uses of nuclear energy, calls attention to influences beyond the direct regulatory authority confined to the Agency's own projects, deals with the problem of nonproliferation, and refers to the Agency's safeguards system in respect to shipments of radioactive materials and diversion to military purposes, with particular attention to inspections by international civil servants with broad powers of access and investigation. Note is taken that for a growing number of activities IAEA safeguards have been requested either voluntarily or in agreement with a supplier of nuclear assistance.

2875. Willrich, Mason. Global Politics of Nuclear Energy. New York: Praeger, 1971, pp. 212.
Examining the interactions among politics, science, and technology, the author surveys the major challenges of peaceful nuclear energy in terms of international politics and major nuclear policy alternatives. Analyzing the development of new nuclear technologies, the author asks that more attention be paid to political control over the process of technological development.

See also nos. 753, 774-776, 796, 1105, 1106, 1566, 1583, 2569, 2692, 2752, 2839.

AUTHOR INDEX

Note: Numerals after authors' names represent bibliographical entry numbers. The symbol "ann." after an entry number signifies that the author is mentioned in the annotation as the contributor of a paper for a symposium, the provider of the analytical framework for an article or book, the scholar with whom an author takes issue, or a contributor of additional information on the topic with which an article or book deals.

Angell, Robert C., 310, 714,
  1334-A, 1335, 2655
Anglin, Douglas G., 1064
Appleman, Philip, 2622
Apter, David E., 162
Archibald, Kathleen, 434, 442,
  1597, 2120
Arendt, Hannah, 1735, 1741 ann.
Arens, Richard, 1828
Arévalo, Juan Jose, 1336
Arfa, Hassan, 2493
Armour, Anne, 256
Armstrong, Donald, 2673
Armstrong, J.A., 1322
Armstrong, L., 184
Armytage, Frances, 2234
Arnold, Robert R., 453
Aron, Raymond, 190, 490 ann.,
  1646, 1652 ann., 1829, 1868
Aron, Robert, 641
Arons, Leon, 1848
Aronson, Elliot, 286
Aronson, Sidney H., 73 ann.
Arrow, Kenneth J., 208
Asch, S.E., 1766
Ash, Maurice A., 1647
Ashby, Sir Eric, 1979
Ashby, W. R., 88, 89
Asher, Robert E., 729
Ashford, Douglas E., 1026, 2022,
  2347
Asimov, Isaac, 2595
Asinger, F., 1158 ann.
Aspaturian, Vernon V., 604, 1387,
  2153
Atal, Y., 545-A
Aubert, Vilhelm, 1830, 1888, 2192,
  2219
Aubrey, Henry G., 2644
Austin, Dennis, 2348
Austin, John Langshaw, 1747
Aventur, J., 1207
Averch, H., 1889
Avon, Anthony Eden, First Earl of,
  2154
Aydelotte, William O., 193
Ayub Khan, Mohammed, 2023
Azad, John, 1092

Baade, Hans W., 223, 1111
Babbar, M.M., 807
Back, Kurt W., 315, 316
Backstrom, Charles H., 366
Baddour, Abd-el-Fattah Ibrahim
  el-Sayed, 1033
Bader, William B., 2096, 2285
Badurina, Berislav, 2242
Baehr, Peter R., 1930-A
Baerwald, Hans H., 2286
Bagdikian, Ben H., 1117
Bahramy, A.A., 1112
Bailey, N.A., 1598
Baker, James M., 1778
Baker, Ross K., 920
Balabkins, Nicholas, 2287
Baldwin, David A., 1034, 1855-A,
  2704
Baldwin, John, 1648
Bales, Robert F., 313, 379, 384
  ann.
Balintfy, Joseph L., 417
Ball, Harry, 1831
Ball, M. Margaret, 888
Bandura, A., 1695
Banerji, J.K., 2024
Banks, Arthur S., 118 ann., 164,
  166 ann., 173, 517, 1662 ann.
Banks, Michael, 548-A ann.
Banno, Masataka, 1127 ann., 1965
Barber, James, 921
Barber, Willard F., 933
Barclay, G. St. J., 784
Barkun, Michael, 30, 144, 145,
  2215, 2228
Barnett, Richard J., 1519
Barnett, Vincent M., Jr., 2044
Barringer, R.E., 394
Barritt, Denis P., 1233
Barros, James, 1799, 2193
Bartlett, B.R., 2614
Bartlett, Z.W., 2808
Barton, Paul (pseud.), 2490
Bartos, Otomar J., 2112, 2113,
  2126
Barzanti, Sergio, 745
Basi, Raghbir S., 2656
Batchelder, Robert C., 2243
Battaglia, Roberto, 2271
Batten, E.S., 2244

Quirk, James P., 203

Rabow, Jerome, 1285
Raczyński, Edward, Count, 634
Radcliffe-Brown, Alfred R., 117
Radlow, Robert, 1757
Radnor, Michael, 1439-A
Radovanovitch, Lj., 799
Raestad, Arnold, 1953
Rahul, R., 2329
Raiffa, Howard, 438
Rall, J.E., 2599
Ramazani, Rouhollah K., 1081
Ramírez Novoa, Ezequiel, 1373
Ramsey, P., 1049
Randle, Robert, 2317-A
Randolph, Lillian, 2131
Ranney, Austin, 75
Ransom, Harry Howe, 67
Rao, G.N., 2382
Rao, G.R., 2202-A
Rao, V.K.R.V., 2725
Rapacki, Adam, 1543
Rapisardi-Mirabelli, M. Andréa, 1929
Rapoport, Anatol, 288, 441, 442, 443, 444, 1286, 1542, 1597 ann., 1618
Rapoport, David C., 948
Rapp, R.R., 2609
Raser, John R., 68, 176, 422, 423
Rashevsky, N., 205
Rassmuss, J.E., 2852
Ratoosh, P., 330
Ratzel, Friedrich, 2365 ann.
Raven, Bertram H., 1772, 1836
Ravndal, Gabriel Brie, 2069
Rawls, John, 1758
Raymond, A.E., 2780
Read, Thornton, 1671, 2148, 2149, 2168
Reboud, Louis, 1071
Redding, Stephen, 1362
Redelis, Valdis, 2279
Redfield, Alfred C., 2751, 2774
Redford, Emmette Shelburn, 44
Regala, Roberto, 2062
Regan, Mark M., 2418
Reid, A.J.S., 574

Reid, Donald Darnley, 1158 ann.
Reigrotski, E., 1790
Reinken, Donald L., 63 ann.
Reisman, William M., 1845
Reiwald, Paul, 1711
Remington, Robin Alison, 2202-B
Renborg, Bertil A., 2574
Rennell of Rodd, Lord, 2303
Renouvin, Pierre, 1287
Reuber, Grant L., 589
Revelle, Roger, 2616
Reynaud, R., 1403
Reyner, Anthony S., 2383
Reynolds, David R., 2384
Reynolds, J., 918
Reynolds, Philip Alan, 1288
Rhatib, M. Fathalla El, 1358
Rhode, Gotthold, 575
Richards, Peter G., 1316
Richardson, Lewis F., 1255, 1620 ann.
Richardson, Stephen A., 375
Richman, Alvin, 68-A, 1619, 1619-A
Ridgeway, George L., 882
Riecken, Henry W., 276, 382 ann.
Rienow, Robert, 142 ann.
Rieselbach, Leroy N., 9, 376, 700, 1317
Riesman, David, 43
Rifaat, M.A., 875
Rifflet, R., 1404
Riggs, Fred W., 560 ann.
Riggs, Robert E., 69-A
Riker, William H., 701
Rikhye, Indar J., 1582
Rios Gallardo, Conrado, 2106
Rintala, M., 2146
Ristelhueber, René, 2557
Ritchie, Ronald S., 702
Rivkin, Arnold, 1082, 1930
Roa, R., 1544
Robertson, Arthur H., 800
Robin, Geoffrey de Q., 2447
Robinson, Alan D., 1405
Robinson, Hal, 286
Robinson, James A., 328, 329, 334, 377, 424, 679, 1318
Robinson, Jane, 473
Robinson, Kenneth, 562